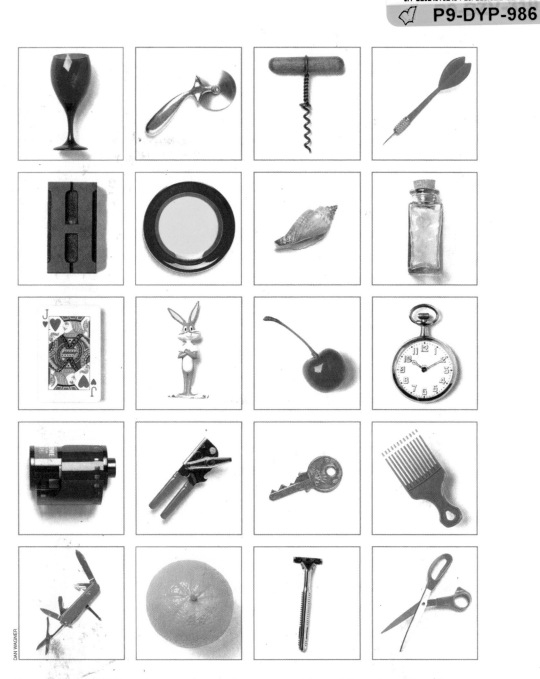

Can you solve it? What do an ancient corkscrew, a watch, and Bugs Bunny have in common? Can't figure it out? See Chapter 16.

Reprinted by permission of Dan Wagner.

DAN WAGNER

SEVENTH EDITION

Cognitive Psychology

Robert L. Solso
University of Nevada, Reno

M. Kimberly MacLin
University of Northern Iowa

Otto H. MacLin
University of Northern Iowa

PEARSON

Boston ● New York ● San Francisco
Mexico City ● Montreal ● Toronto ● London ● Madrid ● Munich ● Paris
Hong Kong ● Singapore ● Tokyo ● Cape Town ● Sydney

Executive Editor: *Karon Bowers*
Editorial Assistant: *Lara Torsky*
Senior Marketing Manager: *Wendy Gordon*
Editorial Production Service: *Omegatype Typography, Inc.*
Manufacturing Buyer: *JoAnne Sweeney*
Cover Administrator: *Linda Knowles*
Electronic Composition: *Omegatype Typography, Inc.*

For related titles and support materials, visit our online catalog at www.ablongman.com.

Between the time Website information is gathered and published, some sites may have closed. Also, the transcription of URLs can result in typographical errors. The publisher would appreciate being notified of any problems with URLs so that they may be corrected in subsequent editions.

Library of Congress Cataloging-in-Publication Data

Solso, Robert L.
  Cognitive psychology / Robert L. Solso, M. Kimberly MacLin, Otto H. MacLin.—7th ed.
    p.   cm.
  Includes bibliographical references and index.
  ISBN 0-205-41030-8
  1. Cognition—Textbooks.   2. Cognitive psychology—Textbooks.   I. MacLin, M.
Kimberly.   II. MacLin, Otto H.   III. Title.

BF311.S653 2005
153—dc22

                                                                              2004043668

Printed in the United States of America

10   9   8   7   6   5   4   3   2   1   09   08   07   06   05   04

This book is lovingly dedicated to our children to whom we entrust the future:

Anne E. Solso
Laird A. Solso
Robert S. Solso
Davis McDonald MacLin
Gage L. MacLin

Contents in Brief

1   **Introduction to Cognitive Psychology**   1

2   **Cognitive Neuroscience**   33

3   **Perception and Attention**   70

4   **Pattern Recognition**   104

5   **States of Consciousness**   140

6   **Memory Processes**   166

7   **Memory Models**   202

8   **Mnemonics and Experts**   234

9   **The Representation of Knowledge**   260

10   **Mental Imagery**   290

11   **Language: Structure and Abstractions**   318

12   **Language: Words and Reading**   352

13   **Cognitive Development**   379

14   **Thinking: Concept Formation, Logic, and Decision Making**   417

15   **Thinking: Problem Solving, Creativity, and Human Intelligence**   451

16   **Computerized Cognition: Artificial Intelligence**   486

Contents

Preface   *xvii*

CHAPTER 1 Introduction to Cognitive Psychology   1

What Is Cognitive Psychology?   2

Information-Processing Model   4

The Domain of Cognitive Psychology   6

Cognitive Neuroscience 6   Sensation/Perception 7   Pattern
Recognition 8   Attention 8   Consciousness 8   Memory 9
Representation of Knowledge 9   Imagery 10   Language 10
Cognitive Development 11   Thinking and Concept Formation 11
Human and Artificial Intelligence 11

A Brief History of Cognitive Psychology 12

Early Thoughts on Thinking 13   Cognition in the Renaissance and
Beyond 14   Cognitive Psychology: The Twentieth Century 16

Conceptual Science and Cognitive Psychology   20

Cognitive Models 22   The Computer Metaphor and Human
Cognition 24   Cognitive Science 25   Neuroscience and Cognitive
Psychology 26   Parallel Distributed Processing (PDP) and Cognitive
Psychology 28   Evolutionary Cognitive Psychology 29

Summary   31

Key Words   32

Recommended Readings   32

CHAPTER 2 · **Cognitive Neuroscience   33**

Exploring the Brain   34

Logbook: The Twenty-First Century—Brain Sciences   34

Mind–Body Issues   35

Cognitive Neuroscience   36

Cognitive Psychology and Neuroscience   37

The Nervous System   38

The Neuron 40   The Brain: From Localization to Mass Action 43
The Anatomy of the Brain 45

Neurophysiological Sensing Techniques   52

CT Scans 53   PET Scans 53   MRI and fMRI 55   MEG 56
TMS 56   Research Using Imaging Techniques: An Example 56

A Tale of Two Hemispheres   60

Cognitive Psychology and Brain Science 67

Summary   68

Key Words   68

Recommended Readings   69

CHAPTER 3 · **Perception and Attention   70**

The Computational Brain   71

Sensation and Perception   72

Illusions 73   Previous Knowledge 74   Sensory-Brain
Predisposition 75   Everything We Know Is Wrong 76

Perceptual Span   77

Iconic Storage   78

Echoic Storage   80

Function of Sensory Stores   81

Attention   82

Attention, Consciousness, and Subliminal Perception 85

Processing Capacity and Selective Attention   86

Auditory Signals   87

Models of Selective Attention   88

The Filter Model: Broadbent 88   The Attenuation Model: Treisman 91

Visual Attention   94

Automatic Processing   96

The Cognitive Neuroscience of Attention   98
Attention and the Human Brain 99   Attention and PET 100

*S*potlight on Cognitive Neuroscience: Visual Attention   100

Summary   102

Key Words   103

Recommended Readings   103

CHAPTER 4 **Pattern Recognition   104**

Perceptual Theories   107

Visual Pattern Recognition   108
Vision 109   Subjective Organization 110

Gestalt Theory   112

Canonic Perspectives   114

Bottom-Up versus Top-Down Processing   117

Template Matching   119
Geon Theory 121   Priming Technique 123

Feature Analysis   125
Eye Movements and Pattern Perception 126

Prototype Matching   127
Abstraction of Visual Information 128   Pseudomemory 130
Prototype Theory: Central Tendency versus Attribute Frequency 132

Form Perception: An Integrated Approach   133

Pattern Recognition among Experts   134
Pattern Recognition in Chess   134

Pattern Recognition—The Role of the Perceiver   136

*S*potlight on Cognitive Neuroscience: Pattern Recognition   137

Summary   138

Key Words   139

Recommended Readings   139

CHAPTER 5   **States of Consciousness   140**

History of Consciousness   142

Consciousness as a Scientific Construct   144

Cognitive Psychology and Consciousness   146

Explicit and Implicit Memory 147   Research with Primes 148
Neurocognitive Studies: Sleep and Amnesia 151   Limited Capacity 154

Metaphors of Consciousness   155

The Novelty Metaphor 155   The Spotlight 155   An Integration
Metaphor: The Theater in the Society of Mind 156

Theories of Consciousness   157

Schacter's Model of Dissociable Interactions and Conscious
Experience (DICE) 158   Baars's Global Workspace Theory 159

Functions of Consciousness   162

*S*potlight on Cognitive Neuroscience: Consciousness in the Brain   164

Summary   164

Key Words   165

Recommended Readings   165

CHAPTER 6   **Memory Processes   166**

Short-Term Memory   167

Cognitive Neuroscience and STM 169   Working Memory 171
Capacity of STM 172   The Coding of Information in STM 175
Retrieval of Information from STM 182

Long-Term Memory   184

Cognitive Neuroscience and LTM 185   LTM: Storage and Structure 186
Very Long-Term Memory (VLTM) 190   Autobiographical Memories 193
The Fallibility of Memory and Eyewitness Identification 198

*S*potlight on Cognitive Neuroscience: Autobiographical Memory   200

Summary   200

Key Words   201

Recommended Readings   201

CHAPTER 7   **Memory Models   202**

Early Studies   203

The Cognitive Neuroscience of Memory   207

Two Memory Stores   209

Memory in the Larger Cognitive Domain   211

Models of Memory   213

Waugh and Norman 213   Atkinson and Shiffrin 214   Level of Recall
(LOR) 216   Levels of Processing (LOP): Craik 217   Self-Reference
Effect (SRE) 221   Episodic and Semantic Memory: Tulving 223
A Connectionist (PDP) Model of Memory: Rumelhart and McClelland 227

*S*potlight on Cognitive Neuroscience: Working Memory   231

Summary   232

Key Words   232

Recommended Readings   233

CHAPTER 8   **Mnemonics and Experts   234**

A King from Texas Matches a Paul Bunyan King from Minnesota   235

Mnemonic Systems   236

Method of Loci 236   Peg Word System 238   Key Word Method 240
Organizational Schemes 241   Recall of Names 243   Recall of Words 244

Extraordinary Memories   245

S.: Luria 245   E.: A Case of Photographic Memory 247   V. P.: Hunt
and Love 248   Others 250

Experts and Expertise   250

H. O.: Case Study of an Artist—Solso; Miall and Tchalenko 252
The Structure of Knowledge and Expertise 255   Theoretical Analysis
of Expertise 257

*S*potlight on Cognitive Neuroscience: Chess Experts   258

Summary   258

Key Words   259

Recommended Readings   259

CHAPTER 9   **The Representation of Knowledge   260**

Semantic Organization   261
Declarative Knowledge and Procedural Knowledge   262

Associationist Approach   263
Organizational Variables: Bower 263

Semantic Memory: Cognitive Models   264
Set-Theoretical Model 266   Semantic Feature-Comparison Model 267
Network Models 269   Propositional Networks 273

Representation of Knowledge—Neurocognitive Considerations   279
The Search for the Elusive Engram 279   What Amnesic Patients Tell
Us When They Forget 279   Knowing *What* and Knowing *That* 281
A Taxonomy of Memory Structure 282

Memory: Consolidation   283

Connectionism and the Representation of Knowledge   284

*S*potlight on Cognitive Neuroscience: Representation of Knowledge   286

Summary   287

Key Words   288

Recommended Readings   289

CHAPTER 10   **Mental Imagery   290**

Historical Overview   291

Imagery and Cognitive Psychology   292
Dual-Coding Hypothesis 294   Conceptual-Propositional Hypothesis 295
Functional-Equivalency Hypothesis 297

Cognitive Neuroscience Evidence   302

Cognitive Maps   308
Mental Maps: Where Am I? 309

Synesthesia: The Sound of Colors   312

*S*potlight on Cognitive Neuroscience: Cognitive Maps   315

Summary   316

Key Words   317

Recommended Readings   317

CHAPTER 11   **Language: Structure and Abstractions   318**

Linguistics   322

Linguistic Hierarchy 322   Phonemes 322   Morphemes 324   Syntax 325

Chomsky's Theory of Grammar   326

Transformational Grammar 327

Psycholinguistic Aspects of Language   329

Innate Properties and Environmental Effects 329
Linguistic-Relativity Hypothesis 330

**Cognitive Psychology and Language: Abstraction
of Linguistic Ideas   332**

"The War of the Ghosts": Bartlett 332   "Ants Ate the Jelly":
Bransford and Franks 335

Knowledge and Comprehension   338

"Soap Opera," "Thieves," and "Police" 339   "Bumper Stickers
and the Cops": Kintsch and van Dijk 341

A Model of Comprehension: Kintsch   343

Propositional Representation of Text and Reading 345

Language and Neurology   346

*S*potlight on Cognitive Neuroscience: Linguistics   349

Summary   350

Key Words   351

Recommended Readings   351

CHAPTER 12   **Language: Words and Reading   352**

Perceptual Span   354

Text Processing: Eye Tracking 358

Lexical-Decision Task (LDT)   364

Word Recognition: A Cognitive-Anatomical Approach   369

Comprehension   371

*S*potlight on Cognitive Neuroscience: Dyslexia   377

Summary   377

Key Words   378

Recommended Readings   378

CHAPTER **13**   **Cognitive Development**   379

Life-Span Development   381

Cognitive Development 381   Neurocognitive Development 381
Comparative Development 381

Developmental Psychology   382

Assimilation and Accommodation: Piaget 382   Mind
in Society: Vygotsky 389   Vygotsky and Piaget 390

Neurocognitive Development   392

Early Neural Developmental 393   Environment and
Neural Development 393   Lateralization Studies 396

Cognitive Development   398

Intelligence and Abilities 398   Development of Information-Acquisition
Skills 400   Memory 405   Higher-Order Cognition in Children 409
Prototype Formation among Children 412

*S*potlight on Cognitive Neuroscience: Cognitive Development   414

Summary   414

Key Words   415

Recommended Readings   416

CHAPTER **14**   **Thinking: Concept Formation, Logic,
and Decision Making**   417

Thinking   418

Concept Formation   419

Association 420   Hypothesis Testing 420

Logic   422

Inferences and Deductive Reasoning 425   Syllogistic Reasoning 427

Decision Making   433

Inductive Reasoning 433   Decision Making in the "Real World" 434
Reasoning and the Brain 438   Estimating Probabilities 440   Decision
Frames 441   Representativeness 443   Bayes's Theorem and Decision
Making 444

Decision Making and Rationality   446

*S*potlight on Cognitive Neuroscience: Decision Making   448

Summary   448

Key Words   449

Recommended Readings   449

CHAPTER 15   **Thinking: Problem Solving, Creativity, and Human Intelligence**   451

Problem Solving   452

Gestalt Psychology and Problem Solving 453   Representation of the Problem 454   Internal Representation and Problem Solving 459

Creativity   462

Creative Process 463   Creativity and Functional Fixedness 464
Investment Theory of Creativity 465   Judging Creativity 466

Human Intelligence   469

The Problem of Definition 469   Cognitive Theories of Intelligence 470
Cognitive Neuroscience and Intelligence 478

*S*potlight on Cognitive Neuroscience: Creative Problem Solving   482

Summary   482

Key Words   483

Recommended Readings   484

CHAPTER 16   **Computerized Cognition: Artificial Intelligence**   486

AI—The Beginnings   489

Computers 489   Computers and AI 491   AI and Human
Cognition 494

**Machines and Minds: The Imitation Game
and the Chinese Room**   496

The Imitation Game, or the Turing Test 498   The Chinese Room 498
The Chinese Room—Refutation 500

Perception and AI   500

Line Analysis 501   Pattern Recognition 502
Recognition of Complex Forms 505

Language and AI   509

ELIZA, *PARRY, and NETtalk* 509   Meaning and AI 513   Continuous Speech Recognition (CSR) 514   Language Understanding Program 515

Problem Solving, Game Playing, and AI   515

Computer Chess 519

AI and the Arts   521

Robots   524

The Future of AI   525

AI and Scientific Inquiry   528

$\mathcal{S}$potlight on Cognitive Neuroscience: Artificial Face Recognition   529

Summary   529

Key Words   530

Recommended Readings   530

Glossary   531

References   542

Name Index   588

Subject Index   595

Preface

To the Student

Those of us who grew up with psychology during the twentieth century saw rapid and important developments about the way people perceive their world, how they form memories, and how thought occurs. These developments are due to the dedicated efforts of numerous cognitive psychologists aided by an improved technology. This combination has yielded a rich harvest of knowledge about perception, memory, thinking, and information processing—indeed, all of human cognition.

Among the important findings in cognition is the establishment of a connection between the thinking mind and its corresponding neurophysiological activities. These advances were pioneered during the last part of the twentieth century. Today, a new epoch in all areas of scientific endeavors is anticipated. It is our aim to catch the spirit of these lively times and to stimulate you to investigate the topic further. It is hoped that the contents of this book will let you know where we cognitive psychologists have been; report accurately the best ideas, theories, and experiments; and prepare you to comprehend future developments.

The book follows a sequential model of human cognition from sensation to perception, to attention, to memory, to higher-order cognition; a bottom-up approach, as it were. That system is easy to grasp and gives an order to what may otherwise seem to be a chaotic lot of information; however, it is noted that cognition–perception, memory, consciousness, language use, problem solving, and other topics engage all processes simultaneously. A comprehensive view of cognitive psychology involves an appreciation of all of its components as they weave their exquisite pattern through the mental life of members of our species.

In most chapters you will find boxes called "Cognition in Everyday Life" and "Try This!" If we know one thing about learning and cognition it is that an involved reader learns material better and probably at a deeper level of understanding. These sections are designed to draw you into one or more themes central to the chapter. We encourage you to allow yourself to be drawn in and interact with the text, and to recognize aspects of cognitive psychology all around (and within) you.

Some students may choose to follow a career in a branch of the cognitive sciences. If the contents of this book stimulate you to work toward continuing the job we psychologists have started, the labor will have been entirely rewarded. Finally, we are interested in what you think about the book and would welcome your reactions and comments (seriously!).

To the Instructor

From the first edition of *Cognitive Psychology* to this seventh edition, the basic organization of the text has changed only a little but the substance has changed considerably. In the earlier editions only perfunctory cross-references were made to what we now call cognitive neuroscience. Now, the prominence of cognitive neuroscience is palpable in all areas of cognitive psychology (and many other areas of psychology) to the extent that other, more traditional fields are beginning to be squeezed out of some textbooks. The remarkable advancements in cognitive neuroscience, not only in technology but also in data and their implications, are fully appreciated in the present edition, gaining ground in the fourth, fifth, and sixth editions; but we are clearly mindful that cognitive psychology is the study of the human mind: its thoughts, its reasoning process, its language, its memory. These subjects (and others) are the topics of cognition that cognitive neuroscience serves to illustrate, explain, and illuminate (in more ways than one). Because cognition is psychology, we have retained many of the conventional studies that have endured the test of time and the empirical test of science and, when appropriate, have added an interesting new study. There is a great temptation to substitute a new study for an old one, and in some instances, when the more recent paper illustrates a new facet of a problem, substitution is justified. However, in many cases an older study is perfectly clear and has been retained. In addition to holding on to the psychological aspects of cognitive psychology, this seventh edition also has a multitude of new studies on cognitive neuroscience that are included as new verification for cognitive theories.

Writing the first edition of *Cognitive Psychology* more than twenty years ago was particularly challenging because I (RLS) had no example to follow except the now classic book of the same title by Ulric Neisser, which was published in 1967, and the hundreds of articles and symposium papers that were unsystematically strewn about my office and home. I did have the good fortune to sit in on Ed Smith's class on cognition at Stanford University in 1974 (a course I later taught). His organization of material is still in the background (although somewhat modified) in the present book as well as in many other texts in cognition, and it seems to me that Ed Smith, who was inducted into the National Academy of Sciences, had a hand in the way cognitive psychology is taught throughout the United States and the world. There are now several dozen textbooks in cognitive psychology and many more that discuss topics as far ranging as cognition and the law, cognition and psychotherapy, cognition and society, and cognition and education, to name but a few. Since those early days of the "cognitive revolution," the sphere of influence of those interested in this topic has expanded greatly, far exceeding what I envisioned decades ago. However, it is my impression that the major topics that formed the discipline during that time are still viable today, although the emphasis has shifted over the past years—such is the dynamic nature of viable sciences. Since writing the first edition more than a quarter century ago through the sixth edition, the writing has been mostly a solo effort by the first author. In this seventh edition you will find the addition of two remarkable scholars, Kim MacLin and Otto MacLin, who have added breadth and depth to the book. Kim and Otto bring fresh writing, insightful scholarship, and an increased comprehensiveness to the book while at the same time retaining the essential philosophy of the original editions. Both are intimately familiar with the contents of the book and had assisted in the sixth edition. In addition, I (RLS) am proud to say that they are both Ph.D. students of mine.

In this seventh edition we have tried to retain the best features of the previous six editions while adding important new material and changing the emphasis of the book to reflect important changes in the field. In particular, we have retained the comprehensive nature of the book. With the field undergoing significant change and development during the past decade, it has become increasingly difficult to cover all areas of cognition reasonably. Although there is a need for specialized books that are written from a specific point of view, we trust that many will welcome a comprehensive book on cognitive psychology.

Those of you who have used *Cognitive Psychology* for the past few years will be pleased to find that for material that presents contradictory findings, an exposition is given, followed by a summary of the results in which certain conclusions are made. This summary was first used in the third edition and is in response to the needs many of you have expressed.

As with previous editions, most chapters begin with a brief review of the historical antecedents of the topic presented. Since the field of cognitive psychology changes so rapidly, we believe it is important for readers to know something of the history of a topic so that they may understand new information within the context of past events. Each chapter correspondingly ends with a recent study in cognitive neuroscience that highlights an aspect of that chapter.

Overview

- Each chapter begins with preview questions we call "Hmmm . . . ?" These are the questions we think capture students' interest and encourage them to wonder about these concepts prior to delving into the chapter material. We know that learning of essential knowledge is facilitated if the student has a clue about what he or she is expected to learn. The addition of several pertinent questions at the beginning of the chapter will direct the student's perspective on the chapter, and in some cases, the questions are designed to pique the interest of the reader.
- Each chapter has been updated, and several chapters have been significantly reworked, often in response to requests from users.
- As mentioned briefly earlier, each chapter ends with a section called "Spotlight on Cognitive Neuroscience." In this section, a recent study is discussed that focuses on a key concept in the chapter from the perspective (either topically or methodologically) of cognitive neuroscience.

- The organization of the chapters and sections follows an information-processing sequence that starts with the perception of signals by the sensory/brain system to higher-order processes such as memory, language, and thinking. This sequence has been one that students and professors find easy to follow although the Information Processing (INFOPRO) model of cognition is not the only model students are exposed to in this book. And it is our opinion that cognition is such that all parts work together more or less simultaneously. While people have little difficulty following a sequential processing model, it should be pointed out that memory without perception is like a beautiful painting without paint.
- We have streamlined the boxed material in this edition in two important ways. First, some of the content has been incorporated directly into the text. We feel this provides more examples to keep the student engaged in the material. Second, the remaining boxes (and some new ones) have been reorganized around two themes: "Cognition in Everyday Life" and "Try This!" These boxes encourage the student to analyze or contemplate the immediate subject matter in terms of an everyday experience or an easy-to-do demonstration or thought experiment.
- New artwork has been added that is both lively and instructive.
- A test bank, instructor's manual, PowerPoint slides, and companion Web site are all available for your use.

In writing a comprehensive book on cognitive psychology, it is our intention to present a work that would be attractive to many professors who prefer to select their favorite topics for coverage in a one-term class. It may be possible to cover all sixteen chapters in one course, but most professors have told us that they select certain chapters and not others. The book has been written so that some chapters may be dropped without losing the continuity of the book. Following are several suggested models:

1. A brief, general introduction to cognition—Chapters 1, 3, 4, 6, 7, 8, 11, 13, 15, and 16.
2. A cognitive neuroscience system—Chapters 1, 2, 3, 4, 5, 6, 7, 9, 10, 12, 15, and 16.
3. An applied approach—Chapters 1, 3, 4, 5, 6, 7, 8, 9, 10, 11, 13, 14, 15, and 16.
4. A thinking/problem-solving emphasis—Chapters 1, 4, 5, 6, 7, 8, 9, 10, 11, 14, 15, and 16.
5. A memory course—Chapters 1, 2, 3, 6, 7, 8, 9, 10, 11, 12, 13, 14, and 15.
6. A cognitive development course—Chapters 1, 2, 3, 4, 6, 7, 8, 9, 10, 11, 12, 13, 14, 15, and 16.

These models are only basic suggestions to which chapters of your own liking and/or specialty may be added.

Many people have contributed to this book, and it is a pleasure for us to recognize them here. Many of you, faithful users over the years, have expressed your opinions of the book in person or by email. Your continued use is most deeply appreciated, and your comments have been most important. Also, the students who have written or given feedback have helped us keep in contact with the most important group—namely, the people to whom the book is directed. Many researchers have kept us informed of their latest discoveries, and to you we are particularly obliged. We acknowledge the reviewers of the fifth and sixth editions. The fifth and sixth editions were made measurably better by the reviews provided by Tom Busey, Indiana University; William S. Cassel, University of New Orleans; Linda D. Chrosniak, George Mason University; Darlene De-Marie-Dreblow, Muskingum College; Doug Eamon, University of Wisconsin–Whitewater; Paul Foos, University of North Carolina–Charlotte; Paul Jose, Loyola University of Chicago; Kristy A. Nielson, Marquette University; Greg Robinson-Riegler, University of St. Thomas; Barbara A. Spellman, University of Virginia; and Laura A. Thompson, New Mexico State University. Thanks also to the reviewers for this edition, especially John Krantz, Hannover College, who spent a great deal of time to provide us with useful, constructive criticism. Thanks are due to several students: Mike Anderson, former graduate student at UNI who spent much of one summer collecting articles, surfing the Internet, and reviewing chapters; and Becky J. Fisher and Scott Shaw, both undergraduates at UNI, who helped us at every turn on the instructor's manual, test bank, and indexing responsibilities. Thanks to our wonderful editor Karon Bowers for her enthusiasm and support, to editorial assistant Lara Torsky for her continuous help with the details, and to the absolutely fantastic staff at Omegatype; to our students, for their guidance and feedback, and to our colleagues, for their encouragement (and some course release time too). And finally, we'd like to thank all of the instructors who have adopted the text for all these years. Without you this seventh edition would not have been possible. We thank you all. Please let us know how we are doing (we mean it!).

R.L.S.   M.K.M.   O.H.M.

CHAPTER **1**

Introduction to Cognitive Psychology

hmmm...?

- **What Is Cognitive Psychology?**
- **Information-Processing Model**
- **The Domain of Cognitive Psychology**
  Cognitive Neuroscience
  Sensation/Perception
  Pattern Recognition
  Attention
  Consciousness
  Memory
  Representation of Knowledge
  Imagery
  Language
  Cognitive Development
  Thinking and Concept Formation
  Human and Artificial Intelligence
- **A Brief History of Cognitive Psychology**
  Early Thoughts on Thinking
  Cognition in the Renaissance and Beyond
  Cognitive Psychology: The Twentieth Century
- **Conceptual Science and Cognitive Psychology**
  Cognitive Models
  The Computer Metaphor and Human Cognition
  Cognitive Science
  Neuroscience and Cognitive Psychology
  Parallel Distributed Processing (PDP)
     and Cognitive Psychology
  Evolutionary Cognitive Psychology

1. What is cognitive psychology?
2. What are the principal components of cognitive psychology?
3. How did cognitive psychology emerge as a major force in psychology?
4. What is a cognitive model, and how have cognitive models been used to understand the mind?
5. How has cognitive neuroscience influenced the study of mind sciences, and what new directions in cognition might emerge because of this influence?
6. How has evolutionary cognitive psychology influenced thinking in cognition?

Thanks to the development of new logical tools, the diverse deployments of the computer, the application of the scientific method to human psychological processes and cultural practices, our deeper and more rigorous understanding of the nature of language, and the many discoveries about the organization and operation of the nervous system, we have attained a more sophisticated grasp on the issues put forth originally by Plato, Descartes, Kant, and Darwin.

—*Howard Gardner*

What Is Cognitive Psychology?

When you read and think about this question, you are engaging in cognition. Cognitive psychology deals with the perception of information (you read the question), it deals with understanding (you comprehend the question), it deals with thought (you ask yourself whether you know the answer), and it deals with the formulation and production of an answer (you may say, "Cognitive psychology is the study of thinking"). You can also think of cognitive psychology as the study of processes underlying mental events. Cognition touches all parts of the perceptual, memory, and thinking processes and is a prominent characteristic of all people.

Cognitive psychology is the scientific study of the thinking mind and is concerned with:

- How we attend to and gain information about the world
- How that information is stored and processed by the brain
- How we solve problems, think, and formulate language

Neisser (1967) summed it up best: ". . . The term 'cognition' refers to all processes by which the sensory input is transformed, reduced, elaborated, stored, recovered, and used . . . it is apparent that cognition is involved in everything a human being might possibly do; that every psychological phenomena is a cognitive phenomena" (p. 4).

Cognitive psychology involves the total range of psychological processes—from sensation to perception, pattern recognition, attention, consciousness, learning, memory, concept formation, thinking, imaging, remembering, language, intelligence, emotions, and developmental processes—and cuts across all the diverse fields of behavior. The course we have charted—the scientific study of the thinking mind—is both ambitious and exciting. Because the scope is great, the range of studies will be diverse, and because the topic deals with viewing the human mind from a new perspective, your views of the intellectual nature of humankind may be changed profoundly.

In this chapter a general picture of cognitive psychology is presented, the history is reviewed, and some current theories of how knowledge is represented in the human mind are summarized.

Before we consider the technical aspects of cognitive psychology, it may be useful to gain some perspective on the assumptions we humans make in processing information. To illustrate the way we interpret information, let's consider, for example, a common event: a motorist asking a police officer for directions. Although the cognitive processes involved seem simple, they are not.

> *Motorist:* Say, I'm new in this town; can you tell me how to get to Computer Super-Store? I'm looking for a thinking program—you know, something that simulates problem solving.
>
> *Police Officer:* Well, they've got that.
>
> *M:* Good!
>
> *P:* Yes, in the software area. So . . . do you know where the coliseum is?
>
> *M:* Is that the building with the kind of cone shape or is that the one that . . .
>
> *P:* No, but you know where that is—that's the Expo site; remember, they had the Expo in 1998.
>
> *M:* Oh yes, I know where the Expo is.
>
> *P:* OK, that's the Expo site. Well, it's kind of hard to get there from there, but if you go down from where you are now, if you go down this street one stoplight and then to the flagpole, turn right one block to another light, and then make a left, go over the train tracks past the lake to the next stoplight near the old mill. . . . Do you know where the old mill is?
>
> *M:* Is that the street on the bridge that says "one-way street" up to the old mill?
>
> *P:* No, it's two-way.

M: Oh, it must be the other bridge. OK, I know which street . . .

P: You can tell it by the large sign that says "Once you have lost a jewel you can never re-place it." Something like that. It's an ad for a night deposit box. I call it the bozo box be-cause it's the Bozwell Bank. Anyway, you'll go by the old mill—that's where La Strada's restaurant is, in the Eldorado—and you turn left—no, right—then one block turn left and that's Virginia. On Virginia Street you can't miss it. It's on the right-hand side of the street.

M: You're kidding. I'm staying in a motel on Virginia Street.

P: Yeh?

M: I was going in the wrong direction. Here I am in the other end of town. Two blocks from my motel room! I could've walked there.

P: What motel are you in?

M: The Oxford Motel.

P: Oh, the Oxford?

M: Well, its not "upscale," but they have a pretty good library.

P: Huh?

The episode described took less than two minutes, yet the amount of information perceived and analyzed by the two people is staggering. A layperson, finding the ex-change mind-boggling, might simplify it to "I asked—he told—I understood." Yet, there is far more to the dialogue than just that. A student of cognitive psychology might want to know what the underlying processes are behind "I asked," "He told," and "I understood."

How might a cognitive psychologist view the process? Although the behaviors themselves are important elements, there are "internal" systems that are behind such actions, and those internal systems are intriguing to cognitive psychologists. It is from just such a standpoint that cognitive psychologists examine the complex phenomena of human behavior.

Using the example beginning on page 3, how might a cognitive psychologist view the process? He or she begins by making certain assumptions about the cognitive char-acteristics possessed by the motorist and the police officer. In the left column of Table 1.1 are the assumptions made; in the right column are the topics in cognitive psychology that deal with those assumptions.

Information-Processing Model

One way these assumptions may be integrated into a larger system, or cognitive model, is in an **information-processing model,** which is generally related to a time-ordered se-quence of events. The model makes sense and is easy to understand. It has been the conventional model used by cognitive psychologists for decades although it is not the *only* way cognition may be characterized, studied, and understood. Another model, for example, the **neuroscience model,** focuses on the underlying brain function that pro-duces cognitive experience.

An information-processing model begins with a set of three assumptions. They are:

- Cognition can be understood by analyzing it into a series of (mostly) sequential stages.

- At each stage unique processes take place on incoming information. The eventual response (for example, saying, "Oh yes, I know where the Expo is") is assumed to

TABLE 1.1

TABLE 1.1

Assumptions about Cognitive Characteristics

Assumption	Topic in Cognitive Psychology
Ability to detect and interpret sensory stimuli (e.g., visual and auditory)	Sensation
Tendency to focus on certain sensory stimuli and to disregard others	Attention
Detailed knowledge of the physical characteristics of the environment	Knowledge
Ability to abstract certain parts of the event and integrate those parts into a well-structured schema that gives meaning to the total episode	Representation of knowledge
Ability to extract meaning from letters and words	Perception, reading, and information processing
Capacity to retain immediate events and to integrate those events into an ongoing sequence	Short-term memory
Ability to form an image of a "cognitive map"	Mental imagery
Understanding the role of the other person	Social cognition
Ability to use "memory tricks" to aid in recall of information	Mnemonics and memory
Tendency to store linguistic information in a general form	Abstraction of linguistic ideas
Ability to solve a problem	Problem solving
General ability to act in a meaningful way	Human intelligence
Inference that the directions can accurately be translated into a complex motor response (driving an automobile)	Language/motor behavior
Ability to recall quickly from long-term memory specific information that is immediately applicable to the present situation	Long-term memory
Ability to translate visual events into spoken language	Language processing
Knowledge that objects have specific names	Semantic memory
Inability to perform perfectly	Forgetting and interference

be the outcome of this series of stages and operations (for example, perception, coding of information, recall of information from memory, concept formulation, judgment, and language production).

- Each stage receives information from preceding stages and then performs its unique function. Because all components of the information-processing model are in some way related to each other, it is difficult to identify an initial stage, but for convenience we can think of the sequence as starting with incoming information.

These pieces of information—the environmental cues in our example—are not directly represented in the police officer's brain but are transformed into meaningful symbols, what some cognitive psychologists have labeled **internal representations.** On the most fundamental level, light (or sound) energy emanating from the perceived information is

Cognition in Everyday Life

Let's Go Shopping!

*T*hroughout this book you will see these boxes where you will be asked to use the knowledge of the current chapter in understanding cognition in your life.

The next time you visit a supermarket or a mall, pause for a few moments and observe the various examples of cognitive psychology that surround you. Pay particular attention to (1) the use of forms and colors to gain atten-

tion, (2) your own reaction to environmental cues (for example, where your eyes focus and how long you look at an object or person), and (3) the use of memory in understanding language, context, and the interpretation of the sights and sounds of your environment. Jot down your impressions of these matters and read them over in about a week. What principles discussed in this chapter apply?

transduced (converted) to neural energy, which in turn is processed through the above-mentioned hypothetical stages to form the internal representation of the perceived object. This internal representation is understood by the police officer and, when combined with other contextual information, provides the basis for his answer to the question posed by the motorist.

Two important questions raised by the information-processing model are the subject of considerable debate among cognitive psychologists:

- What are the stages through which information is processed?
- In what form is information represented in the human mind?

Although there are no easy answers to these questions, a major portion of this book deals with both issues, and it will be useful to keep these questions in mind. One way cognitive psychologists have attempted to answer them is by incorporating into their research the techniques and theories of specific psychological disciplines, of which several are described here.

The Domain of Cognitive Psychology

Modern cognitive psychology freely draws theories and techniques from twelve principal areas of research (see Figure 1.1): cognitive neuroscience, sensation/perception, pattern recognition, attention, consciousness, memory, representation of knowledge, imagery, language, cognitive development, thinking and concept formation, and human and artificial intelligence. Each area is covered in the chapters that follow.

Cognitive Neuroscience

Only within the past few years have cognitive psychologists and cognitive neuroscientists formed a close working relationship. Thus far, this union has produced some of the most provocative developments in the study of our mental character. Cognitive psychol-

FIGURE 1.1

Principal research areas of cognitive psychology.

ogists are seeking neurological explanations for their findings, and neuroscientists are turning to cognitive psychologists to explain observations made in their laboratories. In the earlier example of the befuddled motorist and the police officer, every part of the cognitive process—from sensation to memory to driving—is supported by basic electro-chemical processes taking place in the brain and nervous system.

Sensation/Perception

(The branch of psychology directly involved with the detection and interpretation of sensory stimuli is **sensation and perception.**) From experiments in sensation, we have a good understanding of the sensitivity of the human organism to sensory signals and—more important to cognitive psychology—of the way we interpret sensory signals, in other words, perception.)

The police officer's description of the street scene is essentially dependent on his ability to "see" the pertinent environmental cues. "Seeing," however, is not a simple matter. The sensory information (in this case, largely visual) must be of a certain magnitude to be perceived. That is, if the motorist is to execute the described maneuvers, the cues must be of a certain strength. In addition, the scene is an ever-changing one. As the motorist's location changes, new cues emerge. Several cues become more important than others in the perceptual process. Signposts are distinguishable by their color, location, shape, and so on. Many of these images are in constant flux, and to translate the directions into performance the motorist must make a rapid adjustment in behavior.

The experimental study of sensation and perception has helped identify many of the parts of this process, some of which are discussed in Chapter 3. However, the study of sensation and perception alone does not adequately account for the expected performance; other cognitive systems are involved, including pattern recognition, attention, consciousness, and memory.

Pattern Recognition

Environmental stimuli rarely are perceived as single sensory events; they usually are perceived as part of a more meaningful pattern. The things we sense—see, hear, feel, taste, or smell—are almost always part of a complex pattern of sensory stimuli. Thus, when the police officer tells the motorist to "go over the train tracks past the lake . . . near the old mill," he is using words to describe complex objects (train tracks, lake, old mill). At one point the officer describes a sign and assumes the driver to be literate. But think about the problem of reading. Reading is a complex effort in which the reader is required to form a meaningful pattern from an otherwise meaningless array of lines and curves. By organizing the stimuli that make up letters and words, the reader may then access meaning from his or her memory. The entire process takes place in a fraction of a second, and considering all the neuroanatomical and cognitive systems involved, this feat—performed daily by all sorts of people—is wondrous.

Attention

The number of environmental cues available to the police officer and motorist is overwhelming. If the motorist attended to all or even a sizable number of them, he would never find the computer store. Although we are information-gathering creatures, it is evident that under normal circumstances we are also highly selective in the amount and type of information to which we attend. Our capacity to process information seems to be limited to two levels—sensory and cognitive. If too many sensory clues are imposed on us at any given time, we can become overloaded; if we try to process too many events in memory, we can become overloaded, which may cause a breakdown in performance. If the cartoon shown on page 3 accurately represents the motorist's cognitive map, he is hopelessly confused. All of us have felt the same way at one time or another.

Consciousness

Consciousness is defined as "the current awareness of external or internal circumstances." Although it is a word "worn smooth by a million tongues" (Miller, 1962), it is certainly one of the slipperiest concepts to define operationally. Rejected as being "unscientific" by the behaviorists, the word *consciousness* and the concept it represents simply will not fade away. And the fact that some topics are hard to analyze does not mean they should be disregarded: Science does not study only easy problems. For most people, conscious and unconscious thoughts are very real. For example, when you glance at your watch while studying and it reads "10:42 (P.M.)," you are conscious, or aware, of that external signal, much as the motorist was conscious of the directions given by the police officer and what those directions meant. However, your reading of the time also brings up another conscious thought, one that was initially activated by reading the time but is from "inside." That conscious thought might be, "It's getting late: I'd better finish this chapter and go to bed"—just as the motorist may have thought, "I hope this cop knows where Computer SuperStore is and tells me without giving me a hassle. Oh, where is my car registration? Is my insurance up-to-date? Act calm. Is someone watching us? I remember where the bridge is. I can 'see' the flagpole." All of these conscious thoughts may have flashed through the person's mind in a few seconds. *Consciousness,* the term that will not go away, has gained new respectability recently and now is a concept studied seriously in modern cognitive psychology.

Memory

Could the police officer describe the scene without memory? Certainly not, any more than he could function without perception. In fact, memory and perception work together. In the example, two types of memory contribute to the officer's answer. The first type retains information for a limited time, long enough for him to carry on a conversation. This memory system seems to hold information for only a brief period, when new information displaces it. The entire exchange would have taken only about 120 seconds, and it is unlikely that all the details were permanently retained by either the police officer or the motorist. However, these details were stored in memory long enough for both of them to keep track of the sequence of elements making up the dialogue,[1] and some of the information may have found its way into their permanent memory. This first memory stage is called **short-term memory** (STM) or, in this case, a specialized form of memory called **working memory.**

On the other hand, a great amount of the answer is drawn from the police officer's **long-term memory** (LTM). Most obvious is his knowledge of the language. He didn't refer to the lake as a kumquat, or the Expo site as a rubber tire, or a street as a basketball; he drew words from his LTM and more or less used them correctly. There are additional cues that indicate LTM is involved in his description: ". . . Remember they had the Expo in 1998." In a fleeting second, he was able to recall information about an event of years before. That information did not come from an immediate perceptual experience; it was stored along with a vast number of other facts in his LTM.

The information available to the police officer came from his perception, STM, and LTM. In addition, we can infer that he was a thinking person, that the information was conceptualized in a scheme that "made sense."

Representation of Knowledge

Fundamental to all human cognition is the **representation of knowledge:** how information is symbolized and combined with the things stored in the brain. This part of cognition has two aspects: the conceptual representation of knowledge in the mind and the way the brain stores and processes information.

---

[1]For example, the police officer had to retain briefly that the motorist was looking for "Computer Super-Store," that he knew the location of Expo, even (at least until he finished asking, "What motel are you in?") that the motorist was staying at a motel. Similarly, in the case of the motorist, he had to retain briefly that the officer had asked if he knew the Expo site; that he had to pass the old mill; and so on.

If we are to take literally the thought bubbles over the police officer and the lost motorist in the cartoon on page 3, the two had considerably different conceptual representations. (One of the problems we have in communicating with each other is that the world is never identically represented.) What *you* see, hear, smell, taste, or feel is not the same as what *I* experience and represent in memory; and what I experience and store in memory is not identical to your experience. In spite of these inherent dissimilarities between representations of knowledge, most humans do experience and depict experiences in similar enough ways to get along well in the world.

In addition, we humans share a brain that largely determines the way information is stored. It has taken millions of years for the human brain to evolve; nevertheless, your brain and the brain of your best friend are remarkably similar. Even the differences between your brain and the brain of your professor are slight (in spite of perceived differences—on both sides). Of course, the *content* is hugely different: Your friend may know a great deal about the gear one needs to take on a three-week kayak trip to northern Canada and you may know more about the classification of stellar objects, for example. But our neurological web entraps information and experiences and holds them in structures that are similar in all human brains. When the motorist and the police officer look at each other's face, for example, the same parts of their brains are activated.

Cognitive psychologists are especially interested in the topic of internal representations of knowledge, and a large part of this book deals with this topic in one form or another. The history of knowledge representations is reviewed later in this chapter.

Imagery

To answer the motorist's question, the police officer formed a mental image of the environment. This mental image was in the form of a **cognitive map,** a type of internal representation of the juxtaposed buildings, streets, street signs, stoplights, and so on. From the cognitive map he was able to draw out the significant cues, order them in a meaningful sequence, and transform those images into language that, we hope, would allow the motorist to construct a similar cognitive map. That re-formed cognitive map would then provide the motorist with a reasonable picture of the city, which could be transformed later into the act of driving an automobile along a certain route. Although the experimental study of mental imagery is relatively new to psychology, some significant research has recently been reported; it is discussed in Chapter 10.

Language

To answer the motorist's question successfully, the police officer had to have extensive knowledge of the language. That knowledge involves more than knowing the proper names for the landmarks. Equally importantly, it involves knowing the syntax (the customary arrangement and relationships of the words) of the language. The sequence of words, although it might not satisfy a fussy English professor, does communicate. In nearly every sentence uttered by the police officer, the essential grammatical rules are observed. The officer didn't say, "Got well that they've"; he did say, "Well, they've got that." We all can understand what he meant. In addition to finding the appropriate word in his lexicon and forming grammatically correct sentences, the officer had to coordinate the complicated motor reactions necessary to articulate the message. Also, communication between people is much more than what they say or write. Most obvious is the use of gestures, or body language, to communicate, and it is likely that both motorist and police officer pantomimed much of their meaning as they played out their verbal fugue. Finally, we may appreciate the richness and complexity of the connotative features of language. Reconsider this brief exchange at the end of the conversation: *P:* What motel are you in? *M:* The Oxford Motel. *P:* Oh, the Oxford? *M:* Well, it's not "upscale. . . ."* Something about the intonation of the police officer's rejoinder, "Oh, the Oxford," was a signal read by the motorist as "Why are you staying in such a crummy dump?" Language and communication are far more than words.

Cognitive Development

Interest in how our cognitive abilities develop and change over the lifespan has made cognitive development a major area of study in cognitive psychology. Recent experiments and theories in developmental cognitive psychology have greatly expanded our understanding of how cognitive structures develop. In the example we have been studying, the speakers share developmental experiences that allow them (more or less) to understand each other. Some of these shared experiences include the development of mental manipulation of internal representations of concrete objects; the capacity for abstract thought and logical reasoning; and, not the least of all, the development of a common language, which allows for communication. Chapter 13 deals with cognitive development. As adults, we have all lived through childhood and adolescence and we share maturational experiences with all members of our species.

Thinking and Concept Formation

Throughout this episode the police officer and the motorist exhibited an ability to think and to form concepts. When asked how to get to Computer SuperStore, the officer replied, after some intermediate steps, "Do you know where the coliseum is?" indicating that if the motorist knew this landmark, he could easily be directed to Computer SuperStore. When he didn't, the officer developed another plan for answering the question. Furthermore, the officer's use of some words (such as "train tracks," "old mill," "La Strada's restaurant") indicates that he had formed concepts that were similar to the concepts shared by the motorist. Later in the conversation, the police officer seemed baffled when the motorist told him that the Oxford Motel had "a pretty good library." Motels and libraries generally are incongruous, and knowing this, the officer, as you might have done, implied, "What kind of motel is that?"

Human and Artificial Intelligence

Human Intelligence.   The police officer and the motorist each made certain assumptions about the intelligence of the other. These assumptions included (but were not restricted to) the ability to understand a common language, to follow instructions, to convert verbal descriptions into actions, and to behave according to the rules of their culture. In Chapter 14 some cognitive theories of human intelligence are considered in detail.

Artificial Intelligence.   The motorist is interested in finding "a thinking program," presumably for his personal computer. A program of this sort might emulate human cognition in a problem-solving task. To write a program that simulates thought, it is necessary to understand at least the fundamental attributes of human thought. This is a primary task of cognitive psychology. The specialty within computer science called **artificial intelligence** (AI) has had a major influence on the development of cognitive science, especially because the design of programs requires knowledge of how we process information. A related and fascinating topic (dealt with in detail in Chapter 16) addresses whether a "perfect robot" can simulate human behavior. Imagine, for example, a superrobot that has mastered all the perceptual, memory, thinking, and language abilities of humans. How would it answer the motorist's question? If the robot were identical to a human, the results would be identical, but consider the difficulty of developing a program that would make an error, as the police officer did ("you turn left"), and then, realizing its error, correct it ("no, right").

A Brief History of Cognitive Psychology

During the late summer of 1956, a symposium on information theory was held on the campus of MIT. Many of the leading figures in communication theory were in attendance and listened to talks by Noam Chomsky, Jerome Bruner, Allen Newell and Herbert Simon, and George Miller, among others. The meeting had an indelible effect on many of its participants, and the general feeling was that something new was being created that significantly changed the way psychological processes could be conceptualized. Reflecting on the meeting several years later, George Miller (1979) wrote:

> I went away from the Symposium with a strong conviction, more intuitive than rational, that human experimental psychology, theoretical linguistics, and computer simulation of cognitive processes were all pieces of a larger whole, and that the future would see progressive elaboration and coordination of their shared concerns. . . . I have been working toward a cognitive science for about twenty years, beginning before I knew what to call it. (p. 9)

So profound were the changes in American psychology during the last half of the twentieth century that they have been called the cognitive revolution.

As we have learned, a great portion of cognitive psychology deals with how knowledge is represented in the mind. The lively issue of representational knowledge has evoked the same fundamental questions over centuries: How is knowledge acquired, stored, transformed, and used? What is consciousness, and where do conscious ideas originate? What is the nature of perception and memory? What is thought? How do these abilities develop?

These questions reflect the essential issue of representational knowledge—how ideas, events, and things are stored and schematized in the mind. In this section on the history of cognitive psychology we will review three major periods, although a much more detailed history is available (see Solso & MacLin, 2000; Wilson & Keil, 1999). First, we will deal with traditional ideas from a very early period. Then we touch on the way knowledge and thinking were conceptualized by Renaissance scholars. Finally, we will deal with the modern period with emphasis on current ideas and methods.

Early Thoughts on Thinking

Human and other animal survival is dependent on knowing the important properties of the environment. Without knowing we would not be here.

Where did knowledge come from, and how is it represented in the mind? That eternal question is fundamental to cognitive psychology as it has been through the ages of humankind. Basically, two answers have been proposed. The **empiricists** maintain that knowledge comes from experience (as your knowledge of the Pythagorean Theorem was learned through your experience with high school geometry), and the **nativists** suggest that knowledge is based on innate characteristics of the brain—in today's parlance, that the brain is (partially) "hard wired." For example, you may have learned the Pythagorean Theorem, illustrated in Figure 1.2, in high school: *The sum of the squares of the length of the sides of a right triangle is equal to the square of the length of the hypotenuse.* No doubt your experience led to that "knowledge." But, then, is the "knowledge" of triangles something that existed inside your nervous system before the learning of this theorem? The nativists argue that there are some preexisting categories that order sensory experiences. From a scientific perspective, neither case can be definitively proved, so the argument continues without clear resolution. From a "commonsense" view, it is obvious that experiences lead to information *and* that experiences must have a receptive brain that cogitates on experiences and makes sense out of impressions. Some of the difficulty in this ongoing debate stems from our defining **knowledge** as the

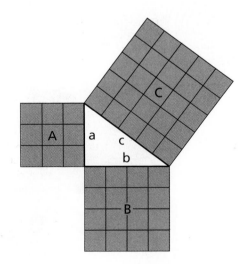

FIGURE 1.2

The sum of the squares in A and B is equal to the number of squares in C.

"storage and organization of information in memory," thus fitting the definition to two sides of the argument: The "storage" side suggests that experiences are important, and the "organization" side suggests that some preexisting structural capacity exists in the nervous system.

With these issues clearly before us, let's consider the way ancient philosophers and early psychologists grappled with the issue. The fascination with knowledge can be traced to the earliest writings. Early theories were concerned with the seat of thought and memory. Ancient Egyptian hieroglyphics suggest their authors believed that knowledge was localized in the heart—a view shared by the early Greek philosopher Aristotle but not by Plato, who held that the brain was the locus of knowledge.

Cognition in the Renaissance and Beyond

Renaissance philosophers and theologians seemed generally satisfied that knowledge was located in the brain. Some even went so far as to render its structure and locus graphically (see Figure 1.3). In the figure, knowledge is shown as acquired not only

FIGURE 1.3

Seventeenth-century view of the structure and workings of the mind.

In the world of knowledge, the essential Form of Good is the limit of our inquiries, and can barely be perceived; but, when perceived, we cannot help concluding that it is in every case the source of all that is bright and beautiful—in the visible world giving birth to light and its master, and in the intellectual world dispensing, immediately and with full authority, truth and reason—and that whosoever would act wisely, either in private or in public, must set this Form of Good before his eyes.

   —*Plato*

All men by nature desire knowledge.

   —*Aristotle*

through the physical senses (*mundus sensibilis*—touch, taste, smell, vision, and hearing) but also from divine sources (*mundus intellectualis*—*Deus*). During the eighteenth century, when philosophic psychology was brought to the point where scientific psychology could assume a role, the British empiricists—George Berkeley, David Hume, and, later, James Mill and his son John Stuart Mill—suggested that internal representation is of three types: (1) direct sensory events (*esse est percipi*, or "perception is reality"); (2) faint copies of percepts, or those that are stored in memory; and (3) transformation of these faint copies, as in associated thought. Hume, writing in 1748, said of the capacity for internal representation: "To form monsters, and join incongruous shapes and appearances, costs the imagination no more trouble than to conceive the most natural and familiar objects." This notion of internal representation and transformation postulates that internal representations are formed according to definable rules, and that such formation and transformation take time and effort—assumptions underlying much of modern cognitive psychology. (The latter assumption is the basis of much current research in cognitive psychology. Participants' reaction times are taken as a measure of the time and effort required to perform internal representations and transformations.) Also, recent findings in cognitive neuroscience have located anatomical structures related to specific psychological processes.

During the nineteenth century, psychologists started to break away from philosophy to form a discipline based on empirical results rather than on speculation. Conspicuous as a factor in this emergence was the activity of the early psychologists—Gustav Fechner, Franz Brentano, Hermann Helmholtz, Wilhelm Wundt, G. E. Müller, Oswald Külpe, Hermann Ebbinghaus, Sir Francis Galton, Edward Titchener, and William James.

By the last half of the nineteenth century, theories of the representation of knowledge were clearly dichotomous: there were those, led by Wundt in Germany and Titchener in the United States, that emphasized the structure of mental representation; and those, led by Brentano[2] in Austria, that emphasized the processes or acts. Brentano considered internal representations to be static entities of little value in psychology. He took

[2]See Boring, *A History of Experimental Psychology* (1950), for a more complete review.

the study of cognitive acts of comparing, judging, and feeling to be the proper subjects of psychology. The rival theories dealt with many of the same issues discussed two thousand years before by Plato and Aristotle. However, unlike the case with previous philosophic speculation, both theories were subjected to testing by experimentation.

About the same time in America, James critically analyzed the new psychology that was developing in Germany. He established the first psychological laboratory in America, wrote the definitive work in psychology in 1890 (*Principles of Psychology*), and developed a well-reasoned model of the mind. James considered the subject matter of psychology to be our experience of external objects. Perhaps James's most direct link with modern cognitive psychology is in his view of memory, in which both structure and process play an important role. (Those ideas and their modern counterparts are discussed in Chapter 6.) F. C. Donders and James Cattell, contemporaries of James, were performing experiments using the perception of brief visual displays as a means of determining the time required for mental operations. Their reports frequently described experiments that dealt with topics we would now call cognitive psychology. The technique, subject matter, procedures, and even the interpretation of results of these early scientists seem to have anticipated the emergence of the discipline a half-century later.

Cognitive Psychology: The Twentieth Century

The representation of knowledge, as we have used this term, took a radical turn with the advent of twentieth-century behaviorism and Gestalt psychology. The behaviorist views of human and animal psychology were cast in a framework of stimulus-response (S-R) psychology, and Gestalt theorists built elaborate conceptualizations of internal representation within the context of **isomorphism**—one-to-one relationship between representation and reality.

Psychological studies of mental processes as conceptualized in the late nineteenth century suddenly became unfashionable, displaced by behaviorism. Studies of internal mental operations and structures—such as attention, consciousness, memory, and thinking—were laid to rest and remained so for about fifty years. To the behaviorists, internal states were subsumed under the label of "intervening variables," which were defined as hypothetical constructs presumed to represent processes that mediated the effects of stimuli on responses and were neglected in favor of making observations on behavior (the things that animals did that could be observed) rather than on the mental processes that were the underpinning of behavior.

In 1932, some years before the cognitive revolution swept across psychology, learning psychologist Edward Tolman from the University of California at Berkeley published *Purposive Behavior in Animals and Men*. In this seminal work, Tolman observed that what rats learn in a maze is the lay of the land rather than simply a series of S-R connections. Tolman, conducting a series of ingenious experiments in which a rat was trained to find food by following a single roundabout pathway, found that, when given the opportunity to go directly to the food, the animal took it. It went directly to the place where the food was rather than following the original pathway. The animal, according to Tolman's interpretation, gradually developed a "picture" of its environment that was later used to find the goal. This picture was called a cognitive map. The rats in Tolman's experiments exhibited their possession of a cognitive map by reaching a goal (the food)

Edward C. Tolman (1886–1959).
Developed the concept of a cognitive map.

Photograph courtesy of Archives of the History
of American Psychology, University of Akron,
Akron, Ohio 44303.

from a number of different starting points. This "internal map" was, in effect, the way information about their environment was represented. It would be unwarranted to suggest that Tolman's research directly affected modern cognitive psychologists, but his postulate about cognitive maps in animals did anticipate the contemporary preoccupation with how knowledge is represented in a cognitive structure.

Also in 1932 Sir Frederick Bartlett from Cambridge University wrote *Remembering* in which he rejected the popular view at the time that memory and forgetting can be studied by means of nonsense syllables, as had been advocated by Ebbinghaus in Germany during the previous century and that was a popular topic in experimental psychology throughout the middle of the twentieth century. In the study of human memory, Bartlett argued, the use of rich and meaningful material under naturalistic conditions would yield far more significant conclusions. To study human memory, Bartlett had participants read a story and then try to recall as much of the story as they could. He found that an important aspect of remembering a story was the participant's attitude toward the story. In Bartlett's words, "The recall is then a construction made largely on the basis of this attitude, and its general effect is that of a justification of the attitude." In effect, what you remember about a story is based on the overall impression created by the story, or the theme of the story. Recall of specific facts then tends to corroborate the principal theme. Bartlett introduced the concept of **schema** as a unifying theme that describes the essence of an experience. Schema theory plays a central role in modern theories of memory.

The fecund ideas of Tolman in America and Bartlett in England ran contrary to the intellectual zeitgeist of the 1930s, which was centered in other accounts of animal and human behavior. Nevertheless, in retrospect, it is possible to appreciate the visionary nature of their work and how much it influenced the thinking of future cognitive psychologists.

In the 1950s interest again began to focus on attention, memory, pattern recognition, images, semantic organization, language processes, thinking, and even consciousness (the most dogmatically eschewed concept), as well as other "cognitive" topics once considered outside the boundary of experimental psychology (vis-à-vis behaviorism). New journals and professional groups were founded as psychologists began more and more to turn to cognitive psychology. As cognitive psychology became established with even greater clarity, it was plain that this was a brand of psychology different from that in vogue during the 1930s and 1940s. In 1956, George Miller published his landmark article entitled "The Magical Number Seven, Plus or Minus Two: Some Limits on Our

© 1974 by Sidney Harris—*American Scientist* magazine.

Capacity for Processing Information," which brought to the forefront the empirical evaluation of cognition. Among the most important forces accounting for this neocognitive revolution were the following:

- *The "failure" of behaviorism.*[3] Behaviorism, which generally studied overt responses to stimuli, failed to account for the diversity of human behavior as in the case of language (see the earlier analysis of the conversation between the police officer and motorist). Furthermore, there were some topics ignored by the behaviorists that seemed to be profoundly related to human psychology. These included memory, attention, consciousness, thinking, and imagery. It was apparent that

[3]It should be noted that behaviorism has had a significant effect on certain types of psychotherapy, especially in what has become known as "behavioral modification," as well as on experimental psychology and operational definitions.

internal mental processes were very real parts of psychology and required investigation. Many psychologists thought that these internal processes could be operationally defined and incorporated within a general study of the mind.

- *The emergence of communication theory.* Communication theory prompted experiments in signal detection, attention, cybernetics, and information theory—areas of significance to cognitive psychology.

- *Modern linguistics.* New ways of viewing language and grammatical structure became incorporated into attitudes concerning cognition.

- *Memory research.* Research in verbal learning and semantic organization provided a sturdy empirical base for theories of memory, which led to the development of models of memory systems and the appearance of testable models of other cognitive processes.

- *Computer science and other technological advances.* Computer science, and especially a subdivision of it—artificial intelligence—caused reexamination of basic postulates of problem solving and memory processing and storage, as well as of language processing and acquisition. Research capabilities were greatly expanded by new experimental devices.

- *Cognitive development.* Psychologists interested in developmental psychology discovered an orderly unfolding of abilities with maturation. Notable among developmental psychologists during this period was Jean Piaget, who described how children develop an appreciation for concepts from infancy to adolescence. Such progress of abilities seems to be natural.

From the earliest concepts of representational knowledge to recent research, knowledge has been thought to rely heavily on sensory inputs. That theme runs from the Greek philosophers, through Renaissance scholars, to contemporary cognitive psychologists. But are internal representations of the world identical to the physical properties of the world? Evidence is increasing that many internal representations of reality are not the same as the external reality—that is, they are not isomorphic. Tolman's work with laboratory animals and Bartlett's work with human participants suggest that information from the senses is stored as an abstract representation. Furthermore, studies of neurology clearly show that information from the outside world is sensed and stored as in a neurochemical code.

A somewhat more analytic approach to the topic of cognitive mapping and internal representation of information has been taken by Norman and Rumelhart (1975). In one experiment they asked residents of college housing to sketch floor plans of their apartments. As expected, the students were able to identify the prominent architectural features—the location of rooms, major utilities, and appliances. There were, however, omissions and errors. For example, many drew a balcony flush with the exterior of the building, although in fact it extended beyond. From the errors made in reconstructing the floor plan, we can learn a great deal about a person's internal representation of information. Norman and Rumelhart conclude:

> The memory representation is not simply an accurate rendition of real life, but in fact is a combination of information, inference, and reconstruction from knowledge about buildings and the world in general. It is important to note that when the mistake was pointed out, all the students were surprised at what they had drawn.

Don Norman. His inventive studies in memory representations and artificial intelligence introduced new ways of conceptualizing cognition.

An important principle of cognitive psychology is introduced by these examples. The most evident is that our representation of the world is not necessarily identical to the actual nature of the world. The representation of information is, of course, related to the stimulation received through our sensory apparatus, but it is also modified. This modification of information seems to be related to our past experiences, which have resulted in a rich and complex network of knowledge. Thus, incoming information is abstracted (and to some degree distorted) and stored within the person's memory system. Such a notion does not deny that some sensory events are directly analogous to their internal representations, but it does suggest that the storage of sensory stimuli may be (and frequently is) subject to abstraction and modification as a function of a person's rich and complex web of previously structured knowledge.

Conceptual Science and Cognitive Psychology

Two ideas that are used frequently throughout this book are the notions of conceptual science and cognitive models. Although related, they differ in the sense that conceptual science is a very general concept, whereas cognitive models refer to a specific class of conceptual science.

From observation of objects and events, both experimentally controlled and in nature, scientists develop concepts in order to:

Organize observations
Make observations meaningful
Relate the elements deriving from their observations
Develop hypotheses
Direct subsequent observations
Predict unobserved events
Communicate with others

Cognitive models are specialized forms of scientific concepts and have the same purposes. Although they have been variously defined, we will define a cognitive model as a metaphor, based on observations and on inferences, that describes the detection, storage, and use of information. For example, memory can be thought of in terms of file cabinets, computers, puzzles, or VCRs. Each of these metaphors provides a framework to conceptualize the structure and function of memory.

Scientists may find a useful metaphor that elegantly structures their concepts, but then new research may prove the model wrong, requiring its revision or abandonment. Sometimes the model may be so useful as a framework for research that, even though not perfect, it is maintained. For example, although cognitive psychologists have conceptualized the previously mentioned two types of memory, short-term and long-term, some evidence exists that suggests that dichotomy misrepresents the reality of memory systems. Nevertheless, the metaphor is still useful to conceptualizing cognitive processes for analytic purposes. When models lose their vitality as analytical or descriptive tools, they are abandoned. In the next section, both conceptual science and cognitive models are more thoroughly discussed.

One way to mark the development of science is by the concepts that emerge through experimentation and observation. The scientist does not change nature (except in a limited sense), but observation of nature does change the way a scientist conceptualizes it. In turn, our conceptualization of nature directs our observations! Cognitive models, as well as other models of **conceptual science,** are the consequence of observations and, to some degree, are the determinant of observations. The issue is related to the above-mentioned one of how knowledge is represented by the human observer. As we learned, many times the internal representation of information does not coincide perfectly with external reality. Our internal representation of percepts may distort reality. One means of bringing the external reality into clearer focus is use of the scientific method, as well as precise instrumentation. In effect, there is a constant effort to transcribe the observation of nature into cognitive structures that are accurate representations of nature and, at the same time, compatible with the observer's sense of reason and comprehension. The numerous concepts discussed in this book—from visual perception, to memory structure, to semantic memory—are all based on this logic.

The logic of conceptual science can be illustrated by consideration of developments in the physical sciences. For example, it is generally acknowledged that matter is composed of elements whose existence is independent of direct human observation. The way elements are classified, however, greatly influences the way scientists perceive the physical world. One classification scheme divided the "elements" of the world into the categories *earth, air, fire,* and *water.* When this rudimentary taxonomy of alchemy gave way to more critical observation, elements—such as oxygen, carbon, hydrogen, sodium, and gold—were "discovered," and it became possible to study the characteristics of elements as they combined with each other. Hundreds of diverse laws about the combining properties of the elements were discovered. Because elements seemed to combine in an orderly fashion, some thought that the elements could be arranged in a pattern that would make the scattered laws of atomic chemistry meaningful. One scientist who thought this was Dmitri Mendeleev, a young Russian who wrote the name and atomic weight of all the elements then known on a series of cards—one element to a card. By arranging and rearranging the cards time and again, he finally hit on a meaningful pattern, now well known as the periodic table of elements. Mendeleev's procedure is an example of how information is structured by the mind so that it both accurately portrays nature and is understandable. It is important to understand that the periodic arrangement of the elements is subject to different interpretations. Mendeleev's interpretation may not be the only one possible, or even the best (and there may not even *be* a natural order), but the order suggested does help us to understand one part of the physical universe and seems compatible with the "real" nature.

Conceptual cognitive psychology has much in common with Mendeleev's structuring of elements. The raw observation of how knowledge is acquired, stored, and used lacks formal structure. Like physical scientists, cognitive scientists seek out schemes that will be intellectually compatible and scientifically valid.

Cognitive Models

As we have said, conceptual science, including cognitive psychology, is metaphorical in character. Models of nature, including cognitive models, are abstract organizational ideas derived from inferences based on observations. The structure of the elements may be classified into a periodic table, as Mendeleev suggested, but it is important to realize that the classification scheme is a metaphor. Asserting that conceptual science is metaphorical does not reduce its utility. Indeed, one of the purposes of building models is to make observations more comprehensible. Other needs are served by conceptual science; it provides researchers with a structure within which specific hypotheses can be tested, and it enables them to predict events on the basis of the model. These functions were elegantly served by the periodic table. On the basis of the arrangements of elements in it, scientists, rather than performing the endless helter-skelter experiments involving chemical combinations, could accurately hypothesize chemical combination and displacement laws. Furthermore, elements not yet discovered could be predicted and their characteristics inferred, even though no direct physical proof of their properties existed. As you approach cognitive models, keep in mind the analogy of Mendeleev's model, since cognitive models, like those in the physical sciences, are based on inferential logic and are useful in our understanding of cognitive psychology.

In summary, a model is based on inferences drawn from observations. Its purpose is to provide an understandable representation of the character of the observation and, in developing hypotheses, to aid in making predictions. We now consider a few models in cognitive psychology.

We begin our discussion of cognitive models on an austere level, dividing the cognitive process into only three components: the detection of stimuli, the storage and transformation of stimuli, and the production of responses.

$$\text{Detection of stimuli} \quad \rightarrow \quad \text{Storage, transformation of stimuli} \quad \rightarrow \quad \text{Production of responses}$$

This sequential processing model, close to the S-R model mentioned earlier, was frequently used in some form in the early conceptualizations of psychological processes. Even though the model seems to express the basic stages of cognitive psychology, it offers so little detail that it does little to enhance our understanding of the processes. It is equally inadequate in its capacity to inspire hypotheses or predict behavior. This primitive model is roughly analogous to early conceptualization of the universe as being composed of earth, air, fire, and water. The taxonomy does represent one way to view the phenomena, but it belies their complexity.

One of the first and most frequently cited cognitive models dealt with memory. In 1890 James expanded the concept of memory to include primary memory and secondary memory. Primary memory was hypothesized to deal with immediate events, and secondary memory with permanent, "indestructible" vestiges of experience. The model was as follows:

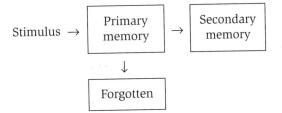

A later revision of the model by Waugh and Norman (1965) satisfied many of the demands for an acceptable model. It is comprehensible and it is a source of hypothesis and prediction; however, it, too, is overly simplistic. Can *all* human memory processes and storage systems be accurately described by this model? Hardly, and it was inevitable that more complex models would evolve.

A modified and expanded model of the Waugh and Norman model is shown in Figure 1.4. Notice that a new storage system and several new routines have been added. However, even this model is incomplete and needs to be expanded.

During the emergence of cognitive psychology, model making became a favorite pastime of psychologists, and some of their creations are truly wonderful. The common solution to the problem of too simple models is to add another box, another routine, another storage system, another component to be tested and analyzed. Such creative effort seems justified in light of what we presently know about the vastness of the human cognitive system.

By now you may have concluded that model making in cognitive psychology is as out of control as was the sorcerer's apprentice. That conclusion is not entirely justified,

FIGURE 1.4

Modified Waugh and Norman cognitive model. Adapted from Waugh and Norman (1965).

for the task is so vast—analysis of how information is detected, represented, and transformed as knowledge, and how knowledge is used—that, were we to confine our conceptual metaphors to simplistic models, we would fail to elucidate the involved and comprehensive domain of cognitive psychology.

These models have one element in common: they are based on a sequence of events. A stimulus is presented, we detect it through the sensory system, we store and transform it in memory, and we react to it. Models of human cognition bear some similarities to the sequential steps involved in computer processing; indeed, the patterning of human information processing was constructed along the lines of a computer metaphor.

The Computer Metaphor and Human Cognition

Although Pascal, Descartes, and others dreamed of computing machines centuries ago, it was not until the development of computers about fifty years ago that practical machines were invented. These machines gained enormous acceptance and are presently used in virtually every aspect of modern life. Curiously, they also have had an impact on the way humans view their own minds, in addition to being an important tool for scientists interested in the study of cognition. Originally, such devices were thought to be wonderful number crunchers capable of performing a multitude of complex mathematical operations in a fraction of the time required by humans. However, it was quickly discovered that they could perform functions that resembled human problem solving. This discovery hinted that the long-awaited intelligent robot might be just around the corner, and perhaps, ominously, Aldous Huxley's "brave new world" might be more of a reality than originally feared. (For further discussion of thinking machines, refer to the final chapter of this book.)

In 1955 Herbert Simon, a professor at the Carnegie Institute of Technology (now Carnegie Mellon University) in Pittsburgh, is said to have announced to his class, "Over Christmas, Allen Newell and I invented a thinking machine." Shortly after that announcement, Simon and Newell's computer (dubbed "Johniac" after John von Neumann[4]) was capable of working out a proof of a mathematical theorem. The real breakthrough, however, was conceptual rather than computational. Simon and Newell had shown not only that a computer was capable of simulating one limited aspect of human thought but also that computers and their multifarious internal networks could provide a model of the way humans think. Although Simon and Newell pursued topics of problem solving at a more general level, and not a theory of neural or electronic mechanisms for information processing, the idea that computers could model human cognition greatly excited psychologists. A new metaphor had been born.

The logic of the new metaphor was "Give me a dozen healthy computers, with their own special programs, and I will produce the thinking of a doctor, lawyer, merchant, and even beggarman and thief." In effect, if computer programs could operate according to the same rules and procedures as the human mind, then they should be able to perform functions indistinguishable from those performed by humans. Computers could do things that appear to be intelligent, thus the label "artificial intelligence" or "AI." The marriage between cognitive psychologists and computer scientists seemed destined for

---

[4]John von Neumann was a mathematician who authored the notion that it was possible to store a program within a computer's internal memory, thus avoiding reprogramming each time a procedure was to be performed. See Chapter 16 for more details.

Allen Newell (left) 1927–1992 and Herbert Simon. Pioneers in the field of artificial intelligence and "thinking machines."

utter bliss. Psychologists could provide the rules and procedures we follow when we perceive, store information in memory, and think, while computer scientists could write programs that would mimic these functions.

However, the honeymoon was less than euphoric. Unfortunately, what computers do well (perform high-speed mathematical functions and abide by rule-governed logic) humans do poorly, relatively speaking. And what humans do well (form generalizations, make inferences, understand complex patterns, and have emotions) computers do stupidly, or not at all. For example, if we ask you to find the square root of 2.19 by hand, it will probably take you several minutes; a computer can solve the problem in milliseconds. However, if we ask you if you know Connie Diamond, who lives in Ridgecrest, is studying for a master's degree in cellular biology, you might say, "Yes, I know who you're talking about, but her name is Connie Jewel and she lives on Crestview and she's working on a Ph.D. in physiology." Computers just can't do that . . . yet.

However, the marriage is not over, and a second generation of cognitive-computer scientists is working toward building computers that look something like a brain. These are complete with layers of interconnected electronic surrogate neurons, whose organizational "hardware" mimics the "wetware" of the brain, and they contain programs that mimic the functions of organic neural networks. These new computers are sometimes called neural networks and act more like humans than the earlier versions. They are able to make generalizations and understand complex visual patterns, are slow at math, and make witless mistakes. Although they still do not have emotions, they are nevertheless a mark of success.

The computer analogy has lurked in the background of cognitive psychology for most of its brief history. Occasionally the analogy got mixed up: computers were not modeled after the way humans thought, but rather people began to think that the brain was really a very complex computer. We now know that there are fundamental differences between the internal workings of computers and the internal workings of the brain. Nevertheless, the computer metaphor continues to have a profound and generally positive impact on the development of cognitive psychology.

Cognitive Science

Three powerful areas of scientific development—computer science, neuroscience, and cognitive psychology—converge to create a new science called cognitive science. The boundaries between these disciplines are sometimes hard to distinguish: some cognitive psychologists may be closer to neuroscience, others to computer science. One thing is clear, however; the science of human cognition is undergoing a radical transformation as a result of major changes in computer technology and brain science. Our subject is cognitive psychology, but we will make full use of recent discoveries in neuroscience and computer science that illuminate the cognitive properties of the human species.

As with most emerging sciences, new models appear frequently. Some stand the test of empirical research; others do not. One model has received an unusual amount of attention. This model is known by several interchangeable labels, including **parallel distributed processing (PDP), connectionism,** and **neural network systems.** The main features of this model are described next and in Chapter 2.

Neuroscience and Cognitive Psychology

During the early stages of cognitive psychology, little attention was given to physiological psychology or neuroanatomy. It was quite enough to establish a new way of conceptualizing the mind, and besides, the **information-processing model** and computer metaphor seemed adequate. Moreover, students of neurophysiology and related areas seemed to be absorbed with microscopic structures bearing little resemblance to broad cognitive topics such as perception, memory, and thinking.

Much of the early information on the brain and its functions resulted from head traumas incurred during wars and accidents. For example, during World War I, neurosurgeons treating victims of shrapnel wounds to the brain learned a great deal about the specialized functions of that organ (for example, which areas were associated with vision, speech, hearing, and so on) as well as the general functions. The central issue neurologists struggled with was whether the brain was a holistic organ, with operations distributed throughout its infrastructure, or whether activities were localized and tied to specific regions. For example, did learning a specific act take place in a localized area of the brain, or was learning distributed throughout many parts of the brain? Among the most prominent of the scientists who wrestled with these issues was Karl Lashley (1929). In his experiments, Lashley destroyed specific parts of the brains of rats that had learned to run a maze. He showed that performance declined according to the total amount of the brain destroyed but was not related to the location of the lesions (see Chapter 2 for more on Lashley's work).

Recently, progress has been made in the field of neuroscience, which comprises both the structural aspects of the brain and its peripheral components, as well as the functional aspects. In the 1960s researchers found structural elements that would later have a direct impact on cognitive psychology. Some of these discoveries were made at the Johns Hopkins School of Medicine by Vernon Mountcastle, whose work dealt with the **cerebral cortex**—the top layer of the brain, thought to be involved in higher mental functions. Mountcastle (1979) discovered that connections among the cells of the cortex, or **neurons,** are many times more numerous than had been thought. (Neurons are the basic cells of the nervous system that conduct neural information.) Perhaps most intriguing was the discovery that the system of neural connections appeared to be distributed in a parallel array in addition to serial pathways. The network of parallel neural connections seems to range over a large territory, with functions occurring at the same time in several locations. This type of processing is in contrast to serial or sequential processing, in which one nerve impulse is passed on to another nerve, and then on to another. Mountcastle writes, "These connective subsets are distributed systems, each composed of modular elements in several or many brain regions, connected in both parallel and serial arrays. They form the neuronal pathways for distributed and parallel processing within the brain" (cited in Restak, 1988, p. 22). The way the brain functions, according to this view, is that processing networks are distributed throughout the cortex rather than localized. Thus, there is no master **homunculus** guiding the activities of neural processing, or "ghost neuron" concealed in the background to oversee action. Localized parts of the brain associated with vision, speech, motor actions, and so on are specialized only in the sense that they receive inputs and make outputs associated with those functions.

Additionally, some studies have found that many functions are actually distributed throughout the brain. Thus, a psychological function, such as retrieving something from memory, is distributed throughout the brain and accomplished through parallel routines at several sites.

These discoveries seemed to offer a solution to one of the toughest problems faced by the young science of cognition: how relatively slow neurotransmission can produce such diverse and fast cognition. Consider this example: A skilled pianist is given an intricate piece of music to play, and she does so with dazzling dexterity. If the "neuro-machinery" operated in a sequential way—an impulse from one neuron jumping to another and then on to another—by the time the pianist would be able to respond to one note, it would be well past the time she should respond to another. Cognitive psychologists study just such phenomena and have discovered that the interstroke interval (ISI), the time elapsed between the playing of one note and the playing of a second, is about 50 milliseconds.[5] Compensating for the sluggish neurosystem with which we are all endowed, we process information (such as notes on a page that are to be translated into finger movements) in several different subsystems, all acting more or less at the same time. The simultaneous processing of information in several subsystems suggests a parallel processing of information: both cognitive psychologists and neuroscientists recognize this and have incorporated the notion of parallel processing into their models of psychology and neurology—a topic to be considered in the next section.

With the beginning of the twenty-first century, cognitive psychology seems poised to make another paradigm shift. While the traditional topics of perception, memory, language, problem solving, and thinking and the method of experimental analysis are still central to the cognitive story, the use of neurocognitive imagery promises to become a major means (if not *the* major means) of investigating cognitive functions in this century. The reasons for this possible shift in emphasis are easy to see (no pun intended!). Imaging techniques, which have been developing very rapidly in the past several decades, allow us to see deeper and more clearly into the brain—and the brain is believed to be the engine of cognition. It follows then that to find the source of cognition and understand its functioning is to gain insight to the age-old questions of how humans perceive, store information in memory, use information in making decisions about everyday life, and formulate activities consistent with our thoughts. As we shall

[5]One millisecond (msec.) equals 1/1000 second. Fifty milliseconds equal 1/20 second, or about the time of an eye blink.

discover throughout this book, virtually every area of cognition has been investigated with neurocognitive techniques. These techniques, MRI, PET, EEG, and the like (see Chapter 2), show not only the structures of cognition but also the processes involved. And, in many instances, the results have been remarkable. While this trend is likely to continue and grow, it is important to recognize the central themes in cognition mentioned previously. At the end of each chapter we will highlight how cognitive neuroscience has informed those particular topic areas.

Parallel Distributed Processing (PDP) and Cognitive Psychology

Many people have been associated with this model of human cognition, but David Rumelhart and James McClelland have done the most to formalize the theory (see especially their two-volume *Parallel Distributed Processing*, 1986). There are many components to the theory; this section addresses only the basic ones.

Essentially, the model is neurally inspired, concerned with the kind of processing mechanism that is the human mind. Is it a type of von Neumann computer—a Johniac—in which information is processed in sequential steps? Alternatively, might the human mind process information in a massively distributed, mutually interactive parallel system in which various activities are carried out simultaneously through excitation and/or inhibition of neural cells? PDPers opt for the latter explanation. "These [PDP] models assume that information processing takes place through the interactions of a large number of simple processing elements called units, each sending excitatory and inhibitory signals to other units" (McClelland, Rumelhart, & Hinton, 1986, p. 10). These units may stand for possible guesses about letters in a string of words or notes on a score. In other situations, the units may stand for possible goals and actions, such as reading a particular letter or playing a specific note. Proponents suggest that the PDP models are concerned with the description of the internal structure of larger units of cognitive activity, such as reading, perceiving, processing sentences, and so on. The theory is comparable to atomic theory in physics; the basic units correspond to subatomic particles, which may document the internal structures of atoms that form the constituents of larger units of chemical structure. By studying the basic units, we may better understand the properties of larger units of psychological activity.

David Rumelhart (left) and James McClelland. Formalized the neurally inspired PDP model.

One of the appeals of the PDP model is that it is tied to neuroanatomical functioning. It has been reasonably well established that human thought takes place in the brain, which consists of tens of billions of interconnected neurons. These relatively simple neurons, which interact with hundreds of thousands of other neurons, are basic to the complex processing of information. While most human brains are capable of involved thought, the nature of neural transmission places constraints on the speed with which processing can take place. PDP modelers consider this factor in their theory and have developed an explanation as to how complex processes, such as the visual identification of a common object, can take place in a short period of time. As an example of the types of constraints imposed by the brain on the processing of information, consider the speed with which neural transmission takes place. Neural transmission is a relatively sluggish, "noisy" affair (to use computer argot), with some neurons requiring 3 milliseconds to fire.[6] If neural activities, which logically underlie all cognitive functions, require a relatively long period of time to function, then what processing mechanism would allow us to make complex decisions in a brief period of time?

Let's illustrate the point made earlier. Suppose you are shopping in a supermarket, actively thinking about the ingredients you must select to make a Greek salad, and out of the corner of your eye you see and recognize your professor of cognitive psychology. How long does the recognition process take? Not long at all. Experiments conducted under well-controlled laboratory conditions show that from the onset of a complex visual stimulus until the recognition and response to that stimulus, about 300 milliseconds elapse—less than one-third of a second! How is that possible, given the slothful speed of neurotransmission? The answer suggests that the brain processes visual information, as well as other stimuli, by means of massive parallelism.

The brain does not store memory in any single neuron or probably even in any local set, but it does store memory in an entire ensemble of neurons distributed throughout several parts of the brain. If two neurons are simultaneously activated, the bond between them is strengthened. On the other hand, if one is activated and another inhibited, the bond is weakened. Memory in such a system, then, is in the pattern of activated and inhibited networks distributed throughout the system rather than located in a specific subsystem. One theory of PDP views memory and retrieval of information from memory in a model that is similar to the way neural networks work.

Thus far, PDP models seem consistent with the basic structure and processing of the brain, but that alone is not sufficient reason to accept PDP as a psychological theory. Its importance as a psychological theory will ultimately be tested by observations that will either confirm or deny the validity of the model. At this time the model is creating new excitement among its advocates, who are working toward cognitive theories based on massive parallel processing. More is reported on PDP in other parts of this book.

Evolutionary Cognitive Psychology

A broad new field of inquiry into the psychological nature of humankind has emerged within the past decade or so—**evolutionary cognitive psychology.** This field is based on

---

[6]The time required to close a circuit in a computer is approximately 1 million times faster and is measured in nanoseconds. A nanosecond is one-billionth of a second.

the idea that cognition—perception, memory, language, thinking, and the like—are best understood within the context of human physical and social evolution. The approach is conspicuously Darwinian in foundation, but it is beyond the nineteenth-century scheme in that all cognition, as well as brain structures that undergird the process, are viewed within the framework of biological evolution and universal environmental forces. Thus, all major topics discussed in this book, from sensation, to perception, to pattern analysis, to language, to problem solving, to thinking, and so on, are interpreted in terms of the long-term biological and evolutionary history of the species. Take any common event, say the chance encounter with an acquaintance of the opposite sex. Your ability to perceive, evaluate, and remember his or her characteristics is based on our long-standing evolutionary history at work. Thus, cognition (for example, memory) and emotions (for example, lust) are understandable in humans' quest for procreation and survival.

Among the proponents of an evolutionary view of cognition are the anthropologists John Tooby and Leda Cosmides and a number of well-known cognitive psychologists such as Steve Pinker and Roger Shepard who, in general, fault traditional psychology (including cognitive psychology, behaviorism, clinical psychology, and other social sciences) for studying psychological phenomena in isolation. Because of this narrow view of psychology (and other social sciences) theories and attributes are developed that are inconsistent with the long view of evolution in which all species, including our own, are the consequence of millions of years of cohabitation with the physical and environmental effects of the universe. The result of this narrow-minded view of human psychology is that it leads to the invention of psychological processes that are inconsistent with what is known about evolution and adaptation.

A major premise of evolutionary psychology is the supposition that there are universal human cognitive attributes and that these common and widely shared attributes of the mind are the result of evolved psychological mechanisms, not a matter of social interaction. While social actions are undoubtedly powerful forces in the daily lives of all creatures who inhabit the planet, they may be better understood by looking at the deep, underlying determinants of behavior and thought that are imbedded in the long evolution of sensory, perceptual, cognitive, and emotional reaction to consistent environmental forces such as gravity, reflected light, temperature changes, and other universally experienced phenomena, which were the conditions under which all organic creatures happened.

In a section entitled "Evolution of a Mesh between Principles of the Mind and Regularities of the World" Roger Shepard (1987) formulates the theme of evolutionary psychology:

> I seek general psychological laws that underlie all specific mental processes and behaviors, despite their apparent variation between individuals, cultures, or species. Moreover, I seek an evolutionary origin of such general psychological laws in the properties of the world that have been so pervasive and enduring as to be relevant for a broad spec-

*M*ind and world . . . have evolved together, and in consequence are something of a mutual fit.
—*William James*

trum of species. I reason that in the evolutionary long run, these general properties of the world would tend to be even more deeply internalized than the more local and transitory properties peculiar to any particular ecological niche. Each individual would then not have to learn about each property *de novo* by trial and possible fatal error. (p. 254)

Shepard goes on to identify several enduring regularities of the world that appear to have been internalized over the long course of evolution and directs the interested reader to the original sources. One could rationally argue that evolutionary cognitive psychology has been around for a long time, and indeed, in the basic writings of Charles Darwin and other nineteenth-century psychobiologists one may find ample support for the idea.

SUMMARY

The purpose of this chapter is to set the stage for the rest of the book by introducing you to cognitive psychology. Many important and varied aspects of cognitive psychology are discussed in this chapter. Some of the main features include the following:

1 Cognitive psychology is concerned with how we acquire, transform, represent, store, and retrieve knowledge, and with how that knowledge directs what we attend to and how we respond.

2 One commonly adopted model is the information-processing model, which assumes that information is processed through a series of stages, each of which performs a unique function.

3 Two questions raised by the information-processing model are:
   (a) What are the stages through which information is processed?
   (b) In what form is knowledge represented?

4 Cognitive psychology uses research and theoretical approaches from major areas of psychology, including neuroscience, perception, pattern perception, attention and consciousness, memory, representation of knowledge, imagery, language, developmental psychology, thinking and concept formation, human intelligence, and artificial intelligence.

5 Historical antecedents of modern cognitive psychology include Greek philosophy; eighteenth-century empiricism; nineteenth-century structuralism; and the neocognitive revolution influenced by modern developments in communication theory, linguistics, memory research, and computer technology.

6 The main theme of the cognitive revolution is that internal processes are the subject matter of psychology. This is in contrast with behaviorism, which proposes that response or behavior is the true subject matter of psychology.

7 Conceptual science is a useful metaphor devised by humans to help comprehend "reality." Psychologists devise conceptual models in cognitive psychology with the aim of developing a system that reflects the nature of human perception, thought, and understanding of the world.

8 Cognitive models are based on observations that describe the structure and processes of cognition. Model building can make observations more comprehensible.

9   The information-processing model has dominated cognitive psychology, but other models, occurring in computer science and in neuroscience, have been combined with cognitive psychology to form cognitive science.

10   Parallel distributed processing (PDP) is a model of cognition in which information is thought to be processed in a way similar to neurological networks. Those networks suggest that neural processing occurs simultaneously, in different regions, with simple connections being either strengthened or weakened.

11   Evolutionary cognitive psychology is an approach to cognition that draws on evolutional psychology and biological psychology in a unitary system of knowledge.

KEY WORDS

artificial intelligence	knowledge
cerebral cortex	long-term memory
cognitive map	nativists
cognitive model	neuron
conceptual science	neuronetwork systems
connectionism	neuroscience model
consciousness	parallel distributed processing (PDP)
empiricists	perception
evolutionary cognitive psychology	representation of knowledge
homunculus	schema
information-processing model	short-term memory
internal representation	working memory
isomorphism	

RECOMMENDED READINGS

● Howard Gardner has written a lively history of cognitive science in *The Mind's New Science*, which is highly recommended. Karl Pribram, a neurophysiologist, has a thoughtful article in *American Psychologist* entitled "The Cognitive Revolution and Mind/Brain Issues." Posner (ed.), *Foundations of Cognitive Science*, and Neisser, *Cognition and Reality: Principles and Implications of Cognitive Psychology*, will serve to introduce several issues in cognitive psychology. The best source to gain a perspective on American psychology, including the emergence of cognitive psychology, is Ernest Hilgard's *Psychology in America: A Historical Survey*. A good account of the schism between behaviorism and cognitive psychology can be found in the lively book by Bernard Baars, *The Cognitive Revolution in Psychology*. Interesting new views on adaptive cognition may be found in Barkow, Cosmides, and Tooby, eds., *The Adapted Mind: Evolutionary Psychology and the Generation of Culture*, and Gazzaniga, ed., *The Cognitive Neurosciences* (especially Section X) and *The New Cognitive Neurosciences*. Some useful entries may be found in *The MIT Encyclopedia of the Cognitive Sciences*, edited by Wilson and Keil.

C H A P T E R **2**

Cognitive Neuroscience

hmmm...?

- **Exploring the Brain**
- **Logbook: The Twenty-First Century—Brain Sciences**
- **Mind–Body Issues**
- **Cognitive Neuroscience**
  Cognitive Psychology and Neuroscience
- **The Nervous System**
  The Neuron
  The Brain: From Localization to Mass Action
  The Anatomy of the Brain
- **Neurophysiological Sensing Techniques**
  CT Scans
  PET Scans
  MRI and fMRI
  MEG
  TMS
  Research Using Imaging Techniques: An Example
- **A Tale of Two Hemispheres**
  Cognitive Psychology and Brain Science

1. What is the mind–body issue?
2. What is the basic tenet of cognitive neuroscience?
3. Why has cognition turned to the neurosciences?
4. Identify the major parts of the central nervous system.
5. Describe the basic anatomy and functions of the brain.
6. How did early studies of the brain lead to an understanding of functions and location?
7. What are the imaging techniques in use today?
8. How has split-brain research increased our understanding of cognitive neuroscience?

*I*n all of modern science, no field is developing more rapidly, attracting more interest, and promising more insight into ourselves than the study of the nervous system. Whether you are a beginning student who is intrigued by what you read about the brain in newspapers and magazines and see on television programs, or a science student with experience in conducting experiments and reading scientific articles, this . . . [chapter] . . . invites you to join in learning about the most interesting and important organ in the world.

—*Gordon M. Shepherd*

Exploring the Brain

Cognitive neuroscience is the brain-based approach to cognitive psychology. Developments in cognitive neuroscience have changed the way cognitive psychology is being done at the beginning of the twenty-first century.

Humans have always wondered what was over the next hill, what was in the valley, and where the river began. And, in the past, the great explorers of the world—Columbus, Lewis and Clark, and Erhardt—have seen wondrous new things. Today, scientists are exploring an even more fundamental territory than the geography of the earth, one that it is far more intimate, is far more enigmatic, and is far more stubborn in giving up its secrets. That world is the domain of the human brain.

While the dimensions of the globe are vast and its climate complex, the brain is small in size (its gelatinous mass weighs only about three pounds) and its processing capacity is enormous. We can state it simply: The intricate network of neurons in the human brain and their interconnections make up the most complicated system known to humankind. The capacity of the human brain for the computational analysis of sensory signals and the understanding of itself and the universe are staggeringly complex. Everything we experience—from love to hate, and everything we do, from swinging a baseball bat to playing classical guitar—arises out of the activity of neurons. Let us look into this wonderful computational system and its physical and functional properties.

While the gross geography of the human brain has been known for a very long time (it is likely that ancient people saw far more human brains spilled out before them than we do), the specific geography and functions of the brain are still being reported in the scientific literature. This exploration of the new world of the brain has been aided by imaging technology that allows us to see through the solid wall of the skull. Like the ancient mariner who charted dangerous seas, safe lagoons, and "widow-maker" reefs, cartographers of the mind are mapping areas in which visual processing, semantic analysis, auditory interpretation, and a myriad of other cognitive functions take place. This chapter is a logbook of the geography, maps, and processes of the brain.

Logbook: The Twenty-First Century—Brain Sciences

Cognitive Neuroscience. Much of the excitement in cognitive psychology is due to new developments in a discipline that combines cognitive psychology and neuro-

*T*he brain is the last and greatest frontier . . . the most complex thing we have yet discovered in our universe.

—*James Watson*

science, a specialty called **cognitive neuroscience.** The scientific field of cognitive neuroscience received its name in the late 1970s in the back seat of a New York taxi. Michael Gazzaniga, a leader in "split-brain" research, was riding with the great cognitive psychologist George A. Miller on the way to a dinner meeting for scientists from Rockefeller University and Cornell University who were to study how the brain enables the mind . . . a topic in need of a name. Out of that taxi ride came the term *cognitive neuroscience.* Before discussing the details of cognitive neuroscience, let's briefly consider the larger question of how cognitive neuroscience fits into the mind–body dichotomy contemplated by scientists and philosophers for centuries and recently reexamined by cognitive neuroscientists equipped with a dazzling mélange of scientific instruments.

Mind–Body Issues

Everything psychological is simultaneously neurological. Remarkably, we humans occupy these two worlds at the same time.

The first is the physical world of things that exist in time and space. These things have physical properties that follow physical laws, such as the laws of gravity, which govern falling bodies; the laws of centrifugal force, which control the action of rotating objects; or the neurological laws, which regulate the transmission of an impulse from one neuron to another (neurotransmission).

The second world is populated by memories, ideas, thoughts, images, and so on. These are also governed by laws, although sometimes finding them is more difficult than finding those that govern the physical world.

Because, traditionally, we have set out to find rules in the two worlds using different techniques, many philosophers and scientists have thought that these worlds are fundamentally different and fundamentally separate. This dichotomous conclusion is based on the assumption that one world is focused on the physical universe, or body, while the other is centered on the mental universe, or mind. The separation of mind from body is intuitively logical, or self-evident, but the interaction between the worlds is equally self-evident. Your mental inability to concentrate on a test may be related to the physical harm you inflicted on your body at last night's toga party.

Some philosophers of science argue that the only real world is the world of the mind and that the physical world is an illusion. Conversely, some argue that the only real world is the physical world and that the mind is ultimately a function of the brain. A frequent criticism of the latter position is that it robs humanity of its lofty, idealistic spirit.

One basic problem the mind–body dualists have is trying to figure out how the mind is connected to the body and vice versa. There are various ideas about the connection.

The following is a succinct interpretation of the **mind–body issue.** When we talk of *mind,* we are talking about the things that are done by the brain; for example, thinking, holding things in memory, perceiving, judging, as well as being in love, feeling pain, plotting schemes to rule the world, composing music, and making jokes. The mind, in this sense, comprises the processes carried out by the brain.

The brain has physical properties (discussed in some detail later in this chapter) that are in a constant state of flux. The brain never rests totally but is always teeming with electrochemical activity. However, the general architecture; the network of neurons; the location of major landmarks on the cortex; the areas of the brain that are related to functions such as sensory feelings, motor control, vision, and so on are generally stable and change little. What takes place in the brain—the brain processes—changes more readily. Minds tend to be more dynamic than brains. We can change our thoughts rapidly and without much obvious structural (architectural) change in the brain, even though the pattern of electrochemical transmissions may be extremely changeable. Our conscious thoughts may shift swiftly from the ridiculous to the sublime, from inner space to outer space, and from sacred to profane in less time than it takes to read this sentence. The physical changes in neural activity cause changes in the mind.

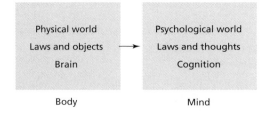

However, even though minds tend to be dynamic, they also have their consistencies; our general mode of thinking, our attitudes toward religion, our aspirations, our view of the family, and so on are reasonably stable. This chapter is about both mind and brain and about how cognitive psychology and neuroscience have, after centuries of debate, for the first time in the intellectual history of our species, shed some light on the topic that is both reliable and scientifically valid.

Our recent, and unusual, attention to the brain and cognition is based on a fundamental tenet: All cognition is the result of neurological activity. That means that pattern recognition, reading, attention, memory, imagery, consciousness, thinking, and the use of language, as well as all other forms of cognition, are a reflection of the activity of neurons, mostly those that are concentrated in the brain's cerebral cortex. Because the things we do—speak, solve problems, operate machines, and so on—are based on cognition, all behavior is likewise predicated on neural activity.

Cognitive Neuroscience

Out of neuroscience and cognitive psychology a new science has been fashioned called **cognitive neuroscience,** defined as "the study of the relationships between neuroscience and cognitive psychology, especially those theories of the mind dealing with memory, sensation and perception, problem solving, language processing, motor functions, and cognition." Neuroscientists are scientists who study neuroscience, or the branch of science that encompasses the study of neuroanatomy, neurophysiology, brain functions, and related psychological and computer models. Because of the efforts of neuroscientists, hypothetical constructs such as memory types and language processing are no longer so intangible but seem to have specific neurophysiological correlates. Furthermore, microscopic structures of the brain, when viewed as neural networks, seem to be related to larger components of human cognition, such as memory, perception, problem solving, and the like.

Perhaps another generation will view such gross demonstrations of cortical neural activity, which correspond to equally gross categories of thinking, as a primitive attempt to use knowledge from two previously disparate sciences to understand the central mechanisms of human cognition. This early work will be remembered as a turning point in both cognitive psychology and neuroscience, and the exciting part for contemporary students of cognition is that they will witness and, in some cases, create a new science of the mind. It's a wonderful time to be alive!

Cognitive Psychology and Neuroscience

There are several reasons contemporary psychologists are using information and techniques from neuroscience and neuroscientists are using cognitive psychology. These include:

- *The demand to find physical evidence for theoretical structures of the mind.* The search for the properties of the human mind stretches back to the beginning of history, if not before, but has been constantly frustrated because of the tenuous nature of the supporting evidence. The development of sophisticated equipment has made it possible to materially identify the presence of important psychological processes such as language, perception, form identification, thinking, memory, and other cognitive functions.

- *The need on the part of neuroscientists to relate their findings to more comprehensive models of the brain and cognition.* Even if it were possible to identify every minute detail of neurological functions, this would tell us little about the network and systems properties that are essential to the understanding of cognitive effects and the way we humans perform everyday activities, from the profound to the profane.

- *The clinical goal to find correlates between brain pathology and behavior.* For generations neurologists have been concerned with the way in which brain traumas, lesions, infarctions, thrombosis, and tumors affect behavior and with the procedures that might alleviate related symptoms. These concerns require a precise understanding of brain functioning and psychology. Conversely, psychologists interested in the psychological treatment of organically impaired patients require better understanding of the physical causes of such behavior.

- *The increased involvement of neurological functions in models of the mind.* Specifically, cognitive psychologists interested in parallel distributed processing (PDP), also called *connectionism* or *neuronetwork systems,* are interested in finding psychological models consistent with neurological structures and functions.

Evolution has encased the brain in a rock-hard vault of bone, wrapped it in layers of tough membrane, and cushioned it in a viscous bath of cerebral spinal fluid. These protective shields pose particularly difficult challenges for scientists who would like to observe human brain activity directly.

—*Gordon Bower*

- *The work of computer scientists who are attempting to simulate human cognition and intelligence by developing computers that behave in a way that is similar to the way in which the human brain behaves.* These approaches to brain and computer are sometimes called *neuronet architectures.* They include the subspecialty of **perceptrons,**[1] which is the simulation of neural networks in computer architecture. Such developments of computer architecture and function require detailed understanding of brain architecture and function.
- *The development of techniques that allow scientists to peer into the human brain and that reveal structures and processes never before seen.* These include positron emission tomography (PET) scans, computed axial tomography (CT) scans, magnetic resonance imaging (MRI), and electroencephalography (EEG). These largely noninvasive tools are possible because of advances in computer technology and brain-scanning techniques.

Because neuroscience has become increasingly important in the study of cognitive psychology, an introduction to some of the elementary aspects of human neurology follows. We start from the elementary part of the central nervous system (CNS) and build our way up to the brain and its functions.

The Nervous System

The **central nervous system (CNS)** consists of the spinal cord and brain. Our discussion focuses on the brain, with particular attention to the structures and processes that bear on neurally inspired cognitive models.

The basic building block of the nervous system is the **neuron,** a specialized cell that transmits neural information throughout the nervous system. The human brain is densely packed with neurons. Some estimates place the number at more than 100 billion (about the number of stars in the Milky Way), each of which is capable of receiving and passing nerve impulses to sometimes thousands of other neurons and is more complex than any other known system, terrestrial or extraterrestrial. Each cubic inch of the human cerebral cortex contains about ten thousand miles of nerve fibers, which connect the cells together (Blakemore, 1977). Figure 2.1 presents a view of the tangled mass of neurons in the hu-

---

[1]The word *perceptron* was first used in 1957 by a Cornell Aeronautical Laboratory scientist, Frank Rosenblatt, who built one of the first neuralnets. In 1968 Minsky and Papert published a book entitled *Perceptrons.*

A schematic drawing of brain cells.
By the renowned Spanish anatomist
Santiago Ramón y Cajal, who won
the Nobel Prize for his pioneering
neurological work, this drawing of brain
cells was made from careful observations
through a microscope and shows the
complex network of nerve cells in
the human brain.

man brain. Compare this drawing with the diagram of a neuron (see Figure 2.2), and try
to locate the dendrites and axons. At any given time, many of the cortical neurons are active, and it is thought that cognitive functions such as perceiving, thinking, awareness,
and memory are carried out by the simultaneous firing of neurons located throughout

Drawing of a neuron.

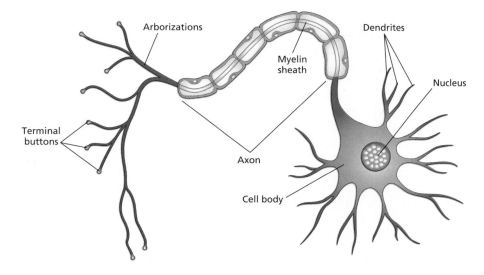

this complex neural network. It is difficult to imagine the vast number of neurons that are simultaneously activated and the intricate infrastructure that supports the system. Therein lies a paradox: Because the brain is so complex, it may never fully understand itself no matter how hard we try. The idea is something like an imaginary conference on dog physiology convened by dogs—no matter how hard they try to understand themselves, they can't quite do so. However pessimistic these thoughts may seem, an alternate view is that with new techniques the twenty-first century may solve most of the important issues of the mind–brain problem.

The Neuron

There are perhaps as many as a thousand different types of neurons (see Kandel, Schwartz, & Jessell, 1991), each of which carries out specialized functions in a variety of locations (see Figure 2.2). The main morphological regions of the neuron include:

1. The **dendrites,** which gather neural impulses from other neurons. Dendrites are highly arborized, suggesting the branches and twigs of a tree.
2. The **cell body,** where nutrients and waste products are filtered in and out through the permeable cell wall.
3. The **axon,** a long, tubular transmitting pathway in which signals from the cell body are passed along to other cells by means of junctures known as synapses. Axons in the brain may be tiny or may reach up to 1 meter or more in length. Large axons are surrounded by a fatty substance called the **myelin sheath,** which acts as a type of insulation for the neuron.
4. The **presynaptic terminals,** or buttons, found at the ends of the fine branches at the terminus of the axon. They are near the receptive surface of other neurons at a juncture, or synapse, and transmit information to other neurons.

At the **synapse** (see Figure 2.3) the axon terminal on one side releases a chemical, which acts on the membrane of the dendrite of another neuron. This chemical neurotransmitter changes the polarity, or electrical potential, of the receiving dendrite. A **neurotransmitter** is a chemical message that acts on the membrane of the dendrite of the receiving neuron. One class of neurotransmitter has an inhibitory effect, which tends to make the next neuron less likely to fire. Another class has an excitatory effect, which makes the next neuron more likely to fire. Currently, as many as 60 different chemical substances are known or suspected of functioning as neurotransmitters. Some seem to perform ordinary functions, such as maintaining the physical integrity of the cells; others, such as acetylcholine, seem to be related to learning and memory.

At birth, not all synaptic connections are complete, nor are all neurons completely myelinated; however, most neurons are present. In adulthood all synapses are grown in completely, and all appropriate cells are myelinated. In adults, synapses do not propagate. In adults, the average cell body and dendrite have the capacity to receive about one thousand synapses from other neurons, and the average axon has the capacity to send synapses to about one thousand other neurons.

The speed with which impulses move along the axon is related to size. In the smallest axon, neurotransmission creeps along at about 0.5 meter per second (about 1 mile

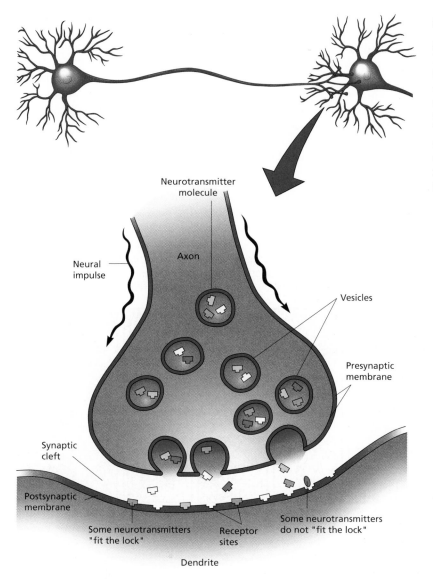

FIGURE 2.3

Synaptic transmission.
Neurotransmitters in
the axon of one neuron
are released into the
synaptic gap by means
of a neural impulse.
These neurotransmitters
stimulate receptor mole-
cules embedded in the
membrane of the post-
synaptic neuron.

per hour), while in the largest axons the rate is 120 meters per second (about 270 miles
per hour). (These speeds are many thousands of times slower than transmission and
switching speeds in a computer.) The brain is always alive with electrochemical activity,
and an excited neuron may fire as often as one thousand times per second. The more
times a neuron fires, the more effect it will have on the cells to which it synapses. These
firings can be observed by means of **electroencephalography (EEG)** and event-related
potential (ERP) recordings, which measure the electrical activities of regions of the

brain, or by single-cell recordings of activities in individual neurons of animals. In some instances (for example, the perception of a particular visual pattern), it is possible to detect single-cell firings and translate them into auditory signals. The sound is reminiscent of a distant machine gun firing rapid volleys.

Human knowledge is not localized in any single neuron. It is believed that human cognition takes place in the large patterns of neural activity that are distributed throughout the brain, function in parallel, and operate by means of excitatory or inhibitory connections, or "switches." A number of different theories, including the influential theory of Donald Hebb (1949), have been proposed that address the issue of the connection strengths between units (See Figure 2.4). In a simplified version of a connectionist model, when unit A and unit B are simultaneously excited, the strength of the connection between them increases. When units are not mutually excited, the connection be-

FIGURE 2.4

Neural networks from birth to 2 years of age. A human baby has almost all of its neurons at birth. However, the connections among neurons continue to grow, reaching astronomical numbers. A small sample is shown here.

Birth   1 month   2 months   6 months   15 months   2 years

Donald O. Hebb (1904–1985). Early researcher in neurocognition whose seminal ideas are frequently used in connectionistic models.

tween them weakens. It is no coincidence that the basic assumptions underlying these parallel distributed processing (PDP) models are similar to these neural models.

The Brain: From Localization to Mass Action

For centuries the brain has been a puzzle. It is less so now because of the tenacious work of numerous researchers over several decades, but it still has its secrets.

Early scholars believed that the brain had nothing to do with thought and perception. Aristotle, for one, ascribed such functions to the heart. Much later, the pseudoscience of **phrenology** held that character, personality, perception, intelligence, and so on were exactly localized in the brain (see Figure 2.5). Phrenologists believed that personal character, aptitude, and emotions could be measured by examining the bumps on the outer

FIGURE 2.5

Phrenological map of the brain.

*W*hen an axon of cell A is near enough to excite cell B . . . some growth or metabolic change takes place in both cells such that A's efficiency, as one of the cells firing B, is increased.

—*Donald O. Hebb*

surface of the skull (Figure 2.6). This view received early scientific support from neurologists, who discovered that some brain functions were related to specific areas.

As we learned in the first chapter, the focus of research in brain science for more than a century has been to find specific brain regions that correspond to specific behaviors. Important findings were made that confirmed the notion of **localization;** that is, some functions, such as motor activities, language processing, and sensing, are each associated with a specific area of the brain. The theory of localization reached its zenith among the phrenologists, who claimed to locate in the brain such attributes as generosity, mother love, secretiveness, combativeness, and even Republicanism. However, one French neurologist, Pierre Flourens, considered this a lot of nonsense. In his investigations, he excised portions of the human brain and examined the effect of the surgery on behavior. He concluded that motor and sensory functions are not a matter of simple localization in specific regions, as suggested by other researchers, but that these functions are also distributed in other parts of the brain. Traumas or injuries to the brain seemed to affect all higher functions equally. This position was later called the **aggregate field theory.**

Localization is contrasted with the view that the brain operates as a holistic organ, with cognitive processes distributed throughout. There is a compromise view, which seems consistent with the best knowledge in the field. It holds that some mental attributes are localizable to specific regions, or constellations of regions, within the brain. These include control of motor responses, sensory terminals, vision, and some language processing. However, many functions—especially higher-order cognitive processes such as memory, perception, thinking, and problem solving—are divided into subfunctions, which are distributed throughout the brain. We will briefly trace the development of this argument, beginning with an overview of the brain and its functions.

FIGURE 2.6

Early phrenological mechanical measuring device.

The Anatomy of the Brain

The anatomy of one hemisphere of the brain is shown in Figure 2.7. The brain is divided into two similar structures, the right and left **cerebral hemispheres.** The hemispheres are covered by the **cerebral cortex,** a thin, gray, moist material densely packed with the cell bodies of neurons and short unmyelinated axons. The cerebral cortex is only about 1.5 to 5 millimeters (¼ inch) thick. Because it is deeply convoluted, the surface area of the cortex is greater than it appears. The ridges between the folds are called **gyri** (singular, *gyrus*), and the grooves are called **sulci** (singular, *sulcus*). Deep and prominent sulci are called **fissures.** If the cortex were spread out, it would measure about 324 square inches, or about three times the amount seen on the surface. The convoluted cortex, with its characteristic walnut appearance, increases the surface area of the brain without increasing the size of the skull, a clever biological solution that enables the human animal to retain its mobility and thus survive, unencumbered by a monstrous cranium. It is within the cerebral cortex that human thought, sensation, language processes, and other cognitive functions take place.

The brain processes information contralaterally. That is, sensory information from the spinal cord (for example, the sense of touch) that enters the left side of the body

FIGURE 2.7

Structures of the forebrain, midbrain, and hindbrain.

Cerebral cortex
(controls thinking and sensing functions, voluntary movement)

Thalamus
(relays sensory information to cerebral cortex)

Midbrain
(reticular activating system: carries messages about sleep and arousal)

Corpus callosum
(relays information between the two cerebral hemispheres)

Hypothalamus
(regulates temperature, eating, sleeping, and endocrine system)

Pons
(relays information between cerebral cortex and cerebellum)

Pituitary gland
(master gland of the endocrine system)

Cerebellum
(coordinates fine muscle movement, balance)

Medulla
(regulates heartbeat, breathing)

Spinal cord
(relays nerve impulses between brain and body, controls simple reflexes)

crosses over and is initially processed in the right hemisphere. Also, the motor areas of each hemisphere control movements of the opposite side of the body.

The surface of each hemisphere is divided into four major sections, some of which are marked off by major convolutions or fissures. These four areas are the **frontal, temporal, parietal,** and **occipital** lobes. Although each lobe is associated with specific functions, it is likely that many functions are distributed throughout the brain.

The Cerebral Cortex.   The cerebral cortex has been the focus of attention for over a hundred years because it seems to be the site of thinking and cognition. While cognition (perception, memory, problem solving, language processing, and memory) engages many sections of the brain, the cerebral cortex, that thin veneer of densely packed cells, is what we commonly think of as "the brain," although one should note that many intricate and necessary body and cognitive functions rely on other parts of the brain.

The cortex is the most recent of the brain structures to evolve. Some creatures, such as fish, have no cortex; others, such as reptiles and birds, have a less complex cerebral cortex. On the other hand, mammals such as dogs, horses, cats (contrary to the belief of some dog lovers), and especially primates have well-developed, complex, cerebral cortexes. In humans the cortex is involved in perception, speech, complex actions, thinking, language processing and production, and other processes that make us cognizant.

Sensory-Motor Areas.   The sensory-motor areas of the brain were among the first regions of the brain to be mapped. The principal sensory and motor projections (areas that are associated with functions and "mapped" on the surface of the brain) are shown in Figure 2.8 along with the major lobes of the brain.

Scientific work on the motor areas of the brain may be traced to the nineteenth century when studies of electrical stimulation to various parts of the cortex of lightly anesthetized dogs resulted in twitching reactions, as a mild current to the frontal lobe led to a reflexive reaction in the forelimb. **Countralaterality** (that is, stimulation of the left hemisphere led to right body responses and vice versa) was also empirically demonstrated in these early experiments. Mapping of the sensory and motor areas of the brain in other mammals, including humans, soon followed, and a general picture of topographic size and function emerged. The more important a function, such as the forepaw manipulation in raccoons (raccoons depend on forepaw activity for eating and building), the greater the size of the motor cortex allocated to this part of the anatomy. The raccoon has a relatively large motor cortex devoted to the forepaws, say, in comparison to a dog. (See Welker, Johnson, and Pubols, 1964.) Mapping of the sensory area has shown that delicate electrical stimulation of various parts of the regions shown in Figure 2.9 is associated with corresponding sensations in the opposite side of the body associated with the sensory cortex being aroused. Stimulation in the somatosensory area associated with the hand, for example, might create a tingling sensation in the hand on the opposite side of the body. As with motor allocation, parts of the body rich in sensory functions, such as the human tongue, occupy a large part of the sensory cortex.

Association Areas of the Cerebral Cortex.   While the sensory and motor parts of the cortex occupy considerable space (about 25 percent of the surface) and their functions are substantial, the rest of the cortex is involved in what are called the **association** areas. These meandering areas of the brain are involved in cognition, memory, language

FIGURE 2.8

The major areas of the human cerebral cortex. Here the frontal, parietal, occipital, and temporal lobes are shown. The primary motor cortex is shown (shaded) and also the primary somatic sensory cortex (dark shading). Two important functional areas used for generating words and understanding speech are shown: Broca's area (anterior to the primary motor cortex) involved in speech production, and Wernicke's area (posterior to the sensory cortex) involved in comprehension of spoken words.

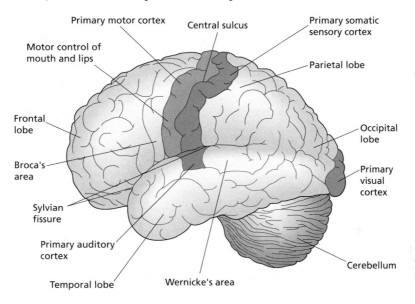

processing, and the like. People have known about some of the relationships between cognition and the brain for centuries through patients who have suffered lesions, tumors, hemorrhages, strokes, and other pathologies. Alas, the link between brain and thought was usually made postmortally after opening the skull of a recently deceased patient and then reconstructing his or her curious behavior with brain anomalies. Now, fully functioning, live participants are used to show what parts of the brain are functioning when specific cognitive activities are practiced. More on that later, but now a brief history of some early discoveries.

Early Functional Neurology.   Early knowledge about the specialized functions of the brain can be traced to the nineteenth century. Especially important is the work of the French neurologist Pierre Paul Broca, who studied aphasia, a language disorder in which the patient has difficulty speaking. This disorder is commonly found in stroke victims. Postmortem examination of aphasics' brains revealed lesions in the area now called Broca's area (see Figure 2.9). In 1876 the young German neurologist Karl Wernicke described a new type of aphasia, which was characterized by the inability to comprehend rather than the inability to speak. In fact, the speech was fluent, but made no sense.

Gary Larson pokes fun at Fritsch and Hitzig's classic experiment.

THE FAR SIDE® BY GARY LARSON

"Whoa! *That* was a good one! Try it, Hobbs—just poke his brain right where my finger is."

Wernicke agreed with earlier scholars that certain mental functions are localized but that these are, for the most part, concerned with simple perceptual and motor activities. Complex intellectual processes such as thinking, memory, and understanding result from the interactions among perceptual and motor areas. Support for this position came around the turn of the century, when the Spanish physiologist Santiago Ramón y Cajal showed that the nervous system is made up of discrete elements, or neurons.

What had been a mosaic concept of the mind (conceptually not far removed from the phrenological view, without the bump readings) was now a connectionist concept: complex cognitive functions take place and can be understood in terms of the network of links among neurons. Furthermore, Wernicke suggested that some functions are processed in parallel in different parts of the brain. Wernicke's hypothesis about the brain and its functions proved to be important to modern cognitive psychologists.

Redundant processing of information, as suggested by the parallel processing theory, might appear wasteful and contrary to the view that animal systems are efficient to the point of parsimony. However, it is arguable that involved biological systems are

Areas of the brain involved in aphasia and language.

	Language Symptomology in Aphasia			
	TYPE OF APHASIA	SPONTANEOUS SPEECH	PARAPHASIA	COMPREHENSION
	Broca's aphasia	Nonfluent	Uncommon	Good
	Wernicke's aphasia	Fluent but makes no sense	Common	Poor
	Conduction aphasia	Fluent	Common	Good
	Global aphasia	Nonfluent	Variable	Poor
	Subcorticle aphasia	Fluent or nonfluent	Common	Variable

usually redundant. Certainly this is true in the case of reproduction, where many times more eggs are produced than are fertilized and, among many species, many times more offspring are spawned than grow to maturity. Redundancy in nature is likely to play a central role in survival and adaptability. Perhaps redundant and parallel processing of neural information by humans increases our chances for survival and procreation. Thinking, and the science of cognition we now enjoy, are the serendipitous by-products of these primary functions.

The theories of Flourens, Broca, and Wernicke on the relationship between the brain and behavior were expanded by the American psychologist Karl Lashley of Harvard University. Lashley, however, was not concerned with aphasia in humans but with the locus of learning in rats. In his influential book *Brain Mechanisms and Intelligence* (1929), Lashley expressed his interest in brain injuries and behavior, with the aim of shedding light on the issue of localization versus generalization of functions. To study

Karl Lashley (1890–1958). Founded the principle of mass action. APA president, 1929.

Photo courtesy of Harvard University Archives.

such phenomena, he examined lesions in the brains of rats to determine their effects on the animals' ability to master a complex maze. Small areas of damage to a rat's brain did not have much effect on maze performance. Because no specific area seemed tied directly to learning, Lashley concluded that learning was not confined to specific neurons. Lashley developed a theory called **mass action,** in which the importance of individual neurons is minimized and memories seem to be distributed throughout the brain. Lashley (1950) concluded that "There are no special cells reserved for special memories." The importance of his ideas lies in their suggestion that the brain operates in a holistic rather than compartmentalized manner. (About the same time, Alexander Luria was developing similar ideas in Russia.)

Recent studies of memory and blood activity (which is thought to reflect neural activity) suggest that some memory functions may be associated with certain areas of the brain but perhaps not to the precise degree suggested by earlier data (see Penfield, 1959, for example).[2] We now believe that the brain contains areas associated with specific functions (such as motor reactions) but that the complete processing of this class of information also engages other parts of the brain. Other functions (like thinking) seem to be widely distributed throughout the brain.

Space restrictions require that we examine only a sample of the existing experimental and clinical studies of brain structure and processes. Nonetheless, some general conclusions and their implications are in order:

- Many mental functions seem to be localized to specific regions or constellations in the brain, such as motor regions and sensory terminals. However, in addition to the regional concentration of these functions, further processing appears to take place in different sites.

- Many higher-order mental functions (thinking, learning, and memory, among others) seem to involve several different areas of the cerebral cortex. Neural processing of this class of information is redundant in the sense that it is distributed throughout the brain and processed in parallel at many locations.

- Damage to the brain does not always lead to a diminution of cognitive performance. This may be due to several factors. In the first place, the damage may be to parts of

[2]This is not to suggest that Penfield's observations are erroneous but that they are difficult to replicate.

the brain that are related to performance in subtle ways or in areas of the brain that perform redundant functions. Also, cognition may be unaffected because the intact connections can take over the original function or the intact connections can be rearranged in a way that allows them to accomplish the primary task.

Consider a model of neural processing that is consistent with the existing clinical, experimental, and psychological knowledge. This model of neural processing proposes that neurons process information in a serial way, somewhat analogous to the von Neumann computer mentioned earlier.

In this model (see Figure 2.10A), information from one neuron is passed to another neuron, then to another neuron, and so forth. Although this model may be consistent with some of the experimental evidence, it seems too simple to account for some findings, especially the work of Lashley, which would suggest that a break in the link does not (altogether) interfere with the process. Another possibility is that the processing of complex, higher-order, intellectual tasks is accomplished through a series of functional links in a parallel network (see Figure 2.10B). In this model, information is processed in parallel as well as in series. Thus, if part of the pathway is destroyed, the system does not necessarily break down completely, but it allows alternative pathways to take over some functions. The latter theory seems to be more consistent with the data and has influenced current thinking in cognitive psychology.

Many recent models of the brain have been made possible because of technical developments in the field of neuroscience that have allowed a clearer view of the physical structures and internal workings of the human organism. Following is a brief review of those developments that have had an impact on cognitive psychology.

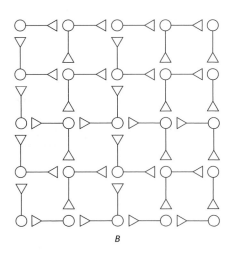

A

B

FIGURE 2.10

A. A cellular connection model in which neurons are connected in series.

B. A cellular connection model in which chains of neurons are connected in series and in parallel. When a neural link is broken, the system typically does not fail completely because of the possibility of parallel processing.

Adapted with permission from W. R. Uttal, *The Psychobiology of the Mind*, Lawrence Erlbaum Associates, 1978.

Neurophysiological Sensing Techniques

Fifty years ago, neurologists had only a few tools and techniques to use in the direct observation and exploration of the human brain. These included excising of tissue, electrical probes, EEG recordings, postmortem examinations, and animal studies. Psychologists, on the other hand, invented a whole arsenal of techniques in which the mind revealed itself, such as the momentary presentation of stimuli and measuring of reaction time. Recently, however, new instruments have been invented that have profoundly accelerated our understanding of the brain and, for our purposes, spun off a new breed of scientist who is part neurologist and part cognitive psychologist. The new technology was originally developed for the diagnosis of brain disorders, but it has now become a valuable research tool. These methods have already led to important new discoveries in the study of human cognition and are an integral part of the future of cognitive science.

EEG (electroencephalograph) records electrical signals from the brain via electrodes placed on the scalp. These electrodes pick up the electrical signals and send them to instruments that detect the signals and in turn are hooked up to "pens," which trace signals on the constantly moving graph paper. This is the oldest of the sensing techniques of the brain, having been developed by Hans Berger in the 1920s. EEGs can show us how long it takes the brain to process stimuli, but they cannot show us structures, anatomy, or functional regions of the brain.

Alan Gevins and his colleagues of the EEG Systems Laboratory in San Francisco developed a "super" EEG system, called Mental Activity Network Scanner (MANSCAN), which can record as many as 250 images of cerebral activity per second. EEG recordings are also lightning fast—as fast as one-thousandth of a second, which is a real advantage over other imaging techniques that, in some instances, require many seconds to capture an image.

For many years conventional EEG recordings have been used to record the minute electrical signals originating in the brain. Studies of traditional EEG recordings led to the discovery of low-amplitude beta waves, which were associated with alertness and attentiveness, and slower, larger alpha waves, which were associated with tranquility and relaxation. In MANSCAN a soft helmet with 124 electrodes is placed on the participant's head, and computers track the shifting centers of electrical activities. The tiny electrical impulses detected by the electrodes are plotted on a high-resolution MRI map of the brain, giving a dynamic impression of, as Gevins calls it, "shadows of thought." In Figure 2.11, brain scans of five people are shown (see Gevins & Cutillo, 1993). In the left figure, participants are waiting for a single number to appear. In the right figure, participants must remember two digits while waiting for a third to occur. As shown, in the more complex task much greater communication between different areas of the brain takes place as contrasted with the relatively simple EEG activity associated with the simple task. It may be that keeping something in mind while monitoring other events requires diverse mental operations.

Many of these new techniques allow us to see the brain in one way or another, with apparatuses similar to that shown in Figure 2.12A. In such procedures a patient is placed in the center of the scanning instrument, which records impressions from within the cranium or other parts of the body. The scan produces a cross-sectional image of the brain or other body part. The impression is first enhanced by a computer, then color

FIGURE 2.11

Five brain scans.

Reprinted with permission of Alan Gevins.

coded, and finally displayed on a video terminal. Photographs and/or hard copies of the display are often made.

There are several types of brain scans in general use: the computed axial tomography (CT) scan, the positron emission tomography (PET) scan, magnetic resonance imaging (MRI), and magnetoencephalography (MEG).

CT Scans

Computed axial tomography is the process of using computers to generate a three-dimensional image from flat (in other two-dimensional) X-ray pictures. A CT scan also provides a still image that shows the structure of the brain. The machine rotates around the skull, bombarding it with thin, fan-shaped X-ray beams (see Figure 2.12B). The beams are recorded on sensitive detectors on the opposite side of their source. This procedure is different from a conventional X-ray examination, which gives only one view of the body part. Also, with conventional X rays, large molecules (such as calcium in the skull) absorb the rays and partially occlude the organs behind them. The CT scan rotates the X-ray beam 180 degrees, resulting in numerous "pictures" of the same organ and producing an internal cross section, or "slice," of the body part. This graphic cross section, called a **tomogram** (literally, "section writing"), has become critical in medical diagnosis. An even more sophisticated version of the CT technique, the dynamic spatial reconstructor (DSR), shows internal structures in three dimensions. One advantage of CT is the ubiquity of machines. As of the mid-1990s, more than 10,000 scanners were in use in American hospitals. Also, recent technology has helped solve one of the problems with this technique. The temporal resolution, or shutter speed, had been about 1 second, with the result that dynamic processes (even the heart beat) appeared blurred. Now, an ultrafast CT has been developed that speeds up processing so that previously blurred images are now clear.

PET Scans

Positron emission tomography (PET) scans for glucose use in the brain. PET scans (Figure 2.13) differ from CT scans in that they use detectors to measure radioactive particles

FIGURE 2.12

Brain scanning techniques.

A. Overall procedure for obtaining brain scans with a video display.

B. CT scan procedure in which low-intensity X-ray beams scan the brain.

C. PET scan procedure, in which radioactive tracers are detected by peripheral sensors.

(A) Scanning the brain

(B) CT scan procedure   (C) PET scan procedure

in the bloodstream. Active parts of the brain require greater blood flow; hence, more radioactive tracers amass in operative areas. These tracers emit rays, which can be converted into visual maps. The computer codes the glucose absorption data to show varying levels of activity in a color-coded "map." Red usually indicates more active areas and blue usually indicates less active areas. The application of PET scans to cognitive neuropsychology has been particularly useful. At Lund University in Sweden, the re-

Functional MRI **PET**

Resting state

Blood flow

Hemoglobin
Oxygen

Radioactive
water

Activated state

FIGURE 2.13

Blood flow to the brain provides the signals detected by functional MRI and PET. When resting neurons (top) become active (bottom), blood flow to them increases. MRI (left) detects changes in oxygen levels, which rise in the nearby blood vessels when they are activated. PET (right) relies on the increased delivery of injected radioactive water, which diffuses out of the vessels to reach all parts of the brain.

Raichle, *Scientific American*, April 1994. Reprinted with permission from Jared Schneidman Design.

search scientists Jarl Risberg and David Ingvar (see Lassen, Ingvar, & Skinhoj, 1979),[3] working in collaboration with Steve Petersen, Michael Posner, Marcus Raichle, and Endel Tulving, have pioneered the use of PET scans in cognitive psychology (see Posner et al., 1988). PET technology has provided some very interesting results (some of which are presented in this book), but the widespread research application is handicapped because of very high costs and because the time for images to be recorded is long (at present about 20 seconds).

The early PET studies measuring regional cerebral blood flow were based on the inhalation of 133xenon, which was used as the tracer substance. Risberg and Ingvar have successfully used 195mgold, administered intravenously. With this tracing material, high-resolution "maps" can be made in a very few seconds (Risberg, 1987, 1989; and Tulving, 1989a, 1989b), thus giving the researcher considerable latitude in collecting cognitive data.

MRI and fMRI

Magnetic resonance imaging (MRI) scans provide still images of structures of the brain. In the MRI technique the body is surrounded with very powerful electromagnets that align the nuclei of hydrogen atoms found in water. From these measures, it is possible to infer varying densities of hydrogen atoms and their interaction with surrounding tissues. Since hydrogen reflects water content, it is possible to use the MRI for diagnostic and research purposes. One of the main drawbacks of the technique, until recently, has

[3]See also *Scientific American*, September 1992, a special issue on "Mind and the Brain," and *Newsweek*, April 20, 1992, for readable accounts of brain function, blood flow, and imaging techniques.

been the time it takes to form images using MRI technology. Because it required long exposure time, the technique was acceptable for viewing static biological structures. However, it was nearly useless for rapidly changing functions, those associated with cognition. It is now possible to apply high-performance data acquisition techniques that make it possible to capture an image in as little as 30 milliseconds, which is brief enough to record fast-acting cognitive functions. fMRI (functional magnetic resonance imaging) detects increased blood flow to activated areas of the brain, thus displaying function and structure. For more detailed information, see Schneider, Noll, & Cohen, 1993; and Cohen, Rosen, & Brady, 1992.

MEG

MEG, or magnetoencephalography, uses a machine that measures brain activity from the outside of the head by detecting the faint magnetic fields that the brain activity produces. MEG produces an "activity map" or "functional image" of the brain. MEG scans can help answer questions such as *What activity is the brain producing and where in the brain does it come from? Which part of the brain undertakes different tasks?* Of all the brain scanning methods, MEG provides the most accurate resolution of nerve cell activity (to the millisecond).

TMS

A new technique called transcranial magnetic stimulation (TMS) is used in conjunction with EEG or MEG to evaluate the effects of changes in brain electrical activity on perceiving and thinking. A magnetic charge is directed via a wand placed on the head and pointed to a specific location in the brain for a very short period of time. This charge alters the neural functioning; these effects on brain functioning can be seen in the output of the EEG or MEG, as well as in terms of the participant's responses to the cognitive and perceptual tasks he or she is engaged in at the time.

Research Using Imaging Techniques: An Example

Of particular interest to cognitive psychologists is the use of cortical blood-flow patterns in memory research.[4] Tulving has been developing a theory of memory that posits two unique types: episodic and semantic, or memory for personal events and memory for general knowledge, respectively. In one experiment (Tulving, 1989a), the participant was asked to think silently about an episodic (personal) event and then to think about something general. The research was conducted with a high-resolution Cortexplorer 256-HR system, which was developed by Risberg. For the tracer, a small amount of radioactive gold with a half-life of only 30 seconds was injected into the participant's bloodstream. Blood flow was monitored by measuring the number of tracers approximately 7 or 8 seconds after injection of the radioactive gold. The number of tracers in

---

[4]Although in several subsequent chapters memory research is discussed in detail, at this time we will consider a few topics in memory specifically related to brain tomography.

*T*he microscope and telescope opened vast domains of unexpected scientific discovery. Now that new imaging methods can visualize the brain systems used for normal and pathological thought, a similar opportunity may be available for human cognition.

—*Michael I. Posner*

each area was measured by a battery of 254 extracranial gamma-ray detectors that snugly encircled the participant's head. Each detector scanned an area of approximately 1 square centimeter and produced a colored, two-dimensional map of the brain, which consisted of 3,000 pixels. Several measurements were made over a period of 2.4 seconds, and, with the assistance of appropriate computer transformations, they were made visible. The results of one participant's rCBF are shown in color on the inside front cover (top).

These photographs require some study to understand them, but initially we can see general differences in the patterns of blood flow, namely, neural activity, associated with different regions of the brain. Basically, it appears that episodic (personal) retrieval is accompanied by greater activation of the anterior portion of the cerebral cortex, and semantic (general) retrieval is accompanied by greater activation of the posterior regions. Further work is needed before definitive theoretical statements can be made, but it seems safe to conclude that episodic and semantic memory systems involve different brain processes and that each has its own location. This in turn suggests that we may have multiple memory systems. Such observations are also consistent with pathological studies of lesions and subsequent loss of episodic memory (see Milner, Petrides, & Smith, 1985; and Schacter, 1987, for details).

In another attempt to find a direct correlation between cognitive processes and brain activity, Michael Posner, Steven Petersen, and their colleagues at the McDonnell Center for Higher Brain Functions at Washington University conducted a series of significant experiments dealing with the processing of words by the normal, healthy brain. Using PET scanners, Petersen, Fox, Posner, Mintun, and Raichle (1988) injected short-lived radioactive isotopes in participants to trace blood flow in the brain. There were

Steven Petersen. Along with colleagues at Washington University (St. Louis), Petersen has done pioneering work with PET and cognitive processes.

four stages in one experiment in this group: (1) a resting stage, (2) the appearance of a single word on a screen, (3) the reading of the word aloud, and (4) the production of a use for each word (see Figure 2.14). Each of these stages produced its own visual "signature"; see the color illustration on the inside cover (bottom). (Datum from "hearing" is from another experiment.)

In this experiment, when a participant looked at a word on a screen, the occipital region of the cortex was activated; when the participant was hearing a word, the central part of the cortex was activated; when speaking a word, motor regions were activated; and when asked to produce related words (for example, if the word *cake* appeared, the participant was to produce a verb that went with the word, such as *eat*), the associative

FIGURE 2.14

Are words processed in the same place in the brain? Not at all, according to PET studies of word processing. When participants are presented with a word to view, parts of the occipital region are activated (A). When they are listening to words, the superior temporal cortex is activated (B); when they are speaking, parts of the primary motor cortex (C) are activated; and when they are generating verbs, the frontal lobe and middle temporal cortex are implicated (D) (after Petersen et al., 1988).

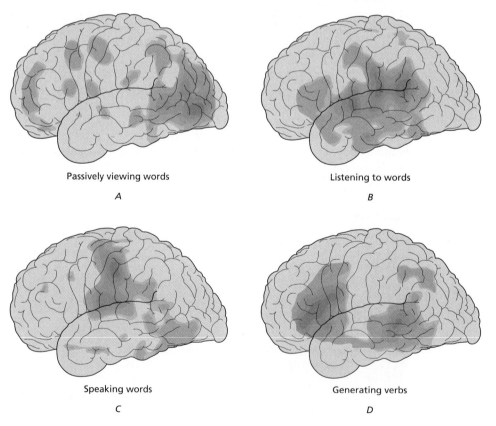

Passively viewing words

A

Listening to words

B

Speaking words

C

Generating verbs

D

region produced the greatest amount of activity, but other general activity throughout the cortex was also observed.

The specificity of memory operations was recently investigated by Daniel Schacter of Harvard University in an experiment that dealt with memory categories (see chapters on memory and the representation of knowledge). Suppose you are asked to read the following list of words: *CANDY, CAKE, SUGAR, TASTE.* Now, turn to page 69. Please do this before you go on reading the text.

If you incorrectly identified one of the items as being on the list (cognitive psychologists call that a "false alarm") or did not recognize one of the previous words (a "miss"), you demonstrated the fallibility of memory. (Of course, the same thing frequently happens when one takes a test.) You also may have correctly recognized one or more of the above words that you just read. That correct recognition is called a "hit." Do hits and false alarms occur in the same part of the brain? To answer this question, participants were read a series of words that were categorically related, as was the preceding set, and then ten minutes later they were shown the lists and asked if the words were previously heard or not. As the participants were thinking about their decision, their brain activity was being monitored by PET measures. In Figure 2.15 we see the results.

The medial temporal lobe is activated during hits and false alarms, but only the temporal parietal region (right) where sounds are processed is active during hits. It is known that true memories tend to be related to more physical and sensory details than are false memories, which tend to show activity in the frontal cerebral cortex, where decision making and associative memory seem to be located. It is almost as if false memories are related to a search for sensory evidence. The cerebral migration in creating a false alarm originates in the medial temporal lobe, which is active when general recall takes place, and then moves to higher-order associative regions. During the reconstruction process similar memories may be mistaken for real memories. The findings have broad implications for the so-called "false memory syndrome," which has been the focus of many court trials involving eyewitness credibility during the past decade.

Even though PET technology is still in its infancy and will probably be refined in the future, it has proved to have a palpable effect on the mapping of brain functions. In addition, other technologies are likely to emerge. Even at this stage, the early results

FIGURE 2.15

The medial temporal lobe is active during both true (left) and false (center) memories. But only true memories show activity in the temporal parietal region (right), where sounds are processed.

have already had a significant impact on cognitive psychology and related sciences. For example, the question of the localization of brain functions so widely touted by the phrenologists may have some credibility, although we hasten to add that the techniques and general theory of phrenology are *not* about to gain scientific respectability! Nor is the notion that many of the brain's functions require the cooperative integration of widely distributed areas in doubt. However, what does seem to be true, given the impressive initial studies, is that there is a surprising number of region-specific activities involved in complex cognitive tasks, such as specific types of language processing and attention matters. For example, it has been found that when we pay attention to real words, such as the text you are reading, specific posterior brain areas are activated.

Nonsense words, however, do not activate these centers. Additionally, specific frontal and temporal areas of the brain are activated when participants are asked to indicate the use of a noun (for example, hammer-pound) or its classification into a category (hammer-tool). (See McCarthy et al., 1993; Petersen et al., 1990; Petersen & Fiez, 1993; Posner, 1992; and Posner et al., 1994.)

The preceding studies make use of recent advances in the neurosciences that tell us something about cognition, thought, and memory as well as the nature of the brain and its functions. We now turn our attention to the topic of the specialization of cerebral hemispheres.

A Tale of Two Hemispheres

If you removed the cranium from any person, you would see a brain with two plainly visible parts, each about the size of a fist, known as the right and left hemispheres of the cerebral cortex. Even though they appear identical, the two parts of the cortex differ widely in function. This difference in humans has been known for centuries, and it has also been observed in most mammals and in many vertebrates.

The earliest written reference to the brain is found in Egyptian hieroglyphs written during the seventeenth century B.C. The hieroglyphic character for brain is shown here as *'ys.* According to the eminent Egyptologist James Breasted, it has been found eight times in ancient writings. In one source, known as "The Edwin Smith Surgical Papyrus," found in the rare-book room of the New York Academy of Medicine, the author describes the symptoms, diagnoses, and prognoses of two patients with head wounds. The early Egyptians knew that injuries to one side of the brain caused an affliction in the opposite side of the body.

The purpose of contralaterality is still not completely understood but has contributed to the theory that the two hemispheres carry out distinctively different functions. There has been a profusion of scientific (see Kandel, Schwartz, & Jessell, 1991; Kupferman, 1981; and Sperry, 1982) and popular (see Ornstein, 1972) ideas about the functions of the hemispheres. (One even proposes that Eastern mysticism and Western rationalism are associated with the right and left hemispheres, respectively.)

Clinical evidence for contralaterality was first recorded by the ancient Egyptians, but the scientific confirmation of opposing functions emerged during the last century, when brain surgeons noted that tumors and excisions in the left hemisphere produced different effects from similar pathology in the right hemisphere. Left-hemisphere damage resulted in language impairment, while patients with damage to the right hemisphere were observed to have difficulties dressing themselves. Further indications of functional asymmetry appeared in the 1950s, when physicians treating patients with severe epilepsy cut the **corpus callosum**—the massive bundle of nerves that connects the two hemispheres (see Bogen & Vogel, 1962). By severing the connective tissue between the two main structures of the brain (a procedure called **cerebral commissurotomy**) surgeons hoped to confine the effects of an epileptic seizure to one hemisphere. Apparently, this worked. (Such radical surgery is not commonly done today.)

Split-Brain Research.   Also in the 1950s, Roger Sperry at the California Institute of Technology conducted research on animals concerning the effect of the so-called split-brain procedure. The main thrust of this work was to determine the different functions associated with each hemisphere. Of particular interest was the finding by Myers and Sperry (1953) that cats that had undergone this procedure behaved as if they had two brains, each of which was capable of attending to, learning, and remembering information independent of the other.

Sperry and his colleagues, notably Michael Gazzaniga, had an opportunity to study human patients who had undergone commissurotomies. In one study (Gazzaniga, Bogen, & Sperry, 1965), they observed that a patient who was given a common object, such as a coin or comb, in his right hand could identify it verbally, since information from the right side crosses over to the left hemisphere, where language processing is centralized. However, if given a common object in the left hand, the patient could not describe it verbally; he could point to it, but only with his left hand.

The studies conducted by this group and others indicated that, indeed, the left hemisphere is associated with special functions such as language, conceptualization, analysis, and classification. The right hemisphere is associated with integration of information over time, as in art and music; spatial processing; recognition of faces and shapes; and such mundane tasks as knowing our way around a city or getting dressed. These findings tend to support the argument for localization of functions. However, subsequent work indicated that the right hemisphere was capable of more linguistic processing, especially written language, than was initially believed. In addition, younger patients exhibited well-developed capacities in both hemispheres (Gazzaniga, 1983). Overall, these observations suggest that there is considerable plasticity in the developing human brain and that functions are not as clearly separated as they once were believed to be but rather are shared by various regions and hemispheres.

Roger Sperry (1924–1994), Nobel Laureate, introduced split-brain research, which opened a new area of research with far-reaching implications regarding the brain.

Eye Movements and Hemispheric Processing

*T*ry this little experiment. Ask a friend to answer this question: "What does it mean when we say, 'Facts are the abridgment of knowledge?'" Did your friend's eyes move to the right? Now ask, "Imagine your home and count the number of windows." Did the eyes look to the left? In general, especially among right-handed people, activation of left-hemisphere functions—those associated with language processing—are accompanied with right-body activities or right-sided orientations, while right-hemisphere functions—those associated with visual and/or spacial tasks—are accompanied with left-body activities.

Much of the current work in the field of hemisphere specialization has dealt with visual perception, which has a unique system of processing contralateral information. Consider the visual system's anatomy in relation to the hemispheres (see Figure 2.16).

FIGURE 2.16

Schematic drawing of the neural pathways between the retinas and the right and left cerebral hemispheres. Note that some of the nerve fibers from each eye cross over to the opposite hemisphere at the optic chiasm and some do not.

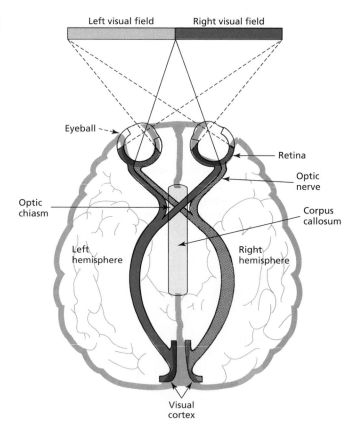

As shown, the processing of visual information follows the crossover principle, at least partly. Light information (for example, the light's reflecting off the text you are now reading) is picked up initially by the receptor neurons in the eyes. The system of nerve pathways from each eye to the brain is more complicated than that of other sensory systems. About half the nerve fibers from each eye follow the principle of contralaterality, but the remaining half do not; that is, they terminate on the same side as detected. Consider the left eye as shown in Figure 2.16. Information detected by the right side of its **retina** (the light-sensing membrane at the back of the eye, shaded gray) is connected to the right hemisphere, and information detected by the left side of its retina is connected to the left hemisphere. The same type of routing holds for the right eye.

If the corpus callosum is cut, as in the split-brain procedure, then information detected by, say, the right retina of the right eye would be "trapped" in the right hemisphere, since the corpus callosum is the conduit between the hemispheres. Likewise, information detected by the left retina of the left eye would be limited to the left hemisphere. Experiments in this area have produced fascinating results. If a split-brain person is blindfolded, given a common object (such as a ball or a pair of scissors) in one hand, and then asked to retrieve that object by touch alone, the person can do it, but only with the same hand that initially touched the object. If asked to retrieve the object with the opposite hand, the results show that the person can do so with accuracy no greater than chance.

The ability to synthesize information is lost after split-brain surgery (see Figure 2.17). One hemisphere of a patient was flashed a card with the word "bow"; the other hemisphere saw "arrow." Because the patient drew a bow and arrow, it was assumed that the two hemispheres were still able to communicate with each other—despite the severing of the corpus callosum—and had integrated the words into a meaningful composite.

The next test proved this theory. "Sky" was flashed to one hemisphere, "scraper" to the other. The resulting image revealed that the patient was not synthesizing information: sky atop a comblike scraper was drawn, rather than a tall building. One hemisphere drew what it had seen, then the other drew its word. In the case of bow and arrow, the superposition of the two images misled us because the picture appeared integrated. Could each hemisphere, on its own, integrate words? "Fire" and then "arm" were flashed to the right hemisphere. The left hand drew a rifle rather than an arm on fire, so it was clear that each hemisphere was capable of synthesis (Gazzaniga, 1998).

In a similar line of inquiry, a participant gazes at a particular point. It is then possible to present a visual stimulus that has been positioned so as to be detected by either the right or left side of the retina. Figure 2.18 illustrates the apparatus used in these types of studies. In a typical experiment, a commissurotomized patient receives a stimulus, such as a picture or word, to the right or left of the fixation point so that the information is recorded in either the right or left hemisphere. If a picture (for example, a pair of scissors) is flashed momentarily to the left of the participant's fixation point (to be recorded and processed in the right hemisphere) and then the participant is asked to select the object by sight or touch, he or she can do so using the left hand, but not the right.

An equally impressive demonstration of the bilateral nature of the hemispheres is found in an often-cited article by Levy, Trevarthen, and Sperry (1972). In this experiment, a split-brain patient was asked to look at a fixation point. A "chimeric" face (half man and half woman) was momentarily flashed on the screen in a position that favored

FIGURE 2.17

Split-brain test results.

From Gazzaniga, M. S. (1998).

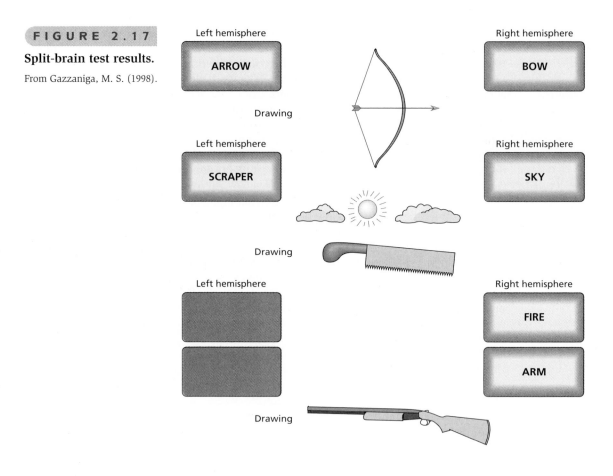

Left hemisphere | Right hemisphere

ARROW | BOW

Drawing

Left hemisphere | Right hemisphere

SCRAPER | SKY

Drawing

Left hemisphere | Right hemisphere

FIRE

ARM

Drawing

FIGURE 2.18

Apparatus used to study split-brain patients. The participant looks at a fixed point on a screen. A picture or word is momentarily presented on the screen, so that one hemisphere can process it. The participant is then asked to pick up the object, which is out of sight.

the processing of the woman's face in the right hemisphere and the man's face in the left (see Figure 2.19).

The participant did not report anything unusual about the composite, even though each hemisphere perceives a different face. When asked to tell about the face, the participant verbally described a man's features, which supports the concentration of verbal information in the left side of the brain. However, when asked to select the face from an array of photographs, the participant picked the woman's, which supports the concentration of pictorial information in the right side of the brain (see Bradshaw &

(A) Chimeric stimuli

(B) Left hemisphere

Vocal naming

(C) Right hemisphere

Visual recognition

FIGURE 2.19

Display of chimeric face (A) used with commissurotomized patients. Each hemisphere appears to register separate images: the left (B) records a man's face, the right (C) a woman's. When asked to describe the face, the participant verbally labels it as a man's, but when asked to point out the face among a display of faces, the participant selects the woman's face.

Nettleton, 1981; and Springer & Deutsch, 1984, for a thorough discussion of cerebral specialization).

Cognitive Studies with Participants with Intact Corpus Callosums. Because of the curious neural pathways involved in visual processing (see Figure 2.17), it is possible to do lateralization experiments with participants whose corpus callosum is intact. Obviously, it is far easier to find unimpaired participants than commissurotomized ones, and, as a consequence, a great number of cognitive experiments have been done with this population. Also, the procedure is relatively straightforward, and the apparatus is conventional. Typically, a person, screened for handedness and gender, is asked to look at a central viewing point presented on a computer screen or tachistoscope. A word, a color, or some other type of visual information is then momentarily presented either to the right or left of the fixation point. Information presented to the right of the fixation point crosses over to the left hemisphere, and information to the left crosses over to the right hemisphere. The participant is then typically asked to make some type of decision about the visual information (for example, was it a word?), and his or her reaction time is recorded. The rationale behind the design is that if information is normally processed in one or the other hemisphere, then access to that information should be fast; if information is initially processed in the "wrong" hemisphere, it must pass over to the "correct" hemisphere to be processed, an operation that takes time. It should be noted that the amount of time involved in these experiments is very brief indeed, and a difference of 50 milliseconds is considered large. Of course, very precise timing instruments are necessary for this type of research.

Researchers have successfully used the technique of presenting a momentary stimulus to the right or left visual field to evaluate information processing. For an overview of these results, see Table 2.1. It is noted that results in this area are often equivocal as a result of faulty research design, participant variables, and failure to replicate previous experiments. Nevertheless, in general, these findings have confirmed that words and letters produce left-hemisphere superiorities, while faces and slanted lines produce right-hemisphere superiorities. Other studies have indicated differences in gender (Boles, 1984), in auditory processing (Ivry & Lebby, 1993), during sustained visual attention (Whitehead, 1991), in prototype formation (Rees, Kim, & Solso, 1993), and in handedness (Annett, 1982). These studies have also suggested that the type of visual stimuli has differential effects depending on the hemisphere in which the material is processed (Boles, 1987). (See Bradshaw & Nettleton, 1981; Chiarello, 1988; Kosslyn, Sokolov, & Chen, 1989; and Springer & Deutsch, 1981, for overviews of the topic.)

The reason for laterality is less clearly understood than the fact that it does appear consistently, especially in humans. One intriguing hypothesis by Corballis (1989) gives the phenomenon an evolutionary basis: human evolutionary history reveals that right-handedness, tool use, and the development of left-hemispheric mechanisms for language use developed in hominids as long as 2 or 3 million years ago and set the stage for the development of more complex functions. Corballis (1989) writes, "Beginning some 1.5 million years ago with the emergence of the larger brained H. erectus, tool culture became more complex. However, a truly flexible tool culture and the rapid, flexible speech of modern humans may not have developed until later still, perhaps 150,000 years ago, when H. sapiens sapiens emerged in Africa, to subsequently populate the globe" (p. 499). According to Corballis, the evolution of hemisphere specialization may

TABLE 2.1

Summary of Research on Cerebral Functions

Function	Left Hemisphere	Right Hemisphere
Auditory system	Sounds related to language	Music, environmental sounds
Spatial processes	Unknown	Geometry, direction sense, mental rotation of geometric forms
Somatosensory system	Unknown	Tactile recognition, Braille detection
Memory	Verbal memory	Nonverbal memory
Language processing	Speech, reading, writing, arithmetic	Metered prosody
Visual system	Letters, words, surrealistic art	Geometric patterns, faces, realistic art
Movement	Complex voluntary movement	Spatial-pattern movements

be associated with flexibility of thought and generativity or the ability to combine elements using rules to create new associations—be they words, sentences, or more complex tools. Generativity may be uniquely human and is associated with the left cerebral hemisphere. Corballis's theory is fascinating, but it should be considered in light of studies done on language processing and tool use by chimpanzees and apes (see Gardner & Gardner, 1969). Further developments in this area are worth watching.

Impressive as they are, these experiments regarding the dissimilar nature of the hemispheres need to be considered in a larger context. Although a sizable number of careful experiments and demonstrations have indicated that some functions are located in specific areas of the cortex, it is likely that cerebral processing is also distributed throughout other places in the brain. Even in the case of hemisphere specialization, the brain seems to operate as a holistic organ. It should be noted that many of the research paradigms reported here involved patients whose corpora callosa had been severed and were designed to demonstrate the bilateral nature of the human brain. In normal humans the connective tissues are intact, and the two hemispheres operate cooperatively with massive "communication" between them.

Cognitive Psychology and Brain Science

In an effort to understand the human mind better, cognitive psychologists have become more interested in the organ of the mind—the brain. Their interest in the brain sciences has been matched by that of brain scientists looking to cognitive psychology to provide models of human information processing. We have seen that specialization as well as diversity of functions can be found in the human brain. The nervous system appears to be a massive parallel processing system, which is thought to be necessary for the rapid, complex, and creative processing of information.

Discoveries from brain science have had a direct impact on cognitive psychology and computer science. Theories of information processing have embodied knowledge from neuroscience. An example of this is the recent interest in neurally inspired PDP models. In the field of computer science, we see renewed interest in the modeling of computers, not only to perform humanoid functions but also to mimic neuronetworks in their architecture.

At the end of all the following chapters, look for a section called "Spotlight on Cognitive Neuroscience." This section will highlight a particular aspect of each chapter as it relates to cognitive neuroscience.

SUMMARY

1   The mind–body issue has been debated for centuries. The term *mind* refers to the functions of the body, specifically the brain.

2   Using studies of regional cerebral blood flow (rCBF), Tulving found specific regions of the brain that are active during episodic memory processing and other regions that are active during semantic memory processing.

3   Neurocognition is the scientific study of the relationships between cognitive psychology and neuroscience. Several reasons exist for the alliance between psychology and neuroscience. These include the need to find physical evidence for theoretical properties of the mind, the need among neuroscientists to find more comprehensive models of brain and behavior, the need to find relationships between brain pathology and behavior, the increased use of neurally inspired models of cognitive science, the increased use of computers to model neurological functions, and the invention of techniques that enhance the ability to depict brain structures more clearly.

4   The basic building block of the nervous system is the neuron, whose principal parts are the dendrites, cell body, axon, and synaptic juncture where neurotransmission takes place.

5   Neurologists have long debated whether the functions of the brain could be localized. The conclusion is that some gross functions are localized (for example, speech) but that functions are generally distributed throughout the brain.

6   Recently, brain scientists have developed techniques that allow high-resolution graphic depictions of brain activity. These techniques include MRI, PET, and CT scans as well as other imaging procedures.

7   Split-brain and cognitive research has indicated that processing of information in the right hemisphere differs from that in the left hemisphere.

KEY WORDS

aggregate field theory	cell body
association	central nervous system
axon	cerebral commissurotomy

cerebral cortex

cerebral hemispheres

cognitive neuroscience

contralaterality

corpus callosum

dendrites

electroencephalography (EEG)

fissures

frontal

gyri

localization

mass action

mind–body issue

myelin sheath

neuron

neurotransmitters

occipital

parietal

perceptrons

phrenology

presynaptic terminals

retina

sulci

synapse

temporal

tomogram

Recommended Readings

● The field of neurocognition is relatively recent, and some of the best references are to be found in current issues of journals. Germane periodicals include *Science, Brain and Behavioral Sciences, Cortex, Journal of Neurophysiology, Psychobiology, Nature, Brain,* and *Brain and Cognition,* among others. Corballis's article "Laterality and Human Evolution" appears in *Psychological Review* (1989), and Land and Fernald is in the *Annual Review of Neuroscience,* Volume 15.

● Some books of interest are Restak, *The Mind;* Blakemore, *Mechanics of the Mind;* Ornstein, *The Psychology of Consciousness;* and Benson and Zaidel, eds., *The Dual Brain: Hemispheric Specialization in Humans.* More specialized, but highly recommended, are Kandel, Schwartz, and Jessell, *Principles of Neural Science* (3rd edition); Thompson, *The Brain: A Neuroscience Primer* (2nd edition); and Squire and Butters, eds., *Neuropsychology of Memory* and an edited behemoth by Gazzaniga called *The Cognitive Neurosciences.* Of particular interest in the Gazzaniga volume are introductory chapters on memory, by Tulving; on consciousness, by Schacter; on language, by Pinker; on thought and imagery, by Kosslyn; and on attention, by Posner.

Which word(s) were among those you just read?

BLOOD, SWEET, SUGAR.

How sure are you of your choice(s)?

Perception and Attention

hmmm...?

● **The Computational Brain**

● **Sensation and Perception**
Illusions
Previous Knowledge
Sensory-Brain Predisposition
Everything We Know Is Wrong

● **Perceptual Span**

● **Iconic Storage**

● **Echoic Storage**

● **Function of Sensory Stores**

● **Attention**
Attention, Consciousness, and Subliminal Perception

● **Processing Capacity and Selective Attention**

● **Auditory Signals**

● **Models of Selective Attention**
The Filter Model: Broadbent
The Attenuation Model: Treisman

● **Visual Attention**

● **Automatic Processing**

● **The Cognitive Neuroscience of Attention**
Attention and the Human Brain
Attention and PET

1. When we talk about the "computational brain," what do we mean, and how does that relate to the survival of the human species?

2. Why are sensation and perception important topics to cognitive psychologists?

3. How do illusions help us understand the relationship between the things sensed and the things hypothesized?

4. What are iconic storage and echoic storage, and how do they help us understand the "real" world?

5. How do cognitive psychologists define *attention*? Name several examples of attention in everyday life.

6. What are the major theories of attention and the experimental support for them?

7. What do we mean when we talk about "processing capacity" and "selective attention"?

8. What is "automatic processing"? Give some examples of automatic processing from your everyday life experiences.

9. What have cerebral imaging techniques told us about attention?

As you woke today, you fired up your cognitive computer, which had been turned off for the night. When you were jolted out of an unconscious state by the ringing of an alarm clock, you sensed the auditory world; when you opened your eyes, you caught sight of the visual world; when you splashed water on your face, you sensed the tactile world; when you inhaled the rich aroma of freshly brewed coffee, you enjoyed the olfactory world; and when you nibbled on a fresh roll, you savored the gustatory world. Five senses—five windows to the world—only five ways to know the world. Yet, contained within those five conduits to the "real world" are the basic means by which we comprehend everything from Picasso to punk rock, not to mention the ocean's mist, Bach, perfume, Dostoevski, peppermint candy, sunsets, and physical intimacy.

In this chapter we will find out how we humans use the **computational brain** to:

- *Perceive* information about the environment.
- *Attend* to the world.
- *Process information* during the initial stages.

We begin by examining the perception of sensory signals because this is the initial step in the processing of information. At the heart of this process is the brain, whose task it is to understand and, in effect, make sense out of the things being fed into it from the **peripheral nervous system.** That system is made up of nerves that lie outside the spinal cord and the brain and are involved in sensation and perception.

The Computational Brain

The peripheral nervous system and brain are largely designed to perceive and cogitate— to see and understand, for example. Steve Pinker expressed it well in his book *How the Mind Works:* "The mind is a system of organs of computation, designed by natural selection to solve the kinds of problems our ancestors faced in their foraging way of life, in particular, understanding and outmaneuvering objects, animals, plants, and other people" (1997, p. 21). We see, hear, smell, taste, and feel the sensations of the world as the first link in a chain of events that subsequently involves coding stimuli; storing information; transforming material; thinking; and, finally, reacting to knowledge.

The concept of the computational brain is based on the idea that the mind is what the brain does—the mind processes information. When we engage in "higher-order cognition"—thinking about the way an apple and America are alike or figuring out how to meet our friend Jean in Chile—we are doing a type of computation.

As shown in Figure 3.1, physical energy that falls within the limited range of human detection stimulates the sensory system, is transduced (converted to neural energy), is

FIGURE 3.1

The stages of information processing showing external phenomena and
internal processes and structures.

briefly held in a sensory storage, is subjected to further processing by the central nervous
system (CNS) and coded, and may be passed on to memory systems for processing. The
results can initiate responses that become part of the stimulus field for further processing.
(A large portion of the remainder of this book deals with the very complex and abstract
processing of information that takes place in the memory systems and the computation of
that information.)

It is useful to keep in mind that the flowchart shown in Figure 3.1 is just a representation of the hypothetical stages through which information is processed. It is certainly not
the case that the brain is arranged more or less as shown in the illustration, but this model
has value as a visual conceptualization of the various stages of information processing
postulated in cognitive psychology. What is key in cognitive psychology is the capability
to see the activation of the brain as information is being processed. These techniques,
mentioned in the previous chapter, suggest that the stages shown in this figure are analogous to actual physiological processes. With these viewing techniques, the dream of scientists throughout the twentieth century to observe the locus of brain activities associated
with cognitive processes is rapidly becoming a reality. Some of these findings and trends
are shown in this chapter and in later chapters on memory and higher-order cognition.

Sensation and Perception

The point of contact between the inner world and the external reality is centered in the
sensory system. The study of the relationship between the physical changes of the world
and the psychological experiences associated with these changes is called **psychophysics.**

The term **sensation** refers to the initial detection of energy from the physical world.
The study of sensation generally deals with the structure and processes of the sensory
mechanism and the stimuli that affect those mechanisms (see Table 3.1).

The term **perception,** on the other hand, involves higher-order cognition in the interpretation of the sensory information. *Sensation* refers to the initial detection of stimuli; *perception* to an interpretation of the things we sense. When we read a book, hear a
concert, have a massage, smell cologne, or taste caviar, we experience far more than the

TABLE 3.1

The Five Senses

Sense	Structure	Stimulus	Receptor
Vision	Eye	Light waves	Rods and cones
Hearing	Ear	Sound waves	Hair cells
Taste	Tongue	Chemicals	Taste buds
Smell	Nose	Chemicals	Hair cells
Touch	Skin	Pressure	Nerve cells

immediate sensory stimulation. Each of these sensory events is processed within the context of our knowledge of the world; our previous experiences give meaning to simple sensory experiences—that is perception.

Illusions

The distinction between sensations and the perceived interpretation of those experiences—in effect between what our sensory system receives and what the mind interprets—has occupied a central position in perception and cognition. It also poses a fascinating question: Why does the mind distort reality?

One line of research uses measurement of the physical and psychological quality of the same sensory stimuli. Sometimes the two measures of reality, the "real" and the perceived, do not match, as in the case of perceptual illusion. A well-known example is the Müller-Lyer illusion (see Figure 3.2), in which two equal segments of a line seem unequal. The explanation of this illusion is probably partly influenced by our past experiences, which have taught us to expect that certain shapes are far away and others close. On the other hand, some argue that this illusion (and many more like it) reflects deep-seated invariant structures of the brain. See the discussion on illusory contours in Chapter 4. A more involved type of illusion is that in the drawing by M. C. Escher shown in Figure 3.3. Here the visual cues of proximity and distance and of the behavior of running water do not appear consistent with each other.

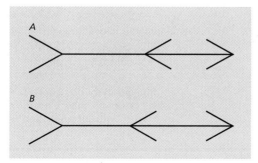

FIGURE 3.2

The Müller-Lyer illusion. The line segments in A are of equal length; those in B, which appear equal, are actually unequal.

Previous Knowledge

The relationship between perception and previous knowledge of the world is manifested
not only in simple geometric illusions but also in the interpretation of scientific data.
Figure 3.4A shows post holes found in an archaeological dig. If your knowledge of the
tribe in question led you to the hypothesis that the huts had been rectangular, you
would tend to "see," or interpret, the post hole data as shown in Figure 3.4B. Conversely, other hypotheses might lead you to interpret the pattern of post holes differently, as in Figure 3.4C. Suppose you had reason to believe that the huts were triangular.
Attempt an outline along those lines, selecting "relevant" and "irrelevant" post holes.

FIGURE 3.4

Plans of huts hypothesized from the positions of post holes found in an archaeological dig.
A. Pattern of holes (black shapes). B and C. Hypothetical plans of huts.

A   B   C

Perceptions are influenced by past knowledge, previous hypotheses, and prejudices, as well as sensory signals.

So, the way we perceive the primary information of the world is greatly influenced by the way the sensory system and brain are initially structured—we are "hard-wired" to perceive the world in a certain way—*and* by our past experiences, which give abundant meaning to the initial sensation of stimuli. If past learning did not influence our perception, the curious lines on this page you are now reading, which we call letters, would not be perceived as parts of words and the words would be devoid of meaning. We learn what visual (and auditory, tactical, gustatory, and olfactory) signals mean.

Sensory-Brain Predisposition

There is another side to the sensory and perceptual process that is supported by studies of the physical makeup of the sensory system and the brain. The sensory system is composed of the receptors and connecting neurons of the five senses (hearing, sight, touch, taste, and smell). Each of these senses has, to a greater or lesser degree, yielded its secrets through the effort of physiologists, physicians, and physiological psychologists throughout the past 150 years. Knowledge about the brain and its role in perception, on the other hand, has been slow to develop, partly because of the brain's inaccessibility. Direct observation of the workings of the brain typically involved the removal of a portion of its hard calcified case, which had evolved over millennia for the very purpose of keeping the brain from harm's way, or the postmortem scrutiny of brains by physicians interested in finding the neurological basis for symptoms. These studies indicated some gross features, such as the well-known contralaterality of the brain, which dictates that cerebral damage to one hemisphere will result in a deficiency in the opposite side of the body. Other traumatic episodes, such as getting rapped on the back of the head in the region called the occipital lobe, result in "seeing stars." We "see" bright flashes, and yet the eye does not detect such things. Through the direct stimulation of the occipital cortex, a visual perception occurs in that part of the brain. Brain scientists have been able to observe the sensory, perceptual, and cognitive processes of the brain without removing the skull or clobbering people on the cranium. These techniques involve both behavioral data, such as reaction time experiments, and imaging technology, as discussed in the previous chapter (PET, CT, MRI, and the like). Now it is really possible to see the workings of the brain as it perceives information about the world and how those perceptions are routed through the labyrinth of the brain.

The processing of sensory signals by the computational brain plays a role in **episte-mology,** or the study of the origin and nature of knowledge. Some of these thoughts pose this question: What is the rationale for our sensory, perceptual, and cognitive system as a reflection of the world? The windows of the mind, the human sensory system, emerged with the physical changes that occurred in our evolving planet. Very simple organisms developed specialized cells that reacted to light, and over millions of years, those cells became more and more specific in operation until, in time, something like an eye emerged in the limpet (see Figure 3.5.). With the evolution of the eye, the brain also emerged. After all, it's nice to see the world, but it's even nicer to understand what the world means! The eye and other sensory organs are as stupid as the brain is wise. Conversely, a wise brain without sensory input is devoid of essential knowledge of the world. Sensations of the world and what they mean are as much a function of the biologically fixed mechanisms as they are of the past history of the observer.

Everything We Know Is Wrong

It is useful to think of the various elements of the sensory system as channels that are open to external reality. Only the sensations that are detected by our receptors are available for higher-level processing, and because the system is limited in its receptivity, our knowledge is necessarily restricted. It is likely that we overemphasize the importance of the features of our physical universe that we can detect, while underemphasizing the importance of those we do not perceive or that require special filters to facilitate their

FIGURE 3.5

A. The eye pit of a limpet.
B. The pinhole eye of a nautilus showing rudimentary receptions and nerve fibers.

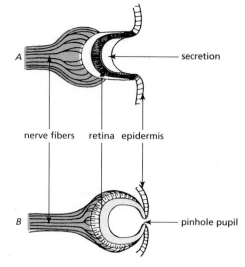

transduction. Consider how our view of "reality" would change if our eyes could "see" infrared radiation but could not "see" the normally visible part of the spectrum. Would our day and night schedules be the same? What would be the effect on history, on marketing, on fashions, on philosophy—indeed, on the whole of society? Most importantly, consider the effect on how we conceptualize reality. Because we apprehend reality through such limited (hence, distorting) channels, we are forced to conclude that everything we know is wrong. However, within the limits of our sensory apparatus, we are able to rough out a descriptive system of how we process the immense amount of information that we can detect, being mindful that the reality of our immediate world is many times more bustling than that sensed.

Our view of the perceptual process, then, is that the detection and interpretation of sensory signals is determined by:

- Stimulus energy sensed by the sensory systems and brain
- Knowledge stored in memory prior to an experience.

A large portion of cognitive research is concerned with the question of how the sensory systems and brain distort sensory information. It now seems that the things stored in our memory are abstract representations of reality. The apple you see, of course, is not stored in your head. The apple is abstracted such that all the information you need to know (that is, what it looks like, smells like, feels like, tastes like, and all the other information you know about apples) is stored in your memory. The key to the processing of sensory information and its cognitive interpretation seems to be the abstraction of information. At the sensory level, information is very specific, whereas on the interpretation level, information is commonly abstract. Our view of the world is determined by the integration of what we know (in an abstract sense) with what we sense (in a specific sense). Now, we turn to another aspect of perception—the question of how much information can be detected in a moment's glance.

Perceptual Span

How much we can experience at a brief exposure is called **perceptual span,** an early component in the processing of information. We know that the world is teeming with stimuli, a huge number of which are within the range of sensory detection. How many of these sensations are available for further processing? Much of the confusion in considering human perceptual span resulted from the failure to discriminate between two hypothetical structures—preperceptual sensory store and short-term memory.

We apparently have a sensory store that is capable of quick decisions based on brief exposure to events. Common knowledge confirms this notion. If we close our eyes, we continue to "see" the world; if a piece of music ceases, we still "hear" it; if we remove our hand from a textured surface, we still "feel" it. Each of these sensory memories fades rapidly, however, and most are soon forgotten. What are the boundaries of these transitory impressions? How long do they last? How much can be perceived in how short a time?

The first experiment investigating perceptual span dealt with vision, not only because vision is an important sense but also because it is somewhat easier to exercise experimental control over visual than over other stimuli (touch or taste, for example). Visual studies also had a practical side in that they were related to the rapidly developing research in reading. (Many early studies of the perceptual span were concerned with the amount of information that could be apprehended in a brief period.) Javal (1878) had observed that reading was not done by smoothly scanning a line of text but was a matter of jumping from one fixation point to another. Reading, or the gathering in of textual material, took place at the fixation points, not during the jumps, or **saccades** (Cattell, 1886a, 1886b; Erdmann & Dodge, 1898).

These early studies indicated that the most information that could be gathered during a single exposure was about four or five letters of unconnected matter. It is important to recognize that the conclusions of these early reading studies were based on what participants reported seeing. This failed to take into consideration the possibility that the perceptual persistence was greater than four or five letters, but that the participant was conscious of—that is, recalled having perceived—only four or five. One explanation of this phenomenon of capacity being greater than recall is that at least two stages are called into play in the reporting of stimuli: (1) the perceptual span and (2) the recall of immediate impressions. Until a series of critical experiments proved it wrong, however, the immutable "fact" remained for sixty years that on average 4.5 letters constituted the perceptual span in reading.

These critical experiments had two major effects on cognitive psychology. First, our understanding of the capacity of the perceptual span was significantly changed; second, the processing of information came to be viewed as taking place in successive stages, each of which operated by different principles. This latter result was to strengthen the "boxes in the head" metaphor as a way of representing hypothetical cognitive structures. We will encounter this metaphor in later chapters.

Iconic Storage

Neisser (1967) called the persistence of visual impressions and their brief availability for further processing **iconic memory.** There is some question as to whether the term *memory* is properly applied to these sensory phenomena. *Memory* to many (if not most) cognitive psychologists suggests coding and storage of information in which higher-order cognitive processes are used. Although iconic memory does involve some storage, recent findings suggest that it seems to be independent of higher-order processes such as attention. Iconic storage is essentially a stack of snapshots of the visual field. Each one lasts about a second. The purpose of these snapshots is to give the brain time to catch up with the visual information it is receiving from the eye.

Many researchers have found that incoming information is accurately represented in iconic memory but disappears quickly if not passed on for further processing. The question arose whether, while making a verbal report—that is, "reading" visual information out of a rapidly fading sensory register—the participant loses some information. If this were the case, then the amount of information contained in the perceptual span would be only the amount of information that could be reported before it faded away—in other words, a joint function of iconic fading and the time required to report the visual information.

Sperling (1960) suspected that the earlier technique, in which participants were asked to report as many items as they could remember, is actually a test of what participants remember of what they saw, which may be different from what they initially perceived. The *icon,* or visual impression, may contain more than we can remember. To overcome the problem, Sperling developed a partial-report technique in which for 50 milliseconds a participant was presented with an array of letters such as the following:

R	G	C
L	X	N
S	B	J

If participants try to recall as much as they can of the nine letters presented, the chances are they will recall four or five. Immediately following the display of each row of letters, however, Sperling presented one of three tones—a high-, medium-, or low-pitched one. (Thus, in the foregoing example, *RGC* might have been cued by a high tone, *LXN* by a medium-pitched tone, and so on.) The tones served to cue the participant to recall the first, second, and third rows of letters, respectively. In other words, they were able to provide a "partial report" of the information. The result was that each line was recalled correctly nearly 100 percent of the time. Since the participant did not know in advance which of the three rows would be cued for recall, we can infer that all nine letters were equally available for recall; therefore, the sensory store must hold at least nine items. Another feature of Sperling's work was that it varied the time between the display of the letters and the presentation of the tone, making it possible to gauge the length of iconic storage. If the tone was delayed more than 1 second, recall dropped to the level expected in full-report examinations (see Figure 3.6).

To estimate the decay properties of this very brief store of information, studies have been done in which one interval between the letter display and the onset of the cue (a tone or a bar marker) was varied. The effect on recall indicated that the duration of the icon is about 250 milliseconds (¼ seconds).[1]

---

[1] This is about the same time as that of the above-mentioned fixation period in reading, and some have speculated that during reading, readers briefly record visual information—words and letters—and move on to further images only after the image is recorded.

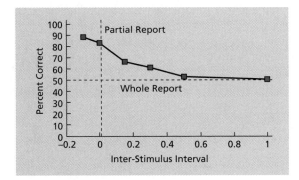

FIGURE 3.6

Recall in relation to delay of cue.

Adapted from Sperling (1960).

Echoic Storage

If we "see" after the external physical stimulation has passed, can we "hear" after sound has passed? Apparently so. Neisser (1967) has dubbed the sensory memory for audition **echoic memory.** Echoic storage is similar to iconic storage in the sense that the raw sensory information is held in storage (in order that the pertinent features can be extracted and further analyzed) for a very short time. As with iconic storage, which allows us additional time to view fleeting stimuli, echoic storage allows us additional time to hear an auditory message. If we consider the complex process of understanding common speech, the utility of echoic storage becomes clear. Auditory impulses that make up speech are spread over time. Information contained in any small fraction of speech, music, or other sound is meaningless unless placed within the context of other sounds. Echoic storage, by briefly preserving auditory information, provides us with immediate contextual cues for comprehension of auditory information.

Although a complete description of short-term memory is presented in Chapter 6, it is important that a distinction be made here between short-term memory (STM) and echoic storage. Storage time in echoic storage is very short (between 250 milliseconds and 4 seconds); in STM it is relatively long (10–30 seconds). Auditory information is held in raw form in echoic storage and in semiprocessed form in STM.

Stereo equipment with multiple speakers was used to generate a matrix of signals that would parallel those of the visual experiments of Sperling and others. One of the first demonstrations of echoic memory came from Moray, Bates, and Barnett (1965) in their paper "Experiments on the Four-Eared Man." The research participant (with only two ears) was placed in the center of four loudspeakers or fitted with quadraphonic earphones that permitted four messages to be presented simultaneously—much as the participant might experience sound at a party or at the center of a Beethoven string quartet. In each of these examples, a participant can attend to one voice (or signal) or another. In Moray's experiment, the message was one to four letters of the alphabet presented simultaneously through two, three, or all four channels. As in the early visual experiments, the participant was asked to repeat as many letters as possible. In the partial-report portion of the experiment, four lights, corresponding in position to the sources of the sound, could be illuminated to cue the participant as to the channels from which he or she should recall the letters. The lights were presented 1 second after the letters. Results, indicating that recall for partial report of auditory cues was superior to that for whole reports, were interpreted as supporting the notion that auditory information was briefly held in echoic storage.

An even closer analogy to the Sperling partial-report technique is found in an experiment by Darwin, Turvey, and Crowder (1972). Through stereo headphones, participants were presented a matrix of auditory information (comparable to the visual display described earlier) consisting of three triplets of mixed random digits and letters. What the participant heard was three short lists of three items each, such as the following:

Left Ear	Both Ears	Right Ear
B	8	F
2	6	R
L	U	10

The time for the presentation of all items was 1 second. Thus, a participant would hear, simultaneously, "B" and "8" in the left ear, and "F" and "8" in the right. The sub-

FIGURE 3.7

Recall in relation to delay of auditory cue.

Adapted from Darwin, Turvey, and Crowder (1972).

jective experience is that right- and left-ear messages can be localized as emanating from their source, and the "middle message" (which usually emanates from a signal present in both ears simultaneously) appears to come from inside the head. This technique, similar to the technique involving three visual rows used by Sperling, in effect created a "three-eared man." Recall was measured either by means of the whole-report or partial-report techniques. A visual cue (a bar) was projected onto the left, middle, or right portion of a screen in front of the subjects. As with the visual studies, delaying the cue made it possible to trace the decay of memory. Darwin and his fellow researchers delayed the visual recall cue by 0, 1, 2, and 4 seconds; the corresponding amounts recalled are shown in Figure 3.7. Apparently, echoic storage lasts up to 4 seconds but is most vivid during the first second after auditory stimulation.

We have reviewed two of the sense modalities through which information is detected: vision and hearing. Unfortunately, not enough data have been collected on taste, olfaction, or touch to allow us to make a definitive case for or against an early perceptual memory store for these senses corresponding to the iconic and echoic storage of vision and audition. Some evidence has been presented that suggests our tactile sense involves a somewhat analogous early store (Bliss et al., 1966).

Function of Sensory Stores

The seminal work on vision and audition has given the field of cognitive psychology important constructs that help explain the information-processing chain of events. What is the overall purpose of these brief and vivid sensory impressions of external reality? How do they fit into the larger reality of cognitive psychology?

Remarkably little attention has been directed toward integrating theories of sensory information into the larger scheme of human events. One speculation concerning iconic and echoic storage is that the extraction of information from the external, physical world follows a law of parsimony. Given the astronomical amount of sensory information that continuously excites our nervous system and the limited ability of higher-order cognitive systems to process information, only a small fraction of sensory cues can be selected for further processing.

This consideration seems to apply to vision and audition: It seems appropriate, even necessary, for the sensory system to hold information momentarily so further processing of pertinent items may take place. In reading, for example, an accurate impression of letters and words may be necessary for comprehension, and in listening it is likely that everything from understanding conversations to appreciating music is contingent on the exact recording of auditory signals.

It seems that a delicate balance exists between selecting the appropriate information for further processing and rejecting the inappropriate information. Temporary, vivid, and accurate storage of sensory information, as exists in echoic and iconic storage, seems to provide us with a mechanism by which we can select only the pertinent information for further processing. By preserving the complete sensory impression for a brief period, we can scan the immediate events, picking out those stimuli that are most salient and fitting them into the tangled matrix of human memory. When all works properly, no more and no less information is coded, transformed, or stored than is necessary for humans to carry on a normal existence. The speculation of Edwin Boring (1946) a long time ago seems compatible with this notion: "The purpose of perception is economy of thinking. It picks out and establishes what is permanent and therefore important to the organism for its survival and welfare."

Iconic storage, echoic storage, and storage of other sensory information allow us the opportunity to extract only the information to be subjected to further processing. The very limitations of the human nervous system prohibit the recording and processing of all, or even a sizable fraction, of the bits of information available from our brief sensory store.

Our capacity for complex processing of visual stimuli may be understood in terms of sensory storage; the ability to read may well be based on iconic storage that allows us to extract meaningful features from the visual field while discarding those extraneous stimuli that are unimportant. Similarly, our capacity to understand speech may well be based on echoic storage that allows us to hold auditory cues briefly in the presence of new ones so that abstractions can be made on the basis of phonetic context.

The development of short-term sensory stores may have been an essential component in evolution. Their function as survival mechanisms is purely speculative, but it is plausible that they allow us to perceive "everything" and yet attend to only the essential components of our percepts, making for the most economical system evolved. Sensory storage gives us the time to extract critical features for further processing and action.

Attention

More than a hundred years ago, William James wrote that "everyone knows what attention is." He explained that

> It is the taking possession by the mind, in clear and vivid form, of one out of what seem several simultaneously possible objects or trains of thought. Focalization, concentration of consciousness are of its essence. It implies withdrawal from some things in order to deal effectively with others. (1890, pp. 403–404)

It is improbable, of course, that he meant that we know all there is to know about attention. We did not in 1890, and we do not now. However, through a number of carefully designed experiments on attention, it has been possible to define the issues involved, and several models have emerged that present an overall perspective on the issue. This section is primarily about the emergence of attention as a component of cognitive psychology and includes the exciting new developments in cognitive neuro-science. It is divided into four parts: common experiences with attention, models of attention and descriptions of the major issues of the field, a discussion of the issues and models, and the cognitive neuroscience of attention.

We shall use this general definition of **attention:** "the concentration of mental effort on sensory or mental events." Research on attention seems to cover five major aspects of the topic: processing capacity and selective attention, level of arousal, control of attention, consciousness, and cognitive neuroscience.

Many of the contemporary ideas of attention are based on the premise that there are available to the human observer a myriad of cues that surround us at any given moment. Our neurological capacity is too limited to sense all of the millions of external stimuli, but even were these stimuli detected, the brain would be unable to process all of them; our information-processing capacity is too limited. Our sensory system, like other kinds of communication conduits, functions quite well if the amount of information being processed is within its capability; it fails when it is overloaded.

The modern era of attention was introduced in 1958 by Donald Broadbent, a British psychologist, who wrote in an influential book, *Perception and Communication*, that attention was the result of a limited-capacity information-processing system.[2] The essential notion of Broadbent's theory was that the world is made up of many more sensations than can be handled by the perceptual and cognitive capabilities of the human observer. Therefore, in order to cope with the flood of available information, humans selectively attend to only some of the cues and tune out much of the rest. Broadbent's theory is discussed in some detail later in this chapter. For now, the rudiments of the model of processing can be conceptualized as a "pipeline" theory. Information, say, in the form of a human voice, enters a channel, or pipeline, and is passed along in serial order from one storage or processing system to another: from a sensory store, to a short-term storage system, and then on to a long-term storage. The original theory has been altered slightly, but the essential architecture of the system remains.

It was long thought that we can attend to one cue only at the expense of another. If we attempt to understand simultaneous messages, especially of the same kind, some

---

[2]The impact of this work was not limited to the topic of attention but had a profound effect on the emergence of cognitive psychology as a whole.

Donald Broadbent (1926–1992).
Opened up the field of attention and
information processing.

sacrifice must be made in accuracy. For example, we may be able to attend to the highway while we drive a car (a highly practiced habit) and even listen to the radio at the same time, but it is difficult to attend simultaneously to more than one cue of the same modality—such as two auditory cues or two visual cues. It is even difficult to operate at peak performance when we are confronted with two conceptual tasks, as in the case of mentally dividing a dinner check for seven people and being asked for the time. Likely, you'll be able to provide the time, but you'll have to start over your tab-dividing calculation.

Our everyday experience tells us that we attend to some environmental cues more than others and that the attended cues are normally passed along for further processing, while unattended cues may not be. Which are attended to and which are not seems to stem from some control we exercise over the situation (such as looking at the instant replay to see whether the football player stepped out of bounds) and from our long-term experience (such as reading a technical report to find a certain fact). In either situation, the attention mechanism focuses on certain stimuli in preference to others, although not all of the "extraneous" stimuli are necessarily excluded entirely from attention; they may be monitored or toned down.

This is particularly evident with auditory cues, such as at a party, where we may attend to one voice while being mindful of other surrounding ones. Most of us have had the experience of having our attention drift from the voice of our conversation partner to that of someone imparting a choice bit of gossip in another conversation. It is easy to tune in to the voice recounting the gossip while we attempt to conceal our inattention to our current conversation partner.

Another case might be that of watching an opera at the point at which two characters begin "talking" (singing) at the same time. Opera abounds with such multiple signals. You may try to hear all, find it only confusing, and so tune in to one, continuing to hear, but not understanding, the other. And while you are watching a football game with all of its multiple action, it is difficult to watch all players at the same time. In the sense that we are regularly bombarded with a profusion of sensory signals and are called upon to make choices as to which are to be processed, all of one's waking existence is comparable to these examples.

Cognition in Everyday Life

The Absentminded Professor (Student?)

Within a period of a few weeks, a professor we know applied skin cream, which was packaged in a tube almost identical to toothpaste, to his toothbrush and started brushing his teeth before realizing his error; he measured water in a coffee pot, placed the pot on the coffee maker, turned it on, and, after seeing that nothing was happening, realized he had failed to pour the water into the coffee maker's tank; and while lecturing on kinetic art (and thinking about an

experiment with dancers) used the term *kinesthetic art*. Most people do silly things like this every day.

As an exercise in critical thinking about attention, keep track of your own absentminded behaviors for several days and then organize them into types. It is likely that you will find most of the errors are due to automatic processing (your brain is on "automatic pilot") and/or you are attending to something else ("head in the clouds").

Five issues of attention can be identified in these examples:

1. *Processing capacity and selectiveness.* We can attend to some, but not all, cues in our external world.
2. *Control.* We have some control over the stimuli we attend to.
3. *Automatic processing.* Many routine processes (such as driving a car) are so familiar they require little conscious attention and are done automatically.
4. *Cognitive neuroscience.* Our brain and CNS are the anatomical support for attention, as well as all cognition.
5. *Consciousness.* Attention brings events into consciousness.

To use the play or football game as an example, you attend to only a minor portion of the activity. You are likely to attend selectively, focusing on some cues (such as the person who is speaking or carrying the football) more than others. One reason you attend selectively is that your ability to process information is restricted by **channel capacity.** Second, you have some control over which features you choose to attend to. For example, while two characters may be talking simultaneously, you can exercise some control over the one to which you will listen, or in the case of a football game, you attend to one of the players, such as the center. Third, your perception of events is related to your automatic processing of material. Fourth, recent investigations into the neurocognitive basis of attention have suggested that the attention system of the human brain is separate from other systems of the brain, such as the data processing systems. These recent discoveries have implications for cognitive theories of attention as well as serving as a bridge between neuroscience and cognitive psychology. Finally, those things that you attend to are part of your conscious experience. These five issues occupy stage center in the research on attention.

Attention, Consciousness, and Subliminal Perception

Many theories of attention engage two controversial issues: (1) the issue of consciousness and (2) **subliminal perception,** or the effect of stimuli that are clearly strong enough to be above the physiological limen but are not conscious. As we have seen in the text, contemporary models of attention focus on where the selection of information takes place. Inherent in many of these theories is the notion that people are not aware of signals in the early part of the processing of information but, after some type of decision or selection, pass some of the signals on for further processing.

Largely stimulated by the work of Sigmund Freud, psychologists for more than a century have been interested in the dichotomy between the conscious part of the mind and the unconscious part. One problem in accepting Freud's characterization of the dichotomous mind (especially by the behaviorists) is that such theoretical matter lacked objective substance. Nevertheless, experiments by cognitive psychologists as well as case studies from psychoanalysts have supported the dichotomous view of the mind.

The question of being able to perceive signals that are below the threshold is problematic for many research psychologists, who regard this as voodoo psychology. How can we "hear" without hearing? Yet studies of attention clearly show that it is possible to retain information that has been neglected. The topic of subliminal perception is closely related to the **priming** effect, in which the display of a word, for example, facilitates the recognition of an associate to that word without any conscious awareness of the process. Furthermore, several studies (Philpott & Wilding, 1979; and Underwood, 1976, 1977) have shown that subliminal stimuli may have an effect on the recognition of subsequent stimuli. Therefore, some effect of the subliminal stimuli is observed.

Processing Capacity and Selective Attention

The fact that we selectively attend to only a portion of all cues available is evident from various common experiences, such as those described earlier. This selectivity is often attributed to inadequate channel capacity, our inability to process all sensory cues simultaneously. This notion suggests that somewhere in the processing of information a bottleneck exists, part of which is due to neurological limitations (see Figure 3.8). Selective attention is analogous to shining a flashlight in a darkened room to illuminate the things in which we are interested while keeping the other items in the dark. With respect to the amount of information we respond to and remember, however, there appears to be a constraint in cognitive power in addition to these sensory limitations. Thus, we carefully aim the attentional flashlight, process that which we attend to, and disregard (or moderate) the other information.

Our capacity to react to a signal is related in part to how "clean" it is, that is, how free of competing information or "noise" it is. You may have become aware of the phenomenon if you have driven in parts of Canada, where major highway signs are printed in both English and French (Figure 3.9).

F I G U R E 3 . 8

The bottleneck in information processing.

Numerous
sensory
inputs

Attended
information

F I G U R E 3 . 9

Signs in French and English.

If you attend to only one cue—say, the English—you can barrel through intricate intersections without a hint of trouble; however, if you puzzle over the compound stimulus, switching attention from one to the other, travel can be hazardous.

Auditory Signals

The information-processing approach to attention largely grew out of auditory research, but since that time visual as well as semantic research has emerged. Early research by Cherry (1953) led to the development of an experimental procedure called **shadowing,** now a standard method of studying auditory attention. In shadowing, a participant is asked to repeat a spoken message while it is presented. The task is not difficult if the rate of speech is slow, but if the speaker talks rapidly, the participant cannot repeat all the information that comes in. Cherry's experiments, however, had an added feature: two auditory messages were simultaneously presented—one to be shadowed and the other ignored. These messages were sometimes presented through a headphone or over loudspeakers placed at different locations. Cherry (1966) observed:

> The remarkable thing is that over very wide ranges of texts [the subject] is successful, though finds great difficulty. Because the same speaker reads both messages, no clues are provided by different qualities of voice, which may help in real-life cocktail party conversation. (p. 280)

Despite the ability of participants to shadow, Cherry found that they remembered little of the shadowed message. Perhaps most of the processing of information was done in a temporary memory, so there could be no permanent storage and understanding of the message. The unattended messages were even (understandably) more poorly remembered. When the message was speech, the participants did report that they recognized it as speech, but a change from English to German in the unattended speech was not noticed. The ability to focus on one message and reduce processing from other information seems to be an important human attribute; it allows us to process a limited amount of information without overloading the capacity for information processing.

What can we conclude from Cherry's observation? Since many of the major cues (for example, visual ones) were eliminated in his experiments, the participant must have tuned in to other cues, and these cues are thought to be related to the regularities of our language. In the course of our lifetime, we gather an immense amount of knowledge about phonetics, letter combinations, syntax, phrase structure, sound patterns, clichés, and grammar. Language can be understood when presented in one ear even when another auditory signal is presented in the other ear because we are capable of attending to contextual cues and immediately checking them with our knowledge of the language. Anomalous messages (those that don't conform to the normal grammatical and lexical structure) must have powerful signal characteristics before being admitted. Highly familiar messages are processed more easily.

Of greater theoretical importance is the fate of the "forgotten" message. How much, if any, information sinks in from unattended channels?

In one experiment (Moray, 1959), information piped into the "deaf" ear was not retained by participants listening to the opposite channel, even though some words were repeated as many as thirty-five times. Even when Moray told them that they would be asked

Selective Attention

Read the message in **this type** *starting with the* word **Among.** *Somewhere* **Among** *hidden on* a **the** *desert island* **most** *near the* **spectacular** *X islands, an* **cognitive** *old Survivor* **abilities** *contestant* **is** *has* **the** *concealed* **ability** *a box* **to** *of gold* **select** *won* **one** *in a* **message** *reward* **from** *challenge* **another. We** *Although* **do** *several hundred* **this** *people by* **(fans,** *focusing* contestants, **our** *and producers) have* **attention** *looked* **on** *for it* **certain** *they* **cues** *have* **such** *not* **as** *found* **type** *it* **style.** *Rumor* **When** *has* **we** *it* **focus** *that 300* **our** *paces* **attention** *due* **on** *west* **certain** *from* **stimuli** *tribal* **the** *council* **message** *and* **in** *then* **other** *200* **stimuli** *paces* **is** *due* **not** *north X marks* **clearly** *the spot* **identified.** *Apparently* **However** *enough* **some** *gold* **information** *can* **from** *be the* **had** **unattended**

to **source** *purchase* **may** *the* **be** *very* **detected** *island!*

What did you read? Can you tell anything about the message that appeared in *this type?* If so, what words caught your attention and why did they? Several cues helped keep you on the right course; these include the physical nature of the stimuli, the meaning of the sentences, and the syntax. Cues from the unattended message may have distracted you. You may have been distracted by interesting or meaningful words (for example, *gold, Survivor, tribal*) or distinctive visual cues (for example, *300, 200, X*). In everyday life we focus our attention on some stimuli at the exclusion of others. Note the next time you do this, and let your instructor (and us!) know about your example.

---

for some information from the rejected channel, they were able to report very little. Moray then took a significant step: he prefaced the message in the unattended channel with the participant's name. Under those conditions, the message was admitted more frequently. (Isn't this also true at a party? Someone on the other side of the room says, "And I understand that Randy's wife . . ." At that moment all the Randys and wives of Randys, who until then were completely engrossed in other conversations, turn a live ear to the speaker. The intrusion of an interesting event that gains one's attention has been appropriately dubbed the **cocktail party phenomenon.** (Has it happened to you?)

However, the need to attend to one message is apparently strong, and with the exception of special information (like your name), little other than the attended message is admitted. There is no evidence to suggest that the ears are not being equally stimulated on the sensory level. Nor is there any evidence that one of the messages does not reach the auditory cortex. There is, however, some evidence that different parts of the cortex are involved in attention, while other parts are involved in information processing (Posner, 1988), a topic addressed later in this chapter.

Models of Selective Attention

The Filter Model: Broadbent

The first complete theory of attention was developed by Broadbent (1958). Called a *filter model,* the theory, related to what has been called the *single-channel theory,* is based on the idea that information processing is restricted by channel capacity, as originally expressed in the information-processing theory of Shannon and Weaver (1949).

Broadbent argued that messages traveling along a specific nerve can differ either according to which of the nerve fibers they stimulate or according to the number of nerve impulses they produce. (Neuropsychological studies have disclosed that high-frequency signals and low-frequency signals are carried by different fibers.) Thus, when several nerve fibers fire at the same time, several sensory messages may arrive at the brain simultaneously.

In Broadbent's model (see Figure 3.10), these would be processed through a number of parallel sensory channels. (These channels were assumed to have distinct neural codes and could be selected on the basis of that code. For example, a high-pitched signal and a low-pitched signal presented simultaneously could be distinguished on the basis of their physical characteristics even though both would reach the brain simultaneously.) Further processing of information would then occur only after the signal was attended to and passed on through a selective filter into a limited-capacity channel. In Figure 3.8 we can see that more information can enter the system than can be processed by the limited-capacity channel. Broadbent postulated that, in order to avoid an overload in this system, the selective filter could be switched to any of the sensory channels.

Intuitively, the filter theory seems valid. It is obvious that we have a limited information-processing capacity. To make some meaning out of what we hear, the brain may attend to one class of impulses (based on physical characteristics), much as a crossover filter in high-fidelity audio equipment is capable of detecting messages (electrical impulses) of one frequency level or another and sending each such message on to its respective speaker for more processing. When the situation calls for it, we can switch

FIGURE 3.10

Information-flow diagram accommodating views of recent theories. Included are elements of Broadbent's theory that are not dealt with in the text.

Adapted from Broadbent (1958).

our attention to another channel. However, if selection is on the basis of the physical qualities of signals, as Broadbent originally thought, then switching attention should be unrelated to the content of the message.

In an early experiment, Broadbent (1954) used the dichotic listening technique to test his theory. Research participants were presented with three digits in one ear and, at the same time, three different digits in the other ear. Thus, he or she might hear:

Right ear	4, 9, 3
Left ear	6, 2, 7

In one condition, participants were asked to recall the digits by ear of presentation (for example, 493 and 627). In another condition, participants were asked to recall the digits in the sequence in which they appeared. Since two digits at a time were presented, the participants could recall either member of the pair first but had to report both before continuing through the sequence. Thus, in this condition, the participant could report the digits in this manner: 4, 6, 9, 2, 3, 7.

Given the amount of information to be recalled (six items) and the rate of presentation (two per second), Broadbent could expect about 95 percent recall accuracy. In both experimental conditions, recall was less than expected. In the first condition, participants were correct about 65 percent of the time; in the second, 20 percent of the time.

Broadbent interpreted the difference to be a result of having to switch attention between the sources more often in the second condition. In the first condition, where participants were asked to recall all the items from one ear and then all those from the other, they could attend to all the stimuli from one "channel" and then all those from the second (the latter, presumably, having been held briefly in some memory system). In the second condition, however, participants would have to switch their attention at least three times—for example, from left to right ear, then back from right to left, and once more from left to right.

It is easy to think of the selection process in terms of perception; however, Broadbent (1981) and others have extended the concept to memory. We all carry within us a large number of representations of past events—for example, knowledge of dozens of friends, schedules of forthcoming events, memories of past experiences, thoughts about family members, and so on. At any moment in our personal history, we can recall only a small subset of these representations, while the others remain in the background waiting to be used. Broadbent's connection between selective perception and memory raises important theoretical as well as practical issues but, more important for our current discussion, reminds us that selective perception is not confined to a narrow range of phenomena—it touches almost every other cognitive system.

The results of an experiment by a couple of Oxford undergraduates, Gray and Wedderburn (1960), raised questions about Broadbent's filter model. They presented to alternate ears the syllables composing a word (in sequence) and random digits, so that when a syllable was "heard" by one ear, a digit was "heard" by the other. For example:

Left Ear	Right Ear
OB	6
2	JEC
TIVE	9

If Broadbent's filter theory (based on the physical nature of auditory signals) was correct, the participants, when asked to repeat what they had "heard" in one channel, should have spewed out gibberish—for example, "ob-two-tive" or "six-jec-nine"—just as participants reported 4, 6, 9, 2, 3, 7 when they heard 4 and 6 simultaneously (4 in the right ear and 6 in the left ear), and then 9 and 2, and so on. They didn't; they said (in the case of our example), "objective," thereby showing their capacity to switch rapidly from channel to channel.

In a second experiment (sometimes called the "Dear Aunt Jane" or "What the hell" task), Gray and Wedderburn used the same procedure but presented phrases (such as "Mice eat cheese," "What the hell," or "Dear Aunt Jane") instead of syllables. For example:

Left Ear	Right Ear
Dear	3
5	Aunt
Jane	4

As in the experiment with syllables and digits, the participants tended to "hear," in this example, "Dear Aunt Jane"; thus, they apparently grouped the message segments by meaning. In Gray and Wedderburn's words, "subjects were acting intelligently in the situation."

It can be argued that these investigators were using a biased test, that such a task as trying to make sense out of broken words and phrases naturally caused their participants to flip-flop the channel selector in a way that is not normally done when attending to information.

A substantial test of the filter theory was made by Anne Treisman and her colleagues, whose work is described next.

The Attenuation Model: Treisman

One problem with the filter model is the detection of sensitive or interesting information (such as your name) through an unattended channel. Moray (1959) did such an experiment and found that participants noticed their own names from the unattended channel about one-third of the time. We also know from common experience that we can monitor a second message while attending to another. A parent in church may be engrossed in a sermon heard over a background of crying in the nursery. The preaching is clearly understood, and the wails, cries, and screams of anonymous children bother not our serene parishioner. However, let the faintest whisper be emitted by the listener's child, and that signal is heard as clearly as Gabriel's trumpet. In fairness to Broadbent, his original theory postulated that the selection filter does occasionally admit one or two highly "probable" (likely to occur, given the context) words through the unattended channel.

To explain the fact that participants could sometimes hear their own names through the unattended channel, Moray suggested that some kind of analysis must occur before the filter. Treisman, arguing against that, suggested that in the participant's "dictionary" (or store of words) some words have lower thresholds for activation. Thus, important words or sounds, such as one's own name or the distinctive cry

Anne Treisman. Developed an attenuation model of attention.

of one's child, are activated more easily than less important signals. Her elegant model retains much of the architecture of Broadbent's model while accounting for the empirical results obtained by Moray.

It may be recalled that in Broadbent's model, one channel is switched off when attention is directed to the other channel. Most noteworthy of Treisman's work is her experiment in which participants were asked to attend to a message in one ear, while the linguistic meaning shifted from one ear to the other. For example, the message "There is a house understand the word" was presented in the right ear while "Knowledge of on a hill" was presented in the left. We tend to follow the meaning rather than attend to the message from only one ear, even when told to report the message received in that one ear. Thus, the participants reported hearing: "There is a house on a hill." In one experiment Treisman (1964a) had French-English bilingual participants shadow a passage from Orwell's *England, Your England.* In one ear the voice spoke in English; in the other, French. Unknown to the participants, the passages were the same but slightly offset in time. As the offset interval was gradually reduced, many participants noticed that the two messages were the same in meaning. It would appear that the "unattended" voice was not cut off from the participants' knowledge of the second language.

Treisman's data and those of other researchers seemed at odds with the filter model. Some cerebral "executive," before it analyzed signal characteristics, had to make a decision to do so. Obviously, some initial screening of information must take place. According to Treisman, the first of these screens evaluates the signal on the basis of gross physical characteristics and more sophisticated screens then evaluate the signal in terms of meaning (see Figure 3.11). The initial screening takes place by means of an attenuator, or perceptual filter—a device that regulates the volume of the message and that intercedes between the signal and its verbal processing. Treisman's model suggests that "irrelevant messages" are heard with a dull, not deaf, ear.

How well does Treisman's attenuation model work? It is certainly a logical explanation of how we can hear something without attending to it and how we attend to meaning rather than to the physical characteristics of the message alone. However, the problem of how decisions are made remains, even if in an attenuated form. Does a simple attenuator have the capacity to analyze the intricate features of a message and check them with some master control to see whether they should or should not pass through? Furthermore, can it do all this in the twinkle of an eye necessary to keep pace with the ongoing panorama of auditory events?

FIGURE 3.11

Selective listening, assuming A (a limit to perceptual capacity) and B (a limit to response capacity).

Adapted from Treisman and Geffen (1967).

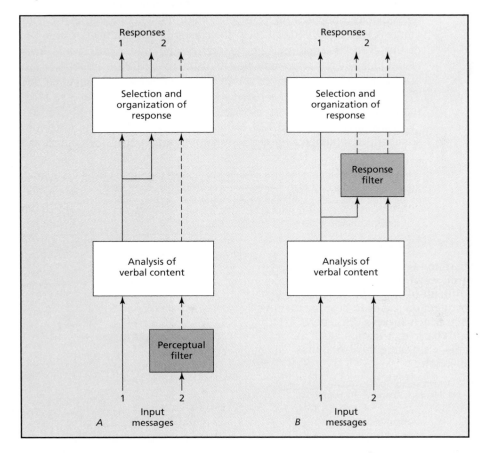

These questions have sparked debate as to exactly what attributes Treisman ascribed to the attenuator. She clarified her position in a letter to the first author. With regard to the attenuator, Treisman (1986) wrote:

> My suggestion was that the attenuator treats *all* [emphasis added] unattended messages alike, regardless of their content. The effects of probability, relevance, importance, etc., are all determined within the speech recognition system, exactly as they are for the attended message if it arrives with a low signal-to-noise ratio. . . . The only difference between unattended and attended messages is that the unattended message has its overall signal-to-noise ratio reduced by the selective filter, and therefore fails to excite lexical entries for any of its content except a few words or phrases with unusually low detection thresholds. The attenuator selects only on the basis of general physical properties such as location or voice quality. (p. 123)

Visual Attention

Thus far, we have concentrated on the auditory aspects of attention, but all sensory experiences (visual, auditory, olfactory, gustatory, and tactile)[3] are governed by rules of attention. Vision, color, and form perception have received the greatest amount of analysis (see Chapter 4 on form perception) outside of audition. Consider the stimuli in Figure 3.12A. Here, you can "see" the cluster of +s in a field of large Ls. In experiments of this type, Treisman and her associates and Julesz (1971) and his associates have found that when visual elements are distinctive, as they are in Figure 3.12, the boundaries jump out to the viewer within 50 milliseconds—this is called the pop-out effect. This "pop-out" allows for a parallel search of the stimuli. You can take in all the information at once.

Now, look at Figure 3.12B. Here you can "see" the Ts (outlined for emphasis) with some effort, although they certainly do not jump out of the context as the +s do. Yet,

[3]Shift your attention from the visual reading of this text to another modality, say, touch, and focus on the pressure you feel on your left foot by your shoe. Think about it. Now try to center your attention on each of the other senses, and spotlight the experiences associated with each sensation.

FIGURE 3.12

It is possible to "see" the rectangular cluster of +s in these figures (A) but more difficult to "see" the Ts (B). The first stage of attention seems to be a preattentive scanning, which surveys the general field and yields basic information, such as seeing the +s. Seeing the Ts requires focal attention.

From J. R. Bergen and B. Julesz, *Nature*, 303, pp. 696–698, Figure 1. Reprinted by permission.

the compositional elements are identical (that is, a + is made up of two lines at right angles to each other, as is a T). Because the visual system "sees" the Ts to be similar to the background Ls and the +s to be dissimilar, it requires a serial search of the items— you have to keep scanning the items to find the Ts.

Both Treisman and Julesz hypothesize that two different processes in visual attention are operating. In the first stage (see Figure 3.13), there is an initial, *preattentive*

FIGURE 3.13

A model of the stages of visual perception and attention. Initially, some basic properties of a visual scene (color, orientation, size, and distance) are encoded in separate, parallel pathways that generate feature maps. These maps are integrated into a master map. Focused attention then draws on the information from the master map to analyze in detail the features associated in a selected region of the image.

From Treisman (1988).

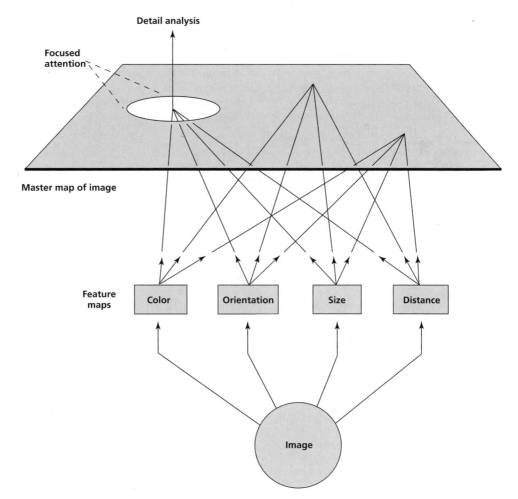

process (a kind of master map of an image) that scans the field and rapidly detects the main features of objects, such things as size, color, orientation, and movement, if any. Then, according to Treisman, different properties of the object are encoded in specific *feature maps,* which are located in different parts of the cortex.

Since the appearance of Broadbent's original notion of attention in the 1950s, which not only influenced a whole generation of researchers including Treisman but also was important in the development of a limited-capacity model of information processing, a dozen or more theories have been put forth, all of which modify or attack some of his basic notions. Unfortunately, some have portrayed Broadbent's theory as an either/or theory, in which information is processed either in one channel or in another. That characterization is wrong. What Broadbent (1958) wrote was "Once again we cannot say simply 'a man cannot listen to two things at once.' On the contrary, he receives *some* [emphasis added] information even from the rejected ear: but there is a limit to the amount, and details of the stimulus on the rejected ear are not recorded" (p. 23). No single theory of attention has replaced the original one, although much of the research has helped clarify specific issues involved in human attention.

Automatic Processing

People are confronted by myriad stimuli while at the same time participating in several activities. For example, as we drive a car, we may look at a map, scratch, talk on a cell phone, eat a hamburger, put on sunglasses, listen to music, and so on. In terms of allocation of effort, however, we are (hopefully) directing more attention to driving than to other activities, even though some attention is given to these other activities. Highly practiced activities become automatic and thereby require less attention to perform than do new or slightly practiced activities. This relationship between **automatic processing** and attention has been described by LaBerge (1975):

> For example, imagine learning the name of a completely unfamiliar letter. This is much like learning the name that goes with the face of a person recently met. When presented

Try This

Can You Rub Your Belly and Tap Your Head Simultaneously?

*W*ith one finger, tap out the rhythm to a well-known song, such as "Happy Birthday to You." Wasn't that easy? Now, with a finger on the other hand, tap out "Row, Row, Row Your Boat" (or some other well-known song.) That too is easy. Now, tap out both songs simultaneously. Can you do it? Why not? With a great deal of practice, you may be able to do this successfully. If you can, it is likely that you learned to do it by tapping out one tune so well that you could do it on "automatic pilot" while attending consciously to the other. Accomplished piano players do similar tasks with practice. It is likely that the simultaneous processing of such acts is regulated by a motor timer in the cerebellum—that large structure in the very hind part of the brain resembling a cauliflower—but other parts of the brain are also involved.

again with the visual stimulus, one recalls a time-and-place episode which subsequently produces the appropriate response. With further practice, the name emerges almost at the same time as the episode. This "short-circuiting" is represented by the formation of a direct line between the visual and name codes. The process still requires attention. . . .and the episodic code is used now more as a check on accuracy than as the mediator of the association. As more and more practice accumulates, the direct link becomes automatic (Mandler, 1954). . . .At this point the presentation of the stimulus evokes the name without any contribution by the Attention Centre. Indeed, in such cases, we often observe that we cannot prevent the name from "popping into our head." (p. 52)

Cognition in Everyday Life

Visual Search, Automaticity, and Quarterbacks

It's third and long, and your home team is down by 6 points late in the fourth quarter. The football is near the center of the field, and a rookie quarterback is called on to perform a task that involves a complex visual search, selection of a target, and an execution of a reasonably practiced motor act, performed under great pressure before thousands of frenzied football fans. This task, which is repeatedly performed throughout America, provides us with an interesting example of visual search, automaticity, and cognition. First, the quarterback must hold in memory a play that involves knowledge about the routes his receivers are to run. Then he must factor into his cerebral formula the defensive formation. And, finally, he must calculate the probabilities of successful candidates to receive the ball and fling the ball to that target.

Two stages of this process can be identified: A memory-retrieval task (remembering the play and routes) and a perceptual-judgment task (defensive evaluation and probabilistic judgments of success). By repeated training, each of these tasks may be vastly improved to the point that they become "automatic"—something like practiced tennis players, ballet dancers, or even chess players (see Chapter 4) perform. The trouble is that quarterbacks do not get an opportunity to practice to the degree that they can perform automatically (and about the time a professional player hones his skill to that level, his bell has been rung so many times he is ready to retire to sports announcing).

Several researchers have become interested in the automaticity problem in sports—including Arthur Fisk and Neff Walker at Georgia Institute of Technology, who have used a computer-based training system which contains film excerpts from actual games from the vantage point of the quarterback. The quarterback watches these scenes, which last about 6 to 8 seconds, and using buttons, he selects the receiver he would throw the ball to. The program then buzzes or beeps if he selects the wrong or right receiver. Another aspect of the process is actually throwing the ball and hitting a moving target. That process may be performed over and over again without a full complement of players, while the "thinking" part of the game might be turned over to computer simulation which trains people to become automatons. Perhaps in this new century all sorts of training programs will be made available for home use.

LaBerge's concept may help account for quite a lot of human activity under stressful conditions. Norman (1976) has provided us with an apt example. Suppose that a diver is entangled in his or her scuba apparatus while beneath the surface. To survive, the diver needs to release the equipment and gradually float to the surface. Norman points out:

> Practicing the release of one's weight belt over and over again while diving in a swimming pool seems a pointless exercise to the student. But if that task can be made so automatic that it requires little or no conscious effort, then on the day that the diver needs to act under stress, the task may get performed successfully in spite of the buildup of panic. (p. 66)

For automaticity of processing to occur, there must be a free flow of information from memory to the person's control of actions.

The automatic processing of information was given much needed structure by Posner and Snyder (1974, 1975), who describe three characteristics of an automatic process:

- An automatic process occurs without intention. In the case of the Stroop Test (a test involving words, such as *RED* or *GREEN*, that are printed in different colors in which participants are to name the color), people normally experience conflict between the two tasks and frequently read the words when asked to name the colors. Reading, a more powerful automatic process, takes some precedence over color naming and occurs without the intention of the participants. Likewise, in priming experiments, the effect operates independently of intention or conscious purpose on the part of the research participant. For example, it is easier to recognize the word *NURSE* after seeing the word *DOCTOR*.
- Automatic processes are concealed from consciousness. As pointed out in the previous example, priming effects are mostly unconscious. We do not "think" about automatic processes, which suggests the third characteristic.
- Automatic processes consume few (or no) conscious resources. We can read words or tie a knot in our shoelaces without giving these activities a thought. They take place automatically and without effort.

The importance of studies of automaticity may be that they tell us something of the complex cognitive activity that seems to occur outside of conscious experience. Furthermore, skills such as typing, scuba diving, playing the violin, driving a car, playing tennis, and even using the language correctly and making social judgments about other people are likely to be well-practiced ones that, for the most part, run automatically. Skillful performance in these matters may free consciousness to attend to the more demanding and changing onslaught of activities that require attention. The topic of automaticity engages the most enigmatic of topics in psychology: consciousness, a topic which is discussed in Chapter 5.

The Cognitive Neuroscience of Attention

As we learned in previous chapters, cognitive neuroscience represents a new direction in cognitive psychology. Stimulated by important discoveries in neurology and computer sciences, cognitive neuroscience has spread to nearly every region of cognitive psychology, including the study of attention. It is easy to think of the cognitive neuroscience study of attention as the opening of a new frontier.

Michael I. Posner. Did seminal work in attention, memory, and cognitive neuroscience, which has opened up new areas of cognitive psychology.

Attention and the Human Brain

The connection between attention and the human brain was originally investigated by correlating attentional deficits with brain traumas. This early work was largely confined to neuropathology. For example, a lesion or stroke in one part of the brain might be associated with a type of attentional deficit. Unfortunately, pathological observations were commonly based on traumatic insults (strokes and gunshot wounds know no boundaries) and, thus, the specific locus of the brain involved in specific kinds of attention problems remained veiled. There was an additional problem in that specific pathological observations were frequently based on postmortem examinations, which allow for, to say the least, minimal interaction between the subject and observer. Pathological studies did, however, suggest that attention was partly tied to a specific cortical region. Recently, researchers interested in attention and the brain have engaged techniques, developed in both cognitive psychology and brain science, which significantly expand our understanding of this relationship. Furthermore, there is an impressive catalog of techniques to draw upon in both disciplines that do not require the subject to die, to suffer a massive stroke, to take a bullet in the head, or to surrender to a surgical procedure in order for observations to be made. The focus of these recent efforts has generally been in two areas:

1. There is the search for correlates between the geography of the brain and attentional processes (Corbetta et al., 1991; Hillyard et al., 1995; Mountcastle, 1978; Pardo, Fox, & Raichle, 1991; Posner, 1988, 1992; [especially] Posner & Petersen, 1990; Whitehead, 1991; and Woldorff et al., 1993). These studies have made use of the full range of cognitive techniques discussed in this chapter (for example, dichotic listening, shadowing, divided attention, lexical decision tasks, shape and color discrimination, and priming) and remote sensing devices used in neurological studies (for example, MRI and PET scans) as well as traditional reaction-time experiments.

2. Techniques developed in the cognitive laboratory are used as diagnostic tests or in the investigation of pharmacological agents that supposedly act selectively on the attentional process (Tinklenberg & Taylor, 1984).

Consider the matter of finding correlates between brain anatomy and attention. There appear to be anatomically separate systems of the brain that deal with attention and other systems, such as the data processing systems, that perform operations on specific inputs even when attention is directed elsewhere (Posner, 1992). In one sense, the attention system is similar to other systems (the motor and sensory systems, for example) in that it interacts with many other parts of the brain but maintains its own identity. Evidence for this conclusion can be found in patients with brain damage who demonstrate attentional problems but not processing deficits (or vice versa).

Attention and PET

Current research on attention has used brain imaging technology (mainly PET), and although it is impossible to report all of the recent studies (or even a reasonable cross section, so numerous are the new data in this field), it is possible to give a glimpse of some work being done in this important area of neurocognitive research by some of its foremost scientists. The basic methodological technique for PET investigations is discussed in Chapter 2. Although an explanation of the technique is not repeated here, it is important to remember that this is a procedure in which blood flow rates in the brain are evaluated by means of radioactive tracers. As the brain metabolizes nourishment through use, more blood is called for. These actions are monitored by means of radioactive sensors and transposed by a computer into a geographic map of the cortex in which "hot spots," regions of concentrated blood flow, are identified.

Typical of these experiments is the work of Petersen and his colleagues (Petersen et al., 1990) in which research participants were shown words, nonwords that resembled words, and consonant strings. As shown in Figure 3.14, the areas activated for words and regular nonwords (but not consonant strings) were the ones shown with an oval (left figures). Curiously, patients who suffer lesions to these areas frequently are unable to read words but may read letter by letter. For example, shown the word *sand,* these patients cannot read it but can say the letters one by one (*s-a-n-d*). Through this action, the string is (probably) represented into an auditory code. Other areas of the brain take over the functioning, and these patients can say what the word is. Additional studies of the brain by means of PET show other areas involved in specific types of attention, as shown in Figure 3.14. Each of these designated areas of the brain is involved in selective attention in different ways, and to thoroughly understand the nature of the brain in attention, it is necessary to consider the topic of awareness and consciousness. The current state of knowledge of the role of the cerebral cortex in awareness and attention is that the attentional system produces the contents of awareness in the same way as other parts of the brain, such as the visual system, and organizes the way other sensations are processed, such as how the visual world is perceived.

Spotlight on Cognitive Neuroscience

Visual Attention

Paul Downing, Jia Liu, and Nancy Kanwisher (2001) use fMRI and MEG to study visual attention. Not only do they focus on finding the neural correlates of this type of cognitive

FIGURE 3.14

The areas of the cerebral cortex of the human brain involved in attention.
Attentional networks are shown by solid-colored shapes on the lateral (outside) and
medial (cross-sectional) surfaces of the right and left hemispheres. It appears that the
parietal lobes are involved in the attentional network (see square); the right frontal
lobes are related to vigilance; and the diamonds are part of the anterior attention
network. The oval and circle are word processing systems, which are related to visual
word form (ellipse) and semantic associations (circle).

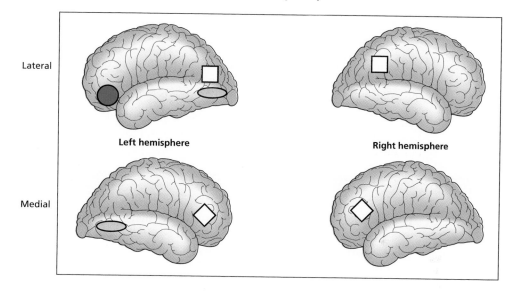

function, but they also then use that information to test theories of attention. The spatial
and temporal resolution of fMRI and MEG afford the opportunity to pinpoint the neural
locations of activity resulting from particular stimuli and task activities. Downing and his
colleagues capitalize on previous research that has shown that the fusiform face area
(FFA) of the brain responds selectively to faces and the parahippocampal place area
(PPA) responds to places and houses. Using this information, they conducted a study to
evaluate object-based attention. Using activity in FFA and PPA as dependent variables,
they had participants focus their attention to either the direction of a moving stimulus or
to the position of a still item. The stimuli were a transparent house and a transparent face
superimposed one over the other. The moving stimulus was sometimes the face and
sometimes the house (with the corresponding still stimulus being the opposite). So half
of the time the participants were told to pay attention to the house and the other half of
the time to the face. They found that when participants attended to a moving house, activity was higher in the PPA, compared to a moving face. Alternatively, when participants
attended to a moving face, activity was higher in the FFA, compared to a moving house.
When they were instructed to attend to the still item, the reverse occurred: When attending to the static face while the house was moving, activity was higher in the FFA, and
when attending to the static house while the face was moving, activity was higher in the

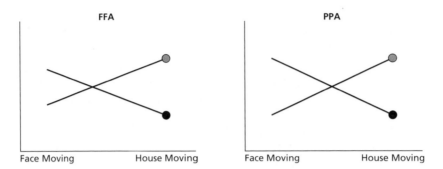

PPA. They conclude that "task-irrelevant features in each display received more attention when they were associated with the attended object, compared to an ignored object at the same location, implicating object-based selection uniquely" (p. 1334).

Downing, P., Liu, J., and Kanwisher, N. (2001). Testing cognitive models of visual attention with fMRI and MEG. *Neuropsychologia, 39*(12), 1329–1342.

Summary

1 Cognitive psychologists are interested in perception because cognition is presumed to be a consequence of external events, sensory detection is influenced by previous experiences, and knowledge about sensory experience may tell us how information is abstracted at the cognitive level.

2 *Sensation* refers to the relationship between the physical world and its detection through the sensory system whereas *perception* involves higher-order cognition in the interpretation of sensory signals.

3 Illusions occur when one's perception of reality is different from "reality." Illusions are often caused by expectations based on past experiences.

4 The perceptual process consists of the detection and interpretation of reality as determined by the stimulus sensed, the structure of the sensory system and brain, and previous knowledge.

5 Studies of perceptual span concern the basic question of how much we can experience from a brief exposure.

6 Reporting stimuli perceived from a brief presentation is a dual-stage process: (1) the perception, or actual sensory registration, and (2) the recall, or ability to report what was registered before it fades.

7 Partial-report techniques address the problem of confounding sensory capacity with recall ability.

8 Iconic storage holds visual input and appears to be independent of subject control factors (for example, attention). Capacity is estimated to be at least nine items with a duration of approximately 250 milliseconds. Echoic storage holds auditory input with a duration of about 4 seconds.

9 Iconic and echoic storage may allow us to select relevant information for further processing, thus providing one type of solution to the problem of capacity limitations inherent in the information-processing system.

10 Attention is the concentration of mental effort on sensory or mental events. Many contemporary ideas about attention are based on the premise that an information-processing system's capacity to handle the flow of input is determined by the limitations of that system.

11 Research on attention covers five major aspects: processing capacity and selectiveness, control of attention, automatic processing, the cognitive neuroscience of attention, and consciousness.

12 Capacity limits and selective attention imply a structural bottleneck in information processing. One model locates it at or just prior to perceptual analysis (Broadbent).

13 The attenuation model of selective attention proposes a perceptual filter, located between signal and verbal analyses, which screens input by selectively regulating the "volume" of the message. Stimuli are assumed to have different activation thresholds, a provision that explains how we can hear without attending.

14 Recent work in cognitive neuroscience has studied attention and has sought correlates between parts of the brain and attentional mechanisms.

KEY WORDS

attention
automatic processing
channel capacity
cocktail party phenomenon
computational brain
echoic memory
epistemology
iconic memory
perception

perceptual span
peripheral nervous system
priming
psychophysics
saccade
sensation
shadowing
subliminal perception

RECOMMENDED READINGS

● Historically, Broadbent's *Perception and Communication* is an important work and still makes interesting reading. Gregory's *The Oxford Companion to the Mind* is an intellectual tour de force to be enjoyed by anyone interested in ideas, cognition, and attention. Highly recommended papers include Kihlstrom's article "The Cognitive Unconscious" in *Science;* Cowan's article in *Psychological Bulletin;* Posner and Petersen's chapter, "The Attention System of the Human Brain," in the *Annual Review of Neuroscience;* Pashler's "Doing Two Things at the Same Time" in *American Scientist;* and, for a touch of automaticity and PDP, Cohen, Servan-Schreiber, and McClelland's article (1992). Gazzinaga's edited volume, *The Cognitive Neurosciences,* contains some detailed chapters by leading authorities in the field. Recent issues of *Perception and Psychophysics, Cognitive Psychology, American Journal of Psychology, Journal of Experimental Psychology: Human Perception and Performance,* and *Memory and Cognition* frequently carry reports on the subjects discussed in this chapter.

CHAPTER **4**

Pattern Recognition

hmmm...?

● **Perceptual Theories**

● **Visual Pattern Recognition**
Vision
Subjective Organization

● **Gestalt Theory**

● **Canonic Perspectives**

● **Bottom-Up versus Top-Down Processing**

● **Template Matching**
Geon Theory
Priming Technique

● **Feature Analysis**
Eye Movements and Pattern Perception

● **Prototype Matching**
Abstraction of Visual Information
Pseudomemory
Prototype Theory: Central Tendency
    versus Attribute Frequency

● **Form Perception: An Integrated Approach**

● **Pattern Recognition among Experts**
Pattern Recognition in Chess

● **Pattern Recognition—The Role of the Perceiver**

1. What are the main issues regarding pattern perception?

2. What is constructive perception? Direct perception?

3. Identify several illusions and explain them.

4. What is Gestalt psychology, and how does the theory account for perception?

5. Give several examples of canonic perspectives.

6. What are the main features of the following ideas regarding pattern recognition: template matching, geon theory, feature analysis, and prototype formation?

7. What is priming, and why is it considered important in modern cognitive psychology?

8. How do experts (such as chess masters) organize visual patterns?

The lowest form of thinking is the bare recognition of the object. The highest, the comprehensive intuition of the man who sees all things as part of a system.

—*Plato*

What familiar objects did you see today? If you are like most people, the number of things you saw and identified was enormous. Now, for the harder question: How were you able to recognize so many objects rapidly and accurately?

Our ability to recognize familiar types of things is a spectacular human characteristic. This attribute allows us to recognize an old friend in a sea of faces, to identify a song from a few notes, to read words, to enjoy the taste of a vintage wine, or to appreciate the smell of a rose. It is a cognitive endowment that we mostly perform seamlessly, rapidly, and without much effort. In our everyday life, we use pattern recognition all the time, yet the cognitive structures that support pattern recognition are only recently understood. How, for example, do you recognize your grandmother? Do you do it by means of "a grandmother template" that no other grandmother will fit? Do you have a grandmother prototype that epitomizes your grandmother but will still allow you to recognize her when she has her glasses on, or even when she has her hair done differently? Alternatively, do you perform a hasty scan of her features and check each item against a master feature list for "my grandmother"? Although our discussion deals exclusively with visual pattern recognition, other forms of patterns—auditory, tactile, and so on—also affect our behavior. These have been less frequently investigated than visual pattern recognition, and this chapter reflects that disparity. As we shall see, even everyday **pattern recognition** involves a complex interaction between sensation, perception, STM, LTM, and a cognitive search for identification of stimuli. As complex as the process of object recognition is, it is also performed more or less accurately within a fraction of a second. From both laboratory studies and common knowledge, we know several things about pattern recognition. These include the human capacity to:

Principle	Example
• Recognize familiar patterns promptly and with a high degree of accuracy.	• We easily recognize the faces of our friends, the interior of our house, and street signs.
• Evaluate and understand unfamiliar objects.	• Even though we may have never seen an unusual shape (an unusual *S,* for example), our visual-perceptual system can analyze it.
• Accurately perceive objects that are placed or rotated at different angles.	• We recognize a coffee cup, even though it may be upside down.
• Identify objects partly hidden from view, occluded, or in some other way "noisy."	• We infer that hidden parts of objects exist, as in the case of the lower torso and legs of TV reporters.
• Perform pattern recognition quickly, with subjective ease, and automatically.	• We move through a world in which shapes and objects are constantly changing, and yet we process this information swiftly and without undue effort.

Cognition in Everyday Life

Form Perception

At this moment two American spacecraft called *Voyager* are hurtling through space on their way to the stars. These space vehicles are extraordinary in that attached to each is a gold-coated phonograph record, which, when decoded by creatures from some distant civilization, will tell about our planet and culture. Each record has about 90 minutes of music, sounds from the earth, greetings in 60 languages, and 118 "photographs" of people and planet. What, if anything, might intelligent inhabitants from a distant civilization make of this information? More important for human cognitive psychologists, what assumptions about human perception and information processing are embodied in this task?

Photographs 61 and 62 have been reproduced to illustrate the assumptions we make about human and alien perception of complex forms. In photograph 62 (below left) a Bushman hunter and (presumably) his son are hunting a small, horned, four-legged animal. Most humans easily discern that the animal is larger than the absolute size in the photograph. In photograph 61 (below right) scientists created a silhouette of the three principal forms in the photograph along with measurements of the animal and the boy. It was anticipated that an alien would be able to use these measures to understand the concept of depth perception, which we humans take for granted. However, when we consider the probably unique evolutionary history of homo sapiens and other creatures, it is unlikely that even these cues would be sufficient for complete and immediate understanding. We humans bring to form perception a myriad of cognitive and physiological attributes that produce a singular impression that, as far as we know, is special among intelligent beings.

Diagram by Jon Lomberg. From *Murmurs of Earth: The Voyager Interstellar Record*, by Carl Sagan, F. D. Drake, Ann Drugen, I. Ferris, Jon Lomberg, and L. S. Sagan. Random House, Inc. Photography by N. R. Farbman, *Life Magazine*, Time, Inc., in Sagan et al. (1978).

Perceptual Theories

Perceptual psychologists have developed two major theories of how the world is perceived by humans. One theory, **constructive perception,** holds that people "construct" perceptions by actively selecting stimuli and merging sensations with memory. Another theory, **direct perception,** holds that perception consists of the direct acquisition of information from the environment. First consider the constructivist position.

The theory of constructive perception is based on the notion that during perception we form and test hypotheses regarding percepts based on both what we sense and what we know. Thus, perception is the combined effect of what comes in through our sensory system and what we have learned about the world through experience. When you see a friend approaching from a distance, you recognize him because his features, his nose, his eyes, his hair and so on, are sensed by your eye *and* because you have knowledge that he usually can be seen at this time at this place. You may even be able to recognize him in spite of the fact that he may have grown a goatee recently or changed his hair styling or is wearing sunglasses. According to the constuctivists, these changes in the pattern of the original stimuli still allow you to recognize him accurately because of **unconscious inference,** a process by which we spontaneously integrate information from several sources to construct a perception. We see, according to the constructivists, as much with the brain and its rich supply of knowledge about the world as with the eyes (and other sensory organs) that provide us with the raw sensory input. The theory is closely aligned with a "top-down" view of sensory processing (which is considered in the next section) and is consistent with the view of many cognitive psychologists working on problems in visual pattern recognition, such as Jerome Bruner, Richard Gregory, and Irvin Rock. The theory may be traced back to the classic work of Hermann von Helmholtz writing at the turn of the twentieth century.

Direct perception holds that information in the stimuli is the important element in perception and that learning and cognition are unnecessary in perception. The leading proponent of the theory was the late James Gibson (1966, 1979) and his followers at Cornell University including James Cutting (1986, 1993) who stated that "Direct perception assumes that the richness of the optic array just matches the richness of the world" (p. 247). The idea, which has gained support among ecologically minded psychologists, is that the stimulus contains enough information for correct perception and does not require internal representations for perception. The perceiver does minimal work in perception because the world offers so much information, leaving slight demand to construct perception and draw inferences. Perception consists of the direct acquisition of information from the environment. Consider an example not from vision but from audition. If you listened to a piece played on a piano in the key of G and then the same piece played in the key of C, you would probably recognize the second piece as being similar to the first, and if there were sufficient time between the renditions, you might conclude that they were identical. Even though the notes in one piece differed from the notes in the other piece, the relationships between them would be constant or invariant. Similar invariants may be seen in visual perception.

Gibson reasoned that visual cues, such as linear perspective, relative size, and so on, are not relevant for depth perception in real-world scenes. He found support for his notion when he was involved in pilot selection during World War II and found that those pilots who performed well on depth-perception tests were no better at flying a plane, which requires a high level of performance as well as depth perception, than those who scored poorly on such tests. He concluded that the traditional set of cues for depth was not adequate for real-world perception. The direct perception view shares many features of the "bottom-up" theory of form perception, which will be discussed shortly.

Each of these two theories of perception has a legion of ardent supporters and, at least on the surface, seems to represent directly opposing and irreconcilable propositions. Yet, at another level of analysis the theories can be seen as complementary rather than contradictory. The constructive view of perception is intuitively appealing as, after all, when you perceive the words on this page as you are reading, you "understand" their meaning *because* you have semantic knowledge of what they mean; when you look at a piece of art you perceive its significance because of your information about the artist, the materials used, and its context. These examples of "perception" seem to rely on knowledge, experience, and learning—all of which direct our attention to and meld with internal representations of the mind. On the other hand, what could be more natural than perception that emphasizes the completeness of the information in the receptors and suggests that perception occurs simply, naturally, and directly without complicated internal representations and circuitous information processing routines?

Our view is that both theories work well to explain perception but they focus on different phases of the process. The direct-perception view is important for our understanding of perception for two reasons: It calls to attention the significance of sensory stimuli, suggesting that the processing of these is simple and direct and that cognition and perception are natural, ecologically based phenomena—a position harmonious with the newly repackaged cognitive evolutionary view discussed in Chapter 1. While direct perception may help us understand some of the early perception of sensory impressions, the constructive-perception theory is useful in understanding how sensory impressions are comprehended by the thinking brain. The deductive attribute of humans (and other animals) in perceiving "reality" is not only useful in the comprehension of stimuli that are *not* complete (e.g., seeing your friend without his goatee) but are necessary for the survival of the species.

Visual Pattern Recognition

What, then, are the cognitive processes that account for our ability to classify and understand visual patterns? The question has been approached from several theoretical positions; each of the following is considered in this chapter:

Gestalt Theory. Pattern recognition is based on the perception of the whole pattern of stimuli. Parts of the entire configuration derive their meaning from their membership in the whole.

Bottom-Up and Top-Down Processing. Pattern recognition is initiated by the parts of the pattern (bottom-up) that, when summed, lead to the recognition of the whole pattern; alternatively, recognition of the whole leads to recognition of the components (top-down).

Template Matching. Pattern recognition occurs when a match is made between sensory stimuli and a corresponding internal mental form.

Feature Analysis. Pattern recognition occurs after incoming stimuli have been analyzed according to their simple features (similar to bottom-up processing).

Prototype Theory. Pattern recognition occurs when a match is made between a perceived pattern and an abstracted or idealized mental pattern.

Form Perception. Pattern perception is examined from various theoretical positions.

Pattern Recognition among Experts. Pattern recognition among specialists in a variety of fields is examined.

It should be recognized that each of these viewpoints may share some theoretical features with other viewpoints; the distinctions provide an organizational scheme for our following discussion.

Vision

Vision, the act of sensing electromagnetic waves, is made possible because of the eye's unique structure, which is precisely designed to detect photopic energy. Light rays enter the eye through the cornea and lens, which focus an image on the retina. The recognition of a pattern, whether a simple two-dimensional black-and-white form or a complex three-dimensional colored form, is always represented on the retina as a two-dimensional[1] form. From these two-dimensional representations on the retina, higher-order perception—including the illusion of three-dimensionality—is made possible when the impulses are passed along to the visual cortex and, when combined with existing knowledge, lead to the recognition of, say, our grandmother when we see her. The magic that has surrounded the visual process for centuries has, at last, given way to scientific understanding.

The visual system is the most complex of all sensory systems. The human eye has about 7 million cones, which are sensitive to well-illuminated stimuli, and 125 million rods, which are sensitive to poorly illuminated stimuli. This distribution of rods and cones in the retina is not even. Cones are concentrated in the **fovea,** and rods are spread away from the fovea. Despite the uneven distribution of sensory neurons in the eye, many models of visual perception, especially those built on a computer metaphor, conceptualize the visual system as a type of matrix that can be described geometrically as conforming to an x and y grid. In addition to the number of sensory cells and their geographic location, another factor in understanding visual perception is the intensity of stimuli, or how bright an object is, and what influence that has on sensation. It has been discovered that bright objects and dark objects are similarly represented.

Several ongoing projects are attempting to emulate human vision using computers, which have been built on the information just presented. At this time it is impossible to build an artificial eye with millions of sensors. What has been built is a television "eye" with a 512 × 512 array (which has 262,144 pixels, or "picture elements") that crudely simulates the human eye. The pixels can be turned on or off, and light intensity can be further simulated by computer programs. Identifying visual boundaries of real objects has also been successfully simulated (see Marr, 1982, for details). We shall return to

---

[1]The image that falls on the retina occurs over a period of time, which some might consider another dimension.

computer vision in Chapter 15, but now we will turn our attention to models of human visual information processing.

Subjective Organization

An intriguing feature of human vision is the tendency to "see" things in the physical world that do not exist. These illusions are the result of not only the sensations from the outer world but also the predisposition of the visual/cognitive system in distorting what really exists in the real world; these distortions are called *illusions.* Illusions are erroneous perceptions of reality that are generally shared by all people. While such a dogmatic definition begs the question of "What is reality?" we will leave that question to philosophic debate. All of us have been "fooled" by these perceptual curiosities as in the familiar Müller-Lyer illusion and the illustration by M. C. Escher we encountered in the last chapter. By studying illusions, cognitive psychologists are able to understand the relationships between external physical phenomena and the way the mind organizes such stimuli in "internal representations."

One class of illusions that illustrates the way the mind naturally organizes visual stimuli is called *illusory contours.* These are visual perceptions in which contours are seen even though they are not physically present. In Figure 4.1 an example of an illusory contour is shown. Illusory contours are percepts of forms where the forms exist in the perceptual-cognitive system, not in the stimulus. They appear to be in the figure, rather than the ground (or background), and have a real perceptual presence, although the observer seems to have the feeling that they are not really "real." (This last notion is an intriguing problem, yet very little research has been focused on it. Perhaps some enterprising reader will correct this deficit in the literature.)

Look at Figure 4.1. What do you see? It is likely that your "mind's eye" sees a hovering equilateral triangle in the center *even though there is not a physical triangle.* Yet, you see it! Furthermore, the illusionary triangle has well-defined features; for example, it is whiter than the surrounding area and it tends to float above the background. Furthermore, the lines of the illusory triangle appear even though only a fraction is de-

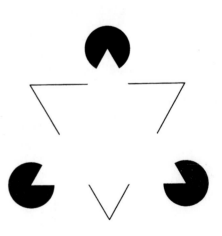

Can you see a floating white triangle? Does it physically exist or does it exist only in your mind's eye?

fined by the slits in the three defining circles. The illusion of the triangle is so compelling that after one views it for several seconds and then covers the outer black circles the *triangle persists.* Perhaps the persistence of the triangle is caused by *lateral inhibition,* or the tendency of adjacent neural elements of the retina to inhibit surrounding cells, thus accentuating contours. (For more information see Coren, 1991; Kanizsa, 1976; Lesher, 1995; and Lesher & Mingolla, 1993.) Even though one can create the phantom triangle, there is a feeling that this figure is an illusion and not a physical triangle.

The clarity with which edges are perceived and the lightness of the figure seem to be a function of the density of the inducing features as shown in Figure 4.2. Here we see that the right-hand figure creates a very strong, floating illusion that is clearly defined, whereas the middle form is less well defined and more difficult to create (though still possible).

There are a number of explanations for these illusions. From an evolutionary perspective, the need to see forms, edges, and motions (as well as faces, some might add) was an imperative necessary for survival. Thus, even in the absence of real lines or forms, our sensory-cognitive system used partial information to fabricate these forms in an effort to make comprehensible a seemingly chaotic world. This explanation is rooted in the evolution of survival mechanisms, and creatures who evolved the ability to perceive these types of figures were able to disambiguate figure from ground when an important figure was nearly the same color or luminance as the background. Some theorists (for example, Ramachandran, 1987) propose that the perception of illusory contours is a means for canceling the effects of camouflage.

On another level, there is some evidence that illusory contours do activate cells in the visual cortex (areas identified as V1 and V2). Gestalt psychologists, whom we will consider in the next section, argue that we create subjective illusions because of the tendency to see simple, familiar or "good" figures (**Pragnanz**) in our environment. In effect, this "good figure" explanation answers the question "What is the most likely visual organization of environmental stimuli?" Each of these explanations focuses on one aspect of the perplexing problem of perception.

FIGURE 4.2

Some illusory contours are better defined when the contrast between the figure and ground is greatest.

Reprinted from *Vision Research,* Vol. 33, G. W. Lesher and E. Mingolia, "The role of edges and line-ends in illusory contour formation," pp. 2253–2270, © 1993, with permission from Elsevier.

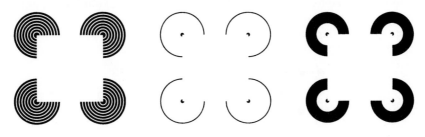

Gestalt jokesters test an illusion.

Gestalt Theory

Some patterns of stimuli seem to be classified the same way by many people. For example, if shown this pattern of visual stimuli,

most people would recognize it and label it a square. The way we organize and classify visual stimuli was studied by adherents of **Gestalt psychology** during the early part of the twentieth century. **Pattern organization** to these early Gestalt psychologists involved all stimuli working together to produce an impression that went beyond the sum total of all sensations.

Some patterns of stimuli, according to Wertheimer (1923), tend to be naturally (or "spontaneously") organized. For example, in all likelihood your impression of the following is of a series of eight dots.

● ● ● ● ● ● ● ●

If the dots form the pattern,

● ●   ● ●   ● ●   ● ●

you tend to see four sets of two-dot patterns because of **similarity,** and it is quite difficult to rearrange the pattern mentally so you see the first dot alone, the second and third dots together, the fourth and fifth dots together, the sixth and seventh dots together, and the eighth dot alone. The same eight dots arranged as follows:

will tend to be seen as a square, a circle, and an abstract form, respectively.

Consider also the way the eye "naturally" organizes the direction in which the triangles are pointed[2] in Figure 4.3. Look at this figure for several seconds, and you will see the orientation shift from one direction to another and yet another. One explanation of this change is that the mind's eye is constantly searching for alternate perceptual organization. In this instance, the stimuli that impinge on the retina are identical, but the interpretation is different. Although the reorganization may occur spontaneously, it can also be voluntarily controlled. Such demonstrations show the influence of higher-order mental processes on visual perception.

The influence of past memories on form perception can also be seen in Figure 4.4. Examine the two figures briefly. What do you see? In Figure 4.4A, people generally see a stable two-dimensional object, and in Figure 4.4B an unstable three-dimensional one. However, if you look closely, you will see that both figures are identical except that they are misaligned by 45 degrees. Why do we have this radically different perception of two nearly identical patterns? One constructivist reason is that through past experience we see boxes positioned in the orientation shown in Figure 4.4B. This reminds us of a box that has three dimensions. The form in Figure 4.4A is unboxlike. At best, it would be an odd orientation for a box. We do not easily see the dimensionality associated with a box, but we do see a symmetrical two-dimensional object that appears to be two squares held up by a frame. Although this powerful illusion may be particularly compelling for people growing up in Western civilization, would the illusion hold for people who might not come into contact with boxes or angular forms in their everyday lives? Probably not. (See Deregowski, 1980, for further discussion.)

A conspicuous assumption of the early Gestalt psychologists—especially Köhler (1947)—was that spontaneous organization of a pattern was a natural function of the stimulus itself and only minimally related to past experience with the object. Although

[2]For a much more detailed analysis, see Palmer (1989, 1999).

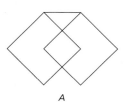

FIGURE 4.3

Look at this display of triangles. In which direction do they point? Look again. Does the direction change? Can you control the direction?

FIGURE 4.4

Effect of orientation on perception. Which of these forms appears to be three-dimensional?

A   B

Cognition in Everyday Life

Common Grouping in the Real World

*G*raphic designers have known the powerful influence that Gestalt principles have on conveying a message. Consider the example below of common grouping.

Here the background shading exerts a powerful influence over the message being read. It is likely that common regions help organize the text.

the controversy about the source of "natural organization" continues, a considerable number of experimental reports (some based on cross-cultural observation) support the notion that "natural organization" of patterns is directly tied to the perceptual history of the human subject.

Study of pattern recognition by cognitive psychologists has extended the work of the early Gestalt psychologists. Some recent cognitive psychologists have concentrated on the "internal" structures and processes that are associated with complex pattern recognition rather than emphasizing the characteristics of simple stimuli. Following are some of these models and the patterns on which they are based.

Canonic Perspectives

One extension of the ideas expressed by the Gestaltists can be seen in the work with canonic perspectives. **Canonic perspectives** are views that best represent an object or are the images that first come to mind when you recall a form. If we ask you to think of a common object, say, a blender, the image that comes to mind is likely to be the canonic perspective. Research in this area is important, since it combines findings from Gestalt psychology with prototype formation, a topic that is covered in some detail later in this chapter.

If your canonic perspective of a blender is the same as ours, you conjured up a view of a blender that is generally from the front, rotated to the left a few degrees, and viewed from a slightly elevated position. You did not "see" it from directly above, from the back, with a large cookie jar occluding part of it, or from the perspective of a tiny ant crawling over the buttons. However, each of these perspectives is possible. (Much more is reported on visual imagery in Chapter 8.)

Canonic representations may be formed through experience with like members of a category (called exemplars) although some suggest that they represent idealized forms which are part of people's collective unconscious. As interesting (if not entertaining) as these views might be, they fall outside the confines of empirical science. For several years we have been asking people all around the world to "draw a cup and saucer," and some of the renditions are shown in Figure 4.5. There is some variation in the drawings, as a result of varied artistic ability and personal idiosyncrasies, but the remarkable feature of this little experiment is that most people—from Palo Alto, California, to Waterloo, Iowa, to Chicago, to London, to Istanbul—drew basically the same "cup and saucer." The first author's drawing of a "cup and saucer," a bird's-eye view of those objects shown in Figure 4.6, meets the criterion of the task and, when identified, is easily recognized. It is also conspicuously different from the other sketches because it is not canonic; yet, when you are told what it is, you "see it" easily.

One theoretical explanation of the generality of canonic perspectives is that, through common experience with objects, we develop permanent memories of the most representational view of an object and of a view that discloses the greatest amount of information about it. Thus, studies of canonic perspectives tell us something about form perception, but they tell us much more about human information processing, prototype formation (or

FIGURE 4.5

Canonic cup caper connected cognitively.

FIGURE 4.6

Cup and saucer—bird's-eye view.

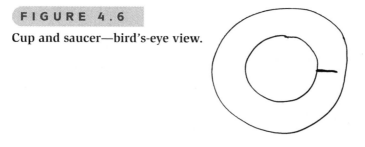

the typicality of objects as represented in memory), and economy of thinking and, in the above-mentioned case of the cup caper, efficiency in communication. We store superordinates and use a type of visual shorthand to tell others of our impressions.

Experimental data have supported these conclusions. Palmer, Rosch, and Chase (1981) photographed a series of horses from different perspectives (see Figure 4.7). Participants rated the perspectives for typicality and familiarity. In a second part of the ex-

FIGURE 4.7

Twelve perspective views of a horse. Used in Palmer, Rosch, and Chase experiment (1981) with mean "goodness" ratings.

Reprinted by permission of Sylan Kornblum.

periment, subjects were shown the photographs of the horse and other objects (for example, a camera, a car, a piano, or so on) that had been similarly evaluated and were asked to name the objects as rapidly as they could. Not surprisingly, the canonic views were identified most quickly, with reaction times increasing as a function of the rated distance away from canonicality. It should also be noted that the visual system still operates with a reasonable degree of efficiency, even when evaluating less than "perfect" figures.

There are several probable reasons that reaction times are generally longer for less canonic pictures: (1) Fewer parts of the object may be discernible. Look at the back view in Figure 4.7. How much of the horse can you see by looking at its rear? Not much. (2) The best (canonic) view (figure in the upper left) is one that is most commonly experienced. We "see" blenders, chairs, cars, telephones, and horses from one orientation more than others and, therefore, that view is more familiar to us. (3) The canonic view is an idealized, or best, view of the object. Through endless impressions of the world, we form a mental picture of a class of objects in which the epitome of the class is represented in memory. When we ask you to imagine a blender, it is likely that your impression is one of a garden-variety blender, not one of an unconventional model with a weird shape. The same principle works for recalling dogs, horses, sports cars, and birds. This view is consistent with theories of prototype formation, which are discussed shortly.

Bottom-Up versus Top-Down Processing

How do we recognize a pattern? Do we identify a dog because we have first recognized its furry coat, its four legs, its eyes, ears, and so on, or do we recognize these parts because we have first identified a dog? This problem—whether the recognition process is initiated by the parts of the pattern, which serve as the basis for the recognition of the whole (**bottom-up processing**), or whether it is primarily initiated by a hypothesis about the whole, which leads to its identification and subsequent recognition of the parts (**top-down processing**)—is called the parsing paradox.

Some theorists (for example, Palmer, 1975a) have suggested that, under most circumstances, the interpretation of parts and wholes takes place in top-down and bottom-up directions simultaneously. As an example of the interactions of part-to-whole and whole-to-part strategies, Palmer cites the recognition of parts of a face with context and without context. As shown in Figure 4.8, the parts of a face that can easily be recognized in context are somewhat ambiguous when seen alone, although recognizable when more detail or information is supplied.

We expect to see certain objects in various contexts, for example, a stethoscope in a physician's office, silverware in a kitchen, a computer in an office, and a hydrant in a street scene. It is likely that this world knowledge is what facilitates identification of objects in familiar contexts and hinders identification of objects in inappropriate ones. Several investigations of this "context effect" by Biederman and his associates (Biederman, 1972; Biederman, Glass, & Stacy, 1973; also see the section entitled "Geon Theory" later in this chapter) have shown that, when a person searches for objects in real-world scenes (for example, objects in a campus scene or street scene), recognition,

FIGURE 4.8

Facial features. Recognizable in the context of a whole face in profile (A) are less recognizable out of context (B). Differentiated more fully and realistically (C), the features are more recognizable.

From Palmer (1975a).

*L*ook at the figures below. If you were shopping for a matched set of chairs, which two would you buy? How did you come to that conclusion? What factors entered into your decision? See discussions of template matching, priming, and feature analysis for additional thoughts.

Cognition in Everyday Life

Pattern Recognition

accuracy, and time required to identify objects are related to the appropriateness of the objects' location in the scene.

From these and similar studies on word and letter identification in context, it is clear that the perception of objects is greatly influenced by the person's expectation as determined by the context.

Template Matching

One idea of how the brain recognizes shapes and patterns is called **template matching.** A template in our context of human pattern recognition refers to an internal construct that, when matched by sensory stimuli, leads to the recognition of an object. This idea of pattern recognition holds that a great number of templates have been created by our life experience, each template being associated with a meaning. Thus, the visual identification of a shape—say, a geometric form—would occur as follows: The light energy emanating from the form falls on the retina and is transduced to neural energy, which is transmitted to the brain. A search is made among existing templates. If a template is found that matches the neural pattern, then the person recognizes it. After a match between the object and its template is made, further processing and interpretation of the object may occur.

Template matching, as a theory of pattern recognition, has some strength as well as some weakness. On the positive side, it seems apparent that to recognize a shape, a letter, or some visual forms, some contact with a comparable internal form is necessary. On some level of abstraction, the objects in the external reality need to be recognized as matching a memory in the long-term memory. On the negative side, a literal interpretation of the template matching theory meets with some difficulty. For example, if recognition is possible only when a 1:1 match is found between the external object and its internal representation, then an object with even slight misalignment between itself and the template would not be recognized. Such a rigorous interpretation of the theory would imply that countless millions of templates need to be formed to correspond to each of the varied geometric forms we see and recognize.

The ease with which we identify visual patterns in our daily life may lead us to think that the process is simple, but if we try to duplicate pattern recognition by some artificial means, we find success elusive. Take, for example, the recognition of a letter

Cognition in Everyday Life
The Remarkable Versatility of Human Form Perception

Shown here is a diverse collection of letters, which we easily recognize as variations of the letter S. However, it is unlikely that we have seen and formed a precise memory for all of these versions. We can do this task, and many other similar pattern recognition tasks, because we have formed an impression of various classes of objects, such as an S, and are able to apply that information to a wide class of similar forms.

and the development of word recognition. Although it may take several years to become a skilled reader, once we have learned to identify the orthographic configuration that makes up a word, we can immediately recognize that word in various contexts, pronounce it, and recall its meaning. How would you simulate the initial process of letter recognition in a machine or computer? One way would be to have each of the twenty-six letters stored in a computer memory. Then, each time a letter was scanned by an optical device, the perceived visual configuration would key the memory (template) associated with that letter. Thus, the word *CARD* would be analyzed as C-A-R-D, with *C* fitted into the slot in memory corresponding to the configuration *C*. *A* would find a match in the *A* slot, and so on. "Voilà!" our computer may exclaim, "I'm reading letters." However, what if we ask it to recognize the letters in *card*? There are no lowercase configurations in its memory. The solution is simple, you might assert: increase the memory to include lowercase letters. However, how would our computer read (as we can) the letters in ꓛꓥꓤꓷ or *Card* or *C A R D* or ꓛꓮꓤꓷ? Of course, the process of reading involves a much more complex process than simple letter identification. The technique used by computers (of matching specific letter configurations against specific configurations in its memory) is called template matching, and it works something as a key in a lock does. A key's configuration of ridges and slots needs to correspond exactly to a lock's configuration if it is to release the lock. In template matching, if the visual configuration corresponds to a compatible memory representation, information, in terms of pattern recognition, is released. In the preceding example of the computer, the method of template matching to recognize various anomalies in the word *CARD* encountered difficulties, much as a bent key might in releasing a lock.

Cognition in Everyday Life

Template Matching in Computers

*T*emplate matching is the basis of many coding systems that are part of everyday living. For example, nearly all banks in the United States use a system of identifying accounts by groupings of special digits (the ABA number) printed at

the bottom of checks, and many markets use similar codes printed on packages for speeding the checkout process and maintaining inventory. (The bar code identifies the item for which

the computer supplies the price, which is then entered on the cash register tape.) Both types of codes are read by means of template matching. An ABA number has distinctive features that make it possible for a computer to distinguish between the characters, and a bar code is read on the basis of the position, width, and spacing of the lines. Codes are converted by the scanner into electrical impulses, which constitute the patterns of signals that are transmitted to the computer. The computer identifies the pattern by matching it with an analogue (template) that is in its memory.

MATTHEW A. SWANN
18 Chelsea Place
New York, N.Y. 10011

American STATE BANK

NO.   159

PAY TO THE ORDER OF

DOLLARS

Thus, template matching is a simple pattern recognition procedure based on fitting the exact configuration of sensory information to a corresponding configuration in the brain and, despite its restricted capacity, has some useful conceptual and practical applications. We deal with the conceptual issues raised by template matching later; the practical applications are numerous.

For human pattern recognition, then, a strict interpretation of the model would mean that millions of separate templates need to be formed, each corresponding to a specific visual pattern. If we were to store that many templates, our brain would be so bulky we would need a wheelbarrow to cart it; the feat seems to be neurologically impossible. Even if it were possible, gaining access in memory to untold millions of templates would require a time-consuming search that our rapid recognition of numerous patterns suggests does not exist. Finally, our ability to recognize unfamiliar shapes and forms (for example, a novel letter *S*) also makes the process unlikely.

Geon Theory

An alternative to an unyielding template model, which requires countless millions of forms to match the everyday sights of the world, is a theory that posits that the human information processing system has a limited number of simple geometric "primitives" that may be applied to complex shapes. One theory, which also bears some resemblance to feature analysis (discussed later in the chapter), was developed by Irving Biederman of the University of Southern California and adopts such an idea. Biederman's concept of form perception is based on the concept of the **geon,** which stands for "geometrical ions." It proposes that all complex forms are composed of geons. For example, a cup is composed of two geons: a cylinder (for the container portion) and a ellipse (for the handle). (See Figure 4.9 for examples of geons and objects.) Geon theory, as espoused by Biederman (see Biederman, 1985, 1987, 1990; Biederman & Cooper, 1991; Biederman & Gerhardstein, 1993; and Cooper & Biederman, 1993) proposes that the recognition of an object, such as a telephone, a suitcase, or even more complex forms, consists of *recognition by components* (RBC) in which simple forms are found in complex forms. Geons are 24 distinct forms and, like the letters of the alphabet, make up a type of system. When combined, they fabricate more complex forms, much as the words on this page are composed of letters. The number of different forms that can be generated by

Irving Biederman has advanced our understanding of object recognition through innovative experiments and theories, especially geon theory.

FIGURE 4.9

Geons and objects. Objects are
represented as configurations of geons,
which are simple visual volumes.

From Biederman (1990). Reprinted by permission
of MIT Press.

combining primitive shapes is astronomical. For example, three geons arranged in all
possible combinations yield a total of 1.4 billion three-geon objects! However, we use
only a fraction of the total possible number of complex forms. Biederman estimates that
we use only about 30,000, of which we have names for only 3,000.

One test of geon theory is in the use of degraded forms, as shown in Figure 4.10.
Which of these figures (A or B) is easier to identify?

In the illustration, 65 percent of the contour has been removed from a common object. In the cup on the left (A), the lines from the middles of the segments were removed, which still allows the viewer to see how the basic segments are related. In the
cup on the right (B), the deleted lines are from the vertices, which include critical corners that relate segments one to another. Biederman presented objects of this type to
participants for 100 milliseconds. He found that when the connecting lines were removed (A), a correct identification was made about 70 percent of the time; when the
vertices were deleted (B), the number of correct identifications was about 50 percent.
Thus, consistent with a theory that holds that object identification is grounded on seeing basic forms, the removal of critical relational information made the object harder to
see than when such information was provided.

FIGURE 4.10

**Sixty-five percent of the contour has been
removed from a cup.** Centered at either
midsegments (A) or vertices (B).

From I. Biederman, "Human Image Understanding: Recent
Research and a Theory" in *Computer Vision, Graphics and
Image Processing,* 1985, 32, 29-73. Copyright 1985 Elsevier.
Reprinted by permission.

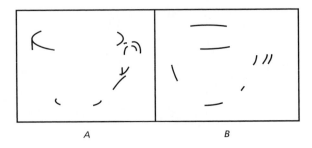

A   B

Priming Technique

In other experiments involving object classification tasks, Biederman and others used a priming technique in which a stimulus is briefly presented (a prime) and then, after a delay, a second stimulus is presented and a participant is asked to make some judgment regarding the second stimulus, such as, "Is the second stimulus the 'same' as the first?" The technique has been used by cognitive psychologists for several generations, and a type of simple priming (cueing participants to make a response) can be found in the early history of experimental psychology, dating back to the nineteenth century. With the advent of the tachistoscope (a device that allows the brief presentation of stimuli and measures response time), computers, and, more recently, brain imaging technology, priming experiments have become increasingly popular. The rationale behind priming experiments, especially those designed to test semantic effects, is that by activating one item that may be related to another item, the acceptability of the second item is enhanced. This effect is called the **semantic priming** effect and is discussed in some detail in Chapter 12. If, for example, you see a bright-red square patch, you will recognize the word *"BLOOD"* faster than if you saw no stimulus or if you saw a bright-green square patch (see Solso & Short, 1979).

A second type of effect called the *object priming effect* is similar to semantic priming. Typically, there are two stages. The first stage consists of the presentation of an object, say, a line drawing of an airplane, followed by an interval that may be as brief as 100 milliseconds or as long as months. In the second stage, a second object, similar to the original but commonly changed, rotated, elaborated, or degraded in some way (for example, some of the contours may be left out), is presented and the participant's accuracy and (sometimes) reaction time are measured. In some instances, the reverse procedure is used; that is, the participant sees a degraded form and then is asked to identify a completed object. Control participants get the same treatment but without the presentation of the first item. (See Tulving & Schacter, 1990, for further details.)

Consider the typical priming experiment shown in Figure 4.11 in which a participant is given a cue followed by a stimulus, a mask (to suppress after-image effects), and a second stimulus. In a number of experiments using visual material, priming of an object with a similar form measurably enhances perception of a form. The use of priming techniques raises an important issue for cognitive psychology; that is, the presentation of the prime, or initial, stimulus seems to activate a whole range of response tendencies

Cognition in Everyday Life

Geons and Art?

*P*ablo Picasso, the great abstract painter, was influenced by Paul Cézanne, the great impressionist painter. Cézanne encouraged Picasso to examine the nature of "cones, cylinders, and spheres" as he believed that complex paintings should be organized around these "basic" forms. Picasso took the advice seriously and experimented with assembling a painting with these basic forms, which eventually led to cubistic renditions.

Sequence of events on a 0° orientation difference. "Different" trial with familiar objects in the same-different task. Only if the two exemplars of the chair were the same, whatever the orientation in depth, were the participants to respond "same." (The designation of orientation on different trials was arbitrary.)

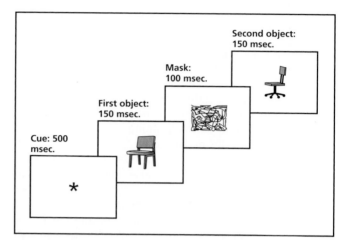

of which the observer is not conscious. This nonconscious activation is called *implicit memory* as contrasted with *explicit memory*, which involves the conscious recall of previous experiences. In the example shown in Figure 4.11, it is unlikely that participants consciously thought about the second type of chair when they saw the first. For this reason, the type of memory being tested is called implicit memory.

An application of the priming technique in which a component theory of object recognition was tested can be found in Biederman and Cooper (1991). To test the recognition of common forms (for example, a piano, a flashlight, or a padlock), participants were first primed with outline drawings of figures in which parts of the lines were missing. For each of these a corresponding drawing was shown in which the name of the object was the same as the prime, but the type of object differed (for example, the prime was a grand piano, but the object was an upright piano—see Figure 4.12). The results indicated that the **priming effect** was visual rather than conceptual. This is consistent with other findings in studies of short-term memory (see discussion of Posner and colleagues in Chapter 6).

Example of prime and object used in Biederman and Cooper (1991).

Complementary Image 2

Same Name, Different Exemplar

Feature Analysis

Another approach to the problem of how we extract information from complex stimuli is **feature analysis.** This notion holds that pattern perception is a high-order processing of information that is preceded by a step in which complex incoming stimuli are identified according to their simpler **features.** Thus, according to this approach, before the full-blown pattern of visual information is appreciated, its components are minimally analyzed. On a simple visual level, a word (for example, *ARROW*) is not immediately translated into its definitional or imaginal representation in our memory (for example, "a pointed shaft shot from a bow" or "→"). Neither is it read as "arrow," nor are the individual letters perceived as (A-R-R-O-W), but rather the features, or components, of each character are detected and analyzed. Thus, the *A* of *arrow* may be fractured into two diagonal lines (/ \), one horizontal line (—), a pointed head (^), an open bottom (/—\), and so on. If the recognition process is based on feature analysis (and there is good evidence to support this), the earliest stages of information processing are more complex than we might first guess.[3]

Two lines of research—neurological and behavioral—have supported the featural-analysis hypothesis. First, we will take up experiments by Hubel and Wiesel (1959, 1963)[4] and Hubel (1963b) that give direct evidence of the type of information coded in the visual cortex. These researchers inserted small wires, or microelectrodes, in the visual cortex of a lightly anesthetized cat or monkey and then studied the neural activity that resulted as simple patterns of light were projected onto a screen directly in front of the animal's eyes. By recording excitation of single nerve cells and amplifying the resulting electrical impulse, they found that some cells respond only to horizontal forms, while others respond only to vertical ones. In other experiments they found that some cells are sensitive to edges of visual stimuli, some to lines, and still others to right angles. Figure 4.13 shows the amplified brain activity in a cortical cell of a very young (and visually inexperienced) kitten correlated with specific orientations of a light slit (A to E) that was presented on a screen within the vision of the animal. Horizontal bars above each activity recorded indicate periods when light was visible. Hubel (1963b) concluded that the development of these cortical codes of perceptual forms was innate and specific to each cell.

One can now begin to grasp the significance of the great number of cells in the visual cortex. Each cell seems to have its own specific duties; it takes care of one restricted part of the retina, and it responds best to one particular shape of stimulus and to one particular orientation. Let's look at the problem from the opposite direction. For each stimulus— each area of the retina stimulated, each type of line (edge, slit, or bar), and each orientation of stimulus—there is a particular set of simple cortical cells that will respond. Changing any of the stimulus arrangements will cause a whole new population of cells to

---

[3]To appreciate the complex sensory and perceptual (and motor) apparatus necessary for "simple" perception and reaction, think of what is involved in hitting a tennis ball in flight. In a fraction of a second, we are able to judge its shape, size, speed, color, trajectory, spin, and anticipated location. Our brain must translate all of this information (which is recorded in only two dimensions on the retina) into a motor reaction, which, if successful, allows us to return the ball. In addition to the fact that this takes place in only a flash of time, much of the information is constantly changing (for example, the ball's relative size, speed, and trajectory).

[4]Hubel and Wiesel shared the Nobel prize with Sperry in 1981.

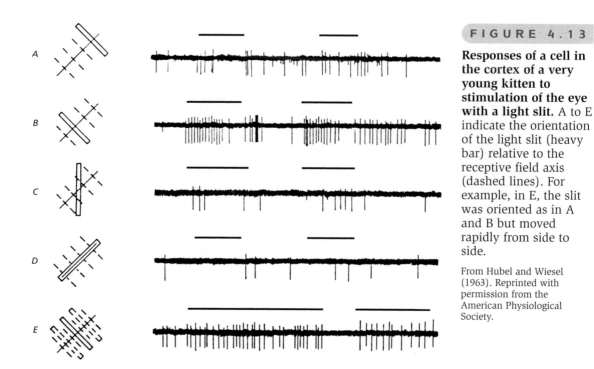

FIGURE 4.13

Responses of a cell in the cortex of a very young kitten to stimulation of the eye with a light slit. A to E indicate the orientation of the light slit (heavy bar) relative to the receptive field axis (dashed lines). For example, in E, the slit was oriented as in A and B but moved rapidly from side to side.

From Hubel and Wiesel (1963). Reprinted with permission from the American Physiological Society.

respond. The number of populations responding successively as the eye watches a slowly rotating propeller is scarcely imaginable.

The complex and awkward mechanism of breaking patterns into simpler features, then, may be not only within the realm of neurological possibilities but also neurologically necessary. That is, feature analysis may be a stage in informational analysis that must occur before higher-level pattern analysis can take place.

Eye Movements and Pattern Perception

A direct approach to feature analysis is observation of eye movements and eye fixation. This line of research presumes that if you gaze for a relatively long time at a certain feature in a pattern, you are extracting more information from it than from a feature only cursorily viewed. The results of the fixation experiments by Yarbus (1967), a Russian psychologist, are shown in Figure 4.14. Yarbus suggests that the more information carried by a feature (for example, the people or relationships in the illustrations shown), the longer the eyes stay fixed on it. He also concludes that the distribution of fixation points is a function of the participant's purpose. In one series, the participant was asked to make certain estimates regarding the complex pattern (for example, the material circumstances of the family and the ages of the people). Under these circumstances the focus tends to be on those features most important to the participant's purpose. Thus, the perception of features within complex patterns seems not only to depend on the nature of the physical stimuli but also to engage higher-order cognitive processes, such as attention and purpose.

FIGURE 4.14

Records of eye movements of participant examining picture at upper left. Trace 1 was made when participant examined picture at will. Subsequent traces were made after participant was asked to estimate the economic level of the people shown (Trace 2); judge their ages (3); guess what they had been doing before arrival of the "visitor" (4); remember their clothing (5); remember their positions (and those of objects) in the room (6); and estimate how long the "visitor" had not seen the "family" (7).

From Yarbus (1967). Reprinted by permission from Kluwer Academic.

Prototype Matching

An alternative to template matching and feature analysis as a means of recognizing patterns is **prototype** formation. It seems likely that, rather than form specific templates or even features for the numerous different patterns we are called upon to recognize, some kind of abstraction of patterns is stored in LTM and that abstraction serves as a prototype.

A pattern would then be checked against the prototype and, if a resemblance were found, the pattern would be recognized. The prototypical-matching hypothesis in humans seems to be more compatible with neurological economy and memory search processes than template matching, and it also allows for recognition of patterns that are "unusual" but in some way related to the prototype. In this system, we may, for example, form a prototype of the idealized letter *S*, against which all other *S*s are evaluated in terms of how closely they fit the model. Where the degree of mismatch is great, as in the case of letters other than *S*, we recognize the lack of a match and reject the letter as an *S*; we may then search for a prototype that fits the letter better.

Evidence for **prototype recognition** is all around us, and the hypothesis has a strong intuitive credibility. For example, we recognize a Volkswagen, even though it may be of a different color or shape or have a lot of fancy doodads that are at odds with the idealized model in our head. A prototype in this sense is not only an abstraction of a set of stimuli, but it is also the epitome or the "best" representation of the pattern.[5]

Although the argument seems to favor prototype matching over template matching, you might ask whether an exact match between image and template is necessary or whether templates only serve as an approximation of the image that unlocks the memory. If the latter were the case, however, how could you make the fine distinctions necessary for common visual discrimination? Consider, for example, the close featural similarity of *O* and *Q*, and *B*, *P*, and *R*. Although these visual patterns are similar, we seldom confuse them. In effect, then, templates cannot be sloppy, for if they were, we would make many errors in pattern recognition—and we seemingly do not.

As a theory of pattern recognition, then, template matching has utility in computer programs (check-code reading and so on) but, in its rigid form, inadequately accounts for the diversity, accuracy, and economy of human pattern recognition. To sum up, pattern recognition presumes an operation conducted in memory. At the simplest level, it is safe to assert that a pattern is identified by some process that matches sensory information with some trace held in a repository of information.

Abstraction of Visual Information

As we have suggested, template matching may occur at one level of visual recognition, but at another level prototypes may be used. This view holds that a prototype is an abstraction of a set of stimuli that embodies many similar forms of the same pattern. A prototype allows us to recognize a pattern even though it may not be identical (only similar) to the prototype. For example, we recognize a diverse number of *S*s, not because they fit neatly into cerebral slots but because the members of the class *S* have some common properties.

The empirical studies seeking evidence concerning prototypes as a means of pattern recognition have largely addressed the questions of how prototypes develop and by what process new exemplars are quickly classified. The question is not new; Bishop Berkeley (cited in Calfee, 1975) worried about it a long time ago:

> In his mind's eye all images of triangles seemed to have rather specific properties. They were equilateral or isosceles or right triangles, and he searched in vain for a mental

---

[5]In a civilization in which physical glamour is prized, the prototypes of womanhood and manhood may be the currently "hot" movie stars, and our evaluation of each other may in some way be related to how closely one approximates the prototypical ideal.

image of the "universal triangle." Although it is easy to define verbally what we mean by a triangle, it is not clear what the "perfect" triangle looks like. We see lots of different kinds of triangles; from this variety what do we create in our mind as the basis for recognizing a triangle? (p. 222)

Berkeley's speculative odyssey for the "perfect" triangle spanned several centuries and was finally empirically studied, in what has itself become a prototypical experiment, by Posner, Goldsmith, and Welton (1967). They searched for the prototype of a triangle (and other forms) and then measured participants' reaction to other forms that were something like the prototypical one. In the first part of their experiment, they developed a series of prototypes (see Figure 4.15) formed by placing nine dots in a 30 × 30 matrix (standard, 20-squares-per-inch graph paper). These formed either a triangle, a letter, or a random arrangement, which served as prototypes. Four distortions of each of these original forms were made by shifting dots from their original positions. (Figure 4.15 also shows the distortions of the triangle pattern.) Participants were shown each of the four distortions one at a time and asked to classify the pattern by prototype. After participants classified each pattern (by pressing a response button that indicated how they classified the pattern), they were told which of their choices had been correct; the prototype was not presented.

From this first experiment it was evident that the participants had learned to classify distorted patterns of a specific prototype into a common category, while other patterns, derived from another prototype, were sorted into another common category. The original task was followed with a transfer task, in which participants were asked to classify a series of patterns into one of the three previous categories. The new sets of patterns were composed of (1) old distortions, (2) new distortions (based on the original prototypes), and (3) the prototypes themselves. The old distortions were easily correctly classified (with an accuracy level of about 87 percent). More importantly, the prototypes (which the participants had never seen or classified) were correctly classified about

FIGURE 4.15

The four prototypical patterns and four distortions of the triangle pattern used by Posner, Goldsmith, and Welton in their study.

Adapted from Posner, Goldsmith, and Welton (1967).

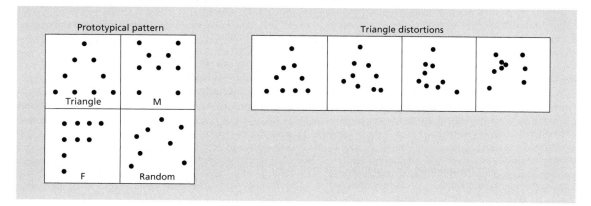

equally well. The new distortions were classified less well than the other two types. Because the prototypes were as accurately classified as the old distortions, it would seem the participants had actually learned something about the prototypes—even though they had never seen anything but distortions of them.

The remarkable feature of this experiment is that the prototype was classified correctly about as frequently as the original learned distortion and more frequently than the new (control) distortion. Posner and his colleagues argue that information about the prototype was abstracted from the stored information (based on the distortion) with a high degree of efficiency. Not only are prototypes abstracted from distorted exemplars, but also the process of pattern learning involves knowledge about variability. The possibility that the correct classification of the prototype was based on the familiarity of the prototype (triangle, *F*, and *M*) in the experience of most people was dealt with in an experiment by Petersen et al. (1973). Their results indicated that prototypes and minimally distorted test patterns of highly meaningful configurations were more easily identified than meaningless prototypes and minimally distorted test patterns. However, where the degree of distortion was great, the opposite was true; that is, the highly meaningful prototype was less often identified than the one with low meaningfulness. Their results are not inconsistent with Posner and his team but tease out the interaction between what Berkeley may have called the "universal triangle" and its distortion. Apparently, we abstract prototypes on the basis of stored information. Well-learned forms do not seem to accommodate as wide a range of distortion as less well-learned forms. Bishop Berkeley's search for the perfect triangle has led to the conclusion that all triangles are equal, but some are more equilateral!

Pseudomemory

In an experiment of prototype formation that embodied the Franks and Bransford procedure, Solso and McCarthy (1981a) found that participants falsely recognized the prototype as a previously seen figure with greater confidence than they identified previously seen figures. This phenomenon is called **pseudomemory.** They hypothesized that a prototype is formed on the basis of frequently experienced features. These features, such as individual lines in a figure or parts of a human face, are stored in memory. A general index of the strength of the memory for features can be determined by the frequency of exposure to the feature. Frequently perceived features are, in general, more likely to be permanently stored in memory than are rarely perceived features. Furthermore, it may be that the rules that govern the relationships between features in a pattern are not as well incorporated in memory as the memory for features themselves. Thus, we can conceptualize the process of acquiring knowledge about a pattern as consisting of two stages: acquisition of information about the features of the pattern and acquisition about the relationships between the features. Perhaps the most intriguing part of the puzzle of prototype formation is the evidence that the two stages appear to develop at different rates as we acquire knowledge about a pattern. It is something like a race in which two runners run at different rates. The faster runner is analogous to feature learning, and the slower runner is analogous to learning relationships.

In the Solso and McCarthy experiment, a prototype face was composed from an Identikit, a face-identification device used in police work that consists of a series of plastic templates, each representing a facial characteristic such as hair, eyes, nose, chin, and mouth. From each of the three prototype faces selected, a series of exemplar faces was derived ranging in similarity to the prototype face (see Figure 4.16). Participants were shown exemplar faces and then a second set of faces, which contained some of the original faces, some new faces that were scaled in their similarity to the prototype face, and the prototype face. The participants were asked to judge the faces as being members of the previously seen set or new faces and to rate the confidence of their impression. As can be seen in Figure 4.17, not only did participants rate the prototype faces as an old

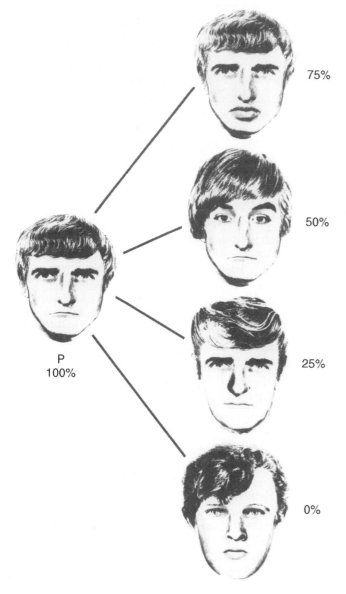

75%

50%

25%

P
100%

0%

FIGURE 4.16

Prototype face and exemplar faces used in Solso and McCarthy (1981a). The 75 percent face has all the same features as the prototype face except the mouth; the 50 percent face has different hair and eyes; the 25 percent face has only the eyes in common; and the 0 percent face has no features in common with the prototype face.

Confidence ratings for prototype face, old faces, and new faces.

From Solso and McCarthy (1981a).

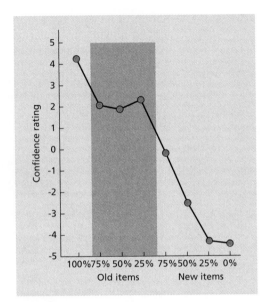

(previously seen) face, but they also gave those faces the highest confidence ratings (an example of pseudomemory).

From the foregoing we can draw some conclusions about visual prototype formation and use. The previously cited research indicates that we (1) form a prototype on the basis of averaging the characteristics of its exemplars; (2) acquire some specific information about prototypes when we deal only with exemplars; (3) acquire some general information about the common properties of prototypes, with well-known prototypes yielding less generous inclusiveness than less familiar (or recently learned) prototypes; (4) judge exemplars in terms of their transformational proximity to prototypes; and (5) form prototypes on the basis of abstractions from exemplars and then evaluate the relationship between forms of the prototypes on the basis of their distance from the prototype as well as from other individual examples.

Prototype Theory: Central Tendency versus Attribute Frequency

From the above-mentioned experiments and many other studies, two theoretical models of prototype formation have emerged. In one model, called the **central-tendency model,** a prototype is conceptualized as representing the average or mean of a set of exemplars. The research of Posner and his colleagues (1967) tends to support this model. Posner and Keele (1968), for example, believe that a prototype is represented mathematically by a hypothetical point in multidimensional space at which the means of the distances along all attributes intersect. We can see in the Posner and Reed experiments how people form a prototype that is an abstraction of a figure. Thus, the prototype is an abstraction stored in memory that represents the central tendency of the category.

The second model, called the **attribute-frequency model,** suggests that a prototype represents the mode or most frequently experienced combination of attributes. The experiments of Franks and Bransford, Neumann (1977), and Solso and McCarthy support this model. In this model a prototype is synonymous with the "best example" of a set of patterns. A prototype is a pattern that incorporates the most frequently experienced features expressed in a series of exemplars. While the prototype is often unique because it is made up of a unique combination of attributes (think of the unique geometric forms in Frank and Bransford's experiment or the unique face in Solso and McCarthy's experiment), the features themselves have been previously experienced. The features (the geometric components, or face parts) are the building blocks of the prototype. Each time a person looks at a pattern, he or she records both the features in the pattern and the relationship between the features. However, according to the attribute-frequency model, upon the introduction of a prototype (which incorporates many of the previously perceived attributes), an individual believes he or she has previously seen the figure because the attributes have been stored in memory. Since the relationships between the features have been seen fewer times than the features (in most experiments the exemplars are shown only once), knowledge about the relationships of features is less well stored in memory than is the knowledge about features.

Form Perception: An Integrated Approach

Up to this point we have considered several hypotheses about pattern recognition in humans. First we considered the human visual system with its enormous capacity—and its limitations. Then we considered some topics in Gestalt psychology, which suggested that visual patterns are "naturally" organized in predictable ways. Next we discussed the topics of top-down and bottom-up processing, and we learned of the importance of contextual cues on form perception. Three models of form perception were discussed: template matching, feature analysis, and prototype formation. In developing the different approaches to form perception, it may appear to the reader that the problem is as confusing as the one facing the seven blind men who are asked to describe an elephant. One grabs hold of the tail and depicts the creature as a great rope; another holds its trunk and portrays it as a serpent; the next feels the elephant's side, which appears to be like a wall; and so on.

Each of our various theories of form perception seems to lay hold of only one aspect of the entire picture without integration. Quite the contrary is true. Each theory is essentially correct, but each also needs support from the others. For example, at a simple level of processing, some type of feature detection operates, as the experiments by Hubel and Wiesel demonstrate. However, a comprehensive view of form perception is more expansive than simple bar identifiers. Conceptually, some type of match between things in memory and things seen, as suggested by the template model, seems reasonable. Nevertheless, this theory also fails to account for the diversity of pattern recognition. Perhaps the geon theory will account for both the diversity and adaptability of the human eye and mind to understand a world filled with complex forms that require rapid and accurate identification. The prototype concept, although well documented, must, at some level, turn to other models to account for the initial stages of perception. Thus, the many theories of form perception are complementary rather than antagonistic. Form perception is a complicated affair, and at present, no single comprehensive theory has been developed to account for all of its components.

Pattern Recognition among Experts

Pattern Recognition in Chess

So far our perceptual displays have been simple; even Reed's deadpan faces are stripped of complexity. How are more complex patterns viewed? Chase and Simon (1973a, 1973b) studied this problem by analyzing the complex pattern made by pieces on a chessboard and the way chess masters differed from ordinary players. Intuition may tell us that the cognitive differences between the two are a matter of how many moves ahead the master player can think. The intuition is wrong, at least according to the research of de Groot (1965, 1966), who found that master players and weaker players thought ahead about the same number of moves, considered about the same number of moves, and had a similar search for patterns of moves. It may be that master players even consider fewer alternative moves, while the weaker player wastes time looking at alternatives that are totally inappropriate. What is the difference? One is the master's ability to reconstruct a pattern of chess pieces after viewing if for only a few seconds; the weak player has great difficulty in doing so. The key to this observation is in the nature of the pattern: it must make sense. If the pieces are arranged in a random order, or illogically, then both masters and beginners do equally poorly. Perhaps the masters put together several chess pieces into chunks or patterns, much as we might put together letters to form words, and words to form sentences. Experienced masters, then, would seem to have greater capacity to reproduce the pattern because they are able to encode the bits and pieces into chess schemata.

Chase and Simon checked this hypothesis using three types of participants—a master, a Class A player (a very strong player), and a beginner. In one experiment their participants were asked to reconstruct twenty chess patterns in plain view—half from the middle games and half from end games selected from chess books and magazines (see Figure 4.18). In this task, two chessboards were placed side by side and the participant was to reconstruct on one chessboard the arrangement of chess pieces shown on the other. In a second experiment, participants scanned a chess pattern for five seconds and then reconstructed it from memory. Chase and Simon found that scanning time was about the same for the master and the Class A player and the beginner, but that the time spent in reconstructing was much less for the master than for the others (Figure 4.19); Figure 4.20 shows the number of pieces correctly placed. Further analysis of these data indicated that the ability to see chunks, or meaningful clusters, of chess pieces made it possible for the better players to gather more information in the given time.

The Chase and Simon experiment has significant theoretical implications. Chunks of information held together by abstract relationships may constitute the basis for a theory of pattern syntax. Bits of information without any meaningful context or grouping are hard to encode, be they letters, geometric forms, notes, or chess pieces; however,

FIGURE 4.18

Example of a chess middle and end game and its randomized counterparts.

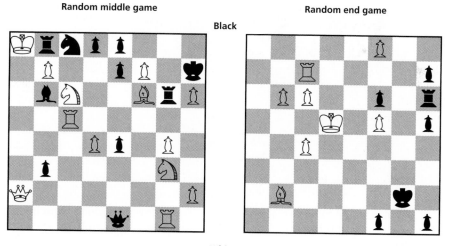

when fitted into a meaningful structure (such as poetry, architecture, music, an elegant chess defense), they become significant because they are easily abstracted in terms of a common grammar. Modern information theorists have developed pristine models of the mind based on structural levels. We have witnessed the growth of structural grammar in language (discussed further in Chapter 11), in music, in body responses, in graphic tasks, and in chess problems. A prevalent human attribute, applicable to all sensory forms, may be the tendency to code information into higher-order abstractions of reality

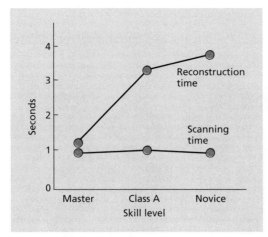

FIGURE 4.19

Scanning and reconstruction times for chess players of three levels of skill.

Adapted from Chase and Simon (1973a).

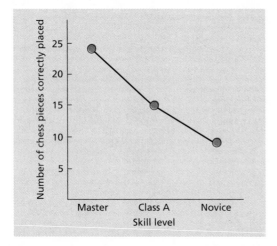

FIGURE 4.20

Distribution of correct placement of chess pieces by players of three levels of skill. Players were shown original pattern for 5 seconds.

Adapted from Chase and Simon (1973a).

into which new information is fitted. The above-mentioned experiments on chess perception, and other experiments in which immediate stimuli are abstracted, support this postulate.

Pattern Recognition—The Role of the Perceiver

We have covered quite a lot of territory in this chapter on pattern recognition: bottom-up and top-down processing; template matching; computer simulation of pattern recognition; feature analysis; physiological components in pattern recognition; prototype matching; cognitive structure; letter identification; and forms, faces, and chess problems. In most of these topics it has been hard to isolate specific functions of pattern recognition without calling on other cognitive systems. Throughout our discussion, we have occasionally considered the influence that context and redundancy have on pattern recognition and learned that both of these factors bear directly on the recognition of sensory stimuli. These topics are covered in greater detail in the section on language in Chapter 11 as they relate to the perception of letters and words. The one system that seems to crop up time and again is memory. Pattern recognition seems to involve several lower-order systems, such as visual storage, analysis of features, synthesis of features, and prototypical matching. However, pattern recognition in humans also involves memory. In our natural environment the world is filled with sensory stimuli, which, when organized and classified, create a recognition of a pattern. The stimuli themselves are empty of meaning, existing in their primitive form whether or not we perceive them. They do become meaningful when analyzed into higher-order patterns. Look and listen to your immediate environment. What do you see and hear? What do you smell, taste, or feel? Certainly, you do not perceive raw, vacuous stimuli (even though we are confident that these stimuli excite our sensory system), but you do sense things that mean something to you. The bell in the distance, the tree outside a window, the series of letters on this page, and the smell of fresh bread are all examples of stimuli that, when recognized by the brain, take on a fuller meaning than the physical structures that they excite. That meaning is provided by our memory for these events, which casts immediate experiences in a larger realm of reality. The meaning of sensory stimuli is provided by the perceiver.

In one of the adventures of Sherlock Holmes, the eminent detective is able to portray accurately the life and style of a certain character through a series of brilliant deductions based on a few clues, which are, in effect, cues to memory and association. The cues, which were equally available to his companion, Dr. Watson, were coded and structured in Holmes's mind in such a way that the deductions seemed "elementary" to him, but not to Watson. After Holmes explains what the cues mean, he reproaches his companion by saying, "You 'see' but you do not 'observe'!" All normal humans "see," but the ability to abstract the things we see into meaningful patterns is, to a large extent, a function of the previous structure and knowledge of past experiences.

In Chapter 11 on language, we discuss the perception and human analysis of letters and words within an information-processing context. In that chapter we shall see, as we have in this one, that our experiences, as they are represented in memory, play a major role in what and how we see.

Spotlight on Cognitive Neuroscience

Pattern Recognition

It is known that the two hemispheres of the brain have different "specialities" or, in other words, functional asymmetries. Fine motor control and language use tend to be focused in the left hemisphere (of right-handed people). Spatial abilities tend to be focused in the right hemisphere. Margaret Funnell, Paul Corballis, and Michael Gazzaniga were interested in demonstrating that the right hemisphere is specialized for processing spatial information. To do this, they solicited the help of J. W., a 45-year-old, right-handed man, who had received a callosotomy (severing of the corpus collosum) at age

25 to control severe epilepsy. By using a "split-brained" patient, they were uniquely able to determine the functioning properties of each side of the brain, because the hemispheres are unable to communicate with one another as can someone who has an intact corpus collosum. Using a variety of stimuli (colored images of objects, black-and-white line drawings of objects, and abstract geometric forms), they found that both hemispheres were able to encode the stimuli but that the left hemisphere was poor at recognizing spatial differences in the stimuli (for example, if an object was presented next to its mirror image, the left hemisphere did not notice the difference). They concluded that the left hemisphere is directed more toward pattern recognition, and the right hemisphere is directed more toward the analysis of spatial information (like understanding that the object and its mirror image were different images due to orientation).

Funnell, M. G., Corballis, P. M., and Gazzaniga, M. S. (1999). A deficit in perceptual matching in the left hemisphere of a callosotomy patient. *Neuropsychologia, 37*(10), 1143–1154.

SUMMARY

1   The ability to identify and process visual patterns has been approached from several theoretical positions: Gestalt psychology, bottom-up versus top-down processing, template matching, feature analysis, and prototype recognition.

2   Gestalt psychologists proposed the perception of visual patterns to be organized according to the principles of proximity, similarity, and spontaneous organization.

3   Pattern recognition may be initiated by the parts of the pattern, which are then summed (bottom-up processing), or as a hypothesis held by the perceiver, which leads to recognition of the whole and subsequent recognition of the components (top-down processing).

4   Experimental work indicates that object perception is greatly influenced by contextually derived hypotheses.

5   Template matching holds that pattern recognition occurs when an exact match is made between sensory stimuli and a corresponding internal form. This position has conceptual and practical utility, but it is unlikely as an explanation for many complex cognitive processes, such as our ability to interpret unfamiliar shapes and forms correctly.

6   Feature analysis asserts that pattern recognition occurs only after stimuli have been analyzed according to their simple components. Data from neurological and behavioral experiments lend support to this hypothesis.

7   Prototype formation asserts that pattern perception occurs as a result of abstractions of stimuli, which are stored in memory and serve as idealized forms against which patterns are evaluated. Two models proposed by prototype theory are the central-tendency model, which states that a prototype presents the mean or an average of a set of exemplars, and the attribute-frequency model, which states that a prototype represents the mode or a summation of the most frequently experienced attributes.

8   Visual pattern recognition in humans involves visual analysis of input stimuli and long-term memory storage.

*K*EY *W*ORDS

attribute-frequency model
bottom-up processing
canonic perspective
central-tendency model
constructive perception
direct perception
feature
feature analysis
fovea
geon
Gestalt psychology
pattern organization

pattern recognition
Pragnanz
priming effect
prototype
prototype recognition
pseudomemory
semantic priming
similarity
template matching
top-down processing
unconscious inference

*R*ECOMMENDED *R*EADINGS

● Most of the readings recommended for Chapter 3 are relevant to this chapter. Other sources include Reed, *Psychological Processes in Pattern Recognition;* Humphreys (Ed.), *Understanding Vision;* Murch, *Visual and Auditory Perception;* and McBurney and Collings, *Introduction to Sensation/Perception.* Rock's book *The Logic of Perception* is an important addition to the field. Lesher's article on illusionary contours in *Psychonomic Bulletin & Review* (1995) is excellent.

CHAPTER 5

States of Consciousness

hmmm...?

● **History of Consciousness**

● **Consciousness as a Scientific Construct**

● **Cognitive Psychology and Consciousness**
Explicit and Implicit Memory
Research with Primes
Neurocognitive Studies: Sleep and Amnesia
Limited Capacity

● **Metaphors of Consciousness**
The Novelty Metaphor
The Spotlight
An Integration Metaphor: The Theater
    in the Society of Mind

● **Theories of Consciousness**
Schacter's Model of Dissociable Interactions and
    Conscious Experience (DICE)
Baars's Global Workspace Theory

● **Functions of Consciousness**

1. What are you consciously aware of at this instant? Now define *consciousness*. How does your definition compare with the text's definition?

2. What important historical events led to the contemporary studies of consciousness?

3. What is a "prime," and how has priming research told us about conscious and unconscious processes?

4. Distinguish between explicit and implicit memory.

5. How can consciousness be studied scientifically?

6. What are the stages of sleep?

7. What are some theories of consciousness?

8. What function does consciousness serve in everyday life as well as for our species?

*S*omething about the topic of consciousness makes people, like the White Queen in *Through the Looking Glass,* believe six impossible things before breakfast. Could most animals really be unconscious—sleepwalkers, zombies, automata, out cold? Hath not a dog senses, affections, passions? If you prick them, do they not feel pain? And was Moses really unable to taste salt or see or enjoy sex? Do children learn to become conscious in the same way that they learn to wear baseball caps turned around?

    —*Stephen Pinker*

Consciousness, once central to psychology then banished as unscientific, has now returned in full glory. It is a topic that simply will not disappear, and for good reasons. This last great mystery of science spans psychology, philosophy, and neuroscience. Topics such as subjective experience, awareness, dreams, drugs, and meditation all fall in the realm of the study of consciousness. We spend most of our waking lives engaged in conscious activity, and even during sleep some murmur of awareness is present. Otherwise, how do we wake to the alarm, the cry of our own baby, or a bucket of cold water in the face? When full consciousness returns from deep sleep, a massive change in electrical activity takes place all over the brain, as the fast, small, and irregular waves of waking EEG replace the large, slow, and regular hills and valleys of deep sleep. At the same time, we humans report a rich and varied array of conscious experiences: colors and sounds, feelings and smells, images and dreams, the rich pageant of everyday reality. Because these reports of conscious experience are so perfectly synchronized with brain activity, psychologists infer that they reflect a single underlying reality, the reality of waking consciousness. We begin this chapter with the following definition: **Consciousness** is the awareness of environmental and cognitive events such as the sights and sounds of the world as well as of one's memories, thoughts, feelings, and bodily sensations. By this definition consciousness has two sides:

- Consciousness includes a realization of environmental stimuli. For example, you might suddenly become mindful of a bird's song, a sharp toothache, or the visual recognition of an old friend.

- Consciousness also includes one's cognizance of mental events—those thoughts that result from memories and your own internal sense of awareness and self. For example, you might think of the name of the bird, the telephone number of your dentist, or how shy you get in large groups.

These internal, often private thoughts are every bit as important as external stimuli are in determining who we are and what we think. Throughout the day, we all have a myriad of conscious experiences caused by the sights and sounds of the world and an untold number of internal conscious experiences caused by our inner thoughts which privately unmask our personal reactions and feelings.

    What conscious thought are you aware of now? What is its source? Does anyone else know your thoughts? Have you ever concealed your thoughts from someone else? If so, why? These are the types of questions that have kept consciousness, shall we say, always in mind.

All that we are is the result of what we have thought. The mind is everything. What we think, we become.

—*Buddha (563–483 BCE)*

For scientists interested in consciousness, a fundamental question centers on how the mind emerges from brain activity. While brain activity is observable by others, the "mind is observable only to its owner" (Damasio, 1999, p. 4). This fascinating conundrum has led scientists to study consciousness from the smallest pulse of brain activity to the complexity of the subjective experience of smelling a rose. The fear that some have is, as Damasio (1999) has pointed out, that somehow by uncovering the neurological basis of conscious experience that we cheapen the wonder of the mind and all that makes us human. Not so. "By understanding the mind at a deeper level, we will see it as nature's most complex set of biological phenomena rather than as a mystery with an unknown nature. The mind will survive explanation, just as a rose's perfume, its molecular structure deduced, will still smell as sweet" (Damasio, 1999, p. 9).

History of Consciousness

No one recorded the early events of evolution, but had some biographer been there, it is likely that person would have observed the development of consciousness very early in the mental life of developing creatures. Furthermore, human concerns with the topic of consciousness were closely related to fundamental concerns of people, such as "Who am I?" "Why do I think the thoughts I do?" and "What happens to 'me' when I sleep or die?"—topics mixed with religious and superstitious matters. The topic of consciousness was part of the early philosophic concerns from ancient times to modern times, and a portion of that history is recounted in Chapter 1.

Scientific psychology began in the nineteenth century as the study of conscious experience. In the famous words of William James, "Psychology is the science of mental life," by which he meant *conscious* mental life (James, 1890/1983, p. 15). James was not alone in this definition of psychology. Even before him, Europeans, including Hermann Ebbinghaus (the memory expert whom we shall study in the Chapter 7) and Sigmund Freud (who turned the world on its head with his ideas about consciousness and especially the unconscious determinants of human thought and behavior), were exploring elements of consciousness for half a century. Some of this work we can readily rec-

My unconscious knows more about the consciousness of the psychologist than his consciousness knows about my unconscious.

—*Karl Kraus*

ognize. For example, psychophysical laws were discovered in the middle of the nineteenth century. There had been many explorations of hypnosis and sensory processes; memory and intelligence were beginning to be studied; the laws of associative learning were being worked out. And almost everyone believed that consciousness was the key to these mental events.

That changed about 1900, with Ivan Pavlov, John Watson, and similarly inclined people who felt it was scientifically improper to deal with personal consciousness, since we can only observe physical behavior. For most of the twentieth century, human personal experience was almost a taboo subject in science. There were some practical reasons for this. It is plainly difficult in many cases to be sure about someone else's personal experience, so that it can be hard to test and retest evidence in the way necessary in science. Yet psychologists have found clever ways to test hypotheses about short-term memory, implicit cognition, and mental imagery, which are not readily observable. Could the same strategies be applied to consciousness? Why not treat the experience of others as an inferential construct, based on observable evidence, just as scientists deal with electrons and the speed of light? The methodological problems in studying consciousness seem difficult but not impossible.

There is also a great philosophical problem that has made it difficult for scientists to explore consciousness in the way we routinely study memory or perception. It is called the mind–body problem (see Chapter 2) and has been discussed by philosophers since the beginnings of written thought. The mind–body issue considers whether our world is basically mental or physical. Can all conscious experiences be explained by neurons? Or are neurons themselves only ideas in the minds of scientists?

In ordinary language we are always switching back and forth between mental and physical ways of describing reality. "I took a [physical] aspirin for a splitting [mental] headache." "I walked to the [physical] refrigerator because I had a [mental] craving for ice cream." How do mental experiences cause physical actions, and vice versa? Common sense doesn't care. It just jumps back and forth between the realms of the mind and the body. Common sense psychology is *dualistic*.

However, the situation gets more complicated when we try to think carefully about the relationship between our private experiences and the public world we share. In the realm of aspirins and refrigerators, ordinary causality explains how things happen. Ice cream can melt because of heat, and bottles of aspirin be spoiled by too much moisture. These phenomena follow causal regularities of the physical world. But mental events are affected by goals, emotions, and cognitive processes, which seem to follow different laws.

In Western philosophy the human soul was thought to have only such mental properties, and in the 1600s René Descartes, the French philosopher and mathematician, concluded that the conscious soul touches the physical brain in only one spot: the tiny pineal gland, hanging from the bottom of the brain. He could imagine no other way to explain how the mindful soul related to the physical body. Most Western philosophers were *mentalists*, believing that the conscious soul was the basis of all reality. Asian philosophers were generally mentalistic too.

The beginning of the twentieth century, however, saw a change. Possibly the main reason for the scientific rejection of consciousness about 1900 is that scientists thought mentalism was incompatible with established sciences like chemistry and physics. Therefore, a little after 1900 there occurred a widespread movement in science toward *physicalism*—the idea that all conscious experiences can be explained by neurons or, psychologically, by observable stimuli (inputs) and responses (outputs).

In psychology this *behavioristic* philosophy was popularized by I. P. Pavlov and John Watson starting about 1910 and maintained by B. F. Skinner and many other psychologists well into the 1970s. For most of the twentieth century, human conscious experience was avoided because it was thought to be essentially mentalistic.

Gradually, however, learning theories were being challenged by theories of memory, perception, and internal representations of mental processes. *Information processing* and *cognition* became buzz words, and consciousness—a topic that simply would not go away no matter how scorned by the behaviorists—began to creep into the psychological literature after a half century of neglect. And the scientists experimenting with the concept were not the psychedelic-loving beatniks of Haight-Asbury attempting to reach higher and higher levels of "consciousness." The 1990s proved to be a crowning decade for the study of consciousness with a "surge" of publications and scientific interest (Zeman, 2001). Interest in the topic continues to grow.

Consciousness as a Scientific Construct

George Mandler (1984) has pointed out that as scientists dealing with public evidence and shared reasoning, we observe only the *reports* people make about their conscious experience. The implication of this is that your subjective report of a conscious event may not be the same as mine. (When you say, "I love to watch *Saturday Night Live*," I presume your emotional reaction to *SNL* is a different experience from the one you describe when you say "I love to make out with my boyfriend.") On the other hand, we do make reliable inferences about human experience based on such public reports; otherwise, our world would be even more chaotic than it already is.

In studying perception, in practice we always treat verbal reports as descriptions of conscious experience. We know that perceptual reports correspond with exquisite sensitivity to the physical stimulus array. Entire domains of research depend upon this methodology. *Unconscious* processes can also be inferred from public observations, though people cannot act on them deliberately. The simplest example is the great multitude of memories that are currently unconscious. You may recall this morning's breakfast. But what happened to that memory before it was brought to mind? It was still represented in the nervous system, though not consciously, and there's the rub. By what cerebral command does the invisible become noticed? For example, unconscious memories can influence other processes without ever coming to mind. If you had orange juice for breakfast today, you may try milk tomorrow, even without bringing today's juice to mind.

A case can be made for unconscious representation of habituated stimuli, memories before and after recall, automatic skills, implicit learning, the rules of syntax, unattended speech, presupposed knowledge, preconscious input processing, and many other phenomena. Researchers still argue about the particulars of some of these cases, but it is widely agreed that given adequate evidence, unconscious representations may be inferred. It is crucial to treat both conscious and unconscious representations as inferred constructs, for only then can we treat consciousness as a variable, so that we can talk about consciousness *as such*. As in the case of Newtonian gravity, we can compare a state with its absence. This is a bit more abstract than the familiar experimental method, because we are comparing two *inferred* entities, rather than two direct observations. But the principle of treating consciousness as a variable to be studied is the same. It is useful to form a type of taxonomy in which some events are associated with consciousness and some with unconsciousness as a first step in the scientific analysis of these phenomena. In Table 5.1 psychological characteristics are classified into one or the other camp as a basis for distinction as well as a starting place for empirical research. As a general guide to building a framework for the scientific study of consciousness, the following four categories are inspired by Zeman and revised here (2001):

- Waking state—when we are awake we are able to perceive and interact
- Experience—our moment-to-moment awareness of what is going on around us
- Possession of a mental state—beliefs, hopes, intentions, desires, etc.
- Sense of self-self recognition, self-knowledge, feeling ownership over the ideas, thoughts, and feelings that are in your head

TABLE 5.1

Some Widely Studied Polarities between Matched Conscious and Unconscious Phenomena

Associated with Consciousness	Associated with Unconsciousness
1. Explicit cognition	1. Implicit cognition
2. Immediate memory	2. Long-term memory
3. Novel, informative, and significant stimuli	3. Routine, predictable, and nonsignificant stimuli
4. Attended input	4. Unattended imput
5. Focal contents	5. Fringe events (for example, familiarity)
6. Declarative memory	6. Procedural memory
7. Supraliminal stimulation	7. Subliminal stimulation
8. Effortful processes	8. Spontaneous/automatic processes
9. Remembering	9. Knowing
10. Available information	10. Unavailable information
11. Strategic control	11. Automatic control
12. Patterned stimulus series	12. Implicitly learned structures
13. Intact reticular formation and intralaminar nuclei	13. Lesions to reticular formation and bilateral intralaminar nuclei
14. Rehearsed item in working memory	14. Unrehearsed item in working memory
15. Waking and dreaming	15. Deep sleep, coma, sedation
16. Explicit inferences	16. Automatic inferences
17. Episodic memory	17. Semantic memory
18. Autonoetic memory (Tulving)	18. Noetic memory

Cognitive Psychology and Consciousness

Several important lines of research helped reintroduce the topic of consciousness into mainstream psychology. Two central approaches have been used by cognitive psychologists in the current investigation. One is psychological and the other neurological.

> *Research with primes.* It was observed that people's ability to recognize a word, for example, was measurably enhanced if they had a single experience with that word or even a related word. For example, if you were asked to recognize *psychedelic* as a word, the chances are that you would do so easily. However, if you had not read a preceding paragraph, in which the word *psychedelics* was used, the task might take you a little bit longer. Why? Your level of consciousness for that word would be elevated, greater than if you had not read that section. We humans do this all the time, and it seemed that good empirical data could be gathered on this phenomenon.

Try This

Consciousness Craze

*R*ecently, a search in Medline and PsycINFO for the keyword "consciousness" each turned up more than 17,000 entries. Our rapacious appetite for all sorts of topics related to consciousness is understandable when we consider that everything we do or think is somehow related to the topic. At the beginning of the twenty-first century, a search of the Internet turned up over 5 million pages! Granted, people (scientists included!) use the word consciousness to mean a variety of things. Finding over 5 million Internet sites attests to the broad interest this topic sparks. Just one site (www.u.arizona.edu/~chalmers) had 1,284 online papers, mostly scholarly cognitive works. Check it out! Here are some of the popular sites for consciousness on the Internet:

Consciousness
www.u.arizona.edu/~chalmers
Large index of online papers on consciousness and related topics. Topics include the concepts of consciousness, and dualism and materialism.

Consciousness
www.lycaeum.org/drugs/other/brain
Diverse range of articles and links covering topics such as behavioral and cognitive sciences, and psychology.

The Hare Krishna Home Page
www.webcom.com/~ara

Journal of Consciousness Studies
www.zynet.co.uk/imprint/jcs.html
Professional organization for those with an interest in mythic consciousness.

Center for Consciousness Studies
www.consciousness.arizona.edu
University of Arizona research group supports the development of a science of consciousness. Read about current research and upcoming events.

Descriptions of Religions, Faith Groups & Ethical Systems
www.religioustolerance.org/var_rel.htm
From Wicca to Judaism, the Ontario Consultants on Religious Tolerance offer essays on the origin, history, beliefs, and practices of sixty-three different faiths.

Neurocognitive studies: Sleep and amnesia. The most obvious distinction between unconscious and conscious states is in sleep and wake states. The extensive research on sleep, much of it done with electroencephalograph (EEG) recordings of people in various stages of sleep, has provided a glimpse into this type of unconsciousness. In addition it has been shown that some amnesic patients, suffering from neurological problems (such as a brain trauma), cannot consciously recall events, even simple things like their own name, the name of their hometown, their school song, the faces of their children, and their social security number (three out of five is acceptable). But they can learn and recall other types of tasks, such as motor learning tasks. Because conscious recall was related to neurological injury, it appeared that consciousness seemed to have a neurological basis.

Explicit and Implicit Memory

Explicit memory refers to the conscious recall of information, the type of memory you might use when answering a question on an examination. For example, if you were asked to recall the U.S. president who preceded Bill Clinton, you would answer, "George Bush." You are consciously making an association between the cue, or question, and the answer. We use explicit memory for answering direct questions. **Implicit memory,** on the other hand, is more germane to our discussion of consciousness because it refers to memory that is measured through a performance change related to some previous experience, as in the case of priming experiments discussed earlier.

In many cases, implicit memory is revealed when previous information facilitates task performance and does not require conscious recall of those experiences. If you were asked to recall the capital of France, you actively and consciously search your memory to find Paris; this is an example of explicit memory. If you are shown a badly

Raising Your Level of Consciousness

𝒴ou know how it is—your friend tells you about a favorite new car, restaurant, or clothing style. And all of sudden you see that thing everywhere! Were these things not there before? Of course they were, but your level of awareness of them was raised by the conversation with your friend and now you notice these elements in your environment when you didn't before. Let's see if we can raise your level of consciousness of the following list of words. Read this list and form an impression of each item:

In the next few days note how some of these words have an uncanny way of entering your consciousness. How is this exercise in critical thinking related to priming experiments? Why did these concepts "pop into your head"? What is the relationship between memory and consciousness? Can you now reverse the process so you *cannot* have these words and their associates intrude on your conscious thought? How might other words and activities raise your level of consciousness?

BOOKSTORE   PERFUME
TV ANCHOR   TRAFFIC LIGHT
DOG FOOD   FUNNY HAIR
CRYING BABY

degraded figure and then shown the whole figure and asked to identify it, you are able to recognize the figure faster than if the prime (the degraded figure) is not shown. Yet, your conscious awareness of the influence of the prime is likely to be absent. Or try this one: Here is a fragmented word:

p_y_h_d_l_c.

What is it? The answer simply popped into your head (implicitly)! Yet, if you ask a friend to solve this word problem who had not been primed by reading *psychedelic* several paragraphs ago, it is likely that the solution time would be considerably longer. Try it.

The use of primes that activated mental associations just below the level of consciousness became all the rage in psychology in the 1980s and 1990s (see Roediger & McDermott, 1993, for an excellent review), and it seemed that one could not pick up a journal in experimental psychology during this period without reading about a new wrinkle on the topic. Now, those who are passionate about putting human heads in the "magnet" (as the MRI machine is affectionately called) are beginning to isolate some of the structures implicated in the bijou of the brain—consciousness.[1]

Research with Primes

Cognitive psychologists began investigating the influence of briefly presented words on subsequent recognition of other words as early as early as the 1970s (see Meyer & Schvaneveldt, 1971, 1976; and Meyer, Schvaneveldt, & Ruddy, 1974a, as discussed in Chapter 12) and unwittingly opened up a can of worms still not clearly understood. The experimental paradigm of these early studies was simple enough and has remained little changed to this day. A research participant is shown a word, say *COLLEGE,* and then is shown an associate of the word, say *UNIVERSITY.* He or she is asked to identify the second word as a real word as fast as he can. Another participant is shown a word such as *JELLY* and is asked to identify *UNIVERSITY* as a real word. If primed with *COLLEGE,* a participant identifies *UNIVERSITY* faster than if primed with *JELLY.*

The matter got more complicated when a different type of prime was used by Richard Nisbett and Lee Ross (1980) at the University of Michigan in a social psychological experiment that involved showing participants words that were associated such as *OCEAN* and *MOON.* Then, when asked to *free-associate* (a term made popular by Sigmund Freud and his disciples) to the words, participants did not know why they responded with the words they used. For example, a person might say *detergent* and invent a reason like "My mom used Tide to do the laundry." By now, it was becoming clear that primes had an effect on subsequent performance *even when the participant was unaware of the cause.* The topic raised the possibility of **subliminal priming,** or the effect of a prime that is presented below the **sensory threshold,** level of conscious awareness. Several interesting experiments were published on the topic.

Figure 5.1, which illustrates subliminal priming, is based on some of the work done in England (see next section) and has been used as a successful class demonstra-

---

[1]Such a statement is true of the aspirations of many brain scientists who are actively seeking "centers of consciousness." However, it may be they are like the feckless lover who was "looking for love in all the wrong places" in that consciousness (and other higher-order cognitive processes) may be so widely distributed throughout the brain that trying to find "centers" may be a slippery matter indeed.

tion. One half of the class looked at a picture such as the one in Figure 5.1A, and the other half at 5.1B. (The pictures were presented on an overhead projector for about 100 ms.) Then all students were shown the boy in Figure 5.1C and asked to draw the face and make a judgment about the character of the boy. Students who saw A, even momentarily presented, had a tendency to see and draw the boy as somewhat devilish and use words such as *naughty* or *mischievous*. Those who saw B tended to draw and describe the boy using words like *angelic* or *nice*. The surprising part of the story is that students were not (generally) aware of the character of the prime picture. When allowed to study the prime, they remarked, "My gosh, the kid looks like a little devil complete with horns" or "I did not see how innocent the guy appeared." It appears that in this example, a stimulus prime presented subliminally (that is, below the level of conscious recognition) has an influence on subsequent evaluation of a similar picture. A more closely controlled experiment is presented now.

What has become an archetypal experiment in subliminal priming is a study by Tony Marcel of Cambridge University. In the first phase of the experiment a group of participants were presented with a word very briefly (20 to 110 milliseconds), which was followed by a visual mark (such as a series of XXXXs) that blocks the image of the word staying on the retina and, thus, the participant sees a continuing procession. The presentations were so brief that the participants did not report seeing the words. They were presented at a subliminal rate and their guess as to the word presented was no better than chance. Having established the level of presentation at which participants could no longer identify the word, they were then presented with a word at a subliminal rate, which was a prime of another word (BREAD) or a word that was not a prime (see Figure 5.2). The participants were to decide whether the second word (SANDWICH), the target word, was a legal word or not. This task is called a lexical decision task (LDT) and will be discussed further in the section on words. Reaction times were made to make a decision as to whether or not the string of letters actually made up a word. The results showed that, if primed with an associate, reaction time was faster than if not primed with an associate.

Several researchers have reported similar results. However, strong reactions have been called forth in others (see Holender, 1986, for an overview). Some critics argue that when the criterion for a perceptual threshold is set by a participant—that is, when a participant reports that he can or cannot "see" the prime—then the effect appears. On the other hand, if the threshold exposure time is set by an objective measure, the effect of subliminal priming does not occur. Several conclusions may be derived from this and many similar experiments.

- Under certain specific conditions, subliminal priming happens.
- If a stimulus prime is presented below the sensory threshold (defined as the lowest energy required to activate a neural response), subliminal priming cannot occur.

FIGURE 5.2

Paradigm for testing subliminal perception. Participants are shown a word presented under the level of conscious perception. In one case the word (*bread*) is an associate of the target word (*sandwich*) and in the other case the word is not an associate (*truck*) of the target word. Followed by a mask (XXXX) to inhibit further sensory processing of the word, a lexical decision task (LDT) is done in which the particpant is asked simply to report if the string of letters in the second set (*sandwich*) form a word. The presentation of a subthreshold word that was an associate of the target word (*bread*) influenced the reaction time of the LDT but the nonassociated word (*truck*) had no effect.

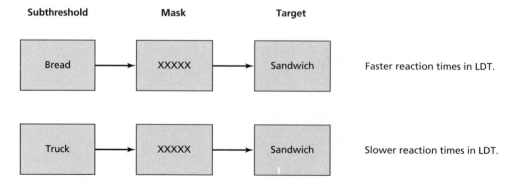

- In the case in which subliminal priming was effective, it is likely that some fragment of the priming word or picture was perceived but the level of subjective confidence was too low to be reported. It seems indefensible to argue that stimuli below the sensory threshold (by which it is meant below the level that external stimuli fire sensory neurons) influence cognitive phenomena, such as enhancing recall or recognition of a subsequent event. Nevertheless, in several experiments, the weak detection of a priming word was sufficiently strong to enhance the detection of a related word. It appears that at some low level of sensation, in which the participant does not report being consciously aware of the sensation, some partial information is detected and stored. We need to separate what a participant actually (physically) experiences from what a participant reports experiencing.

- The issue raises an important philosophic as well as empirical question: How reliable are subjective reports of unconscious and conscious experiences? This may lie at the crux of the problem. One issue is the observer's internal criteria for accepting sensations as reaching a level of strength to be considered "conscious." The matter is related to the theory of signal detection, and the interested reader may find related material under that topic. Philosophically, studies of consciousness involve questions of reality and illusion that regrettably, will not be disentangled here.

- Finally, the study of consciousness seems to appeal to some who attempt to find nonempirical explanations for their beliefs. It is easy to find those who speculate about "psychic powers," "cosmic consciousness," sleep learning, extrasensory perception, subliminal perception (used here to suggest the perception of stimuli below the limen, or threshold, of consciousness), and even reincarnation, clairvoyance, the soul, free will, and the collective unconscious. While such topics are not taboo to cognitive psychology, and some may deserve close empirical investigation, we believe that extraordinary theories of consciousness—a prominent diamond in cognition's tiara—require extraordinary evidence, especially when such notions require that the fundamental laws of cognitive neuroscience, as well as what is known about the nature of the physical universe, be revised if not abandoned.

Neurocognitive Studies: Sleep and Amnesia

Sleep.   The clearest distinction between consciousness and unconsciousness is seen when one is awake or asleep, and experiments with sleeping people have been favored by researchers of consciousness. The preferred tool has been the electroencephalograph (EEG) because it is reasonably nonrestrictive (if one does not mind wearing a harness of snakelike wires hanging from one's head like Medusa) and good temporal data can be collected. It is possible to get brain waves throughout the sleeping period. During the

*W*hat if everything is an illusion and nothing exists? In that case, I definitely overpaid for my carpet.

—*Woody Allen*

day, we interact and are constantly in an attentive state—looking here, listening to one message, or smelling a new odor. But while we are asleep, the attentive mechanisms are profoundly reduced and personal interaction is almost nonexistent. There are also noticeable changes in EEG recordings which confirm that we humans normally go through various "stages" of sleep. In Figure 5.3, five characteristic brain waves show the electrical activity of humans awake and during the four stages of sleep.

When we are in a relaxed state, awake with our eyes closed, we exhibit alpha waves in which the electrical potential shows a fairly regular pattern of 8 to 12 cycles per second. Stage I sleep is the lightest of the four stages and happens when we first doze off. During this stage there are short periods of theta activity (4 to 7 Hz) indicative of drowsiness. Stage II sleep is characterized by sleep "spindles," which are rhythmic

FIGURE 5 . 3

An example of EEG recordings as a person goes from wakefulness to deep sleep.
In the first level, the person is awake and exhibits a low-amplitude rapid pattern of activity that becomes the higher-voltage, slow delta wave patterns of deep sleep. During this stage, consciousness is markedly reduced. This deep sleep is replaced by rapid eye movement (REM) sleep when dreaming occurs as the person returns to a state of consciousness.

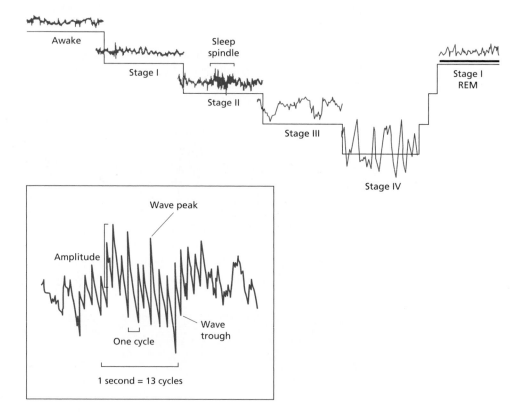

bursts of 12 to 15 Hz of EEG activity. During Stage III sleep, we observe some very low frequency (1 to 4 Hz) delta waves in addition to the spindling pattern, and in Stage IV sleep, the EEG recordings are similar to those of the previous stage, but more extensive delta waves are noted. Stage IV sleep is the deepest of sleep states, from which arousal is most difficult. The behavioral characteristics of each stage, as well as an indication of **rapid eye movement (REM) sleep,** which is sleep characterized by rapid eye movements and dreaming, are shown in Figure 5.4.

In the study of sleep, it is possible to see the change from a state of consciousness to unconsciousness and then a return to consciousness. Furthermore, through EEG recordings and other instrumentation, we can tie levels of consciousness to physiological measures of brain activity.

Amnesia.　A second major event that helped reintroduce consciousness to psychology came from research studies on the hippocampus (that part of the limbic system which is involved in learning and memory). In experimental tests it was found that some types of memory were profoundly affected by lesions; but, more interestingly, some other types of memories were *not.* Thus, it appeared, that (at least) two types of fundamental memory systems existed.

These results helped researchers understand a clinical group of patients called amnesiacs. Profoundly amnesic patients seem to be unable to recall almost everything in

FIGURE 5.4

Sleep cycle. The stages of sleep as indicated by behavioral representations as well as EEG characteristics are shown. Here, the person goes from wakefulness and slumber (he tosses and turns) to quiet, deep sleep to REM (rapid eye movement) sleep and a return to more conscious activity.

their past or to learn anything new. Yet, Brenda Milner[2] (1966) found that even profoundly amnesic people could learn sensorimotor skills—the type of actions one might learn when throwing darts at a dart board or practicing mirror drawing. Also, some patients could recover information about words or pictures if cued properly.

The relationship of these findings to the newly reemerging study of consciousness was that patients did not seem to respond to the recall cue by *consciously* recalling the word picture, but they simply gave the first response that the cue brought to mind. When performing the "recall" task, amnesiacs did not report a sense of familiarity (for example, "Yah, I remember that that cue was associated with my response"), but they simply responded with the first thing that they thought of (for example, "I don't know why I gave the response. It simply popped into my head," a response similar to that of my students who were primed with the devilish-angelic boy). In concluding this section, we can note several points. From a procedural side, we can see that experimental studies of brain structures have had a direct impact on the understanding of amnesic patients. From a psychological side, we have further empirical evidence that (at least) two types of memory exist. Finally, some memories seem to involve conscious recall and others do not. Thus, a series of rigorous investigations, in both experimental and clinical psychology, demonstrated that the role of consciousness was too important to be ignored.

Limited Capacity

Many psychologists have noted the limitations on moment-to-moment conscious capacity. In each conscious moment, we tend to be conscious of only a single thing, for ex-

[2]See Chapter 6 for details.

Too many people trying to pass through a limited gate! From the flood of sensory impressions in the environment, only a few can be processed at a time.

ample, a scene, an intention, or a daydream. In everyday life, we know that we cannot do two things at one time, such as have a heated argument and drive in downtown traffic. If one task does not require much conscious involvement, we can carry on two activities at a time, probably by switching rapidly between the two tasks. The number and duration of items currently rehearsed in working memory is similarly limited; classically, we talk about 7 ± 2 words or numbers in short-term memory, but that number drops to 3 or 4 when we are unable to rehearse them. Likewise intentional (controlled) actions can only be carried out serially, one at a time, while automatic processes can be carried out concurrently (LaBerge, 1980). In carefully studied dual-task situations, consciously controlled tasks interfere with each other, causing errors and delay. But when one or both tasks become automated through practice, the interference declines and can disappear entirely.

Metaphors of Consciousness

The Novelty Metaphor

One line of thought about consciousness holds that consciousness is focused on novelty—or a type of "antihabit," in which there is a mismatch between our expectations and reality (Mandler, 1984). There is ample evidence that people and animals seek novel and informative stimulation; consciousness seems to have a preference for "news." Repetitive, predictable, "old" stimuli tend to fade from consciousness regardless of their sensory modality, degree of abstractness, or physical intensity. *Novelty* can be defined as change in the physical environment (dishabituation), disconfirmation of expectation (surprise), or violation of skilled routines (choice-points in the otherwise routine flow of action). The *novelty metaphor* captures one central function of consciousness—its ability to direct resources toward adaptation to novel and significant events. In the language of Piaget, consciousness comes into play more when we need to accommodate to unexpected events than when we readily assimilate to predictable ones.

However, the novelty hypothesis is obviously not enough. We can be conscious of routine matters if they are important enough personally or biologically, for example, of our repetitive need to eat, without getting habituated or bored.

The Spotlight

One of the ancient idioms embedded in many languages regards consciousness as something that casts a light on things so as to clarify and enlighten one's understanding. (Ah, I see!) The image of casting light is discussed as far back as Plato. The searchlight, or spotlight, metaphor is our modern way of expressing these ideas (see, for example, Lindsay & Norman, 1977; and Crick, 1984). It is an attractive metaphor, embodying in a single image the selective function of consciousness and the flow of conscious contents across numerous domains of memory, perception, imagery, thought, and action. Crick's neurobiological version also captures what is known about the thalamocortical complex, the fact that the thalamus, nestled like an egg in the cocoon of each hemisphere, maps point-to-point into the corresponding parts of the cerebral cortex, almost like a

Spotlight metaphor of selective attention and consciousness.

miniature brain within the brain. The searchlight of attention can be imagined as shining out from the thalamus to the corresponding regions of the cortex.

It must be relevant that the thalamus contains two nuclei (the reticular and intralaminar) whose lesioning uniquely abolishes consciousness. Cortical lesions, on the other hand, abolish only the contents of consciousness, not consciousness itself. Crick's thalamocortical spotlight is an elegant image, and one that may yet turn out to be true.

Both psychological and neurobiological searchlight theories are open to two unanswered questions: (1) How is the *particular* focus selected? That is, what determines whether the searchlight shines on *this* content or cortical area and not some other? And (2) once something is selected to be in focus, what happens to that information? What does it mean for that content to *be* conscious? Is it conveyed to a self-system, as suggested by the executive metaphor? Does it go to motor systems, to prepare them for voluntary action? Or does it go to semantic processors, which encode the meaning of the event? One can imagine a real searchlight operating in full darkness, so that one can see the light and its target, but not the people who control its aim or the audience that is looking at it. What is happening in these dark spaces? Without filling them in, the metaphor is missing some essentials. The theater metaphor makes a stab at an answer.

An Integration Metaphor: The Theater in the Society of Mind

The theater metaphor likens conscious experience to the brightly lit stage in a darkened auditorium. Whatever is on stage is disseminated to a large audience, as well as to the director, playwright, costume designers, and stagehands behind the scenes. The focus of this metaphor is a publicity function in a vast array of specialized systems, which constitutes the audience. Events on stage are privileged; they are made available to all the listeners in the auditorium.

A Cartesian theater of consciousness.

Dennett and Kinsbourne (1992) have criticized a particular version of this metaphor, which they call the Cartesian theater, "a single place in the brain where 'it all comes together,' " much like the tiny, centrally located pineal gland in Descartes' description of the brain. This is a bit of a red herring, however. No current model suggests that conscious contents may be found in a single, tiny point, the discrete finish line of competing potential contents. There are many other ways to bring multiple sources of information together, for example, by coordinating the dozens of perceptual maps in the nervous system. The thalamus may be in an ideal situation to do that.

Modern theater metaphors bypass these Cartesian paradoxes. In recent versions, consciousness is not identified with any single locus. Rather the contents of consciousness are whatever is being widely disseminated throughout the brain (Newman & Baars, 1993).

Combining the Metaphors into a Single Coherent Theory.   We can combine all metaphors into a single, integrated "supermetaphor." The theater can be visualized to include useful aspects of the threshold, searchlight, novelty, and the executive notions. As such a supermetaphor becomes enriched, it can gradually take on the features of a genuine theory. The theoretical proposals described later can be seen as steps in that direction.

With consciousness gaining scientific respectability and a number of well-designed experimental studies from both the physiological and psychological side, it was time for a model to be born which would summarize the findings in consciousness. Several will now be considered.

Theories of Consciousness

Now that we've presented some definitions, the various scientific approaches, and the metaphors for consciousness, we will present some theories of consciousness.

Schacter's Model of Dissociable Interactions and Conscious Experience (DICE)

Accumulating evidence regarding neuropsychological disconnections of processing from consciousness, particularly implicit memory and anosognosia (unawareness of one's cognitive deficits) led Schacter to propose his Dissociable Interactions and Conscious Experience (DICE) model. "The basic idea motivating the DICE model . . . is that the processes that mediate conscious identification and recognition—that is, phenomenal awareness in different domains—should be sharply distinguished from modular systems that operate on linguistic, perceptual, and other kinds of information" (1990, pp. 160–161). In Figure 5.5 the basic components of DICE are shown.

In this model, when information is processed, the systems or modules are changed and perceptual residual is left behind—a type of engram in our brain. Schacter (1996) defines *engrams* as "the transient or enduring changes in our brains that result from encoding and experience" (p. 58). The neurons of the brain record an event by strengthening the connections between groups of neurons involved in encoding events. Different parts of the brain specialize in different kinds of sensory events. For example,

FIGURE 5.5

A schematic depiction of DICE: Dissociable Interactions and Conscious Experience model.

From Schacter (1987). Reprinted by permission.

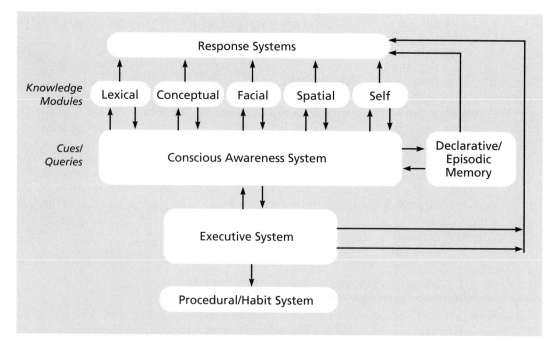

the occipital lobe is involved in visual experiences; the auditory cortex, the processing of sound; and so on, as described in Chapter 2.

Each memory is associated with millions of neural cells being activated in thousands of engrams in your brain. For the most part, these memories and associations that lie dormant may be activated and brought into active consciousness in an astoundingly brief interval. For example, if you are asked what clothes you wore yesterday, in a matter of seconds you could activate a previously latent engram. This unconscious trace might otherwise lie inactive for a lifetime. Or if you are asked to recall the name of your fifth-grade teacher, in a moment that name becomes conscious. (Even more remarkable is the likelihood that even if you cannot recall your teacher's name, you might recognize it faster simply by being asked the question!)

Schacter's DICE model assumes independent memory modules and a lack of conscious access to the details of skilled/procedural knowledge. It is primarily designed to account for memory dissociations in normally functioning and damaged brains. With the exception of coma patients, failures of awareness in neuropsychological cases are usually restricted to the domain of their impairment; there is no difficulty generally in gaining conscious access to other knowledge sources. Amnesic patients do not usually have trouble reading words, while alexic individuals don't necessarily have memory problems. However, implicit (nonconscious) memory for unavailable knowledge has been demonstrated in many conditions. For example, name recognition is facilitated in prosopagnosic patients, that is, patients with brain damage who have difficulty in facial recognition, when the name is accompanied by a matching face—even though the patient does not consciously recognize the face.

Numerous examples of implicit knowledge in neuropsychological patients who do not have deliberate, conscious access to the information are known (see Milner & Rugg, 1992). These findings suggest an architecture in which various sources of knowledge function somewhat separately, since they can be selectively lost; these knowledge sources are not accessible to consciousness, even though they continue to shape voluntary action.

In offering DICE, Schacter has given additional support to the idea of a conscious capacity in a system of separable knowledge sources, specifically to explain spared implicit knowledge in patients with brain damage. DICE does not aim to explain the limited capacity of consciousness or the problem of selecting among potential inputs. The DICE model suggests that the primary role of consciousness is to mediate voluntary action under the control of an executive. However, the details of these abilities are not spelled out, and other plausible functions are not addressed.

Baars's Global Workspace Theory

The theater metaphor is the best way to approach Baars's global workspace (GW) theory (Baars, 1983, 1988). Consciousness is associated with a global "broadcasting system" that disseminates information widely throughout the brain. If this is true, then conscious capacity limits may be the price paid for the ability to make single momentary messages available to the entire system for purposes of coordination and control. Since at any moment there is only one "whole system," a global dissemination facility must be limited to one momentary content. (There is evidence that each conscious "moment" may be on

Bernard Baars. Developed
a comprehensive theory of
consciousness.

the order of 100 milliseconds, a tenth of a second.) Baars develops these ideas through
seven increasingly detailed models of a global workspace architecture (see Figure 5.6) in
which many parallel, unconscious experts interact via a serial, conscious, and internally
consistent global workspace (or its functional equivalent).

GW theory relies on three theoretical constructs: expert processors, a global workspace, and contexts. The first construct is the specialized unconscious processor, the
"expert." We know of hundreds of types of "experts" in the brain. They may be single
cells, such as cortical feature detectors for color, line orientation, or faces, but also entire networks and systems of neurons, such as cortical columns, functional areas like
Broca's or Wernicke's, large nuclei such as locus ceruleus, and so on. Like human experts, unconscious expert processors may sometimes be quite narrow-minded. They are
extremely efficient in limited task domains, able to act independently or in coalition
with each other. Working as a coalition, they do not have the narrow capacity limitations of consciousness. They can receive global messages, and if they can mobilize a
coalition of other experts, they may be able to control a perceptual processor that can
place a mental image, phrase of inner speech, or even perceptual content in consciousness. For routine missions they may work autonomously, without conscious involvement, or they may display their output in the global workspace. Answering a question
like "What is your mother's maiden name?" requires a mission-specific coalition of unconscious experts, which report their answer to consciousness.

The second construct is the global workspace (GW) itself. A GW is an architectural
capability for system-wide integration and dissemination of information. A global
workspace is much like the podium at a scientific meeting. Groups of experts may interact locally around conference tables, but in order to effect change, any expert must
compete with others, perhaps supported by a coalition of experts, to reach the podium,
whence global messages can be broadcast. New links between experts are made possible by global interaction via the podium and can then spin off to become new local
processors. The podium allows novel expert coalitions to form, to work on new or difficult problems that cannot be solved by established experts and committees. Tentative
solutions to problems can then be globally disseminated, scrutinized, and modified.
The argument presented in Figure 5.6 falls into place by the assumption that information in the global workspace corresponds to conscious contents. Since conscious experience seems to have a great perceptual bias, it is convenient to imagine that perceptual
processors—visual, auditory, or multimodal—can compete for access to a brain version

FIGURE 5.6

Global workspace theory of conscious and unconscious processes.

From *In the Theatre of Consciousness: The Workspace of the Mind* by Bernard J. Baars, copyright © 1997 Oxford University Press, Inc. Used by permission of Oxford University Press, Inc.

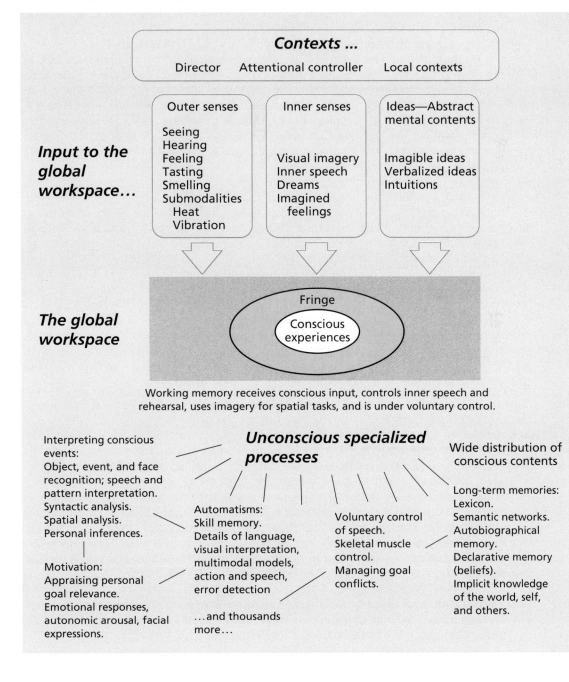

of a GW but, of course, perceptual input systems may in turn be controlled by coalitions of other experts. Clearly, the abstract GW architecture can be realized in a number of different ways in the brain, and we do not know at this point which brain structures provide the best candidates. While the brain correlates are unclear at this time, there are possible neural analogues, including the reticular and intralaminar nuclei of the thalamus, one or more layers of cortex, or an active loop between sensory projection areas of the cortex and the corresponding thalamic relay nuclei. Like other aspects of GW theory, such neural candidates provide testable hypotheses (Newman & Baars, 1993).

Context, the third construct in GW theory, refers to the powers behind the scenes of the theater of mind. Contexts are coalitions of expert processors that provide the director, playwright, and stagehands behind the scenes of the theater of mind. They can be defined functionally as *structures that constrain conscious contents without being conscious themselves,* just as the playwrite determines the words and actions of the actors on stage without being visible. Conceptually, contexts are defined as preestablished expert coalitions that can evoke, shape, and guide global messages without themselves entering the global workspace.

Contexts may be momentary, as in the way the meaning of the first word in a sentence shapes an interpretation of a later word, or they may be long-lasting, as with lifelong expectations about love, beauty, relationships, fate, pride, and all the other things people care about. While contextual influences shape conscious experience without being conscious, contexts can be established by conscious events. The word *tennis* before *set* shapes the interpretation of *set,* even when *tennis* is already gone from consciousness. But *tennis* was initially conscious and needed to be conscious in order to create the unconscious context that made sense of the word *set.* Thus, conscious events can establish unconscious contexts. The reader's ideas about consciousness from years ago may influence his or her current experience of this chapter, even if the memories of the earlier thoughts do not become conscious again. Earlier experiences typically influence current experiences as contexts, rather than being brought to mind. It is believed, for example, that a shocking or traumatic event earlier in life can set up largely unconscious expectations that may shape subsequent experiences.

Functions of Consciousness

William James wrote that "The particulars of the distribution of consciousness, so far as we know them, point to its being efficacious" (1890/1983, Vol. I, pp. 141–142). If consciousness is a major biological adaptation, it may have not just one but a number of functions. The bloodstream circulates oxygen and glucose to all the body cells, takes away waste products, provides a channel for hormones, carries the white cells of the immune system, plays a role in temperature regulation, and much more. Fundamental biological adaptations tend to accrue multiple functions. The evidence suggests at least the following functions for conscious experience.

Definitional and Context-Setting Function.   By relating global input to its contextual conditions, the system underlying consciousness acts to define a stimulus and remove ambiguities in its perception and understanding.

Adaptation and Learning Function.   The more novelty the nervous system must adapt to, the more conscious involvement is required for successful learning and problem solving.

Prioritizing and Access Control Function.   Attentional mechanisms exercise selective control over what will become conscious. By consciously relating some event to higher-level goals, we can raise its access priority, making it conscious more often and therefore increasing the chances of successful adaptation to it. By persuading smokers that the apparently innocuous act of lighting a cigarette is life-threatening over the long term, the medical profession has raised smokers' conscious involvement with smoking and created the possibility for more creative problem solving in that respect.

Recruitment and Control of Mental and Physical Actions.   Conscious goals can recruit subgoals and motor systems in order to organize and carry out voluntary actions.

Decision Making and Executive Function.   While the global workspace is not an executive system, executive access to the GW creates the opportunity for controlling any part of the nervous system, as shown by the extraordinary range of neural populations that can be controlled with conscious biofeedback. When automatic systems cannot resolve every choice-point in the flow of action, making a choice-point conscious helps to recruit knowledge sources able to help make the proper decision. In the case of indecision, we can make a goal conscious to allow widespread recruitment of conscious and unconscious resources acting for or against the goal.

Error-Detection and Editing Function.   Conscious goals and plans are monitored by unconscious rule systems, which will act to interrupt execution if errors are detected. Though we often become aware of making an error in a general way, the detailed description of what makes an error an error is almost always unconscious.

Reflective and Self-Monitoring Function.   Through conscious inner speech and imagery, we can reflect on and to some extent control our conscious and unconscious functioning.

Optimizing the Trade-Off between Organization and Flexibility.   Automatized, "canned" responses are highly adaptive in predictable situations. However, in facing unpredictable conditions, the capacity of consciousness to recruit and reconfigure specialized knowledge sources is indispensable.

In sum, consciousness appears to be the major way in which the nervous system adapts to novel, challenging, and informative events in the world. A vast array of solid evidence is beginning to reveal the role of consciousness in the nervous system, at least in broad outline. Conscious experience seems to create and access multiple, independent knowledge sources. While organization of coherent percepts and control over novel, voluntary actions may have been primary in the phylogenetic evolution of consciousness, it seems also to have acquired other functions which can be seen as contributing to adaptive action in a complex world, such as self-monitoring and self-reflection, symbolic representation of experience, control over novel actions, and mental rehearsal. Scientists no doubt will continue to strive to discover the inner workings of the brain in hopes of uncovering the mysteries of the mind.

Spotlight on Cognitive Neuroscience

Consciousness in the Brain

Consciousness can be thought of as a waking state, experience, or "mind," and as aspects as self-consciousness, such as self-recognition and self-knowledge, to name just a few. Areas as diverse as philosophy, neuroscience, cognitive psychology, and artificial intelligence have all contributed theories and methodologies to the exploration of consciousness. Adam Zeman reviews his own and others' work on consciousness and provides a comprehensive summary of the important theories, methods, and new directions for the study of consciousness. The goal of this research is to figure out how the activity of the brain results in mental states. In trying to achieve this goal, research is conducted on the electrical correlates of sleep and wakefulness and in the brain structures that control these states (particularly in the brainstem and diencephalon). The science of consciousness is focused on the "neurology of experience." By studying how the brain's neurological activity changes when there is no corresponding change in external stimuli gives insight into conscious awareness. Functional imaging and EEG techniques have changed the way researchers can tackle the "hard" problem of consciousness. Although the "rich texture of experience" may not be readily accessible to the scientist, the corresponding "revealable" neurological activity is.

Zeman, A. (2001). Consciousness. *Brain*, 124, 1263–1289.

SUMMARY

1   Consciousness is the awareness of environmental and internal cognitive events.

2   Human interest in consciousness is as old as humankind, but the scientific study of consciousness is only about one hundred years old.

3   The topic of consciousness is associated with philosophical topics including the mind–body issue.

4   Two lines of scientific research established consciousness as legitimate cognitive topics: research on implicit memory and physiological studies of the hippocampus and amnesic patients.

5   The study of consciousness and unconscious phenomena can be divided into two classes of topics. In the conscious group, we find explicit cognition, immediate memory, novel stimuli, declarative memory, remembering, effortful processery, and so on, while in the unconscious group we find implicit cognition, long-term memory, procedural memory, subliminal stimulation, knowing, automatic processing, semantic memory, and so on.

6   Consciousness may be treated as a scientific construct that allows us to do valid experiments on the topic.

7 Consciousness has, over its history, been treated in terms of an activation threshold, a novelty metaphor, a spotlight, and an integrated metaphor.

8 Some of the most influential contemporary models of consciousness are Schacter's DICE and Baars's global workspace theory.

9 The functions of consciousness include definitional attributes, adaptation, prioritization of information, control of actions, decision making, editing functions, self-monitoring functions, management of internal organization, and flexibility.

*K*EY *W*ORDS

consciousness
explicit memory
implicit memory
rapid eye movement (REM) sleep

sensory threshold
sentience
subliminal priming

*R*ECOMMENDED *R*EADINGS

● There are more than ten thousand entries in data banks on *consciousness,* so the interested reader may have to extend his or her lifetime to plow through the literature. Our job here is to narrow the number of sources at the cost of excluding some fine references. Several general works are recommended, including a new book by Baars, *In the Theater of Consciousness: The Workspace of the Mind,* and another book by Dennett, *Consciousness Explained.* A slightly earlier book by Baars, *A Cognitive Theory of Consciousness,* is also recommended. Some more technical sources include *The Cognitive Neurosciences* (Gazzaniga, ed.), especially section XI, "Consciousness," edited by Daniel Schacter. Francis Crick, a Nobel laureate, has written *The Astonishing Hypothesis: The Scientific Search for the Soul,* which will awaken even the most somnolent of brain cells. There are far too many good chapters and articles by distinguished workers to be listed here, but we would recommend the works of Kinsborne, Searle (for a contrary view), Churchland (both Patricia and Paul), Weiskrantz, Moscovitch, Squire, and Schacter. Finally, in a book edited by Solso, *Mind and Brain Sciences in the 21st Century,* you will find a collection of papers by outstanding thinkers of the twentieth century, such as Carl Sagan, Endel Tulving, Edward Smith, Karl Pribram, Henry Roediger III, Michael Gazzaniga, Bernard Baars, Michael Posner, Richard Thompson, and others, in which consciousness is a central theme.

CHAPTER 6

Memory Processes

hmmm...?

● **Short-Term Memory**
Cognitive Neuroscience and STM
Working Memory
Capacity of STM
The Coding of Information in STM
Retrieval of Information from STM

● **Long-Term Memory**
Cognitive Neuroscience and LTM
LTM: Storage and Structure
Very Long-Term Memory (VLTM)
Autobiographical Memories
The Fallibility of Memory
    and Eyewitness Identification

1. What types of memory do you have?

2. What important experiments opened the field of memory and helped shape the cognitive revolution?

3. How much information can you hold in STM?

4. What is "chunking" of information, and how does it increase our capacity for storing knowledge?

5. How is information coded and retrieved from STM?

6. How is information stored and organized in LTM?

7. What have studies of LTM told us about its permanence?

8. What have memory studies told us about the fallibility of memory, especially as it relates to eyewitness identification of criminal events?

*L*ife can only be lived in forward but understood in retrospect.

—*Kierkegaard*

No other topic has been more thoroughly studied by cognitive psychologists than memory, and in the early days of the cognitive revolution in psychology, memory research defined cognitive psychology. Memory was also prominent in the writings of early investigators—William James in America and Hermann Ebbinghaus in Germany—but then was neglected when American psychology became consumed with an interest in human and animal learning. Out of the learning laboratories of the first half of the twentieth century evolved an interest in how things learned were stored and transformed. Interest in memory captivated the attention of experimental psychologists, who formulated elaborate theories of mental representations of how information was stored. One of the more enduring models of memory was that originally proposed by William James, although the model has undergone significant elaboration. That model maintained that memory was dichotomous in nature: Some things are perceived and enter memory and then are lost, and other things stay in memory forever. The concept of short-term memory (STM) and long-term memory (LTM), which is the theme of this chapter, was born.

Before proceeding, and without looking back, try to answer these questions:

Who was the author of the quote at the beginning of the last chapter?
Name the two early psychologists who were interested in memory.
What are the two types of memory mentioned above?

In the preceding example, it is likely that you could recall some things but not others. Why? One part of the puzzle is that some facts stay in long-term memory while the others are temporally processed in short-term memory and forgotten. Let's see how much of the following material will remain . . . at least, until the next examination.

Short-Term Memory

Between the receptors (which gather countless thousands of stimuli from our environment) and the expansive repository of information and knowledge (long-term memory, or LTM) is short-term memory (STM). (Tiny in capacity but huge in importance, it seems more clearly than any other memory system to be where we first process the stimuli originating from the environment.) Its minimal storage capacity is matched by limited processing capacity, and some think that there is a constant trade-off between storage capacity and processing capabilities.

James's concept of primary memory and Ebbinghaus's forgetting curve of more than a hundred years ago (see Chapter 7) set the stage for a remarkably simple yet highly significant discovery. In 1959 Lloyd Peterson and Margaret Intons-Peterson demonstrated that our capacity to store information in a temporary memory bank is severely limited and susceptible to gross forgetting if we do not have the opportunity to rehearse

167

**Lloyd Peterson and
Margaret Intons-Peterson.**
Discovered the duration
of short-term memory.

the information.)Their experiment represented a turning point in our experimental conceptualization of short-term retention and, along with other seminal experiments, books, and studies, helped launch what was to become the cognitive revolution. Their experiment was an important one. Prior to this time the distinction between STM and LTM had been made on the bases of neurological structures (see Hebb, 1949) and psychological concepts (see James, 1890).

In the experiment done by the Petersons, participants were read a three-letter cluster and asked to recall it after varying periods. During these periods (between hearing the letters and attempting to recall), participants counted backward by threes from a three-digit number presented immediately after the three-letter cluster, as here:

Experimenter says: CHJ/506

Participant responds: 506, 503, 500, 497, 494, and so on

Thus, the time between representation of the letters and recall was filled with the subtraction task, which prevented rehearsal of the letter sequence. The dramatic effects are noted in Figure 6.1, which shows that recall seriously eroded in the absence of rehearsal.

[1]A similar discovery was made by J. Brown (1958) working in England; hence, the designation **Brown-Peterson technique.**

FIGURE 6.1

Recall as a function of recall interval where rehearsal was prevented.

Adapted from Peterson and Peterson (1959).

These results suggested that some memory system could store information, but that if the information was not rehearsed, it dropped out of memory. These findings implied that there was a transitory memory (STM) that had characteristics quite unlike the permanent repository of information (LTM); hundreds of experiments have given us a good picture of its characteristics. In this chapter we review some of these distinguishing features of STM and how that structure fits into an overall information-processing theory, touching occasionally on some of the controversy that still surrounds STM.

The reasons supporting the arguments for two memory stores can be summarized as follows:

- Casual introspection suggests that some things are remembered for a short time and others for a long time.

- Physiological studies indicate that short-term functions can be interrupted, whereas long-term functions seem to remain intact.

- Psychological experiments suggest that the retrieval of some information in memory is characteristic of a short-term function whereas retrieval of other information is characteristic of a long-term function, for example, primacy and recency data.

Cognitive Neuroscience and STM

Neurophysiological findings suggest that a separate memory store could be located structurally within the human brain. The original studies appeared about the same time as the famous Peterson and Peterson psychological experiment, but they dealt with clinical patients who experienced some form of physical trauma or brain lesion. The most famous case, that of H. M., was presented by Brenda Milner (1966), a researcher in Canada (where much celebrated work in cognitive neuroscience developed[2]). The patient complained of severe epilepsy, and following a medical workup, a bilateral surgical excision (of the medial temporal region) was done to relieve him of the symptoms. The procedure removed parts of the temporal lobe, including the hippocampus. Although the patient's epilepsy was improved, he became profoundly amnesic and could not seem to store new information in LTM; yet his STM was unimpaired. He could recall a series of numbers momentarily presented but could not retain similar information over long periods of time. His long-term memories formed before the operation were normal, and he even performed well on standard IQ tests, yet he could not learn the names or faces of people he saw regularly. He could converse normally with Milner when she visited him but not recall her previous visits. H. M.'s STM seemed intact, but his ability to form new LTMs was wanting. Because the lesions took place in the temporal lobe and hippocampus, it is apparent that these sites contain important memory structures. Specifically it seems that the hippocampus is an interim depository for long-term memory in which early experienced information is processed and then transferred to the cerebral cortex for more permanent storage. Then Milner made a startling discovery that changed the way STM and LTM were conceptualized. Patients, such as H. M., with temporal lobe lesions can learn implicit types of tasks that involve perceptual and motor

---

[2]Craik, Hebb, Milner, Moscovitch, Penfield, Roberts, Sergent, Tulving, and many others did their principal work in Canada.

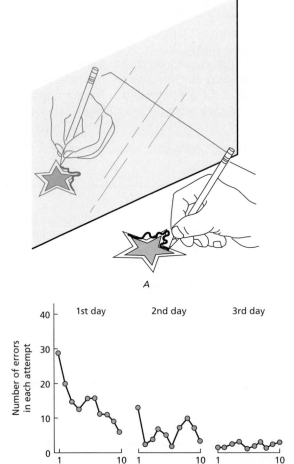

A

Test of Skill. A. In this test, the participant's task is to trace between the two outlines of the star while viewing his or her hand in a mirror. The reversing effect of the mirror makes this a difficult task initially. Crossing a line constitutes an error.

B. H. M. shows clear improvement in motor tasks on the star test, which is a procedural memory.

From Blakemore (1977).

skills. Furthermore, these patients can retain the memory of these tasks for long periods of time. H. M., for example, could learn to draw an image in a mirror and retain that skill over time (see Figure 6.2A).

As shown in Figure 6.2B, H. M.'s learning improved over trials, but he had no knowledge of performing the task. Thus, his procedural memory seemed to function normally, but his ability to learn new information was deficient.

There is also the case of K. F., studied by Elizabeth Warrington and Tom Shallice (1969), who performed oppositely; he had great difficulty learning a series of digits (he could recall only one digit reliably), but his LTM and his ability to learn new material for a long period of time seemed to be intact. This brief sample, augmented by research on dozens of other physically damaged patients (see Kandel, Schwartz, & Jessell, 1991; Martin, 1993; Pinel, 1993; Shallice & Vallar, 1990; and Squire, 1987, for further information), suggests that there are anatomical structures involved in two types of memory. The larger question, however, concerns the storage and processing of information. That part of the puzzle is still largely unknown.

Working Memory

The case of H. M., presented by Milner, and the formulation of the Brown-Peterson paradigm firmly entrenched the concept of STM as a distinct memory system. Not only was STM seen as behaviorally separate from LTM, but also, it had a physiological basis as confirmed through neurological studies of brain-damaged patients. Still, the notion of a clearly dichotomized memory system that simply divided memory into LTM on one hand and STM on the other, without any further embellishment, was soon to be challenged by Alan Baddeley and his colleagues (Baddeley & Hitch, 1974; Baddeley, 1986, 1990, 1992). The type of early memory Baddeley proposed actually includes a specialized part of LTM but also shares some features of STM. This type of memory is called **working memory,** which is defined as a system that temporarily holds and manipulates information as we perform cognitive tasks. Thus, when you are asked to multiply 53 by 78, you might begin by saying to yourself "eight times three is twenty-four; hold the four in memory, and add the two to the sum of eight times five, which is forty, or forty-two. . . ." Or if I ask you to remember a lot of words such as *Albuquerque, Cincinnati,* and *Sacramento,* you might say, subvocally, "Al bu quer que, Cin cin at i. . . ." And, if I gave you another list such as *Tucson, Fargo,* and *Austin,* you would do the same, but the amount of time required to subvocalize *Tucson* in working memory would be less than that needed to subvocalize *Albuquerque.*

Working memory can be conceptualized as a type of workbench in which new and old information is constantly being transformed, combined, and transformed. Working memory challenges the view that STM is simply another "box" in the head—a simple station along the way to either being forgotten or sent on to LTM—in which information is passively deposited. It submits that our working memory is teaming with activity.

The concept of working memory also challenges the idea that the capacity of STM is limited to about seven items (see the next section). Baddeley argues that the span of memory is determined by the speed with which we rehearse information. In the case of verbal material, he proposed that we have an articulatory loop in which we can maintain as much information as we can rehearse in a fixed duration. Take the following example. Read the following five words and try to repeat them without looking back at them:

WIT, SUM, HARM, BAY, TOP

How did you do? Most people are very good at this task. Now try these:

UNIVERSITY, OPPORTUNITY, ALUMINUM, CONSTITUTIONAL, AUDITORIUM

Here, the task is much harder, and on average, only 2.6 items are recalled. The important factor, according to Baddeley, is that the latter group requires more time to say the word. The gist of the idea is that we can rehearse in working memory only a limited amount of information and one determinant is the time to vocalize the word in what is called the **phonological loop** (see Figure 6.3). The phonological loop is a rehearsal circuit that holds inner speech for verbal comprehension. There is also a **visuospatial**

Diagram illustrating Baddeley's working memory model.
Input information is processed by the central executive
system, which has access to two short-term "slave" systems.
One system, the articulary loop, processes verbal information,
and the other, the visuospatial scratchpad, processes visual
and spatial information. The central executive also interacts
with long-term memory.

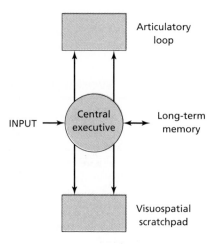

scratchpad that is responsible for rehearsing images and holding them briefly. These processes are regulated by a **central executive,** which coordinates attentional activities and governs responses. The central executive acts much like a supervisor who decides which issues deserve attention and which will be ignored.)

Shortly after the working memory model was introduced, researchers concentrated on finding out more about the phonological loop, the visuospatial working memory, and the nature of the central executive using conventional psychological measures. Lately, however, neurocognitive measures have been applied to the model with considerable success. Cabeza and Nyberg (1997) have shown that the phonological loop, which is involved in maintaining speech-related information, is related to bilateral activation of the frontal and parietal lobes as measured by PET measures. (And, in a study done by Haxby, Ungerleider, Horwitz, Rapoport, and Grady (1995), the visuospatial scratchpad activates different areas of the cortex. Here it was found that shorter intervals activate the occipital and right frontal lobes while longer intervals implicate areas of the parietal and left frontal lobes) Increasingly, observations made possible by brain-imaging technology are being applied to models of memory, and more and more parts of the puzzle of memory are being solved.

Capacity of STM

The amount of information stored in STM is small compared with the vast amount stored in LTM. The earliest recorded evidence of the limited capacity of STM (or "immediate" memory) seems to have come from Sir William Hamilton, a nineteenth-century philosopher, who is said to have observed: "If you throw a handful of marbles on the floor, you will find it difficult to view at once more than six, or seven at the most, without confusion" (cited by Miller, 1956). Whether Hamilton actually did this experiment is unknown, but a similar one was done in 1887 by Jacobs (cited in Miller, 1956), who read aloud a sequence of numbers, in no particular order, and asked his listeners to

Sir William Hamilton
pondered the capacity of
STM as early as the 1800s.

BERNARDA
BRYSON

write down immediately as many as they could recall. In his influential paper on the magical number seven, Miller (1956) stated:

> My problem is that I have been persecuted by an integer. For seven years this number has followed me around, has intruded in my most private data, and has assaulted me from the pages of our most public journals. This number assumes a variety of disguises, being sometimes a little larger and sometimes a little smaller than usual, but never changing so much as to be unrecognizable. The persistence with which this number plagues me is far more than a random accident. There is, to quote a famous senator, a design behind it, some pattern governing its appearances. Either there really is something unusual about the number or else I am suffering from delusions of persecution. (p. 81)

Well, he certainly wasn't suffering from delusions. His work and others' works have demonstrated that the maximum amount of numbers able to be recalled is about seven. Using dots, beans, nonsense syllables, numbers, words, and letters, experiments of this type have been conducted throughout this century with consistent results: immediate memory seems to be limited to about seven units.

STM and Chunking.   That STM holds seven units regardless of the type of data involved seems paradoxical. Obviously, a string of words has greater information content than a string of letters. For example, chances are that, presented the string *T, V, K, A, M, Q, B, R, J, L, E, W,* you could recall about seven letters, and presented the string *towel, music, boss, target, salad, church, money, helium, sugar, parrot, music, chicken,* you would again recall about seven items (depending on the rate of presentation). However,

George Miller. His book *Language and Communication* (1951) shaped the direction of psycholinguistics and cognitive psychology. APA president, 1969.

by inspecting the amount of information recall (at least in terms of letters), it is obvious that more information is recalled in the latter condition than in the former. Miller (1956b) offered an explanation as to how items are coded in STM. He postulated a model of memory in which seven units of information could be held. Individual letters represented individual pieces of information, and, as such, each letter would fill a slot. The letters that composed a word, however, were "chunked" into one word unit, so that each of these word units also occupied one slot in STM. Thus, the increased capacity (in terms of numbers of letters) of STM was achieved through the coding of letter sequences into word units. So, even though our immediate memory capacity seems to be limited to seven units of information, **chunking** (or coding single units into larger units) greatly expands our capacity. For Miller, this kind of linguistic recoding seemed to be "the very lifeblood of the thought process." At the very least, chunking is important because it offers an explanation of how so much information is processed through STM, which, if restricted to seven units, would pose a bottleneck in the information-processing sequence.

STM, LTM, and Chunking.   The capability of STM to handle a vast amount of information, then, is facilitated by our ability to chunk information. However, chunking cannot occur until some information in LTM is activated. Our extensive knowledge can impose a structure on seemingly unrelated material once a match occurs between the incoming items and their LTM representation.

The link between LTM and chunking was nicely illustrated in an experiment by Bower and Springston (1970), in which participants were read a letter sequence and asked to recall the letters. In one condition (A) the experimenters read the letters so that they formed no well-known group (hence, not in LTM); in another condition (B) they read the letters so that they formed well-known groups. Note the following example:

Condition A   FB . . . IPH . . . DTW . . . AIB . . . M
Condition B   FBI . . . PHD . . . TWA . . . IBM

There can be little doubt that the letters read in the second condition (B), which were more readily recalled, are clustered along the lines of abbreviations well known to most college students. In effect, the pause after FBI, PHD, and so on allowed them to "look it up" in their mental lexicon and thereby encode the letters in a chunk, much as you are now forming word chunks out of the letters on this page. The capacity of STM, then, may be limited to seven units, but the density of information in a unit can vary enormously.

The Coding of Information in STM

Auditory Code. (STM seems to operate by means of an auditory code) even if the information is detected by a nonauditory code such as a visual one. Although recent evidence suggests some overlap in codes, the predominant coding of information in STM seems to be auditory.

Because science is suspicious of commonsense answers (at least until they are empirically demonstrated), differences in storage properties as a means of distinguishing between STM and LTM have been examined extensively in the laboratory. Some important results are summarized in the next sections.

In an often-cited early experiment, R. Conrad (1963, 1964) found that STM errors were made on the basis of auditory rather than visual characteristics. Conrad's experiment had two stages. In the first he measured the recall of errors made on a set of letters that was visually presented; in the second he measured the errors made by participants to whom the same set of letters was read over a background of white noise. Each set in the first stage consisted of six letters. Some were letters that sounded alike, for example, *C, V; M, N; S, F.* Each of the six letters was displayed for 0.75 second. The participants were to recall the order of the items. The results indicated that even though the letters were visually presented, the errors were made on the basis of their sound. For example, *B* was frequently recalled as *P, V* as *P,* and *S* as *X.*

Although there seems to be a strong case for the acoustic nature of STM, there are some challenging alternative theories, which we cover in the next section.

Visual Code. A number of experiments question the inferences that STM codes information only by means of an auditory code. Some evidence suggests that STM may also code information by means of a visual code, while others suggest that STM may code information by means of a semantic code.

Cognition in Everyday Life

Make That Call

You call directory assistance to get a friend's phone number. The electronic voice gives you a telephone number, say, 969-1391. Presumably that number must be retained in STM until you can complete the call. How do you keep it alive? Chances are (if you don't write it down) that you repeat it to yourself either aloud, or subvocally (in your head) "969-1391, 969-1391," and so on. This practice is one of maintaining an auditory representation of the digits in STM.

Thus, from the standpoint of common sense, we hold information in STM by auditory rehearsal. You may argue, however, that the source of the information (the electronic voice) was auditory, which biased the nature of STM storage. In fact, the same auditory rehearsal is likely to occur even if you find the number in a directory, which is a visual stimulus. In whatever manner the information may be represented, storage in STM seems to be auditory.

Posner and his colleagues (Posner, 1969; Posner et al., 1969; and Posner & Keele, 1967) found that, at least part of the time, information is coded visually in STM. In their experiment, participants were shown two letters, the second to the right of and simultaneously with, or a brief time after, the first. Participants were to indicate, by pressing a button (and, thereby, recording their reaction time), whether the two letters were the same. The second letter was identical to the first in name and form (AA), or the same in name but different in form (Aa), or different (AB or Ab); and it appeared simultaneously with, or 0.5, 1, or 2 seconds after, the first. (Table 6.1 shows the format of the experiment.)

Reaction time in the second condition (Aa) was longer than in the first (AA). One explanation for the difference is that identical letters are judged on the basis of their physical (or visual) characteristics, while letters having the same name but different visual characteristics are compared in terms of their verbal characteristics; the latter process, it is hypothesized, takes more time. As far as our discussion of codes in STM is concerned, the important conclusion is that apparently the AA match was made at least partly on the basis of a physical (or visual) code. This advantage (as shown in Figure 6.4) lasts only a brief period.

Having established that visual codes can exist in STM (in addition to auditory codes), Posner set out to describe the steps involved. To test a hypothesis that coding of some information in STM is first visual and then based on the name, Posner et al. (1969) and Boies, Posner, and Taylor (1968) used the reaction-time model shown in Figure 6.4. As may be recalled, one of the intervals of presentation of letter pairs was zero. The rationale for this was that if coding involves visual aspects first, then the reaction time for physically (visually) identical stimuli simultaneously presented should be very brief. If name coding occurred slightly after visual coding, then the reaction time for name-identical (but not physically identical) stimuli simultaneously presented should be relatively long. As shown in Figure 6.4, during the very early part of STM processing the identical code takes much less time than the name code, but that effect disappears after 1 or 2 seconds when the name code takes over. However, Boles (1994) has raised questions about these experiments, presenting data that show that phonemic representations of letters play a small, if any, role in the early processing of letters.

The extent to which information is processed in STM was demonstrated in an experiment by Solso and Short (1979) that was procedurally similar to the reaction-time experiments presented previously. We hypothesized that shortly after information is perceived, it is simultaneously coded in different systems. Solso and Short used physical

TABLE 6.1

Reaction Time Format Used by Posner and Keele (1967)

Condition	Exemplar Letters*	Correct Response
Visual and name match	A A	Same
Name match	A a	Same
Visual and name mismatch	A B	Different
Visual and name mismatch	A b	Different

*Interval of presentation: 0–2 sec.

FIGURE 6.4

Reaction time. A function of interval for visual and name matches in mixed lists and for visual matches in pure lists. The two experiments were highly similar, except that in Experiment 2 intervals between stimuli were longer.

Adapted from Posner et al. (1969) and Boies, Posner, and Taylor (1968).

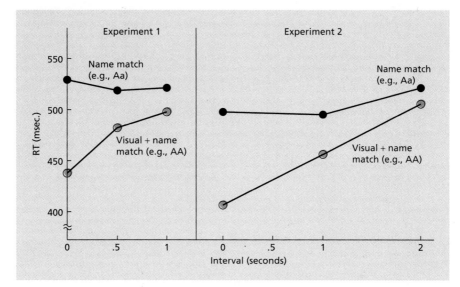

colors (green, blue, red, yellow, brown, and purple) because these stimuli seem particularly rich in their ability to be coded. The research was predicated on the assumption that colors are represented in short-term memory in at least three distinctive codes. One code is physical (for example, the color *red*), another is the name of the color (for example, *red*), and the third is conceptual (for example, an associate of the color *red*, such as *blood*). Participants in this experiment were asked to respond by pressing a key if the color presented "matched" (physically, by name, or by associate) a color, a name of a color, or an associate of the color. After the color was presented, the color, name, or associate were presented simultaneously or delayed 500 or 1,500 milliseconds.

The average reaction times are presented in Figure 6.5. As might be expected, the reaction time for a color-color match was faster than between a color and its name or between a color and its associate when there was no delay between the presentation of stimuli. As the delay between the stimuli increased, however, the differences between the reaction times decreased. In the color-color matching condition, the reaction times were actually greater when the delay between the two stimuli was increased from 500 milliseconds to 1,500 milliseconds (see Figure 6.5). From these data it seems that the emergence of a color code occurs prior to the name code or associate code. However, after about 500 milliseconds a name code begins to emerge, and after about 1,500 milliseconds an associate code emerges.

These experiments (Posner et al., 1969; Solso & Short, 1979) suggest that the processing of information in a short-term store is achieved through a type of parallel processing of

Reaction times. Matching colors to colors, color names, and color associates.

From Solso and Short (1979).

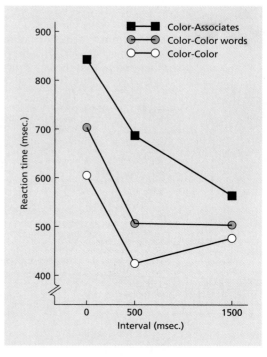

stimuli (a model is shown in Figure 6.6 for colors). It seems that things perceived (colors, for example) initially are passed on from the sensory system to be simultaneously coded in memory. In the case of colors and letters, the first code to reach a level of operable strength (strong enough to be measured reliably) is a physical code—color-color or A-A, for example. This code seems to reach full strength in the first 500 milliseconds after the stimulus has been detected and perhaps decays slightly. A name code is initiated in parallel and reaches full strength after about 500 milliseconds. An associate code, initially weak, increases in strength at least through 1,500 milliseconds. In these experiments the participants did not know what type of code would be presented for their reaction until after the second stimulus appeared. Therefore, if we presume other types of codes were also activated, these experiments may give an estimate of the many codes triggered by a single brief exposure to a stimulus. Such findings suggest that the initial processing of information is many times more capacious than first suspected.

In summary, information would appear to be represented in STM auditorially and visually. Consider next the possibility that semantic codes also function in STM.

Semantic Code. Semantic codes are those that are related to meaning. The question addressed in this section is whether semantic (hence, meaningful) information can be represented in STM. Several experiments indicate that it can. The first of these was conducted by the late Delos Wickens and his colleagues (Wickens, 1970, 1972; Wickens, Born, & Allen, 1963; Wickens et al., 1968; and Wickens & Engle, 1970). Many experiments were done to demonstrate that word meanings are a bundle of attributes and, as such, are of importance in our understanding of the complex seman-

FIGURE 6.6

Development of cognitive codes to the color *red*.

From Solso and Short (1979).

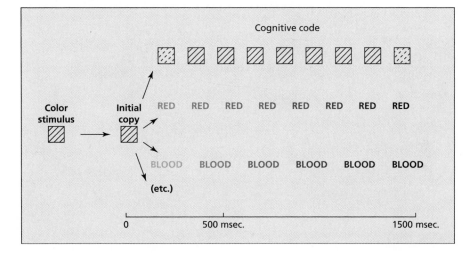

tic nature of LTM. They also provide us with an interesting glimpse of how semantic codes may influence STM. Most of the experiments by Wickens and his colleagues are based on use of a proactive inhibition (PI) design. PI designates the reduced capability to recall later members of a series following the learning of the earlier members. For example, if a participant is asked to learn a series of related words (say, the names of dogs) with recall tested after each set of three names, recall is usually best during the first set and gradually poorer with each subsequent set. If a new set of related items (say, the names of flowers) were to be introduced after PI was built up in the first series (dogs), recall of the names of flowers would be better than for the last set of dogs. Wickens has identified that phenomenon as a "release from PI." The experimental format used in many of the release-from-PI experiments is a modified version of the technique used by Brown and Peterson, in which a stimulus (for example, a trigram such as *KLZ*) is followed by a distractor task (for example, counting backward by threes).

An example of a release-from-PI experiment was done by Wickens, the set up for which is shown in Figure 6.7. In Trial 1, the participant is shown a series (set) of three related words, next does a rehearsal (prevention-of-distractor task) for 20 seconds, and then tries to recall the three words. Following recall, another set of three items from the same category is presented (Trial 2) with another distractor task and recall. This procedure is followed through four sets, except that for the experimental group, the last (fourth) trial uses a set made up of words from a different category, while the control group continues to receive words from the original category.

The results of Wickens's experiments, using huge samples of participants, indicated that the new class of words is recalled better than the old one. A graph of typical data from release-from-PI experiments is shown in Figure 6.8. Trials 1 through 3 show strong

FIGURE 6.7

Experimental procedure for release-from-PI studies.

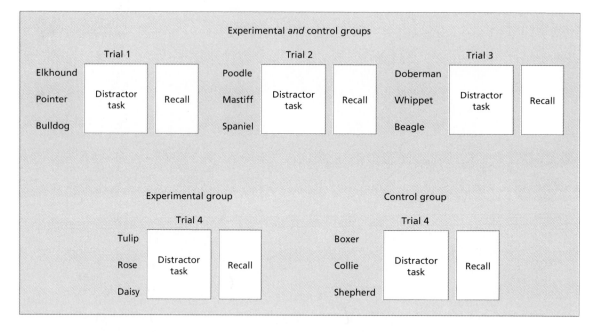

evidence for the buildup of PI. In the fourth trial there is evidence for a continued buildup of PI in the control group and a release from PI in the experimental group. It seems that the participants used some type of semantic organization (for example, names of dogs and flowers) in their storage of the words. Had they not, PI buildup would probably have continued after the shift to the new set of words at Trial 4. Wickens's experiments include a wide variety of categories (for example, professions, meats, flowers, vegetables, words and numbers, taxonomic, sense impression, and masculine and feminine), all with similar results.

Some have criticized Wickens's experiments on several counts. First, for proactive interference effects to take place, the participant's LTM should be engaged in a direct way. Knowledge of dogs, for example, is necessary for canine PI to develop, and the participant, in these experiments, would have to be cognizant of the concept of "dogness" to be released from it. This first criticism is a kind of "straw man." No one has suggested that STM and LTM operate in a vacuum. There is a constant interplay between the two hypothetical memory stores, and most theorists acknowledge the interaction between LTM and STM. All memory operations, it seems, are guided and influenced by long-term memory and goals, including the processing of information in STM. The second criticism is more problematic. In a typical release-from-PI experiment, participants are given several groups of information (such as the three sets of dogs in the previous example) before the "releasing" set is presented. The time spanned by this procedure may take up to several minutes, which may be outside the range of STM. PI, its buildup, and its re-

FIGURE 6.8

Results from typical release-from-PI experiments.

From Wickens (1973).

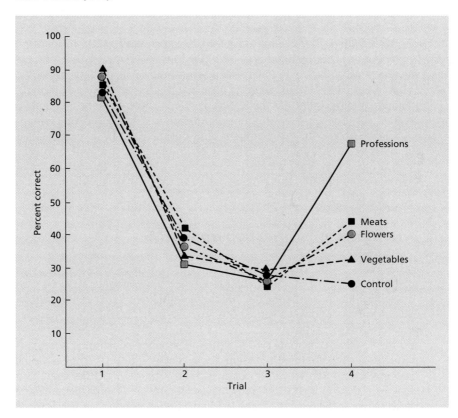

lease may all be LTM processes, which, although interesting, tell us little about the nature of semantic processing in STM.

However, other research has presented convincing evidence that semantic processing does occur in STM. One study by Solso, Heck, and Mearns (1987) not only demonstrates semantic processing in STM but also serves as an introduction to the Sternberg paradigm, which is discussed in detail in the next section. For our present purposes, it is enough to know that the Sternberg paradigm is a technique used to measure the means used to access information in STM.

Consider this problem. Suppose the following words are individually presented to you at the rate of 1.2 seconds each.

SPHERE
MOON
PLANET
GLOBE

Then suppose you are given the following words, individually presented, and asked whether or not they were members of the original set.

MOON
STEEL
EARTH

How would you predict the performance of particpants in identifying the second set of words as being members of the previous set? If you guessed that people correctly identify *MOON* as a previously seen word and correctly reject *STEEL,* you are right. What about *EARTH?* This word is clearly not a member of the original set, yet participants frequently "false alarmed" on this word. They misidentified it as a member of the original set. The basis of this misidentification is related to the semantic relationship that *EARTH* has with the members of the original set. Most important for our present discussion of STM and semantic codes is the fact that the entire process takes place in about 12 seconds, well within the parameters of STM. In addition to showing the semantic nature of STM, these data suggest that a form of abstraction, or prototype learning, can occur in STM.

Retrieval of Information from STM

In this section, we deal with how stored information is retrieved.

The modern era of information processing was significantly influenced by an experimental technique developed by Saul Sternberg (1966, 1967, 1969), whose name it bears. This technique involves a serial scanning task in which the participant is shown a series of items such as numbers, each for 1.2 seconds. It is presumed that these items become recorded in the participant's STM. The entire series constitutes a memory set. After the participant is satisfied that the items are available in his or her memory, he or she pushes a button and is immediately presented with a probe digit that may or may not be the same as a digit in his or her immediate memory set. The participant's task is simply to signal whether the digit is among the items in the memory set. Each new trial contains a different memory set. The experimenter may vary the size of the memory set from one to six items, which is well within the immediate memory span of participants. Few errors are made, and the principal data are the times between the presentation of the probe and the participant's response. The **Sternberg paradigm** is presented in Figure 6.9.

Reaction time should reflect the time it takes to search through the memory set and may serve as a basis for delineating STM structure and laws of retrieval of information from the structure. We are not surprised that the larger the memory set, the greater the reaction time; more information in STM requires more time to access. Two other findings, however, are surprising. One is that the reaction times changed uniformly according to the number of items in a set (see Figure 6.10). Each new item in the memory set seemed to require a fixed amount of processing time, and that amount of time was cumulative with other processing times. In one experiment (Sternberg, 1966), the amount of time required to process additional memory set items was about 38 milliseconds per item.

The second surprise has a far-reaching impact on views of how we recover information from STM. The reaction-time characteristics were nearly identical for items that were in the memory set and those that were not. It would seem obvious, however, that if *7,* the first item in the memory set of Figure 6.9, is also the **probe item** and if we

FIGURE 6.9

The Sternberg paradigm.

process STM information in order, then we ought to be able to respond more rapidly than if *8* is the probe item. In the latter case we would have to scan the entire set—not just the first item—to make a decision. If the probe item is *8,* serial scanning time of the set for a match should be equal to the time required to determine that there is no match (because *8* is preceded by all the other digits in the string). Since the position of the matching items was distributed in each of the positions, we can assume that the average position would be in the middle of the set. Thus, if participants used a serial search of their STM, finding probed items that were in the set would take (on the average) half the time needed to probe items not in it. (Probing the latter would require a search of the complete set.) Hence, the slope of a curve of reaction time versus set size should be twice as steep for probes not in the set.

Similar results have been observed over a wide range of stimulus material, including letters, words, colors, faces, and phonemes, with the slope of the reaction function sometimes more steep or less steep, but the relationship between the yes and no responses remaining invariant. Composition of the test group has little influence on the main results. They hold for children, schizophrenics, college students, alcoholics, and people stoned on marijuana. (Although the last have a reaction-time curve higher, not steeper, than normal, leading one wag to comment that marijuana does not make you steeper, only higher.)

These remarkable demonstrations of search characteristics in STM suggest that, given the constraints of the paradigm, the search seems to be exhaustive rather than self-terminating.

Reaction time as a function of number of items in a series.

Adapted from Sternberg (1969).

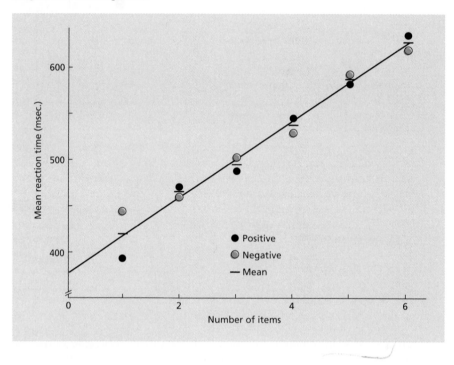

Long-Term Memory

If we "live" in our short-term memory, then the repository of knowledge that gives meaning to our immediate existence resides in the long-term memory. Our ability to deal with the tiny slice of sensory events that constitutes the present in the ongoing continuum of time seems to be the main function of our transitory STM, while our ability to deal with the past and to use that information to understand the present is the function of our LTM. In one sense, our LTM allows us to live in two worlds simultaneously (the past and the present) and, by so doing, allows us to understand the ceaseless flood of immediate experience.

LTM's most distinguishing feature is its diversity—of codes, abstraction of information, structure, capacity, and permanence; other memory stores we have discussed are relatively limited in these features. Thus, our discussion of LTM begins as we contrast it with sensory memory and STM, two memory systems that store information for a very brief time and do not abstract and store it in an involved structure.

The capacity of LTM seems limitless, and its duration virtually endless. To understand this, we consider first the neurological aspects of LTM, then the types of information held in LTM, and finally its general architecture or organization.

Cognitive Neuroscience and LTM

For centuries scientists have known that the brain is involved in memory; without a brain we would be senseless, mindless, and without memory. The tricky part is to determine where memories reside and how the brain stores information in long-term memory— simple questions to the most complicated phenomena known to humans. Nevertheless, determined researchers have made impressive discoveries regarding both questions.

Having One's Cake and Eating It Too. The answer to the first question about the location of memories is that memories are "located"[3] in specialized areas *and* throughout the brain. For example, recent PET investigations show that the frontal area of the brain is involved in the deep processing of information, such as determining whether a word describes a living or nonliving thing (see the work of Kapur et al., 1994; and Tulving et al., 1994), which would suggest that that type of memory operation is highly specialized. However, other regions of the brain are also involved, only to a less specialized degree, and this principle of specialization and generalization seems to apply to other types of memory operations and storage systems (see Zola-Morgan & Squire, 1990).

Some brain regions seem to be essential in the formation of memories. These regions include the hippocampus and the adjacent cortex and thalamus, as indicated through study of clinical patients who suffer damage from these areas. However, the hippocampus itself does not provide permanent long-term memories; if it did, then H. M. (discussed in the first part of this chapter) would not have had old LTM. Many permanent long-term memories seem to be stored (and processed) in the cerebral cortex. It is well established that sensory information is passed along to specific brain regions. Information from the eyes and ears, for example, is passed to the visual cortex and auditory cortex, respectively. It is likely that long-term memories for these types of sensory experiences are also stored in or near these sites. However, and this is one of the many complicating issues in brain science, sensory experiences are cerebrally multifarious. When you read the words in the preceding sentence, the information from your eyes is processed in the visual cortex (no doubt about it), but when you consider the meaning of the word *multifarious,* you use other parts of the brain, perhaps even to the point of subvocalizing or actually saying the word and thereby activating regions associated with auditory memories.

How the Brain Works—Simple and Sweet. How the brain stores information in LTM is the second difficult simple question. Even though the brain is the universe's most complicated thing, some answers are beginning to emerge from the neurocognitive laboratory. One explanation of how long-term memories are formed is based on the early pioneering work done by Donald Hebb, whom we have encountered several times in this book. The simplified version of his notion of long-term memory is that information in short-term memory is converted in LTM if it remains in STM long enough. This

---

[3]The use of the word *located* tends to muddy the issue. Memories are not like black socks, which may appear on one's feet, or behind the dryer, or neatly folded in a dresser drawer. Memories are organic and involve neurological connections between a myriad of neurons. Location, in this sense, is as meaningless as trying to find the wind . . . it is found in some places more than others, but it is distributed throughout the planet.

is because in STM a *reverberating circuit* of neural activity takes place in the brain, with a self-exciting loop of neurons. If the circuit remains active for a period (a type of self-stimulation), then some chemical and/or structural change occurs and the memory is permanently stored. From the cognitive literature, we know that merely holding information in STM does not assure its permanence (see, for example, the research of Craik & Watkins, discussed in the next chapter). However, if information is combined with other, existing, meaningful memories, then long-term memorability is enhanced.

The next section is called "Sugarcoated Golden Memories." You will find it has nothing to do with endearing memories experienced by old geezers (as you might initially think) but is a subtle mnemonic for glucose, a sugar, that has been shown to be related to enhanced learning. That fact is now more likely to persist in your memory because it has been variously associated with other well-entrenched, and perhaps even emotional, memories.

Sugarcoated Golden Memories.   Some experiences are remembered better than others. Exciting, ego-involving, or even traumatic experiences seem to stick in memory better than complicated political theories, for example. Animal studies have indicated that when an exciting event occurs, the adrenal medulla increases its secretion into the bloodstream of epinephrine (adrenaline), which has now been demonstrated to enhance consolidation of a memory (McGaugh, 1990). It is likely that epinephrine does not directly stimulate the brain's synapses (there is the matter of crossing the blood–brain barrier), but it converts stored glycogen to glucose (a sugar), thereby raising the blood level of glucose, which nourishes the brain. Some experimental research supports the notion that directly injecting glucose after learning enhances future memory of the event (Gold, 1987; and Hall & Gold, 1990). This *petit tour* of the cognitive neuroscience of LTM is in itself only a sweet sample of the burgeoning literature on the topic. Surely, new developments will be reported on this exciting topic in the near future and bear watching.

LTM: Storage and Structure

Codes.   In our discussion of STM, we saw that information is stored acoustically, visually, and semantically, but the type of code used is sometimes questioned. We have no comparable difficulty in describing the coding mechanisms in LTM, although there is some disagreement about their relative importance. In LTM, information is clearly coded acoustically, visually, and semantically. The multidimensional coding of information in LTM can be easily illustrated. For example, as Solso recalls, "a black-and-white bird sometimes perches outside my window. I know it's a western magpie when it makes a sound like one, or when I see it, or when I read about a western magpie and I associate that information with other semantic information about birds—feathered creatures, wildlife, and so on."[4] In addition to the common knowledge about acoustical, visual, and semantic codes operating in LTM, an impressive number of research articles has validated its complex coding system. In general, we can think of LTM as the

---

[4]Solso has never tasted, smelled, or felt a western magpie, but if he had he would also probably be able to recognize one by these sensations. Gustatory, olfactory, and tactile codes seem to operate in LTM, although relatively little research has been done on them.

repository of all things in memory that are not currently being used but are potentially retrievable. A very general list suggested by Bower (1975) of some of the classes of information contained in LTM includes the following:

- Our spatial model of the world surrounding us—symbolic structures corresponding to images of our house, city, country, and planet and information about where significant objects are located in that cognitive map.
- Our knowledge of physical laws, of cosmology, and of the properties of objects and things.
- Our beliefs about people, about ourselves, and about how to behave in various social situations.
- Our values and the social goals that we seek.
- Our motor skills for driving, bicycling, shooting pool, and so on. Our problem-solving skills for various domains. Our plans for how to achieve various things.
- Our perceptual skills in understanding language or interpreting paintings or music. (From Bower, 1975, p. 56)

Despite the diversity, emphasis in the literature has been on the semantic code in LTM, and this emphasis is reflected in this book.

Organization.   Perhaps the most pervasive assumption about LTM is that information in it is organized in some orderly way. This assumption is so widely accepted that researchers rarely ask whether information in LTM is organized. The question more often asked is how information in LTM is organized. A moment of introspection is enough to validate the assumption. If you are asked to recall what you were doing on a certain day—say, July 7, 1999—how do you go about finding an answer? Chances are you search for some easily identifiable information that is related to and near that time and work backward or forward to July 7. It is likely that the events on that day are somehow related to and organized with other information. Perhaps a birthday, other anniversary, or a particular national holiday was near that date. You might try to remember what you did during the summer of 1999 or to locate the day of the week on which the date fell. You might remember that on the last day of June you paid your rent. The information you settle on, then, provides a cue for finding what you were doing on July 7. On the other hand, imagine how you might answer the question if your memory was not systematically organized. You might randomly sample information from your LTM in something of this manner: Bank of Chicago, 3.14, LS/MFT, Monica Lewinsky, Lake Tahoe, 361–2849, ESP, Kunta Kinte, Mars, and so on. Of course, this is a silly lot of information, but it is equally silly to imagine an unorganized LTM. The fanciful representation of LTM suggests that within it items are linked in a way similar to that of an intricate telephone network. Retrieval of specific information occurs by means of entering the network, which is capable of calling up other related information until the desired information is contacted. The network of interrelated and associated information is far more complex than can be depicted. In any case, the way we recall common information suggests that LTM is organized.

There is a growing body of knowledge that suggests specific information is recorded within a well-structured and highly practical network. This concept implies that new information entering LTM does not require synthesis of a new network (which would defeat the utility of organization, as each event would require its own system), with an endless number of minor organization schemes the result. Instead, new information is recorded within existing organizations. Much of the research in semantic organization, which is described in Chapter 9, shows that the network can be remarkably sparse.

Cognition in Everyday Life

Making Modular Memories

The brain's real estate keeps getting subdivided. Neuroscientists have been busy for the past three decades parceling up the visual cortex, where the brain starts to process signals coming in from the eyes, into ever-smaller, specialized plots. Some of these areas respond to color, some to shape, and some to movement. But when we think about objects, we recall all of these qualities, so it seemed logical for scientists to assume that, higher up in the brain, this disparate information gets spliced together in areas where memories are formed and cognition takes place. But now a team from Yale University has shown that similar subdivisions exist even in the prefrontal cortex, which is involved in forming temporary, working memories. Some areas chiefly respond to "what" an object was, while others respond to "where" it was located.

"Memory is modular; it's not all in one device," says neuroscientist Patricia Goldman-Rakic, one of the researchers. "This is the first physiological evidence separating out those modules." She and her colleagues Fraser A. Wilson and Séamas P. Ó. Scalaidhe report that neurons in two regions in monkeys' prefrontal cortex respond to different visual cues. Neurons in an area known as the inferior convexity (IC) retain information about an object's color and shape for a short period after the object has disappeared from view. Neurons in an adjacent area encode an object's location.

"This is really right on the forefront" of memory research, says Jon Kaas, a neuroscientist at Vanderbilt University in Nashville, Tennessee. Kaas notes that these results are the first good functional evidence showing that separate perceptual pathways continue into the prefrontal cortex. And if further studies reveal working memory centers tied to the other senses, Kaas believes it would suggest that memories are divided up by their qualities much like image qualities—motion and shape, for example—are divided up in other cortical regions. "But that is a big if," he says.

Finding that working memory is specialized in at least two ways, say other scientists, shows that such memories appear to form in a parallel fashion, and that there's no central memory manager putting everything together. "The assumption in the past has sort of been that there will be a next level [of processing] that will reintegrate everything," says John Allman, a neurophysiologist at the California Institute of Technology. "But there just isn't much evidence for that."

Memory maps. Areas in the prefrontal cortex seem to recall different aspects of an image.

Spatial memory area

Feature memory area

Reprinted with permission from "Making Modular Memories," Science 260:1876. Copyright © 1993 AAAS.

Capacity and Duration.   It is hard to imagine the volume and duration of information contained in LTM, but we can make some reasonable estimates of these characteristics. Even the most obscure information is readily available to us. For example, you can remember and "see" the exact spot you dropped your hunting knife in the creek, the license number of your dad's car, the precise details of a bracelet you gave to a girlfriend, the location of an oil can tucked away in a remote corner of a garage cabinet, and yet many of these events have likely *not* been in your consciousness for quite some time. Even in an era when the information capacity of computers is prodigious, the capacity of the human brain for storing detailed information over long periods (and in so small a space) remains unequaled.

How can we remember so much? One revealing answer to that question is suggested in the way college students tried to remember the names of their fourth-grade teacher. It is plausible that each student had plenty of opportunity to encode the teacher's name, although most admitted that they had not thought of him or her in years. Some of their introspections about the retrieval process follow:

Student K. S.

1. Remember what school I went to. What year did I change to Lowell School? Second or third grade?
2. Location of classroom
3. Visualize teacher—tall and thin
4. Same teacher as third grade
5. Miss Bell?
6. She was friendly with my sixth- and seventh-grade teacher.
7. If I entered Lowell School in the third grade, then the classroom was on the East end. If this was my second classroom in Lowell School, it was on the West end.
8. Yes, Miss Bell.

Student J. C.

1. First thing I thought of was a nun or lay teacher: nun—sister.
2. Second thing I thought of was a most common name that nuns have, almost a surname—Sister Mary.
3. Third thing I thought about was all the grief I had with that nun in fourth grade.
4. Fourth thing I remembered is that her name began with an A, then I remembered Al, then I thought of Alvira—Sister Mary Alvira.
5. Wrong last name, remembered a province in Canada—Sister Mary Alberta.

From these examples and other more rigidly controlled experiments, we can gain some appreciation of the multitude of memory traces we easily store over a long period. Of course, we cannot remember all events of the past as if they happened only yesterday. That loss of recall may be attributed to interference (the intervention of information that blocks the recall of old memory traces) or decay (the weakening of a memory trace through disuse).

Very Long-Term Memory (VLTM)

Some interesting data have been gathered on the fate of very long-term memories (VLTM), or memories more than three months old.

High School Classmates. A landmark of VLTM research is that of Bahrick, Bahrick, and Wittlinger (1975). In their ambitious effort to trace the longevity of memory, they tested 392 high school graduates for memory of names and portraits of classmates selected from old yearbooks. The nine retention intervals tested ranged in length from 3.3 months to almost 48 years! The sample (almost 50 classmates in each of the nine groups) was huge, and an involved testing procedure was developed. First, participants were asked to free-recall or list the names of all the members of their graduating class whom they could remember. Then a picture recognition task was given in which photographs were selected from the participant's yearbook and presented in random order for identification along with some other photographs. A third task was to identify names similarly (name recognition). The fourth and fifth tasks were to match pictures with names and names with pictures, respectively. Finally, a picture-cueing task was given in which the participant was to recall the name of one classmate from his or her picture.

The overall results are portrayed in Figure 6.11. It is noteworthy that the recognition level for the faces of former classmates was astonishingly high (about 90 percent over 34 years), while name recognition and name matching declined after 15 years. The sharp decline in recognition and recall data after about 35 years of stability may reflect some degenerative process of advancing age. The ability to match names with faces and picture recognition remains the same over a very long period, about 90 percent from 3.3 months to 34 years. The data gathered by Bahrick and his colleagues confirm the notion that VLTM does, indeed, last for a very long term, and the invariance of recognition memory over such a long time is surprising. The results suggest that recognition memory for distant events is affected by the degree of initial encoding and the distribution of rehearsal. In the foregoing example, the initial learning of facts about classmates was very thorough, taking place, in most instances, over years. Also, throughout the years intervening between graduation and the experiment, the participants may have had occasion to think about "the good ol' days," attend class reunions, or in some way reminisce about a distant but precious face.

VLTM for Spanish—Evidence for Permastore? How long will your memory for a foreign language last? In another ambitious study done by Bahrick (1984; also see Bahrick & Phelps, 1987), the maintenance of Spanish over a span of 50 years was examined. The participants in this massive study were 773 people who had learned Spanish in high school. They provided such data as the amount of original training, their grades, and how often they had used the language after study. Tests of reading comprehension and recall and recognition tests for vocabulary, grammar, and idioms were given. In general, Bahrick found that the more thoroughly Spanish had been learned, the better the performance on the subsequent test—a finding that should surprise no one. However, the degree of very long-term retention is, if not surprising, gratifying to all who plan to live a long life. Knowledge of Spanish, in general, declined most sharply during the first 3 years and then seemed to reach a stable state, for about another 30 years. Some drop-off of knowledge, especially in reading comprehension, was noted after about 25 years. However, much of the originally learned knowledge was still usable after 50 years! This "per-

FIGURE 6.11

Adjusted mean retention scores for subjects tested in six categories.

Adapted from Bahrick, Bahrick, and Wittlinger (1975).

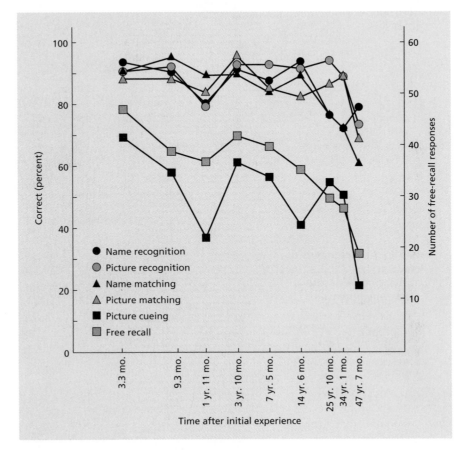

manent" memory was called **permastore,** and it would seem that knowledge of Spanish, and presumably other foreign languages, remains reasonably viable for a very long time.

VLTM and Cognitive Psychology.   Assuming you are reading this book for a course in cognitive psychology, perhaps you have asked yourself, "How much of this information will stay in my LTM?" An answer to that question can be found in an article by Conway, Cohen, and Stanhope (1991) called "On the Very Long-Term Retention of Knowledge Acquired Through Formal Education: Twelve Years of Cognitive Psychology." The experimenters sampled a large number of students (N = 373) who had completed a course in cognitive psychology as long ago as 12 years. The former students were asked to complete a memory test designed to assess their retention of material learned a long time ago. The test consisted of memory for proper names of researchers and concepts. The results are shown in Figure 6.12.

FIGURE 6.12

A. Mean percentages of correctly recognized names and concepts across retention intervals.

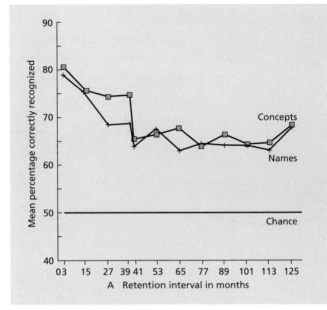

A   Retention interval in months

B. Mean percentages of correctly recalled names and concepts across retention intervals.

From the *Journal of Experimental Psychology: General*, 120, 155–165. Copyright © 1991 by the American Psychological Association. Reprinted with permission.

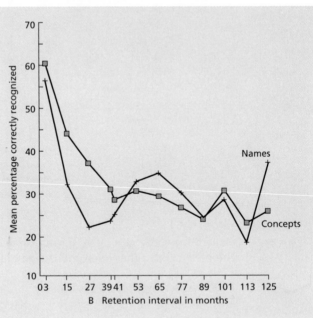

B   Retention interval in months

Retention of names showed a slightly more rapid decline than the recall and recognition of concepts, a finding consistent with what many professors of cognitive psychology (and we suspect other subjects) see in much shorter retention intervals. As shown in Figure 6.12A, the recognition of both names and concepts follows the same trend. In Figure 6.12B we see a much sharper initial decline in the recall of names and concepts. An interesting, if not altogether expected, finding was a high relationship between grades and VLTM scores. It pays to study or, an alternative hypothesis, it pays to have a good memory.

These data are consistent with the landmark experiments of Bahrick and his colleagues in the sense that VLTM for information, (be it old class chums or STM/LTM dichotomy, declines rapidly at first and then levels off and remains at a sustained level, above chance, for many years.) The finding that concepts are retained longer than names) needs some interpretation. It is likely that new names, which the student is (presumably) poorly motivated to commit to LTM (what value is it to know, in the long run, that Bahrick, Bahrick, and Wittlinger collected important data on VLTM?), would be variously associated with other memories of the principle of VLTM, namely, that people tend to forget rapidly at first and then not much. Ebbinghaus, (a name (like his nonsense syllables) likely to be forgotten) continues to be right. Finally, one has to suspect that the emphasis placed on names versus concepts by individual professors, and perhaps even the emphasis placed on these things in the text used, might influence the results, although we hasten to add that the results are entirely consistent with previous studies of VLTM and support the main conclusions found by others.

Memory for Pictures.   A remarkable demonstration of the ability to recognize pictures over a very long time was given by Shepard (1967). From a large number of highly memorable pictures (for example, advertisements in magazines), he selected 612. The pictures were projected one at a time onto a screen at a rate set by the participant. After the participant viewed the 612 individual pictures, a recognition test was given in which 68 of the 612 were shown paired with one new picture each. The participants were to indicate which of each pair was the picture they had previously viewed. The immediate-recognition task yielded a very high percentage of "hits," 96.7 percent. Two hours later, in the part of the experiment particularly germane to our discussion of VLTM, the participants were again asked to judge another set of old/new pairs of photographs. This time 99.7 percent of the pictures that had already been seen were recognized. Participants were subsequently given recognition memory tasks of the same sort after 3 days, 7 days, and 120 days. As can be seen in Figure 6.13, participants were able to recognize the already viewed pictures very well, even after a week. Similar results have been reported by Nickerson (1965, 1968) and Standing (1973) using 10,000 pictures. Standing, Conezio, and Haber (1970) presented 2,560 color slides to participants and found that recognition ranged from 97 percent to about 63 percent over a year. Somewhat more interesting is the decline in recognition scores after about 4 months. Did memory for the picture fade, or did other images intervene and confuse the participants? The data gathered after 3 days and 7 days would suggest that the memory for pictures was encoded in the participants' LTM and that the decline of recognition memory after 4 months would appear to be a function of the intervention of confusing images. In the next section we consider the effects of loss of information or the inability to recall information from memory.

Autobiographical Memories

(**Autobiographical memories** are memories of an individual's past history.) Although personal memories have always been a topic of interest among nonspecialists, they also have been the subject of several interesting psychological studies. One reason these types of memories are interesting is that they are about the individual and his or her

FIGURE 6.13

Results of Shepard's recognition test.

Adapted from Shepard (1967).

unique history. The person—you, your friend, or anyone—is the focus of autobiographical memories. The individual is the expert, since no one knows his or her life better. These memories also can tell us quite a lot about an individual's personality and concept of self.

The contents of personal memory do not comprise an even collection of sensory impressions. Our LTM does not record information unintelligently, but rather it is highly selective in choosing its contents. We remember close relatives, the look of our first car, the first time we had sex, school colors, the name of our hometown, heroes, bullies, and villains, a few cute things our children did, the floor plan of our home, and mother's good china. Contrary to our best intentions, we do not "remember this night forever," or "never forget you," or "think about you every day." We forget a lot of things, and sometimes those things that are very dear to us at the moment fade rapidly. Others remain forever. The contents of one's personal memory are not unlike the contents of one's attic—more a selective collection of important and odd memories than an indiscriminate stowing of all sensory impressions in our cerebral warehouse.

Autobiographical memories, if not perfect, are generally quite good. Objective data on this topic are hard to come by (after all, who can contest a personal memory?), but some researchers (for example, Field, 1981) have interviewed various members of the same family, the "facts" of whose personal history could be validated by other members of the family. Such recollections as "I'm sure I had tonsillitis on July 3, as it was just before the Fourth of July and I had to miss the parade on Main Street" can be verified by checking with other family members and consulting medical records. Validating studies show a correlation of about +0.88 between family members when asked factual questions. A much lower correlation of about +0.43 is reported for emotions and attitudes (Field, 1981). Of course, we all know families in which the correlation between family members' attitudes is negative.

Diary Studies of Autobiographical Memory.   Fortunately, some enterprising psychologists have undertaken the herculean task of keeping a record of their daily activities and then sampling their memories of these activities. One of these studies by Linton (1982; also see Wagenaar, 1986) concentrated on the recollection of episodic experiences over a 6-year period. Each day she wrote on cards a brief description of at least two events that happened on that day. Every month she selected two cards at random; she then tried to recall the events written on the cards and fix the date of the events. She also rated the memory for its saliency, or importance, and for emotionality, both at the time of recall and at the time of writing the card. Linton's results (see Figure 6.14) contained a few surprises. The rate of forgetting was linear, not curvilinear, as many forgetting curves from the time of Ebbinghaus onward have been. From this, we can infer the significant conclusion that memory for everyday, episodic events over a long period of time becomes gradually less available and that the ability to retrieve these items deteriorates at a steady rate. Linton noted two types of forgetting. One was associated with events repeated over time, such as attending committee meetings. In memory, meetings

FIGURE 6.14

Percent of items forgotten during six years.

From Linton (1982).

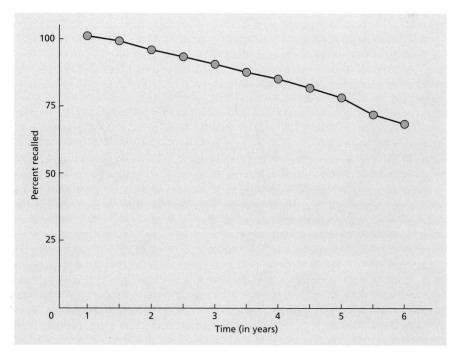

merged with other meetings. A second type of forgetting was associated with events that she simply forgot) One surprise was the failure to find a strong relationship between the rated importance and emotionality of a memory and its recallability. This finding is contrary to "common knowledge" and some other studies, but it is consistent with the "I'll never forget this night" pledge and the subsequent inability to recall the night.

(Another technique used to access the contents of one's bag of memories is to recall thematic life events) In another ambitious study, Sehulster (1989) tried to recall information about opera performances at the Metropolitan Opera spanning 25 years. Sehulster, the lucky patron of the Met for more than a quarter of a century, attempted to free-recall the details about the dates and casting of 284 performances. Validation of Sehulster's memory was done by checking the programs. Unlike the Linton self-study,(Sehulster found primacy and recency effects; that is, opera performances seen toward the first and last part of the 25-year span were recalled better than those in the middle. Sehulster also found that the importance (or intensity) of the opera also contributed significantly to its recallability. Significant performances were, understandably, better recalled than pedes-

Try This

Vintage Memories

*T*hroughout our lifetime we gather countless impressions of our world and carefully store many as treasured memories. Elderly people seem to have an especially rich store of preserved impressions, and like discovering a flower pressed between the pages of a cherished book, once-vivid impressions can be recovered from the pages of memory. In talking with elderly people, it is almost as if they draw a book from memory, open it, and begin to recount its contents; then they turn to another section, tell of its contents, and, finally, carefully return the book to its original place so that it can be found again. Take a moment to call a grandparent and ask him or her to tell you about his or her childhood. Jot down the memories.

One of us once asked members of a cognitive psychology class to visit with elderly neighbors or relatives to record some very long-term memories. The following is a brief sample of one of the papers:

"I was born in 1885. . . . My mother died when I was 8 years old so I lived back and forth with relatives and went sometimes to school in the city of Kahoka, Mo., which consisted of about 5 rooms and sometimes to the country school named Star, which was only 1 room where more than one grade was taught. Star School had windows all around looking out on the trees, a blackboard at the front and a little porch and cloakroom where you entered. . . . For entertainment we had the county fair, exhibiting all the local products. There were rides such as the Ferris wheel and merry-go-round, and pony rides. They sold ice cream cones and had lemonade stands. These items sold for 5 cents each. . . . I remember my Uncle John taking me to these events as well as one time when he took me to a show which featured hypnosis. . . . When we were sick they would give us a spoonful of Ayres sarsaparilla, a patent medicine bought at the drug store. . . . I hope this information will help you with your school project, and that you'll come and see me soon. Your Great-grandmother Menke." (Thanks to Scott Menke. May 24, 1987)

Notice that Great-grandmother Menke recounted "important" events from her childhood that were important to her: pony rides, ice cream cones, and lemonade stands. She also had a strong visual memory as evidenced by her accurate recall of the floor plan of her early school.

What were the important events in your grandparent's life? What will yours be?

trian ones. Nevertheless, some performances stuck out in Sehulster's memory. Finally, the more times Sehulster rehearsed the information, for example, listened to records of those operas he attended, the greater the likelihood of recall.

Thus far, our review of personal memories has concentrated on individual accounts of private experiences. These matters have also been studied from the perspective of group data. In a series of studies, David Rubin of Duke University has shown that people remember some periods of their lives better than others and that for most people the recall of past times is remarkably similar. Rubin (1987, 2000; and Rubin, Wetzler & Nebes, 1986) found, for example, that people who reach their middle years (50s and beyond) tend to remember more episodes from their youth and early adult years than from more recent years (see Figure 6.15).

"It seems to be that reminiscence flows more freely about the period in life that comes to define you: the time of your first date, marriage, job, child," Rubin explains. Our relative inability to remember events that happened between the ages of 40 and 55 may not be due to the dullness of those years but to the increased stability and routine nature of life during that period. In the sameness of life, one memory becomes merged

FIGURE 6 . 1 5

Memory tends to be selective for events as well as for periods. Especially interesting is the tendency of the middle years to be less recallable. By the age of 70, people remember more from their 20s, while those in their 50s recall more from their teens.

From Rubin (1987).

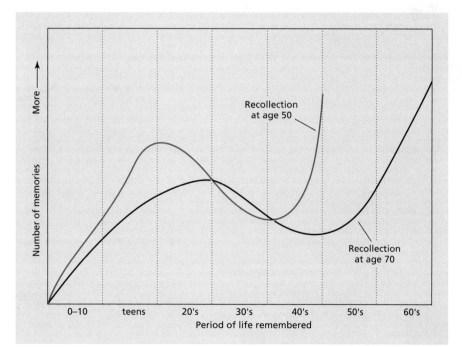

with another and thus becomes less memorable. The period that seems inaccessible is before the age of 4. While some psychoanalysts may contend that childhood repression of sexual desires accounts for this amnesia, another, more cognitive view is that these memories were not well integrated into a larger concept of personal history.

The Fallibility of Memory and Eyewitness Identification

If personal memories are less than perfect, what about other types of memory? Imagine that you are a juror in a case involving a robbery of a local bank. The robber enters, brandishes a handgun, points it at the teller, and demands all the money in her till. A 37-year-old white male bystander, conducting business at the next window, not more than 8 feet away, gets a clear look at the perpetrator who is an African American in his late twenties. A week after the robbery a suspect is arrested in his car along with a large amount of money and a handgun. The suspect claims he was watching a TV program with his girlfriend at the time of the robbery and upon unprompted questioning was able to tell the details of the TV program. His girlfriend also confirmed his alibi. The eyewitness to the crime positively identified the man as the same person he saw rob the bank, and he testifies under oath of his confidence in his recollection. Under these circumstances, how much weight would you give to the eyewitness account? If you are like most other people, the testimony of an eyewitness would predominate over most other circumstances. The effect of an eyewitness's testimony in persuading a jury of the guilt or innocence of a defendant is usually overwhelming. However, until recently, the credibility of eyewitness testimony was unchallenged. In a series of carefully controlled experiments, Elizabeth Loftus and her colleagues have presented evidence of their own that people's memory is susceptible to distortion. In one of her experiments, college students were asked to view a videotape of an automobile and then answer a series of questions based on what they had seen. Half the participants were asked, "How fast was the white sports car going while traveling along the country road?" The other half was asked, "How fast was the white sports car going when it passed the barn while traveling along the country road?" Notice that in the second condition *barn* was introduced in the question, although the film contained no barn. One week later the participants were asked whether they had seen a barn in the videotape. In the second condition 17 percent of the participants reported seeing a barn, which of course did not exist in the film, as contrasted with only 3 percent in the first condition.

In a related experiment Loftus, Miller, and Burns (1978) showed participants a series of slides in which a sports car stopped at an intersection and then turned and hit a pedestrian. Half the students saw a slide with a yield sign at the corner; the other half saw a slide with a stop sign. In subsequent questioning, opposite information regarding the critical yield and stop signs was introduced. That is, for some of the students who saw the stop sign, new information calling the sign a yield sign was introduced, and for some the yield sign was called a stop sign. Later, participants were asked to select from a pair of slides which one they recognized as being part of the original set. Of the group of participants who had not been given the misleading information, 75 percent selected the correct slide; for those who had been given incorrect information, the correct slide was chosen only 41 percent of the time. What has happened to the original memory? It probably got blended in with other memories.

Elizabeth Loftus. Her work on malleability of memory has been frequently applied to eyewitness identification cases.

Loftus has demonstrated that it is possible to create something as huge as a barn and as important as a yield sign instead of a stop sign (or stop sign instead of a yield sign) for some participants.

Memory for events is not simply **reconstructive,** by which it is meant that one consumes facts about the world and then regurgitates them exactly as they were ingested. In real life, memory and recall are **constructive,** by which it is meant that prior experience, postevent information, perceptual factors, and even one's desire to remember certain events over others influence what we recall. We all do this. Take the telling of a sporting event in which one's team actually played poorly: According to an account of the event by an ardent booster, the team performed like titans.

In the case of the eyewitness to a bank robbery, there are several factors that may cause a juror to question the credibility of the witness. Memory for everyday events involve three stages: perception, memory, and recall. In the first stage, the witness may have been, at least partly, traumatized by witnessing the holdup and seeing the weapon; in the memory stage he may have integrated other memories and stereotypes with his perception; and in the recall stage, he may have been encouraged to identify the suspect so the case could go to court and enforce the laws. In addition, there are several studies that indicate that cross-racial identification is particularly susceptible to inaccuracy (see Shapiro & Penrod, 1986; and Bothwell, Brigham & Malpass, 1989). The number of wrongfully convicted people based on eyewitness testimony is as many as ten thousand a year (see Cutler & Penrod, 1995; and Loftus & Ketcham, 1991). While it is difficult to establish exact data on the innocence of convicted felons ("There are no criminals in prison, only those who had crummy lawyers"), we know that many people are falsely imprisoned because of the fallibility of someone's memory. It is even more tragic that some are executed on the same basis.

Loftus's work has extended to the include **repressed memories,** in which a person might exclude from consciousness a particularly painful memory, as in the case of a woman who, as a child, was sexually molested. Under psychotherapy these memories may be consciously recalled.

While some repressed memories of traumatic childhood events are undoubtably real, it is argued by Loftus and others that some "recovered" memories are actually **false memories,** or reconstructed stories about events that did not occur but are invented (perhaps without awareness) to satisfy the demands of a therapist (see Loftus, 1993; and Loftus & Ketcham, 1991). Even though careful experimental research has been presented to support her position, Loftus has been the subject of criticism. She has questioned the credibility of some types of psychotherapy that focus on past traumatic experiences. While some early traumatic experiences are based in fact, others are the result of postevent blending of events and the encouragement of the therapist. The efficacy of such therapies in uncovering true childhood experiences without contaminating the patient's memory is also questioned. The experimental and applied work of Loftus and others has added an important chapter to our understanding of memory in addition to having a significant impact on the credibility of the memory of eyewitnesses to criminal events. While such accounts are now treated with greater suspicion, it should be noted that not *all* eyewitness accounts or *all* accounts of repressed memories are invalid. The debate continues, and the interested reader will find a great deal of literature on both sides.

Spotlight on Cognitive Neuroscience

Autobiographical Memory

Autobiographical memory can be thought of in terms of lifetime periods and general events within those lifetime periods. There are several brain sites that when injured produce disruption in autobiographical memory. This has led researchers to believe that autobiographical memory is a sequence process distributed across the brain and that is why a brain trauma in a variety of locations produces autobiographical memory deficits. Analysis of retrograde amnesiac patients (who have known areas of brain injury) resulted in a cognitive model of autobiographical memory that demonstrates this complex sequence process. Specific events appear to be represented in the posterior regions that are accessed by the autobiographical, "superordinate" memory system, via networks in the frontal and temporal lobes. This superordinate process can be disrupted at any point along that temporal sequence process. Therefore, loss of autobiographical memory is not a loss of the memory itself but is due to problems in the process of accessing that memory.

Conway, M. A. and Fthenaki, A. (2000). Disruption and loss of autobiographical memory. In F. Boller and J. Grafman (Eds.), *Handbook of Neuropsychology*, 2nd ed., Volume 2.

Summary

1 Memory can be categorized as STM and LTM and working memory. Each has distinctive features.

2 Short-term memory capacity is limited to about seven items, but the density or amount of information per item can be increased by chunking (for example, regrouping letters into words).

3 Patients with lesions to the temporal lobe of the hippocampus show that these structures are involved in the storage of long-term memories.

4 Chunking procedures in short-term memory require accessing information from long-term memory.

5 Coding of information in short-term memory involves at least visual, acoustic, and semantic codes. Evidence suggests visual coding occurs before acoustic and semantic coding.

6 High-speed short-term memory retrieval appears to operate by means of an exhaustive rather than a self-terminating process.

7 Memories seem to be stored locally and generally.

8 The neurocognitive view of long-term memory storage suggests that activation of neural circuits results in an electrochemical change and structural change in neural circuitry.

9 Coding in long-term memory is presumably multidimensional and most likely involves a semantic code as well as codes based on all sensory modalities. The literature has primarily emphasized semantic coding.

10 Capacity and duration of long-term memory are practically limitless.

11 Studies of memory indicate that it is susceptible to change, which has affected the credibility of eyewitness accounts.

KEY WORDS

autobiographical memories
Brown-Peterson technique
central executive
chunking
constructive memories
false memories
permastore

phonological loop
probe item
reconstructive memories
repressed memories
Sternberg paradigm
visuospatial scratchpad
working memory

RECOMMENDED READINGS

Among the most readable books that contain lively discussions of STM are Klatzky, *Human Memory: Structures and Processes;* Baddeley, *The Psychology of Memory;* Lindsay and Norman, *Human Information Processing;* and Norman, *Memory and Attention* (1st or 2nd ed.).

On a more advanced level are Tulving's chapter "Episodic and Semantic Memory" in his *Organization of Memory: Quo Vadis?* and Kennedy and Wilkes, eds., *Studies in Long Term Memory.*

Neisser's *Memory Observed* and Tulving's *Elements of Episodic Memory* are also recommended highly. Klatzky's book *Memory and Awareness* is a highly readable account of memory research from an information-processing perspective. *Practical Aspects of Memory,* by Gruneberg, Morris, and Sykes, has some interesting chapters. Cohen has written a fascinating memory book called *Memory in the Real World,* which is recommended.

See also *Memory & Cognition,* Vol. 21, 1993, which is largely devoted to the topic of short-term memory.

C H A P T E R **7**

Memory Models

hmmm...?

● **Early Studies**

● **The Cognitive Neuroscience of Memory**

● **Two Memory Stores**

● **Memory in the Larger Cognitive Domain**

● **Models of Memory**
Waugh and Norman
Atkinson and Shiffrin
Level of Recall (LOR)
Levels of Processing (LOP): Craik
Self-Reference Effect (SRE)
Episodic and Semantic Memory: Tulving
A Connectionist (PDP) Model of Memory:
   Rumelhart and McClelland

1. What contributions to memory did Ebbinghaus and James make?

2. What is procedural memory? declarative memory?

3. What evidence is there for a two-memory model?

4. What is meant by *level of recall, levels of processing,* and *self-reference effect?*

5. What is episodic and semantic memory?

6. How does a connectionist (PDP) model handle memory?

Of the great challenges that cognitive psychologists face as we begin the twenty-first century none is more vital to our understanding of who we are than the nature of the brain and how memories are organized therein. Compressed within each of our skulls, weighing only about 1.5 kilograms, is a spectacular memory instrument. The human brain is the executive of our life, guiding our actions; it is the terminus of sensations, from which knowledge is fashioned; it is the locus of language, giving voice to thought; it is the repository of memory, from which meaning is derived; and it is the heart of our emotions, giving life feeling. However, of all the frontiers that have yielded to exploration and civilization, understanding the seat of knowledge is only the beginning. But what a beginning! We have learned more about the brain and memory in the past several decades than in all the time before, and current studies of the neurological basis of memory, aided by powerful new techniques, are reshaping our views of this enchanting topic.

Software:Hardware::Psychology:Neurology The scientific study of human memory is currently approached from two positions. One group emphasizes the psychological components of memory, emphasizing its structural-processing elements by conventional means (for example, having participants learn some material, such as the contents of this chapter, and then testing for recall on the next test). Another group is interested in the neurological basis of memory, as in the case of using brain imaging technology to investigate memory changes of specialized types of pathology (as might occur with patients who have experienced a brain lesion in a specific part of the brain) or through the administration of pharmacological agents that affect neurotransmission. Metaphorically, we can think of the first group as the "software" group in the sense that its members are pursuing the way memory works, sometimes in everyday life, and the second group the "hardware" group in the sense that its members are investigating the network of neurons and their interconnections that are associated with memory processes. In actual practice, the two groups work cooperatively on memory issues and our understanding of memory is enhanced by the combined effort.

Early Studies

It is unlikely that Hermann Ebbinghaus, who lived in Germany and who wrote the first scientific account of memory experiments (*On Memory*, 1885), could have foreseen the impact his work would have throughout the history of learning and memory. Consider the circumstances that prevailed during his time. Even though everyone "knew" what

Hermann Ebbinghaus (1850–1909).
The first to present systematic
studies of memory and forgetting.
Wrote *On Memory* in 1885.

memory was and philosophers had speculated about its purpose for years, no systematic formulation of memory structure had been tested, no sophisticated analytic apparatus was available, and no database of previous experimentation existed. Thus his exploration of the unknown properties of memory was undertaken with little information and limited tested apparatus to guide him. He did have a hunch that sensations, feelings, and ideas that had at one time been conscious remained hidden somewhere in memory. His view of the contents of memory and its accessibility is eloquently expressed in the following passage, in which he speaks of once-conscious sensations, feelings, and ideas.

> Although the inwardly-turned look may no longer be able to find them, nevertheless they have not been utterly destroyed and annulled, but in a certain manner they continue to exist, stored up, so to speak, in the memory. We cannot, of course, directly observe their present existence, but it is revealed by the effects which come to our knowledge with a certainty like that with which we infer the existence of the stars below the horizon. . . . (p. 2)

The zeitgeist in which Ebbinghaus worked deemed that learning and memory could be understood by looking at formed ideas and then working backward to find their source. Ebbinghaus reversed the procedure; he studied how memory developed and, by so doing, was able to bring under scientific control the variables that were previously inseparable from the memory. Equipped with the most improbable of candles, the nonsense syllable, he ventured into the darkness of inaccessible memory. Although he shed little light on that subject, Ebbinghaus did emerge with a method to study learning that is still used. His search for the answer to the question of how memory is formed required that he develop a task that was unknown to his experimental subject. Since Ebbinghaus was not only the chief theorist and experimenter but also his own subject, he faced the problem of finding something to teach himself that he didn't already know, hence his use of **nonsense syllables**—nonword, three-letter consonant-vowel-consonant sequences. The nonmemorable terms *ZAT, BOK,* and *QUJ* were born to be forgotten and so they were. Ebbinghaus tenaciously rehearsed list after list of nonsense syllables and then tried to recall them after 20 minutes, 1 hour, 8–9 hours, 1 day, 2 days, 6 days, and 31 days. Figure 7.1 shows just how much he forgot. Included in his experimental studies of memory were the effects of list length on learning time, the effects of practice on learning, and the learning and memory of serially ordered items. This technique of serial learning had its origin with Ebbinghaus and became a standard

FIGURE 7.1

Ebbinghaus's forgetting curve for nonsense syllables.

technique that was used for years. Serial learning acquired prominence not only as a learning procedure (as originally proposed by Ebbinghaus) but also as a method of distinguishing short-term memory from long-term memory. Unfortunately, Ebbinghaus himself never discovered his "stars below the horizon." It is likely that he would be pleased with the type of research being done in today's laboratories. There are even some answers to the questions he raised more than a hundred years ago as to how sensation, feelings, and ideas, once conscious but now inaccessible, can be recalled.

Although Ebbinghaus's search for the hidden stars of memory was not entirely successful, it did not dissuade Harvard's William James from continuing the search for the structure of memory. James's work was to have a direct influence on information-processing theories and modern memory theories.

Shortly after Ebbinghaus wrote *On Memory*, James published his two-volume classic *Principles of Psychology* (1890). James takes note of Ebbinghaus's heroic series of daily reading of nonsense syllables and lauds his exact measurement of memory. In a metaphorical style that is similar to Ebbinghaus's, James adds his own speculation as to lost thoughts:

> [The task] which lies before us deals with the way in which we paint the remote past, as it were, upon a canvas in our memory, and yet we often imagine that we have direct visions of its depths. The stream of thought flows on; but most of its segments fall into the bottomless abyss of oblivion. Of some, no memory survives the instant of their passage. Of others, it is confined to a few moments, hours, or days. Others, again, leave vestiges

William James (1842–1910).
Philosopher, physician, psychologist whose dual-memory concept served as the basis of modern theories of memory. Author of *Principles of Psychology,* 1890.

which are indestructible, and by means of which they may be recalled as long as life endures. Can we explain these differences? (p. 643)

James thought that we could. The ongoing panorama of conscious experience is too transitory to be considered memory. For James, recollection from memory requires effort and should be distinguished from the recovery of something from direct conscious experience. He distinguished between the immediate memory, which he called *primary,* and the indirect memory, which he called *secondary.* James based much of his depiction of the structure of memory on introspection, and he viewed secondary memory as the dark repository of information once experienced but no longer easily accessible. There is a remarkable parallel between the two states of consciousness—primary and secondary memory—that he postulated and an idea that was about to boil over in Vienna and spread throughout the world. Few people had heard of Sigmund Freud in 1890, and his concept of the unconscious mind was still in the formative stage and two decades away from being fashionable.[1]

According to James, **primary memory,** closely related but not identical to what is now called short-term memory, never left consciousness and gave a faithful rendition of events just perceived. **Secondary memory,** or permanent memory, was conceptualized as paths, etched in the brain tissue of people but with wide individual differences. As James (1890) stated, "some minds are like wax under a seal—no impression, however disconnected with others, is wiped out. Others, like jelly, vibrate to every touch, but under usual conditions retain no permanent mark" (p. 659). Thus, memory was dualistic in character: permanent and transitory. However, little scientific evidence was presented, other than the unreliable data from introspection, to distinguish operationally between the two systems. That happened about seventy-five years later, when the relationship between primary memory and secondary memory was described by Waugh and Norman (1965), as shown in Figure 7.2. (This is considered later in this chapter.) In their model, a verbal item enters primary memory and then may be held there by rehearsal or may be forgotten. With rehearsal, the item may enter secondary memory and become part of the permanent memory of the subject.

The early theories of Ebbinghaus and James about the deep structure of memory were laid to rest for a long time, while their influence in other areas of psychology proved

---

[1]James did not cite Freud in his two-volume work, *Principles of Psychology,* published in 1890, but the two did meet.

FIGURE 7.2

Model of primary and secondary memory systems.

Adapted from Waugh and Norman (1965).

to be more palatable to the analytic and functional psychology that was rapidly emerging in the United States. It was not until the recent emergence of cognitive psychology and cognitive neuroscience that these early psychologists were recognized for their adventuresome exploration of the structural properties of memory. Another venture is currently underway in America and other countries that may turn out to be the most exciting of all our journeys into the human mind—the neurocognitive search for memory.

The Cognitive Neuroscience of Memory

The current studies into the cognitive neuroscience of memory are straightforward in content. They involve the plotting of functions on the topography of the brain, the routing of memory traces, and the identification of the neural changes in the brain associated with memory formation and change. Many of the techniques used in these studies have been discussed earlier and, in general, include the use of brain imaging technology (for example, PET scans, MRI, and EEG recordings), electrical probes of the brain (for example, use of minute electrical stimulation for the prompting of memories), the use of chemicals and drugs that affect neurotransmission at the synapse (for example, the use of pharmaceutical agents in the treatment or study of memory enhancement or reduction), and the study of pathological types presenting unusual memory deficits.

In the case of the mapping of the areas of the brain associated with specific memories and memory functions, three sites seem to be directly involved, although it should be emphasized that memory functions are distributed throughout the brain. As shown in Figure 7.3, these sites are the cortex, the outer surface of the brain thought to be involved in higher-order cognition such as thinking, problem solving, and remembering; the cerebellum, the cauliflower-looking structure at the base of the brain involved in the regulation of motor functions and motor memory; and the hippocampus, an S-shaped structure deep inside both cerebral hemispheres that is believed to process new information and route it to parts of the cortex for permanent storage. (It is likely that the hippocampus was

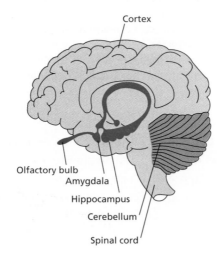

Cortex

Olfactory bulb
Amygdala
Hippocampus
Cerebellum
Spinal cord

FIGURE 7.3

The hippocampus below the two main cerebral hemispheres. Appears to process and route incoming information that is stored in the cortex and cerebellum.

damaged in C.W.'s case, discussed on pages 279–280, since past memories were intact but new memories were difficult to form.) Studies of the brain now suggest that two types of memories, **procedural memory** and **declarative memory,** are associated with these major structures. Procedural memory deals with motor skills, such as handwriting, typing skill, and (probably) our ability to ride a bicycle; it resides primarily in the cerebellum. Declarative memory consists of information and knowledge of the world, such as the name of a favorite aunt, the location of the nearest pizza parlor, and the meaning of words, plus a vast lot of other information; it is stored in the cerebral cortex.

Through the use of new techniques, the structural architecture of the human brain is becoming better known. Of even greater interest to cognitive psychologists are discoveries of the functional properties of the brain; their interrelationships; and their relationship to memory, perception, emotions, language, and other cognitive processes. As a result of these discoveries, psychologists have hypothesized that two types of memory exist: short-term and long-term memories. A wealth of psychological data supports such a notion, but now it appears that additional physiological evidence exists based on the structural and processing characteristics of the brain.

Also, it is becoming evident that sensory information is routed to the cortex soon after it is experienced. There temporary links are formed among neurons and persist only briefly, but long enough for uncomplicated actions to take place, such as remembering a telephone number long enough to dial. In order for these impressions to become permanent a process called **long-term potentiation (LTP)** must occur. This is the tendency of nerve cells that have been exposed to a rapidly repeated stimulus to enhance their response tendencies for an extended period of time. LTP has been observed at hippocampal synapses in mammals. One theory suggests that the dendrites stimulated in this way sprout new growth, which facilitates long-term memories. Long-term declarative memories are thought to begin as the cerebral cortex sends information to the hippocampus, a process that strengthens the memory by rapidly and repeatedly exciting the neural circuit in the cortex. The strengthening of long-term memory may be achieved through voluntary actions, such as repeating a telephone number over and over again, or, in some instances, through involuntary actions, such as might occur in the case of a traumatic or emotional experience. For example, we may vividly recall the details of an automobile accident without conscious rehearsal of the event.

In summary, although much yet remains to be learned about the neurobiology of memory, some things are established. Physical events from the external world, such as light and sound energy, are detected by the sensory system, transduced to nerve impulses, and transmitted to the brain. From there they are initially analyzed and simulta-

*U*ntil recently, attempts to identify brain regions participating in human memory were limited by lack of experimental techniques; case studies of brain-damaged patients provided the principal means of neuroanatomical investigation in humans. The development of noninvasive functional brain-imaging techniques such as PET makes possible unprecedented advances in understanding the neuroanatomical basis of memory and other cognitive processes.

—*Adina L. Roskins (1994)*

neously routed to other centers, including the hippocampus area where, among other functions, their emotional content is assessed. This trace (sometimes called an **engram**) is further rerouted to the cortex and other locations where neurochemicals are activated, sometimes leading to the formation of permanent memory traces so that when the same or similar sensory impression is perceived, the memory trace may be activated. With this basic understanding of the neurocognitive structure of memory, we now turn to the traditional psychological studies and theories of memory.

Two Memory Stores

William James's **dualistic memory theory** made good sense from an introspective standpoint. It also seems valid from the standpoint of the structural and processing features of the brain. Consider the details of the preceding paragraph. Unless you are blessed (cursed?) with a photographic memory, it is not likely that you can remember all of the specific details in that paragraph. Nevertheless, at the time you read it, it was accurately represented in your consciousness. Some facts remain and will be available for recall in the future. Your common sense tells you that two types of memory exist— one brief and one long.

Evidence for two memory states also comes from physiological studies. Performance by animals in learning trials is poorer when the trials are followed immediately by electroconvulsive shock (ECS). That this is the case (while earlier learning is unaffected) suggests that transfer from a transitory memory to a permanent memory may be interfered with (Weiskrantz, 1966). Persons who suffer from amnesia caused by a head trauma frequently indicate no recall of the few seconds preceding the trauma. This condition, called short retrograde amnesia, is distinguished from the loss of memory for longer events, called long retrograde amnesia. For those who suffer from the latter condition, immediate events are completely lost, while the events preceding the trauma by minutes and hours are frequently retained. In addition, a large number of lesion, PET, and trauma studies support the dualist theory of memory (see above and later sections).

Actually, recall directly after trauma seems unaffected. The results of a study by Lynch and Yarnell (1973) support this. These researchers interviewed football players who had received head traumas. The interviews, after a brief neurological examination, were conducted within 30 seconds after the injury. The players were also interviewed 3 to 5 minutes after and (as the situation permitted) every 5 to 20 minutes thereafter. (Uninjured players served as controls.) In the interviews immediately after the trauma, the players accurately recalled the circumstances. For example, "[I was hit] from the front while I was blocking on the punt." However, 5 minutes later they were unable to recall any of the details of the play. For example, "I don't remember what happened. I don't remember what play it was or what I was doing. It was something about a punt." It seems that the details of occurrences just prior to an amnesia-inducing event are stored temporarily in memory but are not passed on to (or consolidated in) permanent memory.

Finally, there is a large body of behavioral evidence—from the earliest experiments on memory to the most recent reports in the psychological literature—that supports a dualistic theory. If Ebbinghaus had pursued serial free recall of items, he might have found those elusive stars that he sensed existed but that remained below the perceptual horizon for so long. When a person learns a series of items and then recalls them without attempting to keep them in order, the "primacy" and "recency" functions emerge. That is, very recent items seem to be readily recalled (recency effects); earlier items are more poorly recalled; and earliest items, again, more readily recalled (primacy). Such data are consistent with a dual-memory concept. The characteristic U-shaped curve of free recall of serial items is shown in Figure 7.4. In this curve we can see that the most recent events are most likely to be recalled, the first items are next most likely, and the middle items are least likely to be recalled. Remember asking what kind of ice cream was available when you were a child? It is likely you selected the last flavor named or the first.

A primacy and recency effect for paired associates was discovered by Mary Calkins, a student of William James. Calkins was studying paired associations by pairing colored cards with those containing black numbers printed on a white background. After learning the paired associations, observers were presented with the color and asked to recall the corresponding number. In her studies examining primacy and recency, Calkins would, for example, present the color blue twice in a series but with a different number each time to determine which number would be recalled during the testing. In a recency test, when the color was presented in the middle and at the end of the series, the observer would recall the number presented at the end of the series about 54 percent of the time compared to about 26 percent of the time when presented in the middle. When the color was presented in beginning and the middle of the series, Calkins found that most of the observers would recall the first number. However, she found this effect to vary across individuals for longer series.

FIGURE 7.4

Free recall in a serial task.

Mary Whiton Calkins.

Primacy and recency effects had been known for a long time, and their incorporation into a two-process theory of memory seemed a logical step. In such a scheme, information gathered by our sensory system is rapidly transferred to a primary-memory store and is either replaced by other incoming information or held there by rehearsal. With a lot of other information coming in, as in serial learning, information held in the short-term store is bumped out by new information. In a free-recall procedure, the items that occurred immediately prior to the free recall (presumably held in short-term memory) are easily remembered (they haven't been bumped out), while a few items deposited in secondary memory are available, but less so. The serial position curve fits well into a dual-memory theory, but how can we account for the primacy effects? It is thought that, because the early items are held longer, they receive more rehearsal, which enhances their availability in a free-recall procedure.

If we assume two memory stores, then it appears that, during free recall, participants spew out those items they have just experienced, that is, those in short-term memory. We can trace the storage capacity of STM by identifying the point at which the recent curve begins to emerge. The number of items in that span is rarely larger than eight, so memory dualists conclude that two stores exist, with STM having a capacity of less than eight items.

The issue of whether memory is based on one or on two stores remains open to debate. Powerful arguments are voiced by both sides, and closure of the issue must await further research.

Memory in the Larger Cognitive Domain

As we learned in Chapter 3, the amount of information that can be detected by our sensory system (even with its limited sensitivity) is enormous. Much of the information is uninteresting to us or simply outstrips our capacity to handle it. Only a little information is processed to the level of our STM, and with appropriate processing, some of this may eventually be held in LTM.

Sensory (iconic, and so forth) memory stores nothing, unless you count the few hundred milliseconds of neural activity; short-term memory is capable of holding some information; and long-term memory is nearly limitless in its storage capacity. The longevity of memory within these three hypothetical structures mirrors their storage capabilities. Some characteristics of these hypothetical components are outlined in Table 7.1, which should be taken as a general guide to storage systems.

TABLE 7.1

Characteristics of Components of Cognitive Storage Systems

| Storage Structure | Processes | | | | Cause of Failure to Recall |
	Code[*]	Capacity	Duration	Retrieval	
Sensory "store"	Sensory features	12–20 items[†] to huge	250 msec–4 sec	Complete, given proper cueing	Masking or decay
Short-term memory	Acoustic, visual, semantic, sensory features identified and named	7 ± 2 items	About 12 sec; longer with rehearsal	Complete, with each item being retrieved every 35 msec	Displacement, interference, decay
Long-term memory	Semantic, visual knowledge; abstractions; meaningful images	Enormous, virtually unlimited	Indefinite	Specific and general information available, given proper cueing	Interference, organic dysfunctioning, inappropriate cues

*How information is represented

†Estimated

The development of a cognitive system involves a great deal of guesswork. Even though the systems depicted in this section are the consequence of many painstaking experiments, they still represent an inferential leap from what can be observed to the nature of the underlying structures. Many cognitive scientists are unwilling to make the leap from data to hypothetical constructs; many others who are willing have drawn different conclusions from the data (and, hence, envision different structures).

Cognition in Everyday Life

Attention and Memory

"You'll never learn anything if you don't pay attention!" admonished many a third-grade teacher—more than once. While it is possible to learn things without conscious attention, a phenomenon called incidental learning, it is true that learning and memory are enhanced if we pay attention.

In everyday life, we are constantly being bombarded with stimuli, usually in the form of advertising and news headlines, that de-mand our attention and frequently create a need in us to buy. It is almost as if advertisers and newspaper editors equate attention with memory and, in order to attract our attention, present outlandish, paradoxical, or incongruous themes. Take a few minutes each day for a week to record these provocative events. Consider some of the issues raised in the previous chapter regarding attention and its influence on memory.

Models of Memory

Up to this point we have focused on experiments that helped solve a portion of the puzzle of memory and, from these studies, have learned that some experiences are held in memory for a short time while others seem to last a long time. By the 1960s research in memory had reached a high state of activity, and it was about this time that some formalized comprehensive theories of memory were beginning to be formulated. This section considers a few of the more viable memory theories of that time.

Waugh and Norman

The first modern behavioral model to travel down memory lane, and one whose concept of primary memory has served as a departure point for most modern theories, was developed by Waugh and Norman (1965). The theory is dualistic; primary memory (PM), a short-term storage system, is conceptualized as being independent of secondary memory (SM), a longer-term storage system. Waugh and Norman borrowed freely from William James's dichotomy of primary and secondary memory and illustrated their theory by means of the model shown in Figure 7.2, which encouraged the memory metaphor of boxes in the head that soon proliferated in the literature of cognitive psychology.

What Waugh and Norman did that James never attempted was to quantify properties of primary memory. This short-term storage system was taken to have very limited capacity, so that loss of information from it was postulated to occur not as a simple function of time but (once the storage capacity was exhausted) by displacement of old items by new ones. PM could be conceptualized as a storage compartment much like a vertical file, in which information is stored in a slot or, if all the slots are filled, displaces an item occupying one of the slots.

Waugh and Norman traced the fate of items in PM by using lists of sixteen digits, that were read to participants at the rate of one digit per second or four digits per second. The sixteenth (or "probe") digit was a repeated digit, one that had appeared in either the third, fifth, seventh, ninth, tenth, eleventh, twelfth, thirteen, or fourteenth position. The probe digit, accompanied by a tone, was the cue for the participant to recall the item that followed the probe digit the first time it occurred. A typical series of digits might be

7 9 5 1 2 9 3 8 0 4 6 3 7 0 6 0 2 (tone)

The correct recall in this case would be *9* (the digit following the first presentation of *2*). In this instance, ten items intervene between the initial presentation and the probe. Since participants did not know which digit would be cued, they could not focus their attention on any one digit and rehearse it. The purpose of presenting digits every second or quarter second was to determine whether forgetting was a function of **decay** (presumed to be due to time) or interference in PM. If forgetting was a function of decay, then less recall could be expected with the slower rate (one digit per second); if forgetting was a function of interference in PM, then no difference in recall could be expected according to the presentation rate. The same amount of information is presented at both presentation rates, which, by Waugh and Norman's logic, allows the same time for decay to occur. It might be argued that even at one item per second, participants would allow extra experimental information to enter their PM, but later experimentation (Norman, 1966a) in

FIGURE 7.5

Results of a probe-digit experiment.

Adapted from Waugh and Norman (1965).

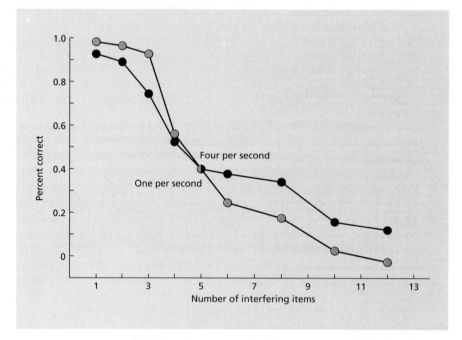

which presentation rates varied from one to ten digits (for a given period), yielded data consistent with a rate of forgetting expected from the original model. As can be seen in Figure 7.5, the rate of forgetting for the two presentation rates is similar. Interference seems to be a greater factor than decay in forgetting in PM.

Waugh and Norman's system makes good sense. PM holds verbal information and is available for verbatim recall; this is true in our ordinary conversation. We can recall that last part of a sentence we have just heard with complete accuracy, even if we were barely paying attention to what was said. However, to recall the same information sometime later is impossible unless we rehearse it, which makes it available through SM.

Atkinson and Shiffrin

The proliferation of the boxes-in-the-head explanation of human memory was well under way when Atkinson and Shiffrin (1968) reported their system,[2] the framework of which was based on the notion that memory structures are fixed and control processes variable. They share the dualist concept of memory described by Waugh and Norman but postulate far more subsystems within STM and LTM. It is as if Waugh and Norman

---

[2]Atkinson and Shiffrin developed the rudiments of their theory in 1965, when they described mathematical models for memory and learning in a technical report.

proposed the elements of earth, air, fire, and water, and Atkinson and Shiffrin proposed the elements found in the periodic table—the latter notion being more complex, dynamic, comprehensive, and better able to explain a wider variety of phenomena. Atkinson and Shiffrin noted that a simplistic notion of memory was not powerful enough to handle the complexities of attention, comparison, retrieval control, transfer from STM to LTM, imagery, coding sensory memory, and so on. The only solution was to divide and conquer, that is, to conceptualize memory properties and to develop empirical rules for differentiating them.

In their model, as shown in Figure 7.6, memory has three stores: (1) the sensory register, (2) the short-term store (STS), and (3) the long-term store (LTS). A stimulus is immediately registered within the appropriate sensory dimension and is either lost or

FIGURE 7.6

Model of memory system with control process expanded. Solid arrows indicate paths of information transfer; dashed arrows are connections permitting comparison with information arrays as well as potential paths for signals that activate transfer, rehearsal mechanisms, and so forth. Long-term store is postulated to be permanent; short-term store, no more than 30 seconds (without rehearsal); and the sensory register, a few hundred milliseconds.

Adapted from Shiffrin and Atkinson (1969).

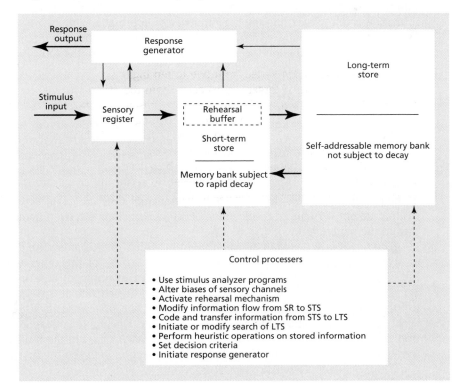

passed on for further processing. A subcomponent of the sensory register is the visual system, which corresponds to iconic storage discussed in detail in Chapter 3. Its properties are well defined; it is rich in information and fast to decay. Although when Atkinson and Shiffrin developed their model systems for other sensory modalities that were less clearly known than today (they still hold many secrets), they provided space for them in their model in anticipation that future research would disclose the unknown features.

Atkinson and Shiffrin make an important distinction between the concepts of memory and memory stores; they use the term *memory* to refer to the data being retained, while *store* refers to the structural component that contains the information. Simply indicating how long an item has been retained does not necessarily reveal where it is located in the structure of memory. Thus, in their system, information can be admitted to LTS shortly after it has been presented, while other information can be held for several minutes in STS and never enter LTS.

The short-term store was regarded as the working system, in which entering information decays and disappears rapidly (but not as rapidly as from the sensory register). Information in the STS may be in a different form than it was originally (for example, a word presented visually may be represented aurally in the short-term store).

Information contained in the third system, the long-term store, was envisioned as relatively permanent, even though it might be inaccessible because of the interference of incoming information. The function of the LTS was to monitor stimuli in the sensory register (controlling those stimuli that enter the STS) and to provide storage space for information from the STS.

Information processing from one store to another is largely controlled by the person. Information briefly held in the sensory register is scanned by the person, and selected information is introduced into the STS. Transfer of information from the STS was regarded as capable of taking place so long as it was held there. Atkinson and Shiffrin postulated that information might enter the long-term store directly from the sensory register.

Level of Recall (LOR)

In a report (not widely known in the West) by P. I. Zinchenko (1962, 1981), a Russian psychologist, the matter of how a person interacts with the material to be learned and committed to memory was introduced. The basic notion was that words encoded by deep means would be retained in incidental memory better than if encoded by other, superficial means. Thus, the memorability of words was profoundly influenced by the goal of the person at the time the material was presented. Different goals were thought to activate different systems of connections because participants have different orientations toward the material.

The thesis was tested in an experiment in which participants were given ten series of words. The first word was to be connected to one of the other words, but the instructions varied for each of three groups. An example of a series is *HOUSE— WINDOW—BUILDING—FISH*. In the first condition the participants were asked to identify the word whose meaning was different from the first word (*HOUSE—FISH*). In a second condition participants were asked to make a concrete connection between the first word and one of the other words (*HOUSE—WINDOW*). In the third condition the participants were asked to make a "logical" connection between the first word and one

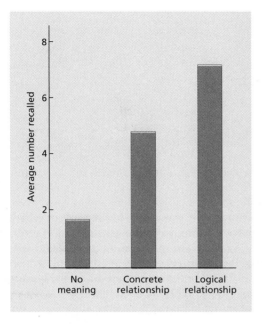

FIGURE 7.7

Recall of words under three different instructions.

Data from Zinchenko (1962, 1981).

of the other three words (*HOUSE—BUILDING*). Zinchenko thought that by altering the instructions the participants would not only have different goals toward the material but also be required to examine each item for meaning. After a brief interrupting task, the participants were asked to recall the items. The data are shown in Figure 7.7. In the condition in which participants formed logical connections between the first word and another word, recall of the target word occurred with greater frequency than the other conditions. Recall of the concrete relationship words was greater than the no-meaning condition.

Thus, the level of recall (LOR), as Zinchenko called it, is determined by the goal of an action. In the experiment cited, we can see that when participants were given a learning set, or instructions to process material at different levels (to use contemporary jargon), recall of the material was affected greatly. Because the original paper was published in Russian and not widely distributed, it has not been incorporated into the larger framework of memory models. Nevertheless, as we shall see, the experiment presented by Zinchenko, because of its theoretical importance to the concept of levels of processing, which has had a profound influence on cognitive psychology, has important consequences for our conceptualization of human memory.

Levels of Processing (LOP): Craik

It is likely that progress in the early stages of scientific development is made more by reaction and counterreaction than by the discovery of great immutable truths. Craik and Lockhart's (1972) **levels-of-processing (LOP) model,** as a reaction against the

Fergus Craik. Challenged traditional ideas of memory with the concept of levels of processing.

boxes-in-the-head scheme of memory, is consistent with that view. They take the position that data can be better described by a concept of memory based on levels of processing. The general idea is that incoming stimuli are subjected to a series of analyses starting with shallow sensory analysis and proceeding to deeper, more complex, abstract, and semantic analyses. Whether a stimulus is processed at a shallow or deep stage depends on the nature of the stimulus and the time available for processing. An item processed at a deep level is less likely to be forgotten than one processed at a shallow level. At the earliest level, incoming stimuli are subjected to sensory and featural analyses; at a deeper level, the item may be recognized by means of pattern recognition and extraction of meaning; at a still deeper level, it may engage the person's long-term associations. With deeper processing a greater degree of semantic or cognitive analysis is undertaken. Consider word recognition, for example. At the preliminary stages, the visual configuration may be analyzed according to such physical or sensory features as lines and angles. Later stages are concerned with matching the stimuli with stored information—for example, recognition that one of the letters corresponds to the pattern identified as *A*. At the highest level, the recognized pattern "may trigger associations, images or stories on the basis of the subject's past experience with the word" (Craik & Lockhart, 1972, p. 675).

The significant issue, in Craik and Lockhart's view, is that we are capable of perceiving at meaningful levels *before* we analyze information at a more primitive level. Thus, levels of processing are more a "spread" of processing, with highly familiar, meaningful stimuli more likely to be processed at a deeper level than less meaningful stimuli.

That we can perceive at a deeper level before analyzing at a shallow level casts grave doubts on the original levels-of-processing formulation. Perhaps we are dealing simply with different types of processing, with the types not following any constant sequence. If all types are equally accessible to the incoming stimulus, then the notion of levels could be replaced by a system that drops the notion of levels or depth but retains some of Craik and Lockhart's ideas about rehearsal and about the formation of memory traces. A model that is closer to their original idea but that avoids the box notion is shown in Figure 7.8. This figure depicts the memory activation involved in proofreading a passage as contrasted with that involved in reading the same passage for the gist of the material. Proofreading, that is, looking at the surface of the passage, involves elaborate shallow processing and minimal semantic processing. Reading for gist, that is, trying to get the essential points, involves minimal shallow processing, or "maintenance

FIGURE 7.8

Memory activation in two kinds of reading.

Figure based on drawing kindly supplied by F. I. M. Craik.

rehearsal" (held in memory without elaboration), but elaborate semantic processing.[3] As a result of some studies (Craik & Watkins, 1973; and Lockhart, Craik, & Jacoby, 1975), the idea that stimuli are always processed through an unvarying sequence of stages was abandoned, while the general principle that some sensory processing must precede semantic analysis was retained.

Levels of Processing versus Information Processing. Information-processing models of memory have generally stressed structural components (for example, sensory store, STM, and LTM) dealing with processing (for example, attention, coding, rehearsal, transformation of information, and forgetting) as operations that are tied (sometimes uniquely) to the structural components. However, another approach is to postulate process and then to formulate a memory system in terms of these operations. Craik and Lockhart have taken just such a position, and their implicit criticism of the information-processing model (along with Neisser, 1976) suggests that it is falling on hard times.

Where information-processing models of memory stress the sequence of stages through which information is moved and processed, this alternate viewpoint argues that memory traces are formed as a by-product of perceptual processing. Thus, the durability of memory is conceptualized as a function of the depth of processing. Information

---

[3]Another example of this latter kind of memory activity would be a typist who concentrates on responding to letter sequences but has very little understanding of the material being typed. A third example is one that will also serve as an introduction to an experiment by Craik and Watkins. We asked the members of a seminar group studying cognitive psychology to recall as many of their elementary-school teachers as they could. They did remarkably well. Then we asked them to try for the earliest article of clothing they could recall wearing, and everyone recalled some favorite garment. Finally we asked them to recall all the articles of clothing they had ever owned. Some of the procedures were quite ingenious, including complex organization matrices—for example, dress clothes; sportswear; sloppy clothes; clothes by age, color, function; and so on. Even though some aggressively pursued this task for several weeks, all agreed that they could not retrieve the memory for all clothes, despite the fact that they had undoubtedly been highly familiar with each article of clothing. The ability to recall some things from memory (teachers' names, favorite clothing) and not others (all clothing) may represent the level of processing to which certain objects are subject; "special" objects may be more deeply processed than mundane ones. (An alternate explanation might be that the students' memory of the other clothing was affected by interference.)

that is not given full attention and is analyzed only to a shallow level is soon forgotten; information that is deeply processed—attended to, fully analyzed, and enriched by associations or images—is long lasting. The levels-of-processing model is not free of criticism (see Craik & Tulving, 1975; and Baddeley, 1978). The criticism includes that (1) it seems to say little more than that meaningful events are well remembered, a mundane conclusion; (2) it is vague and generally untestable; and (3) it is circular in that any events that are well remembered are designated "deeply processed," with no objective and independent index of depth available.

One clear difference between the boxes-in-the-head theory (Waugh and Norman, and Atkinson and Shiffrin) and the levels-of-processing theory (Craik and Lockhart) is their respective notions concerning rehearsal. In the former, rehearsal, or repetition, of information in STM serves the function of transferring it to a longer-lasting memory store; in the latter, rehearsal is conceptualized as either maintaining information at one level of analysis or elaborating information by processing it to a deeper level. The first type, maintenance rehearsal, will not lead to better retention.

Craik and Tulving (1975) tested the idea that words that are deeply processed should be recalled better than those that are less so. They did this by having participants simply rate words as to their structural, phonemic, or semantic aspects. Typical of questions used are the following:

Structural: Is the word in capital letters?
Phonemic: Does the word rhyme with *WEIGHT?*
Semantic: Would the word fit the sentence
              "He met a _____ in the street"?

Craik and Tulving measured both the time to make a decision and recognition of the rated words. (In another experiment, recall was also measured.) The data obtained (Figure 7.9) are interpreted as showing that (1) deeper processing takes longer to accomplish and (2) recognition of encoded words increases as a function of the level to which they are processed, with those words engaging semantic aspects better recognized than those engaging only the phonological or structural aspects. Using slightly different tasks, D'Agostino, O'Neill, and Paivio (1977); Klein and Saltz (1976); and Schulman (1974) obtained similar results.

The previous studies support the idea that memory is a function of how initial information is first encoded; semantically encoded information is better recalled than perceptually encoded information. Adopting a neurocognitive perspective on this topic (some philosophers refer to this perspective as "biological reductionism"), one searches for the anatomic substrata of the strong memory effect associated with levels of processing. Fortunately, just such an investigation has been done by Kapur, Craik, Tulving, Wilson, Hoyle, and Brown (1994) using PET imaging technology with exhilarating results. The task used in the experiment conducted by Kapur and his colleagues was similar to the studies mentioned previously. In one condition participants were asked simply to detect the presence or absence of a letter in a word (for example, Does the word contain the letter a?), and in another condition different participants studied each word and were asked whether it represented something that was living or nonliving. In the first condition, the processing was considered to be shallow; in the second, deep. Behavioral responses (yes or no) to these questions were recorded by means of clicking a computer mouse, but the momentous data were the activation of specific brain areas as recorded by PET images using O_{15}-labeled water that were gathered during the per-

FIGURE 7.9

Initial decision latency and recognition performance for words as a function of the initial task.

From Craik and Tulving (1975).

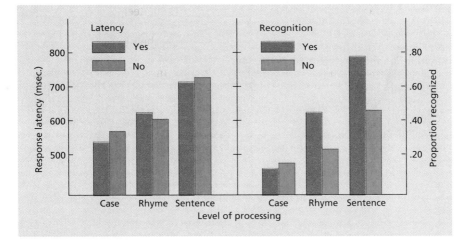

formance of these two tasks. The behavioral data indicated that participants had substantially better recognition memory for the words processed at the deep level (living or nonliving thing) than for words processed at the shallow level (*a* or no *a*). The results of the PET images are shown in Figure 7.10.

Here the differences between the two groups showed a significant increase in cerebral activation in the left inferior prefrontal cortex during the semantic deep task as compared with the perceptual shallow task. In the present study it appears that the left prefrontal region, which was associated with enhanced memory performance, may be the locus of this type of memory storage. The complete understanding of memory process, of course, must consider cognitive processes, neural activity, and memory performance integrated into an overall theory of memory.

Self-Reference Effect (SRE)

New light was shed on the levels-of-processing concept when Rogers, Kuiper, and Kirker (1977) showed that self-reference is a powerful method variable. Using a method similar to that of Craik and Tulving (1975), they asked participants to evaluate a list of forty adjectives on one of four tasks hypothesized to vary in depth, or semantic richness. Included were structural, phonemic, semantic, and self-reference tasks. Typical cue questions were as follows:

Structural task: Big letters? (Adjective presented in the same size type as rest of question or twice the size.)

Phonemic task: Rhymes with? (Word did or did not rhyme with presented adjective.)

FIGURE 7.10

**The regions of the brain that show
increased cerebral blood flow in deep
processing (living and nonliving)
condition.** The upper-left figure is a
side view, with the frontal areas to
the right and occipital lobe to the left.
The upper-right figure is a vertical
cross section. The grid and numbers
represent standard coordinate spaces.
VPC is a vertical line through the
posterior commissure, and VAC is
a vertical line through the anterior
commissure.

Semantic task: Means same as? (Word was or was not synonymous with
                        presented adjective.)
Self-reference task: Describes you?

As in the Craik and Tulving study, it was assumed that words more deeply coded
during rating should be recalled better than those words with shallow coding. After the
participants rated the words, they were asked to free-recall as many of the words they
had rated as possible. Recall was poorest for words rated structurally and ascended
through those phonemically rated and semantically rated. Self-reference words were recalled best. Figure 7.11 shows the recall data from the study by Rogers and his colleagues. From these data, it is clear that words rated on a self-reference task lead to
greater recall, which suggests that self-rating functions are a powerful coding device.

Whether or not these self-rating memories are stored in different parts of the brain
remains a question.

The Narcissistic Trait. Modifications of the original experiment have been conducted in several laboratories with the results being about the same. Some have argued
that self-reference tasks are stored in some special memory system. Certainly, if you are
asked to evaluate a personality trait as being self-descriptive, such as greedy, loving, or
angry, you are engaging a very powerful **self-schema,** an organized system of internal
attributes that is constellated around the topic of "I, me, mine." We also call this the
narcissistic trait. Since we all know a great deal about ourselves (and are emotionally,
if not intellectually, deeply invested in ourselves), we have a rich and elaborate internal
network available for storing self-information. Because of these complex internal self-
structures, we can more easily organize new information as it might refer to ourselves

FIGURE 7.11

Mean recall for both yes and no ratings as a function of rating tasks.

Data from Rogers, Kuiper, and Kirker (1977).

Cognition in Everyday Life

Had Your Feelings Hurt Lately? You Probably Gained a Memory

*A*ll of us may have overheard an inconsiderate remark made about us, such as "she has bad breath" or "he is money-grubbing." Sometimes the remark is an ethnic or racial slur or refers to one's sexual preference. The affront may be related to our own deepest self-doubts: He or she is ugly; is too tall; has a long neck; has a homely nose; is poor; has AIDS; is bald; is alcoholic; is a slut; and one that is particularly prevalent in America, is fat! These "self-reference" caustic remarks have one thing in common: They are memorable, even if they are not true. Think about your own offensive remarks directed toward another person. How long will the memory of these remarks last? Why do we burn these sometimes careless statements so deeply into our personality? What are the cognitive reasons behind the memorability of personally abusive statements?

than other, more mundane information (see Bellezza, 1992, for several important studies on this theme). Whether or not these self-rating memories are stored in different parts of the brain remains a question, but it is a good hunch that plenty of precious brain space is given over to the narcissistic trait.

Episodic and Semantic Memory: Tulving

Tulving (1972, 1983, 1986, 1989a, 1989b, 1993) classified memory into two types: episodic and semantic. Tulving's classification is important. While it is commonly assumed that a single memory state exists in LTM, Tulving distinguishes two forms as a means of orienting research and theoretical development.

Episodic memory is a "neurocognitive memory system that enables people to remember past happenings" (Tulving, 1993, p. 67). Thus, memories of a particular

Endel Tulving. Hypothesized two types of memory, episodic and semantic, and demonstrated different cortical activity associated with each.

experience (for example, seeing the ocean, getting kissed for the first time, going to a good Chinese restaurant in San Francisco) constitute episodic memory events. These events are always stored in terms of "autobiographical reference." Episodic memory is quite susceptible to change and loss, but it is important in forming the basis of recognizing events (for example, people and places) encountered in the past. These memories lack much of the formal structure that we impose on other information, notably that stored in semantic memory.

Semantic memory is the memory of words, concepts, rules, and abstract ideas and is necessary for the use of language. In Tulving's words:

> It is a mental thesaurus, organized knowledge a person possesses about words and other verbal symbols, their meaning and referents, about relations among them, and about rules, formulas, and algorithms for the manipulation of these symbols, concepts, and relations. Semantic memory does not register perceptible properties of inputs, but rather cognitive referents of input signals. (p. 217)

When we use the word *blue*, we probably do not refer to a specific episode in our memory in which this word was used, but rather to the general meaning of the word. In our daily life we frequently retrieve information from semantic memory that is used in conversation, in solving problems, and in reading a book. Our capacity to process diverse information in rapid succession is attributable to a highly effective retrieval process and well-organized information in semantic memory.

Semantic memory and episodic memory differ not only in their contents but also in their susceptibility to forgetting. The information in episodic memory is lost rapidly as new information is constantly coming in. The retrieval process itself is part of the flow of information into episodic memory. For example, asked to multiply 37 × 3 (which calls on information in semantic memory) or to recall what you ate for breakfast (which calls on information in episodic memory), you must first enter those retrieval questions (as "events") in your episodic memory. You may also record in episodic memory that you multiplied 37 × 3 and that you recalled what you had for breakfast. Episodic memory gets a constant workout (and changes as a consequence of it), whereas semantic memory is activated less often and remains relatively stable over time.

Tulving's hypothesis about memory systems is a stimulating challenge to traditional information-processing models. In a paper entitled "How Many Memory Systems Are There?" (1985a), he depicts memory as consisting of a number of systems, each of which serves a different purpose and operates with different principles. The combination of systems and principles makes up what we call memory. Let's consider the details of this challenging hypothesis.

One Memory System or Multiple Memory Systems. As we have seen in this chapter, the number of systems of memory necessary to account for observations in the field of memory ranges from one to many. Tulving suggests five reasons that we should consider multiple memory systems:

1. So far no profound generalizations can be made about memory as a whole.

2. Memory is believed to develop through a long evolutionary history, a process that is characterized by uneven growth. Human memory, as a natural phenomenon, is thought also to reflect such evolutionary quirks.

3. Studies of brain functioning have shown that different brain mechanisms exist for different types of environmental excitation.

4. Most of our assumptions about mental processes are wrong and will be replaced by better theories.

5. Profoundly different learning and memory processes (for example, making motor adaptation to distorting lenses versus remembering the funeral of a close friend) are beyond the ken of a single unitary theory of memory. (1985a, p. 197)

According to Tulving, the system of memory that best accounts for the complexity and adaptability of the human creature is a three-part classification system: procedural, semantic, and episodic memory. (The latter two components have been described previously.)

These three systems are thought to be monohierarchical in that the lowest system, procedural memory, contains the next system, semantic memory, as its single entity, while semantic memory contains episodic memory as its single specialized subsystem. Although each of the higher systems depends on and is supported by the lower system(s), each system has unique capabilities.

Procedural memory, the lowest form of memory, retains connections between stimuli and responses and is comparable to what Oakley (1981) referred to as associative memory. Semantic memory has the additional capability of representing internal events that are not present, while episodic memory allows the additional capability of acquiring and retaining knowledge of personally experienced events.

*T*he (memory) theory holds that episodic and semantic memory are two of the five major human memory systems for which reasonably adequate evidence is now available. The other three systems are procedural, perceptual representation, and short-term memory. Although each system serves particular functions that other systems cannot serve . . .several systems usually interact in the performance of tasks in everyday life as well as in the memory laboratory.

—*Endel Tulving (1993)*

Supporting evidence for semantic and episodic memory has been dramatically demonstrated by Tulving (see the discussion in Chapter 2; Tulving 1989a, 1989b; and Tulving et al., 1994), who has presented physical documentation for memory systems. Two types of studies have been reported. In one Tulving describes the case of a man known as "K. C.," who suffered brain damage from a motorcycle accident.

In the fall of 1980, a thirty-year-old man, identified in the literature as "K. C.," suffered a serious motorcycle accident while returning from work to his home in Toronto. This unfortunate accident has provided psychology with a vivid example of the organic nature of episodic and semantic memory. As a result of the accident, K. C. knows many things but cannot remember anything.

Episodic memory stores information about personal experiences and allows us to travel back in personal time. If you try to recall what movie you saw last night, you are tapping episodic memory.

Semantic memory enables us to assimilate knowledge and information in a general sense. When you think about something you know, such as the influence of economic conditions on political candidates or how to play chess, you are using semantic memory.

K. C. seems to have semantic memory but not episodic memory. He knows, for example, that his family has a summer cottage and where it is located. He can even point out its location on a map. He knows that he spends some weekends there but cannot remember a single occasion when he was at the cottage or a single event that happened there. He knows how to play chess but cannot recall having played chess before with anyone. He knows he has a car and knows its make and year, but he cannot remember a single trip he took in it. Equally deficient is his ability to conjure up images about his future. Alas, K. C. seems to be frozen in a cognitive world that knows no past and anticipates no future.

The regions of the brain most severely injured included the left frontal-parietal and right parietal-occipital areas. K. C. remains densely amnesic, but the type of amnesia is remarkable. He has difficulty remembering normal, everyday, conscious experiences. He cannot bring back to conscious awareness "a single thing that he has ever done or experienced" (1989a). However, he is not mentally retarded, he is able to carry on what

K.C. can play chess, but he cannot remember playing anyone.

appears to be a normal conversation, he can read and write, he can recognize familiar objects and photographs, and he is aware of what he has done for a minute or two after he has done it. Apparently, K. C.'s accident caused serious damage to the part of the brain necessary for the functioning of episodic memory and, to a much lesser extent, the semantic system.

The second type of study indicates the cortical locus of semantic and episodic memory by measuring regional cerebral blood flow (rCBF). Because the technique and findings were discussed in Chapter 2 and briefly at the beginning of this chapter, they are not repeated here, except in summary. By measuring the flow of blood in the cortex (which is interpreted as an indication of localized neural activity) with a modified PET scanning procedure, it was possible to create a cortical map of the brain during different memory operations. When a person engaged in semantic memory activities, specific regions of the brain "lit up," whereas episodic activities led to the activation of other areas of the cortex.

A Connectionist (PDP) Model of Memory: Rumelhart and McClelland

The approach to memory espoused by Tulving in the preceding section found direct correlates between neural activities and types of memory. The connectionist (or PDP) model, developed by Rumelhart and McClelland and others (1986), is also neurally inspired but attempts to describe memory from the even finer-grained analysis of processing units, which resemble neurons. Furthermore, since Tulving's model is derived from observations of brain activities, the connectionist model is based on the development of laws that govern the representation of knowledge in memory. One additional feature of the PDP model of memory is that it is not just a model of memory; it is also a model for action and the representation of knowledge. The rudiments of the PDP model are discussed in Chapter 1.

A fundamental assumption of the PDP model is that mental processes take place through a system of highly interconnected units, which take on activation values and communicate with other units. Units are simple processing elements that stand for possible hypotheses about the nature of things, such as letters in a display, the rules that govern syntax, and goals or actions (for example, the goal of typing a letter on a keyboard or playing a note on the piano). Units can be compared to atoms, in that both are building blocks for more complex structures and combine with others of their kind to form larger networks. A neuron in the brain is a type of unit that combines with other neurons in a parallel processing mode to form larger systems.

Units are organized into modules, much as atoms are organized into molecules. Figure 7.12 shows a simple information-processing module. In this highly oversimplified representation of a module (in fact, the number of units per module would range from thousands to millions), each unit receives information from other modules (left) through the input lines and, after processing, passes information to other modules through the output lines (right).

In this model, information is received, is permeated throughout the model, and leaves traces behind when it has passed through. These traces change in the strength (sometimes called weight) of the connections between individual units in the model. A memory trace, such as a friend's name, may be distributed over many different connections. The storage of information (for example, a friend's name) is thought to be content addressable—that is, we can access the information in memory on the basis of its

FIGURE 7.12

A simplified version of a processing module. Contains eight processing units. Each unit is connected to all other units, as indicated by the branches of the output lines that circle back onto the input lines leading into each unit.

Adapted from McClelland and Rumelhart (1985).

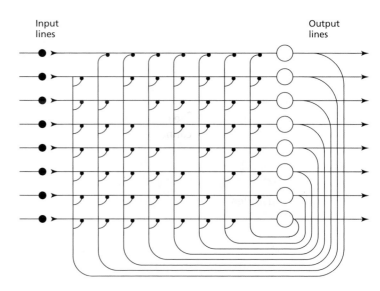

Input lines

Output lines

attributes. You can recall your friend's name if we show you a picture of him, tell you where he lives, or describe what he does. All of these attributes may be used to access the name in memory. Of course, some cues are better than others.

Even though the theory is abstract, it touches real-life activities. To continue with the example of your friend's name, suppose we ask, "What is the name of the man you play tennis with?" Such an inquiry gives at least two content-addressable cues: man and tennis partner. If you play tennis with only one man (and you know his name), then the answer should be easy. If you have many partners who are men, then the answer may be impossible. Additional information (for example, the man with the beard, the left-handed player, the guy with red tennis shorts, the dude with the rocketlike serve, the chap with the Boston terrier, and so forth) may easily focus the search. You can imagine how very narrow the search would be if all of these attributes were associated with only one person: the man you play tennis with has a beard, is left-handed, wears red tennis shorts, has a hot serve, and has a terrier. In real life, each of these attributes may be associated with more than one person. You may know several people who have a hot serve or have a beard. If that is the case, it is possible to recall names other than the intended one. However, if the categories are specific and mutually exclusive, retrieval is likely to be accurate. How can a PDP modular concept of memory keep these interfering components from running into each other?

According to this model, information is represented in memory in terms of numerous connections with other units. If an attribute is part of a number of different memories and is activated (for example, What was your friend's name . . . ?), then it will tend to excite all the memories in which the attribute is a part. One way interfering components are kept from overrunning the system is to conceptualize the relationship between units as being subject to inhibitory laws. Thus, when we identify the person you play tennis with as a man, in theory we inhibit all searches for people who are women. When we add that he has a Boston terrier, then we do not search for the names of people with whom you do not play tennis and who do not own a Boston terrier.

Jets and Sharks.   Memory systems of the sort just described have been studied by McClelland (1981) and McClelland and Rumelhart (1985), who illustrate how this system of content-addressable memory would work in a PDP model. In Table 7.2 are the names of several nefarious (and hypothetical) characters who live in a bad neighborhood (also make-believe). A subset of the units that represent this information is shown in Figure 7.13.

In this figure, the groupings on the periphery enclose mutually exclusive information. (For example, Art cannot also be Rick.) All of the characters' attributes are connected in a

TABLE 7.2

Attributes of Members Belonging to Two Gangs, Jets and Sharks

Name	Gang	Age	Education	Marital Status	Occupation
Art	Jets	40s	J.H.	Sing.	Pusher
Al	Jets	30s	J.H.	Mar.	Burglar
Sam	Jets	20s	Col.	Sing.	Bookie
Clyde	Jets	40s	J.H.	Sing.	Bookie
Mike	Jets	30s	J.H.	Sing.	Bookie
Jim	Jets	20s	J.H.	Div.	Burglar
Greg	Jets	20s	H.S.	Mar.	Pusher
John	Jets	20s	J.H.	Mar.	Burglar
Doug	Jets	30s	H.S.	Sing.	Bookie
Lance	Jets	20s	J.H.	Mar.	Burglar
George	Jets	20s	J.H.	Div.	Burglar
Pete	Jets	20s	H.S.	Sing.	Bookie
Fred	Jets	20s	H.S.	Sing.	Pusher
Gene	Jets	20s	Col.	Sing.	Pusher
Ralph	Jets	30s	J.H.	Sing.	Pusher
Phil	Sharks	30s	Col.	Mar.	Pusher
Ike	Sharks	30s	J.H.	Sing.	Bookie
Nick	Sharks	30s	H.S.	Sing.	Pusher
Don	Sharks	30s	Col.	Mar.	Burglar
Ned	Sharks	30s	Col.	Mar.	Bookie
Karl	Sharks	40s	H.S.	Mar.	Bookie
Ken	Sharks	20s	H.S.	Sing.	Burglar
Earl	Sharks	40s	H.S.	Mar.	Burglar
Rick	Sharks	30s	H.S.	Div.	Burglar
Ol	Sharks	30s	Col.	Mar.	Pusher
Neal	Sharks	30s	H.S.	Sing.	Bookie
Dave	Sharks	30s	H.S.	Div.	Pusher

From McClelland (1981). Reprinted by permission.

F I G U R E   7 . 1 3

Sample of units and connections needed to represent the characters in Table 7.2. Bidirectional arrows indicate that units are mutually excitatory. Units within each cloud are mutually exclusive (that is, one cannot belong to both the Jets and the Sharks).

From McClelland (1981). Reprinted by permission.

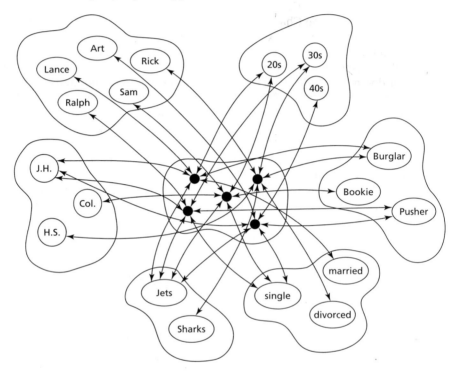

mutually excitatory network. If the network is well practiced, that is, if the connections between units are established, then we can retrieve the properties of a given individual.

Suppose you want to retrieve the attributes of Ralph. By probing the system with Ralph (there is only one Ralph in the system), you can recall that he is a Jet, in his thirties, attended junior high school, is single, and is a drug pusher. In effect, we have recalled a representation of Ralph. In other words, Ralph is what he is. However, if we access the system from another angle and with less than complete information, we would end up with ambiguous results. For example, if we search for a person who is a Jet, is in his thirties, attended junior high school, and is single, we retrieve two names—Ralph and Mike. In this example, more information would be needed to be specific. (Police investigations are conducted with a similar network of inclusiveness and exclusiveness.)

One of the qualities of the connectionist model of memory is that it can account for complex learning, the type of memory operations we encounter in everyday life. These operations might involve the learning of a category or prototype formation (see Chapter 5). These processes are far more involved than the learning of nonsense syllables, as originally done by Ebbinghaus and reported in the beginning of this chapter.

A Boy and His Dog.   Consider the following example of prototype learning, suggested by McClelland and Rumelhart (1986). A small boy sees many different dogs, each only once and each with a different name. All the dogs have slightly different features but can be considered a variation of the prototype dog, the epitome of "dogness." Just as in the case of Solso and McCarthy's prototype face, which was formed through experience with exemplar faces (see Chapter 4), the boy forms a memory for a prototypical dog on the basis of experience with exemplar dogs. As in the case of faces, the boy is likely to recognize the prototype dog as a dog, even if he has never seen it. Of course, the boy is not likely to remember the names of each of the individual dogs, though the most recently seen dog may still be in memory. The rationale offered by the connectionist model for prototype formation is somewhat similar to the example presented for the members of the Jets and the Sharks. In the case of the boy and his (prototype) dog, the connectionist model assumes that each time the boy sees a dog, a visual pattern of activation is produced over several of the units in the module. In contrast, the name of the dog produces a reduced pattern of activation. The combined activation of all exemplar dogs sums to the prototype dog, which may be the stable memory representation. Thus, the model, more detailed than presented here, seems to account for this form of memory quite nicely.

The connectionist model of memory has won many disciples in the past few years. Its popularity is due in part to its elegant mathematical models, its relationship to neural networks, and its flexibility in accounting for diverse forms of memories.

Spotlight on Cognitive Neuroscience

Working Memory

Recall that working memory allows for the continued maintenance of information so that it can be used. This active retention of information is known to involve the prefrontal, premotor, and parietal cortical regions. Axel Mecklinger and his colleagues used fMRI to evaluate whether these cortical areas are specialized to particular content or processes. Using transformed MS Word font (Klinzhai) to create "Klingon" letters, as well as pictures of butterflies and unfamiliar faces as stimuli, they had participants memorize the locations of these objects on a computer screen. Then when the items were presented again, they had to indicate whether they were in the same location or not. This working memory task was done while the participant was in a fMRI scanner. They found that maintaining the contents of working memory is achieved by activation of motor and perceptual networks controlled by inferior frontal regions. The posterior parietal regions appear to have the perceptual representation of objects, while the premotor regions have the response representations. This perceptual and response information is then linked by the inferior frontal region. Their results suggest that the prefrontal cortex is not solely content or process oriented, but also it is a strategic processing center for task management.

Mecklinger, A., Bosch, V., Gruenewald, C., Bentin, S., and von Cramon, D. Y. (2000). What have Klingon letters and faces in common? An fMRI study on content-specific working memory systems. *Human Brain Mapping*, 11, 146–161.

SUMMARY

1 The first detailed scientific account of memory experiments was done by Hermann Ebbinghaus.

2 William James's early distinction between primary and secondary memory was a forerunner of modern dualistic memory theories.

3 Modern brain imaging technology (for example, PET) has been useful in identifying specific brain structures associated with memories.

4 The cognitive neuroscience of memory shows that the cerebral cortex, the cerebellum, and the hippocampus are all involved in memory storage and processing.

5 Evidence for the existence of two memory stores is provided by physiological (for example, ECS), clinical (for example, amnesia), and behavioral (for example, free-recall) studies.

6 The first modern dualistic memory model was developed by Waugh and Norman, who also provided evidence suggesting that forgetting in STM is influenced more by interference than by decay.

7 Atkinson and Shiffrin proposed an information-processing model of memory that assumes fixed memory structures, each having a number of subsystems, and variable control processes with activation determined by the demand characteristics of the task.

8 The levels-of-processing theory holds that memory is a by-product of analyses performed on incoming stimuli, with memory trace durability a function of the complexity or depth of those analyses.

9 Analysis of PET data indicates that the left prefrontal area of the brain is involved in deeper processing.

10 Information-processing models and the levels-of-processing position differ with respect to the importance of structure and process and to the nature of rehearsal. Information-processing theories generally emphasize structure and maintenance rehearsal, whereas the levels-of-processing position stresses processing and elaborative rehearsal.

11 Tulving emphasizes memory as a multiple system involving both systems and principles and proposes a three-part classification that includes procedural, semantic, and episodic memories. Recent observations have suggested that semantic and episodic memories are associated with localized cerebral activity.

12 The PDP model of memory postulates processing units that bear some resemblance to neurons. Mental processes, including memory, take place through a system of interconnecting units.

KEY WORDS

decay

declarative memory

dualistic memory theory

engram

episodic memory	primary memory
levels-of-processing (LOP) model	procedural memory
long-term potentiation (LTP)	secondary memory
narcissistic trait	self-schema
nonsense syllable	semantic memory

RECOMMENDED READINGS

◉ A popular book by Baddeley called *Your Memory: A User's Guide* is a good place to begin your reading. Historically interesting is the first book on memory by Ebbinghaus (1885), which has been translated from German to English and is available as a paperback. A classic in psychology is William James's, *Principles of Psychology,* also recently reprinted; it is recommended not only because of its historical significance but also because some of James's speculations have become an integral part of the contemporary literature in cognitive psychology.

◉ Several books that give an excellent overview of memory are Parking's *Memory* and Baddeley's, *The Psychology of Memory;* Adams's, *Learning and Memory;* and Daniel L. Schacter's popular book *Searching for Memory.* Rubin's edited book *Autobiographical Memory* also has many good chapters.

◉ Most authoritative for particular models of memory are the original sources. These are generally more technical than the summary presented in this chapter, but they are understandable with some effort. Suggested are Waugh and Norman's article in *Psychological Review;* Atkinson and Shiffrin in Spence and Spence, eds., *The Psychology of Learning and Motivation: Advances in Research and Theory;* Craik and Lockhart's article in *Journal of Verbal Learning and Verbal Behavior;* Tulving in Tulving and Donaldson, eds., *Organization of Memory;* and Tulving's article in *The Behavioral and Brain Sciences. Varieties of Memory and Consciousness: Essays in Honor of Endel Tulving,* edited by Roediger and Craik, and *Current Issues in Cognitive Processes: The Tulane Flowerree Symposium on Cognition,* edited by Izawa, are recommended.

◉ Some current studies on the neurocognition of memory are particularly suggested, including Petersen et al. in *Nature;* Petersen et al. in *Science;* and most of the *Proceedings of the National Academy of Sciences,* Volume 91, 1994, which is largely devoted to the work of Tulving and his associates.

CHAPTER 8

Mnemonics and Experts

hmmm...?

- **A King from Texas Matches a Paul Bunyan King from Minnesota**
- **Mnemonic Systems**
  Method of Loci
  Peg Word System
  Key Word Method
  Organizational Schemes
  Recall of Names
  Recall of Words
- **Extraordinary Memories**
  S.: Luria
  E.: A Case of Photographic Memory
  V. P.: Hunt and Love
  Others
- **Experts and Expertise**
  H. O.: Case Study of an Artist—Solso;
     Miall and Tchalenko
  The Structure of Knowledge and Expertise
  Theoretical Analysis of Expertise

1. Have you ever made up or used a memory system (such as remembering the names of the spaces and lines on a musical score—FACE and EGBDF)? What was it? Was it effective? Why do you think it might have made recall better?

2. What are some of the commonly used mnemonic systems, and why do they work?

3. Describe some people you know who have extraordinary memories.

4. What are the characteristics of experts?

5. What neurological and psychological measures were made of the artist H. O.?

6. What principles account for skilled memory as it relates to long-term memory?

People have long been concerned with memory and have long sought means to improve it—and for good reasons. Success, as commonly defined in business, law, medicine, schoolwork, music, athletics, and interpersonal relationships, is to a large measure dependent on the ability to recall specific information. Many people have capitalized on our concern for memory by selling memory courses, books, and even pills that promise to increase memory in a few "easy lessons." Some of these systems will be considered.

A King from Texas Matches a Paul Bunyan King from Minnesota

Solso recounts a memory story: My family, like many others, would gather together after dinner for a board game or some other common amusement—in the days before we became obsessed with mindless TV programs or the Internet. One very "low-tech" game was the card-matching game "memory," played with an ordinary deck of cards all spread around face down. The trick was to match the values of the cards. If you picked up one king and then found another, you kept the cards and continued to select pairs until you failed to find a match.

The game gets easier as it continues because the number of cards left in the pool diminishes (which increases the statistical probability of success) and the player's familiarity with previously exposed cards improves. My mother was a whiz at the game (as she was at all sorts of mathematical and verbal games), my children were pretty good, but I (whose major professional work was in memory!) usually came in a disgruntled last. After walking away from the game a poor loser one time too often, I came up with a scheme that has elevated me into the bronze-metal play of card matching (a trick that was to improve my circumstances after I moved to Nevada) and was a first effort to convert theoretical knowledge about memory into a winning hand.

This memory trick, or "mnemonic system," was based on the idea that memory for items, individuals, exemplars, units, numbers, words, dates, cards, or other scattered bits of information could be improved *if* the information was systematically *organized* in some purposeful network.

What was needed was a purposeful network, or easy-to-learn mnemonic. A system that worked, at least better than rote memorization of cards and their location, was to visualize the arrangement of cards as being placed on a map of the United States and to sort individual cards into class memberships. The face cards—the king, queen, and jack—are one group, distinguished by pictures, rank, and color. The aces form another group; because they stand out, their distinctiveness serves as a memory marker (a phenomenon called the **von Restorff effect**). The 5s and 10s formed another category; the 7s were lucky cards; and the rest of the cards were classified roughly into small cards (2, 3, 4) and big cards (6, 8, 9). If a 9 was exposed in the upper-right quadrant, it could be categorized as "a naughty nine from New York," and if another 9 showed up at the left, it was "a 'forty-niner' from California." An ace in the center, from Nebraska, was "an 'ace' football team" and its match from adjacent Kansas was "another 'ace' team." A king from Minnesota was "a Paul Bunyan King," and when another king showed up, in Texas . . . well, you get the idea. How well did the scheme work? You wouldn't be reading about it if it had failed. Was it perfect? No, but by giving a small edge based on associative geography, it was better than brute memorization.

This "card shark plot" is but one example of how many of us use memory devices to enhance our memory capacity. Many of these organizational schemes are so rapidly and naturally employed that the user is unaware of them. Let's consider some of these techniques and the cognitive principles that they illustrate.

A **mnemonic** (the m is silent: ne-mahn'-ick) is a technique or device, such as a rhyme or an image, that uses familiar associations to enhance the storage and the recall of information in memory. Three important parts are incorporated into this definition: (1) the use of familiar associations, (2) the storage, or coding, of information, and (3) the remembering of information that is stored. The most successful techniques assist in all three. We first review some of the common mnemonic techniques, then discuss the intellectual faculties involved in mnemonic activity, and, finally, present some cases of extraordinary memory. The chapter ends with a review of experts, those people who have extraordinary skill in special areas.

Mnemonic Systems

In Greek mythology, Mnemosyne (from which the word *mnemonic* is derived) was the mother of the nine muses of arts and sciences. Memory was considered the oldest and most revered of all mental skills, from which all others are derived. It was believed that if we had no memory, we would have no science, no art, no logic.

There are dozens of devices to aid (or in some cases replace) memory. Speeches are normally delivered from notes; television performers use teleprompters; salesclerks retrieve items from stock with the help of visual indexes; physicians check symptoms in handbooks; and students even compose "crib cards." Early Greek and Roman orators used a technique called the method of loci; religious people have used beads or prayer wheels to facilitate the recitation of formal prayers; generations of Native Americans passed on their rituals and philosophy through memorized stories; and the oral folk history of numerous groups is filled with vivid imagery, which enhances memory.[1]

Method of Loci

Among the best documented of the early mnemonic devices is the **method of loci.** It has been told that Greek senators used the Greek columns as thematic reminders for their speeches. Thus, Deomonticus, representing a western district, might begin his oration by looking at the left column which had "written" on it *THEATER*, which would remind

[1]The late Alex Haley, author of *Roots,* indicated that much of the oral history preserved among his ancestors was rich in imagery.

him to recall the much discussed Greek theater which was under construction. On the next column would be "written" *FISH*, which would be a cue to talk about the need for increasing the scope of fishing, while in the right column the word *WAR* might be impressed, which would prompt him to speak on that topic.

Perhaps you have used this technique to recall an answer on a test by trying to imagine where the professor wrote it on the chalkboard or visualizing the PowerPoint slide or your own notes.

The method of loci consists of:

- Identification of familiar places sequentially arranged.
- Creation of images of the to-be-recalled (TBR) items that are associated with the places.
- Recall by means of "revisiting" the places, which serves as a cue for the TBR items.

Does the system work? There is abundant casual evidence and some empirical evidence to indicate that it does. Gordon Bower (1970b, 1972) of Stanford University has analyzed the method of loci and illustrated the way this technique might be used to remember a shopping list.

Suppose the shopping list (left column) and loci (right column) are as follows:

hot dogs	driveway
cat food	garage interior
tomatoes	front door
bananas	coat closet shelf
whiskey	kitchen sink

The loci are arranged in a familiar sequence, one easy to imagine moving through. The next step is to create some bizarre imagery in which the items on the shopping list are associated with the loci. Bower illustrates this process in the following way: The first image is a "giant *hot dog* rolling down the *driveway*"; the second, "a *cat* eating noisily in the *garage*"; the third, "ripe *tomatoes* splattering over the *front door*"; the fourth, "bunches of *bananas* swinging from the *closet shelf*"; the fifth, a "bottle of *whiskey* gurgling down the *kitchen sink*"; and, finally, recall of the list activated by mentally touring the familiar places, which cues the items on the list.

Peg Word System

The **peg word system,** or peg list system, has several forms, but the basic idea is that one learns a set of words that serve as "pegs" on which items to be memorized are "hung," much as a hat rack has pegs on which hats, scarves, and coats may be hung. In one variation of this basic system, you learn a series of rhyming pairs, such as the following:

one is a bun	six is a stick
two is a shoe	seven is a heaven
three is a tree	eight is a gate
four is a door	nine is a line
five is a hive	ten is a hen

TABLE 8.1

Mnemonic Techniques

Mnemonic	Characteristic	Example
Loci	Visualize TBR items on familiar landmarks.	To learn the kings and queens of England, imagine a walk around campus. On distinctive landmarks, associate a concept. For example, with the carillon you might associate Henry VIII; with an eighteenth-century building, Victoria and so on.
Peg word	Associate new words or concepts with a list of words you already know.	Learn a rhyme, such as "One is a bun; two is a shoe," and associate kings and queens of England with the known words, for example, Henry VIII had big buns, Victoria had many children living in a shoe, and so on.
Key word	Form an interactive bridge between the sound of a word and a familiar word.	Take the Russian word *kacca*, pronounced "kassa," which sounds like "caught ya," and means "cashier." And when you pay the bill, they "gotcha."
Organizational schemes	Knowledge is structure in some meaningful relationship	A list of words or concepts are hierarchically organized as in the case of kings and queens of England might be organized by period of history or conquests. Or, monarchs could be woven into a story, or rhyme, or sing-song narrative ("Old King Sol was a merry old soul . . .").
Additional techniques Acronym Acrostic	Use the first letter of a word (acronym) or phrase (acrostic) as a cue for recall.	Acronym: **POLKA. P** stands for Peg Word; **O** for Organizational Schemes, **L** for Loci; **K** for Key Word; **A** for Acrostic: **Pa O**bserved **L**ice **K**issing **A**nts.

After the peg list has been learned, you "hook" a set of items to the pegs. One way this can be done is by imagining an interaction between the peg word and the TBR word. For example, if the first word in a series of TBR words is *elephant,* it can be imagined to interact with *bun* (remember "one is a bun") in some way. If the interaction is bizarre, it seems that the effect is better than if the interaction is commonplace. In this example, you might think of an "elephant burger" in which a great elephant is squeezed into a small hamburger bun. If the next TBR item is *lion,* you might associate it with the peg word *shoe* by imagining a lion's wearing tennis shoes or thinking of enormous "cat's paws" outfitted with shoes. The use of peg word mnemonics in the memorization of a shopping list is illustrated in Figure 8.1.

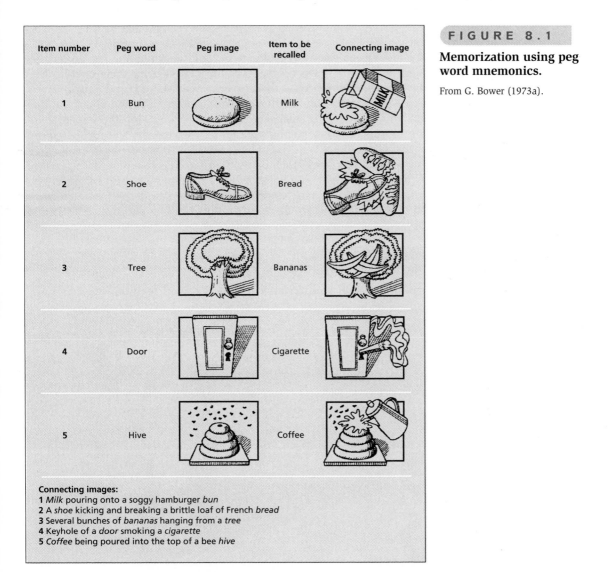

Item number	Peg word	Peg image	Item to be recalled	Connecting image
1	Bun		Milk	
2	Shoe		Bread	
3	Tree		Bananas	
4	Door		Cigarette	
5	Hive		Coffee	

Connecting images:
1 *Milk* pouring onto a soggy hamburger *bun*
2 A *shoe* kicking and breaking a brittle loaf of French *bread*
3 Several bunches of *bananas* hanging from a *tree*
4 Keyhole of a *door* smoking a *cigarette*
5 *Coffee* being poured into the top of a bee *hive*

FIGURE 8.1

Memorization using peg word mnemonics.

From G. Bower (1973a).

Key Word Method

A slightly different form of the peg word technique is the **key word method,** used by Atkinson (1975), Atkinson and Raugh (1975), and Raugh and Atkinson (1975) in second-language instruction. A key word is an "English word that sounds like some part of the foreign word" (Atkinson, 1975, p. 821). After you associate the spoken foreign word with the key word, you form a mental image of the key word interacting with the English translation. Thus, a chain is formed between the foreign word and its English translation, composed of a key word that is acoustically similar to the foreign word and an imaginal relation between the key word and the actual English word. Consider *pato,* the Spanish word for "duck." *Pato* is similar in sound to "pot-o." Using the word *pot* as the key word, we could image a duck with a pot over its head. Alternatively, consider the Russian word *zvonok,* which means "bell." *Zvonok* sounds something like "zrahn-oak," with emphasis on the last syllable. Using the word *oak* as the key word, we could imagine an oak tree with bells as acorns. Figure 8.2 shows the stages of the process using this example.

How well does this system work? In an experiment by Atkinson and Raugh (1975), participants learned 120 Russian words (40 words per day over a period of 3 days). Prerecorded Russian words were presented through headphones; for the experimental group, key words and English translations were presented visually, and for the control group, only English translations were presented. Three training sessions were given each day. The key word group fared much better than the control group. In fact, participants in the key word group learned more words in two training sessions than comparable control participants did in three. Not only did participants in the key word group initially do better than participants in the control group, but in a surprise recall session

FIGURE 8.2

Steps in learning the Russian word *zvonok* by the key word method.

Adapted from Solso and Johnson (1994).

(Oak tree with bells for acorns)

6 weeks later, the probability of a correct response was 43 percent for key word participants and only 28 percent for control participants. The researchers also found that, in general, it is better to provide the key word rather than have the participant generate it.

Organizational Schemes

There is little doubt that knowledge is structured in a systematic way. The *way* knowledge is structured is the subject of much controversy, but few challenge the notion that some structure exists. All mnemonic systems are based on the structuring of information so that it is easily memorized and retrieved. These **organizational schemes** may be based on places, time, orthography, sounds, imagery, and so on. Another powerful mnemonic technique is to organize information into semantic categories, which are then used as cues for recall.

Suppose that, in an experiment in word recall, one group of participants is given 2 minutes in which to learn by rote the following list of words:

bird	hill	web	smoke
boy	home	hand	wool
bread	nail	glass	vegetable
church	nurse	apple	train
feet	queen	hair	carpet
tiger	pepper	grass	star

After the 2 minutes, the participants are asked to add columns of digits for 4 minutes. They then try to recall the words on the list.

Three other groups are given the same words, the same study time, and the same distractor task (adding digits), but with certain other conditions. The second group is also given a line drawing of the object designated by each word and asked to visualize the objects. The third group is asked to memorize the same words by rereading the following story, into which they are incorporated.

The Fantastic Trip

Instead of being in **church,** where he belonged, the **boy** was hiding on the **hill.** He had bare **feet,** although the **nurse** told him he might step on a **nail.** In his **hand** was an **apple** on which, from time to time, he sprinkled black **pepper.**

While a spider spun its **web** over his head, he dreamed of running away from **home.** The thread of this thought went like this. He would hide on a **train** until he got to the coast. From there he'd fly to a faraway **star** on a magic **carpet** or by rubbing an enchanted **glass.**

Once there he would marry the **queen,** lie on the **grass,** and never comb his **hair** or eat a **vegetable.** If he got bored, he'd hunt a **tiger** for fun and watch the **smoke** shoot from his gun.

But before the boy could finish the daydream, he began to grow tired. As he started to feed **bread** crumbs to a nearby **bird,** he saw a sheep with soft **wool.** He lay down on it and fell asleep.

And finally, the fourth group is asked to memorize the words as they are semantically organized in the following list. (They are given the additional instruction that they can help themselves remember the categories by recalling the name B. F. NAPP, which is made up of the first letters of the category names.)

Body Parts	Foods	Nature
feet	bread	hill
hand	pepper	grass
hair	apple	smoke
nail	vegetable	star
		web

Animal Life	Places	Processed Things
boy	church	glass
nurse	home	wool
queen	train	carpet
bird		
tiger		

These categories can be further represented in a "tree structure" as shown in the figure here:

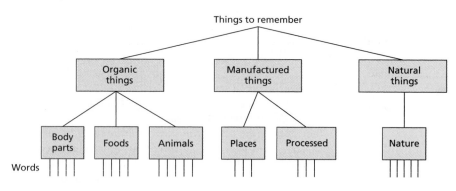

Additional Systems.   There are several additional systems that you have probably used. One is based on **acronyms,** or words formed on the basis of the first letters in a phrase or group of words. *LAN,* in today's parlance, stands for **L**ocal **A**rea **N**etwork. If you were required to learn this list of important cognitive psychologists—Shepard, Craik, Rumelhart, Anderson, Bower, Broadbent, Loftus, Estes, Posner, Luria, Atkinson, Yarbus, Erickson, Rayner, Vygotsky, Intons-Peterson, Piaget, Sternberg—you might form an anagram from the first letters into this acronym: *SCRABBLE PLAYER VIPS.*

Another related system is to form an **acrostic,** or a phrase or sentence in which the first letters are associated with the to-be-recalled words, or otherwise cue those words. Kings Play Chess on Fine Grained Sand is an acrostic many biology students use to remember: kingdom, phylum, class, order, family, genus, species. Sentences that are bizarre, personally meaningful, or visual are easiest to remember. In a moment we will look at how these methods might be used practically, as in the case of remembering the name of a new acquaintance or the recall of words and concepts—hopefully, this material will come in time to help with your next social encounter or examination.

Which mnemonic technique is "best"? Douglas Herrmann (1987) found that some techniques work well for some types of material, while other techniques work well for other types. Specifically, for paired associate learning, imagery mediation worked best; for free-recall learning, the story mnemonic seemed to be superior; while for serial learning, the method of loci worked well. In another assessment of mnemonic techniques, Garcia and Diener (1993) found that when tested over a week the methods of loci, peg word, and acrostics proved to be about equal in effectiveness.

Recall of Names

According to Lorayne and Lucas (1974), who wrote the popular *The Memory Book,* the learning of a name in association with a face involves three steps. The first, remembering the name, may be done by paying close attention to the way the name is pronounced and then by forming a substitute name or phrase for it.[2] For example, the name *Antesiewicz,* pronounced something like "Ante-sevage," can be remembered as "Auntie-save-itch"; *Caruthers* as a "car with udders"; and *Eberhardt* as "ever hard"; and so on. These substitute names are rich in their imaginal properties. All of us can make up an image of these substitute names, some of them most bizarre.

The second step involves searching for an outstanding feature in the person's face—a high forehead, a beard, unusual glasses, a crooked nose, full cheeks, warts, dimples.

The final stage involves associating a substitute word with an outstanding feature. Thus, if you are introduced to a man whose name is Wally Kelly, whose distinguishing features are a receding hairline and ample belly, the *W* made by his hairline may serve as a cue for Wally, and the belly, a cue for Kelly. Of course, if you forget the code, you may mistakenly call him Walter Stomach.[3] Another example is the hockey player Esposito. The name suggests "expose a toe," which can then be associated with his nose, which may look like an exposed toe. Then there is Tony Bennett, whose name might suggest "bend net," a shape you can associate with the Golden Gate Bridge, which could be further associated with Bennett's rendition of "I Left My Heart in San Francisco."

Unless relevant information is attended to (in the cases just mentioned, this refers to the name and the person's physiognomy), even the best mnemonic technique is useless. It seems that the first step in the successful encoding of information is focusing our attention on the information we want to hold in our memory. Attention, also an important part of memory for other items (such as dates, words, ideas, and places), is the key initial stage in the memory process. Where it is not exercised, even the best mnemonic technique will fail.

---

[2]Note the similarities between this technique and the research by Atkinson (1975) and Atkinson and Raugh (1975)

[3]This brings to mind a footnote in Kausler's (1974) *Psychology of Verbal Learning and Memory:*

> Strengthening your imagery muscle forms the core of "how to improve your memory" training programs. Long before imagery's present scientific fad, the first author matriculated in such a mail-order program. Lesson 1 consisted of vignettes on the uses, and potential misuses, of bizarre visual images. For example, there was the young man who learned each new body-name association by creating an image of the body that exaggerated a prominent physical feature. The trick was to select a feature that would, in turn, decode verbally into the person's name. The system worked well until he was introduced to a Mrs. Humach. Her most prominent feature was a rather generous stomach. Upon encountering her again several months later, he greeted her with a friendly, "Nice to see you again, Mrs. Kelly."

Recall of Words

Some of the better-known initial-letter mnemonic devices follow.

The names of the cranial nerves are learned by anatomy students according to this rhyme:

> On Old Olympia's Towering Top
> A Finn and German Vault and Hop

The nerves are olfactory, optic, oculomotor, trochlear, trigeminal, abducens, facial, auditory, glossopharyngeal, vagus, accessory, and hypoglossal. (Of course, going from the G in *German* to *glossopharyngeal* is another matter!) Every student of music has probably learned "*Every Good Boy Does Fine*" for the lines and "*FACE*" for the spaces of the musical staff. Some of us learned to spell *arithmetic* and *geography* by learning, respectively, "*A Rat In Tom's House Might Eat Tom's Ice Cream*" and "*George Elliot's Old Grandfather Rode A Pig Home Yesterday.*" The names of the nine muses can be prompted by the phrase "See, see, my Puttee," which can signify the code *CCMPUTTEE*, translatable to Calliope, Clio, Melpomene, Polyhymnia, Urania, Thalia, Terpsichore, Erato, and Euterpe. The acronym *ROY G BIV* is composed of the initial letters of the names of the spectral colors: *r*ed, *o*range, *y*ellow, *g*reen, *b*lue, *i*ndigo, and *v*iolet.

In these examples the mnemonic uses the first letter of the TBR word. It appears that the initial letter carries the greatest amount of information of any letter in a word, which would suggest that words are coded in LTM according to initial letters—as, for example, in the indexing of a dictionary. The second most important letter tends to be the last one (but the rule is frequently violated in the case of words ending in *s, d,* and *e*—letters that give little information). Crossword puzzle addicts are likely to be familiar with this phenomenon. If the initial letter is cued by a mnemonic system, it is generally the most salient letter cue possible.

Support for the cueing potential of initial letters has been demonstrated by Solso and Biersdorff (1975). Participants were asked to recall a list of words. A word that was not recalled was then cued by either its first letter, something associated with the word in common experience, or a word that rhymed with the TBR word. If the participant still failed to recall the word, dual cues were presented, for example, the first letter *and* an associate. The rhyme, letter, and associate cue all aided the participants in recall, but, most important for our present discussion, if the results due to guessing were compensated for, the initial-letter cue was the best for recall.

Bédard and Chi (1993) state that "the studies (of expertise) have shown that a large, organized body of domain knowledge is a prerequisite to expertise." What is knowledge? Before you read further, formulate your own definition of knowledge and relate it to expertise.

Experts in the field of expertise and knowledge believe that knowledge can be classified in terms of its quantity or its structure. Experts have a greater quantity of domain-specific knowledge—a fact that is self-evident (an expert in carpentry knows far more about his or her craft than a novice). More important, however, is the way experts *organize* their knowledge. Experts organize knowledge in ways that make it more accessible, functional, and efficient.

The use of mnemonic techniques may increase one's specific knowledge base (a prerequisite for expertise), but the organization of knowledge is also vital.

Extraordinary Memories

People with unusual or extraordinary memory may be classified as either professional mnemonists, those who consciously apply a mnemonic technique, or spontaneous mnemonists, those whose capacities seem to have developed more or less naturally without conscious effort and without use of a technique, or trick.

Although there are numerous anecdotal accounts of people with phenomenal memories, they are most difficult to authenticate. There are several accounts of such people, however, about whom much is known, and a few of these people have been studied intensively. Accounts of some of these are presented here.

S.: Luria

The most celebrated case of extraordinary memory (and also one of the best documented) is that of S. (S. V. Shereshevskii), whose capabilities were studied by the distinguished Russian psychologist A. R. Luria (1960, 1968). The semiclinical study began in the mid-1920s when S. was working as a newspaper reporter. He changed jobs several times and finally became a professional mnemonist.

S. was able to recall without error a list of words that was increased to 30, to 50, and to 70. Luria reports that "in order to imprint an impression of a table consisting of twenty numbers, S. needed only 35 to 40 seconds, . . . a table of fifty numbers required somewhat more time . . . 2½ to 3 minutes" (Luria, 1968, p. 21). A typical experiment carried out by Luria is described here:

> [S.] spent 3 min. examining the table I had drawn on a piece of paper (Table 1), stopping intermittently to go over what he had seen in his mind.

Table 1			
6	6	8	0
5	4	3	2
1	6	8	4
7	9	3	5
4	2	3	7
3	8	9	1
1	0	0	2
3	4	5	1
2	7	6	8
1	9	2	6
2	9	6	7
5	5	2	0
X	0	1	X

It took him 40 sec. to reproduce this table (that is, to call off all the numbers in succession). He did this at a rhythmic pace, scarcely pausing between numbers. . . . He read

Alexander Luria (1902–1977). Made basic discoveries in neuropsychology and wrote book on S.

off the numbers which formed the diagonals (the groups of four numbers running zigzag through the chart) in 35 sec, and within 50 sec ran through the numbers that formed the horizontal rows. Altogether he required 1 min, 30 sec to convert all fifty numbers into a single fifty-digit number and read this off. (p. 19)

Several months later when Luria asked S. to recall the list, he did so as accurately as he had on the first occasion. Luria reports:

The only difference in the two performances was that for the later one he needed more time to "revive" the entire situation in which the experiment had originally been carried out: to "see" the room in which he had been sitting; to "hear" my voice; to "reproduce" an image of himself looking at the board. But the actual process of "reading" the table required scarcely any more time than it had earlier. (p. 22)

Luria performed numerous experiments of the same sort with similar results. S. did not seem to forget—even if it involved nonsense material—after days, months, or even years!

Luria observed that S.'s phenomenal memory was accompanied by extreme **synesthesia,** a condition in which sensory information from one modality (for example, auditory) evokes a sensation in another modality) (for example, visual). Most of us have some synesthetic experience; people tend, for example, to associate high-pitched tones with bright, piercing light, and low tones with dark, somber colors. Few, however, are as synesthetic as S., who, when he was mentally "reading" a series of items from memory, would hear noises in the testing area as if they were "puffs of steam" or "splashes," which interfered with his "reading" of the information.

When presented with a tone of 30 cycles per second with an amplitude of 100 decibels, S. reported that he first saw a strip 12 to 14 centimeters wide and the color of old, tarnished silver; a tone of 50 cycles per second with an amplitude of 100 decibels produced the experience of a brown strip against a dark background that had red, tongue-like edges. The experience was also accompanied by a sense of taste "like that of sweet and sour borscht." At 500 cycles per second and 100 decibels, S. saw a "streak of lightning splitting the heavens in two." The same tone at 74 decibels changed to a dense orange color that "made him feel as though a needle had been thrust into his spine." The same responses were obtained when the tones were repeated.

S. also experienced synesthetic responses to voices, once commenting to Luria, "What a crumbly yellow voice you have." His reactions to certain other voices were more flattering; one he described as "though a flame with fibers protruding from it was advancing toward me," adding, "I got so interested in his voice, I couldn't follow what he was saying."

These synesthetic components seemed important in S.'s recall process, since they provided a background for each item to be recalled. The process is described by S.:

> . . . I recognize a word not only by the images it evokes but by a whole complex of feelings that image arouses. It's hard to express . . . it's not a matter of vision or hearing but some overall sense I get. Usually I experience a word's taste and weight, and I don't have to make an effort to remember it—the word seems to recall itself. But it's difficult to describe. What I sense is something oily slipping through my hand . . . or I'm aware of a slight tickling in my left hand caused by a mass of tiny, lightweight points. When that happens I simply remember, without having to make the attempt. . . .

There is also evidence to indicate that S. used the method of loci as a mnemonic. When presented with a series of items to be remembered, he would mentally distribute them along a familiar street in Moscow, starting at Pushkin Square and going down Gorky Street, and then recall the items by taking a mental walk along the same street using familiar landmarks as visual cues for retrieving the items. Errors arose from misperception rather than forgetting, sometimes because the item was not "seen," having been "placed" in some dark corner or because it was very small.[4] An egg, for example, might not be recalled because it had been "placed" against a white surface.

S.'s vivid imagery also tended to interfere with his ability to understand prose, and abstract poetry seemed particularly difficult.[5] He reported that, when listening to a voice, each word spoken elicited an image, which sometimes "collided" with others. When he read, he reported a similar type of imaginal interference. For example, the simple sentence "The work got under way normally" caused this reaction: "as for *work*, I see that work is going on . . . but there's that word *normally*. What I see is a big, ruddy-cheeked woman, a *normal* woman . . . then the expression *got under way*. Who? What is all this? You have industry . . . and this normal woman—but how does it all fit together? How much I have to get rid of to get the simple idea out of the thing!"

It appears that in S.'s case, his enormous capacity and the longevity of information are related to a combination of things, including imagery, synesthesia, and mnemonics.

E.: A Case of Photographic Memory

During most courses in cognitive psychology, a student will inevitably ask something like, "What about photographic memory? Aren't there some people who can look at a page

---

[4]See Kosslyn's work (described in Chapter 10) for a noteworthy discussion of the size of images and the recall of features within the image.

[5]It seems that Shereshevskii sometimes enjoyed demonstrating his unusual ability to students and lay audiences. At one public demonstration the host asked him to memorize a string of numbers. The host went to the blackboard and wrote "36912151821242730333639424548515457." There were a few snickers among the mathematically sophisticated audience as Shereshevskii puzzled over the list for about a half minute. Then he turned away from the blackboard and recited the list perfectly. In the spirit of good fun, the host then told Shereshevskii that most of the people in the audience could do the same because the list was composed of a very simple linear progression of numbers. Shereshevskii was not amused, but the incident further points out the literal nature of his extraordinary memory. The first author learned this story while teaching at Moscow State University as a Fulbright scholar.

and tell you verbatim everything they have seen?" We don't know how our colleagues answer that question, but we usually reply, "If you know of such a person, bring him or her into my lab. Most of us have been looking for someone who has that extraordinary ability for a very long time." It is our experience that stories of people with "photographic memory" are apocryphal. The psychological literature is largely mute on this issue, although the Sunday newspaper supplements and supermarket tabloids are more vocal.

One case of photographic memory is reported by Stromeyer (1970). The subject, Elizabeth, is a very intelligent, skilled artist who teaches at Harvard. She can mentally project an exact image of a picture onto a surface. Her image appears to be an exact copy of the original, and Elizabeth can look at the image and describe it in detail. Psychologists call this **eidetic imagery** (a talent sometimes found in children) rather than the more trendy *photographic memory*. Elizabeth's ability is not restricted to visual images; she can also visualize, say, a poem in a foreign language she had read several years earlier. She can "copy" a line from the top of the poem or bottom equally well by writing as fast as she can, an ability that came in handy in high school examinations.

Is Elizabeth unique? In the two decades since the original report, no other such case has been reported. If there is another Elizabeth out there just waiting to be discovered, please—call!

V. P.: Hunt and Love

In 1971 Hunt and Love (1972) discovered a man (V. P.) whose extraordinary memory rivals that of S. The case of V. P. is particularly interesting to cognitive psychologists for two reasons: V. P. demonstrated an unusually expansive memory, and, perhaps more important, he was systematically examined by a team of contemporary cognitive psychologists who used many of the research techniques discussed in this book.

It is a strange coincidence that V. P. was born in Latvia and spent his early life in a town not far from that of S. By the age of 3½, he could read, and at the age of 5, he had memorized the street map of Riga, a city of 500,000. When he was 10, he memorized 150 poems. After World War II, V. P. lived in displaced-persons camps in Germany until 1950. At the time, because books were in short supply, a great deal of stress was placed on note taking and rote memorization. However, V. P. seems to have had an unusual memory even before this period.

At the time that Hunt and Love observed V. P., he was a store clerk, an avid competition chess player, and sometimes a graduate student. His IQ (Wechsler Adult Intelligence Scale) was 136, with the highest scores obtained on tasks involving memorization and the lowest on mechanical ability. He said of the latter ability that "I even have difficulty putting lead in a pencil."

Hunt and Love had V. P. read Bartlett's (1932) "The War of the Ghosts" twice. After having him count backward by 7s from 253 to 0, they had him recall specific portions of the story after 1 minute, 5 minutes, 30 minutes, and 45 minutes, and the entire story after 1 hour and after 6 weeks. (He was not told he would be expected to recall the story after 6 weeks.) Reproduction of the story after 6 weeks was nearly identical to that after 1 hour, and both performances were superior to the best by ten control subjects.

In a test similar to one by Luria, V. P. was asked to study and recall a list of 48 numbers. He did so perfectly after about 4 minutes of study time and recalled the series with only one transposition error 2 weeks later. Unlike S., V. P. did not seem to rely on un-usual visual memory in this task; an example of the mnemonic he used was to store a row of numbers as a date and then ask himself what he had been doing on that date.

The results suggest that V. P.'s LTM was extraordinary. To test his STM, Hunt and Love used the Brown-Peterson paradigm (see Chapter 6). V. P.'s performance and those of twelve control participants are shown in Figure 8.3. It appears that V. P.'s recall is much better over time than that of the control participants, which would suggest that he is able to retain meaningless trigrams even in the presence of interfering tasks (which are believed to block rehearsal). V. P. did comment that, because of his knowledge of many languages, he was able to associate the meaningless trigrams in the experiment with a meaningful word. If this is the case, then the Brown-Peterson technique may be a test for his ability to store a meaningful chunk of information (a form of organization) over a brief period of time.

In introspecting on his phenomenal memory, V. P. stressed the importance of "con-centration." Hunt and Love comment on this factor:

> In more formal terms, V. P. is much better than most people in creating stimulus codes. There is a conscious effort involved. If he can, V. P. studies the information he

FIGURE 8.3

Recall by V. P. and twelve control subjects of three-consonant trigrams.

Adapted from Hunt and Love (1972).

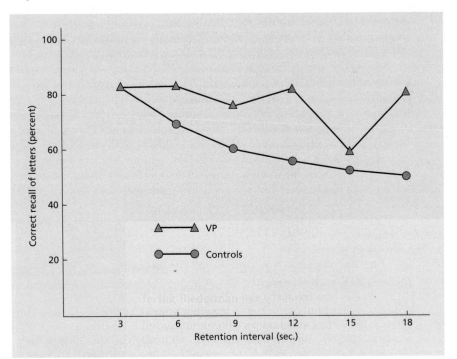

is to remember for a longer time than the average person will spend. When we watched him playing blindfolded chess matches, we could see that, although he was acting with considerable flair, he was also working very hard. He would make "casual" jokes while thinking about his next move, but the veins on his forehead were standing out. The fact that he could joke while calculating moves indicates he has an ability that most of us do not have: he can do a number of mental tasks in parallel. This would perhaps account for his phenomenal performance of the Brown-Peterson task. Unlike most subjects, he seems to be able to repeat numbers backwards while processing information in memory.

Others

Several other cases of extraordinary memory have appeared in the literature. One such is reported by Hunter (1962), who documented the unusual mathematical skill of A. C. Aitken, a professor of mathematics at the University of Edinburgh, Scotland.[6] In 1933 Aitken's memory was tested by presenting him with 25 unrelated words, which he read through twice. Asked to recall the list 27 years later, he began with a few words and then gradually increased the list until all 25 words were correctly recalled. He had also read and memorized a form of "The War of the Ghosts" and recalled it nearly perfectly 27 years later. His memory and retrieval ability were no less spectacular than his numerical ability. On hearing the number *1961*, Aitken immediately recognized it as 37×53, and also $44^2 + 5^2$ and $40^2 + 19^2$.

Another case of extraordinary memory, reported by Coltheart and Glick (1974), is of interest because it deals with iconic memory (see Chapter 3). Sue d'Onim[7] (or O.), had the ability to "talk backward"—that is, to pronounce a normally presented word backward.[8] (Thus, *major* would be "rojam"; *plastic*, "citsalp"; *peppertree*, "eertreppep.") O.'s iconic memory seemed to be considerably greater than would be expected. Shown a row of 8 letters for 100 milliseconds, she was able to report a mean of 7.44, while control subjects reported about 5. Coltheart (1972b) interprets these results to mean that O. can visually encode information about four times faster than normal.

Unfortunately, far too few cases of extraordinary memory have been reported to make more than superficial generalizations about it. Indeed, one observation we can make about the cases described here is that the memory characteristics of the individuals studied are all somewhat different. S. and V. P. seem to have used some type of mnemonic system whose structure was less rigid than others—in S.'s case, imagery, and in V. P.'s, semantic mediation. Aitken's extraordinary memory seems to incorporate some use of images and rhythm but also seems quite different from the others.

Experts and Expertise

We close this chapter with a discussion of **experts,** people who have unusual cognitive abilities, and of expertise, the study of exceptional abilities and skills. There are

---

[6]Some of the following material is from Hunter as reported in Baddeley, *The Psychology of Memory* (1976).

[7]Coltheart's pun for *pseudonym* and probably a takeoff on Freud's famous case study.

[8]An American entertainer called "Dr. Backwards" of many years ago had a nightclub act in which he pronounced and spelled words backward. There is also a current, although obscure, comic who reproduces sounds backward, much as you might hear if you reversed a tape recording.

two parts in this section: the first deals with several observations of experts and their development, while the second part deals with the cognitive interpretation of these observations.

Interest in expertise grew out of artificial intelligence (AI) several years ago and the need to find workable computer programs that could simulate the performance of skilled humans.[9] However, the cognitive study of expertise has recently developed a life of its own. These initial computer programs, sometimes called **expert systems,** were designed to mimic what a human expert knows. The problem is that much of the knowledge an expert knows is not formalized.[10] Nevertheless, these tricks of the trade can tell us a great deal about the way information is structured in the minds of experts and novices. They also have some practical application, as in medical diagnosis by "thinking computers" that simulate the diagnostic procedures used by skilled physicians. We touched on these topics in Chapter 4, when we examined the way grand master chess players perceive a chess display. These investigations of skilled chess players have provided AI scientists with just the type of information they need to build intelligent chess-playing programs—and the results have been spectacular, with computers now able to beat the very best players in the world. The study of expertise, however, is not confined to serving the needs of AI. It is an interesting and worthy topic for cognitive psychologists to study, for both its theoretical and pragmatic value. After all, if we choose to develop talented students to become experts, we need some idea of what the cognitive dimensions are that separate the expert from the novice.

After reviewing a large number of studies of experts, Glaser and Chi (1988) have identified some of the characteristics of experts, which follow:

1. Experts excel mainly in their own domains. Experts in mental calculations, for example, are not likely to be experts in medical diagnosis and vice versa.

2. Experts perceive large meaningful patterns in their domain. Chess masters, radiologists, and architects are able to "see" more meaningful patterns within their specialty than nonspecialists.

3. Experts are fast. Expert typists, chess players, computer programmers, mathematicians, and so on work within their specialty with greater speed than others.

4. Experts seem to utilize STM and LTM effectively. It seems that experts have superior memories, but perhaps they simply utilize their memories better.

5. Experts see and represent a problem in their domain at a deeper level than novices. When experts are asked to sort and analyze problems, they tend to deal with deep issues rather than superficial ones.

6. Experts spend a great deal of time analyzing a problem qualitatively. They tend to look at a problem from several angles before plunging into its solution.

7. Experts have self-monitoring skills. They seem to be aware of their errors and are able to make in-course corrections.

---

[9]Another area intensely studied, especially by the Russians and the "human potential" movement in America, is the concept of "peak experience," as might be attained by an athlete during competition.
[10]Things you don't learn in medical school (but should!): A pediatrician we knew kept his stethoscope in a warm compartment, thus diminishing the shock of placing a cold metal instrument on a fevered little body. Were his measurements more accurate? It's hard to tell without empirical validation, but we're sure his patients were more comfortable.

*O*ne thing that distinguishes us from other creatures is our ability to acquire complex skills. All distinctively human activities—such as mathematics, language, chess, computer programming, sculpture—are acquired skills. . . . People become expert at activities for which there was no possibility of anticipation in our evolutionary history, and the essence of the human genius is just this plasticity.

—*John R. Anderson*

The investigation of experts has focused on finding exceptionally skilled people and examining their talent. A sample of these studies includes:[11]

Actors (Intons-Peterson & Smyth, 1987; Noice, 1991; Noice & Noice, 1993)
Architects (Akin, 1982)
Artists (Solso, 2001)
Auditors (Bédard, 1989)
Baseball players (Chiesi, Spilich, & Voss, 1979)
Bridge players (Charness, 1979)
Chess players (Chase & Simon, 1973a, 1973b; among children see Chi, 1978)
Dancers (Solso et al., 1986; Solso, 1989; Solso & Dallob, 1995)
Those with exceptional memories (for example, S. [Luria, 1974], V. P. [Hunt & Love, 1972], and *JC* [Ericsson & Polson, 1988a&b])
"Geniuses" (for example, in music, chess, science: Hayes, 1986)
Go players (Reitman, 1976)
Mathematicians (for example, A. C. Aitken: Hunter, 1962)
Physicians (Clancey, 1988; Lesgold et al., 1988)
Musicians (Halpern, 1989)
Physics students (Chi, Glaser, & Rees, 1982)
Stockbrokers (Johnson, 1988)
Food servers (Ericsson & Polson, 1988a, 1988b)
Typists (Gentner, 1988)

H. O.: Case Study of an Artist— Solso; Miall and Tchalenko

One of the most complete studies of an expert portrait artist, Humphrey Ocean (H. O.), was recently conducted by Robert Solso at Stanford and Nevada and Chris Miall and John Tchalenko at Oxford. The research was based on the idea that experts in all fields, be it mathematics, music, athletics, or art, demonstrate neurocognitive attributes and performance actions that are markedly different from those of novices. With that premise in mind, a comprehensive study which involved a brain scan and eye-hand movements of an accomplished artist was done by Solso, Miall, and Tchalenko.

H. O. (Humphrey Ocean), a practicing artist for more than twenty years and one of Britain's most distinguished portrait painters, has exhibited at the National Portrait

[11]These well-conducted, interesting studies are recommended reading.

Gallery (London), Wolfson College (Cambridge), and many other galleries. Among his best-known paintings is a portrait of the former Beatle Paul McCartney. He has been the recipient of many awards and has presented numerous exhibitions. In addition to having years of formal training in art, H. O. has spent between three and five hours each day working as an artist or, over his lifetime, has accumulated about 25,000 hours practicing his craft. He was forty-seven years old at the time of the study, a male, and right-handed. The fact that H. O. specializes in portraits was important, as a section of the human cortex seems to be dedicated to facial processing. H. O. agreed to submitting himself to being studied extensively, first by means of MRI and then by means of eye-tracking and motor movements—all data collected on an accomplished artist for the first time.

H. O. and fMRI.   In a study done by Solso (2001), H. O. drew six portraits while lying flat on his back in the confined quarters of the MRI machine. A control participant also participated in this task to provide a contrast for the brain activity of H. O. and a novice. The results of the brain flow activity of H. O. and the novice are shown in Figure 8.4 (and also as a color plate in the inside cover).

As expected there was more activity in the participant's right hemisphere, the sight of geometric and form perception and processing. Notably, the right *posterior parietal* has been implicated in facial perception, and as shown in column A and to some extent B, both the expert and the novice showed considerable activity in that region. However, if you look closely at the differences between the expert and novice, you will see that the novice seems to exhibit *more* blood flow to the right posterior parietal area (column A).

FIGURE 8.4

fMRI scans made on H.O. and a nonartist control participant. Showing right parietal activity for both people (see column A). This area is involved in facial perception, but it appears that the nonartist is demanding more energy to process faces than H.O. In columns C and D, there is an increase in blood flow in the right frontal area of the artist, suggesting a higher-order abstraction of information.

(Solso, 2000, 2001)

H.O.

Novice

A   B   C   D

Why would the expert show *less* blood flow to the face-processing area? The answer may hold one of the key elements to our understanding of experts.

It would appear that experts, in this case an expert portrait painter (who has processed faces for thousands of hours) is so *efficient* in his perception and memory for faces that he shifts his attention to "deeper" forms of cognition that involve a more penetrating analysis of faces. This deeper level may engage a unique form of facial comprehension—what we refer to as **facial cognizance.**[12] Some clue to that deeper processing can be seen in column C where greater activity is shown in the expert's right frontal area than in the novice's. This area is thought to be involved in the more analytic, associative cortex, where abstract thinking takes place. Thus, it appears that our expert artist, H. O., is thinking a portrait as much as he is seeing it. The research, the first of its kind, also opens the door for more experiments on experts as they perform their specialized task. Where is the seat of thinking in the chess master, the astrophysicist, the volley ball champion, the cellist, the psychiatrist, the master carpenter? Answers to these questions, and many more, are within our grasp.

H. O. and Eye-Tracking and Motor Movements.   A second phase of the study of H. O. involved measuring his eye fixations and movements and his hand movements as he drew a portrait of a model. In this phase of the experimental analysis of an artist, Miall and Tchalenko (2001) outfitted (see Figure 8.5) H. O. with an eye camera, which measured eye movements and fixations; a scene camera, which identified the visual scene; and a motion-detector marker, which indicated the movements of the artist's hand. It was possible to do this and, at the same time, allow H. O. to move his head and hands reasonably unimpeded. Thus, it was possible to keep track, over time, of the eye fixations and hand movements of H. O. as he was in the process of drawing a portrait. It will come as no surprise that the final product produced by this celebrated artist was much finer than those of amateurs who also participated in the experiment, but the researchers turned up some additional things, which included the following:

- H. O.'s fixation on the model was different from his "ordinary" looking pattern, which suggested that he assumed a more intense way of viewing when he put on his "artist's hat."

- As the drawing progressed, H.O. shifted his fixations from the model to the canvas, which may mean that as the picture becomes more completely composed, the picture itself serves as a stimulus for further "touch up." In the beginning of the picture, the artist must spend more time looking at the model to record the details of his face.

- The artist's typical fixation time during sketches was 0.6 to 1.0 second, while novices' typical fixation period was about half that time (see Figure 8.6). These results suggest that the artist was locking his gaze onto a single position, studying it in some detail, while the novices fixated on 2 or more positions, sometimes spatially disparate. The latter pattern of looking is not typical of everyday eye movements and was similar to H. O.'s eye fixations when he did not have on his "artist's hat."

- H. O.'s ability to capture visual information and reproduce it seems to be based on a detail-to-detail process rather than a holistic approach. The artist would build a nose, for example, point by point and then an ear and so on.

[12]Such a notion is similar to the analysis of expert chess players mentioned in Chapter 4.

FIGURE 8.5

Technique used to measure H.O.'s eye movements, eye fixations, and hand movements as he drew a portrait.

(Miall & Tchalenko, 2001)

- Finally, when the results of H. O.'s hand movements were recorded, they provided a visual that was more astonishingly similar to the final sketch than had ever been imagined (see Figure 8.7). A fine-grained analysis of hand movements and final drawing shows precisely how the artist proceeded. For example, while the detail work on the subject's right eye absorbed much motor performance, the drawing of the edge of the nose required only one stroke.

For the first time, a very patient artist (and one who unselfishly gave of his time and effort) has been studied under the powerful lens of the fMRI, the eye-tracking device, and the motor movement recorder. Such research opens the way for other studies of experts with modern instrumentation. It is possible that the data collected on H. O. are idiosyncratic and other artists may use different strategies. Certainly, landscape and abstract artists may employ different patterns of eye movements and fixations and motor responses. It may be that different cortical regions would be activated and different eye patterns noted. And perhaps Leonardo da Vinci, Rembrandt, Picasso, and van Gogh would have exhibited different neurocognitive propensities.

The Structure of Knowledge and Expertise

Thus far we have concentrated on a description of expertise. Some of this research has been based on the selection of samples of subjects—some experts, some novices, and

Lengths of eye fixations for H.O. and novice artists. Showing that the expert spent nearly twice as much time fixating on the model during each glance as did the novices.

(Miall & Tchalenko, 2001)

The final result. Left: H.O.'s hand movements (not pencil strokes). Right: Finished portrait.

(Miall & Tchalenko, 2001)

some real tyros, as in the case of the three levels of chess plays described in Chapter 4— and on an evaluation of their knowledge and organization expertise. Two features of the expert (as contrasted with the novice) seem to reappear in the literature. The expert has domain-specific, organized knowledge and knows how to use it efficiently and wisely. For example, it is estimated that a chess master has about 50,000 patterns in memory; a good player, about 1,000; and a beginner, only a few. However, the storage of passive information on any given topic alone does not constitute expertise. Organization of knowledge is important too.

In one important study of the organization of information, Chi, Feltovich, and Glaser (1981) used a card-sorting task to see how experts and novices classified problems. Each card had a diagram and description of a physics problem. The novices sorted problems on the basis of literal, surface features, such as the "problem deals with blocks on an inclined plane"; the experts tended to sort the problems on the basis of the principles used to solve the problem, such as the conservation of energy. This trait (surface analysis versus analysis of principles) holds for a variety of different specialties including mathematics, computer programming, and genetics. The same results are found in the classification and analysis of real-world phenomena such as pictures of dinosaurs, types of cameras, and electronic circuit diagrams. Experts have greater knowledge than novices and tend to organize their knowledge in terms of general principles rather than in terms of surface features.

Theoretical Analysis of Expertise

Are people who have developed extraordinary cognitive abilities an embarrassment to traditional cognitive theory? Take the issue of STM. We learned in previous chapters that STM was restricted to a limited number of items temporarily stored, yet the multiplication of numbers, such as $4,652 \times 93$, seems to require the storage of more than seven items and processing that exceeds STM's capacity. Either the experts introduced in this chapter and others have a different memory system than most of us or they are using existing knowledge, stored in LTM, to expand their working memory capacity.

Chase and Ericsson (1982) have explained extraordinary memory operations in terms of three principles that account for skilled memory and how experts exploit their LTM to perform unusual tasks.

1. The **mnemonic encoding principle** (organization) asserts that experts encode information in terms of a large existing knowledge base. In memorizing a large number of digits, for example, one expert, a long-distance runner, used "good times" for a one-mile run, a marathon, a 3-kilometer run, and so on to remember various chunks of digits. Is his STM capacity larger? It is doubtful. More likely, he is using existing knowledge to chunk new information. (See Bower & Springston, 1970; and the FBI, PHD, IBM, TWA study in Chapter 6.)

2. The **retrieval structure principle** (access) states that experts use their knowledge of a subject (for example, typing, chess, baseball, selection of stocks) to develop abstract, highly specialized mechanisms for systematically encoding and retrieving meaningful patterns from LTM. This ability allows experts to anticipate the informational needs of a familiar task and to store new information in a format that will facilitate its retrieval.

3. The **speed-up principle** (speed) states that practice increases the speed with which experts recognize and encode patterns. In addition, experts are also able to retrieve information from LTM more quickly than novices. If LTM storage and retrieval are facilitated with extensive practice, then the extent to which new information can be processed is seemingly unlimited.

One ingredient almost overlooked in our discussion of experts is practice, the theme of a detailed analysis by Ericsson, Krampe, and Tesch-Römer (1993). It would seem that underlying the development of experts are hours and hours of dedicated practice. The adage "practice makes perfect," although too simplistic to qualify as a scientific principle, is nevertheless of great significance in the nurturing of skill and expertise.[13] Although simple, mindless, brute practice seems counterproductive but distributed, "intelligent" practice is positively related to expertise.

Spotlight on Cognitive Neuroscience

Chess Experts

Volke and colleagues (Volke, Dettmar, Richter, Rudolf, & Buhss, 2002) were interested in evaluating if chess experts differed in brain processing of information during chess play compared to nonexperts. They used EEG recording from 29 different positions on the head. They had 25 men (ages 18–34) of varying expertise solve various chess tasks; in other words, they had to figure out the next move to various chess piece patterns. Statistical analyses revealed that activity in the brain for experts was farther in the back and more in the right hemisphere than the nonexperts. In addition, the experts had higher values (more activity) when they were engaged in the tasks than when they were in the resting (nonplay) conditions as compared to the nonexperts. They interpreted this to mean that the experts' cortical areas were better equipped to integrate information.

Volke, H. J., Dettmar, P., Richter, P., Rudolf, M., and Buhss, U. (2002). On-coupling and off-coupling of neocortical areas in chess experts and novices as revealed by evoked EEG coherence measures and factor-based topological analysis—a pilot study. *Journal of Psychophysiology, 16*(1), 23–36.

SUMMARY

1 A mnemonic is a technique that facilitates storage, or encoding, and the recall of information in memory.

2 A variety of mnemonic techniques have been devised and involve such strategies as imagery and mediation (for example, method of loci and peg word system), phonemic and orthographic characteristics (for example, word and number recall), phonemic cues and imagery mediation (for example, name recall and key word method), and semantic organization.

3 The success of mnemonics in facilitating memory is attributed to their assistance in organizing information.

[13]Several years ago the late Bill Chase gave a talk on experts in which he promised to tell the audience what it would take to become a grand master chess player. His answer: "Practice." After the talk, the first author asked Chase how much practice. "Did I forget to say how much?" he asked quizzically. "Ten thousand hours."

4   Studies of individuals with exceptional memories indicate that their abilities involve a variety of mnemonic technique combinations: method of loci, imagery, and modified peg word system; method of loci, imagery, and synesthesia (for example, S.); and semantic mediation (for example, V. P.).

5   Studies of the expert portrait painter H. O. showed that the part of the brain involved in associative processing was more active than in a novice whereas the novice showed relatively greater activation of the facial-processing area. Also, studies of eye movements and fixations and hand actions of the artist show attributes unique to the expert.

6   Studies of experts show that they excel in their own domain, perceive meaningful patterns, are fast, utilize LTM and STM well, represent a problem at a deep level, analyze a problem qualitatively, and have self-monitoring skills.

7   Some ordinary people have been trained to perform exceptional mathematical computations and remember long strings of numbers. They do so by efficiently utilizing knowledge in LTM.

8   Skilled performance is achieved through organization of material, access to knowledge, speed of encoding patterns, and practice.

KEY WORDS

acronym	mnemonic encoding principle
acrostic	organizational schemes
expert systems	peg word system
experts	retrieval structure principle
facial cognizance	speed-up principle
key word method	synesthesia
method of loci	von Restorff effect
mnemonic	

RECOMMENDED READINGS

● Popular books on mnemonics that are quite good include Cermak, *Improving Your Memory;* Lorayne and Lucas, *The Memory Book;* Yates, *The Art of Memory;* Young and Gibson, *How to Develop an Exceptional Memory;* Hunter, *Memory: Facts and Fallacies;* and Luria, *The Mind of a Mnemonist.* S. B. Smith has written a book about mnemonics called *The Great Mental Calculators: The Psychology, Methods, and Lives of Calculating Prodigies, Past and Present.* Also recommended is *Practical Aspects of Memory* by Gruneberg, Morris, and Sykes; J. R. Anderson's *Cognitive Psychology* and *Cognitive Skills and Their Acquisition;* and *Memory: Interdisciplinary Approaches,* edited by Solomon et al. An edited collection by Chi, Glaser, and Farr, *The Nature of Expertise,* is especially recommended. Jean Bédard and Michelene Chi have an article called "Expertise" in *Current Directions in Psychological Science* (1993), which is a good summary of knowledge and Ericsson, Krampe, and Tesch-Römer have an article in *Psychological Review* (1993) that is one of the best articles on the topic of expert performance and highly recommended as is Ericsson and Charness's article "Expert Performance" in *American Psychologist.*

CHAPTER 9

The Representation of Knowledge

hmmm...?

● **Semantic Organization**
Declarative Knowledge and Procedural Knowledge

● **Associationist Approach**
Organizational Variables: Bower

● **Semantic Memory: Cognitive Models**
Set-Theoretical Model
Semantic Feature-Comparison Model
Network Models
Propositional Networks

● **Representation of Knowledge—Neurocognitive Considerations**
The Search for the Elusive Engram
What Amnesic Patients Tell Us When They Forget
Knowing *What* and Knowing *That*
A Taxonomy of Memory Structure

● **Memory: Consolidation**

● **Connectionism and the Representation of Knowledge**

1. Why has the study of words and language been a favorite topic of psychologists interested in knowledge and its representation?

2. What features identify the following: set-theoretical model; semantic feature-comparison model; network model; propositional networks; neurocognitive model?

3. What is a "linguistic hedge"? Give an example from your everyday life.

4. What are the main features of a "spreading activation theory," and how might it predict results from priming?

5. Distinguish between declarative knowledge and procedural knowledge.

6. What have studies of amnesic patients told us about the structure of memory?

7. How is knowledge represented in PDP models?

This chapter is about the representation of knowledge, which is to some the most important concept in cognitive psychology. Some even go so far as to contend that "Science is organized knowledge" (Spencer, 1864/1981). Before discussing knowledge—also a favorite theme of philosophers, theologians, and poets—it is necessary to understand how this often clouded term is used by psychologists. By *knowledge* we mean "the storage, integration, and organization of information in memory." Information, as we saw in previous chapters, is derived from the senses, but it is not the same as knowledge. Knowledge is organized information; it is part of a system or network of structured information; in a sense, knowledge is digested information. We focus on the representation of semantic information, since it continues to be the dominant theme in this area. In addition, several recent topics that promise to change the way we think about how knowledge is represented and stored in memory are introduced. These topics include neurocognition and connectionism.

Language and Knowledge.   One reason words and language have been studied extensively is that the degree of verbal development in human beings far exceeds that of other species; hence, that attribute serves as a phylogenetic demarcation. Some estimates (Baddeley, 1990) place the number of words a person knows the meaning of at 20,000 to 40,000 and recognition memory many times that number. Another reason, most important for cognitive psychology, is that semantic structure allows us to identify what types of things are stored in the mind and how a stored thing is related to other entities in the mind. Of course, for the cognitive psychologist, words per se are as uninteresting to study as are the bleeps on the oscilloscope. Words derive their vitality not from some intrinsic worth but from the concepts and relationships that they reflect and that make the facts and structures of knowledge come alive with meaning. By studying the ways words seem to be represented in memory, we can learn something about three components of the representation of knowledge: the content, structure, and process involved.

Semantic Organization

Semantic organization is normally conceptualized (in the **clustering model**) as a grouping or clustering of elements that are alike in meaning—for example, Reagan, Clinton, Bush, Nixon, Carter, Kennedy (presidents); Clinton, Carter, Kennedy (Democratic presidents); and Reagan, Nixon, Bush, and Bush (Republican presidents). More complex semantic models deal with the relationship of concepts to one another (for example, Clinton was a governor, Clinton is a Democrat, Clinton has a nose).

Declarative Knowledge and Procedural Knowledge

Thus far we have treated "knowledge" as if it pertained only to information about the world and its properties. Philosophers call this declarative knowledge, in the sense that we have knowledge of the validity of declarative sentences. When we ask you about the meaning of the following sentence: "I put my raincoat in the bathtub because it was wet," you know—that is, you have knowledge—that *it* in the sentence refers to *raincoat,* not *bathtub.* The reason you know what *it* refers to is that you have extensive knowledge about wet raincoats, bathtubs, human behavior, and perhaps certain people who don't want wet raincoats on their immaculate furniture. On the other hand, if you were in a burning building and preparing to make a mad dash for safety through savage flames, *it* might, understandably, refer to *bathtub.* However, traditional epistemology, the branch of philosophy that investigates the nature, origin, and limits of human knowledge, distinguishes between knowing that (*declarative* knowledge) and knowing how (*procedural* knowledge). It seems that some forms of humor are based on "catching" people who have been led to believe one thing and then are surprised by the true intention. We are reminded of a line from Groucho Marx, who said, "I shot an elephant in my pajamas. . . . What he was doing in my pajamas, I'll never know!" In the bathtub example, we know *that* it is used for bathing and, occasionally, for drying out raincoats, but we also know *how* to take a bath. That form of knowledge (procedural) is quite different from declarative knowledge. In any comprehensive theory of the representation of knowledge, then, it is important to include both forms of knowledge.

The Extent of Semantic Knowledge

*R*ead the following sentence: "Last summer Charlee saw Mona Lisa at the Louvre." How confident are you that

1. Mona and Charlee had coffee at a sidewalk cafe on the Left Bank?
2. Mona smiled at Charlee?
3. Charlee had dinner in Paris?
4. Charlee carried French currency?
5. Charlee's IQ is more than 100?
6. Charlee is a male?

From this brief, uncomplicated sentence, a profusion of information is inferred, and it is likely that your inferences (as exhibited in your answers to the preceding questions) are very similar to those of other people.

Today, listen carefully to a simple sentence expressed by another person, and analyze it in terms of the way the words are stored in memory. What model of semantic memory would fit your observations?

Associationist Approach

Organizational Variables: Bower

The study of organizational factors in memory was influenced by a series of papers by Gordon Bower and his associates (Bower, 1970a, 1970b; Lesgold & Bower, 1970; and Bower et al., 1969). In the context of modern cognitive theory, Bower used organizational factors in both traditional and contemporary ways. As in past research, Bower attempted to demonstrate the influence of structural organization on free recall. Bower believes that organization of semantic entities in memory has a much more powerful influence on memory and recall than has been previously demonstrated. In one experiment (Bower et

TABLE 9.1

Organization of Knowledge: "Jennifer played basketball with her friends." Knowledge may be represented in the mind in a number of different ways, including relationships, lexical representations, propositional relations, images, and neurological components.

Relationship	Lexical Representation	Propositional Relationship	Image	Neurological Components
Actions	Jennifer = woman played = action basketball = noun, sport	Played {action}(Jennifer {agent of action}, basketball {object})		Parts of the visual and associative cortex. Perhaps parts of the motor cortex.
Attributes	Jennifer is a woman, she is tall, she is athletic.	Jennifer is a woman. Jennifer is tall. Jennifer is athletic.		Parts of the the visual and associative cortex. Perhaps parts of the right parietal cortex for facial recognition.
Spatial properties	Jennifer holds the basketball.	Jennifer has a basketball in her hands.		Parts of the visual, associative, and motor and sensory cortex.
Class membership	Jennifer is part of the following categories: woman, basketball players, tall people.	Woman a type of which is Jennifer. Basketball players a type of which is Jennifer.		Parts of the associative cortex.

Gordon Bower. Made significant discoveries in memory, mnemonics, mathematical psychology, and language processing.

al., 1969), Bower's group looked at the potent influence on recall of organizational variables by constructing several conceptual hierarchies. An example of a conceptual hierarchy for the word *minerals* is shown in Figure 9.1.

These and many more experiments provided a bridge between an austere view of humankind's intellectual functions and one that envisioned a network of associations connected to other associations, and to other associations, and so on.

Semantic Memory: Cognitive Models

The views of semantic organization described in the previous section were dominated by associationism, the doctrine that there are functional relationships between psychological phenomena. In recent times, the approach to semantic memory has shifted from the associationistic viewpoint to a cognitive viewpoint, which assumes that detailed cognitive structures represent the way semantic information is organized in memory. In the following section, some of these cognitive models are reviewed.

FIGURE 9.1

A conceptual hierarchy of words for the word *minerals*.

Adapted from Bower et al. (1969).

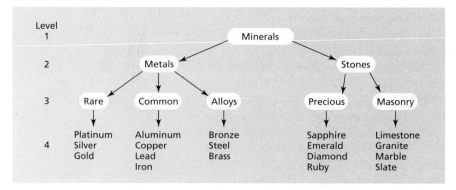

Cognition in Everyday Life
Mind Control

Metacognition: Controlling and Organizing Thoughts

*I*n my laboratory, I have been interested in a region of the prefrontal cortex involved in the supervision of thoughts and memories. This region is called the dorsolateral prefrontal cortex. In psychological terminology, I am interested in *metacognition,* which refers to the ability to monitor, control, and organize mental activity (i.e., cognition). In many instances, our cognitions operate with minimal supervisory control or intervention. For example, you may be able to tell me what you ate for your last meal, without much effort. However, If I asked you to tell me what you ate for lunch 3 days ago, the task now involves mentally monitoring the activities during the past several days and attempting to organize the information. Perhaps, you retrieved the fact that you had lunch with a particular colleague that day, which then cued you into what you had for lunch. In such cases of memory retrieval, it is apparent that a great deal of mental monitoring, controlling, and organizing is involved. It is also likely that your prefrontal cortex attempts to retrieve the information.

The ability to control and monitor thoughts and memories is severely disrupted in patients with lesions in the dorsolateral prefrontal cortex. The patients that I have studied had experienced a stroke that damaged this brain region in either the right or left cerebral hemisphere. These patients have severe impairment in supervisory control, but are not so impaired that they cannot function in daily living. In fact, these patients exhibit normal intellectual and social skills. Their deficit, however, is revealed on tests that require high metacognitive control. For example, in the task above in which you were asked to determine what you had for lunch 3 days ago, it was necessary to organize your thoughts around certain past events and episodes in your life. The construction of your autobiographical time line requires the organization of memories into a chronology with reference to places and time periods. The construction of such timeliness is severely impaired in patients with dorsolateral prefrontal lesions. As a result, they often have difficulty determining the temporal order of past events.

In addition to problems in placing thoughts within a temporal context, these patients also exhibit problems in placing thoughts within a semantic or knowledge-based context. For example, a particularly difficult task for these patients is to list examples from a particular category (e.g., name things you could buy at a supermarket or name as many occupations as you can). Consider the metacognitive demands of this task. After retrieving some obvious examples, it is necessary to monitor the examples that you have already reported, control or inhibit those examples from being reported again, and organize your thoughts to derive other novel examples. On this test, patients performed as if they had a disruption in supervisory control—that is, they often retrieved a few of the most obvious examples, but faltered and repeated the same examples over and over again. Thus, metacognitive control was needed to evaluate (monitor) thoughts and take control of task demands.

Arthur P. Shimamura. His innovative studies have combined cognitive research and neurosciences.

The Representation of Knowledge

The five models of representational knowledge may be summarized as follows:

Clustering Model	Set-Theoretical Model	Semantic Feature-Comparison Model	Network Model	Cognitive Neuroscience Model
Concepts tend to be organized in clusters. Free recall of "unrelated" words indicates that categorically similar words—for example, *camel, donkey, horse; John, Bob, Tom; cabbage, lettuce, spinach*—are recalled together. (Notably the work of Bousfield and Bower.)	Concepts are represented in memory as sets or collections of information. The set can include instances of a category (for example, the category *bird* can include the instances of robins, wrens, eagles, and so on) and also attributes, or properties, of a category (for example, *bird* is characterized by wings, feathers, flight, and so on). (Notably the work of Meyer.)	Concepts are represented in the memory as a set of semantic features. Two distinctive features are associated with an item's meaning: (1) defining features, which are essential components, and (2) characteristic features. (Notably the work of E. Smith and Rosch.)	Knowledge exists in memory as independent units connected in a network. The storage of words is tied to a complex network of relationships; for example, *bird* and *robin* are stored in terms of the relationship between them, that is, a robin is a bird. Specific models include (1) teachable language comprehender (TLC) by Collins and Quillian and (2) human associative memory (HAM) by Anderson and Bower and ACT (adaptive control of thought) by Anderson.	Knowledge is represented in the organization of neural networks. Studies of pathological types, such as amnesic patients, have been done (Squire). Knowledge is in the connections between units (Rumelhart and McClelland).

Set-Theoretical Model

In a **set-theoretical model** of memory, semantic concepts are represented by sets of elements, or collections of information. In this model, unlike the case with the clustering concepts, a word that encompasses a concept may be represented in LTM not only by the exemplars of the concept but also by its attributes. Thus, the concept *birds* may include the names of types of birds—canary, robin, hawk, wren, and so on—as well as the attributes of the concept—sings, flies, has feathers. In a set-theoretical model, memory consists of numerous sets of attributes—or, rather, of constellations of events, attributes, and associations represented by each lexical entity—and retrieval involves verification, that is, a search through two or more sets of information to find overlapping exemplars.

In its simplest form, verification of propositions (for example, "a robin is a bird") is done by comparing only the attributes of one set *(bird)* with the attributes of another set *(robin)*. The degree of overlap of attributes (see Figure 9.2) forms the basis for a decision about the validity of the proposition. As the distance between the sets becomes greater, the reaction time in making a decision should increase, a notion consistent with the research assumption inherent in some network models.

Two types of logical relationships between semantic categories are examined in this model: the universal affirmative (UA) and the particular affirmative (PA). In the UA

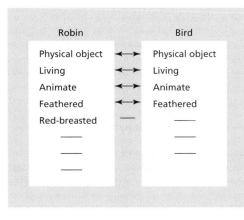

Robin | Bird

Robin		Bird
Physical object	←→	Physical object
Living	←→	Living
Animate	←→	Animate
Feathered	←→	Feathered
Red-breasted	—	—
——		——
——		——
——		

FIGURE 9.2

Attributes of two sets (*bird* and *robin*) with high degree of overlap.

case, all members of one category are subsumed in another category, which is represented as "All *S* are *P*" (for example, "All canaries are birds"); in the PA case, only a portion of the members of one category make up the member of another category—which is represented as "Some *S* are *P*" (for example, "Some animals are birds"). The validity of the statements is determined by the set relationships of the semantic categories. The set relationships, or commonality, are gauged by the number of exemplars the two propositions share. For example, the proposition "Some females are writers" could be represented as "Some *S* are *P*," where *S* represents "female" and *P* represents "writers":

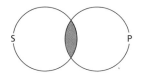

(You may recognize this figure as a Venn diagram, used to illustrate propositional statements.) The degree of validity of the logical assertion "All *S* are *P* (UA) and some *S* are *P*" is contingent on the amount of overlap (shaded area), or the exemplars they have in common.

To understand the model better, consider a typical experimental procedure. A research participant is seated before a screen in which a sentence of the type "All coins are pennies" or "Some coins are pennies" appears. The participant indicates whether the statement is true or false. Statements of the "Some coins are pennies" type (PA) require less reaction time than those of the "All coins are pennies" type (UA). (One might reason that verification of the sentence "Some coins are pennies" would require a search of our memory only until a single instance of a penny's being a coin is found. That is, we would not need to consider *all* pennies.)

Semantic Feature-Comparison Model

The **semantic feature-comparison model** of Smith, Shoben, and Rips (1974) and Rips, Shoben, and Smith (1973) grew out of an attempt to resolve inconsistent predictions of the other models. The feature-comparison model shares a set-theoretical structure with the set-theoretical model but differs in several important assumptions. The first assumption is that "the meaning of a word is not an unanalyzable unit but rather can be represented as a set of semantic features" (Smith, Shoben, & Rips, 1974, p. 216). A broad set of features related to any word varies along a continuum from very important to trivial. A robin, for example, may be described according to these features: has wings, is a biped, has a red breast, perches in trees, likes worms, is untamed, is a harbinger of spring. Some of these are critical defining features (wings, legs, red breast), while others are only characteristic features (perches in trees, likes to eat worms, is untamed, and is a harbinger of spring). Smith and his colleagues propose that the meaning of a lexical unit can be represented by features that are essential, or defining, aspects of the word (**defining features**) and other features that are only accidental, or characteristic, aspects (**characteristic features**).

Take the example "A bat is a bird." Although one defining feature of birds is that they have wings, strictly speaking a bat is not a bird. However, a bat does fly, has wings, and looks something like a bird. Loosely speaking, a bat is a bird. Such terms as *technically speaking, loosely speaking,* or *appear to be* are all examples of linguistic hedges, which we commonly use to expand conceptual representations. As is shown in Table 9.2, a "true statement" would be identified on the basis of both defining and characteristic features; a "technically speaking" statement, on the basis of defining but not characteristic features; and a "loosely speaking" statement, on the basis of characteristic but not defining features (Smith et al., 1974). Validation of a proposition (such as "A robin is a bird"), within the context of two types of features, is based more on the important (defining) features than on the less important (characteristic) features.

The first stage of validation of the statement involves a comparison of both the defining and characteristic features of the two lexical categories (*robin* and *bird*). If

TABLE 9.2

Examples of Linguistic Hedges

Hedge	Statement	Features Represented by Predicate Noun	
		Defining	*Characteristic*
(A true statement)	A robin is a bird.	+	+
	A sparrow is a bird.	+	+
	A parakeet is a bird.	+	+
Technically speaking	A chicken is a bird.	+	−
	A duck is a bird.	+	−
	A goose is a bird.	+	−
Loosely speaking	A bat is a bird.	−	+
	A butterfly is a bird.	−	+
	A moth is a bird.	−	+

there is considerable overlap, then the sentence is validated. If there is no (or only tangential) overlap, then the sentence is judged to be invalid. If there is some overlap, a second-level search is activated in which specific comparisons are made between the two lexical units on the basis of their shared defining features.

Rosch has done research based on the logic that some members are more typical of a category than others. For example, a knife and rifle are typical weapons, while a cannon and club are less so, and a fist and chain are even less weaponlike. Rosch thought that because objects vary in typicality of their categories, the tendency might be to form prototype categories. Consider the category of birds. Most people would agree that a robin is a good example of a bird but that an ostrich and chicken are not so good. When we use the word *bird,* we generally mean something close to the prototype bird or, in this case, something like a robin. In order to test the notion, Rosch (1977) presented participants with sentences that contained the names of categories (for example, *birds* and *fruit*). Some of the sentences might be:

> I saw a bird fly south.
> Birds eat worms.
> There is a bird in a tree.
> I heard a bird chirping on my windowsill.

Rosch then replaced the category name with a member of the category (for example, *bird* was replaced by *robin, eagle, ostrich,* and *chicken*) and asked research participants to rate how sensible the sentences were. In each sentence *robin* was taken to make good sense, and *eagle, ostrich,* and *chicken* less sense. It seems plausible that the typical member of the category is similar to the prototype of the category.

The feature-comparison model seems to account for some of the unresolved issues of the set-theoretical model, but at the same time it has its own shortcomings. Collins and Loftus (1975) have criticized using defining features as if they have absolute properties. No single feature is absolutely necessary to define something (for example, try to define, in legal terms, a "blue" movie by using a single critical feature). A canary is still a bird even if it is blue, or has no wings, or can't fly—that is, no single feature makes a canary. People seem to have difficulty in judging whether a feature is defining or characterizing.

In spite of the unresolved conflict between the set-theoretical model and the feature-comparison model, both models enhance our understanding of semantic memory in several important ways. First, they provide specific information about the multiple dimensions of semantic memory. Second, they use semantically categorized information as a starting point for an overall theory of semantic memory that embraces the vast network of memory functions. Third, because these models involve complex memory operations, they touch on the larger issue of the nature of our representation of knowledge, a principal part of which is the matter of the storage of semantic symbols and the laws that govern their recall.

Network Models

Collins and Quillian.   The best known of the early **network models,** proposed by Allen Collins and Ross Quillian, grew out of an earlier conceptualization of memory organization that was based on a computer program (Quillian, 1968, 1969). The model depicted each word in a configuration of other words in memory, the meaning of any word being represented in relationship to other words (see Figure 9.3). In this example, the information stored with *canary* is "a yellow bird that can sing." *Canary* is a member of the category, or superset, *bird* (as indicated by the arrow from *canary* to *bird*) and has the properties of "can sing" and "is yellow" (arrows from *canary* to these properties). At a higher node, the general properties about birds are nested together ("has wings," "can fly," and "has feathers"), information that need not be stored with each separate kind of bird. Correspondingly, information about fish (for example, "can swim") is stored in another part of the structure. The proposition "A canary can fly" is validated by retrieval of the information that (1) a canary is a member of the superset of birds and (2) a bird has the property "can fly." This system of semantic memory, by means of single rather than redundant entry of elements, minimized the space required for information storage. A model of this sort is considered to be an economical one in computer storage design.

An appealing feature of the Collins and Quillian model is that it makes explicit the means by which information is retrieved from semantic memory. To search our memory for validation of a specific proposition (for example, "A shark can move around"), we must first determine that a shark is a fish, a fish is an animal, and an animal has the property "can move around." This is a rather circuitous route. Another assumption of the model is that all this intrastructural travel takes time. Appropriately, Collins and Quillian tested the model by having participants judge the truth or falsity of a sentence. The principal dependent variable is the time it takes to validate this; the independent variable is the proximity of items in semantic memory.

FIGURE 9.3

Hypothetical memory structure for a three-level hierarchy.

Adapted from Collins and Quillian (1969). Reprinted by permission of Academic Press.

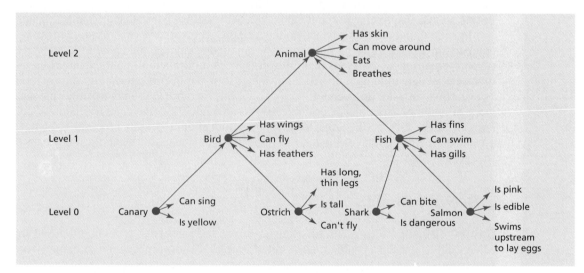

Collins and Quillian's model suggests that semantic memory consists of a vast network of concepts, which are composed of units and properties and are linked by a series of associationistic bonds. In spite of the fact that the model has been criticized on specific attributes, such as that the associationistic strength varies within the network (for example, the subordinate category of wrestling is less easily identified as a sport than baseball) or that some association violates the cognitive economy of the system, it argues for modification of the system, not abandonment of it. Furthermore, in its modifications, the model has provided an effective springboard to subsequent models.

As we have seen, the organization of knowledge in memory has been approached from several vantage points. One is to account for the rapidity with which we answer questions such as those in the list shown here:

Where is Moose Jaw?
Does a fish have eyes?
What is the square root of 50?
Which prime minister was known for the rose he frequently wore?
What is Beethoven's telephone number?
What is the name of Mick Jagger's daughter?
Why do some women wear high-heeled shoes?
Is an apple a porcupine?

How many of these could you answer, how fast were your answers, and what factors influenced your answers? If your access to knowledge is similar to that of others, it is likely that some of the answers were quickly located, others took more time, while others were impossible to know or ridiculous. (What is remarkable is that most of us can answer many of these questions, as well as many others, so quickly.) What model of knowledge representation might account for these differences?

Spreading Activation Theory: Collins and Loftus (1975).   One system, which has become increasingly important (especially among connectionists), is called a **spreading activation theory** of semantic processing, developed by Allan Collins and Elizabeth Loftus (1975); see also J. Anderson (1983b). The model, shown in Figure 9.4, is built on a complex association network in which specific memories are distributed in conceptual space with related concepts that are linked by associations. In Figure 9.4 the concept *red* is shown. The strength of association between concepts is indicated by the length of the connecting lines. Long lines, such as those between *Red* and *Sunrises*, indicate a somewhat remote associate; shorter lines, such as those between *Red* and *Fire*, indicate a closer association. At the heart of many knowledge representation models is the idea that concepts are associated as they are in the Collins and Loftus model. Also, with a bit of imagination, we could conceive a system of neural networks that embody some of the features of this model.

In the Collins and Loftus model, there is a spreading activation among concepts, which may account for the results of priming experiments (the effect of making a word or concept more accessible following the presentation of a related word, or *prime*). For example, if we show you the color *blue*, it is likely that you will be able to recognize the word *BLUE* faster than you would without the prime. Furthermore (see Solso & Short, 1979), if you see the color *blue*, recognition of its associate, for example, the word *sky*, is also enhanced. Presumably, even more distal associates would be activated; for example,

FIGURE 9.4

A spreading activation theory of semantic processing. The ellipses stand for concepts, and the lines are associations. The strength of the relationship between concepts is represented by the length of the line. The assumption that knowledge can be represented as a vastly complex network of associations is a pivotal part of most neural network models of cognition.

From Collins and Loftus (1975).

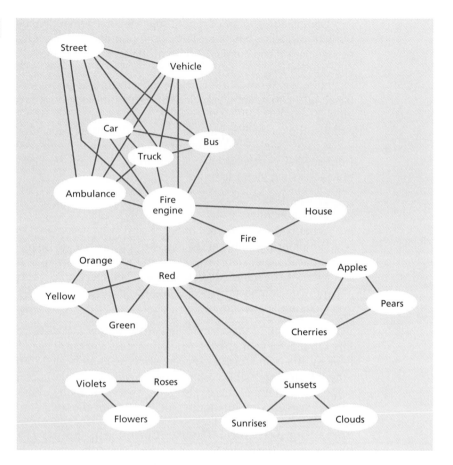

the spread of activation may extend to associates of associates. In the preceding example, the color *blue* primes the word *sky;* however, *sky* may prime the word *cloud,* even though the only relationship between the color *blue* and *cloud* is through *sky.*

(color blue)

In such an extended distributed activation network, an estimate of the capacity for the color *blue* to prime *cloud* (through *sky*) is conceptualized as a function of the algebraic summation of all competing associates. Some effort has been directed toward this end (see Kao, 1990, and Kao & Solso, 1988).

Neural Imaging Techniques and Pathway Activation.   In addition to the traditional behavioral study of activation pathways, recent studies have taken advantage of advanced neural imaging technology to show that physical, phonological, and semantic codes of words activate quite separate neural areas (Posner et al., 1988; and Posner & Rothbart, 1989). Posner and his colleagues distinguish between repetition priming, which comes from repeating the same item twice (such as showing a participant the color *green* as a prime for the same color), and semantic priming, which comes from presenting a semantically related prime and its target (such as showing the color *green* followed by the word *grass*). Behavioral studies have shown that both priming effects yield reliable data and seem to take place automatically, that is, without conscious control or awareness. Are these processes managed by different parts of the brain?

Using positron emission tomography (PET) scans (see Chapter 2 for details), Petersen and his colleagues (1988) evaluated regional blood flow in the cortex as a measure of neural activity associated with different semantic tasks. They found that visual word forms are developed in the ventral occipital lobe, while semantic tasks involve the left-lateralized part of the brain. The word form areas seem to be activated even when the research participant is passive, for example, when the participant is told simply to look at the word. The semantic area is activated only when the participant is asked to process the word actively, for example, when the participant is asked to name the word or to classify it silently. These studies suggest that visual word form is automatic and mostly independent of attention, whereas semantic priming—the type of thing done to rough out the gross properties of representational knowledge—seems to work very closely with attentional factors that are both behavioral and, as we now know because of recent discoveries of brain flow, cortical. In addition to verifying the neural basis of cognition, these studies tell us more about the possible relationship between attentional factors and the representation of knowledge.

Propositional Networks

Representation of semantic knowledge in propositional terms is both the oldest and the newest game in town. The notion that complex ideas can be expressed in terms of simple relationships was central to ancient Greek thought, was a fundamental premise of nineteenth-century associationism, and has experienced unusual popularity among contemporary cognitive theorists. A **proposition** is defined by Anderson (1985) as the "smallest unit of knowledge that can stand as a separate assertion." Propositions are the smallest units that are meaningful. Many theorists subscribe to the concept of propositional representation of knowledge (see Anderson & Bower, 1973; Anderson, 1976, 1983a; Kintsch, 1974; and Norman & Rumelhart, 1975), and yet each interprets the concept somewhat differently.

HAM and the Representation of Knowledge. Anderson and Bower (1973) saw the representation of knowledge within a network of semantic associations called HAM, or human associative memory, as a principal issue in cognitive psychology:

> The most fundamental problem confronting cognitive psychology today is how to represent theoretically the knowledge that a person has: what are the primitive symbols or concepts, how are they related, how are they to be concatenated and constructed into larger knowledge-structures, and how is this "information file" to be accessed, searched, and utilized in solving the mundane problems of daily living. (p. 151)

John R. Anderson. Developed influential theory of associative memory (HAM, ACT).

To find the nexus between the problems of daily living and the representation of knowledge, they use propositions, which are statements or assertions about the nature of the world. A proposition is an abstraction resembling a sentence, a kind of remote structure that ties together ideas or concepts. Propositions are mostly illustrated with semantic examples, but other forms of information, for example, visual representation, can also be depicted in memory by proposition.

The purpose of LTM is to record information about the world and provide accessibility to the stored information. In propositional representations, the principal structure for recording information is the subject-predicate construction. Simple declarative sentences illustrate the point:

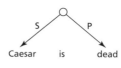

The sentence "Caesar is dead" is represented as having two components, the subject (*S*) and predicate (*P*), both sprouting from a "fact node," which represents the idea being asserted.

More involved sentences, such as "Diana married Charles," that contain a subject, a verb, an object (*O*), and a relation (*R*) to a modifying clause are represented in HAM the following way:

Many sentences involve context, for example (to borrow from Anderson and Bower), "During the night in the park the hippie touched the debutante."

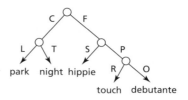

Here, time (*T*), location (*L*), and context (*C*) are added to a fact-idea (*F*) statement. Branches of the tree structures are joined by conceptual nodes, which are presumed to exist in memory before the encoding of a sentence. Nodes represent ideas and the linear association between ideas; therefore, understanding of a specific fact may be contingent upon the relationship to other conceptual facts.

The basic content is "wired" together in an associative web of more and more complex structures, but all can be broken down to sets of two or fewer items emanating from a single node.

ACT. HAM was the basic associationistic model developed by Anderson and Bower (1973). A comprehensive model of knowledge representation and information processing was developed by Anderson called **ACT (adaptive control of thought).** It has gone through several iterations (from ACT* to the current ACT-R). We begin our discussion of this influential theory by describing its general framework (see Figure 9.5). Stimuli are encoded into working memory from the outside world and spin around the system; and outputs, in the form of "performances," are manifest in some actions. It is what happens when information "spins around the system" that is interesting.

In this framework there are three types of memories: working, declarative, and productive. These are defined as follows:

Working memory, a kind of enterprising short-term memory, contains information the system can access currently, including information retrieved from long-term declarative

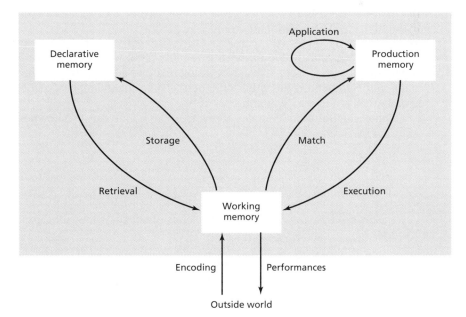

memory. Essentially, working memory refers to active memory, as shown in Figure 9.5. It is central to most of the processes involved.

Declarative memory is the knowledge we possess about the world (for example, knowing that good wine is produced in California and France or being able to recall some of the contents of your last cognitive psychology class). It seems that in Anderson's view, episodic and semantic information is included in declarative memory. Declarative representation of knowledge comes into the system in chunks, or cognitive units, comprising such things as propositions (such as, "Beth loves Boris"), strings (such as, "one, two, three"), or even spatial images ("A circle is above the square"). From these basic elements new information is stored in declarative memory by means of working memory. The retrieval of information from declarative memory into working memory resembles the calling up of information from the permanent memory of a computer—data stored on a hard disk in a computer are temporarily held for processing in a working memory.

Production memory is the final major component in the system. Production memory is very close to procedural knowledge, which refers to the knowledge required to do things, such as tie shoes, do mathematics, or order food in a restaurant. The difference between procedural and declarative knowledge is the difference between knowing how and knowing what. (The concepts of declarative and procedural representations are commonly used ideas in discussions of knowledge, and we expand on these concepts later in the chapter.)

At the foundation of ACT is the concept of **production systems,** or the notion that underlying human cognition is a set of conditional-action pairs called productions. At the simplest level, a production is a pair of IF-THEN clauses, where the IF part specifies some condition that must be met for the second part, the THEN part, to be executed. When a production is applied, its action is placed in working memory. A type of production rule follows:

> IF   *a* is the father of *b* and *b* is the father of *c,*
>
> THEN   *a* is the grandfather of *c.*

This production would function if we substitute names for letters. Thus, if the following propositions were active in working memory—"IF Andrew is the father of Ferdinand and Ferdinand is the father of Robert"—then the inference, "THEN Andrew is the grandfather of Robert," would be possible.

Other slightly more complex forms of productions can be shown in the following addition example:

> 67
> 39
> 72
> ——

In this example the application of a series of subgoals to work through the columns would be:

> IF   the goal is to do an addition problem,
>
> THEN   the subgoal is to iterate through the columns of the problem.

IF   the goal is to iterate through the columns of an addition problem and the rightmost column has not been processed,

THEN   the subgoal is to iterate through the rows of the rightmost column.

and so on. In a similar example, Anderson lists twelve steps involved in a production system. The complexity of steps increases as the problem increases, for example, in the division problem 56 ÷ 4 = _____.

Knowledge Representation in ACT.   Knowledge representation in ACT is central to the theory. Anderson proposes a tricode theory of knowledge representation. The three codes include:

- A *temporal string,* which encodes the order of a set of items, for example, "one, two, three, and so on."
- A *spatial image,* which encodes spatial representations, for example, the coding of a square or triangle.
- An *abstract proposition,* which encodes meaning or semantic information, for example, "Bill, John, hit."

The properties of these three representations and the processes involved are shown in Table 9.3.

The first of these codes, the temporal string, records the sequential structure of events. With it, we can recall the sequence of events in our daily experience. For example,

TABLE 9.3

The Properties of the Three Representations

Process	Temporal String	Spatial Image	Abstract Proposition
Encoding process	Preserves temporal sequence	Preserves configural information	Preserves semantic relationships
Storage process	All or none of phrase units	All or none of image units	All or none of propositions
Retrieval process	All or none of phrase units	All or none of image units	All or none of propositions
Match process			
A. Degree of match	End-anchored at the beginning	Functions of distance and configurations	Function of set overlap
B. Salient properties	Ordering of any two elements, next element	Distance, direction, and overlap	Degree of connectivity
Execution: Construction of new structures	Combination of objects into linear strings, insertion	Synthesis of existing images, rotation	Insertion of objects into relational slots, filling in of missing slots

From Anderson (1983a, p. 47). Reprinted with permission.

we can recall the sequence of events in a movie we recently saw or in a football game. We are less able to fix, in absolute time, the occurrence of these events.

Spatial representations have seemingly been problematic for Anderson.[1] However, in ACT, spatial representations are treated as one of the principal ways information is coded. Configural information, the type of information displayed in a figure, a form, or even a letter, is thought to be encoded in memory, but the size of the configuration is less important. Thus, we may encode the letter *Z* in its correct orientation but not its size. We may recognize *Z* half its size or twice its size, but if rotated 90 degrees, it might resemble an *N*.

The encoding of propositional representations is more abstract than the other types of codes, since it is independent of the sequence of the information. The proposition "Bill, John, hit" does not specify who is the hitter and who is the hittee. What is encoded is that John and Bill are involved in hitting.

The representation of propositional knowledge is similar to our earlier discussion of HAM. Consider how the following sentence would be represented by ACT: "The tall lawyer believed the men were from Mars" (see Figure 9.6). In this figure, propositional representations involve structure, category, and attribute information. A central node stands for the propositional structure, and the links that emanate from it point to various elements, such as the relationship ("believe"), the object ("man from Mars"), and the agent ("tall lawyer").

[1] In Anderson and Bower (1973) and Anderson (1976), the position taken was that the only type of knowledge representation is propositional.

FIGURE 9.6

ACT's proposition encoding of "The tall lawyer believed the men were from Mars."

From Anderson (1983a). Reprinted with permission.

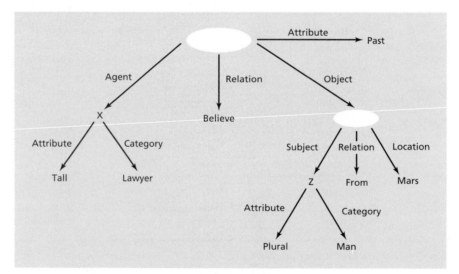

In addition to the general features of ACT described in this section, Anderson has applied the system to a wide range of other conditions and cognitive tasks, including control of cognition, memory for facts, language acquisition, and spread of activation. These topics, all important, are beyond the space we can give to them here. (There is, however, no prohibition against reading the original sources.)

Representation of Knowledge—Neurocognitive Considerations

It is self-evident to say that people learn from experience. What is less obvious is that those experiences modify the nervous system and that the ways in which it is modified form the neurological basis for the representation of knowledge. One approach to the neurological basis of memory is through the study of the molecular and cellular biology of individual neurons and their synapses (Squire, 1986). Although such efforts have told us a great deal about the physiology of neurons, they beg the larger question of how these microscopic entities are related to knowledge representation. Recent cognitive neuroscience studies have tried to integrate findings in neurophysiology with theories in cognitive psychology. One direction these studies have taken is to search for the location of memory.

The Search for the Elusive Engram

The controversy surrounding the locus of memory in the brain is presented in Chapter 2. A traditionally important issue is whether memory and knowledge are distributed or localized in the cortex. One element central to this discussion is the search for the elusive *engram* (literally, "a trace," or, in the present context, a collection of neural charges that represents memory). Some areas of the brain are associated with specific functions (such as vision), yet functions such as memory seem to engage various locations, each of which may function simultaneously, or in parallel, with other locations. Larry Squire (1986) suggested that information storage may be more localized than thought earlier and that memory may be stored as changes in the same neural systems that participate in perception. This hypothesis may seem contrary to the findings of Lashley (see Chapter 2), who concluded that memory is widely distributed throughout the brain. However, Squire argues that Lashley's views are consistent with his own if one considers complex learning (for example, a rat's learning to traverse a maze) as the processing of many types of information (such as visual, spatial, and olfactory) in which each type is separately processed and localized. "Thus, memory is localized in the sense that peculiar brain systems represent specific aspects of each event, and it is distributed in the sense that many neural systems participate in representing a whole event" (Squire, 1986, p. 1613).

What Amnesic Patients Tell Us When They Forget

A patient identified as C.W., who was a music producer for the BBC, was stricken by a rare form of encephalitis, a condition in which the brain becomes inflamed. In his case, the result was a memory deficit in which his memory span lasted only a few seconds.

His memory for common events, such as what he just ate for lunch, a song he had just sung, and so on vanished soon after the event. In the words of his wife, he "is trapped forever in the groove of a scratched record." Yet, remarkably, he can remember the words to songs, he can conduct a choir, and his musical ability seems unaffected. It appears that some parts of the brain store facts (names, images, and events) and others store procedures (such as how to do things).

One way theories of representational knowledge can be investigated neurocognitively is through the study of pathological types. Some studies done with amnesic patients (for example, Baddeley & Warrington, 1970; Milner, 1972; and Squire, 1986) show strong evidence for short-term and long-term memory.

Two types of amnesia have been identified: **retrograde amnesia,** which is the inability to recall information acquired prior to the onset of the disorder, and **anterograde amnesia,** which is the loss of information presented after the onset of the memory disorder. Retrograde amnesia is a disorder of the retrieval of information, while anterograde amnesia is a disorder of encoding information. Both types of amnesia can be temporary or permanent.

Temporary retrograde amnesia may develop when a person experiences head trauma, such as a football player who has "had his bell rung." (See Chapter 7 for a discussion of the football player mentioned in Lynch and Yarnell's study.) Sometimes a "ding" on the head produces retrograde amnesia, in which a few seconds or minutes of the person's life are lost to memory. Another form of temporary retrograde amnesia occurs when a patient undergoes **electroconvulsive** (shock) **therapy (ECT)** or suffers a serious head trauma, such as might occur in a severe automobile accident. In these cases, memories acquired over the previous weeks or even months may become unavailable.

Amnesia can also be permanent. Some causes of permanent amnesia include prolonged use of ECT, severe traumas, stroke, or other cerebral vascular ruptures, such as encephalitis and other diseases. Permanent amnesia can also be brought on by massive consumption of alcohol. One disorder brought about by severe alcoholism is called **Korsakoff's syndrome.** It results in bilateral damage to the diencephalon located at the back of the brain. Korsakoff patients may be confused and have difficulty moving and seeing. Many times this is brought on by a final alcoholic bash in which patients "drink themselves blind." If the binge does not end in death, recovery is possible, except for a permanent form of amnesia in which patients have difficulty learning anything new. Both permanent and temporary forms of amnesia have been studied for clues to the neurological basis of cognition.

Cognitive Tasks and Amnesia.   Temporary retrograde amnesic patients (for example, those patients whose memory is temporarily impaired as a result of ECT) can keep a short list of numbers in memory for several minutes with rehearsal but are unable to recall the information after an intervening period of distraction. It seems that temporal information is stored within a brain area unaffected by this form of amnesia, but the capacity for long-term memory may require the operation of other areas that *are* impaired by the disorder.

Another avenue of research has been to use amnesic patients to establish a neurological basis for short-term and long-term memory. In several important early studies (for example, Milner, Corkin, & Teuber, 1968), it was shown that a profoundly amnesic patient, known in the literature as H. M., exhibited considerable learning and retention of perceptual-motor skills. Thus, some complex cognitive ability remained intact in

H. M., while other tasks, which required the recall of episodic events, were seriously impaired. (See Chapter 6.)

These seminal studies led other researchers to consider further cognitive tasks to study with amnesic patients, such as memory operations. In one study Cohen and Squire (1980) found that amnesic patients could acquire the skill involved in reading words from a mirror-reversed display, but when questioned later about the task, they could neither remember the words nor the skill they had practiced. (See also the case of K. C. in Chapter 7.)

Similarly, amnesic patients can learn the best solution to a puzzle, such as the well-known "Tower of Hanoi."[2] (See Cohen & Corkin, 1981.) To solve this puzzle, considerable parts of the cognitive system must be intact and operable. Specifically, it requires that both skill learning and the ability to learn procedures be intact; these comprise one type of mental representation. Amnesic patients, on the other hand, are deficient in their memory for facts and episodes, another type of mental representation. Since the root cause of amnesia lies in neurological disorders, we can conclude that underlying neurological structures support two types of cognitive tasks—those involving skill learning and those involving episodic recall.

Could it be that knowledge is represented in the brain in terms of knowing how (as in skill learning) and knowing what (as in episodic recall)? (More is reported on this in the following section on procedural and declarative knowledge.)

Finally, some studies have investigated the priming effect, or the effect of a cue on subsequent performance, with amnesic patients. In one investigation by Jacoby and Witherspoon (1982), several Korsakoff patients were asked questions such as, "What is an example of a reed instrument?" Later, the participants were asked to spell *read* and *reed*. Normally, we would expect the spelling to be *read*, a much higher-frequency word, but in this experiment both the amnesic and control participants spelled the word *reed*, because of the priming of that word in the question. However, when given a recognition test of previously heard words, the Korsakoff patients were unable to recognize the words they had heard. In contrast, the control participants were able to recognize the words. These results suggest that the process of activation, as exhibited in the priming effect, is unaffected by amnesia, while the ability to recognize a previously heard word is affected. This latter ability may require additional processing of information and cerebral functions. Furthermore, these findings support the notion that an important distinction in the way knowledge is represented may be in terms of the activation of neural pathways and the access of episodic memory.

Knowing *What* and Knowing *That*

Our pursuit of the neurocognitive basis of representational knowledge continues with studies of **declarative** and **procedural** (or nondeclarative) **knowledge.** As previously mentioned, declarative knowledge is explicit and includes facts and episodes, while procedural knowledge is implicit and is accessible through performance. We may know that a bicycle has two wheels, a handlebar, and a frame (declarative knowledge), but we can only demonstrate that we know how to ride it (procedural knowledge) by actually

[2]The "Tower of Hanoi" puzzle contains several rings of descending size stacked on top of each other on a peg. There are also two empty pegs. The task is to move the entire series of rings to one of the other pegs, moving only one ring at a time and always placing a smaller ring on a larger one.

doing so. One way to test for declarative and procedural knowledge is through priming and recognition experiments.

Priming, you may recall, is a test in which a research participant is given a cue, usually a word, that is in some way related to the target, usually an associated word. The prime facilitates the recognition of the target. For example, if we give you the word *TABLE* (the prime), your recognition of the word *CHAIR* (the target) is facilitated. Priming is thought to tap procedural knowledge, because the response is implicit and there is a more or less automatic activation of existing pathways. Therefore, if amnesic patients demonstrate positive performance on a priming task, we could conclude that their procedural knowledge would remain intact; if they performed poorly on a word recall task, we could conclude that their declarative knowledge was impaired. Several experiments have confirmed this hypothesis (for example, Shimamura & Squire, 1984.)

A Taxonomy of Memory Structure

Studies have indicated that declarative and nondeclarative knowledge can be isolated by investigating pathological types. However, the question still remains of whether these types of knowledge are only a part of a larger system of the representation of knowledge in memory. If they are, what is the larger system? One approach to this problem is to try to fit the existing information about representational knowledge into a taxonomy, or an organized scheme. An intriguing taxonomy has been suggested by Squire (1986) and Squire et al. (1990) in which declarative memory and nondeclarative memory are thought to be the two major types of memory (see Figure 9.7).

According to Squire, the experimental evidence supports the idea that the brain is organized around fundamentally different information storage systems, as illustrated in Figure 9.7. Declarative knowledge comprises episodic and semantic memories, and nondeclarative knowledge includes skills, priming, dispositions, and other nonassociative types of representations.

One feature of this system is that it accepts both conscious and unconscious memory as serious topics for research. In addition, information can activate both types of knowledge. For example, take the perception of the word *CHAIR* after seeing the word *TABLE*. From previous priming studies, we know that the perception of *CHAIR* is enhanced if preceded by *TABLE*, and that the effect is largely unconscious and procedural. Priming is also likely to engage declarative knowledge in normal participants. The engagement of declar-

Larry Squire. Cognitive neuroscience studies have helped establish important links between cognitive psychology and neuroscience.

FIGURE 9.7

A tentative taxonomy for the representation of types of memory.
Declarative memory contains episodic and semantic memory, while
nondeclarative memory includes skills, priming, dispositions, and other
types of memories.

From Squire et al. (1990). Reprinted with permission. Copyright © 1990 AAAS.

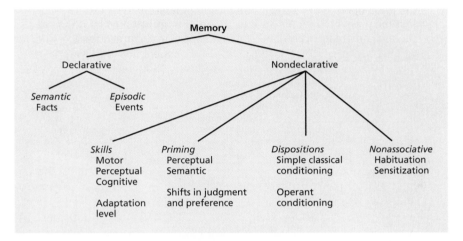

ative knowledge might be to store the word *TABLE* in episodic memory and have it become part of one's conscious experience. Supporting evidence for the model draws on a
wide latitude of studies, including animal studies, the examination of histological sections, human cognitive experiments, and studies of the behavior of amnesic patients.

The importance of the previously mentioned experiments and theories seems to lie
in two domains. First, they address the issue of the structure of knowledge. As such,
they integrate various types of memories in an organized scheme, which accounts for
declarative and nondeclarative knowledge and for conscious and unconscious processes. Second, they provide some of the most eloquent examples of the unification of
brain science and cognitive psychology, especially as related to the central theme of the
organization of knowledge.

Memory: Consolidation

It has been a century since the German researchers Muller and Pilzecker hypothesized a
perseveration-consolidation theory of memory in which they found that memory for
new material was disrupted by the learning of new information shortly after the original
learning. The processes underlying new memories were considered to be fragile and not
entirely consolidated. It was as if memories, like photographic images, need a period of
time to become "fixed." Otherwise, they are not completely developed and fade away.
James McGaugh of the University of California at Irvine, who has been working on the
topic of memory consolidation for several decades, has made important discoveries.

Memory consolidation phases. As shown, the consolidation of new memories into long-term memories is related to time (see *y* axis). Scientific evidence shows that specific drugs can selectively block short-term memory, which lasts from seconds to hours, and other drugs can block long-term memory, which lasts from hours to months. This suggests that the two memory processes are independent and operate in parallel. Long-lasting memories that last a lifetime probably involve an interaction of brain systems in which there is a reorganization and stabilizing of neural connections.

From J. L. McGaugh, *Science, 287,* 2000.

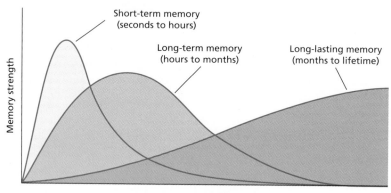

It appears that memory consolidation of short-term memory into long-term memory is not sequentially linked as proposed by the traditional information-processing model (see Figure 9.8).

Studies with nonhuman animals as well as humans (see McGaugh, 2000) show that adrenergic systems and amygdala activation (the part of the brain usually associated with emotional reactions) influence memory consolidation. In one experiment two groups of participants were given a series of photographs and an emotionally arousing story. One group was given an emotion-inhibiting drug while the other was administered a placebo. In the first case recall of the emotionally laden pictures was not enhanced, because of the reduced emotionality of the picture. But in the placebo group recall of the emotionally laden photographs was enhanced. Thus, it appears that in these studies consolidation of short-term memories is altered by emotion-blocking drugs, which have little effect on long-term memories.

Connectionism and the Representation of Knowledge

Connectionism could conceivably be said to date from the ideas of William James. In his treatise called *Psychology: The Briefer Course* (1892), James described the process as follows:

The manner in which trains of imagery and consideration follow each other through our thinking, the restless flight of one idea before the next, the transitions our minds make between things wide as the poles asunder, transitions which at first sight startle us by their abruptness, but which, when scrutinized closely, often reveal intermediating links of perfect naturalness and propriety—all this magical, imponderable streaming has from time immemorial excited the admiration of all whose attention happened to be caught by its omnipresent mystery. [Therefore we should ascertain] between the thoughts which thus appear to sprout one out of the other, principles of connection. . . .

James also anticipated the rule on reinforced synapses that psychologist Donald Hebb would develop fifty years later. In *Psychology: The Briefer Course* James postulated, "Let us then assume as the basis of all our subsequent reasoning this law: When two elementary brain-processes have been active together or in immediate succession, one of them, on recurring, tends to propagate its excitement into the other."

At the same time, James described a mechanism for association that is uncannily like neural networks. Thought *A*, of a dinner party, is composed of details *a, b, c, d,* and *e.* Thought *B*, of walking home afterward, is similarly composed of details *l, m, n, o,* and *p.* All details connect all other details, "discharging into each other," according to James. As a result, then, "the thought of *A* must awaken that of *B*, because *a, b, c, d,* and *e* will each and all discharge into *l* . . . "; and *l* "vibrates in unison" with *m, n, o,* and *p* (from Finkbeiner, 1988).

Connectionism can be defined as a theory of the mind that posits a large set of simple units connected in a parallel distributed network (PDP). Mental operations, such as memory, perception, thinking, and so on, are considered to be distributed throughout a highly complex neural network, which operates in a parallel manner. The theory is based on the assumption that units excite or inhibit each other throughout the system at the same time or in parallel. This is in contrast with serial processing theories, which suggest that processing between units is done only in sequence. The number of pairs of units involved, even in a simple task such as typing a word, may be considerable. It is within the connections between pairs of units that knowledge is distributed throughout the system. How can knowledge, the most complicated of topics thus far encountered, be expressed in terms of simple excitatory and inhibitory connections between units? In this section we try to answer that question.

In many of the previous models of information representation, knowledge was stored as a static copy of a pattern. The position is similar to the concept of isomorphism discussed in Chapter 1. An object, image, or thought is stored in memory with its attributes and connections with other objects, images, and thoughts. When recognition of an item is called for (for example, "Do you know Clyde the Elephant?"), a match is made between the elements of the question and the information stored in memory. Also, the associates of the elements (for example, that elephants are gray), are activated, although the level of activation appears to be far less than for the central items *Clyde* and *elephant.* Still, the way knowledge is represented is more or less static, and the means used to access knowledge is through matching stored information with a cue.

Knowledge representation in connectionistic models of cognition is quite different from models that store objects, images, and so forth. First, in connectionistic models the patterns themselves are not stored; what is stored is the connection strength between units, which allows these patterns to be recreated.

The difference between PDP models and conventional models [of knowledge represen-tation] has enormous implications, both for processing and for learning. . . .The repre-sentation of knowledge is set up in such a way that the knowledge necessarily influences the course of processing. Using knowledge in processing is no longer a mat-ter of finding the relevant information in memory and bringing it to bear; it is part and parcel of the processing itself. (McClelland, Rumelhart, & Hinton, 1986, p. 32)

Second, connectionistic models approach learning differently. In traditional repre-sentational models, the goal of learning is the formation of explicit rules that allow for retrieval of information and generalization of cues. We know that Clyde is an elephant and that, like most other elephants, he is gray and cannot easily fit into your Volkswa-gen. We know these things because we have learned rules. PDP models only assume that learning consists of the acquisition of connection strengths that allow a network of simple units to act as if they knew the rules. Rules are not learned; connections between simple units are. Even though our behavior seems to be rule governed, it is because of the underlying network of connections in the brain that we make these inferences.

Third, it is important to restate that the PDP model is neurally inspired; however, it is not the same as identifying specific neural pathways. Such a model would be imprac-tical, since the model would be as complex as the brain itself. *Neurally inspired* simply means that the metaphor on which the model is based is the brain rather than the com-puter, on which some previous models have been based (see especially Collins and Quillian). The fact that PDP models are neurally inspired bears directly on the represen-tation of knowledge. All knowledge is located in the connections, as might be the case with neural connections. In the computer metaphor, knowledge is thought to be stored in certain units. When we think of knowledge in the conventional sense, we are likely to think of it as being collected and stored someplace. The difference between these per-spectives is considerable. For example, the PDP model suggests that "all knowledge is *implicit* in the structure of the device that carries out the task rather than *explicit* in the states of units themselves" (Rumelhart, Hinton, & McClelland, 1986, p. 75).

To illustrate the notion that all knowledge is in the connections, consider Figure 9.9. In this figure, input units are on the bottom and output units are on the right-hand side. Active units are filled in. Knowledge is stored in the strengths of connections between units, theoretically similar to the way neural networks represent information. The strength of the relations between units is simplified here. In the original system, detailed mathematical statements, which specify the strength of the connections, are given.

Spotlight on Cognitive Neuroscience

Representation of Knowledge

Understanding how knowledge is represented in the brain and how brain activity man-ifests itself in psychological experience is one of the primary goals of cognitive neuro-science. David Boles points out that it is essential to strike a balance between "lumping" and "splitting" if we are to truly develop a science of brain–behavior relationships. "Lumping" occurs when one assumes that a "selected task involves the mental process one thinks it does" or, in other words, when one believes that overtly similar tasks are actually all part of the same sort of processing when, in fact, they may be very different

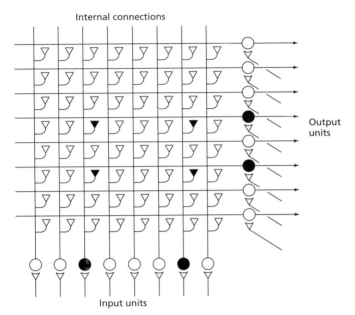

Internal connections

Output units

Input units

FIGURE 9.9

A connectionist association matrix.
Input units are on the bottom, and
output units are along the right side.
The filled circles are active units, and
the filled triangles indicate which
connections would change so that the
input would evoke the output.
Learning of associative relationships
involves changing the strengths
between the input units and the output
units.

Modified from McClelland as suggested by
Schneider (1987). Reprinted with permission.

at the processing level. "Splitting," on the other hand, occurs when variations in brain function for similar tasks are assumed to be indications that they are in fact very different tasks when they may not be at all. An overreliance on lumping and splitting produces "empirical clutter" such that true findings are difficult to discern. David Boles suggests that overlumping can be reduced by using statistical methodologies that identify processes that are in common with various cognitive tasks; oversplitting can be avoided by correlating brain activation with task performance and then focusing on only those areas that indicate a strong relationship. Combining the perspectives of lumping and splitting can ultimately lead to a balance between overgeneralization of results and the temptation to pinpoint brain activity as directly related to task performance in such a way as to advance our understanding of function and the brain.

Boles, D. B. (2000). The "lumping" and "splitting" of function and brain. *Brain and Cognition*, 42, 23–25.

SUMMARY

1   Semantic organization refers to the way concepts are organized and structured in memory.

2   Two principal viewpoints have dominated studies of semantic organization and differ in their respective focuses. The associationist approach has focused on functional relationships between concepts, and the cognitive approach has focused on mental structures that describe the relationship between meaning and memory.

3   Associationist studies examine semantic organization by studying the form of free recall (for example, what words are recalled together), assuming such protocols

provide information about the nature of the organization of concepts and the underlying cognitive structure.

4   Cognitive models organize data from semantic experiments into comprehensive theories of memory and include set-theoretical models, the feature-comparison model, network models, and propositional networks.

5   Set-theoretical models propose that concepts are organized by numerous sets of information, which include categories and attributes.

6   The semantic feature-comparison model assumes a set-theoretical structure but distinguishes attributes either as defining, essential features or as characteristic, descriptive features. Concept validation is presumably based more on defining features.

7   Network models assume that concepts are stored in memory as independent units interrelated by specific and meaningful connections (for example, "A robin is a bird"). Additional assumptions concern memory retrieval by verification of both target and related concepts and the idea that intrastructural movement during retrieval requires time.

8   The spreading activation theory of semantic processing (Collins and Loftus) is based on a complex network in which simple associations (for example, *red* and *fire*) are linked together in conceptual space. The theory is instrumental in accounting for priming effects and the facilitating effects of recovering a word or concept from memory when preceded by a related word.

9   Propositional network models propose that memory is organized by a complex associative network of propositional constructions that are the smallest units of meaningful information (for example, "New York is large").

10 ACT (adaptive control of thought) by Anderson is an associationistic theory of memory in which three types of memories are posited: working memory, declarative representation, and production memory.

11 Recent studies in cognitive neuroscience have tried to integrate findings in neurophysiology with theories in cognitive psychology. For example, studies of amnesic patients have proved quite profitable in the never-ending search for answers about how the brain works.

12 Two types of knowledge have been identified: declarative knowledge and procedural knowledge. Declarative knowledge is explicit and includes facts; procedural knowledge is implicit and may be sampled through performance. A taxonomy of memory structure in which declarative memory and nondeclarative memory are integral parts has been developed by Squire.

13 Knowledge is represented in PDP models as connections between units, which is theoretically similar to the way neural networks represent information.

KEY WORDS

ACT (adaptive control of thought)	characteristic features
anterograde amnesia	clustering model

declarative knowledge

defining features

electroconvulsive therapy (ECT)

Korsakoff's syndrome

network model

procedural (nondeclarative) knowledge

production memory

production system

proposition

retrograde amnesia

semantic feature-comparison model

set-theoretical model

spreading activation theory

RECOMMENDED READINGS

● In addition to those works on memory suggested in previous chapters, there are several good references on semantic memory. The early material on clustering in an associationistic framework is in Kausler, *Psychology of Verbal Learning and Memory*—probably the most authoritative historical review available. For those interested in a psycholinguistic point of view, Edward Smith has a broad, comprehensive review of semantic memory in "Theories of Semantic Memory," which is found in *Handbook of Learning and Cognitive Processes,* edited by Estes. A scholarly approach to semantic memory can be found in Kintsch, *The Representation of Meaning in Memory,* and Miller and Johnson-Laird, *Language and Perception.* Collins and Loftus, "A Spreading Activation Theory of Semantic Processing," in *Psychological Review* gives a current view of their theory.

● Network theories are thoroughly discussed in Anderson and Bower, *Human Associative Memory,* a remarkably ambitious book. In *Language, Memory, and Thought,* Anderson gives a detailed account of a revision of HAM called ACT. Also see *The Architecture of Cognition* by Anderson. *Neuroscience and Connectionist Theory,* edited by Gluck and Rumelhart, although technical in places, is highly recommended. Barsalou's book, *Cognitive Psychology,* stresses semantic memory and is especially recommended for those looking for detailed technical and theoretical discussion of these topics.

Mental Imagery

- **Historical Overview**
- **Imagery and Cognitive Psychology**
  Dual-Coding Hypothesis
  Conceptual-Propositional Hypothesis
  Functional-Equivalency Hypothesis
- **Cognitive Neuroscience Evidence**
- **Cognitive Maps**
  Mental Maps: Where Am I?
- **Synesthesia: The Sound of Colors**

hmmm...?

1. Define mental imagery. Does your definition include all sensory modes?

2. How were the early study of mental imagery and the testing of mental attributes related?

3. What are the main features of (a) the dual-coding hypothesis, (b) the conceptual-propositional hypothesis, and (c) the functional-equivalency hypothesis?

4. If you imagine an elephant standing next to a mouse, which question would you be able to answer faster: Does the elephant have a tail? Does the mouse have a tail? Why?

5. How have neurocognitive experiments made the topic of mental imagery more empirical?

6 How does a person's bias influence the type of mental map he or she might form?

7. Suppose when you hear a high-pitched tone, it reminds you of an electrical spark. What is the word for that experience?

As with some other concepts in cognitive psychology, imagery is what everyone knows it to be (we have all experienced it) and yet its specific cognitive properties are only approximately known. What is a mental image, and what are its properties? How do you "look at" specific features of an image? What is it that you are "seeing" when you look at a mental image? Is the image "real," or is it conjured up from information that is stored in a different modality? Can you differentiate between an imaginary image and one that you have actually experienced? If so, what is different about them? These are some questions that have bemused philosophers for centuries and currently intrigue cognitive psychologists. Recent research has produced some exciting new findings and theories.

Mental imagery is defined in this chapter as a mental representation of a nonpresent object or event. This general definition allows for inclusion of visual images as well as images formed through other senses. Although the definition is broad, the discussion here is restricted to visual imagery, the area in which almost all the contemporary research has been done.

Imagery research is diverse, spanning topics as far-reaching as theoretical issues, neurocognitive findings, sports psychology, psychotherapy, cartography and cognitive maps, and even synesthesia. These disparate topics have been organized in this chapter in three major sections. First, a discussion of the history of imagery and current theories is developed. Then recent cognitive neuroscience evidence for the relationship between sensory processing and imagined processing is presented. The chapter ends with a review of the related areas of cognitive maps and synesthesia.

Historical Overview

We can identify three ages of mental imagery: the philosophic ("prescientific") period, the measurement period, and the cognitive and neurocognitive period.

During the philosophic period, mental images were taken to be a principal ingredient in the composition of the mind and sometimes were believed to be the elements of thought. The topic was an integral part of the philosophies of classic Greek philosophy, notably Aristotle and Plato, and, more recently, the British Empiricists, notably John Locke, George Berkeley, David Hume, and David Hartley.

The quantitative assessment of mental imagery can be traced to Galton (1880, 1883/1907), who circulated a questionnaire to 100 people in which he asked them to recall their breakfast table and answer several questions about the images they had. The results indicated little about the imaginal process except that some people reported images that were as clear as the original percept, while others reported little recollection of the image. Galton developed a measure of imagery that was related to sex, age, and other individual differences. The testing of imagery drew the interest of several researchers, such as Titchener (1909) and Betts (1909). Their investigations consisted in having participants rate their ability to visualize an object such as an apple, the contour of a face, or the sun sinking below the horizon.

Interest in the mental testing of imagery quickly sank below the horizon with the advent of behaviorism, as exemplified in the views of Watson (1913). The behaviorist manifesto—as Woodworth (1948) called it—denounced introspection, which was a critical part of the previously mentioned tests of imagery. Introspection, according to Watson, formed no essential part of psychology. The new science of behavior was committed to the objective observation of overt responses, and terms such as *consciousness, mental states, mind,* and *imagery* should never be used. This rejection of imagery and subjective introspection of mental images as topics worthy of investigation turned many psychologists away from imagery and toward the objective analysis of behavior. As with so many topics in cognitive psychology, research in imagery lay dormant for many years. However, interest in imagery simply would not go away. The subjective experience was profound, and its influence was wide; its dogged pursuit by a few (notably Allan Paivio and Roger Shepard, and later Stephen Kosslyn and Steven Pinker) returned the topic to the mainstream of cognitive research.

Imagery research was reawakened in the late 1960s on two fronts. The first was related to the quantitative assessment of imagery (Sheehan, 1967a) and its use as a therapeutic vehicle. Also related to the assessment of imagery, but with a stronger theoretical bent, was the research of Bugelski (1970) and Paivio (1969). The second contemporary approach to imagery involved incorporation of the concept into a cognitive model in which the internal representation of information was a central element. This view is evident in the research of Shepard (1975); Shepard and Metzler (1971); and, more recently, in the neurocognitive studies by Farah (1988), Kosslyn (1988), and Pinker (1985). Each of these theorists has studied imagery from a unique point of view.

Imagery and Cognitive Psychology

The study of mental imagery engages the broader question of how information is stored and recalled from memory. We could argue that the neurological activity associated with the storage of information is of a specific form. That is, visual information is coded in terms of an internal "picture" that can be reactivated by calling up the picture, as we might in looking at an album. Alternatively, we could argue that visual information is filtered, summarized, and stored as abstract "statements" about the image. Reactivation of the memory then would consist of recalling the abstract code, which in turn would conjure up the subjective image associated with it. Finally, we could argue that some information is stored visually and some in an abstract form, indicating that multiple codes exist in the mind.[1]

---

[1]Some theorists argue that behavioral data are not adequate to settle the issue. Anderson (1976) states:

> At best . . . the imagery-versus-propositional controversy will reduce to . . . a question of which gives the more parsimonious account of which phenomena. Given the earlier results, there is no way to prove one is correct and the other wrong. Moreover, even if parsimony could yield a decision between propositional and imagery theories, there would still remain the possibility that there are other, fundamentally different, representations which are as parsimonious as the preferred member of the propositional-imagery pair. (p. 411)

Try This

"Seeing" Without Sensing

$\mathcal{W}$e see when a visual object is being viewed, but through the curiosity of **visual imagery,** we can also "see" when an object is not being viewed. Humans, and perhaps other animals, can "see" with the mind's eye.

Few dispute that all humans, to some degree, subjectively experience visual images; we can all "see" familiar shapes and forms by thinking of their characteristics.* Consider, for example, this problem: How many windows are there in the house in which you live? In all likelihood the way you answer this question is to form a mental image of your home and then mentally count the windows. Likewise, it appears that we are capable of forming mental representations of other sensory experiences in the absence of the physical stimuli. If we were to ask you to imagine a beach scene on a remote tropical island, you might "see" palm trees, seashells, the sun, and people in various activities, but you might also "hear" the ocean, "feel" the tropical breeze, "smell" the salt air. Some people seem capable of composing very vivid mental images, while others find this task difficult.

Over the next few hours, keep track of your mental representations, visual and otherwise. Which images are the most real, what is the relationship between these images and "reality," and what purpose do images play in one's mental life?

Likewise, we can "hear," "taste," "feel," and "smell" sensations by conjuring up their mental image.

For years, the subject of imagery has been surrounded by controversy. The ancient dispute over whether images are directly represented in the mind (when you imagine a living tree, is there a corresponding tree growing in your head?) or whether images are represented allegorically (when you imagine a tree, is the concept of "treeness" and its attributes represented in your brain?) has been debated for years. The first argument is a radical isomorphic view and, in its extreme form, is essentially foolish—a real tree will not grow in your head no matter how vivid your imagery. The second argument seems, at least, more reasonable (see Pinker, 1984, 1985; Finke, 1985; and Kosslyn, 1994, 1995, for excellent overviews of these topics).

Real progress has been made in the quest for a better understanding of imagery through inventive research techniques and clear-cut results (for example, see the research of Farah, Kosslyn, and Shepard in this chapter). Nevertheless, the subject of imagery remains controversial. Currently the debate is over the question of whether visual imagery is really visual or is governed by general-purpose cognitive processes (as contrasted with specific visual processes) and over knowledge of how the visual system operates. The visual argument holds that mental imagery involves the same representations used in vision, so that when we "see" a tree, specific types of neural processing and representations are activated. When we "image" a tree, the same (or highly similar) processes and representations are activated. The other side of this argument is that the representations used in imagery are not the representations used in real perception. This argument holds that "thinking in pictures" basically involves knowledge best expressed in terms of traditional (that is, propositional or associative) representations of knowledge.

Cognition in Everyday Life

Mental Imagery and Sports

Can mental imagery help athletes perform better? Some research indicates a resounding "yes." Here's how:

[First, immerse] yourself mentally in the sport's environment. If it's basketball, see the gym, the stands, the three-point line, the basket. In skiing, learn the terrain changes, the texture of the snow, where the run starts and finishes and the line you want to take down the mountain.

The second preliminary step is visual imagery. Once you have specified and memorized the task, practice producing a vivid image of the situation, one that uses all your senses. A skier I've worked with imagines riding up in the chairlift, looking over his skis at the top of the hill, seeing the colors of the trees and the other skiers' bright clothing against the whiteness of the snow and feeling the sensation of his skis gliding over the snow. He brings in feelings as well as visual images, recalling the exhilaration and joy he experiences in making a good turn.

Once the task is clear and the images vivid, it's time to start the mental rehearsal itself. Close your eyes and experience the physical activity mentally and emotionally. Everything you visualize should look and feel the same as if you were really on the slopes or on the court.

From May (1989).

The plan of this chapter is to discuss the research on imagery with the theoretical considerations hovering closely in the background. The information is organized around three central themes:

1. The **dual-coding hypothesis,** which suggests that there are two codes and two storage systems—one imaginal, the other verbal—and that information may be coded and stored in either or both (principally the work of Paivio).

2. The **conceptual-propositional hypothesis,** which proposes that visual and verbal information is represented in the form of abstract propositions about objects and their relationships (principally the work of Anderson and Bower as well as Pylyshyn).

3. The **functional-equivalency hypothesis,** which suggests that imagery and perception are highly similar (principally the work of Shepard and Kosslyn).

In addition, there are those who suggest that information can be both visual and spatial (for example, Farah, 1988). We begin our trek through the imagery literature by exploring the dual-coding hypothesis.

Dual-Coding Hypothesis

The original work of Paivio and his associates on imagery was done in a paired-associate learning context, a research paradigm very much in fashion at the time. The first step Paivio (1965) took was to scale the imagery quality of nouns by having a group of college students rate nouns for their capacity to arouse an image, that is, "a mental pic-

TABLE 10.1

Imagery Scores and Scores on Related Attributes for a Representative Sample of Nouns

Noun	Mean Score*			Frequency[†] (per million)
	Imagery	*Concreteness*	*Meaningfulness*	
Beggar	6.40	6.25	6.50	29
Church	6.63	6.59	7.52	AA
Context	2.13	2.73	4.44	1
Deed	3.63	4.19	5.32	A
Elephant	6.83	7.00	6.88	35
Profession	3.83	3.65	5.44	28
Salary	4.70	5.23	5.08	A
Tomahawk	6.57	6.87	6.44	3
Virtue	3.33	1.46	4.87	A

*Ratings were on a scale of 1 to 7; the lower the score, the lower its imagery.
[†]"A" words have a frequency of 50–99 per million words; "AA," 100 or more per million words.
From Paivio, Yuille, and Madigan (1968).

ture, or sound, or other sensory picture." A similar procedure was used by Paivio, Yuille, and Madigan (1968), and Table 10.1 contains a sample of their results, including ratings for concreteness, meaningfulness (the number of associates a word elicits), and frequency (of occurrence of a word in common printed text). These results confirm the obvious: that some words are more imaginal (for example, *elephant, tomahawk,* and *church*) and others less imaginal (for example, *context, deed,* and *virtue*).

Studies by Paivio have led to the dual-coding hypothesis, a major theoretical statement as to how information is represented in memory. The hypothesis is based on the inference that there are two coding systems, or two ways information may be represented in memory: a nonverbal imagery process and a verbal symbolic process. The two codes—imaginal and verbal—may overlap in the processing of information, but greater emphasis is on one or the other. Suppose, for example, that a familiar and easily named picture is coded both imaginally and verbally, but with the verbal code being less available. This may happen because an extra transformation is involved so that, although the verbal code is aroused, it occurs *after* the imaginal code has been activated. On the other hand, while concrete words may be coded both imaginally and verbally, an abstract word is represented by a verbal code only. The availability of coding for different classes of stimuli is shown in Table 10.2.

Conceptual-Propositional Hypothesis

Anderson and Bower were critical of the mental-picture metaphor, stating that "it is not scientifically viable to suppose that memories, or other sorts of knowledge, are carried about in a form like an internal photograph, video tape, or tape recording, which we can

Coding Systems Available According to Stimulus

	Coding System*	
Stimulus	Imagery	Verbal
Picture	+ + +	+ +
Concrete word	+	+ + +
Abstract word	– –	+ + +

*Number of plus signs indicate relative availability.

From Paivio (1971b). Reprinted by permission from Erlbaum.

reactivate and replay in remembering an image" (1973, p. 453). Even though we are capable of a subjective experience of an image, the underlying cognitive component may be of a form much different from imaginal. One reason Anderson and Bower reject the pictures-in-the-head theory is related to a conservation argument, which states that it is useless to postulate storage of full pictures of scenes because such a memory system would require storage and retrieval well beyond the human capability. Some device—a kind of master homunculus—would still be necessary to view and interpret these internal pictures.

The conceptual-propositional hypothesis holds that we store interpretations of events, whether verbal or visual, rather than the imaginal components. Anderson and Bower do not deny that it is easier to learn concrete words than abstract words, but they attribute those results to the supposition that concrete concepts are coded by a rich set of predicates that bind concepts together. They state that "the only difference between the internal representation for a linguistic input and a memory image is detail of information" (p. 460). The following is one of their examples:

> Our words spoken to a listener are like the cryptic directions a playwright provides for a play director, from which a competent director is expected to construct an entire setting, an expressive mood, or an action episode in a drama. To illustrate, in the course of reading a story, you might read the sentence "James Bond ran to his car and drove to the casino." As you read, you can concretize that sentence by bringing to bear all sorts of facts and sensory images about running, about getting into cars, about driving, and so forth. These "fill-ins" would be called upon, for example, if you were to be asked simple questions like "Did James Bond sit in a car? Did he start its motor? Did he move the steering wheel?" Such trivial implications seem immediately available from the referential semantics of the verb phrase "drive a car." What the sentence does is merely mention a couple of signposts (source, instrument, goal) along the way in the description of an event sequence; the listener interpolates or fills in all the interstitial events between the mentioned signposts. Of course, at a later time, the listener is hardly able to say exactly what he heard as compared to what he filled in; if he is asked to tell the story "in his own words," he will probably select slightly different descriptions or signposts to mention in reconstructing the salient episodes. (pp. 460–461)

Anderson and Bower's conceptual-propositional hypothesis is a theoretically elegant point of view and one that is compatible with their theoretical model. However, the hypothesis has some difficulty accounting for some imaginal processes that seem to require an internal structure that is second-order isomorphic to the physical objective. Data that seem to reflect such processes have been presented by Shepard and his students and are considered in the next section.

Functional-Equivalency Hypothesis

Shepard.   Much of the current excitement in the field of mental imagery is due to the demonstration and interpretation of **mental rotation** by Shepard and his colleagues. Using visual cues, Shepard studied mental rotation of visual stimuli in memory. In his experiments participants were asked to judge whether a second stimulus, such as the right-hand one in Figure 10.1, was the same (except for rotation) as the original stimulus (at left). In some cases the second pattern was a mirror image of the first and, therefore, not

FIGURE 10.1

Typical visual forms used by Shepard and Metzler. Form at right is left-hand form rotated 90° counterclockwise.

Adapted from Shepard and Metzler (1971).

Roger Shepard. Studies of mental rotation led to theories in mental imagery.

the "same" as the original stimulus, while in other cases the pattern was identical to the original, but rotated. The degree of rotation ranged from 0 degrees to 180 degrees. The dependent variable was the amount of time required to make a judgment. The results of these experiments indicate that the time required to respond was a linear function of the degree of rotation (see Figure 10.2). That is, a small degree of rotation of the second stimulus was quickly judged, while a large degree of rotation required more time. These data suggest that the participant's internal representation of the images required about 1 second for every 50 degrees of rotation. The results of Shepard's experiments have far-reaching importance for cognitive theory, but for our discussion the relationship between the time required and the degree of rotation suggests that the internal process is an orderly function of the amount of transformation required. Thus, it appears that a close relationship exists between the time required for a specific mental rotation and the actual degrees of rotation involved. If we consider both rotations on two scales—time required for mental rotation and degrees of rotation—the correspondence is evident.

In addition to the reaction data presented in Shepard's elegant experiments, some researchers have presented neurological evidence for mental rotation. One of these studies by Georgopoulos and his colleagues (1989) is particularly interesting. They examined the electrical activity in the brain of a rhesus monkey as it performed a mental rotation task. The monkey was trained to move a handle on a clocklike apparatus in reaction to the location of a light. When the light appeared in one location, the animal would move the handle in a corresponding way. However, the primary interest lay in

F I G U R E   1 0 . 2

Reaction time as a function of degree of rotation of a form.

Adapted from Shepard and Metzler (1971).

what happened in the cortex of the monkey, which the researcher interpreted as mental rotation, just prior to the movement of the handle. During the few milliseconds prior to the response, the animal anticipated the movement. Georgopoulos and his fellow researchers measured minute electrical activity in the monkey's motor cortex during this critical period and, with the assistance of computer graphics, showed that individual cells have directional preferences. The cells that responded most frequently during mental rotation were those that showed a preference for, say, counterclockwise movement. The results provide direct neurological evidence for mental rotation and suggest that the use of "single cell" recordings of neural activity might be a useful supplement to behavioral data in the identification of cognitive operations.

Shepard (1968) and Shepard and Chipman (1970) introduced the term **second-order isomorphism** to represent the relationship between external objects and internal representations of those objects that is not a one-to-one (isomorphic) kind. This position holds that if the relationship between objects in memory is the same as the relationship between those objects in the real world, then the events are second-order isomorphic. The distinction between first-order and second-order isomorphism is a subtle but important one: objects are not directly or structurally represented in our brains, but the way internal relationships work is very similar to the way external relationships work.

From the research findings of Shepard's group, a strong case seems to develop for the existence of images in the mind that are, if not structurally identical to the real-world object, at least functionally related.

Kosslyn.   In a series of inventive experiments, Kosslyn and his colleagues (Kosslyn, 1973, 1975, 1976a, 1977, 1980, 1981, 1994, 1995; Kosslyn & Pomerantz, 1977; Kosslyn et al., 1993) have investigated imagery from the standpoint of its spatial characteristics and, most recently, with the use of brain imaging technology (to be discussed later). In the main, Kosslyn's research has demonstrated that a mental image is similar to the perception of a real object. Most of his experiments are based on the assumption that an image has spatial properties, which may be scanned, and that it takes more time to scan large distances than short distances. In one experiment (1973), Kosslyn asked participants to memorize a set of drawings and then to imagine one at a time. At one time they were asked to "focus" on one end of the object they had imagined (for example, if the object was a speedboat, they were asked to "look at" the rear portion). A possible property of the original picture was named, and the participant was asked to decide whether or not it was in the original. The results indicated that longer times were required to make judgments about properties that involved scanning distances. For example, those

*A*lthough imagery has played a central role in theorizing about the mind since the time of Aristotle, its nature and properties have been surrounded by controversy. Indeed, during the Behaviorist era, its very existence was questioned, and more recently its status as a distinct kind of mental representation has been vigorously debated.

—*Stephen M. Kosslyn*

Stephen Kosslyn. Helped develop the field of mental imagery and cognitive neuroscience.

FIGURE 10.3

Picture for investigating spatial characteristics of imagery.

involving a scan from stern to bow (see Figure 10.3) took longer than those involving one from porthole to bow). Participants who were asked to keep the whole image in mind showed no differences in the time required to identify properties from different locations. It would appear that mental images can be scanned and that the time required to scan them is similar to that needed to scan real pictures.

If images do share some features of real-object perception (that is, scanning time), are there other features common to percepts and images? Kosslyn, using the fact that small objects are generally seen less clearly than large objects, demonstrated that there are. In one experiment (1975), he had participants imagine a target animal (for example, a rabbit) next to a small or large creature (for example, a fly or an elephant). A rabbit next to an elephant is reported by most people to be smaller than one of the same size next to a fly (see Figure 10.4). Participants who were asked to determine the appropriateness of a certain property (for example, ears) to an animal took on the average 211 milliseconds longer to evaluate animals paired with an elephant than those paired with a fly.

To guard against the possibility that such results might derive simply from greater interest in elephants than in flies, Kosslyn tested animals in the context of an elephantine fly and a minuscule elephant. Under these conditions, more time was taken to evaluate the target animal when it was paired with the giant fly than with the tiny elephant.

In yet another experiment, Kosslyn (1975) asked participants to imagine squares of four different sizes—each six times the area of the next smaller one and each identified by a color name. After the participants were able to envision the size of the square on the basis of the color, they were given a color and animal name, such as "green bear" or

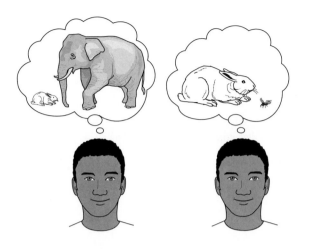

FIGURE 10.4

Typical relationships imagined by participants in Kosslyn's experiment.

Adapted from Kosslyn (1975).

"pink tiger," and asked to summon up an image of the designated animal according to the size of the box linked with the color (see Figure 10.5). After this, a possible property of the animal was presented. The time required to decide whether the property was a characteristic of the animal was much longer for animals in the small boxes than for those in the larger ones (see Figure 10.6).

Taken together, these experiments of Kosslyn and Shepard indicate that visual images seem to reflect internal representations that operate in a way that is analogous to the functioning of the perception of physical objects. On the other hand, not all or even a sizable number of the characteristics of images have been examined.

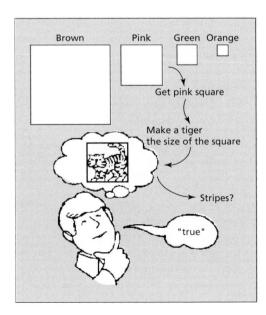

FIGURE 10.5

Process in experiment. Here participants judged appropriateness of a property to an imagined animal paired with boxes of different sizes.

Adapted from Kosslyn (1975).

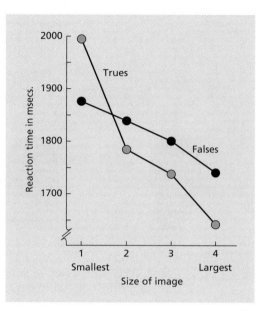

FIGURE 10.6

Times required to determine appropriateness of a property of an animal in experiment depicted in Figure 10.5.

Data from Kosslyn (1975).

Cognitive Neuroscience Evidence

Our analysis of mental imagery has dealt with studies of the psychology of that phenomenon, and thus far, we can cautiously conclude that mental imagery and perception of a real stimulus are seductively alike in many regards. However, to ascertain the completeness of the analogy of perception to imagery, further validation is required in the form of neurological evidence. Fortunately, a large body of data comes from neurological studies (for example, Gazzaniga & Sperry, 1967; Corballis, 1989; and Milner, 1968). Clinical observations by Luria (1976) and Farah (1988, 1995) of neurologically damaged patients show that impairment of the left hemisphere of the brain is associated with disturbances of verbal memory, while right-hemisphere damage is associated with the memory for visual material. These findings tend to support the dual-coding theory of memory: one system for the coding and processing of visual information, another for the coding and processing of verbal information.

The rationale for many experiments dealing with brain activity and imagery is that activation of a cognitive process, such as imagery or verbal thought, is expressed in terms of localized brain activity, which can be measured by regional blood flow (see Chapter 2 for details).

Psychologists have agonized over the question of functional equivalency of images and visual percepts for several decades. The answer may lie within the field of cognitive neuroscience. The logic of this quest is simple. If measurements of regional cerebral blood flow (rCBF) indicate that the same areas of the brain are active when we see an object as when we image an object, then the functional-equivalency position is supported (although not definitely established, since regions could carry on more than a single function). Conversely, if different areas of the brain are activated during perception than during imaging, then the equivalency position is not supported.

First, we consider the matter of uniqueness of imagery and brain activity. Strong objective evidence has been reported showing that all parts of the visual cortex are activated when participants imagine an object or use imagery to solve a problem. Specifically, research by Roland and Friberg (1985) measured rCBF during three cognitive tasks:

1. Mental arithmetic (subtracting by 3s starting with *50*).
2. Memory scanning of an auditory stimulus (mentally jumping every second word in a well-known musical jingle).
3. Visual imagery (visualizing a walk through one's neighborhood, making alternating right and left turns starting at one's front door).

Each task activated different parts of the cortex, but most important for our discussion is the finding that during the visual task, blood flow was most apparent to the posterior regions, which includes the occipital lobe and temporal areas important for higher visual processing and memory. It appears that mental imagery of this sort involves not only visual processing areas but also memory areas.

In a related study, Goldenberg, Podreka, Steiner, Suess, Deeke, and Willmes (1990), using single positron emission computer tomography (PET) scans to trace brain activity, asked participants to answer some questions that required visual imagery and some that did not. For example:

"Is the green of pine trees darker than the green of grass?"
"Is the categorical imperative an ancient grammatical form?"

The results indicated that the first type of question produced high levels of blood flow in the occipital regions and in the posterior parietal and temporal visual processing areas, whereas the second nonimagery condition did not.

A detailed and direct test of the hypothesis about perception and imagery has been reported by Kosslyn and his associates (1993, 1995) in which an often-used test of imagery was used in a PET study. In this case, a task devised by Podgorny and Shepard (1978) consisted of asking participants to view a letter (such as the letter *F*) in a grid (the perceptual condition) or to image the letter in an empty grid (the imaginal condition). Then a mark was presented, and the participants were to indicate whether the mark fell on or off the letter (see Figure 10.7).

In the original experiment, Podgorny and Shepard found that it took participants longer to decide whether the marks were closer to the letter than farther away. The researchers concluded that it's easier to make an evaluation of inclusiveness and exclusiveness if the mark falls well outside the target. However, the main conclusion of the experiment was that similar results were obtained for the perception group and for the imagery group, which lent support for the functional-equivalency hypothesis.

Perception   Imagery

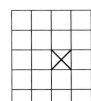

FIGURE 10.7

Example of figure used in the perceptual and imaginal task.

From P. Podgorney and R. M. Shepard (1978). *JEP: HP and P,* 4, pp. 21–35. Copyright © 1978 by the American Psychological Association. Reprinted by permission.

What Kosslyn and his associates found was somewhat surprising. Although they hypothesized that the visual cortex (the structure located at the posterior portion of the cerebral cortex involved in vision) would be activated during the perceptual task and probably activated during the imaginal task, the PET results clearly showed *greater* activation of the visual cortex during image generation than during perception. It is as if this structure, and perhaps other structures involved in visual processing, had to work harder during image generation than during perception. One possible reason for this finding is that during perception the visual cortex receives detailed visual information from the external world (a kind of bottom-up stimulus) and, therefore, operates with the object in view, which requires little effort. In contrast, during image generation, the person must recreate the visual stimulus from memory (a kind of top-down stimulus), which forces it to work harder.

From these studies and many more (see Farah, 1988), several conclusions are appropriate:

1. Studies of brain activity indicate that different areas of the brain are associated with different cognitive tasks.

2. Visual imaginal tasks and vision seem to be situated in similar locations in the brain.

3. Visual imaginal tasks, which require associative knowledge, seem to activate regions of the brain affiliated with memory and vision.

4. Because of their top-down nature, imaginal tasks may require more energy to process than perceptual tasks, which are initially bottom-up tasks.

5. The use of physiological measures of rCBF may resolve some thorny cognitive problems.

One remaining issue has not been addressed in this section. It is the question of whether spatial representations (the type of representations we saw in Shepard's mental rotation experiments) and visual representations (the type of representations dependent on the reconstruction of a visual impression, for example, naming the color of an object such as a football) engage different parts of the brain. In answering this question, we turn to a case study.

In reaction to the argument that the format of mental images is either analogical (positions espoused by those who believe images are functionally equivalent to percepts) or propositional (positions taken by those who reject the idea that images and real perception are highly similar), Martha Farah and her colleagues (Farah, 1988; and Farah et al., 1988) have looked to the evidence from cognitive neuroscience to resolve the issue.

The basic logic of those who have sought cognitive neuroscience explanations of imagery is that by finding specific brain areas associated with imagery and other functions, such as vision, many of the theoretical questions may be resolved. Specifically, the question of mental images being almost the same thing as vision versus part of a more general system of representing spatial information might be clearly resolved if, for example, it were demonstrated that vision and spatial representation occupied different parts of the brain. Thus, the study of neurophysiology bears directly on cognitive theories of imagery.

As shown, the neurophysiology of imagery has been studied through many of the techniques described in Chapter 2, including CT scans, EEG recordings, studies of regional cerebral blood flow, neurosurgery, and the study of patients who have experienced some brain trauma. It is the latter case we turn to next.

Martha Farah. Conducted innovative research in cognitive neuroscience, which has identified neurological sites of cognitive processes.

Farah and her colleagues worked with a brain-damaged patient called L. H, who was a thirty-six-year-old minister working on a second master's degree. When he was eighteen, he sustained a serious injury to his head in an automobile accident. Subsequent surgery (and CT scan confirmation) indicated that the parts of the brain that were damaged involved both temporo-occipital regions, the right temporal lobe, and the right inferior frontal lobe, as shown in Figure 10.8. Although L. H made remarkable recovery and outwardly seemed normal, he was profoundly impaired in visual recognition. For example, he could not reliably recognize his wife or children unless they were wearing

FIGURE 10.8

Areas of damage to L. H's brain (marked with Xs). Areas involved include the right temporal lobe and right inferior frontal lobe (upper figure) and the temporo-occipital regions (lower figure).

From Farah et al. (1988). Reprinted with permission.

distinctive clothes. He also had difficulty recognizing animals, plants, foods, and drawings. Some of the objects L. H could not recognize are shown in Figure 10.9. He could, nevertheless, make reasonable copies of these figures, even though he did not know their identity. He had good elementary visual capabilities.

The experimenters in this case were interested in visual and spatial imagery ability vis-à-vis brain injuries. They argued that:

- Spatial representations are not confined to the visual modality (for example, mental rotations, which are considered to be spatial images, not visual images).
- Visual representations are confined to the visual modality (for example, the naming of a color of a common object such as a football).

In the final stage of the experiment, L. H performed a variety of tasks associated with spatial knowledge and other tasks associated with visual knowledge. Many of the tasks have been described in this chapter.

- *Visual Tasks.* For the visual tasks, animal tails (Does a kangaroo have a long tail?), color identification (What is the color of a football?), size comparison (Which is

FIGURE 10.9

A. Examples of drawings a brain-damaged patient could not recognize.

B. Patient's reproductions of these figures.

From Farah et al. (1988). Reprinted with permission.

A

B

larger, a popsicle or a pack of cigarettes?), and comparison of state shapes (Which states are most similar in shape?) were presented to L. H and to a number of control participants.

- *Spatial Imaginal Tasks.* For the spatial tasks, letter rotation (mental rotation of a letter, similar to form rotation used by Shepard and Metzler), three-dimensional form rotation (see Shepard and Metzler), mental scanning (see Kosslyn), and size scaling (estimates of the same shape of figures regardless of size) were presented to the patient and to control participants.

The results, given in Figure 10.10A, clearly show L. H's performance on visual tasks as being impaired, presumably as the result of destruction of specific brain areas; however, these impairments seem to have left intact his ability to perform spatial tasks (see

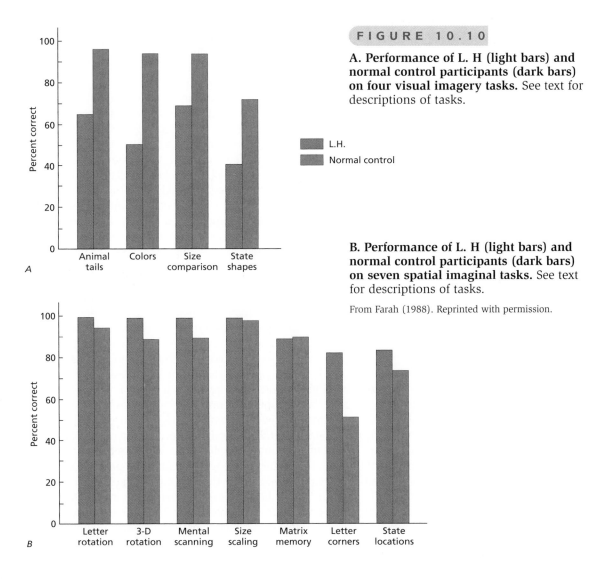

A. Performance of L. H (light bars) and normal control participants (dark bars) on four visual imagery tasks. See text for descriptions of tasks.

B. Performance of L. H (light bars) and normal control participants (dark bars) on seven spatial imaginal tasks. See text for descriptions of tasks.

From Farah (1988). Reprinted with permission.

Figure 10.10B). It would appear, therefore, that these two groups of tasks (visual and spatial) tap different types of mental representation that are neurologically distinct. Because they are neurologically distinct, it follows that different subsystems of imaginal representations exist.

Our understanding of mental imagery is enhanced by this study in three ways. First, cognitive entities such as imagery are shown to be governed by underlying neurological functions, which can be empirically measured. Second, cognitive tasks, such as mental rotation, color identification, and so on, are valuable tools in neurological investigations. Third, mental images are shown to be both visual and spatial.

Cognitive Maps

The human capacity for imagery is a powerful attribute of memory, as we saw in the chapter on mnemonics, but it is also essential in our everyday life as we work and move about in our environment. Humans share the same three-dimensional world as other earth creatures (although not in the same way as fish or birds) and, to survive, must be able to use imagery to navigate through our spatial world and avoid harm.

Psychologists have for a long time been interested in the navigational patterns of animals, and the early work of Tolman led to the concept of the **cognitive map,** which referred to a general spatial knowledge exhibited by rats in a maze. The distinguished naturalist Von Frisch (1967) published a study of honey bees that described the means they used in communicating the location of pollen sources to fellow bees.

One experiment by Thorndyke and Hayes-Roth (1982) concluded that humans use two types of knowledge—route knowledge and survey knowledge—in their effort to learn about the spatial world. Route knowledge is related to the specific pathways used to get from one location to another. If a stranger on campus asked how to find the medical school, We would say something like "You take Virginia to the colosseum; then turn right, go up a hill, and on your left you will see a large, flat building." We would be giving route information. Survey knowledge, on the other hand, deals with more global relationships between environmental cues. We might answer the stranger's question by saying "It's over there, in that general direction." Another, more direct way to form survey knowledge is to study a map. The Thorndyke and Hayes-Roth study took place in the large office complex where they worked. They asked participants in the experiment to study a map and found that after only 20 minutes of study the participants were able to judge distances and locations as well as a group of secretaries who had worked in the building for two years.

In a somewhat related study, B. Tversky (1981) and Taylor and Tversky (1992) examined the distortions of memory for geographic locations. In their interesting work, Tversky suggests that distortions occur because people use conceptual strategies to remember geographic information. We have already seen that people tend to form prototypes when given simple geometric forms to imagine, and it is likely that even more complex forms of abstracted information are part of the cognitive mapping process of humans.

Following this line of thought, it may be that geographic information is structured in memory in terms of abstract generalizations rather than specific images. Such an argument would avoid the difficult question of how we can store so much information in visual memory, since the storage is condensed into larger units. Your home, for example, is part of a neighborhood, which is part of a city, which is part of a township, which is in a

FIGURE 10.11

Geographical distortion. A. Cognitive map of Reno as east of Los Angeles. B. Actual location of Reno—west of Los Angeles.

A

B

region of the state, and so on. When you move from one section to another, say, in your city, the knowledge you use may be in the form of an abstract representation of landmarks rather than a series of discrete visual images. Sometimes these higher structures interfere with decisions made on the local level. For example, if you were asked which city is farther west, Reno or Los Angeles (see Figure 10.11), you would likely answer Los Angeles (see Stevens & Coupe, 1978). Why? Because we know that Los Angeles is in California and that Reno is in Nevada, which is to the east of California. In this case we are relying on strategic information rather than tactical information, and we are misled.

Mental Maps: Where Am I?

It has long been known that we humans enjoy a geocentric view of the universe. Early scientists, with encouragement from the Church, even placed Earth in the center of the solar system (which required an inelegant theory of planetary motion) before Copernicus jolted us out of the vortex and properly placed Earth as the third planet from the sun. It is common, and understandable, that children regard their home as the center of their universe, surrounded by their neighborhood, city, state, and country. Local egocentric impressions of geography are the result of familiarization and provide emotional comfort. (*Home* is one of the most comforting words in our vocabulary.) Some have suggested that maps, which are basically human impressions of geographic reality, are both a reflection of the objective realities of the world and partly a reflection of the subjective interpretation of these impressions.

Can map drawings provide a window to the mind regarding such matters? There is considerable evidence that expressive forms of representation, such as sketches of maps and other graphic figures,[2] mirror our subjective impression of reality (see the Texan's view of the United States in Figure 10.12). Most map-drawing studies have dealt with systematic distortions and accuracies of regional cognitive maps, such as navigating around a college campus or judging the distance between geographic points. Several studies have considered world-scale cognitive maps. Certainly, ancient maps indicated a degree of unavoidable egocentrism. For example, the ancient Babylonians didn't know what lay past the distant hills. However, now almost all schoolchildren know something of the gross geographic boundaries of the world.

Some years ago a mammoth international study of the image of the world by different nationalities was done to broaden our understanding of cultural differences and to foster world peace. The design was simple. Students in a first-year course in geography

---

[2]Our colleagues in clinical psychology have subscribed to this idea for a long time, as shown in their use of projective techniques (for example, Draw-a-Person), which are thought to disclose hidden personality traits.

FIGURE 10.12

A Texan's view of the United States.

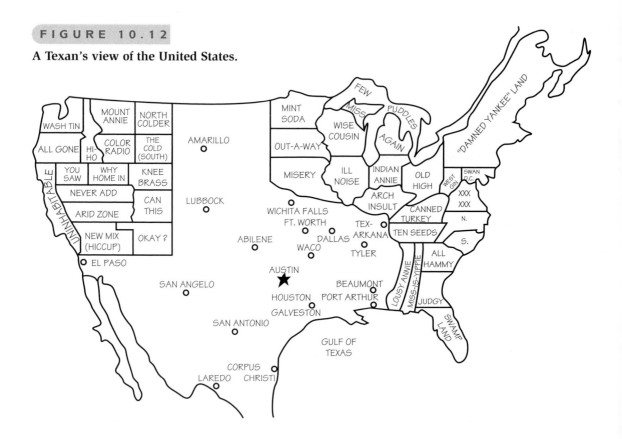

from 71 sites in 49 countries were given a blank sheet of paper and asked to sketch a map of the world. The results were fascinating (Saarinen, 1987). Of the nearly 4,000 maps produced, the majority showed a Eurocentric worldview, even if the person who drew the map was from the periphery, as in the case of students from Hong Kong, Singapore, and Thailand. This is probably due to the wide use of Eurocentric maps for more than 500 years. Some American students drew an Americentric map; an example by a student from Chicago (who seems to have some familiarity with Texas and the Caribbean) is shown in Figure 10.13. Australian students tended to sketch Sinocentric maps, with Australia and Asia in the center; several Down Under students drew maps in which not only was Australia centrally located but also all other countries were shown in the "lower hemisphere," as shown in Figure 10.14. Maps of this orientation are not common in Australia. One would anticipate that students would draw their own country disproportionately larger, but this did not seem to be the case. Prominent countries (the United States and the former USSR, England, France, and so forth) were on most maps. Africa was generally underrepresented, and its countries seemed less well known. American students

FIGURE 10.13

View of the world by a student from Chicago.

FIGURE 10.14

View of the world by a student from Australia.

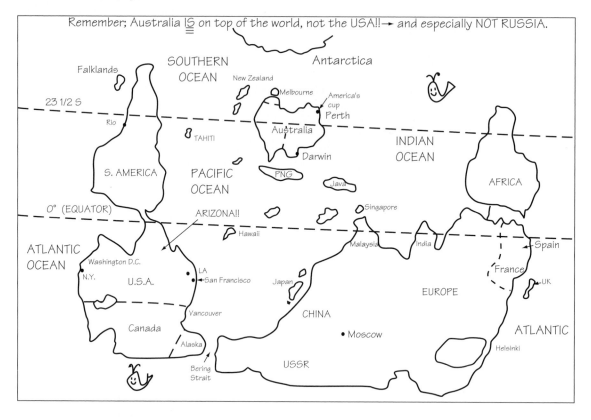

did rather poorly on the task, especially in terms of placing countries correctly. Students from Hungary and the Soviet Union produced some of the most detailed maps.

Synesthesia: The Sound of Colors

Synesthesia is a condition in which sensations from one modality (for example, vision) are experienced in another modality (for example, audition). People may taste shapes, feel sounds, or see numbers or letters in color. In some rare individuals (see the discussion of S. in Chapter 8), the transfer between sensory experiences is extraordinary. In some people, the simultaneous experiencing of sensory events is common. Poetry abounds with metaphors of synesthesia (see the box entitled "Cognition in Everyday Life: Literary Metaphors and Synesthesia"), and artists have confirmed the strong relationship between sights and sounds. The Russian abstract artist Kandinsky (1912) wrote that "the sound of colors is so definite that it would be hard to find anyone who would try to express bright yellow in the bass notes, or [a] dark lake in the treble." However,

Cognition in Everyday Life

Literary Metaphors and Synesthesia

The murmur of the gray twilight—Poe

The sound of coming darkness—Poe

Sunset hovers like the sound of golden horns—Robinson

I could hear the willows weeping sweet smells.—Dickinson

A soft yet glowing light, like lulled music—Shelley

The notes entered my breast like luminous arrows—Gautier

Music bright as the soul of light—Swinburne

both extraordinary synesthesia and ordinary cross-modal transfer remain somewhat mysterious. There are principles that seem to govern synesthesia and research that supports these principles (Marks, 1987a, 1987b).

Synesthesia tends to be rule governed, not random. For example, there is a positive relationship between increasing the pitch of a sound and increased brightness (a sneeze is likely to be "brighter" than a cough).

In one study, Marks (1974) presented to participants a series of tones varying in pitch. The participants were asked to match each tone with a series of colors that differed in brightness. As shown in Figure 10.15, there is a substantial positive relationship

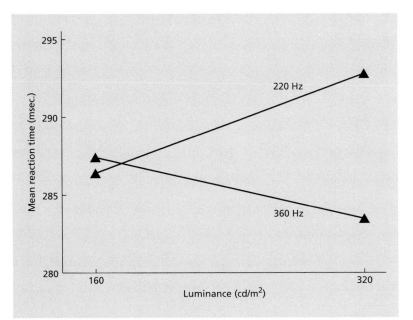

FIGURE 10.15

Ratings of brightness of colors and pitch.

From Marks (1974).

between pitch and brightness. Marks has extended these correlational observations to reaction-time experiments in which a participant is asked to discriminate two auditory values, say, a high and low pitch, by pressing a reaction-time key. On each trial of the experiment, a dim light or a bright light is also turned on. The relationship between the brightness of the light and the pitch of the tones appears random and (the participant is likely to conclude) irrelevant to the main purpose of the experiment. Nevertheless, as shown in Figure 10.16, there is a reliable relationship between pitch and brightness as measured by reaction time. When the luminance is high (320 cd/m^2), reaction time to high-pitched stimuli is relatively fast, while for low-pitched tones the reaction time is relatively slow.

In yet another condition, colors and pitches were found to be predictably related. In evaluating the "sound of colors," it appears that yellow and white are bright, red and green intermediate, and black and brown dark. The pitches associated with these colors correspond almost perfectly with high pitches associated with the bright colors and low pitches with the dark colors (Marks, 1987a). Support for these relationships in literary sources is common. Note for example, "She sang with silvery clarity," "The bass produced rich, dark tones, which set the mood for the entire performance of *Boris Godunov*." Additional experiments confirm these observations.

Our discussion of synesthesia started out with "soft" references (the allegorical character of cross-modal experience—see the box entitled "Cognition in Everyday Life:

FIGURE 10.16

Mean reaction time for tones of different pitches (Hz) and different brightness (cd/m^2).

From Marks (1974).

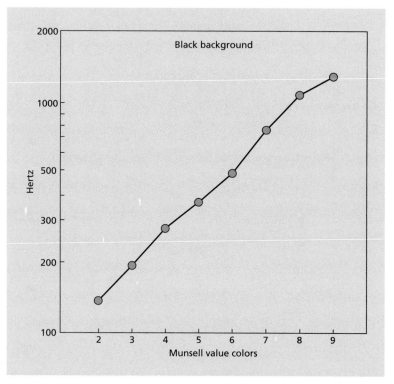

Literary Metaphors and Synthesia") and ended up with "hard" data (the nearly perfect linear relationship between tones and luminance). Perhaps good science and good art are part of a single reality. However, our concern here is to understand synesthesia in the larger context of cognitive psychology.

There are convincing data to suggest that many people have a type of synesthesia in which images and sounds (as well as other sensory experiences) are entwined. Furthermore, synesthesia can be measured, and from these observations lawful statements can be derived. There are also data that suggest that some people are unusually synesthetic. These people experience egregious "cross-talk" among sensory experiences (see the discussion of S. in Chapter 8). What mechanisms might account for these observations?

First, consider the physical character of the natural world. Is there any good reason to link sights and sounds? Are bright objects and high-pitched sounds alike physically? Perhaps, but searching for physical explanations may overlook its important psychological character. Second, consider the perceptual and cognitive nature of synesthesia. It may be that our nervous system is structured in a way that "cross-talk" among cortical neurons is a valuable, "prewired" element in the redundant, parallel processing of information in the human brain. It is possible that connected areas in the brain that have activity simultaneously may give rise to synesthesiatic experiences. In the past, we have had to rely on the mediation of language and reaction-time experiments to find a nexus between sensory experiences. With increased sophistication in the detection of brain activities, studies of synesthesia and brain activity will identify the source and nature of this intriguing issue. Vilayanur Ramachandran of the Brain and Perception Laboratory at UC San Diego says that ". . . normal brains are wired so that concepts, perceptions and names of objects are routinely interconnected, giving rise to widely shared metaphors . . . [like 'loud' shirts and 'sharp' cheddar cheese]" (quoted in *The New York Times,* 4/10/01).

Spotlight on Cognitive Neuroscience

Cognitive Maps

Jeffrey Zacks, Jon Mires, Barbara Tversky, Eliot Hazeltine, and John Gabrieli focus on two different aspects of cognitive maps. The first aspect is object-based spatial transformations, which means rotating in your head a particular object or location. The second is egocentric perspective transformations in which you rotate or translate your point of view. Think of being in your local grocery store. You're pretty familiar with the layout because you shop there at least once a week. You are in one of the frozen food aisles looking at frozen pizza, debating between self-rising and thin crusts. You remember that you want to get some Ben & Jerry's, which is in the next aisle over. If you are engaging in object-based spatial transformation, you would envision the aisle rotating so you could picture where the ice cream was. An egocentric perspective transformation would have you envision yourself moving around the aisle and then facing the ice cream. In each of these types of transformation, some aspects of the world remain fixed while others rotate (you envision the aisle rotating while you remain still, or vice versa). Understanding these types of rotations is important for everyday life (maneuvering between pizza and ice cream at the store) as well as more "technical" areas (air traffic control and architecture, to name two). Zacks and his colleagues' previous research has found that there were different locations in the brain for each of these types of rotations. Their subsequent studies using more traditional cognitive methods of experimentation (mental rotation/visualization tasks as well as paper-and-pencil measures) complemented these findings by showing that there is indeed different processing involved (which corresponds to the different brain regions) for each type of transformation, such that there is an increase in reaction time with object-based transformations but not for egocentric perspective transformations. Their work is a fine example of using multiple methods (neurophysiological and cognitive) to understand important cognitive processes.

Zacks, J. M., Mires, J., Tversky, B., & Hazeltine, E. (2000). Mental spatial transformations of objects and perspective. *Spatial Cognition and Computation,* 2(4), 315–332.

Zacks, J. M., Hazeltine, E., Tversky, B., & Gabrieli, J. D. E. (1999). Event-related fMRI of mental spatial transformations. Paper presented at the Annual Meeting of the Cognitive Neuroscience Society, Washington, DC.

SUMMARY

As we noted in the beginning of this section on imagery, early experimental efforts were frustrating. That remains the case. We have presented three viewpoints on imagery—the dual-coding hypothesis, the conceptual-propositional hypothesis, and the functional-equivalency hypothesis. Each viewpoint is both theoretically elegant and intuitively appealing, so the student of imagery is likely to feel frustrated in choosing the "best" model. It seems that information is imaginally coded at some level of processing, while the same information at another level of processing is conceptually coded. Thus the problem caused by three appealing hypotheses might be resolved by accepting all three, while acknowledging that the coding of information may span several layers of cognitive processes, each of which transcribes information in its unique way.

1   The study of mental imagery is concerned with the issue of how information is represented in memory.

2   Three distinct theoretical positions can be identified regarding how information is stored in memory. They include the dual-coding hypothesis, the conceptual-propositional hypothesis, and the functional-equivalency hypothesis.

3   The dual-coding hypothesis holds that information can be coded and stored in either or both of two systems: verbal and imaginal. Behavioral and neurological data support this position.

4   The conceptual-propositional hypothesis posits that information is stored in an abstract propositional format that specifies objects, events, and their relationships. This position is theoretically elegant, but it has difficulty accounting for the data indicating imaginal processes that involve a second-order isomorphism (for example, Shepard's work).

5   The functional-equivalency hypothesis holds that imagery and perception are highly similar (principally the work of Shepard and Kosslyn).

6   Two types of representation have been proposed to explain imagery: direct representation and allegorical representation. The latter is generally more widely accepted than the former.

7   It is debated whether visual imagery is in fact visual (specific) or whether it is actually a more general-purpose cognitive process.

8   Neurological evidence has been claimed for mental rotation. Modern research on imagery has been polarized between those who believe that mental images are very much like all other sensory impressions from the physical world and those who believe that objects are represented in terms of the person's knowledge base. Some view the situation as being a mixture of these two extreme viewpoints.

9   Researchers using measurements of regional cerebral blood flow (rCBF) to study imagery are operating under the assumption that concentrations of blood in the brain correlate with the amount of functioning happening in that part of the brain. The data seem to show that visual processing and sometimes memory areas of the brain are at work when we imagine.

10   People tend to have an egocentric view of the world concerning their mental maps.

11   Synesthesia is a condition in which sensations usually experienced in a single modality are experienced in two modalities. This phenomenon, and those who experience it, have provided some interesting and informative research. In fact, some very reliable functions have been found in the data.

KEY WORDS

cognitive map	mental rotation
conceptual-propositional hypothesis	second-order isomorphism
dual-coding hypothesis	visual imagery
functional-equivalency hypothesis	

RECOMMENDED READINGS

Relevant readings on imagery can be found in Paivio, *Imagery and Verbal Processes;* Rock, *Perception;* Shepard, "Form, Formation and Transformation of Internal Representations," and Shepard, "The Mental Image," in *American Psychologist.* A definitive account may be found in Pinker, *Visual Cognition.* For a clear description of the "imagery" versus "propositions" argument, Kosslyn and Pomerantz in *Cognitive Psychology* and Pylyshyn in *Psychological Bulletin* and *Psychological Review* are recommended. Also see Kosslyn's *Image and Mind* and his theory in *Psychological Review,* and *Ghosts in the Mind's Machine.* Also, Kosslyn's recent work using PET technology can be found in the *Journal of Cognitive Neuroscience* and *Science* as well as in the book *Image and Brain: The Resolution of the Imagery Debate.* Roger Shepard has a delightful book called *Mind Sights,* which should be read by all those interested in imagery and related topics. The September 1992 issue of *Memory & Cognition* is devoted to mental models and related topics. Volume 2 of Kosslyn and Osherson's series on *An Invitation to Cognitive Science* is on *Visual Cognition.* The entire Section VIII of Gazzaniga's *The Cognitive Neurosciences,* a classic volume, is on thought and imagery and is highly recommended.

CHAPTER 11

Language
Structure and Abstractions

hmmm...?

● **Linguistics**
Linguistic Hierarchy
Phonemes
Morphemes
Syntax

● **Chomsky's Theory of Grammar**
Transformational Grammar

● **Psycholinguistic Aspects of Language**
Innate Properties and Environmental Effects
Linguistic-Relativity Hypothesis

● **Cognitive Psychology and Language: Abstraction of Linguistic Ideas**
"The War of the Ghosts": Bartlett
"Ants Ate the Jelly": Bransford and Franks

● **Knowledge and Comprehension**
"Soap Opera," "Thieves," and "Police"
"Bumper Stickers and the Cops":
 Kintsch and van Dijk

● **A Model of Comprehension: Kintsch**
Propositional Representation of Text and Reading

● **Language and Neurology**

1. How do psychologists differ from linguists in the study of language?

2. What are the basic features of Chomsky's theory of grammar?

3. If you reinforce your child by giving her a kiwi when she says "grape," what theory of language development would be illustrated?

4. What is the linguistic-relativity hypothesis? What support has been given for the hypothesis? And what evidence is against the hypothesis?

5. How have studies on the recall of stories (for example, "The War of the Ghosts") changed the way we think about language and memory?

6. What is a schema, and how does schemata-induced information bias one's memory for stories?

7. What are the main points of Kintsch's model of comprehension?

8. How have cognitive neuroscientists investigated the brain and language, and what are some of the main conclusions of this work?

*L*anguage allows us to know how octopuses make love and how to remove cherry stains and why Tad was heartbroken, and whether the Red Sox will win the World Series without a good relief pitcher and how to build an atom bomb in your basement and how Catherine the Great died, among other things.
—Steve Pinker

As you read this text, you are engaging in one of the mind's most enchanting processes—the way one mind influences another through language. In this process, some cell assemblies in your brain are permanently changed, new thoughts are made, and, in a very real sense, you are changed. A new person is created. Yet, this staggeringly complex operation is done effortlessly thousands of times a day by millions of people. Old men, young children, the president of General Motors, hairdressers in Mexico City, taxi drivers in Denver, shoemakers in Athens, and trappers in Siberia all use language to communicate with others and, if no one is around with whom to converse, will spontaneously start babbling to a caged parakeet, a tree, or a pet dog. With the exception of some religious orders, people talk and otherwise use language incessantly. Language, to cognitive psychologists, is a system of communication in which thoughts are transmitted by means of sounds (as in speech and music) or symbols (as in written words and gestures).

The study of human language is important to cognitive psychologists for the following reasons:

- Human language development represents a unique kind of abstraction, which is basic to cognition. Although other forms of life (bees, birds, dolphins, prairie dogs, and so on) have elaborate means of communicating and apes seem to use a form of language abstraction, the degree of abstraction is much greater among humans.

- Language processing is an important component of information processing and storage.

- Human thinking and problem solving can be conceptualized as processes involving language. Many, if not most, forms of thinking and problem solving are internal, that is, done in the absence of external stimuli. Abstraction of puzzles, for example, into verbal symbols provides a way to think about a solution.

- Language is the main means of human communication, the way in which most information is exchanged.

- Language influences perception, a fundamental aspect of cognition. Some argue that how we perceive the world is affected by the language we use to describe it. On the other hand, language development is at least largely based on our perception of language. So the perceptual-language process is one of interdependency; both significantly influence the other. Language from this point of view operates as a window.

- The processing of words, speech, and semantics seems to engage specific cerebral areas and, thus, provides a meaningful link between neuroanatomical structures and language. In addition, the study of the pathology of the brain has frequently shown manifest changes in language functions, as in the case of aphasia.

For these reasons, language has been extensively studied by cognitive psychologists, *psycholinguists* (specialists who study the relationship between psychology and language), and neuropsychologists, among others.

Overview.   In this chapter the traditional areas of language and psycholinguistics will be covered. In addition, some newer aspects of language research, including cognitive neuroscience of language—that specialty that studies language from the perspective of the neural system—will be introduced. In the past, the study of language by cognitive psychologists has concentrated on two topics: words and grammar. A good portion of Chapter 12 is devoted to a discussion of words and much of this chapter will deal with grammar.

Words and their associated meanings. Consider a common word—the word *barrel,* which we commonly define as a large cylindrical container made of wooden staves (not the holding-off type as in "stave off a decision") cobbled (or coopered) together with hoops (not hoopla). So, when I say "Ben got a barrel of rum," you know, almost immediately (within the constraints of the speed of neurotransmission) a tremendous amount of information because of the many attributes of words and their associations that are stored in your cerebral cortex and within which the perception of the word *barrel* activates an exquisite search-and-associate journey. In this wonderfully complex route, swiftly moving shuttles of electrochemical impulses course through the brain, picking up a connection here, an inference there, and a remote association someplace else, all with massively parallel processing. Thus, when someone hears the sentence about Ben and the barrel, they might think that Ben is about to have a "barrel of fun" and that he might remove the staves and, like the Norwegians of the nineteenth century who invented skiing, slide down a snow-covered hill. The copper rings (not handcuffs) forged by coopers (not Gary, the cowboy actor, or James Fenimore, the *Last of the Mohicans* author) could be used as hula hoops for hoopla. The incredible part of this wild flight of fancy is that it is really not very wild, but is quite conventional—we all do it, all of the time, and without much conscious control. The next time you see or hear *barrel,* your adroitness in recognizing "Gary Cooper," "cops," "ski," or "hula hoop" (either the word or the person or a picture) will be measurably enhanced. There has been a palpable increase in the level of activation of the neural cells connected with these remote associates. While the associates may still remain unconscious (of which you are not aware), nevertheless they remain lurking in the wings awaiting their cue to appear on the stage of consciousness. We can now measure these things by reaction-time experiments and imaging technology (for example, MRI and PET).

We humans know a lot of words; about 60,000 separate entities are stored in our cerebral lexicon, but many more may be understood and are constantly being generated. Such is the dynamic nature of language: words like *snail-mail, Californiaburger, Heaven's gate,* or, as a student remarked about her new boyfriend, "He's kind of a *Jim Carey—Tolstoyesque* guy." Deeply animated.

Grammar. A second area of interest deals with the way words are combined into phrases and sentences. In addition to having lots of words to express our thoughts, we also know the rules of sequencing that allow us to express ideas in an order understood by others. We can combine words in many different legitimate ways and yet express a single thought. Thus, the statement *Joan saw the bear open the refrigerator door and eat strawberries* may be expressed as *The bear who ate the strawberries opened the refrigerator door and was seen by Joan,* or in numerous other possible arrangements while maintaining the meaning. (Technically, the study of grammar embraces the areas of *phonology* (the combinations of sounds of a language), *morphology* (the study of the combinations of bits of words and words into larger units), and **syntax** (the study of the combination of words into phrases and sentences.) Each of these topics will be considered in this chapter.

Neurology. (One of the earliest scientific analyses of language involved neurology, and that inquiry continues today. Since ancient times, physicians have known that cerebral damage to the brain could affect language functions, but a major breakthrough occurred in 1861 when Paul Broca, a young French surgeon, observed a patient who suffered from paralysis of one side of his body as well as the loss of speech. The patient died, and Broca performed a postmortem examination, which showed a lesion in part of the left frontal lobe—an area that subsequently became known as **Broca's area.** Subsequent case histories confirmed the original observation that the left frontal area seemed to be involved in speech production, although at first Broca did not make the association between the left hemisphere and speech. In 1875 Carl Wernicke showed that a lesion in the left temporal lobe, just behind the primary auditory cortex, also affected language processing, but of a different sort than that tied into Broca's area. Where Broca's area seemed to be involved in language production, (**Wernicke's area** (as it was soon to be labeled) was a center of language understanding.) Damage to Wernicke's area left patients able to speak but with reduced understanding of spoken or written words; they could speak fluently, but could not really comprehend what was said to them.) But there is some variability among people, and so these early mapping operations need to be viewed cautiously. It seems that language, which is involved in nearly all acts of thought, is not "located" in a single or even multiple "sights" but is processed by microcircuity at the cellular or even subcellular level.) At these very elementary synaptic levels, presently hidden from even the most advanced imaging technology, basic language processing is likely to take place.

Looking back over a century of brain studies and language processing, we can conclude that language functions are localized in broadly defined regions that are mostly centered in the left hemisphere. This includes the original sites identified by Broca and Wernicke as well as parts of the (left) associative cortex and temporal cortex. However, since language processing and production are so complicated (consider the vast number of subprocessing activities involved in the simple associative response of seeing the word *RED* and saying "blood"—processes that involve vision, feature and word identification, lexical access, word association, motor activities and speech, and perhaps emotional effects among others), it is likely that other parts of the brain whose functions are less than perfectly understood exercise subtle effects. We return to the topic of language and neurology later on in this chapter but now consider the linguistic side of language.

I have been struck with the fact that in my first aphemics the lesion always lay not only in the same part of the brain but also the same side—the left. Since then, from many postmortems, the lesion was always left sided.

—*Paul Broca (1864)*

Linguistics

The study of linguistics is the formal description of the structure of language, including a description of speech sounds, meanings, and grammar.

Language as studied by linguists tends to be competency based (dealing with some ideal potential of the speaker-listener), while psychologists generally view language in terms of performance, or how humans use language. The discipline that incorporates both approaches to the study of language is called **psycholinguistics.**

Linguistic Hierarchy

Linguists are interested in developing a descriptive framework of language. Their approach is, in one respect, similar to that of a cognitive psychologist interested in developing a model of memory. From our discussion of memory, you may recall that a model of memory involved the content of memory, the structure of memory, and the processes that operate within memory (for example, coding operations, retrieval operations, and transformational operations). Similarly, some linguists are concerned with the development of a model of language—its content, structure, and process. However, unlike memory research, linguistic research postulates a hierarchy that ranges from fundamental components to compound components to very complex components—that is, sound units and meaning units in order of growing complexity. Each level is somewhat dependent on a lower level but may interact with any other level.

The development of a writing system that reflects speech and conveys thought is one of the most significant of humanity's hierarchical creations. In the English language, there are only ten symbols for digits and twenty-six letters, some of which are so redundant or infrequently used that they contribute little to the overall structure of the written language. From these few letters and digits, about forty thousand words in our working vocabulary are constructed, and from these words billions and billions of sentences are created. Well, there may not be as many sentences as there are particles in the universe, but given our insatiable need to communicate with others, we are producing a huge number of original sentences every minute and promise to approach that number someday. When we consider the richness of the human experience generated by so few symbols (from literature such as the Song of Solomon to *Mein Kampf*), the hierarchical coding properties of language are staggering.

Phonemes *(basic unit of spoken language)*
(English has 45 phonemes)

The basic unit of spoken language is the **phoneme.** Phonemes, single speech sounds that are represented by a single symbol, are created by an intricate coordination of lungs, vocal cavities, larynx, lips, tongue, and teeth. When all works well, the sound produced is available for rapid perception and understanding by someone familiar with the language being spoken. English uses about forty-five different phonemes, but not equally. Only nine are needed to make up more than half our words, with the most frequently used occurring more than one hundred times more often than the least used. Other languages get by with as few as fifteen phonemes, while some require as many as eighty-five. An analysis of the phonemes of General American English,[1] made by Denes and Pinson (1963), follows:

Vowels

ee as in heat	Λ as in ton
I as in hit	*uh* as in the
ε as in head	*er* as in bird
ae as in had	*oi* as in toil
ah as in father	*au* as in shout
aw as in call	*ei* as in take
u as in put	*ou* as in tone
oo as in cool	*ai* as in might

Consonants

t as in tee	*s* as in see
p as in pea	*sh* as in shell
k as in key	*h* as in he
b as in bee	*v* as in view
d as in dawn	*th* as in then
g as in go	*z* as in zoo
m as in me	*zh* as in garage
n as in no	*l* as in law
ng as in sing	*r* as in red
f as in fee	*y* as in you
θ as in thin	*w* as in we

These few phonemes can be combined in various ways to create thousands of different words that may be phonetically and orthographically similar but occupy distant corners of our semantic reality.

Speech sounds that are produced by a coordinated effort of lungs, thorax, tongue, and so on and that include vibration of the vocal cords are classified as *voiced*—for example, *a* or *z*. Speech sounds that do not use vocal cords—such as the *s* in *hiss*—are called *unvoiced* sounds. Among other sounds—voiced or unvoiced—are *fricatives* (produced by restricting the air passage in the mouth), such as *sh, f, v,* and *th,* and *plosives,* or *stops* (produced by interrupting the flow of air for a brief period), such as *t* and *d.*

Voiceprints. It seemed inevitable that phonetic analysis would surrender some of its secrets to the relentless probing by electronic means. A spectrographic device has been developed that separates the various frequencies composing a phonetic feature. Auditory signals are transmitted to a series of filters, each of which resonates to a range of specific frequencies in principle like a crossover filter in high-fidelity audio equipment, which separates high-frequency from low-frequency sounds so that they can be routed to the appropriate speaker (woofer or tweeter). Impulses from specific filters are recorded on a moving paper. This permits visual analysis of speech sounds and the production of voiceprints. In

---

[1]General American is the dialect of English spoken in midwestern and western areas of the United States and influences an increasing number of Americans. Certain phonemes of other regional dialects (such as southern, British, and so on) are different.

FIGURE 11.1

Voice print for "said."

the print shown in Figure 11.1 (for the word *said*) the trace in the upper left is of the high-frequency phonemes associated with *s*, while the lower frequencies of *aid* are represented in the other trace.

It is possible, by use of the spectrograph, to study in minute detail how the acoustic characteristics of the spoken language vary across time. Not only has the recording of "visual speech" allowed researchers to study acoustic characteristics of the spoken language in detail, but it also has a direct practical application in teaching speech to deaf children. Speech development in normal children involves hearing speech, which serves as a model; from the model, a child produces sounds that he or she also hears, and from the hearing of which corrections can be made. Deaf children lack this feedback loop, but an instantaneous visual feedback system (offered by one spectrograph) may serve as a substitute.

Morphemes (smallest unit of meaning in language)

Phonemes are empty; they have no meaning. The smallest unit of meaning in the language is a morpheme. **Morphemes** may be words, parts of words, prefixes, suffixes, or combinations of these. For example, in the sentence "The old chemist loved joyful sounds," *the* and *old* are free morphemes, which stand alone, while *chemist, joyful,* and *sounds* are the combination of a free morpheme and a bound morpheme. *Chemist* is composed of the morphemes *chem* and *ist; joyful,* of *joy* and *ful;* and *loved,* of *love* and *d.* By combining morphemes, we can generate untold millions of words. In English we have more than one hundred thousand words formed by morpheme combinations, but even with such a vast number the composition of morphemes is tightly governed by linguistic constraints. One of the linguistic constraints of English is that no more than three consonants may start a syllable; usually it is less than two. Another constraint is that certain letters—for example, *q* and *d* or *j* and *z*—never appear together. These and other constraints on morphological formation, plus the built-in redundancy of our language, act to minimize the number of errors in transmission and decoding.

Syntax

The next level in the linguistic hierarchy is that of syntax, or the rules that govern the combination of morphemes in phrases and sentences. In recent years the principles underlying syntax have been extended to include how information can be transformed from one form to another. This extension began with the proposal, made by Noam

Syntax failure and performance anxiety.

THE FAR SIDE®   BY GARY LARSON

Chomsky, of a universal theory of grammar aimed at describing the abstract nature of languages, not just their surface characteristics. The result was not only a theory that changed our conceptualization of linguistics but also one that had a profound effect on psychology, especially psycholinguistics.

The number of different sentences humans can generate is restricted only by time and imagination, both of which are in long supply. In an attempt to understand the structure of language, linguists—those people who study the nature of language—have concentrated their efforts on two aspects: productivity and regularity. *Productivity* refers to the infinite number of sentences, phrases, or utterances that are possible in a language (billions and billions of sentences), and *regularity* refers to the systematic nature of the sentences, phrases, or utterances ("The boy hit the ball" rather than "ball boy The hit the").

Language productivity seems apparent, but the regularity of language is a much more tricky affair. The set of rules that governs the regularity of language is called grammar, and transformational grammar deals with the changes in linguistic forms that may retain the same message. For example:

The cat was chased by the dog.
The dog chased the cat.

Both sentences are correct, convey essentially the same meaning, have similar words, and yet differ somehow in their underlying structure. Apparently, the surface features of a language and the deep structure of a language needed to be separated, and the theories of Chomsky were designed along those lines.

Chomsky's Theory of Grammar

The following points are frequently cited as embodying the most important aspects of Chomsky's thesis:

- Language has much underlying uniformity, and the underlying structure is often more closely related to the meaning of a sentence than are the surface characteristics.
- Language is not a closed system but a generative one.
- Within the underlying structures are elements common to all languages, and these may reflect innate organizing principles of cognition. These organizing principles may directly influence the learning and generation of language.

Noam Chomsky. Changed the way language is viewed with theory of transformational grammar.

Chomsky directed much criticism toward behaviorism and its basis, S-R (stimulus-response) learning (including the learning of language), arguing that the development of language cannot be described simply in terms of operant learning principles and that psychological theory must be concerned with underlying processes rather than surface ones. Even though many psychologists dispute Chomsky's criticism, it is generally agreed that it has had far-reaching implications for psychological theory and cognitive research.

Most interest was in three aspects of Chomsky's theory: surface structure, deep structure, and transformational rules. These terms, to be used throughout the following discussion, are generally defined as follows:[2] **surface structure** is that part of the actual sentence that can be segmented and labeled by conventional parsing; **deep structure** is an underlying form that contains much of the information necessary to the meaning; and *transformational rules* are those that turn one structure into another structure. **Transformational grammar,** a revolutionary component of Chomsky's system, details the laws that govern this transformation of one form of linguistic message into another. Consider the sentences: "The jock pursued the sorority girl" and "The sorority girl was pursued by the jock." Both sentences express the same basic idea, which is contained in the deep structure, but the specific form, or surface structure, differs, and transformational rules relate the two.

Transformational Grammar

In another example, the basic meaning of the simple sentence "The short hippopotamus saw the tall giraffe" may also be expressed as "The tall giraffe was seen by the short hippopotamus" or "It was the short hippopotamus who saw the tall giraffe." Our awareness of the true sense of the sentence prevails, despite the semantic rearrangement and, in some instances, alteration of words or morphemes. The integrity of meaning is maintained in deep structure. As another example, try telling a story about some event in your life, such as, going to a concert. After you have told the story, tell it again, but avoid using the same sentences in the retelling. (You probably wouldn't anyway.) Then, under the same constraints, tell it a third time. There seems to be no real end to the ability of varying the means of saying the same thing. The rules underlying this phenomenon are what modern grammarians call transformational grammar. This task, which

[2]These definitions are simplified versions of those suggested by Chomsky.

Cognition in Everyday Life

Grammatically Correct, Semantically Absurd

Lewis Carroll gave us many examples of grammatically correct and semantically anomalous language nearly a century ago in *Through the Looking Glass*. A fragment of one of his more neologistically wild specimens is the following:

He took his vorpal sword in hand;
Long time the manxome foe he sought—

So rested he by the Tumtum tree,
And stood a while in thought.
And as in uffish thought he stood
The Jabberwock, with eyes of flame,
Came whiffling through the tulgey wood,
And burbled as it came.

even children can easily do, is difficult to explain in S-R terms. Speech and language are rarely a passive, repetitive pattern of activity; rather, human language is a productive, generative system. Each sentence we utter is more or less a creative product, which is also more or less easily understood by the listener even though it is novel to both of you. In Chapter 6 and other parts of this book, we have learned how enormous is the capacity of LTM, but even that capacity would be taxed if it had to hold all the sentences we can produce or understand.

One way of explaining our capacity to generate and understand creative sentences is to use the metaphor of a tree, which represents surface structure and deep structure in an orderly fashion. Using this metaphor, the phrase structure of our earlier example "The short hippopotamus saw the tall giraffe" could be diagrammed as follows, with the sentence at the bottom constituting surface structure, and the network above, deep structure:

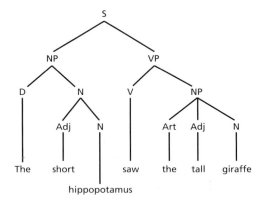

From this simple example, we can identify the fundamental constituents of the sentence, which exist not only on the surface but also on a deeper, abstract level. On the most inclusive level is the sentence (*S*), parsed into the subject and predicate represented as a noun phrase (*NP*) and a verb phrase (*VP*). Contained in the noun phrase (*NP*) are the determiner (*D*) and noun (*N*), which contains an adjective (*Adj*) and a noun (*N*). The verb phrase (*VP*) contains the verb (*V*) and a noun phrase (*NP*) divided into an article (*Art*), adjective (*Adj*), and noun (*N*).

The rules of mathematical transformation seem to offer a basis for representing language in terms in which the specific form may vary while the underlying reality (deep structure) is constant. For example, if $A = B$, then $B = A$; the expression is changed, but the underlying reality is the same. Similarly, $4X = 8$ may be written as $X = 8/4$, and $ab = XY$ $(2X + N)$ may be written as $XY = ab/(2X + N)$. No matter how complex the surface characteristics, the deep structure of underlying reality of the relationship is the

*L*anguage is a process of free creation; its laws and principles are fixed, but the manner in which the principles of generation are used is free and infinitely varied. Even the interpretation and use of words involves a process of free creation.

—*Noam Chomsky*

same. Transformational grammar uses the same kind of logic; sentences, as mathematical equations, may be rewritten in a variety of forms while maintaining their essential meaning. Thus, we can explain our capacity to generate an enormous number of different sentences and several varieties of each sentence not as the result of imitation, which would presume a fantastic memory, but as the result of our innate grasp of certain rules that allow us to form sentences and to transform them into other sentences that express the same meaning. (Chomsky calls this underlying capacity *competence*.) Basic phrase structure rules (using the abbreviations from the tree metaphor just discussed) are as follows:

$$S \quad \rightarrow \quad NP + VP$$

$$NP \quad \rightarrow \quad D + N$$

$$VP \quad \rightarrow \quad Aux \text{ (auxiliary)} + V + NP$$

These rules can be applied to any deep structure to rewrite it in a different and grammatically perfect form while maintaining its true meaning.

The implication of generative grammar is that language analysis should be based on a syntactic level rather than on a phonological or morphological level. It is not that phonological and morphological utterances are unimportant (indeed, they are important) but that a study of linguistics that is limited to only these characteristics fails to account for the variety of linguistic forms that can be rapidly generated and the corresponding ease with which they can be understood. Chomsky illustrates grammatical "correctness" combined with semantic absurdity in the sentence "Colorless green ideas sleep furiously." The grammatical rules for the formation of sentences are limited (again, something does something to something), but the combination of semantic components is limitless. Even in Chomsky's example, if we have an imagination generous enough, the statement is not only grammatically correct but also semantically meaningful.

Psycholinguistic Aspects of Language

Innate Properties and Environmental Effects

Among the most controversial aspects of Chomsky's theory is his assertion that the essential components of language are innate and universal rather than, as argued by B. F. Skinner, learned. Thus, reinforcement—a fundamental element of the Skinnerian (behavioral) view—may determine only the morphological aspects of language development. (For example, a child learns to say "apple" when her request for an apple is reinforced by the object.[3])

To return to a question basic to Chomsky's assertions: How does a child generate a perfectly grammatical sentence he or she has never heard? The innate propensity for language, based on deep structure, is offered as the explanation. Chomsky's position does not hold that a particular grammatical system is innate, but it does argue that we

---

[3]A child given a banana after she said "apple" would undoubtedly form the impression that an apple is a long, yellow fruit fed to chimpanzees and children. Would she understand William Tell, apple cider, Snow White's poisoned apple, and apple pie? Would she ask for an apple split, and how would she interpret the apple picked from the Tree of Knowledge?

have an innate scheme for processing information and forming abstract structures of our language. This may be tied to the biological development of the child.

Several points from our exposition of structural linguistics are important to summarize. From the most general standpoint, we can conceptualize the human brain as a very complex information-processing and storage system. With regard to language, it appears that a great deal of information about language in the form of an abstraction of information (much as we have knowledge of algebra), but we also have specific semantic entities—that is, words. Linguists, especially those subscribing to the ideas of generative grammar, have proposed a description of the abstract character of language and mathematical laws that govern the storage and production of language. Although there is little dispute as to the abstract nature of language, the exact form of abstraction remains debatable.

Another viewpoint (not necessarily antagonistic to the first) is that language and biological maturation go hand in hand, each influencing the other. Both of these positions give us a detailed and expansive paradigm in which to frame a cognitive theory of language.

Linguistic-Relativity Hypothesis

Chomsky's emphasis on linguistic universals is an effort to identify linguistic operations that are common to all languages. As we have seen, it is largely based on deep structure of language and transformations. On the semantic and phonemic level, however, languages are obviously not the same. It is to these surface characteristics that the **linguistic-relativity hypothesis** is principally relevant.

The idea that our language influences our perception and conceptualization of reality has a very long and somewhat stormy history. The modern version has been associated with Benjamin Lee Whorf (1956) who, through his detailed work in the field, has lent his name to the hypothesis (the *Whorfian hypothesis*), although an earlier scholar, Edward Sapir, who was Whorf's professor, is credited with the basic hypothesis. (See Sapir, 1958; Mandelbaum, 1958; and Fishman, 1960, for further details.) Whorf concluded that a thing represented by a word is conceived differently by people whose languages differ and that the nature of the language itself is the cause of those different ways of viewing reality. Whorf studied Native American languages and found that clear translation from one language to another was impossible. In one language, he found that no clear distinction is made between nouns and verbs; in another, past, present, and future are ambiguously expressed; and in yet another, there is no distinction between the colors *gray* and *brown*. However, in English, despite the fact that English speakers have no unique physiological apparatus (to enable them, for example, to see the difference between *gray* and *brown*), we have words that make all these distinctions.

Some linguists have examined how language (and specifically lexical units) influences our conception of reality by studying color names. It is acknowledged that our sensory apparatus is sensitive to a wide range of different colors, yet by labeling various colors, our identification of them is affected. Many years ago Gleason (1961) found that while English divides the color spectrum into purple, blue, green, yellow, orange, and red, plus numerous in-between colors, Shona (spoken in parts of Zimbabwe) and Bassa (spoken in Liberia) identify fewer colors and make the divisions at different points, as shown in Figure 11.2.

Of particular interest in this respect is the fact that all normal persons have the same visual apparatus (that is, the same physiological ability to see colors and make color discriminations). Thus, differences in the mental processing of the colors viewed are suspected of being due to the differences among the different language codes. Some research indicates this to be the case. For example, a color that does not fit into the categories delineated by color name (one that is "between" colors) is likely to be remembered as a member of the color it most resembles. Eskimos have many different names for snow (blowing snow, drifting snow, snow you can make igloos from, and so on), which allows them to "see"—to discriminate—many more different types of snow than we who live in a temperate zone can. Similarly, the Hanuos of the Philippine Islands have ninety-two names for various kinds and states of rice. The Whorfian hypothesis suggests that the physical reality is translated, according to some internal representation of reality, into a perception that is consistent with long-standing cognitive structures. One of the ways information is structured in the brain is apparently related to the specific language codes each of us has developed. These codes differ, as languages differ. This (Whorfian) viewpoint has been strongly opposed by some comparative linguists. Berlin and Kay (1969), for example, examined color names of nearly a hundred languages and concluded that certain basic colors are the same for all languages.

In one experiment they determined the basic color names for twenty languages, and then asked native users of each of the twenty languages to map (that is, to indicate on a series of colors) those they associated with a given color name. Finally, the participants were asked to mark the color they rated as best or most typical of each color name; this was called the *focal color.* Their results indicate that focal colors were very similar for all groups. These results suggest that there is some basic constraint on the

F I G U R E   1 1 . 2

Major divisions of the visible spectrum in three languages.

Adapted from R. Brown (1965).

English	Purple	Blue	Green	Yellow	Orange	Red

Shona	Cips^{w}uka	Citema	Cicena	Cips^{w}uka		

Bassa	Hui		Ziza			

way a participant's experience with colors is coded in language. Thus color names may be more a direct function of perceptual phenomena than a determinant of percepts.

Further evidence in opposition to Whorf's hypothesis has been submitted by Heider (1971, 1972) and Rosch (1973, formerly Heider). She studied New Guinea natives, whose language is Dani. In Dani there are only two color names: *mola*—bright, warm colors—and *mili*—dark, cool colors. By using a recognition test, she found that recognition accuracy was better for focal colors than for nonfocal colors, and yet, if language determines perception, participants whose language has but two names would predictably experience difficulty in recalling focal as well as nonfocal colors. Thus, the case for linguistic determinism (at least of the rigid variety) seems questionable. Anthropologists and psychologists continue to be fascinated by the Whorf hypothesis. Kay and Kempton (1984), writing in *American Anthropologist*, provided a nice review of the empirical research on the hypothesis.

Consider one more question concerning Whorf's view (that language affects the way we conceive reality, process information, and store things in memory and recall): What is the origin of the lexical units? Why does the Eskimo language have so many names for snow and English have so few? Why do we have so many names for types of automobiles and the Laplanders so few (if any)? One answer is that the more significant an experience is to us, the greater the number of ways it is expressed in the language rather than the other way round—that is, that language determines our percepts. The development of specific language codes, therefore, is dependent on cultural needs; the learning of those codes by members of a language group also involves the learning of significant values of the culture, some of which may be related to survival. The consequence of the development of language codes may further determine what information is coded, transformed, and remembered.

Cognitive Psychology and Language: Abstraction of Linguistic Ideas

Up to this point we have covered some of the standard subjects in the psychology of language—a sort of nuts-and-bolts review that has drawn more on the collective wisdom of linguists and anthropologists than on cognitive psychologists. In this section our discussion of language focuses on the cognitive analysis of language, and the theme is the search for underlying, abstract cognitive structures of language. The first idea to be discussed is Bartlett's schema theory.

"The War of the Ghosts": Bartlett

Many investigators have concentrated their efforts on psychological processes involving meaningful prose that closely resembles that of real-life language experiences. The best known of the investigations of complex literary material was done by F. C. Bartlett of Cambridge University and reported in his remarkable book *Remembering: A Study in Experimental and Social Psychology* (1932). In this book Bartlett describes several experiments in which brief stories, prose passages, pictures, and Native American picture writings were used to study the remembering (and forgetting) of meaningful material. The procedures

did exp. where people to recall a story after reading

Sir Frederic Bartlett (1886–1969).
Studied language processing and
memory in a natural context.

were simple. Participants were given a short story or other material. They read it and then
free-recalled what they could remember after a certain period. In other cases a story would
be told to a person, who then retold it to another, who then retold it to another, and so on.
By examining the contents of the reproduced version of the stories, it is possible to analyze
both the nature of the material coded and the nature of the material forgotten. To illustrate
the precise nature of these elements, several participants' protocols are extensively cited.

Here is the original story:

The War of the Ghosts

One night two young men from Egulac went down to the river to hunt seals, and while
they were there it became foggy and calm. Then they heard war-cries, and they thought:
"Maybe this is a war-party." They escaped to the shore, and hid behind a log. Now canoes came up, and they heard the noise of paddles, and saw one canoe coming up to
them. There were five men in the canoe, and they said: "What do you think? We wish to
take you along. We are going up the river to make war on the people."

One of the young men said: "I have no arrows." "Arrows are in the canoe," they said.
"I will not go along. I might be killed. My relatives do not know where I have gone. But
you," he said, turning to the other, "may go with them."

So one of the young men went, but the other returned home. And the warriors went
on up the river to a town on the other side of Kalama. The people came down to the
water, and they began to fight, and many were killed. But presently the young man
heard one of the warriors say: "Quick, let us go home: that Indian has been hit." Now
he thought: "Oh, they are ghosts." He did not feel sick, but they said he had been shot.

So the canoes went back to Egulac, and the young man went ashore to his house, and
made a fire. And he told everybody and said: "Behold I accompanied the ghosts, and we
went to fight. Many of our fellows were killed, and many of those who attacked us were
killed. They said I was hit, and I did not feel sick."

He told it all, and then he became quiet. When the sun rose he fell down. Something
black came out of his mouth. His face became contorted. The people jumped up and
cried.

He was dead.

After about 20 hours, one participant produced a reproduction that in general is
shorter, and the style is more informal. Additionally, there are numerous omissions and
some transformations. Familiar words replace less familiar words—for example, *boat* for
canoe, and *fishing* for *hunting seals.*

Eight days later the same participant recalled the story. This second reproduction was abbreviated. The proper name (*Kalama* in the original) was missing and the excuse "I might get killed" reappeared after being missing from the first retelling.

Six months later another recall measure was made. In this very short version, all unusual terms, all proper names, and references to supernatural powers were dropped.

Finally, one participant was asked to recall the story after 2 years and 6 months. He had not seen the original version in that amount of time and, according to his own statement, had not thought of the story. His account follows:

> Some warriors went to wage war against the ghosts. They fought all day and one of their number was wounded.
>
> They returned home in the evening, bearing their sick comrade. As the day drew to a close, he became rapidly worse and the villagers came round him. At sunset he sighed: something black came out of his mouth. He was dead.

Only the barest rudiments of the story remain. Little elaboration of details can be found, and several themes appear that seem to be related to what the subject thought should happen, rather than what actually did happen in the story. For example, in this passage the wounded man finally dies. When? at sunset . . . naturally! It would appear that this theme is part of the popular folk history of our subject; it certainly isn't in the original version. As we learned from the Bransford and Franks studies, it would appear that fragments of information from a variety of sources (the story and general knowledge) combine to fill out the story in the absence of information of the specific facts.

Bartlett (1932) analyzed this type of information in terms of several categories. These include:

- *Omissions.* Specific information seems to drop out. Also, information that is illogical or does not fit into the subject's expectation is not readily recalled.

- *Rationalization.* Occasionally some information is added that would help explain certain incongruous passages.

- *Dominant theme.* Some themes seem to become prominent, and other features are then related to the dominant theme.

- *Transformation of information.* Unfamiliar words are transformed to more familiar ones.

- *Transformation of sequence.* Some events are characterized as appearing earlier in the story, others later.

- *Subject attitude.* The attitude of a subject toward the material determines the degree of recollection.

In making analyses on these bases, Bartlett used the concept of *schema* to account for his results. (His account, written more than half a century ago, appears as fresh as the latest theory.) Schema, in his view, refers to an active organization of past reactions or past experiences. Incoming stimuli all contribute to the buildup of an organized schema. In Bartlett's words:

> There is not the slightest reason, however, to suppose that each set of incoming impulses, each new group of experiences persists as an isolated member of some passive patchwork. They have to be regarded as constituents of living, momentary settings be-

Linguistic Abstraction

A convincing body of research indicates that when we read a book, a short story, or a poem, we retain only the essence of the work and not many of the details, which are forgotten, unavailable for recall, or melded with other memories to fabricate a distorted memory. Distorted memory from real-life experiences or from written material may be the result of one's previous knowledge, personal aspirations, or seeing the world in light of one's own belief systems. Try this little experiment: Read a short story, and paraphrase its main points in a few sentences as accurately as possible. Have a friend read the same story without writing the main ideas. Several weeks later, ask your friend to tell you the main ideas in the story. Compare your friend's recollection with your notes. Do the same thing with an abstract poem. What differences do you note between the initial factual description and the subsequent recalled accounts? What might contribute to these differences? Are the differences even greater for an abstract poem?

longing to the organism, or to whatever parts of the organism are concerned in making a response of a given kind, and not as a number of individual events somehow strung together and stored within the organism.

Clearly, Bartlett has anticipated the "abstraction of linguistic ideas" that was empirically tested forty years later by Bransford and Franks, Thorndyke, and Kintsch and that has been a recurrent theme in many of the theories of semantic memory mentioned in this book (compare with Rumelhart, Lindsay, & Norman, 1972; Collins & Quillian, 1969; and Neisser, 1976). Some have criticized Bartlett's theory of remembering and schema on the basis that it is too vague and complex to be empirically testable—and with some justification.

The contribution of Bartlett is important for three reasons. First, the notion of abstract memory is introduced in his writings. These abstractions form part of the basis for new learning and later for transformation of new information. Second, he demonstrated that research with real-life stories was possible and led to useful conclusions. Finally, his work provided an important frame of reference for his own students (Broadbent, Brown, and Conrad) and other scholars (Miller, Neisser, and Rumelhart).

In the time since the introduction of Bartlett's notion that stories are coded and remembered by means of schemata, contemporary researchers have proposed ideas that further add to our understanding of the functional properties of narrative memory. Modern theorists have attempted to quantify some of the basic notions of the abstraction of linguistic ideas. Among the best known of these researchers are Bransford and Franks. We consider their work next.

"Ants Ate the Jelly": Bransford and Franks

It has been asserted that beneath the surface structure of our language is a deep structure that follows systematic rules of transformation. The result of this theory has been the proliferation of hypotheses about other hidden cognitive structures. Among the most intriguing of these are those developed by Bransford and Franks (1971, 1972). One of these (Franks & Bransford, 1971) is reported in Chapter 4. In that experiment, participants were shown figures that represented transformation of a prototypical figure and were asked to rate the figure as to whether it was a previously seen pattern. In the recognition portion of that experiment, participants identified, with a high degree of certainty, the prototype that they had never seen. The likely implication is that subjects formed an abstraction, or prototype figure, on the basis of their experience with exemplars. The hypothesis derived from this is that we have a propensity to form abstractions of surface impressions and that these abstractions are the things we store in memory.

Bransford and Franks (1971) also developed a hypothesis concerning the nature of encoding sentences. They composed complex sentences that contained four simple declarative parts, one, two, or three of which could be removed to leave sentences composed, respectively, of three propositions, two propositions, and one proposition. Some of the sentences follow:

Four
The ants in the kitchen ate the sweet jelly which was on the table.

Three
The ants ate the sweet jelly which was on the table.
The ants in the kitchen ate the jelly which was on the table.
The ants in the kitchen ate the sweet jelly.

Two
The ants in the kitchen ate the jelly.
The ants ate the sweet jelly.
The sweet jelly was on the table.
The ants ate the jelly which was on the table.

One
The ants were in the kitchen.
The jelly was on the table.
The jelly was sweet.
The ants ate the jelly.

The experiment consisted of two parts: acquisition of the sentences and a recognition task. During the acquisition part, participants were read 24 sentences, which consisted of one-, two-, and three-proposition sentences. After each sentence was read, the participants were engaged in a color-naming task for 4 seconds and then asked a question about the sentence to ensure that the participants had encoded it. For example, if one of the sentences was "The rock rolled down the mountain," the question might have been "Did what?" After the participants acquired all 24 sentences, the experimenter read aloud additional sentences—some new and some from the original 24. The new sentences contained different parts of the complex idea that had been presented. In order to form a baseline for recognition, some "noncase" sentences were included. These noncase sentences changed the relationship across idea sets. For example, if a reference sentence was "The rock which rolled down the mountain crushed the tiny hut at the edge of the woods" and another sentence was "The ants ate the sweet jelly which was on the table," a noncase sentence might be "The rock which rolled down the mountain crushed the ants eating jelly in the kitchen." Participants were asked to indicate which of the sentences (from among the new, original, and noncase sentences read to them) they had heard during the acquisition stage. Regardless of the response, they were then asked to evaluate their confidence in their judgment on a five-point scale (from very low to very high). The findings were that evaluations were essentially the same for old and for new sentences and that participants' confidence in their recognition corresponded directly to the complexity of the sentence (see Figure 11.3). Thus, sentences that seemed to have four propositions received the highest confidence ratings—in the neighborhood of +3.5 (even though no sentences with four propositions were actually presented)—while those containing three propositions were rated lower and so on through the sentence with only one proposition, which received a negative rating. Few were fooled by the noncase sentences, where confidence was around –4. (This control condition was important in that it shows that participants did not base their confidence on sentence length alone.)

It is likely that participants expressed greater confidence in having experienced complex sentences because they had abstracted a basic idea from the initial sentences to which they were exposed and stored that abstracted entity rather than simply the sentences themselves in a disconnected series. The implication of these data for a theory of cognition and memory is that human memory for sentences is not merely a transcription of words (like a tape recording) but is the result of a dynamic process in which ideas are abstracted. These abstract ideas are, of course, derived from experience with sentences and form the basis of our impression of new and old sentences. Thus, as Chomsky has attempted to describe a structural linguistics in which language capacity is formulated in abstract principles, Bransford and Franks have attempted to describe how information about ideas expressed in sentences is organized in an idea structure that forms the basis for judging new information.

An important conclusion of the Bransford and Franks experiments is that human participants do not isolate sentences (presumably in memory) if the sentences are semantically related. Somehow, information from different sentences is combined into an abstracted form, and we tend to remember the abstraction better than the specific

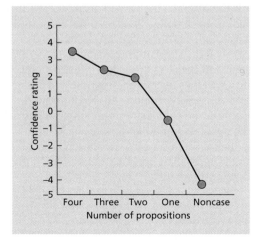

FIGURE 11.3

Confidence in having experienced sentences. Related to the complexity (number of propositions contained) of the sentence.

Adapted from Bransford and Franks (1971).

form. We have seen throughout this book that modern cognitive psychologists seem preoccupied with the building of structures of mental processing that adequately reflect information processing, memory, and thought. The linguistic components of language suggested by Chomsky's theories seem to represent adequately a form of structural components. The research of Bransford and Franks, on the other hand, seems to give considerable insight into the specific kinds of transformations that are likely to occur in the abstraction of sentences.

Quite a different way to look at linguistic processing is to think of narrative information as being structured in the form of a hierarchy in which the most important ideas are supported by less important statements. From an informal perspective, we seem to think of stories in a hierarchical way. If asked to tell what a book (for example, *Crime and Punishment*) is about, we may try to find a single sentence that embodies its essence. When asked to expand our interpretation of the story, we may discuss the theme, the plot, the setting, and the way it turned out. (See Thorndyke, 1977, for an example.)

From the early theories of Bartlett and sentence and story schemata, we have seen a studious progression and development in the scientific analysis of language abstraction. Both the abstraction of linguistic ideas, as shown in the "ants eating the jelly" study, and in story grammar analysis have supported the general notion that there is a hidden, structural processing of sentences and stories. It is precisely within this hidden structure and its top-down effect that significant progress in understanding of language has taken place within the past few years. Our attention is now directed toward the topic of knowledge and text comprehension. Several new ideas are discussed in the next section, including a comprehensive model of language processing developed by Kintsch. As you study these models, keep in mind the previous research on story abstraction and top-down processing and consider its relationship with these models.

Knowledge and Comprehension

We begin with the simple generalization that the greater the knowledge of a reader, the better the comprehension of text. This generalization seems to be valid for readers who have broad knowledge and read colloquial material as well as those who have specialized knowledge and read technical material. One way to account for this generalization is that knowledge can be viewed as an organized collection of information. New information, as might be gathered through reading, can be assimilated more thoroughly when existing cognitive structures and information already exist. Conversely, insufficient knowledge limits comprehension because the reader must develop some structure of knowledge about the material as well as encode the information being read. Comprehension, within this framework, is perceived more as a confirmation of hypotheses about the way the world is thought to be than as a purely original assimilation of new facts. Much, but not all, comprehension is top-down processing. People with specialized knowledge, be it in plumbing, ballet, astrophysics, or motorcar racing, comprehend technical information in their field better than nonspecialists do.[4] Following are several examples of the power of top-down processing.

---

[4]This assumes that all other significant variables (for example, intelligence) are equal.

"Soap Opera," "Thieves," and "Police"

Text comprehension and understanding is influenced by situational information or instructions. In one experiment by Owens, Bower, and Black (1979), which illustrates the "soap opera" effect in story recall, participants were to read a story about a water-skier and the driver of the boat. Half the participants were introduced to the story by a passage that was designed to persuade the reader to identify with the water-skier, and half by a passage to identify with the driver. The test story was the same for both groups. After the groups read the story, a series of questions was asked. Those positively biased toward the water-skier tended to make errors in his behalf. For example, their reaction to the statement "[the skier] . . . reached for the handle [of the rope tow] but it escaped him" was to blame the failure on the boat driver for not coming close enough. On the other hand, those participants positively biased toward the driver tended to believe that the skier was not fast enough to grab the handle. The tendency to ascribe guilt to the "other guy" and innocence to "our guy" demonstrates how understanding of textual material can be based on contextual biases.[5]

In yet another frequently cited study, this one by R. Anderson and Pichert (1978), participants were asked to read a story about the home of a wealthy family from the standpoint of a prospective home buyer or a burglar. Many features about the house and its contents were described, such as its fireplace, musty basement, leaky roof, silverware, coin collection, and television set. The rated importance of these items as well as what was remembered was predictably related to the reader's viewpoints. The would-be thieves seemed to concentrate on the valuable loot, whereas the home buyers focused on the condition of the house. These experiments suggest that understanding or encoding textual material is influenced by contextual information that activates a specific type of schema.

The power of an induced schema on story recall was further illustrated in a study by MacLin and Solso (2004). A "police officer schema" was introduced by having college students complete a police officer entrance exam. A sample question follows:

A patrol officer responds at night to a telephone complaint that a prowler has been observed at a particular location. The patrol officer arrives at the location and notices someone who appears to fit the description of the prowler previously given by the complainant. In approaching this individual, it would be *best* for the patrol officer to:

A. Avoid taking any precautionary measures since the officer has no means of knowing whether any offense has been committed.

B. Consider this individual to be a potentially dangerous criminal.

C. Consider that this individual is probably harmless and is only a "peeping Tom."

D. Fire a warning shot over the individual's head.

After working through 25 such questions, the students were then asked to read a story which contained 66 "idea units," or separate notions, some of which were consistent with a police officer schema and some of which were not. As an example, the sentence "He reached for another cigarette, finding the pack empty" is neutral for a police schema and was generally neutral for the study—although, if you were a person who had

---

[5]These findings tend to substantiate the questions raised by Elizabeth Loftus about the reliability of courtroom witnesses.

schemas related to stopping smoking or you were a tobacco executive, the sentence may have had a particularly trenchant meaning. However, the sentence (from a Tami Hoag novel), "Jay called 911 on his cellular phone and reported a break-in in progress, and then let himself out of the truck, pocketing the keys, careful not to let the door slam" contains several salient ideas that are sure to seize the attention of a police officer or, in the case of the experiment, the attention of someone whose level of police consciousness had been elevated simply by having taken a police entrance examination. The results were significant in that those students who took the police examination recalled two times as many police idea units as did the nonexamination group (schema recall was 15; nonschema recall was 7.88). However, overall, the recall for idea units was about equal for the two groups. By having a brief experience with a police test, a kind of schema seemed to be induced which had a profound effect on the way the story was encoded and recalled.

The power of induced schemas to influence perception and memory was also illustrated by Beal (now MacLin) and Solso (1996) in an experiment in which participants were assigned to a nurse, architect, or police officer schema, or to a control condition. In this experiment participants wrote an essay about the workdays and special skills of the schema assigned to them. A nurse might write that he or she would begin the day by taking the vital statistics on a patient, administering medication, consulting with doctors, and the like. Then the participants were asked to look at a slide show of photos and paintings; this was followed by a memory task. Schema induction increased recall for schema-related questions.

Perhaps even more fascinating was the finding that some of the induced schemas, for example, the police officer and nurse schemas, tended to overestimate the number of schema-consistent components in the pictures. Figure 11.4 shows a rather lurid pulp magazine cover that was shown to all groups. Participants with police- and nurse-induced schema had an inclination not only to focus on the number of weapons and physical injuries but to *exaggerate* the frequency of these things. Thus, perception and memory for schema-related material seem to be the focus of attention, and in some cases, the observer overestimates the magnitude of the related material. Whether of not actual police officers or nurses act that way is unanswered by this research. Incidentally, those participants with the "architect" schema correctly answered the greatest number of questions, which suggests that architects may look at a scene analytically and search for general overall themes, while control-condition participants were the poorest at memory for

If dogs (like humans) had a schema, this is how Snoopy would interpret a story.

PEANUTS reprinted by permission of United Features Syndicate, Inc.

How many guns do you see in this lurid pulp magazine cover? Police-induced schema participants had a tendency to overestimate the number of guns.

scenes. It would appear that having some point of view, even an artificially induced schema, increases memory for scenes and, in some cases, embellishes the memory.

"Bumper Stickers and the Cops": Kintsch and van Dijk

The model of comprehension espoused by Kintsch and van Dijk is important from the bottom-up and top-down perspective. On the level of reading text material, the model is based on propositions, or abstractions of information, drawn from the text base, while on the level of reader intention, the model posits a goal schema that directs the reader's comprehension of text material.

The model (which is discussed in greater detail in the next section) allows researchers interested in the structure of stories to make precise predictions about the memorability of specific types of information. The technique developed by the authors of the experiment is consistent with modern scientific methodology in psychology as contrasted with the subjective method used earlier in the important work of Bartlett.

For purposes of our discussion, we concentrate on the way students go about storing in memory information acquired from an article called "Bumper Stickers and the Cops." In an experiment done by Kintsch and van Dijk (1978), participants were asked to read a nontechnical report that was about 1,300 words long. Following the reading of the report, one-third of the participants were immediately asked to recall and write a summary of it. Another one-third of the participants were tested after 1 month, and the final one-third after 3 months. The procedure is similar to the one conducted by Bartlett.

All of the recall accounts and summaries were organized into statements that could be identified as:

- Reproductions (statements that accurately reflect the comprehension of the text).
- Reconstructions (statements that are plausible inferences from the main theme aided by the participants' world knowledge, such as "Beth went to Vancouver by train," might be expanded to include "She went into the station to buy a ticket").
- Metastatements (participants' comments, opinions, and attitudes on the text).

These components were computer analyzed with specific predictions made by the model. Several important conclusions were made by the authors about text comprehension and memory. As indicated by the data gathered over three different time periods (see Figure 11.5), it appears that participants lost more and more of the specific details of the report over time but retained the gist of the story with about the same degree of fidelity throughout a 3-month period—a finding consistent with the protocol analysis of

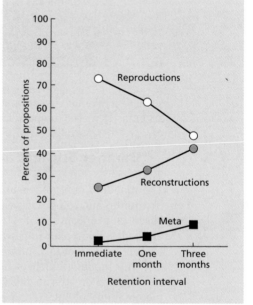

FIGURE 11.5

Proportion of reproductions, reconstructions, and metastatements. In the recall protocols for three retention intervals.

From Kintsch and van Dijk (1978).

Bartlett. Additionally, it seems that the analysis of written material, such as books, stories, and technical reports, is organized in a way that is susceptible to careful empirical study of propositions, which may tell us more about the way text material is organized and how the human mind records and stores in memory written material over time.

This chapter has progressed systematically from very simple linguistic entities (phonemes and morphemes), to syntax and grammar, to psycholinguistic theories, and to the abstraction of linguistic ideas as expressed in the analytic work just presented. One might now wonder whether there are any comprehensive theories of language. Indeed, there are several, but we cannot describe them all. One by Kintsch is particularly significant because it incorporates many bits of wisdom from previous studies and, at the same time, contains a model of the mind. Let's look now at this comprehensive model of language processing.

A Model of Comprehension: Kintsch

In this section we explain the principal components of one influential and extensive model by Kintsch and his coworkers at the University of Colorado (Kintsch, 1974, 1979, 1988, 1990; Kintsch & van Dijk, 1978; Kintsch & Vipond, 1979; J. Miller & Kintsch, 1980; and van Dijk & Kintsch, 1983).

This model of comprehension is more than a system that deals with the way textual information is understood. It is a theory that cuts across many topics in cognitive psychology, including memory and comprehension of the written and spoken language. Comprehension is dependent on two disparate sources that are similar to top-down and bottom-up processing, discussed in some detail throughout this book. At the highest level is the goal schema, which decides what material is relevant. At the opposite extreme of the model is the text.

The model is based on the *proposition,* a term first introduced in our discussion of semantic memory. A proposition is an abstraction, and, as such, it is difficult to define concretely. We can, however, identify some characteristics of propositions: they are abstractions based on observations (such as reading text material or listening to a speaker); they are retained in memory and follow the laws governing memory processes; and, in Kintsch's system, they consist of a predicate and one or more arguments. Predicates

Walter Kintsch. Developed influential theories of language comprehension.

correspond to verbs, adjectives, adverbs, or connectives in the words a person reads or hears. This is called the *surface structure*, a term used by several linguists, including Chomsky. Arguments correspond to nouns, noun phrases, or clauses. The model is illustrated with the following little story:

> The Swazi tribe was at war with a neighboring tribe because of a dispute over some cattle. Among the warriors were two unmarried men, Kakra and his younger brother Gum. Kakra was killed in battle.

The first sentence is divided into five groups, as shown in Figure 11.6. In this figure only three of the factors are in working memory. The predicate "was at war with" is considered the most important part of this sentence insofar as comprehension of the story is concerned. The other parts are clustered around it. A significant feature of the model is that the initial processing of text is assumed to take place in STM, which we know has limited capacity. Because of this constraint, only a portion of the propositions is held in memory. With the reading of the second sentence, some of the propositions from the first sentence are still vital in STM (see Figure 11.7). The reader tries to connect the old and new propositions but finds no match between them. Failing to find a match between the propositions in STM, the reader searches LTM for a possible match. This search of LTM is called *reinstatement search* and is one reason that text material may be hard to read. Text material that flows may be easy to read because the reader is able to retain much of the recent material in STM without having to access LTM. In the example, the lack of a match between propositions in the first and second sentence requires the reader to construct a new network for the ideas and to attempt to relate the two sentences (see Figure 11.6). One inference the reader makes is that the two men were members of the Swazi tribe, a reasonable conclusion even though that fact is not stated directly. With the reading of more sentences, the semantic network begins to get more complicated and interrelated. The reading of the sentence "Among the warriors were two unmarried men, Kakra and his younger brother Gum" retains in memory the names of the men, which can easily be related to the information in the last sentence, "Kakra was killed in battle."

F I G U R E   1 1 . 6

Analysis of the first sentence.

From Kintsch (1979). Copyright 1979 by Division 15 of the American Psychological Association. Reprinted by permission.

FIGURE 11.7

Analysis of the second sentence.

From Kintsch (1979). Copyright 1979 by Division 15 of the American Psychological Association. Reprinted by permission.

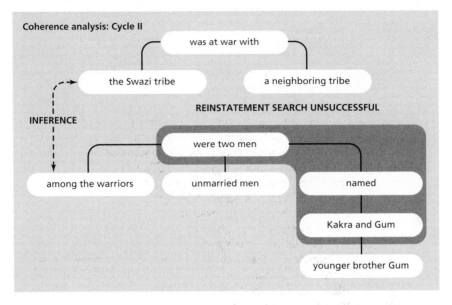

Propositional Representation of Text and Reading
=======

One strength of Kintsch's model is that it is possible to make very precise predictions about the effect of certain types of literature on the reading process. Only one sample of the many experiments is reported here.

You'll recall that the model of comprehension holds that the underlying unit of memory for text material is the proposition. Additionally, the model predicts that sentences of greater propositional complexity are more difficult to comprehend than sentences with simple propositional structure, even if the surface complexity of the two sentences is about the same. Kintsch and Keenan (1973) designed an experiment to test this prediction.

Participants were asked to read ten sentences, all of which had about the same number of words but varied greatly in the number of propositions. Some sentences had as few as four propositions, and others had as many as nine. For example, read the following two sentences:

> Romulus, the legendary founder of Rome, took the women of Sabine by force.
> Cleopatra's downfall lay in her foolish trust in the fickle political figures of the Roman world.

Which sentence was more difficult to read? If you are like the people in Kintsch's and Keenan's experiment, you had more difficulty with the sentence about Cleopatra

FIGURE 11.8

Number of propositions and macrostructures for two sentences.

From Kintsch and Keenan (1973).

than the sentence about Romulus. Even though the surface complexity of the two sentences is about the same, they differ markedly in the number of propositions and the macrostructures that are required to interconnect the propositions. A diagram showing the propositions and macrostructures is shown in Figure 11.8.

In the Kintsch and Keenan experiment, participants were presented with sentences similar to those just discussed by means of slides. The participants were asked to read each sentence and then to write it. They could then advance the slides and see the next sentence. Of interest was the relationship between propositional complexity and the amount of time participants required to read the sentence. The authors found an extraordinarily consistent relationship between the number of propositions and the time required to read the sentences; this relationship is shown in Figure 11.9. The time required to read each sentence is predicted by the formula $t = 6.37 + 0.94p$, where t is time and p is the number of propositions. Therefore, a sentence of the length used in the Kintsch and Keenan experiment would require about 6 seconds to read and about an additional second for each proposition.

All language and comprehension functions mentioned are mediated by the brain, a fact that has long been known but poorly understood. Recently, however, aided by new technology, the brain's role in language processing and production is beginning to be discovered. Some of these recent developments as well as some traditional concepts are presented in the next section.

Language and Neurology

As we have just seen, language is a multifarious affair. It involves letter and word identification, sound patterns, associative networks, speech, comprehension, as well as personal-social considerations. It is a means not only of communication but also of problem

FIGURE 11.9

Reading time as a function of number of propositions per sentence.

From Kintsch and Keenan (1973).

solving and thought. Because language touches so many cognitive functions, the search for one neurological center or even multiple centers might be as fruitless as the search of the feckless lover who is looking in all the wrong places. Rather than thinking of the neurology of language as localized, it is prudent to consider the neurology of language as consisting of a family of capabilities which have centers, but whose full operation is dependent upon a myriad of centers interacting simultaneously. We have good evidence, for example, that the two centers identified earlier (Broca's area and Wernicke's area) are involved in language production and language comprehension. However, clinical results clearly show that profound aphasia may result if the connecting tissues between these sites is severed.

The study of the neurological basis of language has been investigated by several means, including clinical investigations of brain-damaged patients, electrical stimulation of the brain, psychosurgical procedures, pharmaceutical investigations, and imaging technology. We cannot recount, in detail, findings in all areas, but we can give a sample of research.

Electrical Stimulation.   The use of tiny *bipolar electrical probes* has occurred in human and animal experimental work for many decades. In the late 1950s, Penfield (1959) and Penfield and Roberts (1959) stunned the psychological world when they presented verbal protocols of patients undergoing psychosurgery in which low-voltage electrical currents applied to classic language areas, such as Broca's area and Wernicke's area as well as some areas of the motor cortex, interfered with speech production. In one instance, when a probe was placed in the speech zones, the patient (who was awake since the procedure required only local anesthesia) reported, "Oh, I know what it is. That is what you put in your shoes." After the probe was removed, the patient said "foot" (Penfield & Roberts, 1959, p. 123).

More recent experiments using electrical stimulation of the brain by Ojemann (1991) have disclosed some equally interesting data on the brain and language. The technique, which is similar to the one used by Penfield, involves patients who are undergoing a treatment for epilepsy in which a portion of the skull is removed exposing the cerebral cortex. One procedure Ojemann used was to show patients a picture and ask that it be named with the probe turned on and with it turned off. As with the Penfield studies, it was possible to map areas of the cortex that were disabled during the task and to eliminate other areas that were not disabled. The results are shown in Figure 11.10 in which the percentage of participants who showed naming errors is identified in the circled portions. Note that some regions are not affected while in other areas 50 percent to 79 percent of the patients had naming errors while other areas were below 50 percent.

In another task the researcher had patients read a passage such as "The driver will turn at the intersection and then . . . " and complete the sentence. As in the other task, this was done with stimulation and without stimulation to specific areas. In this case the patient sometimes had difficulty reading the sentence, skipped words, or, in some cases, stopped reading completely. In the latter situation, if the probe was moved even slightly (no more than a few millimeters), there was no longer any interference. Thus, it was concluded that in these specific language tasks there were local areas that were critical. Another interesting finding was that the location of sites was highly variable among patients.

PET Scans and Language.   We have reviewed the procedure used in PET scans in Chapters 2 and 9. One advantage of this technology over electrical stimulation is that it is far less intrusive and can be performed on healthy persons; in contrast, electrical stimulation is usually done as an adjunct experiment during psychosurgery with impaired patients. Several PET studies have been done with words, and the field is developing so rapidly it is likely that many more will be reported in the next few years. Of particular interest is a study by Posner and his colleagues (1988) in which visually presented words caused activation in the occipital lobe while spoken words showed activa-

FIGURE   11.10

The results of electrical stimulation of the brain by Ojemann (1991).
The small upper number is the number of patients tested, and the circled number is the percentage of patients who showed naming errors when stimulated at that site.

Reprinted by permission of the Society for Neuroscience.

F I G U R E   1 1 . 1 1

PET scan data showing areas activated in visual reading. The triangles show areas activated in a passive visual task, while the squares refer to the semantic task.

Data from Posner et al. (1988). Copyright © 1988 AAAS. Reprinted with permission from AAAS.

tion in the temporoparietal cortex, a finding entirely consistent with previous neurological studies. These studies are especially revealing when one considers the tasks involved. In one condition, called the semantic task, more complicated processing was examined than was done during the passive viewing of words. In the semantic task, the person was asked to say the use of a noun. For example, to the noun *hammer,* a participant might say "to pound." Such a task requires not just the passive observation of the word, as in the visual condition, but also access to associative-semantic regions of the brain. Posner and his colleagues found an increased blood flow in the anterior left frontal lobe as shown by the squares in Figure 11.11. While in the auditory condition, participants were asked to judge whether or not words, such as *pint* and *lint,* and *row* and *though,* rhymed, which required phonological analysis of visually presented material. The area activated in this task was the left temporal lobe, which is an area normally associated with auditory processing. These experiments suggest that linguistic processing is modality specific, that is, that semantic processing and auditory processing of visually presented material occur in different sites. In the next chapter we shall see how different parts of the brain are associated with words.

In this chapter a general overview of language was presented. The next chapter deals with the specific topics of the perception of words and reading. Some recent findings in that domain are also engaging, and we will find that real progress has been made in furthering our understanding of these cognitive processes.

Spotlight on Cognitive Neuroscience

Linguistics

" 'Liver.' The word rises from the voice box and passes the lips. It beats the air, enters an ear canal, sets nerve cells firing. Electrochemical impulses stream into the auditory cortex of a listener's brain. But then what? How does the brain's neural machinery filter that complex stream of auditory input to extract the uttered word: 'liver'—or was it 'river,' or perhaps 'lever'?" (Gibbs, 2002, p. 26). Wayt Gibbs reports in *Scientific American* magazine on Paul Iverson's work on how your first learned language actually changes the way your brain functions such that you hear other languages differently. He found that while native English speakers can easily distinguish the sounds /l/

and/r/, that native Japanese speakers have difficulties distinguishing the two, which is why these Japanese speakers will sometimes say "river" when they mean "liver," because they actually hear "river" when "liver" is said. Frank Guenther created a neural network to model this idiosyncrasy in the way the sounds of a second language are heard. His findings from this modeling indicate that the brain loses its ability to distinguish similar sounds. Interestingly, infants up to the age of 8 months are able to distinguish between the 869 existing phonemes. After that age, the brain starts to reorganize and becomes sensitized to sounds in the native language. English only has 52 different phonemes from the original 869 that are possible.

Gibbs, W. W. (August, 2002). From mouth to mind: New insights into how language warps the brain. *Scientific American.*

$\mathcal{S}$UMMARY

1   Language is crucial to a wide range of human activities, including communication, thought, perceiving and representing information, higher-order cognition, and neurology.

2   Early neurological studies by Broca and Wernicke established centers of the cortex, mostly located in the left cerebral hemisphere, that are involved in speech production and language comprehension.

3   Linguists conceive of language as a hierarchical structure that ranges from simple to increasingly complex components (for example, phonemes, morphemes, and syntax).

4   One feature of recent theories of transformational grammar is that message content of sentences may remain constant despite changes in linguistic form. One thesis (Chomsky) distinguishes between surface and deep structures and argues for the importance of the underlying uniformity of language, the generative nature of language systems, and commonalities in all languages.

5   Three positions regarding language acquisition can be identified: one position (for example, Chomsky) holds that language is an innate, universal propensity; the second position (for example, Skinner) holds that language is learned via reinforcement contingencies; and a third views language development as a function of biological maturation and interactions with the environment.

6   The linguistic-relativity hypothesis proposes that the nature of a language determines how people see and think about reality (language thought), but evidence indicating that perceptual experience is similar to different language speakers makes a strict interpretation of this position questionable.

7   Comprehension in reading is the process of understanding the meaning of written material. Studies of eye fixations indicate that comprehension is influenced by such factors as rare words, the integration of important clauses, and making inferences. Knowledge, either acquired throughout the history of the individual or situational, also affects comprehension.

8   One model of comprehension (Kintsch) suggests that readers understand text material in terms of propositions and goal schemata.

9   Studies of syntactic constructions show cultural differences in preferred word order (for example, subject-verb-object versus verb-subject-object), although the subject precedes the object in the majority of cases.

10   Some functional properties of memory for narrative prose include the following: sentences are stored in memory in combined, not isolated, form; stories, like sentences, can be parsed into their structural components; memory for narrative information is a function of its structural role; and gist is retained over time, but specific details are forgotten.

11   Studies of the neurology of language suggest that there are specialized areas involved in language processing, but that since language involves so many different subsystems, it is likely that many regions of the brain are engaged simultaneously.

12   The neurology of the brain has been studied by several techniques, including electrical probes and PET scans.

Key Words

Broca's area	psycholinguistics
deep structure	surface structure
linguistic-relativity hypothesis	syntax
morpheme	transformational grammar
phoneme	Wernicke's area

Recommended Readings

● Excellent older books include R. Brown, *Words and Things,* a general and enjoyable book; Miller, *Language and Communication,* somewhat outdated but a classic; and Cherry, *On Human Communication.*

● Original sources on Chomsky's ideas are very specialized, hence difficult for the nonspecialist; more accessible are E. Bach, *Syntactic Theory;* Slobin, *Psycholinguistics;* Kess, *Psycholinguistics: Introductory Perspectives;* and Dale, *Language Development: Structure and Function.* A comprehensive account is H. Clark and E. Clark, *Psychology and Language: An Introduction to Psycholinguistics.*

● Also recommended is G. Miller's excellent book *The Science of Words.* For further treatment of Kintsch's work, read Kintsch and van Dijk in *Psychological Review.* Those interested in the neurology of language are directed to Kolb and Whishaw, *Fundamentals of Human Neuropsychology;* Kandel, Schwartz, and Jessell, *Principles of Neural Science;* and Springer and Deutsch, *Left Brain, Right Brain.* Section VII of Gazzaniga's *The Cognitive Neurosciences* has some good chapters and Pinker's *The Language Instinct* is interesting and a good read, as is his best-selling book *How the Mind Works.*

CHAPTER 12

Language

Words and Reading

hmmm...?

● **Perceptual Span**
Text Processing: Eye Tracking

● **Lexical-Decision Task (LDT)**

● **Word Recognition: A Cognitive-Anatomical Approach**

● **Comprehension**

1. Why are cognitive psychologists interested in words and reading?

2. What is perceptual span?

3. How does the restricted view of foveal vision affect reading?

4. What techniques have been used to study reading scientifically?

5. What are the reading patterns of a dyslexic person?

6. What is reading comprehension and how has it been studied?

7. What parts of the brain have been associated with language processing?

8. What happens visually and cortically when one reads a difficult passage?

In a recent survey of scholars, Johann Gutenberg (1397–1468), the inventor of movable type, was named the most influential person of the last millennium. In a period that saw the likes of Einstein, Galileo, Leonardo da Vinci, Beethoven, Newton, Shakespeare, and Darwin (not to mention Elvis and Bill Gates), why was this humble German printer so highly acclaimed? Gutenberg gave common people letters, which when joined gave us words, which when linked together gave us phrases and sentences, which when combined gave us paragraphs, chapters, and books, which when read and understood gave all of us *Don Quixote, Pride and Prejudice, The Critique of Pure Reason, Principia Mathematica, Les Miserables, The Koran, Crime and Punishment, Moby Dick, Hamlet, The Origin of Species, The Communist Manifesto, The Common Sense Book of Baby and Child Care,* and *The Cat in the Hat* (along with countless others). The printed word was a valuable contribution to the intellectual history of the world, which bestowed upon the brain, a mind; changed civilizations; enlightened the masses; disclosed nature to the curious; and nourished the spirit of all humanity. As we write a chapter about words and reading, in a scientific book on cognition, it is with an uneasy reverence for the topic. Almost all of what we know is because we have access to information that is contained in words. Let's see what psychologists have discovered about this most powerful of media.

The detection of letters and reading is of importance to psychologists for two reasons:

- The process represents, in microcosm, an interaction of stimuli and memory that mirrors the human cognitive process, and so understanding the process may be useful in developing models or theories of cognition—of the interplay between the "thing out there" and the "thing in the head." This is particularly true of reading, where a physical stimulus, devoid of any intrinsic value, is given meaning in an abstract memory system. These theories are developed within the context of the letter and word experiments because we know a great deal about both the nature of the stimuli and the experiences subjects bring with them to the perceptual situation.

- The study of the process involved in letter identification and reading may lead to knowledge that could be used to improve the teaching of reading. The question of what attributes are involved in reading is among the most vexing of educational issues. Some answers to that question may be found by studying the development of reading skills, investigating letter and word identification, and in the neurology of reading.

One phase of the inquiry into the process of letter and word identification started out with determining how much we see in a given fixation—a kind of cognitive snapshot—and ended with finding out how the structure of the visual pattern (for example, words) affects its identification.

Smart Reading

$\mathcal{B}$efore reading ahead try to identify the following words: (1) n_t_r_, (2) m_m_r_, (3) p_rs_n_l_t_. Did you find this too difficult?

It has been determined that word perception is influenced by previous experience. We carry around with us some well-established rules of orthography (letter sequence), grammar, semantics, and word associations—all of which assist us in reading as well as everyday living. How much information did you bring to the decoding of this message, and how much was in the stimuli? Our capacity to "see" letters and words is not a passive process, but rather it is an active process in which we search for perceptual objects that already have their representation in memory. If you had difficulty filling in the blanks, consider the following hints: (1) human, (2) long term, (3) traits. Are there other words that could be formed from the letters given above? Why did you not think of them immediately?

Toward the end of the nineteenth century, when experimental psychology was emerging in laboratories in Germany, England, and the United States, a French scientist, Émile Javal (1878), discovered that during reading the eye did not sweep across a line of print but moved in a series of small jumps—**saccades**—with momentary fixation occurring between them. James McKeen Cattell (1886a, 1886b) undertook to find how much could be read during a single visual fixation. Using a tachistoscope, he estimated the time it takes to identify such things as forms, colors, letters, and sentences. The results of his experiments conformed to those of the earlier studies of range of attention, but of greater interest for Cattell was the fact that reaction times were related to the people's familiarity with the visual material.

By having participants view a display of letters and words for as little as 10 milliseconds (1/100 of a second), he discovered that the capacity to report letters was not so much a function of the number of letters as it was a function of how close the sequence of letters approached a meaningful sequence—as, for example, in a word. A participant exposed to a display of unconnected letters for 10 milliseconds was able to report three or four letters; if the letters made a word, then up to two words (of three or four letters each); and if the words were syntactically related, then the participant could "read" as many as four. Since 10 milliseconds is considerably less than the time required for a saccade,[1] the span of apprehension in the Cattell studies was limited to what might be called (in filmmaking terms) a single frame of perception.

Perceptual Span

Modern cognitive psychologists are as intrigued by the question of **perceptual span** (how much information can be perceived during a brief presentation) as were their

---

[1]A 2-degree saccade takes about 25 milliseconds; a 5-degree saccade, about 35 milliseconds; and a 10-degree saccade, about 45 milliseconds. There is some variation from person to person (L. Young, 1963; Rayner, 1978; and Robinson, 1968).

nineteenth-century counterparts. Following are several questions that dominate current thought on letter and word identification. The answers are discussed in this chapter.

- What are the neurological and physical capabilities in letter and word identification?
- What letter and word characteristics affect recognition?
- What normally is the relationship between stimulus and memory factors?
- What are the effects of context and frequency on word recognition?
- What models of cognition need to be developed to describe the process?

First, consider the question of neurological capabilities in the identification of letters or words. Visual acuity is best for images that fall on the part of the retina called the fovea. This small indentation on the back part of the eye is densely packed with photosensitive neurons called *cones* (see Figure 12.1A). **Foveal vision** encompasses a visual angle of only about 1 to 2 degrees. By fixing your gaze on a single letter of text at a normal viewing distance, you can experience the difference between foveal and peripheral vision. The single letter focused on is very clearly resolved, and some letters on either side may also be seen clearly. However, the letters and words only a few degrees away are quite fuzzy, and letters and words in the periphery are unrecognizable (see Figure 12.1B).

In Figure 12.2 the cone of vision is shown. This illustration is meant to represent a three-dimensional view of normal viewing (in fact, the field of vision is a bit more irregular than shown). We can see that foveal vision occupies only the narrowest of wedges subtending a visual angle of about 2° and parafoveal vision 10°. Peripheral and

F I G U R E   1 2 . 1

A. Distribution of cones in the retina. B. Visual acuity in the retina. Shaded area is the "blind spot" (point of attachment of optic nerve).

A. Adapted from Woodson (1954).   B. Adapted from Ruch and Patton (1965).

FIGURE 12.2

Cone of vision showing foveal, parafoveal, near peripheral, and peripheral vision.
(Here the angles measure the field of vision from one side to the other.)

From Solso (1994).

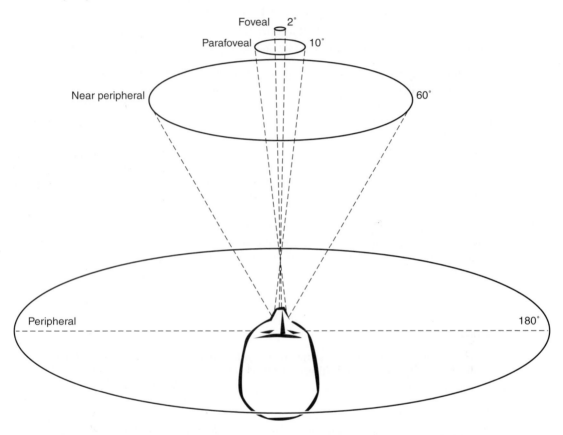

near peripheral vision extends one's field of view considerably but at the cost of decreased resolution. Also, these parameters are sensitive to the type of stimuli being perceived. Stationary objects in the peripheral may go undetected, while moving objects may be "seen" and get our attention. Inherent in this observation are ecological considerations in which the perception of moving prey or predators was related to survival.

Yet, despite the fact that acuity drops off sharply from the fovea, it appears that identification of some letters and words, especially in the normal course of reading, occurs outside foveal vision. To better understand this seeming paradox, consider recent findings about saccadic eye movement. These rapid eye movements, although often studied in association with the reading process, also occur when a person views a visual pattern. (See the discussion of Yarbus's work in Chapter 4.) According to Norton and Stark (1971), during reading there are typically 2 or 3 saccades per second, and these occur so fast that they occupy only about 10 percent of the viewing time. A movement of 10 degrees lasts only about 45 milliseconds and, during the movement, vision seems to be impaired, a condition called visual smear (Haber & Hershenson, 1973). It appears, then, that the recognition of letters and words in the nonfoveal field, which frequently occurs in the reading process, must be partly attributed to something other than the physical stimulation of the retina. That "something" is likely to be the person's great knowledge of letter and word sequencing as well as his or her understanding of the theme of the text. This is particularly evident among so-called speed readers, whose enormous capacity for processing voluminous information seems to be dependent upon their expectation of the material to follow.

Another way to evaluate visual acuity is through eye-tracking experiments that utilize computers. These experiments have been instrumental in identifying eye movement and eye fixation, which are thought to be tied to the processing of information in reading. These techniques and findings are discussed shortly (see the work of McConkie & Rayner and Just & Carpenter). Yet another technique for evaluating visual acuity has been to use a tachistoscope capable of presenting visual stimuli for a short duration. In these types of experiments, while participants gaze at a fixation point, a word or phrase is flashed across the screen for a brief time. The participant may be asked to recall distal letters or words. The results of these types of experiments are summarized in Figure 12.3. As shown, the perceptual span generally takes in about two or three words, or about ten to twenty characters.

Given the constraints of the visual system, what can we infer about the process involved in normal text reading? It is likely that textual information that falls on the fovea is clearly detected and passed on to the brain for further processing. During the saccade, little, if any, textual information is being detected or processed. Textual information that is beyond the fovea, in parafovea or in peripheral vision, is poorly resolved neurologically, and yet this seeming sensory handicap does not impede the normal processing of textual material. Some evidence suggests that letters in the poorly resolved parafoveal vision are detected more clearly if they are surrounded by a space. Estes (1977) reconstructed the process involved in normal reading (shown in Figure 12.4).

An important task of the verbal processing system, which is to make semantic sense out of familiar lines and curves, is to fill in the gaps from the information detected and derive the ultimate meaning intended by the writer. The reading process—from the moment the eyes focus on textual material, to the derivation of meaning to another saccade—is done in a very brief time period. Later we shall learn of some recent techniques that have unraveled some of the mysteries of the process.

William K. Estes. Made significant contributions to many fields of psychology, including learning theory, mathematical psychology, and cognitive psychology. Founding editor of *Cognitive Science.*

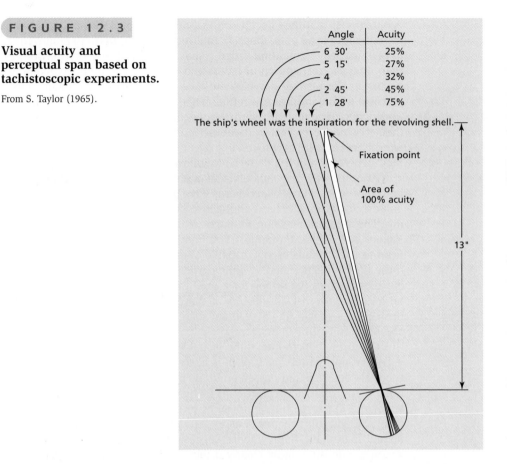

FIGURE 12.3

Visual acuity and perceptual span based on tachistoscopic experiments.

From S. Taylor (1965).

Angle	Acuity
6 30'	25%
5 15'	27%
4	32%
2 45'	45%
1 28'	75%

The ship's wheel was the inspiration for the revolving shell.

Fixation point

Area of 100% acuity

13"

The study of perceptual span in reading allows examination of the processing of information that is frequently not clearly perceived yet is frequently clearly encoded. Studies of the reading process seem to reflect a person's capability to form hypotheses rapidly about text that requires only the confirmation or denial of his or her expectations rather than the detailed featural analysis of each letter. Some of the research related to letter and word recognition is presented in the next section.

Text Processing: Eye Tracking

When we read or view a scene (such as a painting or picture), our eyes make a series of movements, called saccades, and there are periods of time when the eyes stop momentarily, called fixations, which, on average, last about 250 milliseconds, although individual differences both within and between people vary considerably. We do this because vision is sharpest in only a very narrow range, about 1 or 2 degrees. The typical saccade is about eight or nine letter spaces and is not affected by the size of the print, assuming it is not too small or too large. About 10 percent to 15 percent of the time we move our eyes back to review textual material; these are called *regressions.*

FIGURE 12.4

Illustration of fixations and duration (in milliseconds). Also shown is a hypothetical reconstruction of the information perceived during fixations of normal text. Notice that at and near each fixation, letters are clearly perceived, while more distant letters are poorly perceived with the exception of letters surrounded by a space.

From Estes (1977) and Dearborn (1906). Reprinted with permission from W. K. Estes.

As early as 1906 (Dearborn), psychologists were making photographic records of eye movements during reading. Modern eye-tracking systems use videotape recorders and computers to analyze the movement of eyes during reading (see Figure 12.5) or when viewing a picture, and since the mid-1970s there has been a resurgence of interest in studies of eye movements applied to reading (see Inhoff & Tousman, 1990; Just & Carpenter, 1987; Raney & Rayner, 1993; Rayner, 1993; and Rayner et al., 1989, for reviews and recent developments) and perception of art (see Solso, 1994).

Some experimental work on the size of perceptual span has used this system. In this work, when a participant fixates on a portion of textual material, changes can be made in other parts of the display. For example, a display could consist of mutilated and normal text to study visual span of text. In these experiments, when the participant fixates on a line, that part of the display fixated on changes to readable text. When the participant makes a saccade, the readable text changes back to mutilated text and a new display of readable print appears near his new fixation point (see Figure 12.6). The span of readable text can be varied. McConkie and Rayner (1973, 1976) and Rayner (1975, 1993) have found that good readers detect letter and word shape information from a limited area of about seventeen to nineteen character spaces from a fixation point (about 5 degrees of visual angle).

Rayner (1975, 1993) has used a similar technique to study how wide the area is from which a reader picks up information about the text. Some (Goodman, 1970) have suggested that, on the basis of the context of information plus partial information from peripheral vision, subjects generate a "hypothesis" as to what will appear next. This means that when reading text, participants would move their eyes forward to confirm their hypothesis (the more frequent occurrence) or disconfirm their hypothesis (which then requires further processing). A contrary view is expressed by McConkie and Rayner

FIGURE 12.5

A typical eye-tracking experiment. Here the participant is viewing text as presented on a monitor. Her eye movements are recorded by means of a beam reflected off her pupil, which is transmitted to a computer and displayed on a second monitor being observed by the experimenter.

Photo courtesy of EyeTracking, Inc.

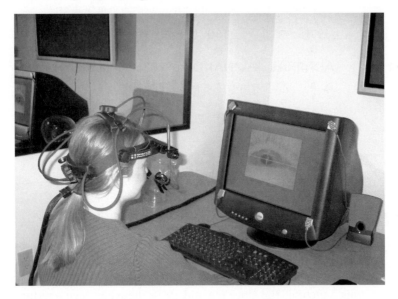

(1973), who assume that participants use the time during fixation to determine the nature of the text rather than hypothesize what is to follow. However, periphery cues are important in a section of certain information (for example, some features and shapes). When participants move their fixation point ahead, the perceived pattern is normally consistent with their partial information. Finally, an innovative feature of Rayner's work is the variability of information presented in participants' peripheral vision. In one experiment Rayner (1975) used a "critical word," which would change to the "word-identical condition" as participants moved their fixation point toward it (see Figure 12.7 for an example). Thus, in the sentence "The rebels guarded the palace with their guns," the critical word *palace* could change (as the eye moved toward it) to *police.*

Critical Word	Condition
Palace	Word-identical.
Police	Semantically and syntactically acceptable word, some of whose letters are the same as W-Ident.
Pcluce	Nonword, with extreme letters and shape the same as W-Ident.
Pyctce	Nonword with altered shape but same initial and end letters.
Qcluec	Nonword with end letters reversed.

Rayner found that a semantic interpretation (that is, meaning) of a word was made one to six character spaces from the fixation point, but beyond that, at seven to twelve

FIGURE 12.6

Examples of the moving-window paradigm. The first line shows a normal line of text with the fixation location marked by an asterisk. The next two lines show an example of two successive fixations with a window of 17 letter spaces. The remaining lines show examples of other types of experimental conditions. In the asymmetric example, the window extends 3 letters to the left of fixation and 8 to the right; in the similar-letters condition, the letters outside the window are replaced by similar letters rather than *X*s; in the no-spaces example, all of the spaces between words are filled in outside the window; in the one-word example, only the fixated word is within the window; and in the two-word example, the fixated word plus the word to the right of fixation is available.

From Rayner (1993). Reprinted by permission of Cambridge University Press.

eyes	do	not	move	smoothly *	across	the	page	of	text	Normal
XXXX	XX	XXX	move	smoothly *	acXXXX	XXX	XXXX	XX	XXXX	
										Moving window
XXXX	XX	XXX	XXXX	XXXothly	across *	the	XXXX	XX	XXXX	
XXXX	XX	XXX	XXXX	smoothly *	acXXXX	XXX	XXXX	XX	XXXX	Asymmetric
cqcr	bc	maf	move	smoothly *	acsarr	fbc	qoyc	at	fcvf	Similar- Letters
XXXXXXXXXXXXmove				smoothly *			acXXXXXXXXXXXXXXXXXXXX			No-spaces
XXXX	XX	XXX	XXXX	smoothly *	XXXXXX	XXX	XXXX	XX	XXXX	One-Word
XXXX	XX	XXX	XXXX	smoothly *	across	XXX	XXXX	XX	XXXX	Two-Word

character spaces, participants were able to pick up only gross visual characteristics, such as word shape and initial and final letters. It appears that information in the near periphery is partially coded, and the extent of the processing is contingent on the distance from the fixation point.

Eye Tracking and Reading of Music. Reading music is similar to reading words. In order to sight-read music, a musician must somehow translate notes on a page to appropriate motor movements and interpret the signals aesthetically. Consider the really complicated task that a pianist has in playing music from a score. At a basic level, the level of a beginning student, there is a direct translation between a note and the striking of a

FIGURE 12.7

An example of the boundary paradigm. The first line shows a line of text prior to a display change with fixation locations marked by asterisks. When the reader's eye movement crosses an invisible boundary (the letter *e* in *the*), an initially displayed word (*date*) is replaced by the target word (*page*). The change occurs during the saccade so that the reader does not see the change.

From Rayner (1993). Reprinted by permission of Cambridge University Press.

eyes	do	not	move	smoothly	across	the	date	of	text	Prechange
*		*		*	*					
eyes	do	not	move	smoothly	across	the	page	of	text	Postchange
								*		

Try This

Can You "Read" This?

*A*occdrnig to a rscheearch at Cmabrigde Uinervtisy, it deosn't mttaer in waht oredr the ltteers in a wrod are, the olny iprmoetnt tihng is taht the frist and lsat ltteer be at the rghit pclae. The rset can be a total mses and you can sitll raed it wouthit porbelm. Tihs is bcuseae the huamn mnid deos not raed ervey lteter by istlef, but the wrod as a wlohe. Amzanig huh?

With little difficulty, you were probably able to decipher the preceding paragraph. People have found this so fascinating that the preceding paragraph often makes the rounds over email, with friends forwarding it to friends, not realizing that they are pondering some important cognitive principles! The paragraph demonstrates the brain's remarkable ability to derive meaning from patterns of symbols (letters) that we are so familiar with, even when those patterns aren't quite right. A bottom-up approach would lead to frustration. But given that reading relies very much on top-down processing, our brain can figure this out quite easily. But just because you can still read this does not mean that you should not spell check your papers!

corresponding key: Read note C; strike C key. But at the virtuoso level, the player looks at a series of notes and merges that immediate information with knowledge held in long-term memory about musical harmonies, global rhythm phrases, and the interpretation of the overall melodic line. In addition, the experienced musician may relate the current piece of music to his or her musical schema. This may be fused with the emotional theme of the music. And these are only a few of the more obvious components inherent in musical playing and interpretation.

In order for all these complicated cognitive processes to occur, it is likely that the skilled musician does not play a piece "note by note" but looks ahead in the score so as to anticipate what comes next—as an experienced reader might do with text material. The question is, "How far ahead does the average skilled player look, in playing a musical piece?"

Several experiments have addressed this point, including a study by Rayner and Pollatsek (1997) in which skilled piano players were asked to sight-read a relatively simple melody by Bartok. The method used was a moving-window technique in which a sequence of notes was presented on a video screen to the player in a "window." The information in the window changed in synchrony with the player's eyes. The results, given in Figure 12.8, show that the player's eyes focused beyond the point being played in the vast majority of cases. Two additional observations are of interest: In a few instances, participants focused *behind* the note being played, which suggests that the player may have been reflecting on the notes just played. And skilled players exhibited a larger perceptual span than less skilled players. The magnitude of the difference was about two beats forward for skilled players versus half a beat for the less skilled players. Skillful performance in reading words, as well as in reading music, seems to exhibit an enhanced perceptual span for experts over novices. Experts are able to "take in" more information in a brief fixation than nonexperts.

Down-the-Garden-Path Experiments.   The method of studying reading by means of eye movements has been used by Carpenter and Dahneman (1981; also see Just & Carpenter, 1987) in whose research brief stories such as follows were read aloud:

> The young man turned his back on the rock concert stage and looked across the resort lake. Tomorrow was the annual one-day fishing contest and fishermen would invade the place. Some of the best bass guitarists in the country would come to this spot.

If you read this passage as most people do, you were led down the garden path in the first few lines, because when you read the word *bass,* you thought of the fish and pronounced it to rhyme with *mass.* The next word, *guitarists,* disconfirms that interpretation. Eye fixations up to *bass* are normal; however, as may be evident to you, the length of time spent on the word *guitarists* is longer than normal. Additionally, people tend to backtrack and look at the previous word.

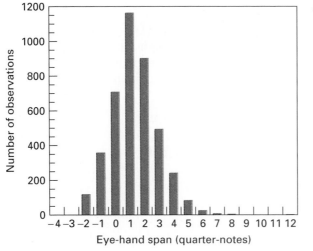

FIGURE 12.8

How far expert piano players look ahead of their hand actions when playing a piece.

From Rayner and Pollatsek (1997).

The garden-path experiments yield significant insights into the reading process as they relate to the processing of textual material, but the results are even more important in our search for the nature of human information processing and consciousness.

- These experiments (along with several others) suggest that the early stages of the comprehension of written material may occur during very brief time intervals. Participants fixed their eyes on *bass* because the meaning of that word, in context, was somehow discordant with the rest of the sentence, and they changed their pattern of reading in a matter of a few hundred milliseconds.

- These findings suggest that from the very beginning of the processing of textual material some sophisticated form of comprehension, that is, the derivation of meaning, takes place. It is likely that, in reading, comprehension is nearly instantaneous with visual perception and need not occur after a trailing, speech-based, short-term memory code. In addition to early and nonspeech-based comprehension, it may be that in reading and other visual experiences we activate a rich chain of associative reactions that are used to understand the thing being perceived.

From the many experiments reviewed in this section, it is clear that the amount of information seen in the perceptual span is rather limited, although the amount of information processed seems to be great. It appears that a portion of the meaning of visual percepts, including letter and word identification, is supplied by readers themselves, a phenomenon that is noted in this and other chapters.

The encoding of a visual symbol involves both the nature of the signal (letter, letter combinations, words) and the expectation of meaning arising from information stored in the long-term memory of each individual. This notion is consistent with signal detection theory, according to which the perceiver brings to a perceptual situation various kinds of sensitivity, comparable to the various frequencies of an electronic receiver (for example, a radio), on each of which only certain transmissions can be received.

Lexical-Decision Task (LDT)

An innovative approach to the problem of contextual effects on word identification has been introduced by Meyer and his colleagues (Meyer & Schvaneveldt, 1971; and Meyer, Schvaneveldt, & Ruddy, 1974a, 1974b). They used a **lexical-decision task (LDT),** a type of priming task, in which the experimenter measured how quickly participants could tell whether paired strings of letters were words. Typical stimuli were as follows:

Associated words	*BREAD-BUTTER*
	NURSE-DOCTOR
Unassociated words	*NURSE-BUTTER*
	BREAD-DOCTOR
Word-nonword	*WINE-PLAME*
	GLOVE-SOAM
Nonword-word	*PLAME-WINE*
	SOAM-GLOVE
Nonword-nonword	*NART-TRIEF*
	PABLE-REAB

Cognition in Everyday Life
The Tortured Reading Patterns of Dyslexic People

Dyslexia is a reading deficiency that afflicts otherwise normal people. Some contend that it is constitutional in origin, while others argue it is social and/or psychological. That issue is not resolved. It is clear, however, that many schoolchildren have difficulty in reading, which profoundly affects their lives. The development of eye-tracking apparatus has made possible the measurement of eye fixations of normal and dyslexic people, which may give us insight into this problem. Samples of reading styles for a normal reader (PP) and a dyslexic (Dave) are shown here. The numbers immediately below the dots are the sequence of eye movements, and the larger numbers further below the dots are the fixation times in milliseconds (1000 milliseconds = 1 second).

PP
As society has become progressively more complex, psychology has

1	2	3	4		5	7		8	9
234	310	188	216		242	188		177	159
							6		
							144		

Dave
As society has become progressively more complex, psychology has

1	2	3	5		6	7	8	9	10		15	12		13	14
311	277	115	412		198	403	266	295	311		193	317		600	312
		4						11				18			
		222						277				206			
												19			
												415			

PP
assumed an increasingly important role in solving human problems.

11		12	13	15	14		16		18
244		317	229	269	196		277		202
	10							17	
	206							144	

Dave
assumed an increasingly important role in solving human problems.

16		21		22	24		25	26	27		28	31		32
369		302		244	310		383	119	487		413	277		366
	17		20		23			29				33		
	415		177		288			200				361		
								30						
								117						

From Rayner and Pollatsek (1989).

In the procedure a participant looks at two fixation points (see Figure 12.9). A series of letters (for example, *NURSE*) appears at the top point. The participant presses a key, indicating whether the letters make a word. As soon as his or her decision is made, the first set of letters disappears and, shortly thereafter, the second set appears. The participant decides whether the second set is a word, and the process continues. This procedure makes it possible to measure word recognition of the second word as a function of the context, or prime, established by the first word. As might be anticipated, Meyer found that reaction time for judging the second word was much faster when it had been paired with an associated rather than nonassociated word (see Figure 12.10).

Again we have an example of the effect of context on word identification. We could interpret those data in terms of a logogen model in which the first word excited the logogen of the second word. Meyer and his associates interpreted them in terms of a general information-processing framework outlined in Figure 12.11, in which the first stage is an encoding operation that creates an internal representation. Following encoding, the sequence of letters is checked against the participant's lexical memory to see whether the item has been previously stored, and, depending on whether a match is made, a decision is executed. Two important assumptions are made by the model regarding memory storage of lexical events: first, the words are stored at various locations in memory, with some words closely associated (for example, *bread-butter*) and some distant (for example, *nurse-butter*); second, retrieving information from a specific memory location produces neural activity that spreads to nearby locations, thereby facilitating the recognition of associated memories. The latter hypothesis is supported by "context" experiments, especially those reported by Meyer and Schvaneveldt, who developed a model (see Figure 12.12) of letter and word recognition. (Although our discussion of this model is in terms of its relation to letter and word identification, the model is also germane to the discussion of semantic memory.) In the model, the recognition process begins when a row of letters enters the visual feature analyzer. The

FIGURE 12.9

Basic procedure on each trial in the lexical-decision task.

Adapted from Meyer, Schvaneveldt, and Ruddy (1974a).

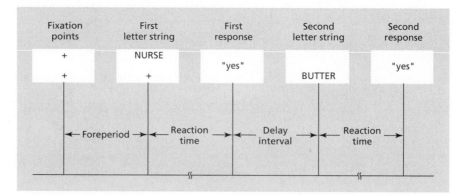

FIGURE 12.10

Effects of semantic context on the time required to identify the second member of word pairs in the lexical-decision task.

Adapted from Meyer, Schvaneveldt, and Ruddy (1974a).

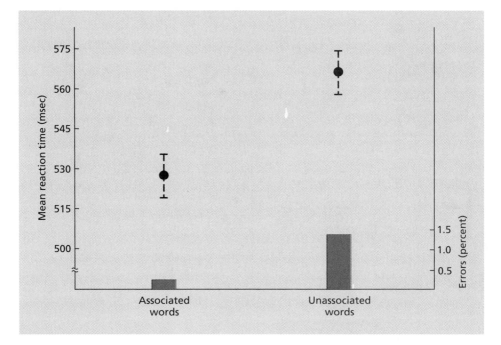

FIGURE 12.11

Possible stages in word recognition. Horizontal arrows show the presumed sequence of operations; vertical arrows, the effects of semantic context and stimulus quality.

Adapted from Meyer, Schvaneveldt, and Ruddy (1974a).

FIGURE 12.12

Hypothetical mechanism for combining sensory and semantic information during word recognition.

Adapted from Meyer and Schvaneveldt (1976).

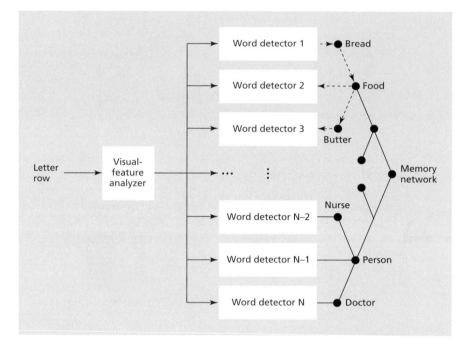

resulting "code," which represents the shape of letters (straight lines, curves, angles), is passed on to word detectors. When sufficient cues are recognized by a word detector, then an affirmative signal is produced to indicate that a certain word has been detected; the detection of a certain word also excites other nearby words. For example, detection of *bread* also activates related words in the participant's memory network. These other words—*food, butter,* and so on—are "sensitized" (my word); this is indicated by the dashed lines in Figure 12.12. The excitation of semantically related words facilitates the subsequent detection of these words. This model takes into account the fact that participants recognize related words faster than unrelated words. This model is noteworthy not only because it accommodates the data, but also because it offers a means of viewing the structure of semantic memory.

The theoretical positions of Meyer and of Morton and connectionism seem not to be antagonistic. Indeed, they appear to be complementary. All address the problem of the effect of context on word identification, and all have concluded that some internal mechanism enhances word identification as a function of context. For Morton, the mechanism is one of elevating a logogen's level of excitation; for Meyer and for Rumelhart and McClelland, it is the spreading of neural activity, which renders similar lexical items more accessible.

Word Recognition: A Cognitive-Anatomical Approach

Our review of the underlying cognitive mechanisms involved in word recognition has covered a wide range of topics—from the contextual effects phases, to logogens, to connectionism, to LDTs. We now turn to some of the evidence on word processing vis-à-vis anatomical structures, which uses some of the advanced technology mentioned in Chapter 2. The research on the cognitive-anatomical foundation of word processing is particularly germane to our present discussion, because some of the cognitive tasks (for example, LDT) have been applied to patients who have sustained brain injuries. The recent neuropsychological journals are overflowing with these types of experiments, which is a harbinger of the direction cognitive science is taking.

(The general direction many of these studies have taken is to locate specific neurological sites involved in specific cognitive functions.) For example, a researcher might be interested in correlating an LDT with specific blood flow observations in an effort to locate cognitive operations in the brain.

Following the work of Meyer and Schvaneveldt just reported, some researchers (for example, Petersen and Posner) have combined several word processing paradigms, including the *DOCTOR-NURSE* task, with advanced imaging technology to isolate the anatomical systems activated by words and their associates in healthy people (see Petersen et al., 1988; Posner et al., 1988; and Posner et al., 1989).

In one study (Petersen et al., 1988) of regional blood flow, participants were asked to participate in three common lexical tasks. Each task differed from the other by a small number of processing operations. At the same time, the researchers monitored data from PET scans with particular attention to the visual and auditory portions of the cortex. The experimental paradigm is shown in Table 12.1)

At the simplest level (A), participants examined a fixation point or passively watched visual words. At the more complex level (B), they repeated each word as it occurred. At

TABLE 12.1

Paradigm Design*

Condition	Control State	Stimulated State	Task
A.	Fixation point only	Passive words	Passive sensory processing; modality-specific word-level coding
B.	Passive words	Repeat words	Articulatory coding; motor programming and output
C. Active semantic	Repeat words	Generate uses	Semantic association; selection for action

*Table showing the rationale of the three-levels stepwise paradigm design. At the second and third levels, the control state is the stimulated state from the previous level. Some hypothesized cognitive operations are represented in the third column.

an even more complex level (C), they generated a use for each word. Succinctly stated, different cortical areas were activated by each of the different tasks (see Figure 12.13). Of particular interest in these findings are the portions of the cortex involved in visual word forms (A), which are represented by triangles in Figure 12.13, and those involved in semantic analysis (C), which are identified by circles, suggesting that these different forms of lexical processing are, indeed, handled by different parts of the brain. These data are even more interesting when we consider them in the context of the previously reviewed (connectionist theory (see Rumelhart & McClelland, 1986). In that theory, you may recall, separate levels of feature, letter, and word form analysis were posited. The demonstration of multiple areas of activation in the experiment by Petersen and his colleagues seems to offer tangible support for this part of the puzzle.

These data were supplemented by an experiment by Posner and his team (1989) using essentially the same technique, except that the person participated in a modified LDT (see preceding discussion). In one condition, a visual priming of a word was presented (for example, *DOCTOR-DOCTOR*); in another task, a semantic priming of a word was presented (for example, *DOCTOR-NURSE*); and in a third task, a cueing of visual spatial attention was done (for example, a peripheral cue to the left of the screen followed by a target to the left

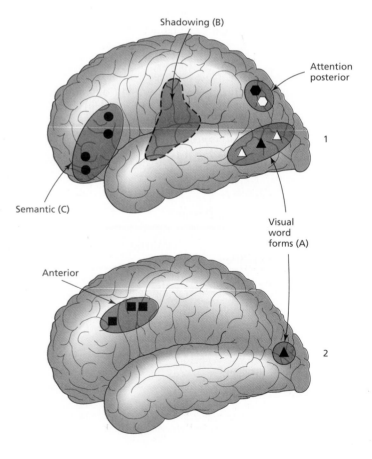

FIGURE 12.13

Data from PET scans studies showing areas of visual and auditory words. Two areas are shown: the lateral sides of the cortex (1) and the medial portions (2). Visual words are shown in triangles (A), semantic analysis in circles (C), and attention in squares or hexagons. Solid figures indicate left hemisphere, and open figures indicate right hemisphere. The area activated by repeating words presented auditorily (such as in shadowing experiments) is encircled by broken lines (B).

From Petersen et al. (1988). Reprinted by permission from *Nature.* Copyright © 1988 Macmillan Magazines Ltd.

for a valid trial or to the right for an invalid trial). The results of the study showed that the area most likely to be involved in the priming of visual features (*DOCTOR-DOCTOR*) is the ventral occipital lobe (identified in Figure 12.13 as visual word forms [A]). Posner and his associates suggest that word primes activate these areas and that an identical target will re-activate the same pathway within the network. Semantic tasks (*DOCTOR-NURSE*) seem to activate two additional areas: the left inferior prefrontal cortex (C) (see circles in Figure 12.13) and the medial frontal lobe (see hexagons in Figure 12.13).

Taken together, these studies advance our understanding of the relationship between cognitive tasks, such as the LDT, and brain functions. Additional work in this area is likely to focus on the role of attention and lexical processing; some data in that area already have been reported (see Posner et al., 1989; and Gazzaniga, 2000). Further application of the work may link the bizarre abnormalities in thought and language among schizophrenics with cortical anatomy, especially abnormalities in the anterior attentional system.

Although linguists have suspected that a word that is processed semantically (what is the meaning of the word?) is processed by a different part of the brain than a word processed perceptually (what is the shape of the word?), until recently, such impressions were scientifically unsubstantiated. John Gabrieli and his colleagues at Stanford University have presented data from fMRI studies that confirm the fundamental difference between these encoding types. In several studies (Gabrieli et al., 1996) participants were asked to evaluate a set of abstract words, such as *TRUST*, and concrete words, such as *CHAIR*. Sometimes the words were presented in uppercase (as shown) and sometimes the words were presented in lowercase (*trust* and *chair*).

In the semantic part of the experiment participants were asked to judge if the words were abstract or concrete, and in the perceptual phase of the experiment they were asked to identify the word as being shown in uppercase or lowercase. (The procedure is similar to one used by Craik & Tulving mentioned in Chapter 7.) In Gabrieli's experiment the participant's brain activity was being monitored by a fMRI (see Chapter 2) scan, which pinpointed the locus of cortical activity in these tasks.

It was found that during the semantic portion of the task, the left inferior prefrontal cortex was more active than for perceptual tasks. These results show that different parts of the brain are implicated in semantic versus perceptual processing of words. In addition, it is possible to use imaging technology to solve some basic problems in language processing.

In this section we have tried to trace the development of lexical processing from both the theoretical and empirical standpoints. The auspicious conclusion is that real progress has been made on both levels, and, fortunately, there seems to be greater mutual support than mutual dissolution. Such a conclusion is, we're sure, a consolation to cognitive and brain scientists who are working on the problem of lexical processing from different perspectives. We now leave this section and turn to the topic of orthography and intention in reading.

Comprehension

Up to this point our discussion of the reading process has concentrated on the recognition of letters and words in and out of context. The reason people read, by and large, is

For a large class of cases—though not for all—in which we employ the word "meaning" it can be defined thus: the meaning of a word is its use in language.

—*Ludwig Wittgenstein*

to extract meaning from material that is conveniently represented in printed form. We use the term *reading comprehension* to describe the process of understanding the meaning of written material. Studies of **comprehension** have yielded nearly as many models and theories as researchers, and although many are meritorious, only a sample of that important work can be reported here.

Consider a simple sentence, such as "The ball is red." From our previous discussion of visual perception and word identification, we know that light reflecting from the printed page received by the sensory neurons is transmitted to the brain, where feature, letter, and word identification is made. Such elementary processes, however, are devoid of meaning, which is presumably the purpose of reading.

When you read the example sentence, it is probable that you understand that (1) a single spherical object is (2) colored red. You comprehend the meaning of the sentence, and that meaning is about the same as the author intended and as most other folks understand. In addition to the basic physical characteristics described, you consciously or unconsciously make many inferences about the object. (For example, most readers infer that the ball is larger than a golf ball and smaller than a basketball.)

Comprehension of the sentence can be validated if you are shown a picture of a red ball and indicate that the meaning of the sentence is the same as the picture, as contrasted with a picture of a green ball or a red box. This seemingly simple task really involves many more operations than are first apparent. In order to understand reading comprehension, some theorists have broken the process into stages, which assumes that there is a sequence of processes that starts with the perception of the written word and leads to the understanding of the meaning of sentences and stories. One model, which incorporates some of the topics discussed in this book, was developed by Just and Carpenter (1980, 1987) and will serve as a representation of contemporary work in this field. The rudiments of the model are shown in Figure 12.14. The process of reading and comprehension in the Just and Carpenter model is conceptualized as the coordinated execution of a series of stages that include extracting physical features of letters, encoding words and accessing the lexicon, assigning case roles, and so on. In this representation the major stages of reading are shown in the left column, while the more permanent cognitive structures and processes are shown in the boxes in the middle and right side of the diagram.

Some of the intriguing features of this model are that it is comprehensive and yet it generates very specific predictions about reading performance that can be empirically measured by eye fixations. The authors assume that words in textual material are structured in larger units, such as clauses, sentences, and topics. A schematic diagram of one example of how a paragraph of scientific material might be conceptualized is shown in Figure 12.15. When a participant encounters a section of written text that demands greater processing of information, he or she may require longer pauses, which can be measured by looking at eye-fixation times.

FIGURE 12.14

A schematic diagram of the major processes and structures in reading comprehension.

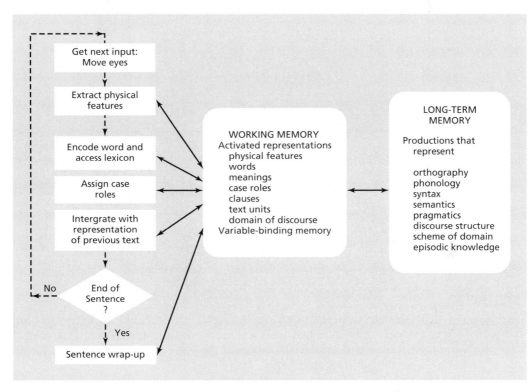

In a test of the model, college students were asked to read scientific texts from *Newsweek* and *Time* magazines while their eye movements and eye fixations were being unobtrusively measured. A sample of one student's performance is shown here:

```
     1        2     3      4       5        6          7
    1566     267   400     83     267      617        767
 Flywheels   are   one   of the  oldest  mechanical  devices
     8        9     1      2       3        5          4        6
    450      450   400    616     517      684        250      317
 known to    man.  Every  internal-combustion engine         contains
     7        8            9               10       11        12
    617      1116         367              467      483       450
 a small   flywheel  that  converts  the  jerky   motion   of the pistons
             13      14     15      16      17             18    19    20     21
             383    284    383     317     283            533   50   366    566
   into      the   smooth  flow    of    energy   that   powers the  drive  shaft.
```

These are the eye fixations of a college student reading a scientific passage. Gazes within each sentence are sequentially numbered above the fixated words with the durations (in msec.) indicated below the sequence number.

FIGURE 12.15

A schematic diagram of the major text-grammatical categories of information in the scientific paragraphs.

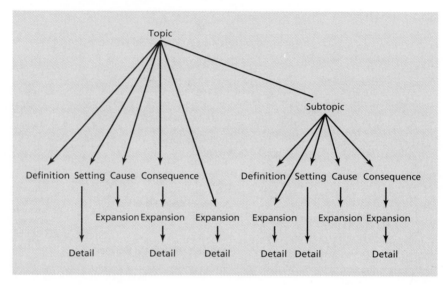

These data suggest that greater processing loads, as shown by eye fixations, occur when readers are confronted with uncommon words, integrating information from important clauses and making inferences at the ends of sentences. The major processing levels are shown in Figure 12.16.

All reading, whether it involves simple sentences (such as "The ball is red") to more involved connected discourse (such as that used by Just and Carpenter), involves the careful coordination of a number of perceptual-cognitive stages. These include feature and letter identification, word encoding, lexical access, semantic extraction, and inferences about the intention of the author that are derived from both the immediate contextual information and the reader's vast knowledge of the world.

As with so many areas of cognition, comprehension has been studied from the standpoint of brain activation. In the previous section we saw that eye fixations of people reading scientific passages tended to be longer when confounded with uncommon words, which suggests that there is a corollary effect of brain computation and activation. In effect, when we read a particularly difficult passage, we may be "thinking harder" than when we read a simpler passage. From what is know about the locus of language processing areas of the cortex (see Chapter 2), one might expect greater involvement in areas such as Broca's area (that part of the cortex involved in language production) and Wernicke's area (that part of the cortex involved in language comprehension) while reading more complicated material than simple material.

To test this notion Just, Carpenter, Keller, Eddy, and Thulborn (1996) developed a series of sentences that varied in structural complexity. After reading the sentences, the participants were asked questions related to their comprehension. All of this was done while fMRI measures were continuously being observed. Take the following sentences ordered in terms of their complexity:

FIGURE 12.16

The major processing levels in the READER model. They operate as the reader fixates on the word *engine* in the text.

Adapted from Just and Carpenter (1987).

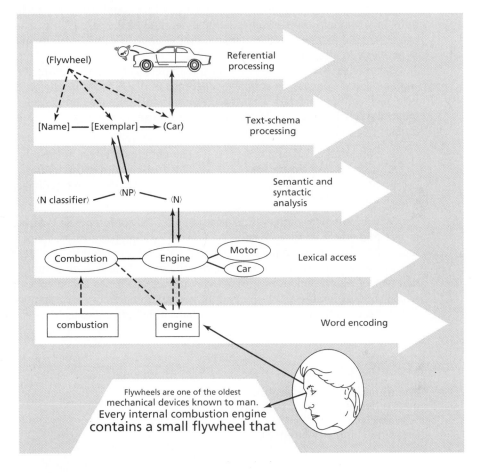

Sentence	Type
"The reporter attacked the senator and admitted the error."	Active conjoined with no embedded clause
"The reporter that attacked the senator admitted the error."	Subject relative clause
"The reporter that the senator attacked admitted the error."	Object relative clause

As you read these three sentences, you may sense that the first is easy to read and understand and the latter two are a bit more difficult. Can such subtle differences in comprehensibility be manifested in different brain activities? The volume of neural tissue activated, that is, the number of **voxels,** was measured in several suspected areas of the brain as participants read and answered questions about sentences of varying complexity. The results of the experiment are shown in Figure 12.17.

As shown, the mean number of voxels activated increased in both Wernicke's area and Broca's area with increased complexity of the sentence. In general, these findings add an important new dimension to our understanding about the brain and language comprehension. The amount of neural activity that cognitive tasks, such as reading, require is dependent on the computational demand of the task. Thus, reading of complicated material places a greater demand on the brain and such activity may be measured by modern imaging technology.

Comprehension of discourse is also a matter of coherence among key concepts in a sentence. And one way to enhance coherence in discourse is by means of a definite article such as the word *the*. Take these examples of sentences on the left, which contain indefinite articles (e.g., *a*) as contrasted with those on the right, which contain definite articles (e.g., *the*).

A grandmother sat at a table.	The grandmother sat at the table.
A husband drove a tractor.	The husband drove the tractor.
Some dark clouds were rapidly accumulating.	The dark clouds were rapidly accumulating.

Which sentences did you find easier to read? To comprehend? Which could you read faster? And which were more coherent? If your reading patterns are like many others you found those sentences on the right to be easier and more comprehensible. You could read them faster and found them to be more coherent. There is even a subtle priming effect that happens with sentences with definite articles. If a series of sentences have been read which contain definite articles (e.g., *the*), recognition memory for a sentence is facilitated if it is preceded by a sentence which contains a definitive article. The reason behind the

FIGURE 12.17

The number of voxels (volume of neural tissue activated. Activated in Wernicke's area and Broca's area for simple to complex sentences.

A. "A" sentences   B. "The" sentences

axial   axial

FIGURE 12.18

The axial projection. Showing the regions of activation for (A) sentences with indefinite articles and (B) sentences with definitive article.

From Robertson et al. (2000).

efficacy of *the* sentences as contrasted with *a* sentences is that a more coherent mental representation is fostered by the definitive article (see Gernsbacher & Robertson, 2000). It seems that this very powerful verbal marker is specifically related to brain functions, as recently discovered by Robertson, Gernsbacher, Guidotti et al. (2000). In a straightforward experiment these researchers asked participants to read the sentences which were displayed with fiber-optic goggles while lying in an MRI scanner. After each block of sentences, participants were asked to recognize if a sentence was an old or a new one.

The results, shown in Figure 12.18, indicated that the comprehension of definite article sentences produced more neural activity in the right than left hemisphere of the frontal lobe, which suggests that the right hemisphere of the frontal lobe is implicated in some form of verbal mapping. The left-hemisphere structures seemed to be associated with "lower-level" reading processes such as word recognition and syntactic processing.

Spotlight on Cognitive Neuroscience

Dyslexia

Eric Nagourney reports on research exploring the origins of dyslexia. Some theories have posited that dyslexia is a hearing disorder, a visual disorder, or a disorder that comprises both modalities. Imaging researchers have discovered that dyslexia may have its origins in a genetic brain defect. Surprisingly, the seriousness of dyslexia may have to do with where you are raised, not just the goings on in your brain. Using PET technology, Eraldo Paulesu studied 72 dyslexic people from three different countries. There were similar abnormalities in brain function across all participants. So what's the point? Well, countries have widely varying incidence rates for the disorder, with the United States having the highest. It is believed that because English has many spellings of the same sounds (*f* and *ph* for the sound *fuh*) and dyslexics have difficulty differentiating between sounds, that English speaking-dyslexics have it tough. Uta Frith has found that dyslexics process words more slowly than nondyslexics. So it appears that "the roots of a language disorder may be in the brain, and on the map" (Nagourney, 2001, p. D7).

Nagourney, E. (2001, April 10). Geography of dyslexia explored. *The New York Times.*

SUMMARY

1   Reading involves an interaction of the detection of symbols and memory and, thus, it mirrors many processes involved in human cognition.

2   Viewing written text is constrained by the characteristics of the visual system, with greatest acuity occurring at the fovea (a visual angle of 1 to 2 degrees), poor resolution in the parafoveal and peripheral areas, and little or no detection during saccades.

3   Studies of perceptual span are used to examine the nature of information processing and include tachistoscopic, eye movement, and fixation procedures.

4   Tachistoscopic studies show that letters and words are more easily recognized when presented in a meaningful sequence.

5   Eye-tracking studies indicate that information in the near periphery (up to twelve character spaces) is partially coded, with the extent of processing determined by the distance from the fovea.

6   Eye behavior changes rapidly (within a few hundred milliseconds) to accommodate discordant contexts, suggesting that sophisticated comprehension processes occur early during text processing.

7   Familiarity and context facilitate word recognition. Increases in both are associated with faster and better recognition.

8   In the interactive activation model, word recognition happens through excitation and inhibition among features, letters, and word levels.

9   Recently a cognitive-anatomical approach has been taken up by some researchers studying word recognition. PET scans are used in such research. Early results indicate that different cortical areas are activated by different word recognition tasks. Such studies help us understand the relationship between cognitive tasks and brain functions.

10   Eye-fixation studies show longer fixations for words that are infrequent, those at the end of sentences, and those in integrating clauses, thus providing support for reading models proposing an interaction between stimulus input and memory.

KEY WORDS

comprehension	perceptual span
foveal vision	saccades
lexical-decision task (LDT)	voxels

RECOMMENDED READINGS

● Studies of word and letter identification can be found in Monty and Senders, eds., *Eye Movement and Psychological Processes;* and Rayner and Pollatsek's *The Psychology of Reading.* Volume 4 (No. 5) of *Psychological Science* contains a series on an interdisciplinary approach to reading research, including PET, eye-tracking, and connectionist articles and is highly recommended. The excellent books by Crowder, *The Psychology of Reading,* and Just and Carpenter, *The Psychology of Reading and Language Comprehension,* are not to be missed by those seeking an overview of the topic as well as detailed analysis of the current state of reading research. Numerous technical journals on the topic may be found in research libraries.

Cognitive Development

hmmm...?

● **Life-Span Development**
Cognitive Development
Neurocognitive Development
Comparative Development

● **Developmental Psychology**
Assimilation and Accommodation: Piaget
Mind in Society: Vygotsky
Vygotsky and Piaget

● **Neurocognitive Development**
Early Neural Development
Environment and Neural Development
Lateralization Studies

● **Cognitive Development**
Intelligence and Abilities
Development of Information-Acquisition Skills
Memory
Higher-Order Cognition in Children
Prototype Formation among Children

1. What is meant by "life-span development"? How is it studied?

2. Who was Jean Piaget, and what were his major contributions? Who was Lev Vygotsky, and what were his major contributions?

3. What have recent studies of twins told us about genetic influences on intelligence?

4. How early do babies attend to faces?

5. At what age do memories last longest?

6. How early do babies form concepts, and how has this been demonstrated?

7. Do children have imagery? Form prototypes?

One of the largest areas in the vast landscape of psychology is developmental psychology. This important topic was once limited to the study of "child" psychology, but now, with the recognition that cognition unfolds throughout the entire life span of people, the topic ranges from the study of the fetus to the study of elderly. And because a greater number of people are living longer, the subspeciality of gerontology has attracted much research attention. It is simply impossible to cover in any detail the main features of this huge area, but it is possible to deal selectively with some very interesting and vital aspects of developmental psychology in this chapter on developmental cognition.

Human cognition, from a developmental perspective, is the result of a long history of growth beginning at the earliest stages. Our perceptions, memories, and language and thought processes are governed by the basic genetic structure we inherit and the changes we experience in response to the demands made during our long and varied interaction with the physical and social environment. The critical feature is that cognition develops—that is, cognition and thinking emerge—in an orderly fashion as individuals progress from infancy to adulthood, and then some cognitive skills may decline in old age. These changes may be caused by:

- Neurological and physical maturation (or deterioration) of the person.
- The family, social, and educational milieu in which the person lives.
- The interaction between a physically changing person and his or her environment.

Some psychologists hold that an infant is largely devoid of naturalistic tendencies— is a kind of *tabula rasa,* or "blank tablet"—upon which the experiences of the world are to be recorded. Other, structurally oriented psychologists hold that infants possess certain invariant neurological and psychological potentials and that cognitive development is a matter of the interaction between these built-in structures and the encouragement and demands of society. The debate between the relative importance of these two views is sometimes called the "nature-nurture debate." While the once popular "nurture" side of the argument was radicalized by some overzealous Skinnerians to the point that *all* behavior was considered to be the result of operant learning, recent findings have demonstrated that there is a large natural (or genetic) component to the developing human. It is safe to conclude that human cognition is determined by both the genetic makeup of the person and his or her environment. Fanaticism on either side misses the main point. Biology provides the voice; learning the utterance. Developmentally, we are a blend of how our biological schematic is constituted and how our experiences are mapped onto the blueprint.

Life-Span Development

Human development over the life span has been approached from several, somewhat independent perspectives: developmental psychology, neurocognitive development, and cognitive development. Cognitive development takes place over the entire life span of humans and other creatures, from before birth to death; however, in this chapter we concentrate on cognitive development during the early parts of life.

Cognitive Development

Interest in the development of cognition throughout a person's life span was initially stimulated by the seminal work of Jean Piaget of Switzerland and the theoretical legacy left by the thoughtful works of Lev S. Vygotsky of Russia. Much has been written and is generally available about the life and times of Piaget. Less is known of the life and theories of Vygotsky, and later in this chapter a brief précis of his life and work is presented. As important as these theories are in terms of establishing a general framework, recent ideas and data have contributed significantly to our current understanding of the forces implicated in cognitive development.

Neurocognitive Development

The neurocognitive approach to developmental cognitive psychology, on the other hand, emphasizes the developing brain and corresponding cognitive changes. The neuroscience approach to the study of developmental psychology has been around for a very long time, but it has been ignored on grounds that it was too physiological for psychological theories. Now, however, we recognize that the biological development of the brain, both prenatal and postnatal, is inherently involved in the cognitive development of the species. In addition to this theoretical reason, the neurocognitive approach to developmental cognitive psychology has become increasingly important because of recent discoveries in the field of brain-imaging technology, some of which are discussed in other chapters of this text.

Comparative Development

Another way cognitive development has been studied is based on animal studies. Here, all sorts of creatures, from fruit flies to chimpanzees, are observed throughout their life spans. Such studies generally have greater latitude as it is possible to keep laboratory animals under close surveillance as well as introduce experimental conditions (such as electrodes in the brain, drugs, or denial of food or water). Such procedures cannot be used in human research, and the use of such conditions with animals should be done guardedly. Some important discoveries have been made by comparative psychologists.

Developmental Psychology

We begin our story by examining two quite different theories of developmental psychology that dominated the thinking in that field throughout most of the twentieth century—first, that of Jean Piaget and then that of Lev Vygotsky.

Assimilation and Accommodation: Piaget

Dissatisfied with attempts of moral philosophers and others to explain human knowledge through rational speculation alone, Jean Piaget adopted a unique and ultimately influential attitude. He decided that since intellect, like all biological functions, is a product of evolutionary **adaptation,** it could best be explained from a biological and evolutionary point of view. The best way to understand the nature of the adult mind was to study mental activity from birth, observing its development and changes in adaptation to the environment.

General Principles.   For Piaget, two major principles operated in intellectual growth as in all biological development: adaptation and organization.

Adaptation is a two-pronged process of **assimilation** and **accommodation.** In eating and digesting an apple, for example, we use certain biological structures and processes—mouth, teeth, stomach, gastric juices—by means of which we take in and convert the apple into forms the body can use. In a sense the body has assimilated an external object and changed it into human biological material. Piaget believed that similar phenomena apply to mental activity, namely, that we possess mental structures that assimilate external events and convert them into mental events or thoughts. Were we to attempt to eat a much bigger apple, we would have to change the way we arranged our mouth and teeth to bite into it, as well as changing other aspects leading to its digestion. In other words, we would have to accommodate our biological structures to meet the problems posed by the new object. In similar fashion we accommodate our mental structures to new and unusual aspects of the mental environment. These two processes, assimilation and accommodation, represent two complementary aspects of the general process of adaptation.

Organization refers to the nature of the mental structures that are adapting. For Piaget the mind is structured, or organized, in increasingly complex and integrated ways,

Jean Piaget (1896–1980). His research and theories form the basis of modern developmental psychology.

the simplest level being the **scheme,** which is a mental representation of some action (physical or mental) that can be performed on an object. For the newborn, sucking, grasping, and looking are schemes; they are the ways the newborn comes to know the world—by acting on the world. Across development, these schemes become progressively integrated and coordinated in an orderly fashion so that eventually they produce the adult mind. Piaget postulates four approximate major periods of development through which the human intellect evolves. Piaget pointed out (1) that changes within a given period were generally quantitative and linear, while differences across periods tended to be qualitative and (2) that there was a necessary sequence of progression through the four periods; that is, a child had to go through each period to get to the next. As we shall see, not all psychologists believe development to be this rigid or lockstep.

Stage 1: The sensorimotor period (birth to 2 years). The sensorimotor period is characterized by several stages of progressive intercoordination of schemes into successively more complex, integrated ones. In the first (reflex) stage, responses are innate and involuntary. In the next stage, reflex schemes are brought under voluntary control. When these primary schemes, such as sucking, looking, and grasping, are truly intercoordinated—that is, when the infant cannot only grasp and look simultaneously but also look at something *to* grasp it—the next stage (secondary schemes) has been reached. In the succeeding stage, the child can carry out a behavior with something other than that behavior as its goal.

Stage 2: The preoperational period (2 to 7 years). In the preoperative period, the young child's behavior shifts from dependence on action to utilization of mental representations of those actions—or what is commonly called thought. The capacity for representation makes possible a number of significant new abilities. Among them is a primitive kind of insight learning, in which the child can merely look at a problem and often solve it without having to perform any overt actions. That is, the child can figure out the answer in his or her head and realize the correct solution. Another advance made possible by representation is the child's ability to pretend and make believe, specifically, to use an object for a purpose for which it was not originally designed. For example, one of Piaget's daughters used a piece of cloth as if it were a pillow. She would pick up the cloth, put her thumb in her mouth, lie down with her head on the cloth, and pretend to go to sleep. Piaget feels that since the child can now relate objects to each other in her head, objects that resemble each other in some way can come to substitute for each other; the child doesn't now need a pillow to lie down—a substitute or make-believe pillow will do just fine. Finally, the capacity for representation underlies and makes possible the child's use of language. Language, for Piaget, comprises symbols (words) that stand for objects and events. Representation involves the creation and evocation, in the head, of symbols for objects. Until the child can truly represent and manipulate symbols, he or she will not be able to use language very effectively. Not surprisingly, the capacity for representation and the child's first multiword utterances emerge at about the same time. For Piaget, there is a causal connection between the two: representation makes possible the acquisition and use of language.

Stage 3: The concrete-operational period (7 to 11 years). The same general transformations that changed the sensorimotor child into the preoperational child are recapitulated to transform the thought structures of the preoperational child into those of the concrete-operational child. According to Piaget the process involves advances in three important domains of intellectual growth: conservation, classification, and seriation and transitivity. The first domain, **conservation,** is depicted in Figure 13.1. Three vessels are placed before you, two identical in dimensions and one higher and narrower. Water is poured into the two shorter vessels to exactly the same level. You confirm that the two contain the same amount of water, perhaps by checking the levels. Now water from one of the short vessels is poured into the tall, narrow one. The water in the latter climbs to a higher level. Is there more water in it than had been in the shorter vessel? Most adults would be surprised at the obviousness of the question. Of course, the amount of water is the same. Nothing was done to change the amount, so it must be the same. Although

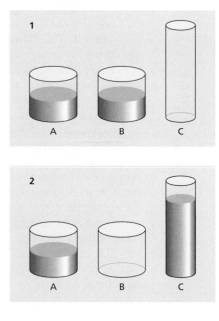

FIGURE 13.1

Arrangement (1) at outset of conservation task and (2) after contents of one vessel have been transferred to narrower and taller vessel.

the answer may seem obvious to adults, Piaget found that children younger than 7 years old typically say that the tall, narrow vessel has more water.

This illustrates a competence that Piaget believes is central to intellectual functioning in the school-age child: the concept of conservation—that is, the understanding that certain transformations do not change some basic properties of objects. In the example illustrated by Figure 13.1, the concept of conservation is the understanding that the amount of liquid does not change when the liquid is poured into a vessel of a different shape.

The second skill that develops in the concrete-operational child involves the **classification,** or grouping, of objects. For example, suppose a child is shown four dogs and three cats and is asked whether there are more dogs or more cats. The preoperational child can answer this question correctly. However, asked whether there are more animals or more dogs, she replies that there are more dogs. The concrete-operational child will answer this last question correctly, demonstrating a classification ability called the addition of classes. For Piaget, successful performance involves not only an awareness of some of the subclasses, such as dogs and cats, but a complete knowledge that subclasses added together make up a third class (animals) and that the class can be broken back down into its subclasses. This concrete-operational system, or grouping, is similar to that underlying conservation. The two subclasses (dogs and cats) can be combined (via *transformation*) into a third class (animals), which can be broken back down (via *reversibility*) into the two original subclasses. All this can be done in the head (*interiorization*). In the preoperational child, classification is not yet a fully unified system, with the result that only some aspects of a problem can be correctly identified.

The last major accomplishments we focus on are **seriation** and **transitivity,** which are actually two separate but related skills. Seriation refers to the ability to string together a series of elements according to some underlying relationship. For example, a preoperational child asked to order several sticks (see Figure 13.2) according to length (a typical problem in seriation of length) will be able to do so in a limited fashion, most often ordering two sticks correctly but then not aligning the third stick with the first two, and so on. Complete seriation ability awaits development of the system of concrete operations. Transitivity is related to seriation ability. In the transitivity problem shown in Figure 13.2, a child is first shown a series of sticks, two at a time, and then asked which is longer. Following this, the crucial question is asked: "Is Stick B longer than Stick D?" The preoperational child performs very poorly on this task, according to Piaget, whereas the concrete-operational child performs correctly. The crucial ability for Piaget is the ability to cross the bridge between B and D. Clearly, the child must be able to seriate the sticks in order to do this. In addition, however, he or she must be able to coordinate the two isolated relationships (B > C and C > D) into a system to make the transitive inference that B > D. For Piaget the preoperational child knows that B > C and that C > D but cannot put these two relationships together via the middle linking term C to create a concrete-operational system.

In 1928 Albert Einstein posed a question to Piaget: In what order do children acquire the concepts of time and velocity? The question was prompted by an issue within physics. Within Newtonian theory, time is a basic quality and velocity is defined in terms of it (velocity = distance/time). Within relative theory, in contrast, time and velocity are defined in terms of each other, with neither concept being more basic. Einstein wanted to know whether understanding of either or both concepts was present from birth; whether children understood one before the other; and if so, how initial understanding of one influenced subsequent understanding of the other.

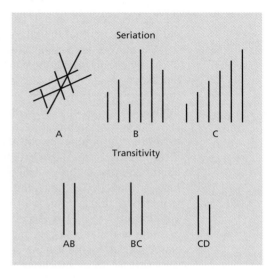

FIGURE 13.2

Above, seriation task (A) and performances on it by preoperational (B) and concrete-operational (C) children. Below, pairs of sticks such as would be presented in a transitivity task. After a child determines that A and B are the same length, that B is longer than C, and that C is longer than D, he or she is asked whether B is longer than D.

Almost twenty years later, Piaget published a two-volume, five-hundred-page reply to Einstein's query. Piaget concluded that children did not understand time, distance, or velocity in infancy or early childhood. Only in the concrete-operational period would they finally grasp the three concepts (Siegler, 1986).

Stage 4: The formal-operational period (adolescence and adulthood). Although the concrete-operational child has made a number of significant leaps in cognitive functioning, for Piaget there are still some definite limits on those capabilities. The limitation is perhaps best summarized by the name he gave to the period, that is, *concrete operations.* The child during this period is limited to coordinating concrete things in an actual situation. What the child cannot yet do is to coordinate possible things in a hypothetical or more abstract formalized situation. The concrete-operational child can coordinate various physical dimensions (for example, height and width of a jar of water) and thereby show conservation of liquid quantity. In a like manner, the child can conserve mass, number, volume, distance, weight—in short, most dimensions of the concrete physical reality in front of him or her. Figure 13.3 shows a problem useful in illustrating this last level of development. Consider a balance beam with various weights that can be placed in a variety of positions on either side of the beam. The goal—to balance the

FIGURE 13.3

Typical arrangement of weights in balance-beam problem. The child must decide whether a beam (initially locked in balance position) will be in balance when released.

Stages of Cognitive Development—Piaget

Stage	Age	Characteristics
Sensorimotor	0–2	World of here and now No language, no thought in early stages Understanding of objective reality absent
Preoperative	2–7 years	Egocentric thought Reason dominated by perception Intuitive rather than logical thought No ability to conserve
Concrete operation	7–11 or 12	Ability to conserve Classes and relations ability Number understanding Concrete thinking Development of reversibility in thought
Formal operations	11–12 14–15	Complete generality of thought Propositional thinking Ability to deal with the hypothetical Development of strong idealism

beam—can be accomplished by changing weights on either side of the beam or by moving weights closer to or farther from the central balance point (fulcrum).

The concrete-operational child can solve the balance problem easily when working with only one dimension. For example, the child will quickly learn that, where one side has more weights than the other, he can restore the balance by removing the extra weight on one side or adding a weight to the other. Similarly, he or she can figure out the effect of moving weights different distances from the fulcrum. However, the concrete-operational child does not understand how these two systems of operations are related. He or she does not know, for example, that adding weight to one side can be compensated for by moving the weights on the other side farther away from the fulcrum. In short, the child cannot coordinate these two systems into a higher-order "system of systems."

This coordination is precisely the goal of the formal-operational period—namely, coordination of previously isolated systems of concrete operations.

A direct outcome of the ability to coordinate systems of thought into higher systems is the ability to move beyond the actual world of physical reality to hypothetical worlds or other realities, to evoke systems of thought not immediately given by reality. Questions such as "What if the sun ceased to exist?" and "What if gravity disappeared?" that are so characteristic of adolescent thought stem directly from the ability to bring new, hypothetical dimensions to an otherwise concrete reality. This propensity toward hypothetical thinking is closely allied to the burgeoning tendency to think at a very abstract level; the formal-operational adolescent can consider general issues such as morality, love, existence.

For Piaget, formal-operational thought marks the end of intellectual growth. The child has clearly come a long way from the simple reflexes of the newborn to the sophisticated thoughts of the adolescent and adult. The striking feature of Piaget's theory is that it postulates the natural, logical progression of this development according to a unified set of theoretical principles.

Critique of the Piagetian Perspective.   Piaget's ideas have not gone unchallenged, and in recent years, many criticisms have emerged. Some focus on minor aspects of Piaget's methodology, but others are directed toward the substance of his theory.

Evidence has been presented by Jean Mandler (1998, 2000) and her colleagues that raises another question about how Piaget and his followers view the thinking ability of young infants. Simply stated, the Piagetian view of young infants is that they go through a period—especially the sensorimotor stage—during which they cannot "think." (This means that they can learn to do simple things—such as recognize common objects, crawl, and manipulate objects—but do not develop concepts or ideas.) Infants in the sensorimotor stage rely largely on procedural knowledge (see Chapter 9), the type of cognitive ability involved in moving around and manipulating objects. Mandler suggests that the development of conceptual knowledge is far more extensive than originally proposed by Piaget. There is evidence for the existence of perceptual conceptualization at an early age. In one experiment (Spelke, 1979) two films depicting complex events accompanied by a single sound track were shown to 4-month-old infants. Infants preferred to view the film that matched the sound. (Also see Mandler & Bauer, 1988; and Meltzoff & Borton, 1979.)

Even infants only 1 month old seem to be able to recognize objects only felt in their mouths (see Meltzoff & Borton, 1979). In one study, 1-month-old infants were given a pacifier with either a knobby surface or smooth surface (see Figure 13.4). After they were able to habituate to the pacifier without being able to see it, the pacifier was removed. Then the infant was shown both pacifiers. The infants spent more time looking at the pacifier they had only felt in their mouths before, which is taken as support for the view that some central processing of two similar patterns of information is accomplished.

Mandler suggests that some of the evidence for conceptual ability gathered by child psychologists has been based on motor behavior and that what may appear to be conceptual incompetence may be motor incompetence. (See also later in this chapter a discussion of inductive inference in infancy.) These areas of criticism, and others, argue that the child may possess sophisticated logical operations far earlier than thought by Piaget. They also suggest that other processes may be critical in determining whether a child will demonstrate a particular competence (such as conservation). Nevertheless,

Jean Mandler. Conducted inventive experiments that have shed new light on thinking in young children.

FIGURE 13.4

Two types of pacifiers used in the Meltzoff and Borton study. After habituation with one type of pacifier without being able to see it, infants tended to look at the pacifier they felt in their mouth.

After Meltzoff & Borton (1979), as reported by Mandler (1990).

supporters of Piaget could argue that the studies just cited show only that the basic processes that determine cognitive advance occur earlier than anticipated. The basic operational schemes and the fundamental sequence of progressive integration and coordination remain as reasonable explanations for the child's cognitive growth. However, even this basic tenet has been challenged.

Mind in Society: Vygotsky

Between the cities of Minsk in Belarus and Smolensk in Russia, in the town of Orsha, Lev Vygotsky was born in 1896. A bright, energetic, curious lad, he won a gold medal for his scholarship upon completing gymnasium. Perhaps only in his fantasy did he imagine that he would be selected to attend "Lomonosov's University" (Moscow State University); few Jewish boys from remote towns were selected (a quota of 3 percent had been established for Moscow and St. Petersburg universities). Also, even if his talent was conspicuous and his grades impeccable, a new rule was being tried out whereby Jewish applicants were to be selected by casting lots (Dobkin in Levitin, 1982). Nevertheless, in some undistinguished pedagogical bureau, fate fell down on the side of schoolboy Vygotsky. By the luck of the draw, he won (and lost a bet with a friend, paying him off with a "good book") and commenced on an intellectual career unparalleled in the history of Russian psychology.

Counted among his early students and coworkers are the most illustrious psychologists in the former Soviet Union, including Alexander Luria (the most frequently cited Russian psychologist by Western psychologists; see Solso, 1985), Alexei Leontiev (the

Lev Vygotsky (1896–1934). Made significant observations and proposed theories of child language development.

most frequently cited Russian psychologist by Russian psychologists), Zaporozhets, Zinchencho, Elkonin, Galperin, and Bozhovich.

Vygotsky's creative talents were not confined to psychology. They included philosophy (his works on Marx and Hegel are classics, and a book on Spinoza is still to be published [see Kozulin, 1984]), art criticism (his dissertation and first book were called *The Psychology of Art*), literary research (he founded the journal *Verask* and befriended the poet Mandelstam), and law and medicine (his first degree was in law, he was working on a medical degree, and, among other achievements, he left an important mark on clinical and developmental psychology). He died in 1934 at the age of thirty-seven; the cause of his early death was tuberculosis. Today, Russians enjoy calling him the Mozart of psychology. Vygotsky's original works deserve careful reading. In this next section we focus on his basic ideas as they bear on the topic of developmental psychology.

Vygotsky and Piaget

Although Vygotsky and Piaget were contemporaries (the leading developmental psychologists of the century) and lived in Europe, they never met. They did know of each other's work, however; Vygotsky knew of Piaget well before Piaget knew of Vygotsky.[1] There are similarities and differences between the theories.

Vygotsky considered Piaget's work to be "revolutionary" (a description not to be taken lightly in Russia during the 1920s), but he felt its trail-blazing qualities suffered from a duality—the dispute between materialistic and idealistic conceptions. As psychology of the intellectual development of the mind was being tested by scientific materialism, an inevitable conflict between the factual substance of that technique was at odds with the theoretical and idealistic nature of human intellect. The dispute is a serious one, especially in the zeitgeist of the 1920s and 1930s, because the growth of experimental psychology posed a real threat to the idealistic, nonmaterialistic, philosophic branch of psychology.

Stages of Development.   For Piaget, modes of thinking in the child developed from "autistic" to egocentric to socialized thought. Vygotsky accepted the general stages of development but rejected the underlying genetically determined sequence. Succinctly stated, Piaget believed that development precedes learning; Vygotsky believed that learning precedes development.

A second point of difference between the theorists is on the nature and function of speech. For Piaget, egocentric speech, which the child uses when "thinking aloud," gives way to social speech in which the child recognizes the laws of experience and uses speech to communicate. For Vygotsky, the child's mind is inherently social in nature, and egocentric speech is social in origin and social in purpose: children learn egocentric speech from others and use it to communicate with others. This position represents a major schism between the theorists and reveals the principal theory of child development according to Vygotsky.

The development of speech, which is tied to the development of thought in the child, proceeds along the following course. First and foremost, the primary purpose of

---

[1]Piaget did not know the details of Vygotsky's criticisms of his works until about 1962, when he received an abridged translation of *Thought and Language.* He did publish an interesting critique on Vygotsky's position and his own in *Comments on Vygotsky's Critical Remarks* (L. Graham, 1972).

speech (not only for children but also for adults) is communication, which is motivated by our basic need for social contact. Thus the earliest speech is essentially social. Speech becomes "egocentric" (and here Vygotsky accepts the stages of development according to Piaget but differs in explanation) when the child "transfers social collaborative forms of behavior to the sphere of the inner-personal psychic functions" (Vygotsky, 1934/1962). The development of thinking therefore is not from the individual to society but from society to the individual.

Phenomenon of Internalization.   Internalization is the process by which external actions (roughly speaking, *behavior*) are transformed into internal psychological functions (roughly speaking, *processes*). On this point Vygotsky and Piaget agree on a descriptive level but not on the origin of internalization. Vygotsky's position is similar to the writings of Émile Durkheim and Pierre Janet (and was undoubtedly influenced by them through his familiarity with the French sociological school). Human consciousness, from this direction, consisted of internalized social, interpersonal relationships. The importance of this position for developmental psychology is that children tend to use the same form of behavior in relation to themselves as others have expressed toward them. This is achieved by the child following the adult's example and gradually developing the ability to do certain tasks without help or assistance. The difference between what the child can do with help and without help is what Vygotsky termed the *zone of proximal development.*

Developmental Stages.   Vygotsky observed the way children sort objects, such as blocks differing in size, color, and shape. Older children, aged 6 and up, seemed to select a single quality such as color: all the green boxes were grouped together, as were the blue boxes, and so on. Younger children, below the age of 6, used chain concepts, by which Vygotsky meant that the classification changed throughout the selection process. A child may pick up, say, a few blue boxes and then notice a triangular block. This would lead to the selection of another triangular block, and so on, until some other type of block caught the child's attention, such as rounded blocks, which were then abandoned for another type. The selection process seemed to be chained and changeable.

Preschoolers seemed to organize objects thematically rather than taxonomically. For example, older children and normal adults might put animals in one category, furniture in another, and toys in yet a third group (taxonomic classification), while a very young child might classify a cat with a chair, a toy with a bookcase, and a dog with a Frisbee because cats sit on chairs, toys are stored in a bookcase, and dogs play with a Frisbee (thematic classification). From similar observations, Vygotsky thought that children pass through three stages of conceptual development:

1. The formation of thematic concepts in which relationships between objects are important.
2. The formation of chain concepts (just discussed).
3. The formation of abstract concepts similar to adult concept formation.

Unlike Piaget, Vygotsky had an opportunity in his brief, intellectually crowded life to test a few of his hypotheses under well-controlled laboratory conditions. We will now turn to the important matter of the development of thought—a central thesis of Vygotsky's theory.

Vygotsky's Theory of Language

Stage	Function
Social (external) (Up to age 3)	Controls the behavior of others Expresses simple thoughts and emotions
Egocentric (Ages 3–7)	Bridge between external and inner speech Serves to control behavior, but spoken out loud
Inner (7 and older)	Self-talk that makes possible the direction of thinking Language is involved in all higher mental functioning

Development of Thought and the Internalization of Speech.   The development of thought in the child is most evident in language development. At one point Vygotsky (1934/1962) wrote, "Language is a merger between outer speech the child hears and inner speech he thinks with." It is easy to conclude that language and thought are therefore dual entities of a common phenomenon. Carried to its logical conclusion, this notion would force us to deduce that without language there can be no thought, that thinking is dependent on language. Although some developmental psychologists subscribe to this idea, Lev Vygotsky does not. For Vygotsky, if a prelinguistic child thinks, as sufficient evidence suggests is the case, then we must find different roots for speech and thought. A fundamental tenet of Vygotsky's psychology is that thought and speech have different genetic roots and that the rates of development for each are different. The growth curves for thought and speech may "cross and recross" but always diverge. The source of thought is in the biological development of the child; the source of language in his or her social milieu. Even though language and thought have a different genus, they intertwine once the child comes to the realization that every object has a name. After this realization, thought and language are inseparable. Thus, the internalization of language causes thoughts to be expressed in inner speech.

Neurocognitive Development

Cognitive processes—perception, memory, imagery, language, and thinking and problem solving, for example—are all based on underlying neurological structures and processes, an idea frequently visited throughout these pages. Certainly, the study of the development of cognition would be incomplete without some understanding of the basic nature of developmental neuropsychology. The purpose of this section is to understand better the function of the nervous system throughout the life span of humans. Four different approaches to developmental neuropsychology have been used:

- Physical studies of the development of the nervous system correlated with cognitive changes.
- Cognitive studies over the life span of individuals from which inferences about neurological maturation are made.

- The study of neurological pathology or damage in which changes in cognition are noted.

- Experimental studies in which the brain is altered (mostly animal studies) or some independent variable is introduced and brain activity observed, as in the case of PET studies.

Each of these methodologies has strengths and weaknesses (see Kolb & Whishaw, 1990, for details), and a complete analysis is beyond the scope of the current text. We can, however, make some summary remarks.

Early Neural Development

The brain develops prenatality over the gestation period as is shown in Figure 13.5. In the very early stages of development, the brain is in the rudimentary stages of growth, but by the beginning of the second trimester, the cerebral cortex is becoming differentiated from the spinal cord. By 7 months many of the principal lobes are being formed. By 9 months the lobes are distinguishable and a number of invaginations are seen. As far as can be told, even with this noticeable and various growth of brain cells, cognition—perception, language processing, thinking, and memory—is still in an embryonic state throughout prenatal growth. Indeed, full cognitive development seems not to occur until late adolescence. (Some overzealous parents even believe an offspring must graduate from college, marry, have three children, and make a decent income before full maturity is achieved, but such a notion is not scientifically supported.)

If one examines synaptic (recall that the *synapse* is where two neurons meet) formation, which is closely related to a cognitively functional brain, we find that the density increases until about 2 years of age. Then, perhaps surprisingly, there is a *shedding* of synapses in which about 50 percent are lost by the age of 16 (which all parents know). Some interpret these findings as meaning that favorable environmental influences may deter the loss of synapses rather than influence their initial formation (see Kolb & Whishaw, 1990). Recent studies have questioned the idea that neural development is arrested early in childhood (Thompson & Nelson, 2001; see Figure 13.6).

In Figure 13.7, we see the effects of a nonstimulated (left) and stimulated (right) brain cell taken from rats. As shown, the hairlike dendrites are small, uncomplicated, and few in the left example, while the dendrites in the other example on the right are large, complex, and numerous; they are "well arborized," like the branches of a healthy tree or bush. The stimulated rats were allowed to explore a variety of objects that were changed daily (Rosenzweig & Bennett, 1996).

Environment and Neural Development

Environment does affect cognitive and brain development. Evidence for this can be found in animal studies where, typically, an animal is reared in some type of sensory isolation and then found to be unable to develop normally when placed in a normal or even an enriched environment. Brain size seems also to be affected by environment as evidenced by the fact that some domestic animals have certain cortical areas that are 10 to 20 percent smaller than comparable animals raised in the wild. Human babies raised in impoverished

Prenatal development of the brain. Showing a series of embryonic and fetal stages.

Adapted from W. M. Cowan (1979). Reprinted with permission.

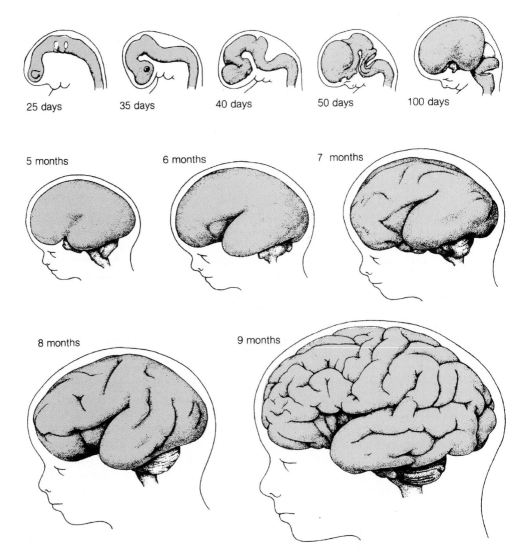

environments, such as the famous case of a child raised by wolves (see Singh & Zingg, 1940), seem unable to overcome their early experiences, although, contrary to common belief, there is no evidence they are destined to become werewolves or disc jockeys.

The effect of early stimulation of cognitive functions is, of course, important, and the term *functional validation* is used to express the notion that for the neural system to

FIGURE 13.6

The developmental course of human brain development.

Note: This graph illustrates the importance of prenatal events, such as the formation of the neural tube (nuerulation) and cell migration; critical aspects of synapse formation and myelination beyond age 3; and the formation of synapses based on experience, as well as neurogenesis in a key region of the hippocampus (the dentate gyrus), throughout much of life.

From Thompson & Nelson (2001).

FIGURE 13.7

Early stimulation and neuron growth.

become fully functional, stimulation is required. Some experiments show an enriched environment increases brain size in the neocortex. Other cases, which are well documented, do suggest that children are remarkably resilient beings, and that some forms of early cognitive impoverishment may be overcome by changing environments.

Lateralization Studies

Lateralization of cognitive functions is likely to produce theoretically important results. For example, it may show that information processing is progressively organized into different areas (such as language processing taking place in the left hemisphere). Or it may be that the brain is formed early in its development and that the processing of certain types of material (language, for example) is inflexibly routed to a predetermined site for processing. The results of these studies might address the larger question of the relative influence of nature (neurology, in this instance) and nurture (type of information, in this instance). In spite of experimental difficulties in studying vision and lateralization in very young children (it's hard to collect reliable data with children because of a number of obvious problems), a number of well-controlled experiments have been done with children and cerebral asymmetry.

Koenig, Reiss, and Kosslyn (1990) tested for lateralization in 5- and 7-year-olds. They asked children (and adult control participants) to play the role of a baseball umpire who was to call the location of a ball (a dot) as being above or below, or in or out (see Figure 13.8). The dot was presented to the right or left of the visual fixation point so that it would be processed in the opposite cerebral hemisphere as a result of the crossover of

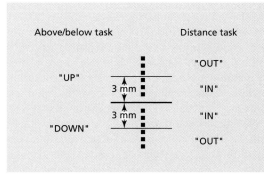

F I G U R E   1 3 . 8

The "baseball" could appear in any one of the 12 positions relative to the "bat." The criterion in the above/below task was whether the ball was "up" or "down." The criterion in the distance task was whether the ball was closer to the line than 3 mm.

From Koenig, Reiss, and Kosslyn (1990). Reprinted with permission from Elsevier.

neural pathways from the eye to the brain (see Chapter 2). The children's decisions were measured by means of a reaction time key. As shown in Figure 13.9, children responded faster to stimuli presented initially to the left hemisphere in the above/below task, and to stimuli presented initially to the right hemisphere in the distance task. The finding presents evidence for the existence of distinct hemispheric subsystems for children as young as 5 years of age. Lateralization effects have been noted in young children by others, and we tentatively conclude that brain structures and processes are formed very early in infancy or even prenatally and are not subject to normal environmental forces.

F I G U R E   1 3 . 9

Response latencies for children and adults. The stimuli were presented initially to the left hemisphere (right visual field), to the right hemisphere (left visual field), or to both hemispheres (central field). The participants decided whether the ball was above or below the bat or greater than 3 mm from the bat. For children and adults, the first trial block only is represented.

From Koenig, Reiss, and Kosslyn (1990). Reprinted with permission from Elsevier.

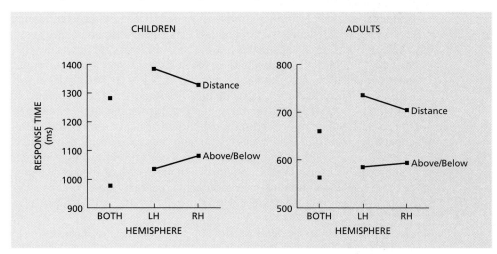

Cognitive Development

The term *cognition* subsumes a large number of individual processes (and structures) such as attention, pattern recognition, sensory registers, cognitive neuroscience, and memory. Thinking, in this context, is actually a product of the complex utilization, manipulation, and organization of these various components. For the developmental psychologist, any one of these processes may change with age. The investigation of age-related changes in cognition has thus required systematic exploration of many different processes. In this section we explore only a portion of these processes, and those within only a limited age range—namely, from preschool through adulthood. In essence we focus on the basic cognitive skills involved in acquiring information from the environment and in storing and manipulating information in memory. Our aim is to illustrate how the cognitive viewpoint is valuable in understanding some important aspects of human development.

Intelligence and Abilities

No area in psychology is more controversial than the nature of intelligence and abilities— a topic that has significant social and political overtones. The topic is frequently in the news, fueled by new books, educational policies, and dubious research findings. Recently, the issue has become even more unsettling with the marketing of "superior genes" by students at leading universities and winners of intellectual prizes (such as Nobel laureates) that are available for harvesting and artificial insemination. The reasoning behind this social phenomenon is "We want our baby to have the best genes money can buy." At the heart of this controversy is how much of a child's intelligence and abilities (such as musical talent, mathematical ability, spatial ability, verbal facility, and so on) can be attributed to his or her genetic disposition and how much can be attributed to environment. Strong arguments rage on both sides, but it is safe to conclude that both genetic makeup and environmental influences play a role in intelligence and abilities. To the more specific question as to the relative importance of each factor, recent research suggests that the radical view of environmentalism, which held that any type of being could be created by simple alterations in the environment, grossly overestimated the influence of one's socialization on intelligence and abilities. One's genes shape components of intellect and abilities to a larger degree than presumed by earlier psychologists.

One method developmental psychologists have used to distinguish the genetic basis from the environmental basis for abilities is to study twins. In this type of research, fraternal twins (or *dizygotic twins*), who carry similar genetic traits, and identical twins (or *monozygotic twins*), who carry identical genetic traits, may be traced over their lifetime in an effort to discover the influence of environment on traits. Another approach has been to look at the relationship between twins, monozygotic or dizygotic, reared in foster homes. Here, correlations between the abilities of the adopted child and his or her birth or adopted parents are made with the idea that biological influences may be seen in contrast with environmental factors. One of the most comprehensive of twin studies is the Colorado Adoption Project[2] directed by John DeFries and Robert

[2]Other prominent sites for twins research are at the University of Minnesota, directed by Thomas J. Bouchard, and at the Karolinska Institute in Stockholm, directed by Nancy L. Pedersen.

Plomin[3] (Plomin & DeFries, 1998). In one study, more than 200 adopted children and their birth and adoptive parents were studied. Correlations for a control group of children raised by their biological parents over several years were made and are shown in Figures 13.10 and 13.11.

In Figure 13.10 we can see that the scores for identical twins are more similar than are the scores for fraternal twins and that that high relationship carries through for the life span of twins from childhood to old age. The relationship holds for verbal as well as spatial ability and suggests that genetic traits are strong and last over a lifetime. In Figure 13.11 we can see that by middle childhood, birth mothers and their children *who were adopted by others* are very similar to control parents and their children on both verbal and spatial abilities. This finding is contrasted with the scores of adopted children, which do not resemble those of their adoptive parents. The data present convincing evidence for the large influence of genetics on mental abilities and intelligence. There is also a development trend, reported in these data, that suggests that there is an

FIGURE 13.10

Twin studies have examined correlations in verbal (*top*) and in spatial (*bottom*) skills of identical twins and of fraternal twins. When the results of the separate studies are put side by side, they demonstrate a substantial genetic influence on specific cognitive abilities from childhood to old age. The scores of identical twins are more alike than those of fraternal twins. These data seem to counter the idea that the influence of genes wanes with time.

From Plomin and DeFries (1998).

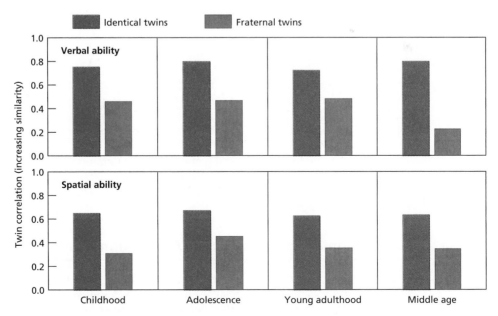

[3]Plomin has moved to the Institute of Psychiatry in London.

FIGURE 1 3 . 1 1

Colorado Adoption Project. Followed participants over time and found that for both verbal (*top*) and spatial (*bottom*) abilities, adopted children come to resemble their birth parents as much as children raised by their birth parents do. In contrast, adopted children do not end up resembling their adoptive parents. The results imply that most of the family resemblance in cognitive skills is caused by genetic factors, not environment.

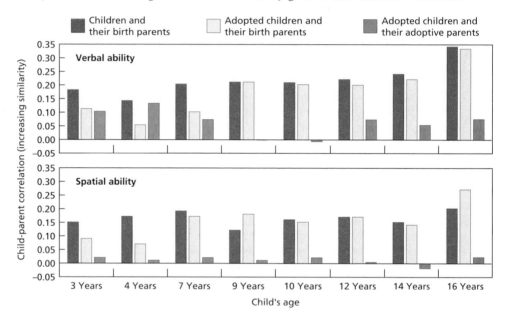

unexpected genetic influence which increases during childhood, so that by a child's mid-teens, the influence of heredity is quite high. It would appear that some genetically activated change in cognitive functions takes place about the age of 9 or 10 years. By the time the child reaches 16, genetic factors account for about 50 percent of the verbal ability and 40 percent of the spatial ability. These results have been corroborated by other twins studies.

It is reasonable to conclude that genetics plays an important role in determining the verbal and spatial ability of children. While such observations are important, it should be noted that the specific shaping of human behavior, especially that of children, is also influenced by the environment in which the child grows.

Development of Information-Acquisition Skills

The initial stages in cognition require that the child be able effectively to attend to, to perceive, and to search out the relevant information in the environment. Successful acquisition of information brings into play such processes as neurological development, the development of sensory registers, focal attention, and speed of processing, as well as

Do you remember T-Rex? How old were you? From *The San Francisco Chronicle*, Dec. 26, 1999.

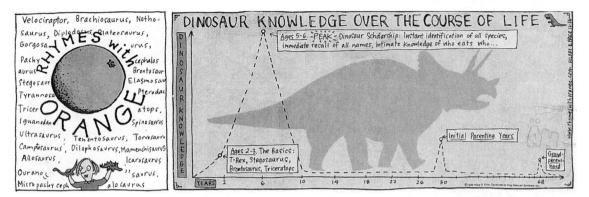

effective strategies for searching out and utilizing information in various portions of the environment. We focus on some of these processes that have been studied developmentally. Most of the modern themes of cognitive psychology, which include selective attention, facial identification, memory, higher-order cognition, and prototype formation, are repeated in the developmental literature.

Selective Attention.   Selective attention (see Chapter 3) refers to the ability to focus on relevant information. The evidence we have suggests that young children are somewhat less able to control their attentional processes than adults are. They are more easily distracted and less flexible in deploying attention among relevant and irrelevant information. In one study (Pick, 1975), children were asked to find all the *A*s, *S*s, and *L*s in a large box of multicolored block letters of the alphabet. Unknown to the children was the fact that all the *A*s, *S*s, and *L*s were the same color. Only the older children noticed this clue and used it to advantage in searching through the pile, displaying their greater attentional flexibility.

Although our knowledge about this process is far from complete, it appears that as children grow older, they become better able to control attention and to adapt to the demands of different tasks. When a high degree of selectivity is called for, older children can better focus on the relevant and ignore the irrelevant. Younger children have greater difficulty in this regard. Likewise, when less selectivity is appropriate, older children can defocus and take in more relevant information. Much of the research on children's attention has dealt with vision.

For some time many professionals believed that newborn infants were functionally blind, a view that has since been discredited. Infants can "see" in the sense that their visual apparatus is functional, but their understanding of what they see—in effect, their perception—is questionable. What is known is that infants tend to look at some objects more than others. Some of the features of infant attention have been identified.

Facial Attention.   One topic of interest among cognitive psychologists is to what features of a visual scene people attend. Because infants become familiar with people's faces

Cognition in Everyday Life

The Developing Brain—Use It or Lose It

"It's crazy," says Pasko Rakic, a Yale neurobiologist. "Americans think kids should not be asked to do difficult things with their brains while they are young: 'Let them play; they'll study at the university.' The problem is, if you don't train them early, it's much harder."*

Early stimulation of the brain, through puzzles, visual displays, music, foreign-language learning, chess, art, scientific exploration, mathematical games, writing, and many other similar activities promotes synaptic connections in the brain. Shortly after birth, the number of

neural connections increases at a phenomenal rate. Then, at about puberty, the number of new connections diminishes and two processes take place: functional validation, in which useful connections are made more permanent, and selective elimination, in which useless connections are eliminated.

Throughout the life span—from infancy to old age—we humans (and other creatures) are endowed with the capacity to expand our mental capacity through use. Disuse, through mindless, passive activities, is likely to dull brain growth.

Cited in Life, July 1994.

(especially the mother's face) at a very tender age, cognitive developmental psychologists have studied facial attention in some detail. You may recall that pioneer work in the field of visual attention was done by Yarbus, who measured eye movements and fixations as subjects viewed a scene (see Chapter 4 for details). Related work has been done with children by Salapatek (1975), who presented infants with a visual display in which one object was placed within another (for example, a circle inside a triangle). Very young infants (up to the age of 2 months) showed an almost total preference for the outer edges of the external figure over the inner figure. After about the age of 2 months, the infants scanned both the outer features and the inner ones. In another study of this type, Haith, Bergman, and Moore (1977) used an eye-tracking device similar to the one shown in Figure 13.12. Of special interest is the use of infrared illuminators, which impinge on the infant's eyes. Rays from this source are beyond the sensory threshold; the infant cannot see them, and they are harmless. Because the position of these lights in the child's visual field is known, the fixation point can be determined by measuring the distance of one of the lights from the center of the pupil. (Similar technology has been used in reading experiments—see Chapter 12.) The infant's eye movements and the exact location of the mother's face are detected by video cameras and combined in a video mixer. It is possible to identify exactly where the infant is looking vis-à-vis the mother's face.

Experiments of these types are helpful in the study of memory and early perceptual organization in addition to the emotional and social development of infants. In the experiment by Haith and his colleagues, three groups of infants were observed. One group was 3 to 5 weeks old; the second group was 7 weeks old, and the third was 9 to 11 weeks old. The mothers' faces were divided into zones, which were used to identify eye fixations (see Figure 13.13). The results of the experiments are shown in Figure 13.14.

It was found that very young infants focus on the peripheral contours (as also reported by Salapatek), but older infants focus on the eyes. It was also found that older infants focus on the nose and mouth more than younger infants. The possible meaning of these findings is that to the infant, the face of the mother is not merely a collection

Drawing of eye-tracking apparatus. Used to record eye movements and fixations of infants.

Zones for mother's face used in eye-tracking study. Zones were individually determined.

From Haith, Bergman, and Moore (1977).

of visual events but a meaningful entity. We can dismiss these findings on the basis of the physical attractiveness of eyes (their color, movement, and contrast), but such argument does not account for the shift in attention over age, nor does it account for the relative lack of attention given to the mouth, which also has these characteristics. It is

FIGURE 13.14

Percentage of time spent on eyes, edges, nose, and mouth by infants of three different ages.

From Haith, Bergman, and Moore (1977).

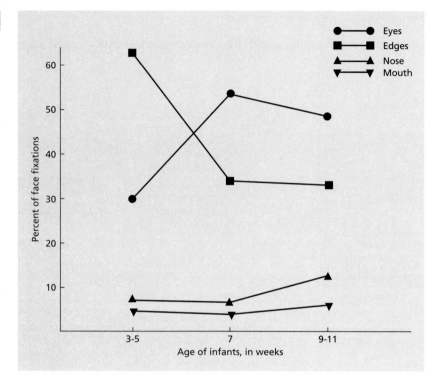

possible that by the seventh week eyes, especially a mother's eyes, take on special social value and are important in social interaction.

The problem of what critical features babies attend to was tackled by Mondloch et al. (1999) in an experiment that used artificial faces and facial features. Some studies indicate that very young babies, neonates, prefer facelike stimuli over non-facelike stimuli (see Valenza, Simion, Cassia, & Umilta, 1996, for example) while others suggest the preference emerges between 2 and 4 months (Dannemiller & Stephens, 1988). In a carefully designed study by Mondloch and her colleagues, very young children whose mean age was 53 minutes were shown a series of standard visual stimuli, which are shown in Figure 13.15. The study also looked at 6-week-old and 12-week-old children. Preference for stimuli was determined by measuring the first look and the duration of the looking.

The results of this experiment show some clear distinctions between viewing preferences of very young babies as contrasted with those of older babies. In the "feature inversion" stimuli, the gross features of a face are shown in an upright or inverted orientation. Newborns overwhelmingly chose to look at the upright image while older babies showed no preference. In the "phase and amplitude reversal" images, in which facial features are somewhat fuzzy contrasted with a more globally defined head, neonates preferred the head while older babies preferred the fuzzy-featured face. In the "contrast reversal" faces, very young babies showed no preference while the 12-week-old babies show a very definite preference for the positive contrast face. From these results we learn that very young children (who have had little opportunity to learn about

FIGURE 13.15

Number of babies who preferred each stimulus over its paired stimulus.

From Mondloch, Lewis, Budreau, Maurer, Dannemiller, Stephens, and Kleiner-Gathercole (1999).

Age	Feature inversion			Phase and amplitude reversal			Contrast reversal		
	Config	Inversion	Neither	Phase of face	Amplitude of face	Neither	Positive contrast	Negative contrast	Neither
Newborns	9*	1	2	0	9*	3	0	0	12
6-week-olds	0	0	12	12**	0	0	3	0	9
12-week-olds	0	1	11	12**	0	0	12**	0	0

*$p < .05$, two-tailed binomial test. **$p < .001$, two-tailed binomial test. All other $ps > .1$.

faces or visual stimuli) have an inborn predisposition to look toward stimuli that resemble facial features. As a child matures other preferences emerge that suggest an increased cortical influence over infants' preferences for faces. From other studies, we know that there are dedicated parts of the human brain implicated in the perception of faces in humans as well as other animals (for example, monkeys). It is consistent with a biological or survival point of view to conclude that facial perception is an important early means of recognizing critical signals during the first few minutes after birth. As a baby matures, the learning of other significant facial signals seems to happen until, in time, a child forms clear facial discriminations and preferences based on frequent exposure to parents, family members, and other caregivers.

We will return to the processing of facial information in a later section on prototype formation in children. Now we consider the topic of short-term memory.

Memory

As we have seen in other parts of this book, memory is among the most important cognitive attributes. Without memory, we would be rudderless, caught in a confusing sea of meaningless events; with memory, events are understood.

Among the most controversial and hotly debated topics in psychology are (1) at what point, in the course of human growth and development, memory first unfolds and (2) how accurate memory is. This was borne out by a spate of court trials involving false-memory syndrome, in which memories of childhood abuse allegedly are the result of reconstructed events encouraged by others, most notably a person's psychotherapist. What do we know about childhood memories?

Infant Memory.   There is considerable common knowledge and scientific evidence that infants have memory for events as well as the ability to form concepts (Mandler & McDonough, 1998). On a basic level, babies show recognition of previously seen stimuli, such as their mother's face, or classically conditioned responses (see Rovee-Collier, 1990, 1999, for details). Imitation and **habituation** are also reliably found in infants. These findings do not suggest, however, that early memories are of the same kind as adult memories (see Eacott, 1999). Early efforts to find the earliest memories have (generally) relied on introspective accounts (for example, "What is your earliest memory?") and found that the average age was 39 to 42 months.

In a well-controlled experiment by Usher and Neisser (1993), childhood memory and its counterpart, childhood amnesia, were tested with 222 college students who were asked questions about four datable events—the birth of a younger sibling, a hospitalization, the death of a family member, and a family move. The events could be checked against reliable records and occurred when the subjects were 1, 2, 3, 4, or 5 years of age. The results are shown in Figure 13.16. Childhood amnesia, or the inability to recall an event that actually happened, ranged from the age of 2 for hospitalization and sibling birth to the age of 3 for death and a family move. The onset of childhood amnesia seems to depend on the nature of the event itself, as the birth of a sibling and hospitalization, potentially traumatic episodes, are significant events likely to be recalled in adulthood.

FIGURE 13.16

Mean recall data for four target events as a function of age at experience.

From J. A. Usher and U. Neisser, "Childhood amnesia and the beginnings of memory for four early life events," *Journal of Experimental Psychology: General,* 122, pp. 155–165. Copyright 1993 by the American Psychological Association. Reprinted by permission of the American Psychological Association.

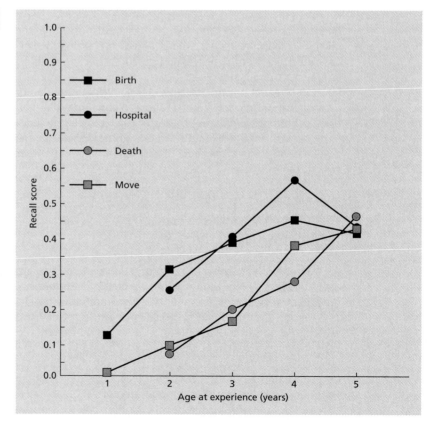

Notice the remarkable cognitive changes in these infants who range in age from 2, 3, 6, 9, 12, 15 months of age.

(Photo compliments of Carolyn Rovee-Collier.)

Conversely, these events may have been recounted throughout the life of the child and early adult (see E. Loftus, 1993, for a rejoinder).

If we consider the memory of older children, into early adulthood, the conclusions about adolescent memory are clear. Evidence abounds that the period between 10 and 30 years of age produces recall of the greatest amount of autobiographical memories. Many times these personal memories—of such things as a special date, a song, an automobile, a dress, a ring, an election, a favorite teacher (or not so favorite teacher), the winner of a movie's Academy Award, a boyfriend, an adventure in an unfamiliar city, an embarrassing moment—are the highlights of what one could call "your time." Many experimental papers address this topic and the conclusion is that those things that happen during adolescence and early adulthood are remembered best. As a sample of this work, consider the data presented in Figure 13.17, based on Holbrook and Schindler (1998) and reported by Rubin, Rahhal, and Poon (1998). Working on the notion that preference

Cognition in Everyday Life

Refuted False Memory Case Wins $500,000

A landmark "recovered memory" trial testing the rights of third parties to sue therapists was decided in a recent case when a father convinced a jury that his daughter's mind was poisoned with false recollections of childhood molestation.

Jurors were asked to decide whether two therapists and a southern California medical center were guilty of malpractice in the case of a young woman who experienced flashbacks

of childhood sexual abuse while being treated for bulimia and depression. The father sued the marriage and family counselor and a psychiatrist charging they had implanted in his daughter false memories of childhood incest.

It was contended that the images were not memories, and the evidence showed that the frightening flashbacks were vague to the point that even the daughter doubted their accuracy.

Based on an article in the San Francisco Chronicle, *May 14, 1994.*

FIGURE 13.17

Distribution of scores.
Shows how much individuals ranging in age from 16 to 86 liked songs as a function of age when the song was popular.

From Rubin, Rahhal, and Poon (1998).

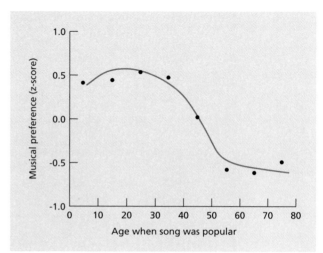

is related to memories, Holbrook and Schindler played 30-second excerpts from 28 songs to 108 people ranging in age from 16 to 86 and asked them to rate each song as to how much they liked it. As shown, the preferences for songs were clustered in the period when the raters were in their early adulthood. Data from other studies conducted here and abroad have corroborated these findings. (See Rubin, Rahhal, & Poon, 1998, for a discussion of theories related to this widely observed phenomenon.)

Organization (Chunking).   The development of sophisticated rehearsal strategies is just one of the factors influencing the growth of memory skills in school-age children. A second, equally important factor involves the ability to recognize and utilize potentially useful higher-order relationships that link various environmental events. (Earlier, we called this *organization,* or *chunking.*) During the school years, the child becomes better able to organize material he or she wants to remember.

Of the following two lists of words, which would you expect to recall more easily?

1. desk, arm, tree, hall, paper, clock, farmer, word, floor
2. apples, oranges, grapes, shirt, pants, shoe, dog, cat, horse

The second list is indeed easier to recall once you realize that the words are composed of three separate categories. By chunking the words into categories, you form a higher-order rule and use the rule to help at the time of recall. Indeed, experiments have shown that recall of categorized lists is much easier than recall of unrelated words. Surprisingly, studies have shown that up to about the third grade, children's recall of categorizable items is not much better than their recall of unrelated items. Older children, on the other hand, recall categorizable items much better than unrelated items (Vaughn, 1968; and Lange, 1973). These findings imply that the older children better recognize and utilize the categorical nature of the stimuli to help their memory performance.

One way to try to help younger children to see the higher-order relationship between stimuli would be to present the categories in a blocked fashion—all items from one category first, the next category second, and so on. An experiment by Yoshimura, Moely, and

Shapiro (1971) presented one group of children who were 4 to 10 years old with categorizable stimuli in a blocked fashion and another group with stimuli in a random fashion. They found that while the older children benefitted from having the items blocked, the younger children did not. Other studies have shown some slight advantage from blocking for younger children (Cole, Frankel, & Sharp, 1971; and Kobasigawa & Middleton, 1972), but, in general, the results reveal that young children appear not to notice or utilize as well the categorical structure of materials presented to them. Furthermore, it appears that if left to their own devices, younger children do not spontaneously use organizational strategies to help them remember. In one study (Liberty & Ornstein, 1973), fourth graders and adults were given twenty-eight words printed on individual cards. They were told to sort the cards in any way they wanted to help them remember. The adults tended to sort and group items that were related semantically, while the fourth graders grouped words in more idiosyncratic and less semantically related ways.

In sum, studies have documented clearly that older children are more likely to notice and utilize higher-order relationships among stimuli and are more likely to group items on that basis. Thus, the development of active, planful, spontaneous organization strategies characterizes the growth of the school-age child's memory abilities.

Higher-Order Cognition in Children

The importance of higher-order cognition in everyday processing of information has been discussed in some detail in previous chapters (with more to come in the following chapters). The question for this chapter is what the corresponding similarities and differences between higher-order cognition in adults and children are. Even though a definitive answer is impossible, a tremendous amount is known about higher-order cognition in both adults and children. One approach is to trace the developmental literature in each of the topics in higher-order cognition—from memory to creativity. Such a procedure requires many volumes; however, we can touch on the highlights here. The curious student is advised of the rich storehouse of information on this topic, and an equally abundant treasure lies ahead in yet undone research awaiting his or her commitment.

Knowledge Structure and Memory. Several features of a comparative study of higher-order cognition are at once apparent. Even the newest-born neonate is capable of storing some information in memory, but, as we learned in the chapters on memory and language, the form in which that information is stored in memory is dependent on several factors. These include the source of the information, the individual's previous knowledge base, and the structural networks that already have been framed. We first consider the way a child might store in memory an experience in his or her life.

Suppose you were to ask a 6-year-old to tell you about her trip to the zoo. She might say something like this: "Let's see. First, we got on a big bus, then I saw elephants, an' big polar bears, an' monkeys, an' then I got an ice cream cone an' come home." From this little story an enormous amount can be learned about the child's knowledge base, the way information is stored, and the story grammar. (Remember the police officer and driver in Chapter 1?)

One way to analyze an episode of this type is to think about the way information is represented. Jean Mandler and her colleagues (Mandler, 1983, 1984, 2000; Mandler &

DeForest, 1979; Mandler & McDonough, 1996) have studied story grammars (as well concept formation) in children and have developed a model that distinguishes between two types of representation. In one, the representation is in terms of what a person knows and how that information is organized in memory (such as a sequential structure or a classification of objects by category). In the other, the representation is in the terms of symbols (such as telling about an episode, or drawing a picture of an event, or writing a story about an experience, or even having an imaginary representation).

In the story of a visit to the zoo, the child organized the episode in terms of a sequence of events ("First . . . then . . . and then . . ." and so on) and in terms of a story schema or grammar (the story had a theme, a subject, a beginning, and an end). The concept is similar to the ideas expressed by Kintsch and others discussed in Chapter 11. Mandler (1983), in discussing children's story grammar, contends that stories have "an underlying structure consisting of a setting component in which the protagonist and background information are introduced, followed by one or more episodes which form the skeletal plot structure of the story. Each episode has some kind of beginning, or initiating, event, to which the protagonist reacts." In one test of the hypothesis that children use a story schema, Mandler and DeForest read a two-episode story to 8-year-olds, 11-year-olds, and adults. In one condition the two episodes were interwoven; that is, the title and story setting of the first episode were presented, and then the title and setting of the second episode were presented. The rest of the story was also presented in a similar way, switching back and forth between the episodes. Some participants were asked to recall the story in the way it was presented (interrelated), and others were asked to recall all of episode one and then episode two. The former "unnatural" story grammar was much more difficult to recall, and in fact, the 8-year-olds found it impossible to recall the episodes in the interrelated way. We can conclude from this and other similar experiments that children at a very young age discover rather sophisticated story schemata, which they use to encode experiences.

Metaphorical Thinking and Imagery.   A beguiling peculiarity of children is their make-believe world. All healthy kids have one. It may be as simple as pretending that a block is a car, or a finger is a gun, or a used cardboard box is a palace, or it may be as elaborate as fantasizing about mystical powers or creating an imaginary playmate. As far as can be told (see Fein, 1979), infants up to 1 year of age are not capable of pretend play, and after the age of 6, children seem to favor (generally) other forms of play and games. Nevertheless, the early normal propensity to create a fantasy world seems to remain an active but poorly understood part of adult human behavior, in spite of important theories on the topic by Piaget and Vygotsky. It seems that the development of intellectual skills, creativity, and imagery is related to metaphorical thinking in children. Sound experimental data on this topic are needed.

Imagery.   A fundamental issue in the study of higher-order cognition in children is the question of how information is represented. In general, the argument is that adults rely more on semantically (meaning-) based representations and children rely more on perceptually based representations. As an example, consider the following question: Can you name the states that are rectangular? Chances are that you formed a mental image of regularly shaped states and then "looked" at them to see which ones were really rectangular. You may have focused on the "four-corner" part of the United States and then "looked" at Colorado, which meets the terms of rectangularity, and then Utah, which comes close but is not quite rectangular enough to meet the criterion, and then Wyoming, and so on. If you were asked to answer the question again, especially if you had repeated familiarization with the question, you may have stored the rectangularity of states in semantic memory (something like "rectangular states [are] Colorado and Wyoming; close to rectangular are New Mexico, North and South Dakota, Kansas, and Oregon"). Then when the question is asked again, you may access the answer from propositional memory rather than from imagery.

Some theorists believe that children use imagery more than propositionally based storage of information to answer questions. For example, consider if we ask an adult and a child the following question: Does a beagle have four legs? Chances are that even though an adult has never been asked this question before, answering correctly is an easy matter of dipping into his or her long-term propositionally stored information bank. However, children under the age of about 7 are poor at this type of logical deduction based on semantically stored information. Kosslyn (1983) suggests that if a child does not have the answer stored as a direct associate, then imagery will be used to answer the question.

As in the case of fantasy, hard data on this subject are difficult to find in the experimental literature, but at least one interesting study conducted by Kosslyn (1980; see also Kosslyn, 1983) sheds some light on the topic. In an experiment done with first graders (about the age of 6), fourth graders (about the age of 10), and adults, he asked the subjects to verify statements (similar to the techniques discussed in Chapter 9) such as "A cat has claws," or "A cat has a head," or "A fish has fur." In one condition, he mentioned the name of the animal and told the subjects to "think about" features of that animal, while in another condition the subjects were asked to "image" the animal. After 5 seconds, they were to decide whether or not the features were part of the animal. For adults, who are supposedly more propositionally inclined, the most expedient way to answer the question would be to retrieve the semantically coded proposition, whereas children, who may rely more on imagery, would answer the question by forming an image of the animal and then "looking" at its features. Reaction time was the dependent variable, and the results are shown in Figure 13.18.

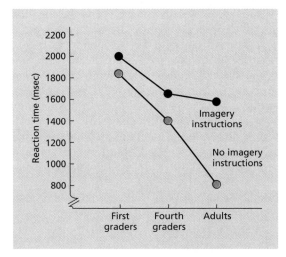

FIGURE 13.18

Average reaction times.
Verify statements with imagery instructions and without imagery instructions.

Data from Kosslyn (1980).

In general Kosslyn found that adults were swifter with the reaction key than children throughout most conditions, but the reaction-time data for the relative reaction times of children and adults are very interesting and deserve close inspection. When we consider the differences between the reaction times for those adults who were given the imagery instructions and those who were not given the imagery instructions, we find that those participants with instructions were much slower in giving an answer than those without instructions. This suggests that adults tend to store this type of information in terms of abstract propositions. These results are in contrast to the children's data, which show only slight differences between the group with instruction and the group without instruction. It may be that the children are using imagery in both conditions.

Many innovative research programs, such as the study of children's imagery, frequently raise more questions than they answer. Why do children rely more on imagery (if indeed they do) than adults? Is it because they have not learned propositionally structured knowledge? Is there a natural sequence of development that begins with sensory memories that give way to abstract semantic memories? Is it inherently more efficient to access propositionally based information than image-based information? Why is there a shift in the way information is stored? What implications does this research have for educational practices? (Isn't it thoughtful of cognitive psychologists to leave so many unanswered questions for you to resolve?)

In the next section we consider only one more example of higher-order cognition among children—the very important problem of prototype formation.

Prototype Formation among Children

The "blooming, buzzing confusions" that William James thought the newborn baby was confronted with is one way of looking at the difficult task that we human information-processing creatures all faced initially. Out of the flood of information that bombards the infant's sensory system, what cognitive means exist for the storage and retrieval of pertinent information? It seems that our storage system—human memory— is limited in the amount of information that can be coded and retained by the limited capacity of the brain. We cannot store everything detected by our sensory system.

One alternative model to a store-everything concept is the idea that we form abstract representations of sensory impressions in the form of prototypes and/or conceptual categories. This necessary proclivity appears very early in infancy, and several experiments have shown that the formation of conceptual categories in infants may develop before language. Ross (1980) did an experiment with 12-, 18-, and 24-month-old infants in which they were shown, one at a time, ten toy objects of the same class, such as types of furniture. Then the infants were shown pairs of objects in which one item was a member of the class (but not originally presented) and the other item was a member of a different category (for example, an apple). Even the youngest of infants in this study spent more time examining the "novel" object, which suggests that they had formed a class representation of, in this case, furniture in which one of the pairs was an "uninteresting" member.

A more direct test of prototype formation in very young (10-month-old) infants was demonstrated by Strauss (1979; see also Strauss & Carter, 1984; and Cohen & Strauss, 1979), who used facial prototypes formed from the plastic templates of an Identikit. The primary purpose of the experiment was to assess infants' abilities to abstract prototypical representations, and if they could, to ascertain whether the prototype was formed on the basis of averaging the values of the exemplar items (feature-averaging model) or on the basis of summing the most commonly experienced values of the exemplar items (modal model).

Infants in Strauss's study were shown a series of fourteen faces that had been designed to represent a prototype formed on the basis of modal, or average, representations. (See the discussion in Chapter 4 for more on the technique and theory of prototypes.) Following this stage, the infants were given pairs of two types of prototypes—one based on an averaging of the features in the first series, and the other based on a modal (or most frequent) number of features in the first series. The dependent variable was time spent looking at one of the faces. It was presumed that infants would spend more time on the novel, or nonprototypic, face than on the prototype face. By using time spent looking at new faces, the experimenter was able to infer which representation was responsible for the formation of a prototype. The most important finding was that very young (10-month-old) infants were able to abstract a prototype face. Strauss also found that infants abstracted information from the faces and formed a prototypical representation on the basis of an averaging of the features of the exemplar faces.

Walton and T. G. R. Bower (1993) reported data that indicated prototype formation in newborn infants, aged 8 to 78 hours, could be achieved. The researchers used infant sucking, which controlled the duration a face would be exposed, as the dependent variable. The faces the infants saw were images of eight female or blended (prototype) images of the faces. The infants looked longer at the composite face than at a composite of unseen faces on the first presentation of each. Walton and Bower argue that newborns do form a mental representation having some of the properties of a schema or prototype and that such representations are formed rapidly.

The work on prototype formation has been extended to include children in the age range of 3 to 6 years in an experiment conducted in 1993 by Inn, Walden, and Solso. This experiment is similar to the abstraction of information discussed in Chapter 4, except the subjects were children. A series of ten exemplar faces were developed from a police identification kit using a prototype face as a base. Initially, only exemplar faces were shown to children. After a child was shown the entire set of ten exemplar faces, he or she was shown a second set. Some of these faces were from the original set (old faces), some were faces not previously seen (new faces), and one of the new faces was the prototype from which the exemplars had been developed. The results are shown in Figure 13.19. As shown, very young children, about 3 or 4 years old, do not form an abstraction of the prototype face. However, by the age of 5 it appears that prototype formation begins, and it is nearly complete at the age of 6, when children's performance on this task is similar to that of college students.

Keep in mind that when a participant identifies a prototype face as an old (previously seen) face, he or she is making a false alarm or error. The face is, in fact, new. Prototype formation may be a sophisticated means of storing frequently experienced features in a single "best example." From these studies and an ever-increasing body of literature on children's cognitive processes, the evidence is beginning to accumulate that points out that abstraction of verbal and visual information (be it conceptualized as schemes, grammars, formation of categories, or prototypes) is as important an attribute of children's information-processing activities as it is among adults.

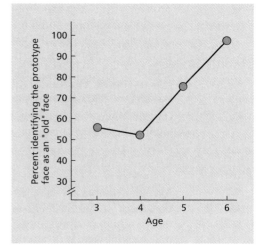

FIGURE 13.19

Percentage of false alarms to prototype face among young children.

Data from Inn, Walden, and Solso (1993).

Spotlight on Cognitive Neuroscience

Cognitive Development

Ross Thompson and Charles Nelson review the literature with regard to media accounts of children's development and the corresponding scientific evidence for those accounts. One particular area that they focus on is the importance of early experiences in brain development. It is known that a newborn's brain has many more synapses than an adult's brain. Furthermore, we know that the number of synapses rapidly decreases as we age. The idea is that various early experiences activate certain brain regions and synapses such that those activated synapses are some of the ones that disappear. This is a widely held belief, and although it has been empirically validated, they caution that more work is needed to understand the influence of genetics and early experiences on particular brain regions and when those experiences should occur for optimal effect (see also Figure 13.6 on p. 395).

Thompson, R. A., & Nelson, C. A. (2001). Developmental science and the media: Early brain development. *American Psychologist, 56*(1), 5–15.

SUMMARY

1   Cognition development concerns changes that occur in a more or less orderly fashion across the life span of individuals. It can be studied from the perspective of developmental psychology, neurocognitive development, and/or cognitive development.

2   One theory of cognitive development (Piaget) proposes that intellectual growth is biologically determined and governed by two processes: adaptation involving cognitive adjustments to the environment (assimilation and accommodation), and organization involving increasingly complex, integrated mental representations of

operations. Cognitive development is characterized by quantitative, linear changes within a stage and qualitative changes across four major stages: sensorimotor, pre-operational, concrete-operational, and formal-operational stages.

3   Another major theory of cognitive development (Vygotsky) rejects a strict biological determinism and proposes that learning precedes development. Thought and language are believed to originate independently, with thought being biologically determined whereas language is socially determined. Integration occurs when the child connects thought, language, and environmental events through naming activity.

4   Developmental cognitive neuroscience is based on the assumption that underlying all cognitive functions are neurological structures and processes.

5   The brain develops from simple to complex throughout the early life of an individual. It is subject to environmental stimulation and biological constraints.

6   Cerebral lateralization has been found among young children, which gives support to the biological nature of this phenomenon.

7   Cognitive development from an information-processing perspective concerns the question of changes in processes such as attention and memory as a function of increasing age.

8   Recent studies of twins suggest that genetics plays an important role in determining verbal and spatial ability in children.

9   Young children and infants have memory capacity, but it is doubtful that reliable memories are formed, or can be retrieved, before the age of 2.

10   The age that the most memorable memories are formed is between 10 and 30.

11   Studies comparing higher-order cognition in children and adults show that children use story schemata in a manner analogous to adults. Adults rely more on semantic representations, whereas children rely more on perceptually based representations (that is, imagery). Conceptual category formation may precede language acquisition with the basis of prototype formation in infants being feature-averaging.

12   Initial information acquisition requires perception of and attention to pertinent information. Research suggests that differences between younger and older subjects with respect to certain abilities, such as selective attention and the ability to respond to task demands, increase with age. Adults and older children use different encoding strategies (for example, multiple versus simple) relative to younger children, and these differences appear as early in the information-processing sequence as the sensory registers.

13   Prototype formation has been observed in very young infants and children.

KEY WORDS

accommodation
adaptation
assimilation
classification
conservation

habituation
scheme
seriation
transitivity

RECOMMENDED READINGS

● Several books by or about Piaget are recommended. They include Piaget, *The Origins of Intelligence in Children;* "Piaget's Theory" in Mussen, ed., *Carmichael's Manual of Child Psychology;* and Piaget and Inhelder, *Memory and Intelligence.* Also see Flavell, *Cognitive Development* and *The Developmental Psychology of Jean Piaget;* and Brainerd, *Piaget's Theory of Intelligence.* Holmes and Morrison, *The Child,* is also recommended, as are P. Ornstein, ed., *Memory Development in Children;* Pick and Saltzman, eds., *Modes of Perceiving and Processing Information;* Siegler ed., *Children's Thinking: What Develops?* Daehler and Bukafko's text *Cognitive Development* is also recommended. Vygotsky's work is now generally available in English. Recommended are *Mind in Society* and *Thought and Language.* Several edited books on the information-processing approach to developmental psychology are also recommended. They include Sternberg, ed., *Mechanisms of Cognitive Development;* Flavell and Markman, eds., *Handbook of Child Psychology: Cognitive Development;* Sophian, ed., *Origins of Cognitive Skills;* and Moscovitch, ed., *Infant Memory.* Flavell's APA Award address, "The Development of Children's Knowledge about the Appearance-Reality Distinction," in *American Psychologist,* is also recommended. For infant memory see Rovee-Collier in A. Diamond, ed., *The Development and Neural Bases of Higher Cognitive Functions.* A somewhat technical, but worthwhile, collection of neurocognitive papers can be found in M. Johnson's *Brain Development and Cognition: A Reader.* Recent issues of journals devoted to developmental psychology are also recommended for current findings.

Thinking

Concept Formation, Logic, and Decision Making

hmmm...?

- **Thinking**
- **Concept Formation**
  Association
  Hypothesis Testing
- **Logic**
  Inferences and Deductive Reasoning
  Syllogistic Reasoning
- **Decision Making**
  Inductive Reasoning
  Decision Making in the "Real World"
  Reasoning and the Brain
  Estimating Probabilities
  Decision Frames
  Representativeness
  Bayes's Theorem and Decision Making
- **Decision Making and Rationality**

1. How do cognitive psychologists define "thinking," and how does thinking differ from concept formation? From logic?

2. Why is logic called the "science of thinking"?

3. What are the major components of a syllogism?

4. What is deductive reasoning, and how is it different from inductive reasoning?

5. How might a conversational argument be separated logically?

6. What are Venn diagrams? Take a basic argument and illustrate it in a Venn diagram.

7. What is a "decision frame," and how does it affect our ability to solve problems?

8. What is the gist of Bayes's theorem?

Thinking is the crown jewel of cognition. It is spectacularly brilliant, in some people; even sublime, among average folks; and, the fact that it happens at all, one of the great wonders of our species. Thinking about thinking, what some call meta-thinking, may seem an insurmountable task, since it seems to engage all of the themes mentioned previously—the detection of external energy, neurophysiology, perception, memory, language, imagery, and the developing person. Advances in cognitive psychology, particularly within the last twenty years, have led to a formidable arsenal of research techniques and theoretical models capable of disclosing some of the facts about thought and casting them in a plausible framework of sound psychological theory. This chapter is the first of two chapters about the thought process and some of the means used to study this fundamental topic.

Thinking

Thinking is experiencing a rebirth as a legitimate topic in psychology. A part of that resurgence may be attributable to experiments on logical thought, reason, and the emergence of neurocognition.

Thinking is a process by which a new mental representation is formed through the transformation of information by complex interaction of the mental attributes of judging, abstracting, reasoning, imagining, and problem solving. Thinking is the most inclusive of the three elements of the thought process and is characterized by comprehensiveness rather than exclusion. When you read a book, information presumably passes through a sequence from a sensory store to a memory store. Then that new information is transformed (in a sense, digested), and the consequence is an original product. The task is, of course, much more complex than is expressed in this example, but it is easy to see that the development of the simple thought depends on judgments, abstraction, reason, imagination, problem solving, and creativity.

There continues to be some dispute as to whether thinking is an internal process or exists only insofar as can be measured behaviorally. For example, a chess player may study his or her next move for several minutes before responding overtly. During the time the player is pondering what action to take, does thinking occur? It seems obvious that it does, and yet some would argue that because no overt behavior is observable, such a conclusion is based not on empirical observation but on speculation. A general definition of thinking might resolve some of the conflict and help guide our discussion. There are three basic ideas about thinking.

- Thinking is cognitive—that is, it occurs "internally," in the mind—but is inferred from behavior. The chess player exhibits thinking in his or her move.
- Thinking is a process that involves some manipulation of knowledge in the cognitive system. While the chess player is contemplating a move, past memories combine with present information to change his or her knowledge of the situation.

- Thinking is directed and results in behavior that "solves" a problem or is directed toward a solution. The next chess move is, in the mind of the player, directed toward winning the game. Not all actions are successful, but generally, in the mind of the player, they are directed toward a solution.

Concept Formation

Concept formation (or concept learning) refers to the discernment of the properties common to a class of objects or ideas. We have dealt with the topic of concept formation as it relates to visual forms and prototypes (see Chapter 4) and semantic items (see Chapter 9). The greater part of our previous discussion specified the components or features of concepts and how concepts were structured in a semantic network. In this section the topic of features is also discussed, but we will concentrate on the rules that relate conceptual features. For example, we all have learned the concept *Volkswagen* by identification of its classic properties (for example, beetle-shaped, no grill) that distinguish it from the other members of the general class of *automobiles,* or we have learned the properties of the more abstract concept *justice* (for example, fairness, morality, equality) that distinguish it from other human qualities. In these instances the "rule" that relates the features to the concept is as follows: The concept is defined in terms of all the features that have been associated with it.

Concept formation, as it is used in this chapter, is more limited in scope than thinking and seems readily susceptible to experimental analysis. It is not surprising, then, that there is a considerable body of knowledge about the laws and processes of concept formation. The early definition of *concept* was "mental images, ideas, or processes." This was normally disclosed through the experimental method of introspection, which was widely accepted as the principal technique of psychology. The decline of introspection as a method and the rise of behaviorism, especially in American psychology, brought about not only revolutionary methodological changes but also corresponding revolutionary changes in the view of the nature of cognitive events—and, consequently, in the definition of *concept.* For our purposes, a concept may be defined in terms of certain critical features and the rules that relate those features. (Occasionally we use the term in its former sense.)

Features, as used here, are characteristics of an object or event that are also characteristic of other objects or events. Mobility, for example, is a feature of automobiles; Ford Escorts have it, Cadillacs have it, and Maseratis have it. However, mobility is also a feature of other objects—trains, birds, and tight ends. From a cognitive viewpoint, the basis for accepting a characteristic as a feature is subjective. Thus, one can imagine automobiles, trains, birds, and tight ends that do *not* share the feature of mobility, and so the determination of "critical features" of an object or idea is a function of the circumstances. In

*T*he only justification for our concepts is that they serve to represent the complex of our experiences . . .

—*Albert Einstein*

this sense, conceptual description is similar to the process involved in signal detection (see Chapter 3), in which acceptability as a feature of a concept is determined by the stringency of criteria. The setting of a criterion, as we have learned, is subject to wide variance, according to the experience of the observer.

A distinction between features can be made on the quantitative basis as well as on the qualitative basis just described. Mobility is a qualitative feature that also can be measured quantitatively. Your Ford Escort automobile may have mobility (a qualitative statement) but may not have as much mobility as someone else's Maserati. Thus, both dimensional (quantitative) features and attributional (qualitative) features enter into conceptual formation; both kinds are investigated.

During the formative periods of most sciences, concept formation played a critical function in the organization of data. In chemistry concept formation is achieved by the organization of the elements in a periodic table; in biology, by the development of phylogenetic order; in art, by the categorization of artists by periods; in Egyptology, by the division of events into dynasties; and in cognitive psychology, by the classification of types of memories—all are examples of concept formation that led to a better understanding of the subject. These complex forms of concept formation, when broken down into their basic components, are actually composed of a series of rather simple (and analyzable) cognitive processes.

Association

The oldest and most influential theory in learning is the principle of association—**associationism.** In its most succinct form, the principle holds that a bond will be formed between two events as those events are repeatedly presented together. Reinforcement, or a reward system, facilitates formation of the bond. The basic model of the principle is cast in terms of stimulus-response (S-R) psychology. Thus, the association principle postulates that the learning of a concept is a result of (1) reinforcing the correct pairing of a stimulus (for example, red boxes) with the response of identifying it as a concept, and (2) nonreinforcing (a form of punishment) the incorrect pairing of a stimulus (for example, red circles) with a response of identifying it as a concept. (Such mechanistic viewpoints leave little room for the concept—prevalent among modern cognitive theorists—of internal structures that select, organize, and transform information.)

Hypothesis Testing

The general notion that people sometimes solve problems and form concepts by formulating and testing hypotheses has long been held in experimental psychology. The direct application of a hypothesis-testing model to concept learning by Bruner, Goodnow, and Austin (1956) in their influential book, *A Study of Thinking,* introduced a thorough methodological analysis of performance in concept formation.

The initial stage in concept attainment is the selection of a hypothesis or a strategy that is consistent with the objectives of our inquiry. Whenever we seek to find out something, the process involves the establishment of priorities, much as a scientist may order a sequence of experiments, a lawyer may ask a series of questions, or a doctor

Jerome Bruner. His seminal work established "thinking" as a legitimate scientific topic.

may develop a set of diagnostic tests. The following from Bruner and his colleagues details the process of selecting strategies:

> A neurologist is interested in the localization of pattern vision in monkeys. More specifically, he is interested in six cortical areas and their bearing on pattern vision. He knows that, with all six areas intact, pattern vision is unimpaired. With all six areas destroyed, pattern vision is absent. His technique of research is extirpation. In planning his research, how shall he proceed? Destroy one area at a time? All but one at a time? In what order shall he do his successive experiments? (p. 56)

The prime question is "What is to be gained by choosing one order as compared to another order of testing instances?"

The first thing to be gained is, of course, an opportunity to obtain information appropriate to the objectives of one's inquiry. One may wish to choose an instance at any given point in concept attainment that can tell one the most about what the concept might be. To sum up, controlling the order of instances tested is to increase or decrease the cognitive strain involved in assimilating information. A well-contrived order of choice—a good "selection strategy"—makes it easier to keep track of what hypotheses have been found tenable or untenable on the basis of information encountered. A third advantage is not at first obvious. By following a certain order of selecting instances for testing one controls the degree of risk involved.

In a typical experiment, Bruner and his associates presented an entire concept universe (that is, all possible variations on a number of dimensions and attributes) to participants and indicated one instance of an exemplar of the concept that the participants were to attain. The participants would pick one of the other instances, be told whether it was a positive or negative instance, then pick another instance, and so on until they attained the criterion (identified the concept).

The strategies participants may select in concept formation include scanning and focusing, each of which has its subtypes as follows:

Simultaneous scanning. Participants start with all possible hypotheses and eliminate the untenable ones.

Successive scanning. Participants begin with a single hypothesis, maintain it if successful, and, where it is unsuccessful, may change it to another that is based on all previous experience.

Conservative focusing. Participants formulate a hypothesis, select a positive instance of it as a focus, and then make a sequence of reformulations (each of

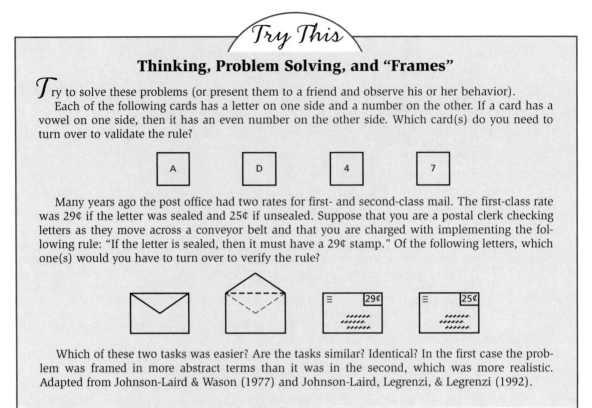

Try This

Thinking, Problem Solving, and "Frames"

*T*ry to solve these problems (or present them to a friend and observe his or her behavior).

Each of the following cards has a letter on one side and a number on the other. If a card has a vowel on one side, then it has an even number on the other side. Which card(s) do you need to turn over to validate the rule?

Many years ago the post office had two rates for first- and second-class mail. The first-class rate was 29¢ if the letter was sealed and 25¢ if unsealed. Suppose that you are a postal clerk checking letters as they move across a conveyor belt and that you are charged with implementing the following rule: "If the letter is sealed, then it must have a 29¢ stamp." Of the following letters, which one(s) would you have to turn over to verify the rule?

Which of these two tasks was easier? Are the tasks similar? Identical? In the first case the problem was framed in more abstract terms than it was in the second, which was more realistic. Adapted from Johnson-Laird & Wason (1977) and Johnson-Laird, Legrenzi, & Legrenzi (1992).

The solutions to the problems are at the end of this chapter.

which changes only one feature), noting each time which turns out to be positive and which negative.

Focus gambling is characterized by changing more than one feature at a time. Although the conservative-focusing technique is methodological and likely to lead to a valid concept, participants may opt for a gamble in the expectation that they may determine the concept more quickly.

Of the strategies described previously, conservative focusing tends to be the most effective (Bourne, 1963); scanning techniques give only marginal success. A difficulty with the Bruner model is that it assumes that participants hold to a single strategy, when, in actuality, some vacilate, shifting from strategy to strategy throughout the task.

Logic

Thought, or *thinking,* refers to the general process of considering an issue in the mind, while **logic** is the science of thinking. Although two people may think about the same thing, their conclusions—both reached through thought—may differ, one being *logical,* the other *illogical.*

In a recent newspaper interview of people on the street, a reporter asked, "Are you in favor of the death penalty?" One person gave the following answer: "I am religious and think that everyone has the right to life. The Bible says 'an eye for an eye,' and if someone does something to another person he should get what he deserves. Besides, it has been proved that some people have defective brains which cannot be changed. Some things are worse than death, like rape." The person was in favor of the death penalty, although it is somewhat difficult to ascertain that conclusion given the reply. The conclusion (favoring the death penalty) seems to be in direct conflict with the opening statement, "I . . . think everyone has the right to life." Perhaps what the person really intended was "Even though people have a given right to life, if an individual violates certain laws of society, he or she should be executed." The justification for execution is supported by biblical teachings, good sense, medical truths, the relative severity of the punishment, and probably a high degree of emotional thought. In this case serious questions can be raised regarding the validity of the argument, but it is, nevertheless, a fairly typical representation of the way many people support a conclusion, which makes life both fascinating and frustrating.

Thinking and logic have been the subject of speculation for a long time. More than two thousand years ago, Aristotle introduced a system of reasoning or of validating arguments that is called the **syllogism.** A syllogism has three steps—a major premise, a minor premise, and a conclusion, in that order. Note the following example:

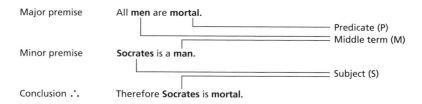

A conclusion reached by means of syllogistic reasoning is considered valid, or true, if the premises are accurate and the form is correct. It is, therefore, possible to use syllogistic logic for the validation of arguments. Illogical conclusions can be determined and their cause isolated. This is a succinct statement of the theoretical basis of much current research on thinking and logic.

Before introducing some of the current research, it is useful to review the laws of formal syllogistic logic. In the outline shown in Figure 14.1 (Erickson, 1974) of the various forms of a syllogism, the predicate of the conclusion is labeled *P*, and the subject of the conclusion is labeled, *S*. The major premise links the predicate of the conclusion (*honest,* in the first example) with a middle term, *M* (*churchgoers*); the minor premise links the subject of the conclusion (*politicians*) with the middle term (*churchgoers*); and the conclusion links the subject (*politicians*) with the predicate of the conclusion (*honest*).

Each syllogism type can be designated on the basis of the kinds of sentences of which it is composed; thus, in the example concerning Socrates and mortality, all of the sentences are of the universal affirmative type (*A*), and so the syllogism is of the AAA type.

The syllogistic figures shown in Figure 14.1 are notations for mediation models, which are commonly used in the study of verbal learning. For example, Figure 1 (forward chain) in the Socrates example would have the following sequence: men-mortal, Socrates-man, Socrates-mortal. The total number of syllogisms possible (a combination

FIGURE 14.1

Forms of a syllogism.

Basic Forms of a Syllogism		
Major Premise	All M are P	All churchgoers are honest.
Minor Premise	All S are M	All politicians are churchgoers
Conclusion	All S are P	Therefore all politicians are honest

Sentence Type Used in a Syllogism			
A	All S are P	All psychologists are wise	(universal affirmative)
E	No S are P	No poor research is published	(universal negative)
I	Some S are P	Some elected officials are truthful	(particular affirmative)
O	Some S are not P	Some professors are not rich	(particular negative)

Syllogistic Figures			
Figure 1 (Forward Chain)	Figure 2 (Stimulus Chain)	Figure 3 Response Equivalence)	Figure 4 (Backward Chain)
M–P	P–M	M–P	P–M
S–M	S–M	M–S	M–S
S–M	S–P	S–P	S–P

*𝐼*NDUCTION

induction, in LOGIC, the process of reasoning from the particular to the general. Francis BACON proposed induction as the logic of scientific discovery and DEDUCTION as the logic of argumentation. In fact, both processes are used together regularly in the empirical sciences: by the observation of particular events (induction) and from already known principles (deduction), new hypothetical principles are formulated and laws induced.

*𝐷*EDUCTION

deduction. 1 In traditional LOGIC, the process of drawing, by reasoning, particular conclusions from more general principles assumed to be true. The Aristotelian SYLLOGISM is the classic example of deductive logic in the tradition.   2 In contemporary logic, any statement derived by a transformed rule upon an axiom; more generally, the term now refers to a process of deriving theorems from axioms, or conclusions from premises, by formal rules (transformation rules).

—*The Concise Columbia Encyclopedia*

of types and figures) is 256, assuming each factor interacts with all other factors, of which only 24 are logical (6 for each figure).

An appealing feature of using syllogistic logic in cognitive research is that it makes it possible to evaluate, or validate, the correctness of the thought process on the basis of its form rather than its content. By using symbols (S and P) to represent the subject and predicate, it is possible to reduce logical thinking to a type of algebra. Instead of saying 8 apples plus 3 apples minus 2 apples yields 9 apples, we can mathematically represent the equation as $a + b - c = b^2$ or $a - c = b^2 - b$, without consideration of the referents designated by these symbols. Similarly, it is possible in syllogistic logic to reduce statements of fact to symbols and manipulate them, as in mathematical equations, without regard to the physical reality they may represent.

Inferences and Deductive Reasoning

If Bill is taller than Jeff and Jeff is shorter than Ryan, then is Bill taller than Ryan? Take a moment and figure this out. Some people work out this problem (which, of course, has no definitive conclusion) by drawing little figures in which the relative height of the Bill, Jeff, and Ryan are depicted.

Your conclusion was reached through a process of reasoning called **deductive reasoning,** which is the logical technique in which particular conclusions are drawn from more general principles. Johnson-Laird (1995) has identified four main issues in the cognitive study of deductive logic.

1. Relational inferences based on the logical properties of such relations as *greater than, on the right of,* and *after.* (In the case of Bill et al. you had to use a "greater than" logic.)

2. Propositional inferences based on negation and on such connectives as *if, or,* and *and.* (For example, you might rephrase the preceding problem as "If Bill is taller . . . ".)

3. Syllogisms based on pairs of premises that each contain a single qualifier, such as *all* or *some.* (In the next section we will study syllogisms that have such qualifiers, such as, "All psychologists are brilliant; some psychologists wear glasses . . . ".)

4. Multiplying of quantified inferences based on premises containing more than one qualifier, such as *Some French poodles are more expensive that any other type of dog.*

These four models, or contingencies involved in decision making, have been formalized by logicians into a type of predicate calculus (*viz.* that branch of symbolic logic that deals with relations between propositions and their internal structure—symbols are used to represent the subject and predicate of a proposition).

As an example of relational inferences and logic consider the following problem.

Suppose a friend of yours visits the Chicago Art Institute and tells you of his visit:
In one room there was a van Gogh, a Renoir, and a Degas.
The van Gogh painting was on the right of the Renoir.
The Degas was on the left of the Renoir.
Was the van Gogh on the right of the Degas?

A moment's thought will confirm your answer. But how did you arrive at that answer, and what are the cognitive rules that describe your logic? One model by Johnson-Laird (1995), which may be generalized to other similar problems, follows.

> For any x, y, if x is on the left of y, then y is on the right of x.
> For any x, y, z, if x is on the right of y, and y is on the right of z, then x is on the right of z.

With these postulates a conclusion may be derived.

> If p then q
> p
> ∴ q

where p and q denote any propositions. The model may be expanded greatly by adding just a few more propositions.

Consider another problem:

Problem A

The cup is on the right of the saucer.
The plate is on the left of the saucer.
The fork is in front of the plate.
The spoon is in front of the cup.
What is the relation between the fork and the spoon?

Try to solve this problem and the other problems in your head before looking at the illustration at the end of the chapter. Now, presume that one premise is changed so the problem now reads (the changed item is in bold):

Problem B

The cup is on the right of the saucer.
The plate is on the left of the *cup.*
The fork is in front of the plate.
The spoon is in front of the cup.
What is the relation between the fork and the spoon?

What is your mental representation of this problem? There are at least two arrangements. Even though the answer is the same, this is a decidedly more difficult problem because both models must be constructed in order to test definitively the validity of the answer. The task may be made even more difficult if the correct response may be made *only* by constructing the models as in this description:

Problem C

The cup is on the right of the saucer.
The plate is on the left of the cup.
The fork is in front of the plate.
The spoon is in front of the *saucer.*
What is the relation between the fork and the spoon?

One can see that the number of items one must hold in immediate memory nearly reaches the limit of short-term memory. Nevertheless, finding the underlying mathe-

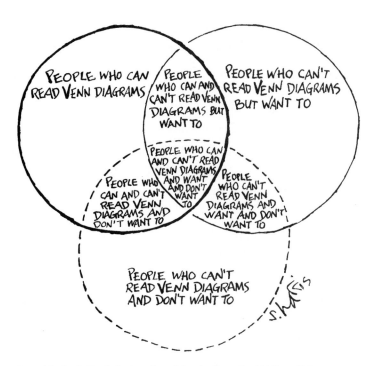

Copyright by S. Harris in *American Scientist* (Sep–Oct 1994), p. 420.

matical models that describe human logic is a worthy endeavor. These are simple little problems that nevertheless require careful attention and concentration to solve mentally. You might try these problems out on your friends and invent some more along the way. What principles of mental problem solving emerge?

Syllogistic Reasoning

Early research using syllogistic reasoning relied on reports by the participant of "what was going on in my head" while solving a problem in logic. Although these introspective techniques lacked the empirical basis science requires, three important independent variables did emerge from them: the form of the argument, the content of the argument, and the participant (individual differences).

Form. Early researchers (Woodworth & Sells, 1935; Sells, 1936; and Chapman & Chapman, 1959) looked at the errors produced in syllogistic reasoning tasks as a consequence of the "mood" or "atmosphere" created by the form of the argument, rather than on the basis of formal logical deduction. A typical case might be:

> All *A* are *B*.
>
> All *C* are *B*.
> ———————————
> Therefore, all *A* are *C*.

Here the term *all* in the major and minor premises seems to suggest a universal affirmative atmosphere, so that when participants come to the conclusion, which mimics the form of the premise, their tendency is to accept it. The obvious invalidity of the argument is evident if we substitute content for the letter abstractions. Thus:

All Republicans are human.
All Democrats are human.
Therefore, all Republicans are Democrats.

Before going on with our discussion of syllogistic logic, try to ascertain the validity of the following statements.

All revolutions are basically economic.
Some economic conditions cause hardships.
Some revolutions cause hardships.
Sam is not the best cook in the world.
The best cook in the world lives in Toronto.
Sam does not live in Toronto.
All nerts are soquerts.
All connets are strequos.
All connets are nerts.

Did you find some of these easy and some difficult? One easy to way to solve syllogisms is to use diagrams, as shown in Figure 14.2. (More is said about this later.) The reason some were more difficult than others may be a function of your previous knowledge and your previous ability to recognize a logical argument when you see it. The first of these effects is called the atmosphere effect, discussed next, and the second is related

FIGURE 14.2

Diagrams in which all and some *A*'s are *B*'s and no or some *A*'s are *B*'s are represented.

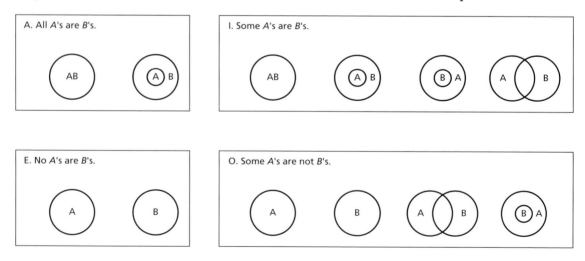

to the validity of an argument that may be the result of formal training but is more likely the result of practice. Also, you may have learned that you need not know the definitions of terms to determine the validity of an argument.

Atmosphere.   The *atmosphere effect* is defined as the tendency to accept or reject an argument on the basis of its form. In other words, merely presenting an argument in a certain way may influence its believability.

Johnson-Laird and his associates (Johnson-Laird & Byrne, 1989, 1991; and Johnson-Laird & Steedman, 1978) have demonstrated that the form of a syllogism exhibits a strong influence on the conclusion drawn. Specifically, a syllogism of the following sort:

Some of the parents are scientists.
All of the scientists are drivers.

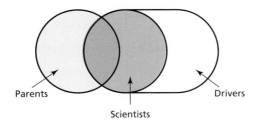

tends to elicit the conclusion "Some of the parents are drivers" in preference to the equally valid conclusion "Some of the drivers are parents." In the symbolic language we have been using, an AB, BC syllogism favors an AC conclusion, while a BA, CB syllogism favors a CA conclusion. Furthermore, the authors report that the phenomenon occurs with audiences at universities as far-flung as Chicago, New York, Edinburgh, London, Padua, and Nijmegen!

A feature of Johnson-Laird and Steedman's research that is particularly interesting to cognitive psychologists is their inferences about the mental representations of syllogistic premises.

For example, one participant represented the statement "All the artists are beekeepers" by first imagining an arbitrary number of artists and tagging each as a beekeeper. One participant, when asked how he performed the task, said, "I thought of all the little

Phillip Johnson-Laird. **Developed important models of human cognition and logic.**

artists in the room and imagined that they all had beekeeper hats on." Thus, the "internal representation" of the premise might be as follows:

artist	artist	artist		
↓	↓	↓		
beekeeper	beekeeper	beekeeper	(beekeeper)	(beekeeper)

Arbitrary numbers of artists are tagged as beekeepers, as are some beekeepers who are not artists. The arrows, in Johnson-Laird and Steedman's theme, represent semantic relationships of class membership. (Here, for example, the arrow represents *is a* in "Each artist is a beekeeper.") The earlier relationship (All *A* are *B*) can be further symbolically illustrated as follows:

a	*a*	
↓	↓	
b	b	(*b*)

which is recognized as an *A* sentence type, or premise. An *I* sentence type, or premise, "Some *A* are *B*," has the following representation:

a	(*a*)
↓	
b	(*b*)

An *E* sentence type, or premise, "No *A* are *B*":

a	*a*
⊥	⊥
b	b

And an *O* sentence type, or premise, "Some *A* are not *B*":

a	(*a*)
⊥	↓
b	(*b*)

If the second premise is "Some of the beekeepers are chemists," the form is:

All of the artists are beekeepers.

Some of the beekeepers are chemists.

or symbolically:

All *A* are *B*	*a*	*a*	
	↓	↓	
Some *B* are *C*	b	b	(*b*)
	↓	↓	
	c	c	(*c*)

which frequently leads to the invalid conclusion:

Some of the artists are chemists.

The formulation of a conclusion calls on the participant to trace a path between the end items in their representation of the parts of a syllogism, much as we might consider a problem in mental mapping (for example, determining the shortest route to Boston to San Francisco to Atlanta). If there is at least one positive path, as in the artists-beekeepers-chemists syllogism, then the invalid conclusion that some artists are chemists is likely to be made.

This work has been extended by Clement and Falmagne (1986) in an interesting study in which world knowledge and mental imagery were related to logical reasoning. Essentially, the experimenters varied the imagery value of the terms and the relatedness of conditional statements in syllogisms. From our discussion of mental imagery (see Chapter 10), you may recall that words differ with regard to their imagery values (for example, *beggar* has higher imagery than *context*). *Relatedness* refers to how easily or naturally two actions form a relationship. An example of a statement used in a logical syllogism that is high in imagery might be "If the man wants plain doughnuts, then . . ." whereas a statement low in imagery might be "If the woman reorganizes the company structure, then . . ." High- and low-relatedness statements might include "If the man wants plain doughnuts, then he walks to the bakery across the intersection" and "If the man walks his golden retriever, then he gets upset about his insect bite." All four possible combinations of statements were used in syllogistic problems (that is, high imagery–high relatedness; high imagery–low relatedness; low imagery–high relatedness; and low imagery–low relatedness). Clement and Falmagne found that syllogisms in which the statements were high in imagery and relatedness were solved significantly better than other forms. That, given what we know about the powerful effects of both imagery and relatedness to form internal representations of reality and the above theoretical model of Johnson-Laird, seems to be a logical conclusion.

The usefulness of diagrams (such as a Venn diagram) and imagery to solve problems in logic has been further demonstrated by Bauer and Johnson-Laird (1993) on complicated deductive logic problems of the following kind:

> Raphael is in Tacoma or Julia is in Atlanta, or both.
> Julia is in Atlanta or Paul is in Philadelphia, or both.

Is the following conclusion valid?

> Julia is in Atlanta, or both Raphael is in Tacoma and Paul is in Philadelphia.

If you are like most participants in the study, you found this difficult to validate. Now, try to visualize the problem with the assistance of the diagram in Figure 14.3. This diagram is a kind of road map in which the participant must travel from the left side to the right side by inserting the shapes (representing people) into the slots in the path (representing places). When a pathway is intact, travel can take place. Thus, if Julia is in Atlanta, traffic could flow through that area. Julia could be in Atlanta or Seattle or neither place. In a study done at Princeton University (Bauer & Johnson-Laird, 1993), it was found that when problems of this sort were presented in diagram form, undergraduate students solved the problems faster and drew many more valid conclusions (about 30 percent more) than when the problems were presented verbally. The important conclusion we may draw from this experiment is that logically untrained people, such as most people are, tend to reason by building models of the situation or drawing diagrams that show relationships clearly.

The research on syllogisms has suggested that people tend to draw conclusions in syllogistic problems (and presumably in less formal ways of logical thinking as well) on

FIGURE 14.3

Diagram representing a double disjunctive problem. Participants were asked to complete a path from the left side to the right side by inserting the shapes corresponding to people into the slots. Thus, Julia could be in Atlanta *or* Seattle but *not* both.

From Bauer and Johnson-Laird (1993).

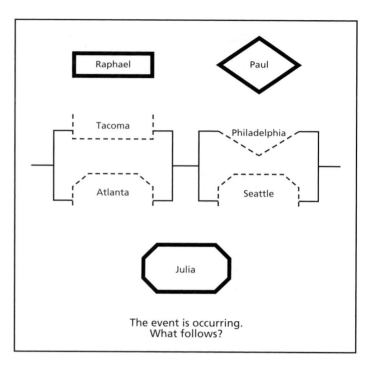

The event is occurring.
What follows?

the basis of first forming internal representations of the premises—sometimes imagined representations. Once these internal representations are formed, it is possible to apply logical thinking to them. If the representation (or heuristic) is biased toward verification (as "All artists are beekeepers"), then the logical test of the conclusion consists of trying to break the pathways between the premises and the conclusion.

Content.   Since it is possible to hold the form of the argument constant while varying the content, the latter has also been a useful tool in the analysis of the thought process. Thus the content of our opening syllogism:

> All men are mortal.
> Socrates is a man.
> Therefore, Socrates is mortal.

may be evaluated by using the same form but different content:

> All men are moral.
> Hitler is a man.
> Therefore, Hitler is moral.

If the premises of these syllogisms are true, then the conclusions are, even though one conclusion may be more difficult to accept than the other.

The effects of content on the judged validity of an argument remind us that the cognitive process is neither simple nor devoid of the considerable impact of knowledge stored in long-term memory. Throughout this book we have seen numerous examples of how that information influences (in many instances, to the degree of determining) the quality of the information perceived, encoded, stored, and transformed. It should not be surprising, then, that the judged validity of syllogistic statements about something we know may be a reflection of the content of the long-term memory.

The tendency to accept the conclusion of an invalid syllogism if the conclusion is consistent with the attitude of the judge was tested by Janis and Frick (1943). In their experiment, graduate students were asked to judge the soundness of arguments, with *soundness* defined as "a conclusion that logically follows from the premises." Some of the items used were as follows:

> Many brightly colored snakes are poisonous.
> The copperhead snake is not brightly colored.
> So the copperhead is not a poisonous snake.

> There is no doubt that some drugs are poisonous.
> All brands of beer contain the drug alcohol.
> Therefore, some brands of beer are poisonous.

> All poisonous things are bitter.
> Arsenic is not bitter.
> Therefore, arsenic is not poisonous.

After the participants had agreed or disagreed with each of the syllogisms, they were asked to reread the conclusion and indicate whether they agreed or disagreed with it. The results indicated that participants' errors tended to be made in the direction of their bias concerning the conclusion. Thus, the bromide "Don't confuse me with the facts; I've already made up my mind" seems to be true for some people under certain circumstances.

There is more than one way to err in making a "logical" deduction. We will consider several.

Decision Making

In the previous section we discussed a type of reasoning in which conclusions could be proved valid through a process of deductive logic. In that form, if the premises of a syllogism are true and the form correct, then the conclusion of an argument is valid—that is, the probability of the conclusion being correct is certain.

Inductive Reasoning

Another form of reasoning is called **inductive reasoning.** In inductive reasoning a conclusion is usually expressed implicitly or explicitly in terms of a probability statement. In our everyday life we commonly make decisions not so much as a result of a well-reasoned syllogistic paradigm, but in terms of inductive reasoning, where decisions are based on past experiences and conclusions are based on what is perceived as the best choice of a number of possible alternatives. Consider the following statements:

> If I work at the library for one week, I will have enough money to go skiing on
>   Saturday.
> I will work at the library for one week.
> Therefore, I will have enough money to go skiing.

The preceding argument is deductively valid. Now, suppose that the second statement was "I will not work at the library for one week." Then the conclusion "I will not have enough money to go skiing" is true given the constraints of syllogistic logic, but it is not necessarily true in real life. For example, your rich Uncle Harry might send you some money. Evaluating the validity of a conclusion based on inductive reasoning may be based on considerations other than the structural form of an argument. In the case just mentioned, it could be based on the likelihood that Uncle Harry will send a gift of money or on other possibilities that some funds will come your way shortly. This type of decision making goes on every day and has recently become the focus of research on the process by cognitive psychologists.

An example of decision making based on inductive reasoning is one that you may have faced when you selected a college. Let us presume that you were accepted into four colleges—a large private university (S), a small private college (T), a medium-sized state university (N), and a large state university (A). How might you go about deciding which college to attend? One method would be to evaluate each of the choices in terms of their relative value on pertinent dimensions. The important dimensions might include (1) the quality of instruction, (2) cost, (3) proximity to home, (4) social opportunities, and (5) prestige. Each dimension will be assigned a value between 0 and 10.

	University S	College T	University N	University A
1. Instruction	9	7	6	7
2. Cost	2	3	9	7
3. Proximity	4	7	8	3
4. Social life	8	7	3	5
5. Prestige	9	10	3	4
Totals	32	34	29	26

If all of these factors are equally important in making your decision and if the values are accurately assigned, then the favored choice is a small, private college. A decision based on some organization of factors may be a practical way to solve a problem but as can easily be deduced from the example of choosing a college, definitive judgments of real problems are not so simple.

In many situations the nature of the problem is not compatible with mathematical analysis. Tversky (1972) suggests that in making decisions we select alternatives by gradually eliminating less attractive choices. He called this notion *elimination by aspects,* since the individual is thought to eliminate less attractive alternatives based on a sequential evaluation of the attributes, or aspects, of the alternatives. If some alternatives do not meet the minimum criterion, then those alternatives are eliminated from the choice set.

Decision Making in the "Real World"

If only the world were as reasonable as the rational logic of Socrates, you might lament, all of our problems would disappear. You have probably been in a heated argument with someone else and felt like saying, "Get real!" (By this, of course, you may actually mean to say "agree with me—never mind the logic and facts.") While not all arguments can be settled objectively, it is possible to parse verbal disagreements so that at least we can better analyze the components of a dispute.

Reasoning Dialogues.   In the "real world" in which we all live, we commonly engage in conversations, or **verbal dialogues,** which may include argumentation. One may make an assertion ("Professor Solso, we would like to have a take-home final"); which is followed by a request for clarification ("Why is a take-home test better than an in-class test?"); which is followed by a justification ("Because in the 'real world' people have access to a variety of materials that will help them answer questions, such as the Internet, books, notes, and the like"); and finally by a refutation ("But, also in the 'real world' one is required to use stored knowledge to answer questions on the spot. We will have the final in class"). This scenario is typical of dozens of little arguments people engage in daily. What are the basic components of reasoning dialogues?

One way an argument may be parsed is to identify the underlying structural components as done by Rips and his associates (Rips, 1998; Rips, Brem, & Bailenson, 1999). Look at the two arguments shown in the box—the first from the O. J. Simpson trial and the other from two children.

Fortunately, many arguments are resolved amicably—some are not so smoothly settled. The components of argumentative dialogues consist of assertions, sometimes followed by concessions, requests for justification, or rebuttals; rebuttals can be followed by concessions or counterrebuttals; and so on. One way to illustrate the complexities of an argument is shown in the diagram in Figure 14.4.

In this figure we see that it is possible to nest arguments and subarguments into their logical components. For example, in the first case the initial claim by Mr. Kelly is met with a challenge, consisting of a justification query ("What is your foundation . . . ?") and that is followed by a paired justification ("She indicated to her mother . . ."). The researchers point out that "what is important in this example, though, is that the claim—the beginning of a new subargunment—can therefore be countered by a *rebutting defeater* (Pollock, 1998) from the judge ('The foundation is

---

Cognition in Everyday Life

Argumentative Dialogues

A. Excerpt from CNN (1997)

MR. KELLY: Your Honor, this is four days before the murder; it [evidence about a book, "Battered Women," that Nicole Simpson was reading] goes directly to her—not only her state of mind, but—

THE COURT: What is your foundation that she wrote these underlined—these things that you say she underlined?

MR. KELLY: She indicated to her mother, she was reading it and marking it up, and showed it to her mother, that she was doing it. At the same time, she said, "I've just started it; I'll give [it] to you afterwards."

And she can identify her handwriting.

THE COURT: I think under 352, the foundation is totally inadequate. I'm going to exclude it.

B. Dispute between two children (from Eisenberg & Garvey, 1981, p. 151)

CHILD 1: You're the mother, I'm the father.

CHILD 2: No, you're the mother, I'm the father.

CHILD 1: Why I'm the mother?

CHILD 2: Because you're—you're a girl.

CHILD 1: I'm not a girl.

FIGURE 14.4

A diagrammatic analysis of the dialogues presented in boxed feature "Cognition in Everyday Life: Argumentative Dialogues."

From Rips, Brem, and Bailenson (1999).

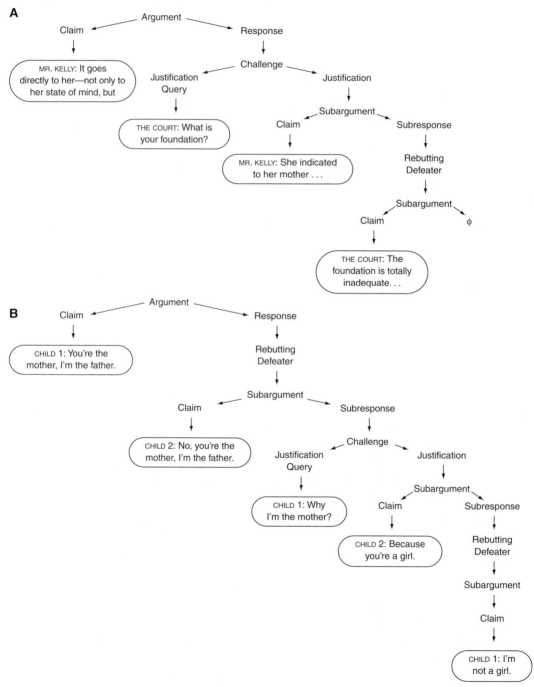

totally inadequate').” The same general analytic approach may be applied to the children's dialogue as well as most other “real-world” conversations.

Let us consider some other ways people fail in logical analysis.

The Fallacy of Reification.   To *reify* an idea is to assume that it is real when, in fact, it may be hypothetical or metaphoric. For example, a student who was having difficulty completing his master's degree said to me, “This university does not want to give me a degree!” He assumed that the university acted as an individual would act, when, in truth, the university did nothing. Possibly, his major advisor did not want to grant him a degree, perhaps for good reasons. Demagogic politicians, rabble-rousers, anarchists, and petit paranoids frequently reify ideas with such expressions as *the government, the newspapers, the unions, the Republicans, the Democrats, big business,* and even *nature* or *the gods.*

Ad Hominem and Personal Arguments.   **Ad hominem** arguments are those that attack a person's character rather than the substance of an argument. American politicians provide good examples. A candidate may present well-reasoned ideas but is rebutted, not for the ideas, but on the basis of his or her moral character. Reviewers of professional matters—be they book reviewers, manuscript reviewers, or judges of fellow professors for tenure or promotion—are admonished to avoid ad hominem arguments in their evaluations. Attack the idea, not the person—such advice is a good policy in everyday life.

Related to ad hominem arguments are those that are validated in terms of an individual's experience or knowledge of an individual's experience. These personal arguments seem to be pervasive among nonscientific thinkers as well as an alarming number of students. The gist of the validation of such an argument is that “it must be true because it happened to me . . . or to my great-uncle Oliver . . . or to my professor.” Scientific progress is ill served by either type of argument.

Arguments That Appeal to Force and Power.   An example of an appeal to power to validate an argument might be, “The United States was justified in entering the Vietnam War because we are a mighty and moral nation.” Might and morality may be virtues, but they also may have nothing to do with treaties and a nation's right to sovereignty. Nevertheless, it is “human” to resort to such arguments.

Appeal to Authority and/or Fame.   A common logical error is made by those who are impressed by authorities and/or famous people in one domain who make statements about another. This practice is common among advertisers who, in the United States especially, use athletes, movie stars, dancers, and singers to endorse products about which they have virtually no special knowledge. Particularly insidious, and offensive to an

“*What* we have here is a failure to communicate.”
—*From the movie* Cool Hand Luke.

academic, is the use of scholars such as Nobel laureates to make proclamations about topics far removed from their field.

The Majority-Must-Be-Right Argument. Here the argument is that if most people do something, it must be right. "Ten million Americans use 'Zapo' deodorant, so it must be good" is the essence of this argument.

The Straw Man Argument. The straw man technique is to set up a weak argument and attribute it to someone else so that you can knock it down. Sometimes the straw man is a caricature of a more modest position taken by another. We sometimes call it the lightning rod argument because a prominent feature is isolated and emphasized, redirecting the main thrust of the argument. For example, while debating about foreign aid to the Philippines, you develop a well-reasoned case based on a multitude of socio-economic forces. These might include, as a minor point, the need to save wild animals in the mountains. Your opponent then attacks the entire argument by citing endless statistics showing that the Luzon tree squirrel actually is in abundant supply. The straw man approach may be somewhat effective, especially among noncritical thinkers, but others felicitously recognize its basis as material commonly found on the ground where cattle trod. It is surprising how often this ploy is used in the academic world by professors and graduate students zealous in attacking the theses of others.

Reasoning and the Brain

The scientific study of the relationship between the brain on the one hand and reasoning and thinking on the other has traditionally been the domain of neurologists (who have concentrated on patients with a variety of neurological problems) and, only recently, cognitive neuropsychologists (who have concentrated on imaging studies with "normal" participants). While the literature abounds with both types of studies, we can present only a sample here.

In the first category, neurologists have devised a series of diagnostic tests that may be administered as part of a neurological assessment. In one of these tests, called the Wisconsin Card Sorting Task, patients are asked to sort cards, one by one, by placing them under one of four target cards (see Figure 14.5). The task is similar to the concept-formation task described earlier in this chapter. The person is not informed as to the rules of sorting, whether sorting is to be on the basis of color, form, or number. He or she must discover the rules as determined by feedback from the person administering the test, who says "right" if the card is sorted by means of a predetermined rule or "wrong" if the card is incorrectly sorted by the same rules. After the person learns to sort by one rule, the game changes. Without her being informed, the sorting is governed by another set of rules.

This test is designed to see if the person can, first of all, find the initial rule of concept formation and, secondly, be flexible enough to abandon a previously reinforced rule and find a new rule. Participants do pretty well on this task, and college students, for example, not only learn the first rule but are also flexible enough in their thinking to "change gears" and learn the second sorting law. However, patients with frontal lesions do not do well on this task. And those patients with bilateral frontal lesions have major

FIGURE 14.5

A concept formation task, such as the Wisconsin Card Sorting Task. A patient with damage to the lateral prefrontal cortex experiences difficulties. Here the patient places the top card of the deck next to one of four target cards. The experimenter says "correct" if the card is correctly placed and "wrong" if incorrectly placed. Through trial and error most normal partipants learn the sorting rule. The tricky part occurs after the participant has learned one sorting rule and then the rule changes.

problems, especially with the switched rule task. Frontal lesioned patients tend to perseverate, or continue to sort by the old rule of sorting. Perseveration is a common symptom of frontal lobe syndrome. This is but one example of the type of reasoning studies used to make a diagnosis with patients suspected of brain damage.

There is little question about the brain as the instrument of thought and reasoning. There are serious questions as to what parts of the brain are involved in the thought process and how the neuropsychology of thinking operates. To know how the brain acts when we are reasoning and thinking is a fundamental issue in current psychology that speaks to an age-old problem in philosophy, and that is that reasoning is exclusively verbal in nature. If, in solving the location of the fork and spoon problem presented earlier in this chapter, you relied on language to arrive at a conclusion, then we might (logically) expect the left hemisphere to be primarily involved and that right hemisphere activity would be minimal. Conversely, if you solved the problem by constructing models within a structural representation—in effect, used nonverbal techniques—in which you imaged the locations of items, then the left hemisphere would be only minimally involved and the right hemisphere would be primarily involved.

The neuropsychological data support this general conclusion, which also bolsters the theory that holds that nonverbal reasoning is a viable idea. In one study (Caramazza et al., 1976) patients with damage to their right hemispheres had difficulty in making inferences in simple deductive problems such as:

John is taller than Bill.
Who is shorter?

And they also performed more poorly when compared to normal controls on more complex problems such as:

Arthur is taller than Bill.
Bill is taller than Charles.
Who is shortest?

In studies of conditioned reasoning, several research papers (see Whitaker et al., 1991) have studied brain-damaged patients' problem-solving ability. One study examined two groups of patients who had undergone brain surgery (a unilateral anterior temporal lobectomy for the purpose of relieving epilepsy). One group had surgery on the right hemisphere and the other on the left hemisphere. Those with right-hemisphere lesions were poorer at reasoning in which false conditional premises were used than those with left-hemisphere damage. Consider the following conditional premise:

If it rained the streets will be dry.
It rained.

The right-hemisphere damaged group had a tendency to conclude:

The streets will be wet.

which, although true in the grand scheme of what we know about rain and wet streets, is nevertheless invalid, *given the premise.*

Thus, it appears that patients who have lost some functions of their right hemisphere are unable to deduce a correct answer of a logic problem which is based on a false premise. While the "location" of reason will be pursued for some time and it is likely that much more will be found out about the various cortical sights involved, these investigations may beg an even more meaningful question and that is "How is the thought process carried out?"

Estimating Probabilities

Whether or not we recognize it, most decisions are related to an estimate of the probability of success. We plan a picnic when we think the sun will shine, we enroll in a course in cognitive psychology expecting certain rewards, we decide to stand with a card count of fourteen when a blackjack dealer shows a six as his or her "up card," we carry an umbrella when we see clouds in the sky, or we buy (or don't buy) an insurance policy before boarding an airplane. In some instances the probability of an event may be calculated on the basis of mathematics, while other events may be determined only by our previous experience. It is likely that we think we are acting rationally in these conditions since our decisions are based roughly on mathematical probabilities, but how accurate are our estimates? Or, in other words, how can we act so stupidly when we think we are acting so rationally? The next section might shed some light on the question.

In a series of studies, Tversky and Kahneman (1973, 1981; Kahneman & Tversky, 1983, 1984; and Kahneman & Miller, 1986) have looked at the way people sometimes arrive at a poor conclusion when their decisions are based on past experience. In one experiment (1974) they asked questions such as the following:

Are there more words in the English language that start with the letter *K* or that have a *K* as their third letter?
Which is the more likely cause of death—breast cancer or diabetes?
If a family has three boys (B) and three girls (G), which sequence of births is more likely—BBBGGG or BGGBGB?

All the preceding questions have factual answers, and yet people's intuition or guesstimates are generally wrong. For example, when asked about the occurrence of the letter

Amos Tversky, **left (1935–1996), and Daniel Kahneman**. Identified strategies people use in solving common problems.

K, more people said that it more frequently started a word than was located in the third position, contrary to actual data. Why do people misjudge these events? According to Tversky and Kahneman, when confronted with this question, people try to generate words that start with the letter *K* and then try to think of words with *K* in the third position. If you try this yourself, you will see why people err in this problem. We tend to overestimate the frequencies of initial letters because the words they generate are more available than are words with that same letter in the third position. It seems that estimates of letter probabilities are derived from a generalization based on a very limited sample of available words that can be generated.

This basic idea was tested in an experiment by Tversky and Kahneman (1973) in which participants were asked to read a list of thirty-nine names of well-known people. One list contained about the same number of men as women (nineteen men and twenty women), but the women were more famous than the men. Another list reversed these conditions; it contained more famous men than women. Then the participants were asked whether the list contained more men or women. In both instances the participants greatly overestimated the frequency of the gender that was more famous. The reason for this behavior, despite the fact that the frequencies were nearly identical, was that the names of the famous people were more available.

Other researchers have used the availability hypothesis to account for errors in the estimate of "everyday" knowledge. In one study Slovic, Fischhoff, and Lichtenstein (1977) asked people to estimate the relative probability of forty-one causes of death. Participants were given two causes of death and asked to judge which was more likely to cause death. The most seriously misjudged choices were causes of death that were well publicized. For example, accidents, cancer, botulism, and tornadoes were judged to be frequent causes of death. The authors reasoned that because these lethal events receive wide media coverage, they were more available than less publicized causes of death.

Decision Frames

A **decision frame** is, according to Tversky and Kahneman (1981), a decision maker's "conception of the acts, outcomes, and contingencies associated with a particular choice." A frame adopted by someone about to make a decision is controlled by the formulation of the problem as well as by the norms, habits, and personal characteristics of the individual. The authors of this concept have clearly demonstrated how powerful a frame can be in determining the conclusion reached by individuals who are given

How Rational Are Your Decisions?

Give your best estimates to the following questions:

1. Billy, a tall, slender, nonathletic 36-year-old has been described by a neighbor as being somewhat shy, intellectual, and withdrawn. He is helpful, tidy, and has a need for order and structure. Is it more likely that Billy is a salesperson or a librarian?
2. Suppose you are in Las Vegas on a gambling junket. (A) Last night you won $1,000 on a hot slot machine. Will you bet more tomorrow than you usually do? (B) Last night you discovered you have $1,000 more in your savings account than you thought. Will you bet more tomorrow than you usually do?

3. (A) You go into a store to buy a portable cassette/radio. It costs $50. You notice an ad for the same item at a store ten blocks away that costs only $25—such a deal! (B) You go into a store to buy a computer that costs $2,545. The same computer can be bought at a store ten blocks away for $2,520. Do you bother to go to the other store?

The solutions are at the end of this chapter.

essentially the same facts, but in different contexts. The effect of different frames is shown in the following example:

> Problem 1 (N = 152): Imagine that the United States is preparing for the outbreak of an unusual Asian disease, which is expected to kill 600 people. Two alternative programs to combat the disease have been proposed. Assume that the exact scientific estimates of the consequences of the programs are as follows:
> If Program A is adopted, 200 people will be saved (72 percent).
> If Program B is adopted, there is a one-third probability that 600 people will be saved and a two-thirds probability that no people will be saved (28 percent).
> Which of the two programs would you favor?

Given the choice in this problem, the majority selected Program A (72 percent), while only 28 percent chose Program B. The prospect of saving 200 lives is more attractive than the more risky alternative. Statistically, however, the alternatives will save the same number of lives.

Another group of participants was given this reformulated version of the same problem:

> Problem 2 (N = 155): Remember, if Program A is adopted, 200 people will be saved (72 percent). If Program C is adopted, there is a one-third probability that nobody will die, and a two-thirds probability that 600 people will die (78 percent).
> Which of the two programs would you favor?

In this frame the majority chose the risk-taking procedure: the certain death of 400 people is less acceptable than the two-in-three chance that 600 will die. These problems illustrate how the influence of the framing of a question, even though the probabilities are identical, leads to different choices. In general, choices involving gains are frequently seen as risk aversive, whereas choices involving losses are perceived as risk taking.

Yet another example of framing, which is perhaps a more realistic problem than the one just discussed, is the following:

> Problem A (N = 183): Imagine that you have decided to see a play for which admission is $10 per ticket. As you enter the theater, you discover that you have lost a $10 bill.
> Would you still pay $10 for a ticket for the play?
> Those who answered affirmatively amounted to 88 percent.

> Problem B (N = 200): Imagine that you have decided to see a play and paid the admission price of $10 per ticket. As you enter the theater, you discover that you have lost the ticket. The seat was not marked, and the ticket cannot be recovered.
> Would you pay $10 for another ticket?

Those who answered yes to this reformulated version amounted to 46 percent. In both instances you are out $10. However, in the first instance, about twice as many people confronted with this problem would buy a ticket as those confronted with a similar condition in which the amount of money lost is identical.[1]

Representativeness

Estimates of the probability of an event are influenced not only by the availability of the event but also by how representative an event is estimated to be in terms of how similar it is to the essential properties of its population. Consider this example from a study by Kahneman and Tversky (1972):

> On each round of a game, 20 marbles are distributed at random among 5 children: Alan, Ben, Carl, Dan, and Ed. Consider the following distributions:

	I		II
Alan	4	Alan	4
Ben	4	Ben	4
Carl	5	Carl	4
Dan	4	Dan	4
Ed	3	Ed	4

> In many rounds of the game, will there be more results of Type I or Type II?

What is your answer? If you selected Type I, your answer is consistent with the majority of participants in this experiment and is, of course, wrong. When participants read the word *random,* they apparently formed the impression that the distribution would be somewhat chaotic or helter-skelter, and when asked to evaluate Types I and II, they thought that the second distribution was too orderly to be random. The same type of error was observed in the sequence of boy and girl birth patterns mentioned earlier.

Another somewhat disturbing finding was that people tend to ignore sample size when estimating probabilities. For example, when asked whether finding 600 boys in a

---

[1]Framing a question can also be used to yield a desirable answer, which reminds us of the following story: Young Brother Gregory had been in the abbey only a few days when he innocently asked the head monk whether it was all right to smoke while saying his prayers. "Of course not," was the answer. A week later the young brother asked the monk, "May I pray while I smoke?"

sample of 1,000 children was as likely as finding 60 boys in a sample of 100 children, participants reported that both samples were equally likely. In fact (if one assumes an equal distribution of the sexes), the first statistic is far less likely than the second.

Bayes's Theorem and Decision Making

We have seen that people may revise their probability estimates when new or different information is presented. When confronted with an equally attractive choice of going to a concert or a movie, we may make a decision tipped in favor of the movie if we learn that the only concert tickets available cost $35. A mathematical model that provides a method for evaluating hypotheses of changing probabilistic values is called **Bayes's theorem** after its author, Thomas Bayes, an eighteenth-century mathematician. Use of this theorem is illustrated in the following decision-making scenario.

Suppose that a long, romantic, and emotional relationship between you and a lover ended in a terrible fight in which you vowed never to see the person again. Several months pass during which you avoid situations in which you might accidentally see your former lover. A mutual friend asks you to a large party. Your decision to go or not to go is based on the perceived probability that the former lover will be in attendance. After considering the situation, you conclude that the mutual friend would probably not be so insensitive as to invite both of you. Furthermore, given past experience with similar situations, you might estimate that the probability of a chance encounter would be about 1 in 20. The hypothesis then could be stated mathematically as follows:

$$P(H) = 1/20$$

The equation is read as "the probability of the hypothesis is equal to 5 percent (or 5 in 100)." The hypothesis is based on prior probabilities, that is, the possibility the event will occur given prior similar circumstances. An alternative hypothesis can also be stated, which is the probability that your lover will not be at the party. It may be stated as follows:

$$P(\overline{H})- = 19/20$$

This equation is read as "the probability of the hypothesis not occurring is 95 percent."

Thomas Bayes (1701–1761). Born into an affluent family, Bayes studied logic and theology at Edinburgh and wrote only two scholarly papers, published after his death. His "theorem" published in 1763 has become increasingly popular and has been applied to psychology and sociology.

If real situations could be reduced to such probabilistic statements, life would be simple and boring. You could weigh the possibilities of an undesirable confrontation against the pleasure of going to a party and then make your decision. In this case, let's say you decide to go to the party. As you approach the house, you notice a yellow Volkswagen parked in the driveway. In a few seconds you calculate the probability that the owner of the car is your former lover (which would further suggest that the person is at the party) and weigh that new information with the previous information about the probability that the host has invited the two of you to the same party. This situation is called a conditional probability—the probability that new information is true if a particular hypothesis is true. In this case, presume that the likelihood that the car belongs to your former lover is 90 percent (the other 10 percent could be attributed to several factors, including the possibility that the car was sold to someone else, the car was loaned to someone else, or this was only a similar car). According to Bayes's theorem, the combined probabilities (1/20 the person was invited plus 9/10 that the car indicated the person was present) can be expressed in the following formula:

$$\frac{P(\overline{H}|E) \;=\; P(E|H) \times P(H)}{P(E|H) \times P(H) \;+\; P(E|\overline{H}) \times P(\overline{H})}$$

where $P(H \mid E)$ is the probability of the hypothesis (H) given the evidence in E, or, in our case, the probability the former lover would be at the party given the initial low probability and the recent new evidence. $P(E \mid H)$ represents the probability that E is true given H (for example, the probability that the car belongs to the former lover = 90 percent). $P(H)$ is the probability of the initial hypothesis ($P = 5$ percent), and the terms $P(E \mid H)$ and $P(H)$ represent the probability the event will not occur (10 percent and 95 percent, respectively). By substituting these values into the formula, we can solve for $P(H \mid E)$.

$$P(H|E) \;=\; \frac{0.9 \times 0.05}{(0.9 \times 0.05) \;+\; (0.1 \times 0.95)} \;=\; 0.32$$

Thus, according to this model the chances of an unhappy encounter at the party is about 1 in 3. Given these odds, you now can make a studied decision on the basis of how aversive such a meeting might be versus how pleasurable the party might be. Perhaps you should drive to the nearest pay phone and call your host.

How closely does Bayes's theorem coincide with real life? It is highly unlikely that if you found yourself in the above circumstance, you would whip out your pocket calculator and determine the value of $P(H|E)$. Some evidence gathered by Edwards (1968) suggests that we tend to judge conditional probability circumstances more conservatively than Bayes's theorem suggests. In one study of the influence of new information on participants' estimates of probabilities, Edwards gave college students two bags that contained 100 poker chips. One bag had 70 red chips and 30 blue chips, and the other bag had 30 red chips and 70 blue chips. One bag was selected at random, and the participants were to determine which bag it was on the basis of drawing out one chip at a time, examining it, returning it to the bag, and then continuing the process. Initially, the probability of drawing a red chip from the mostly red-chip bag would be 70 percent, or from the mostly blue-chip bag, 30 percent. However, if we draw only one chip from one of the bags and it is red, then the probability, according to the theorem, that the composition of the bag is predominantly red is 70 percent. People tend to underestimate the real (mathematical) significance of that observation and guess the content of the bag to be predominantly red with a value of 60 percent. If the second chip is also red, the real probability of the bag being predominantly red is 84 percent. Participants' judgments tend to be conservative in this case as well as with larger samples.

The application of Bayes's theorem to real-world tasks poses special problems because an accurate estimate of the probabilities of events is difficult to ascertain. Consider an event of international world politics. A few years ago considerable tension between the former Soviet Union and the United States existed, which, some would suggest, led to an increased probability of overt aggression, perhaps even all-out war. If all the forces could be accurately assessed and the probability of war determined, then the influence of other events that bear on the likelihood of war (such as a meeting between former Presidents Clinton and Yeltsin) could be integrated into Bayes's formula, and for what it is worth, a probabilistic statistic could be derived. Some ambitious scholars representing the fields of psychology, sociology, and political science have undertaken just such global schemes.

Interest in Bayesian methods has increased over the past few years (Malakoff, 1999). One reason for the increased number of papers is the ubiquitous presence of desktop computers and the development of new algorithms. Some have used the simulation techniques known as Markov Chain Monte Carlo (MCMC to insiders) that use Bayesian mathematics to use prior knowledge to predict everything from nuclear magnetic resonance to who might be a likely suspect in a crime scene. The latter use has been questioned on the basis of "racial profiling."

Decision Making and Rationality

To some, this chapter may seem to have initially represented the human animal as the most rational of creatures. Our discussion of concept formation, after all, showed that all normal beings form concepts using rational rules. In the discussion of syllogistic reasoning, we learned that the validity of an argument could be determined by the rules of logic, even if we tend to be fooled by either the structure or the content of a faulty argument. Finally, in the preceding section on decision making, we learned that the "rational" human race is commonly nonrational when it comes to making a decision about a large class of events.

We think it would be foolish to argue that all people are as rational as we fashion ourselves, but are we, as a species, as nonrational as one might conclude, given the empirical results gathered on decision-making tasks?

The findings of Tversky and Kahneman as well as studies of syllogistic reasoning, when carefully examined, suggest that human beings are less than perfectly rational creatures. Some have objected to these findings on the basis of experimental design and the inevitable philosophic conclusion forced by these experiments. One such critic is L. J. Cohen (1981), of Oxford University, who argues that (1) rationality should be determined by the common people, not in contrived laboratory experiments that are not really designed to illustrate everyday decision making and are largely irrelevant to real performance, (2) it is unreasonable to expect ordinary people to be sophisticated in the laws of probability and statistics that establish the baselines and points of deviation in

Cognition in Everyday Life

The Fido Caper

Suppose that you left your dog Fido at home to guard your house so that burglars would not break in and steal the 10-pound roast that is defrosting on the counter. When you get back, the locks are all in good order, so you know that no burglar has entered. However, the roast is gone. Needless to say, Fido is a prime suspect.

On the basis of past experience, two sessions with the dog psychiatrist, and a certain shifty look in his eye, you judge the probability is 0.95 that Fido did it. However, before convicting Fido, you decide to collect one more piece of evidence. You prepare his ordinary dinner and offer it to him. To your surprise, he gobbles it up to the last crumb. Hardly what you would expect of the thief who just made a 10-pound roast disappear. You estimate that the probability that Fido would do this if he had in fact eaten the roast is only 0.02. Normally, though, he has a good appetite and eats his dinner with a probability of 0.99. How are you to revise your earlier suspicions given the evidence of the readily eaten dinner? Clearly, Bayes's theorem can come to the rescue. Given that he just ate his dinner, the probability that Fido is guilty may be expressed as follows:

$$P(\text{Guilty}|E) = \frac{P(E|\text{Guilty}) \times P(\text{Guilty})}{P(E|\text{Guilty}) \times P(\text{Guilty}) + P(E|\text{Innocent}) \times P(\text{Innocent})}$$

From the story, we know that

$$
\begin{aligned}
P(\text{Guilty}) &= 0.95 \\
P(\text{Innocent}) &= 0.05 \\
P(E|\text{Guilty}) &= 0.02 \\
P(E|\text{Innocent}) &= 0.99
\end{aligned}
$$

Therefore,

$$
\begin{aligned}
P(\text{Guilty}|E) &= \frac{(0.02)(0.95)}{(0.02)(0.95) + (0.99)(0.05)} \\[6pt]
&= \frac{0.0190}{0.0190 + 0.0495} \\[6pt]
&= \frac{0.0190}{0.0685} \\[6pt]
&= 0.28
\end{aligned}
$$

Things looked very bad for Fido before the dinner experiment. However, with the aid of Bayes's theorem, we were able to take the results of the dinner experiment into account and conclude that Fido was probably innocent. Anyone who loves dogs can see the value of Bayes's theorem.

many of the experiments, and (3) the laws of logic and rationality are not relevant to ordinary human behavior. Take the case of the unfortunate individual who tried to avoid a former lover. Using Bayes's theorem, the probability of the encounter, if the person to be avoided went to the party, was 0.32. How does that number bear on the behavior of the individual doing the avoiding? If the enmity between the pair is great ("I wouldn't go within 100 miles of him/her"), the figure is meaningless insofar as predicting behavior is concerned.

Spotlight on Cognitive Neuroscience

Decision Making

Monique Ernst and her colleagues argue that decision making is integral to behavior and that exploring the corresponding brain activity can aid in understanding when decision-making behaviors are maladaptive. To study this they had participants play a computerized gambling card game while in a PET scanner. They had to evaluate rewards and losses, which comprised the risk-taking component of the study. Research participants played two rounds of the gambling card game where they were active in deciding which decks to choose from based on loss and win information (in terms of dollar amounts). By the second round, participants had figured out that two of the four decks yielded larger gains. Another group of participants formed a control group where they played the same game but had no decisions to make (the decks from which they chose cards were chosen for them). They found that brain activity in the orbital and dorsolateral prefrontal cortex, anterior cingulated, insula, inferior parietal cortex, thalamus (right side), and cerebellum (left side) accompanied uninformed decision making (the first round). Guessing demonstrated activity in the sensorimotor associative areas and amygdala (left side). Informed decision making (data from the second round) activated memory areas such as the hippocampus, posterior cingulated, and motor control areas such as the striatum and cerebellum.

Ernst, M., Bolla, K., Mouratidis, M., Contoreggi, C., Matochik, J. A., Kurian, V., Cadet, J. L., Kimes, A. S., & London, E. D. (2002). Decision making in a risk-taking task: A PET study. *Neuropsychopharmacology, 26*(5), 682–691.

SUMMARY

1 Thinking is an internal process in which information is transformed; thinking may be directed and lead to problem solving and, at the structural level, results in the formation of a new mental representation.

2 Concept formation involves discerning features common to a class of objects and discovering rules that relate those conceptual features. Cognitive activities believed important to the process include rule learning, association, and hypothesis testing.

3 Strategies for formulating and testing hypotheses during concept formation include scanning and focusing procedures, with focusing techniques (similar to scientific procedures) being more effective than scanning strategies.

4 Studies of deductive reasoning indicate that conclusions to syllogistic problems are affected by the form of presentation (visual versus verbal), the number of alternatives generated by premises, the argument form (for example, positive versus negative), long-term knowledge relative to the problem presented, and the problem solver's level of intelligence and education.

5 Inductive reasoning results in conclusions often expressed in probability statements and corresponds more to everyday decision making than does syllogistic or deductive reasoning.

6 Studies of decision making show that problem solutions are influenced by memory factors (the availability hypothesis), reference frames that affect problem formulation, failure to consider how similar an event is to its population, and underestimating the mathematical significance of a possible event.

KEY WORDS

ad hominem	inductive reasoning
associationism	logic
Bayes's theorem	simultaneous scanning
concept formation	successive scanning
conservative focusing	syllogism
decision frame	thinking
deductive reasoning	verbal dialogues
focus gambling	

RECOMMENDED READINGS

● The number of books and articles dealing with thinking, problem solving, and decision making has increased sharply during the last decade. For more specialized reading, try Maxwell, *Thinking: The Expanding Frontier;* Gardner, *The Mind's New Science;* and Rubenstein, *Tools for Thinking and Problem Solving.* For decision making in the world context, read Janis and Mann, *Decision Making;* Valenta and Potter, eds., *Soviet Decision Making for National Security;* and Brams has an article called "Theory of Moves" in *American Scientist* that discusses game theory in international conflict situations. Johnson-Laird's chapter "Mental Models, Deductive Reasoning, and the Brain" in Gazzaniga's volume (1995) is excellent.

● Within the past few years several fine books in this field have been published. These books are well written, interesting, and contain a wealth of information about thinking and related topics. These include *Mental Models: Towards a Cognitive Science of Language, Inference, and Consciousness,* by one of the main researchers in the field, Johnson-Laird; and *Deduction* also by Johnson-Laird and Byrne. You might also try a stimulating book by John Hayes, *The Complete Problem Solver* (2nd ed.); and one of our favorite and highly recommended books, Marvin Levine's *Effective Problem Solving* (2nd ed.).

Answer to Try This! Thinking, Problem Solving, and "Frames"
Most people answer the first problem by inferring "A only" or "A and 4." The correct answer is "A and 7." If A does not have an even number on the other side, the rule is false, and if 7 has a vowel on the other side, the rule is false. In the second problem the answer is the first (sealed) envelope and the last, the envelope with the 25¢ stamp on it. More than 90 percent of participants solve the realistic (envelope stamp) problem, and yet only about 30 percent solve the abstract (card-letter) problem.

Possible arrangement of items mentioned in the problems on page 426.

A.

B.   Or

C.   Or

Answers to Try This! How Rational Are Your Decisions?

Problem 1: If you are like most people, you guessed that Billy is a librarian—in fact, about 2 out of 3 people make that judgment in a similar problem. However, if we look at the statistics regarding the likelihood of professions, there are more than 14 million salespeople in America and fewer than 200,000 librarians. On the basis of statistics alone, Billy is 75 times more likely to be a salesperson. Even if one factors into the conclusion the descriptive material, the probability of Billy's being in sales is higher than his being in books.

Problem 2: Most people say they would be more likely to blow the easy money won on the slot machine than the newly discovered hard money in the bank account, yet in both instances you are ahead by the same amount.

Problem 3: In the first instance, about 3 out of 4 people opt to go down the street to buy the cassette/radio for half price, yet only 1 in 5 would do the same for the computer. However, in both instances, the saving is $25. Is such action justified in the first case but not the second?

CHAPTER 15

Thinking

Problem Solving, Creativity, and Human Intelligence

hmmm...?

● **Problem Solving**
   Gestalt Psychology and Problem Solving
   Representation of the Problem
   Internal Representation and Problem Solving

● **Creativity**
   Creative Process
   Creativity and Functional Fixedness
   Investment Theory of Creativity
   Judging Creativity

● **Human Intelligence**
   The Problem of Definition
   Cognitive Theories of Intelligence
   Cognitive Neuroscience and Intelligence

1. How has the topic of problem solving been studied in the past?

2. Why is the way a problem is represented so important?

3. Name some people you consider to be creative. What are the features that define creativity in them?

4. How does functional fixity make creative solutions difficult?

5. How do you define *intelligence*? How do cognitive psychologists define *intelligence*?

6. What recent experiments in genetics portend a new way of looking at intelligence?

In this chapter we present theories and data on three topics considered to be higher cognitive processes; they are problem solving, creativity, and human intelligence. These topics have been investigated by researchers interested in how each fits into the grand scheme of human cognition: they have also caused the philosopher and poet to wax eloquent. Interest in problem solving, creativity, and intelligence can be found among the nitty-gritty, pragmatic types who enjoy mundane topics such as: How do I get from my house to work in the shortest time with the least annoyance? Can I invent a device that will keep cinnamon rolls warm from the time they are baked until they are served? Why does my daughter write better computer programs than English essays?

Problem Solving

Problem solving permeates every corner of human activity and is a common denominator of widely disparate fields—the sciences; law; education; business; sports; medicine; industry; literature; and, as if there weren't enough problem-solving activity in our professional and vocational lives, many forms of recreation. Humans, apes, and many other mammals are curious types who, for reasons seemingly related to survival, seek stimulation and resolve conflict through a lifetime of creative, intelligent problem solving.

A good share of early problem-solving experiments addressed the question: What does a person do when he or she solves a problem? Although this descriptive approach helped define the phenomenon, it did little to enhance our understanding of the cognitive structures and processes involved in problem solving.

Problem solving is "thinking that is directed toward the solving of a specific problem that involves both the formation of responses and the selection among possible responses." We encounter an untold number of problems in our daily lives that cause us to form response strategies, to select potential responses, and to test responses in solving a problem. For example, try to solve these problems: A dog has a 6-foot rope tied to its neck, and a pan of water is 10 feet away. How would the dog reach the pan? The solution to this problem involves the generation of possible responses (of which there are few), the selection and trial of them, and perhaps the discovery of the trick in the problem.[1]

The early experimental technique of introspection was established by European psychologists before the turn of the twentieth century and spread through America about that time. It seemed well suited to an investigation of problem solving. It was held that

---

[1] The dog would walk to it. The rope was tied to its neck.

McGuffin's Problem

"*P*aul McGuffin was born in 1986 in St. Louis. His father was Irish; his mother Native American. Fifty-two years later, he dies while playing chess with Albert Einstein in Nebraska. However, he dies in 1999. How can this be possible?" Try to solve this puzzle. What techniques are you using? Are you trying the same old solution over and over without success? Try a really innovative or creative approach to the problem. Is intelligence involved in your problem-solving efforts? After you give this a good attempt and produce some solutions then look below for some other solutions.

1. In the Native American calendar each year is counted as four years.
2. He was playing chess in room 1999.
3. "1999" is the name of a town in Nebraska.
4. In the year 2038, fifty-two years after his birth, a couple of brilliant scientists perfect a time machine and regress to the year 1999 so they can welcome in the millennium one more time. While passing the time of day, they play chess, but the excitement of time

travel and anticipating the century are too much for Paul's heart and he dies.
5. During a cataclysmic event in the middle of 2022 all particles in the universe began to run in the opposite direction, which had the effect of reversing time. Why 2022? Well, that's another puzzle.
6. The guy moved his chess pieces so slowly that he died in 1999 but no one noticed for thirty-nine years.
7. "However" is the name of Paul's father.

His name was McGuffin, which was a name used by the late filmmaker Alfred Hitchcock for any device or element that deflects attention from other pivotal bits in a mystery film. Here, the "extra" bits of information—that his father was Irish, that he was born in St. Louis, that he was playing with Albert Einstein—are the McGuffin, used to sidetrack your thinking in nonproductive ways. McGuffins abound and sometimes pop up on final examinations. Do you have better "solutions"? Send them to us for future editions.

thinking aloud, or *reflection parlée,* elucidated the mechanics of the thinking process. In early studies the participants were told what was expected of them and what the problem was. During the problem-solving section of the task, participants were to identify the objects they were attending to; the situation as they saw it; what they were trying to accomplish; and, in some instances, the very tentative attempts to solve the problem.

Gestalt Psychology and Problem Solving

Among the early experimentalists concerned with problem solving were the Gestalt psychologists in Germany. (*Gestalt* is roughly translatable as "configuration" or "organized whole." The perspective of Gestalt psychologists is consistent with the word, in that they view behavior in terms of an organized system). Perceptual events are not perceived as a series of individual elements but as a whole configuration made up of these events. According to the gestaltists, problems, especially perceptual problems, exist when tension or stress occurs as a result of some interaction between perception and memory. By thinking about a problem, or by examining it from different angles, the "correct" view can emerge in a moment of insight. The early Gestalt psychologists (Max Wertheimer,

Kurt Koffka, Wolfgang Kohler) demonstrated the perceptional reorganization viewpoint in problem-solving activity (sometimes using apes as experimental subjects). Out of their work emerged the concept of **functional fixedness,** originated by Karl Duncker (1945). This concept, which was to have considerable impact on problem-solving research, held that there is a tendency to perceive things in terms of their familiar uses and that that tendency often makes it difficult to use them in an unfamiliar way (for example, using a brick as a measuring device). In effect, objects or ideas become set in their functions and, when they are part of a problem-solving task that requires that they serve a different function, the subject must overcome that "set."

Although we usually associate the term **set** with the state of mind (habit or attitude) a person brings to a problem-solving task, the original definition of the term includes the idea of any preparatory cognitive activity that precedes thinking and perception. In the context of the latter definition, *set* may enhance the quality of perception or thought through more active participation in the meaning of a stimulus (as in the case of an ambiguous word, the next move in a chess game, or the next response in a social situation). Alternatively, it may inhibit perception or thought (as in a problem in which a participant repeatedly tries a certain nonproductive solution that is related to an earlier experience). For example, Duncker (1945) gave participants three cardboard boxes, matches, thumbtacks, and candles and asked them to devise a plan whereby the candle could be mounted on a screen to serve as a lamp. One group of participants was given the screen; the candles, the tacks, and the matches were each presented in their own box. Another group of participants was given these objects *along* with the three boxes—that is, the objects were not *in* the boxes. The solution to this puzzle was to use the matches to light the candles, drip some wax on a box, stick the candle on it, and thumbtack the box to the screen. When the boxes were modeled ahead of time as containers, participants had much more difficulty in solving this problem than when the boxes were not (see Figure 15.1). Later experimenters (Glucksberg & Danks, 1969) demonstrated that simply labeling an object with a name fixed in the participant's mind a certain set that could either facilitate or impede the solving of a problem.

The types of problems used in the early experiments were of a wide variety, from mechanical to logic problems. The protocols (records of the thought processes as "thought aloud" by the participants) revealed that the problem-solving process had several well-ordered stages. Participants normally seem to begin with what is expected of them. Then hypotheses about possible solutions arise, are tested, and confirmed; if they are not confirmed, new hypotheses emerge (see Figure 15.2). The process, then, seems to be one of trial and error, with a new hypothesis replacing an unsuccessful one. These early experiments said little about how hypotheses originated and made no credible postulates as to the cognitive structures involved in the process.

Representation of the Problem

The work of the Gestalt psychologists focused on the nature of a task and its influence on a person's ability to solve it. Recent scholars have attacked the question of problem solving from several different perspectives, including what modern cognitive psychologists call the process of representation, or how a problem is depicted in the mind. Throughout this book, the topic of internal representation has been a central theme. Material that has

A

FIGURE 15.1

The Candle Problem. Participants were asked to attach a candle to the wall when provided with a box of tacks, candles, and matches (A). The solution is shown (B).

B

Wall

FIGURE 15.2

Stages of problem solving.

already been presented is not repeated here, except to note that the way information is represented in a problem-solving task is important in finding its solution.

The way information is represented in solving a problem seems to follow a well-ordered pattern. For example, let's look at the problem of entering the real world after graduation from college. The stereotypical sequence of problem solving, as suggested by Hayes (1989), takes the following form:

*T*he biggest problem in the world
Could have been solved when it was small.

—*Lao Tsu*

Cognitive Action	Nature of the Problem
1. Identifying the problem	Next May I will graduate from college. It is the end of one phase of my life. (Time to grow up.)
2. Representation of the problem	I will be unemployed and without funds. I must get work. (Can no longer sponge off Mom and Pop.)
3. Planning the solution	I will write a résumé, investigate the job market, and consult with friends and teachers. (See what's out there. I could go to Tibet and become a monk.)
4. Executing the plan	I will make appointments with interesting companies. I will interview with them. (Take the plunge.)
5. Evaluating the plan	I will consider each offer in light of my own needs and desires and make a decision. (Who's offering big bucks, long vacations, and early retirement.)
6. Evaluating the solution	I will reflect on the process of solving this problem and use such knowledge in future problem solving. (Where did I go wrong?)

Perhaps, if you think of the way you have solved problems in your own life, you will find that you have used a sequence similar to the one shown here. The process is almost always unconscious. That is, you do not deliberately say to yourself, "Now, I am in phase three, 'planning the solution,' which means that I . . ."; nevertheless, it is likely that these stages are lurking in the background as you solve daily problems. Consider any problem—either real or imaginary (such as fixing a broken toaster, solving a difficult interpersonal problem, or deciding whether or not to have children)—and work through it following the steps of the sequence. You will find through this process that well-defined problems ("I'm unhappy in my current job") are easier to solve than ill-defined problems ("I hate my life").

Although all stages are important, the representation of a problem appears to be very important, especially the way information is represented in terms of visual imagery. Suppose you are asked to multiply 43 by 3. No big deal, you might say, as you produce the answer easily with few mental operations. However, if I ask you to multiply 563 by 26 mentally, how do you perform the task? If you are like many others, you "see" the problem; that is, you represent it visually and begin the process by multiplying 3 × 6, "see" the 8, carry the 1, then multiply 6 × 6, add the 1, and so on. All of these

Try This

Brazilian Brain-Teaser

You and your companion are walking in a Brazilian rain forest when you come across a gorge. The gorge is 40 feet deep and 60 feet wide and several miles long in each direction. You have a 20-foot ladder, a pair of pliers, a box of matches, a candle, an endless supply of rope, and several rocks and boulders. How do you and your friend cross the chasm?

Fewer than one in 10 people solve this problem. Why did or did you not solve it? Did you use all of the equipment provided? Is the solution "simple minded"? Did you not solve it because you added too many factors? Try this out on your friends and record the means they use to solve the problem. See the discussion of "Representation of the Problem" in the text. The solution is found at the end of this chapter.

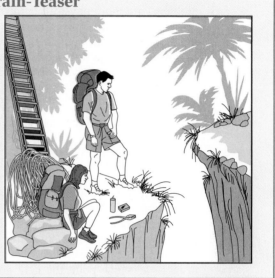

operations are done with the information being represented in imagery. Vision is the dominant sensory modality. So much of our information about the world comes through our visual system. It's no wonder that our mental world is equally visually oriented. It seems that writers have capitalized on this propensity to represent things visually by using prose rich in imagery. Sometimes these are called word pictures, as illustrated in the following passage from Salisbury (1955):

> A tall, lanky serious-faced man strolled toward the datcha with a loose-jointed boyish pace and came up to where I was wielding a paintbrush. We were glassing in the front porch and I was busy in my paint-smeared clothes putting the white trim on the windows. (p. 112)

You can "see" the "loose-jointed boyish" character (who turned out to be George Kennan), and the paint-smeared clothes, and so on. Now consider how the problem of representation influences the following problem.[2]

> Of course, I could go out and buy one, but that would take time and money. I could make one from an old newspaper, or wrapping paper, but the paper must be sturdy. Then there is the matter of use. Streets aren't so good, the beach is perfect, and an open field is also OK. Finally, the weather needs to be good; kind of windy, and definitely no rainstorms (unless you are foolish or interested in physics). (p. 112)

As you read this paragraph, you can undoubtedly understand every word and sentence, and yet you have a gnawing feeling that you really do not understand what is going on. (Try reading this to a friend and then ask what he or she thinks the paragraph is about.)

[2]Inspired by research of Bransford and Johnson (1972).

However, if we tell you that theme of the paragraph is how to make and fly a kite, everything falls into place and you comprehend the entire passage and problem. Representation of information is very important in problem solving.

These examples have dealt with literary expressions of problems, but many of our problems are more physical. For example, we are puzzled by the arrangement of furniture in a room, the shortest route to and from work, which grocery items we should select for greatest efficiency in shopping, and so on. One way some of these problems can be solved is to "go to the extremes," as suggested by Marvin Levine (1993), a leading expert on problem solving. Try to solve one of his problems:

> Two flagpoles are standing, each 100 feet tall. A 150-foot rope is strung from the top of one of the flagpoles to the top of the other and hangs freely between them. The lowest point of the rope is 25 feet above the ground. How far apart are the two flagpoles?

Can you solve the problem? How did you do it? Some of you might have begun with elaborate calculus in which the sag line of a rope is calculated. One other way is to draw a picture of the problem (see Figure 15.3). The solution to the problem is simple and does not require advanced knowledge of geometry—only common sense. Remember, *go to the extremes.* The solution is at the end of the chapter.

These examples have stressed the importance of representing the problem in a way that will enhance your ability to find a solution. In general, the solution to these problems seems to occur in one brilliant moment of awareness—what the Gestalt psychologists call insight—at which point the light goes on and all parts of the puzzle make sense. Frequently, however, problem solving is achieved through the stepwise discovery of small parts of a puzzle. This method, in which the solution to small components of a large problem serves as a means to the end solution, is sometimes called means-end analysis. We discuss this in greater detail later. Now, try to solve a problem which involves means-end analysis. This is the final example in problem solving and knowledge representation. It is shown in the box entitled "Try This! A Problem of Patients—Psychiatrists' and Yours."

At the end of this problem is a matrix to keep track of your inferences and deductions. It is unlikely that you will be able to solve the problem without resorting to some outside representational aid.

FIGURE 15.3

A visual representation of the flagpole problem.

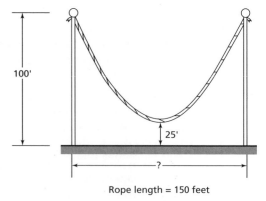

100'

25'

?

Rope length = 150 feet

How far apart are the poles?

A Problem of Patients—Psychiatrists' and Yours

*T*hree married couples, Rubin, Sanchez, and Taylor, have a rather unusual thing in common: all six (three husbands and three wives) are psychiatrists. The six psychiatrists' names are Karen, Laura, Mary, Norman, Omar, Peter. As fate would have it, each doctor has one of the other doctors as a patient (but not his or her own spouse). Several other facts are:

1. Karen is the psychiatrist for one Dr. Rubin; Laura is the psychiatrist of the other.
2. Mary is the patient for one Dr. Taylor; Peter is the patient for the other.
3. Laura is a patient of Dr. Sanchez.
4. Peter has his psychotherapy with Omar.

Given these facts, determine each psychiatrist's full name and who is treating whom. Use

the following table to keep track of your deductions. This mildly difficult problem is unlikely to be solved "in your head," and it is suggested that impossible combinations be marked with an "o." From these marks it will be possible to make inferences about other possible and impossible combinations. Since women cannot be husbands and men cannot be wives, we have marked the intersections with the exclusionary mark "o." Hint: Take clue 1. Since Karen and Laura are psychiatrists for Dr. (Mr.) Rubin and Dr. (Mrs.) Rubin, they (Karen and Laura) cannot be Rubins. Who is Dr. (Mrs.) Rubin? Mark with a ✓. Carry on and good luck. As you work through this problem try to identify the inferential processes you are using.

The solution is at the end of this chapter.

	Rubin Dr. (Mrs.)	Rubin Dr. (Mr.)	Sanchez Dr. (Mrs.)	Sanchez Dr. (Mr.)	Taylor Dr. (Mrs.)	Taylor Dr. (Mr.)
Karen		O		O		O
Laura		O		O		O
Mary		O		O		O
Norman	O		O		O	
Omar	O		O		O	
Peter	O		O		O	

Internal Representation and Problem Solving

Cognitive psychologists seem to focus their greatest efforts on defining the cognitive processes involved in internal representation. Only very recently has there been any systematic search for definite cognitive structures that are engaged during problem-solving activity. The models that have emerged draw heavily on the existing knowledge of memory structure and semantic networks—and for good reasons: the literature in both fields is extensive, and problem solving is certainly related to memory factors as well as to many of those of semantic networks.

Internal Representation Model: Eisenstadt and Kareev. ⸤Eisenstadt and Kareev (1975), exploring some aspects of human problem solving exhibited by people playing board games, developed a network model⸥ They focused their attention on the kind of internal representations of board positions that players form and on representations of knowledge. The board games they dealt with are the traditional Asian games of "Go" and "Gomoku," but presumably the model they postulate is flexible enough to apply to many games. Both "Go" and "Gomoku" are played on a board that contains a grid of nineteen vertical and nineteen horizontal lines. The pieces are small white and black "stones," which are placed on the intersections of the grid. The object is to capture the opponent's stones and occupy space. In "Go," players alternate placing their stones, and, if one player's stone is completely surrounded by the other player's stones, it is considered captured and is removed from the board. "Gomoku" is played on the same board, but here the object is fulfilled by forming an unbroken, straight line of five pieces. The opponent tries to block the formation while building his or her own line. To simplify the game, Eisenstadt and Kareev used a 9 × 9 grid and had participants place stones in the box portion of the grid rather than the intersections.

Game-playing activity was studied with human participants playing against a computer; this gave the researchers some control over the strategy and skill of the opponent, the computer, which plays a good game.

⸤Internal representation in problem-solving tasks (as well as most other tasks) is highly subjective; mental transcription of configurations in the real world are not necessarily perfectly matched by a person's internal representation⸥ For example, when the configuration shown in Figure 15.4A is regarded as a "Gomoku" position, the pattern important to the player (and, hence, the one given internal representation) is that indicated by the superimposed X in Figure 15.4B; however, in "Go" the important represen-

FIGURE 15.4

Board position (A); subject organization of same patterns as a position in a game of "Gomoku" (B); a game of "Go" (C).

Adapted from Eisenstadt and Kareev (1975).

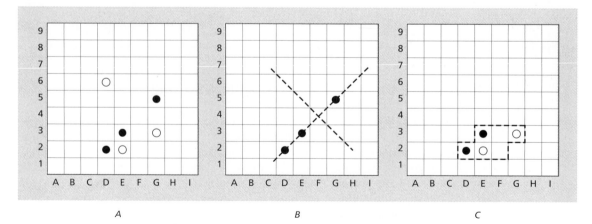

tation would be the possible capture configuration shown in Figure 15.4C. Perceptual organizations of problems, affected by the perceiver's motivation, can and frequently do differ from the physical nature of the task. To demonstrate the disparity between internal representation and real-world events, Eisenstadt and Kareev asked participants to analyze the board positions shown in Figure 15.4A and make the best play for black in a "Gomoku" game. Participants were then asked to reconstruct the positions in the absence of the configuration. Later they were given the board position shown in Figure 15.5B, told to make the best move for white in a "Go" game, and again asked to reconstruct the positions. The boards in Figures 15.5A and B are the same, except that the latter is rotated 90 degrees and reflected across the vertical axis, and the color of the stones is reversed. Therefore, in terms of pieces, essentially the same amount of information was given in both tasks. The researchers identified six pieces critical in "Go" and six pieces critical in "Gomoku"; in essence, these constitute the template for each game. The reconstruction from memory of these pieces was a direct function of the instruction. In other words, if the participants thought it was a "Go" game, they remembered the key "Go" pieces; if they were told the game was "Gomoku," they remembered the key Gomoku positions. Figure 15.6 shows the percentage of critical pieces correctly recalled as a function of the type of game participants believed they were viewing.

Further analysis of game playing indicated that participants played rapidly, suggesting that planning, or anticipating various configurations that might emerge, was neglected. Additionally, participants seemed to examine the board by means of "active searches for specific patterns, as well as by searches that seem to be driven by 'accidental' discovery of new configurations and pieces." Thus, the scanning of a problem seems to suggest that internal representations are formed by an active search. This operation is commonly called *top-down analysis* (a computer science term) and means that the analysis starts followed by a hypothesis, with attempts made to verify it by means of seeking out stimuli (for example, "This problem has stimuli, some of which are critical"). Also a possibility are bottom-up procedures, in which the stimuli are examined and attempts are then made to match them with structural components (for example, "How does this piece figure into the problems?").

Solving a problem is somewhat dependent on the subjective representation stored in memory, and the formation of internal representation is an active process. Planning

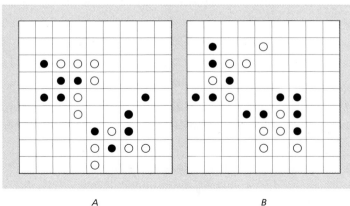

A   B

FIGURE 15.5

Board problems. Positions shown in board B are the same as in board A rotated counterclockwise 90 degrees and reflected across the vertical axis, with colors of pieces reversed.

Adapted from Eisenstadt and Kareev (1975).

Percentage of critical pieces correctly recalled according to which game participants were told they were viewing.

Adapted from Eisenstadt and Kareev (1975).

in board games, according to this viewpoint, involves both top-down and bottom-up processes, as Eisenstadt and Kareev observe:

> When a subject plans ahead, the same kinds of search processes can be used. The placement of "imaginary" pieces within the internal representation of the problem space automatically invokes the planning processes in a bottom-up manner. Determining which pieces to consider in this fashion is, of course, a top-down, hypothesis-driven situation. This helps explain one of the standard observations about human problem-solving behavior: People follow a "progressive deepening" search strategy rather than a depth-first or breadth-first one. Evidently, this results from the fact that once imaginary moves have been considered within the working (short-term) memory, they cannot be erased. Thus, backup in the planning sequence can easily overload the capacity of this memory. As a result, subjects tend to start a search process over rather than to back up a few steps. (p. 32)

Eisenstadt and Kareev, by their careful analysis of board games, have roughed out what seem to be the central mechanisms of problem solving within the domain of modern cognitive psychology. Many questions remain, particularly insofar as specification of the internal processes and structures is concerned.

Creativity

It is reasonable to assume that most people are creative, but the degree of creativity differs widely. The creativity of, for example, Georgia O'Keeffe, Buckminster Fuller, Wolfgang Mozart, or Thomas Jefferson not only is a manifestation of great talent but also is well known. Other creative geniuses surely exist but go unrecognized.

The definition of **creativity** used in this section is that it is "a cognitive activity that results in a new or novel way of viewing a problem or situation." This definition does not restrict creative processes to utilitarian acts, although the examples of creative people are almost always drawn from some useful invention, writing, or theory they have created.

Creative Process

It is ironic that no dominant theory has emerged during the past twenty years that might unify the disparate and sometimes conflicting studies of creativity. The absence of a unified theory points out both the inherent difficulty of the topic and the lack of widespread scientific attention. Nevertheless, creativity is widely heralded as an important part of everyday life and education.

A long time ago in the history of cognitive psychology, Wallas (1926) described the creative process as having four sequential stages:

1. **Preparation.** Formulating the problem and making initial attempts to solve it.
2. **Incubation.** Leaving the problem while considering other things.
3. **Illumination.** Achieving insight to the problem.
4. **Verification.** Testing and/or carrying out the solution.

Empirical evidence for the validity of Wallas's four stages is almost nonexistent; however, the psychological literature abounds with introspective reports from people who have given birth to a creative thought. The most celebrated of these accounts is by Poincaré (1913), a French mathematician who discovered the properties of Fuchsian functions. After working on the equations for a time and after making some important discoveries (the preparation stage), he decided to go on a geologic excursion. While traveling he "forgot" his mathematical work (incubation stage). Poincaré then writes about the dramatic moment of insight. "Having reached Coutances, we entered an omnibus to go some place or other. At the moment when I put my foot on the step the idea came to me, without anything in my former thoughts seeming to have paved the way for it, that the transformations I had used to define the Fuchsian functions were identical with those of non-Euclidian geometry." The author continues to tell us that when he returned to his home, he verified the results at his leisure.

Wallas's four-stage model of the creative process has given us a conceptual framework to analyze creativity. Here we briefly consider each of the stages.

Stage 1: Preparation.   Poincaré mentioned in his notes that he had been working intensively on the problem for fifteen days. During that period he seemed to have thought of several tentative solutions, which he tried out and, for one reason or another, discarded. However, to suggest that the period of preparation was fifteen days is, of course, wrong. All of his professional life as a mathematician and probably a good portion of his childhood could be considered part of the preparation stage.

A common theme in biographies of famous men and women is the notion that even during their early childhood, ideas were being developed, knowledge was being acquired, and tentative thoughts in a specified direction were being tried out. These early ideas frequently shape the ultimate destiny of the creative person. What remains one of the many mysteries of the process is why other individuals who share similar environmental stimulation (or, in many cases, deprivation) fail to be recognized for their creative talent. Maybe more attention should be given to the genetic bases of creativity.

Stage 2: Incubation.   Why is it that a creative breakthrough frequently follows a period in which the problem is allowed to lie fallow? Perhaps the most pragmatic answer is that more of our life is devoted to recreation, watching television, skin diving, playing "Parcheesi," traveling, or lying in the sun watching the clouds drift by than in rock-hard thinking about a problem that needs a creative solution. So creative acts are more likely to follow dormant periods simply because those periods occupy more of our time.

Posner (1973) offers several hypotheses about the incubation phase. One suggestion is that the incubation period allows us to recover from the fatigue associated with problem solving. Also, interruption of an arduous task may allow us to forget inappropriate approaches to a problem. We have already seen that functional fixedness can impede problem solving, and it is possible that during incubation people forget old, unsuccessful solutions to problems. Another reason incubation may help in the creative process is that during this period we may actually work on the problem unconsciously. Such a notion is similar to William James's famous dictum, "We learn to swim in the winter and ice-skate in the summer." Finally, interruption of the problem-solving process may allow for reorganization of material.

Stage 3: Illumination.   Incubation does not always lead to illumination (we all know a lot of people who have been in incubation most of their lives but so far have failed to illuminate). When it does, however, the sensation is unmistakable. Suddenly, the lightbulb is turned on. The creative person may feel a rush of excitement as all the bits and pieces of ideas fall into place. All of the pertinent ideas complement each other, and irrelevant thoughts are discarded. The history of creative breakthroughs is replete with examples of the illumination stage. The discovery of the structure of the DNA molecule, the composition of the benzene ring, the invention of the telephone, the conclusion of a symphony, and the plot of a novel are all examples of how a moment of illumination has flooded the mind with a creative solution to a vexing old problem.

Stage 4: Verification.   Following the euphoria that sometimes accompanies an insightful discovery, the idea is tested. This is the mopping up stage of the creative process in which the creative product is examined to verify its legitimacy. Often a solution first thought to be creative is only an intellectual fool's gold when examined carefully. This stage may be rather brief, as in the case of rechecking one's calculations or seeing whether an invention works; however, in some cases verification may require a lifetime of study, testing, and retesting.

Creativity and Functional Fixedness

Earlier in this chapter we saw how functional fixedness could impede problem solving. Functional fixedness also may obstruct creativity (which points out the similarly between the concepts of problem solving and creativity). People who do the same old thing over and over again or who think the same thoughts are considered to be rather unimaginative, not to mention being socially boring. On the other hand, creative people see novel relationships or unusual connections among seemingly unrelated things, such as the person who slipped an oversized tire over a small tree so when the tree grew it would have a built-in ring seat.

Several years ago some psychologists thought it might be possible to assess creative ability by measuring how well people see novel connections between seemingly unrelated words. One of these tests, invented by Mednick (1967), was called the Remote Associations Test (RAT); it asked people to generate a single word that would be logically associated with three words. Consider the following two groups of three words: *RED, BRIDGE, ANGRY,* and *HEAD, SICK, PORT.* If you said "cross" for the first group, you would be right. What is the common denominator for the second group?

The RAT measures at least one component of creativity, but it probably measures other things too. Additionally, some very creative people might bomb on the test, which illustrates the slippery concept of creativity. Could it be that we are unconsciously creative, by which we mean that we have many associates to stimuli, such as a word or a visual scene or a musical piece, but are not consciously aware of them? The remote associates idea was expanded by Bowers and his colleagues (1990) in a task called the *dyads of triads.* One part of the task is like the RAT in that the words are part of a *coherent* triad, as are those just presented or those in the threesome *GOAT, PASS, GREEN,* all of which constellate around the coherent word *MOUNTAIN.* However, the triad *BIRD, PIPE, ROAD* is considered *incoherent* in that no (likely) common element is apparent. In this study subjects were given sets of coherent and incoherent triads and asked to find the common elements, if they could. Also, they were asked to judge which of the triads were coherent. The results showed that they were able to identify the coherent triads *even if they were unable to come up with the solution.* It was as if the participants knew that there was a common element but could not quite name it. Possibly, people activate part of a solution to a remote associate task, and that may be one phase of a creative solution to a task. Such an idea might be related to the concept of *intuition* (which is defined by the *Oxford English Dictionary* as "the immediate apprehension of an object by the mind without the intervention of any reasoning process"), a frequently defamed term in scientific literature. Human intuition may indeed be an important part of the discovery phase of creative acts.

Investment Theory of Creativity

You may have heard that a wise investment strategy is to buy low and sell high and that fortunes have been made by those who follow that self-evident maxim (as well as lost by those unhappy folks who got the thing turned around). Some have speculated there is a not too subtle a similarity between investment wisdom and human creativity. Shrewd investors, through creativity, wisdom, or financial acumen, know when to buy and when to sell. These people may make an investment in a property or stock when others reject such opportunities. To others, their actions may seem foolish until the worth of the investment rises, and then others jump on the bandwagon. When the investment is worth more, the original investor sells. In effect, people under these circumstances are acting in a creative way.

In science, art, literature, music, and most other fields, creative people "buy low and sell high." That is, they get in on the ground floor in which the initial stages of their endeavor are frequently thought by others to be foolish, ill-advised, or worse. If the idea has merit, then others may join in, but we do not judge those joiners' actions as particularly creative. It's the person or people who *first* dared to try something new that we consider creative. Many times the creative person will "sell high," which means that when the idea is more in vogue, he or she will move on to another problem.[3]

---

[3]See Thomas Kuhn (1962) for an analysis of the development of scientific revolutions in which a similar argument is made.

Sternberg and Lubart (1996) have developed a theory of creativity based on a multivariate approach to the topic, which is built around six attributes. These six facets of creativity are:

- Processes of intelligence
- Intellectual style
- Knowledge
- Personality
- Motivation
- Environmental context

Truly creative performance is rare, not because people are lacking in any one attribute but because it is difficult to get all six attributes working together. These attributes are seen much as an investment portfolio might be seen in a business enterprise. Our creativity portfolio is the basis of creative acts. These six facets of the portfolio can combine to yield creative performances at any stage of life, and the intellectual environment, such as school or home life, has an important early influence on creativity.

The importance of the work of Sternberg and Lubart is that it provides a general theory of creativity specifying particular attributes that can be studied analytically and longitudinally. It is clear that creativity is not a single trait, skill, or ability but a combination of several factors that can be identified and analyzed. Furthermore, assessing human creativity is not a simple matter of identifying the amount of each attribute and adding them together to find a kind of creativity index. Rather, it is a matter of identifying and assessing the strengths of the interactions among attributes. The combination of strengths of attributes and the number of interactions possible poses a complex network that might befuddle some scientists. In fact, the whole idea may appear foolishly complex. It may be that the authors of this theory are investing in what others might call a risky venture. To others, it appears that Sternberg and Lubart have bought low.

Judging Creativity

Whether or not we label it, Americans are fond of judging creative acts and individuals. Everything from the latest Italian sports car to the recent Steven Spielberg film, to the performance of ice-skating champions, to lovemaking is rated for its originality and creative merit. In most cases judging creative acts is a highly subjective affair. Sometimes the standards are set by an authority in the field, such as a noted professor of design, a film critic, a former Olympic skater, or a very discerning person. This approach to psychology sounds more like art than science, and, understandably, many scientifically obsessed psychologists would rather put on a white coat, go to their laboratory, and measure blips on an oscilloscope made by a cat looking at a vertical line than try to evaluate a creative act or person. Yet some bold individuals have rushed in where their angelic colleagues fear to tread.

Divergence Production Test. J. P. Guilford (1967) has spent most of his long and celebrated professional career developing theories and tests of mental ability that includes creativity. He has distinguished between two types of thinking: **convergent**

thinking and **divergent thinking.** Convergent thinking moves in a straightforward manner to a particular conclusion. Much of pedagogy emphasizes convergent thinking, in which students are asked to recall factual information, such as

What is the capital of Bulgaria?

Divergent thinking requires a person to generate many different answers to a question, the "correctness" of the answers being somewhat subjective. For example:

For how many different things can you use a brick?

The convergent answer may be "to make a building or a chimney." A slightly more divergent answer may be "to make a bookcase" or "to serve as a candleholder," while a more off-the-wall divergent answer may be "to serve as emergency rouge," or "to serve as a bon voyage gift—shoes for people who are going to the moon for the first time." Simple productivity of responses is not creative thinking. One could use a brick to make a candy shop, a bakery, a factory, a shoe factory, a shop that sells hand-carved wooden things, a filling station, and so on. Divergent or more creative answers may utilize objects or ideas in more abstract terms. The divergent thinker is more flexible in his or her thinking.

If productivity were a valid measure of creativity, then quantitative assessment of that trait could be achieved by counting the number of responses to brick-type questions. Since it is not, as illustrated in the previous example, subjective evaluations must be used. Most people would agree, we suspect, that bricks as moonshoes is a more creative answer than listing the types of buildings one could make with bricks. The latter answer is, however, more practical.

Cultural Blocks.   Why is it that some people can generate creative uses for objects, such as a brick, and others cannot? Part of the answer may lie in the cultural heritage of the individual. James Adams (1976b) provides an example of a cultural block in the following puzzle:

Exercise: Assume that a steel pipe is embedded in the concrete floor of a bare room, as shown in the illustration. The inside diameter is 0.6 inches larger than the diameter of a

table tennis ball (1.50 inches), which is resting gently at the bottom of the pipe. You are one of a group of six people in the room, along with the following objects:

100 feet of clothesline
A carpenter's hammer
A chisel
A box of Wheaties breakfast cereal
A file
A wire coat hanger
A monkey wrench
A lightbulb

In 5 minutes list as many ways you can think of to get the ball out of the pipe without damaging the ball, the tube, or the floor.

Take a few moments to figure out a creative solution to this problem.

If your creative powers are like ours, you may have thought, "If I could only damage the floor, the ball, or the tube, I could get the ball out in minutes." Then perhaps you might have considered how the inventory of items could be used or fashioned into tools. If you were able to generate a long list of possible uses for the items, you may have been showing your fluency or ability to produce a number of concepts over a period of time. If you were able to generate several diverse ideas, however, you would have shown your flexibility. Creative problem solving may be done by fluency—that is, you may think of enough concepts to find one that will be appropriate—but in many cases fluency does not lead to a solution and may even be a waste of time. More flexible thinking is required.

Did you solve the ball-in-the-pipe problem? Perhaps you thought of making a giant pair of tweezers by separating the coat hanger and flattening the ends. Other, more flexible means might include making a snare from the filaments of the lightbulb. Another possibility would be to have one of the six people pee into the pipe, thereby levitating the ball to the surface. Why didn't you think of this, or if you did, why did you? It is likely that because of a cultural taboo that forbids public urination, this solution (apologies to those who can't stand puns) may not have occurred to you. Since no time limit is specified, you could also make a sticky paste of the Wheaties cereal, dip the clothesline in it, slip it down the pipe, and let it dry on the ball. Then the lightweight ball could be gently removed. Alternatively, the six people may be able to rotate the entire room and concrete floor, letting the ball roll out of the pipe (the directions say only that the pipe is embedded in a concrete floor and that the group of six people are in the room). After all, it could be a very small room easily negotiated by six people. Why didn't you think of that? Perhaps you could invent an antigravity machine with the tools available or transcendentally experience the ball outside the pipe (what is reality, after all?). If you have other ingenious solutions, perhaps you will send them to me. Our ability to think creatively is, in part, determined by our culture and education.

Teaching Creativity.   Insofar as creativity is a function of our culture and education, is it possible to teach creativity? The answer depends on how creativity is defined. It is possible to train people to be more flexible in their thinking, to score higher on tests of creativity, to solve puzzles more creatively, and to probe scientific and philosophic issues more deeply than before. However, it is difficult to prove empirically that through training alone the likes of a Rossini, De Quincey, van Gogh, Einstein, Picasso, Dickinson, or Freud could be fashioned from a randomly selected person.

Hayes (1978) has suggested that creativity can be enhanced by the following means:

- *Developing a knowledge base.* A rich background in science, literature, art, and mathematics seems to give the creative person a larger storehouse of information from which to work his or her creative talents. Each of the previously mentioned creative people spent many years gathering information and perfecting their basic skills. In a study of creative artists and scientists, Anne Roe (1946, 1953) found that the only common denominator among the group she studied was the willingness to work unusually hard. The apple that fell on Newton's head and inspired him to develop a general theory of gravity struck an object filled with information.

- *Creating the right atmosphere for creativity.* Several years ago the technique of brainstorming became fashionable. The gist of brainstorming is that people in a group generate as many ideas as they can without criticism from the other members. Not only can a large number of ideas or solutions to a problem be generated this way, but also the technique can be used on an individual basis to facilitate the development of a creative idea. Frequently, we are inhibited by others or our own constraint from generating bizarre solutions.

- *Searching for analogies.* Several studies have shown that people do not recognize it when a new problem is similar to an old problem that they already know how to solve (see Hayes & Simon, 1976; and Hinsley, Hayes, & Simon, 1977). In formulating a creative solution to a problem, it is important to consider similar problems you may have encountered. In the problem of extracting a table tennis ball from a 4-inch-long pipe, one technique was to make a glue from the Wheaties. If you were confronted with a similar puzzle, perhaps now you would, through analogous thinking, remember the problem with the pipe and table tennis ball and its Wheaties-and-glue solution.

Human Intelligence

The Problem of Definition

In spite of the wide usage of the word **intelligence,** psychologists do not agree on a single definition. Many would agree, however, that all of the topics called higher-order forms of cognition—concept formation, reasoning, problem solving, and creativity, as well as memory and perception—are related to human intelligence. A short time ago, R. Sternberg (1982) asked people to identify the characteristics of an intelligent person, and among the most frequently given responses were "reasons logically and well," "reads widely," "keeps an open mind," and "reads with high comprehension." As a working definition we shall consider *human intelligence* to be "the ability to acquire, recall, and use knowledge to understand concrete and abstract concepts and the relationships among objects and ideas, and to use knowledge in a meaningful way."

The recent interest in artificial intelligence (AI) has caused many psychologists to consider what is uniquely human about human intelligence and what abilities a computer would require to act (humanly) intelligent. Nickerson, Perkins, and Smith (1985) have compiled the following list of abilities that they believe represent human intelligence:

- *The ability to classify patterns.* All humans with normal intelligence seem able to assign nonidentical stimuli to classes. This ability is fundamental to thought and language, since words generally represent categories of information. For example, telephone refers to a wide class of objects used for long-distance electronic communication. Imagine the hassle if you had to treat each telephone as a separate, nonclassified phenomenon.

- *The ability to modify behavior adaptively—to learn.* Many theorists consider adapting to one's environment the most important mark of human intelligence.

- *The ability to reason deductively.* As we considered earlier, deductive reasoning involves making logical inferences from stated premises. If we conclude that "Phil Smith likes wine," given the validity of the premises "All residents of Napa Valley like wine" and "Phil Smith lives in Napa Valley," we infer a degree of deductive reasoning ability.

- *The ability to reason inductively—to generalize.* Inductive reasoning requires that the person go beyond the information given. It requires the reasoner to discover rules and principles from specific instances. If Phil Smith likes wine and lives in Napa Valley, his neighbor also likes wine, and if his neighbor is also inclined to enjoy a bit of the nectar, you might get the impression that the next neighbor is also fond of fermented grapes. It might not be true, but it tends to be "intelligent."

- *The ability to develop and use conceptual models.* This ability means that we form an impression of the way the world is and how it functions and use that model to understand and interpret events. Nickerson and his colleagues use the following example:

  > When you see a ball roll under one end of a couch and then emerge at the other end, how do you know that the ball that came out is the same one that went in? In fact you do not really know for sure that it is, but your conceptual model of the world leads you to make such an inference. . . . Moreover, had the ball, on emerging, been a different color, or a different size, than on entering, you would have had to infer either that the ball that came out was not the one that went in, or that something peculiar was going on under the couch. (p. 321)

  Much of what we "know" we never directly observe, but we infer from our past experiences with other similar things and events. For example, we don't know whether a barber, born and bred in Arizona, can tell time or speak Hindi, but we act as if he can tell time and not speak Hindi whereas a person growing up in a remote village in northeastern India might have an opposite model.

- *The ability to understand.* In general, the ability to understand is related to the ability to see relationships in problems and to appreciate the meaning of these relationships in solving a problem. Validation of understanding is one of the most elusive problems in intelligence testing.

Cognitive Theories of Intelligence

If the processing of information follows a sequence of stages in which at each stage a unique operation is performed, then human intelligence is thought to be a component of human intellect that interacts with the processing of information. Essentially, this is the way intelligence is conceptualized by cognitive psychologists who subscribe to the information-processing theory of cognition. Enthusiasm for the model seemed to start with cognitive psychologists fascinated with computer intelligence (Chapter 16 of this book is devoted to artificial intelligence, or computer simulation of intelligence.) The analogy between human and artificial intelligence is inescapable; information from the external world is perceived or input, it is stored in memory, transformation of the information is performed, and an output is made. Additionally, the processing of information is analogous to programs in computers and intellectual functions, including intelligence, in humans.

Short-Term Memory.   As an example of the type of studies of intelligence done by cognitive psychologists, we first consider the work of Hunt (1978), Hunt, Lunneborg, and Lewis (1975), and Hunt and Lansman (1982) of the University of Washington. One question asked by Hunt and his associates was, "In what way(s) does the processing of information differ in high- and low-ability subjects?" Two groups—one with high-ability students and one with low-ability students—selected on the basis of standardized college entrance examinations such as the Scholastic Aptitude Test (SAT), were asked questions that required searching for common information in their long-term memories. Speed of retrieval was used as the dependent variable.

The test Hunt used to measure reaction times was the letter-matching task developed by Posner and his colleagues (1969), which is discussed in some detail in Chapter 6. The task required subjects to decide whether two letters (for example, *A-A* or *A-a*) matched. In some instances the letters matched physically and in other cases the match was made on the basis of the name of the letters. From the perspective of information processing, the physical match condition required only that the subject get the letters in short-term memory and make a decision. In the name-matching condition, the subject, in addition to getting both terms in STM, had to retrieve the name of the letter (ostensibly stored in LTM), make a decision, and then press a reaction-time key. Hunt assumed that physical matches reflect only structural processes dealing with the encoding and comparison of visual patterns, while name matching reflects the efficiency of encoding information to a level that requires that the physical representation of a letter make contact with the name of that letter in LTM. Crudely put, the speed with which people could retrieve information from LTM was hypothesized to be a measure of verbal ability. In the first condition, involving the physical match (*A-A*), the low- and high-ability

Earl Hunt. Studied intelligence and artificial intelligence within the context of cognitive psychology.

groups did about equally well, in the name-matching condition (*A-a*), the low-ability group, on average, took more time to make a correct decision than the high-ability group. The difference between the groups was in the range of 25 to 50 milliseconds, which may seem to be very brief indeed; however, when we consider the decoding of countless thousands of letters and words in the process of normal reading (such as reading a text-book), the impact of these brief times adds up quickly. These results hold for different participant groups such as university students, 10-year-old children, elderly adults, and mentally retarded persons.

In another study Hunt (1978) used a modified form of the Brown-Peterson task (see Chapter 6) to study differences between those with high verbal ability and those with low verbal ability." This task, as you may recall, requires participants to recall a three-letter syllable after they have counted backward by 3s for a certain length of time. (Hunt used four-letter syllables and had the participants read the digits.) In this experiment the two groups differed significantly in recall of letters. In addition, the retention curves between the two groups were parallel, which suggests that the high-verbal group may be more efficient in encoding verbal information (rather than simply maintaining more information) than the low-verbal group. Finally, Hunt used the (Saul) Sternberg paradigm (see Chapter 6) to identify differences between participants with high-verbal ability and those with low-verbal ability. As might be expected by now, he found that the former group performed better than the latter group on this task.

The studies by Hunt and others are significant for two reasons. First, they indicate that the information-processing paradigm provides many useful procedures for the study of human intelligence. It is feasible that, in addition to verbal ability, other measures of intelligence—such as mathematical ability, spatial ability, or perhaps even general intelligence—may yield some of their enigmatic secrets in terms of reasonably simple cognitive processes and mechanisms. Second, STM is related to verbal components of intelligence, not necessarily because the number of items retained in STM is critically related to intelligence but because simple cognitive processes and operations, such as identification of the name of a letter or the retention of a trigram, that depend on LTM and STM are sensitive to individual intellectual differences.

General Knowledge. General knowledge has, since the development of the earliest tests of intelligence, been considered an integral part of human intelligence, and to this day questions designed to tap an individual's understanding of the world are part of most standard tests. Apparently, knowing that Baghdad is the capital of Iraq, or that hydrogen is lighter than helium, or that the Kirov Ballet performs in Saint Petersburg, or that Tutankhamen's mostly unmolested tomb was discovered by Howard Carter (all of which are examples of passive knowledge—the type of information a simpleminded computer could store) is presumed by test makers to be related to intelligence. However, embarrassingly little attention has been given, either theoretically or pragmatically, to the reason general knowledge is considered a correlate of intelligence. As Siegler and Richards (1982) point out:

> For the same reasons that fish will be the last to discover water, developmental psychologists until recently devoted almost no attention to changes in children's knowledge of specific content. Such changes are so omnipresent that they seemed uninviting as targets for study. Instead of being investigated, improved content knowledge was implicitly dismissed as a by-product of more basic changes in capacities and strategies. (p. 930)

Tests of general information may provide important data on a person's current state of knowledge and ability to retrieve information. This in turn could provide a useful clue to the past intellectual history and predict future performance. Yet, of the many cognitive attributes recently discovered, only a few have been related to human intelligence. It seems that semantic organization is a topic that could be of special interest to people interested in intelligence. In Chapter 9 some of the current theories of semantic organization were discussed, and it would seem that the ability to store semantic information in an organized schema and to access that information efficiently is characteristic of at least one type of intelligence. Perhaps some enterprising student of cognitive psychology will pursue this valuable subject.

One developmental study has shown not only how experiments can be done in this area but also how they can lead to a clear demonstration of the impact of a knowledge base. Chi (1978) examined the effect of a specialized knowledge base on the recall of chess and digit stimuli. For her experiment, she selected 10-year-old children who were skilled chess players and adults who were novices at the game. The task was similar to the one used by Chase and Simon (see Chapter 4) in which chess pieces were arranged in a normal game configuration. Both groups of participants were allowed to view the board and pieces and then were asked to reproduce the arrangement on a second board. A related task, called a metamemory task—which refers to an individual's knowledge about his or her own memory—consisted of asking the children and adults to predict how many trials it would take to reproduce all the pieces. The results, shown in Figure 15.7, revealed that the children not only were better at recalling the arrangement of chess pieces but also were better at predicting their performance—that is, their metamemory was more accurate than that of adults. A standard digit-span task, which is commonly used in intelligence tests, was also administered, and as expected the adults performed better on recalling these digits and predicting their performance than the children. The effect of a knowledge base, independent of age or other types of intelligence (for example, digit-span performance), appears to measurably enhance the ability to recall from working memory specialized information that is directly related to the knowledge base. The issues raised by this experiment, both methodological and theoretical, suggest that in the future many more studies of this type will appear.

Reasoning and Problem Solving. Almost everyone would agree that reasoning and problem solving are important components of human intelligence, and some would suggest that separating these concepts is done only for analytic purposes.

Most prominent among the new generation of cognitive psychologists to tackle the question of human intelligence in relation to reasoning and problem solving is R. Sternberg (1977, 1980a, 1980b, 1982, 1984a, 1984b, 1986a, 1986b, 1989). The theory of human intelligence proposed by Sternberg (1984b, 1985b, 1989) is the *triarchic theory*. It comprises three subtheories that serve as the governing bases for specific models of intelligent human behavior. These parts are:

1. *Componential intelligent behavior.* This subtheory specifies the structures and mechanism that underlie intelligent behavior. Within this subtheory are three information-processing components: (a) learning how to do things, (b) planning what things to do and how to do them, and (c) actually doing the things. People with such ability are generally good test takers and blow the top off standardized

Recall of chess and digit stimuli by children and adults.

From Chi (1978). Reprinted by permission from Erlbaum.

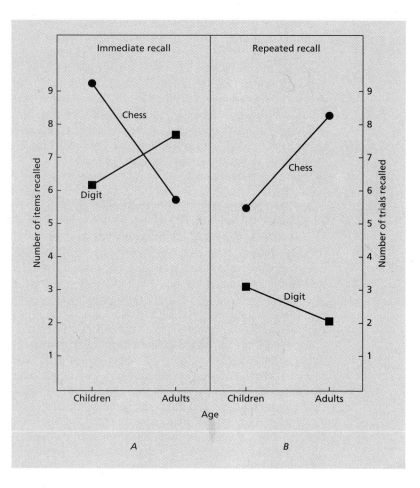

tests. They also do well commenting on other people's work. However, they are not necessarily critical thinkers, nor are they particularly creative.)

2. (*Experiential intelligent behavior.*) This component posits that for a given task or situation, contextually appropriate behavior is not equally "intelligent" at all points along the continuum of experience with that behavior or class of behaviors. This kind of intelligence is best demonstrated when people are confronted with a novel situation or are in the process of automatizing performance on a given task) Those who have this component may not score highest on typical IQ tests, but (they are creative. Such ability is generally predictive of success in a chosen field, be it business, medicine, or carpentry.)

3. (*Contextual intelligent behavior.* This involves (a) adaptation to a present environment, (b) selection of a more nearly optimal environment than the one the individual presently inhabits, or (c) shaping of the present environment to render it a better fit to skills, interests, or values.) Contextual intelligence allows a

Robert J. Sternberg. Developed triarchic theory of intelligence.

person to find a good fit with the environment by changing one or the other or both. We might think of this type of intelligence as instrumental in getting along in your world, whether that world is a slum in Los Angeles, the board room at IBM, the Cattleman's Club in Dallas, the Polo Room at Southampton, or the Laurel Booster Club.

In illustrating these three types of intelligence, Sternberg recalls three idealized graduate students called Alice, Barbara, and Celia, who each exemplified one of the components of intelligence (see Trotter, 1986). The three students are described in the table entitled "Sternberg's Triarchic Theory of Intelligence."

Such revolutionary ideas in the sensitive field of intelligence, which crosses so many areas of human endeavor (educational, political, racial, to name only three), were certain to be met with criticism. Some of the arguments are technical, others are philosophical, and others are pragmatically inspired.[4] One reviewer, H. Eysenck (1984), is critical of the triarchic theory on the basis that it is not so much a theory of intelligence as it is a theory of behavior. The interested reader is directed toward original sources and current literature. At this time, no one—including Sternberg (see 1984b, p. 312)—believes that the final model of intelligence has been developed. At the same time, no one believes that our view of intelligence will remain unchanged.

In Sternberg's scheme, reasoning is characterized as an attempt to combine elements of old information to produce new information. (See the box entitled "Try This! Intelligence Test.") The old information may be external (from books, movies, newspapers), internal (stored in memory), or a combination of both. In inductive reasoning, discussed earlier, the information contained in the premises is insufficient to reach a conclusion; the person must create the correct solution. One technique used by Sternberg is the analogy that can be represented by A is to B as C is to D or, symbolically, A:B::C:D. In some instances the last term (D) is omitted and must be generated by the participant, or in other cases the participants must select from a series of alternative answers, as in the following:

Philology:Languages::Mycology:
(a. Flowering plants, b. Ferns, c. Weeds, d. Fungus)

---

[4]For an excellent collection of Sternberg's theory and criticism of it by leading authorities, see Sternberg (1984b).

Sternberg's Triarchic Theory of Intelligence

Componential

Alice had high test scores and was a whiz at test taking and analytical thinking. Her type of intelligence exemplifies the componential subtheory, which explains the mental components involved in analytical thinking.

Experiential

Barbara didn't have the best test scores, but she was a superbly creative thinker who could combine disparate experiences in insightful ways. She is an example of the experiential subtheory.

Contextual

Celia was street-smart. She learned how to play the game and how to manipulate the environment. Her test scores weren't tops, but she could come out on top in almost any context. She is Sternberg's example of contextual intelligence.

The reasoning ability needed to solve this problem is minimal, but the analogy is nevertheless difficult for many people because they don't know that mycology is the study of fungi and philology is the study of the origin of languages. Analogies of this type measure a form of intelligence related to vocabulary.

In the preceding analogy, the solution is dependent on knowledge of words and reasoning ability. Solving analogies is not as simple a matter, however, as recalling information from memory; it involves several stages. Sternberg suggests that when confronted with a problem of this sort, one should break the analogy down into subproblems, each of which requires solving before the entire problem can be solved. The strategy used is similar to the means-end analysis of Newell and Simon (mentioned earlier), but it differs in that each stage of the information-processing sequence is thought to play an important role in the process. The following problem, adapted from R. Sternberg (1982), is an illustration of some of the stages a person must work through in solving an analogy.

> Lawyer:Client::Doctor:
> (a. Patient, b. Medicine)

In this case the encoding of the words is less problematic than in the previous case because most people are familiar with all the terms. The stages used in solving this problem are as follows:

1. The reasoner encodes the terms of the analogy.
2. The reasoner makes an inference between lawyer and client (for example, a lawyer gives service to a client, a lawyer is paid by a client, and a lawyer may help the client).

Intelligence Test

Sample Test Questions

1. Suppose that all gemstones were made of foam rubber. Which of the following completions would then be correct for the analogy below?

   Wood: Hard::Diamond:

   a. Valuable, b. Soft, c. Brittle, d. Hardest

2. Janet, Barbara, and Elaine are a housewife, lawyer, and physicist, although not necessarily in that order. Janet lives next door to the housewife. Barbara is the physicist's best friend. Elaine once wanted to be a lawyer but decided against it. Janet has seen Barbara within the last two days, but has not seen the physicist.

   Janet, Barbara, and Elaine are, in that order, the

   a. Housewife, physicist, lawyer
   b. Physicist, lawyer, housewife
   c. Physicist, housewife, lawyer
   d. Lawyer, housewife, physicist

3. Josh and Sandy were discussing the Reds and the Blues, two baseball teams. Sandy asked Josh why he thought the Reds had a better chance of winning the pennant this year than did the Blues. Josh replied, "If every man on the Red team is better than every man on the Blue team, then the Reds must be on the better team." Josh is assuming that

   a. Inferences that apply to each part of a whole apply as well to the whole, and this assumption is true.
   b. Inferences that apply to each part of a whole apply as well to the whole, and this assumption is false.
   c. Inferences that apply to a whole apply as well to each part, and this assumption is true.
   d. Inferences that apply to a whole apply as well to each part, and this assumption is false.

4. Select that answer option that represents either a necessary or forbidden property of the italicized word.

   lion

   a. Fierce, b. white, c. mammalian, d. alive

5.

Answers: 1. b, 2. d, 3. b, 4. c, 5. 2

From R. Sternberg (1986a).

3. The reasoner maps the higher-order relationship between the first half of the analogy and the second (both deal with professionals who render service to a patron).

4. The reasoner applies a relationship similar to the inferred one to the second half of the analogy, that is, from the doctor and each of the alternatives (a doctor gives service to a person, not medicine).

5. The reasoner makes his or her response.

Initially the terms of an analogy must be encoded, or translated, into internal representations upon which subsequent operations can be performed. One model of representations used by Sternberg (1977, 1982, 1985b) is based on attributes of the information, which is similar to theories discussed in Chapter 9 on semantic memory. This model is illustrated in the following example:

Washington:1::Lincoln:
(a. 10, b. 5)

- Washington could be encoded as a president (1st), a person whose visage is on currency (one-dollar bill), or a war hero (American Revolution).
- 1 might be encoded as a counting number (1), an ordinal position (1st), or an amount (1 unit).
- Lincoln might be encoded as a president (16th), a person whose visage is on currency (five-dollar bill), or a war hero (Civil War).
- 10 might be encoded as a counting number (10), an ordinal position (10th), or an amount (10 units).
- 5 might be encoded as a counting number (5), an ordinal position (5th), or an amount (5 units).

In addition to the semantic representations shown by these analogies, information in problems can be presented pictorially, as in an analogy that might include a black square inside a white circle, which might be represented in terms of shape, position, or color. (For an example, see question 5 in the box entitled "Try This! Intelligence Test.")

From such problems Sternberg has developed a theory of intelligence that distinguishes five different components by which intelligence can be analyzed: metacomponents, performance components, acquisition components, retention components, and transfer components. *Components* refers to the steps that a person must go through to solve a problem. *Metacomponents* refers to the person's knowledge about how to solve a problem. Because metacomponents are the basis of so many diverse intellectual tasks, Sternberg considers it to be related to general intelligence. He is continuing to investigate how different components are involved in reasoning tasks, such as analogies, and how the components and metacomponents increase in complexity with development. Of particular interest to the student of cognitive science is his overall scheme, which has clearly cast theories of intelligence and tests of intelligence in the cognitive mold.

Cognitive Neuroscience and Intelligence

While psychologists of different orientations, from Binet, to Spearman, Thurstone, Guilford, Cattel, Wechsler, Hunt, and Sternberg (and many others) have sought behavioral answers to the question of intelligence, neuroscientists have also been intrigued by the problem but have sought neurological answers in the brain. Traditionally, the neurological approach has been grounded in medical research and practice and, frequently, the emphasis has been on mental retardation and developmental considerations. Surprisingly little work had been done on the biological development of "normal" intellectual processes. This situation changed with the invention of imaging technology, which allowed researchers to probe into the workings of the brain with effulgent clarity.

Dilbert/ by Scott Adams

DILBERT reprinted by permission of United Features Syndicate, Inc.

From our previous discussion (see Chapter 2) of positron emission tomography (PET) we learned that by measuring minute amounts of radioactive particles—specifically, hydrogen combined with oxygen 15, a radioactive isotope of oxygen—in the bloodstream, it is possible to measure sites in the brain that demand glucose nutrition. Ostensibly, areas that require more energy in the form of glucose are more active than areas that require less and these "hot spots" may be delineated by PET scans. The potential of this work for understanding the location of different types of intellectual work and possibly the way the brain processes intelligence tasks (such as taking an IQ test) is significant and may lead us in new directions regarding our basic concepts of intelligence. But, where to begin?

A logical place to look at the brain and intelligence is at the most general level. In a series of experiments Richard Haier and his colleagues at the University of California, Irvine have addressed this issue by looking at metabolic needs vis-à-vis brain locations, for different groups, such as skilled computer-game players versus nonskilled players; people who score high on abstract, nonverbal reasoning tasks versus base rates for normal performance; individuals with mild mental retardation and Down syndrome versus matched controls; and men versus women performing mathematical reasoning tasks. In one experiment subjects with high scores on abstract, nonverbal reasoning tasks showed reduced energy activity in parts of the brain which otherwise are involved in these tasks. You may recall from Chapter 2 we reported the finding that neural activity for computer-game experts was less than for novices and this finding and the preceding finding suggest that the brain is an efficient organ in the sense that intelligent and practiced brains use less glucose than comparable controls. The brain's glucose metabolic rate (GMR) was less for the people who scored high on the abstract test than for the control group, suggesting that this kind of intelligence is efficient in problem solving.

In yet another experiment related to intelligence a group of people practiced playing the computer game "Tetris" (see Figure 15.8), which requires the player to rotate and move objects in such a way as to create a solid row of blocks. If the player is successful, the speed increases until only real aficionados can keep up with the rapidly falling blocks. In general, Haier and his colleagues have developed an "efficiency model" of intelligence: Intelligence is not a function of how hard the brain works but rather how efficiently it works. In addition, learning may actually decrease brain metabolic works and, one is reminded of the concept of automaticity (see Chapter 3) in which well-practiced routines

FIGURE 15.8

The "Tetris" game in progress from left to right. Participants attempt to manipulate configurations of four square blocks falling from the top of the screen to produce solid rows of blocks. Once a solid row of blocks is completed, it disappears and is replaced by the row above it. Symbol markings show individual shapes that have already been placed. Note the bottom row of the middle panel is complete; in the panel on the right it has disappeared (1 point is scored) and the rows above moved down.

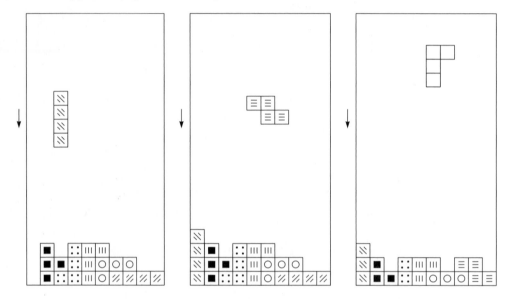

require little attention and run on "auto pilot." An earlier study had participants practicing up to five days a week for several months on the "Tetris" game. They got better by sevenfold, but their cortical and subcortical GMRs *decreased* significantly over their initial metabolic rates. Following this experiment Haier, Siegel, Tang, Abel, and Buchsbaum (1992) administered several standard tests of intelligence (Raven's Progressive Matrices scale and the Wechsler Adult Intelligence Scale). The purpose of the experiment was to establish the relationship between the learning of Tetris and scores on intelligence to determine if high-ability people show the largest GMR decreases as suggested by the brain efficiency hypothesis. The results, indicating that the magnitude of GMR changes and intelligence scores were related, supported the efficiency model.

Additional indication that smart brains are efficient brains comes through a study of brain size, GMR in mild mentally retarded and Down syndrome individuals by Haier et al. (1995) using both PET scans and magnetic resonance imaging (MRI) data. The results of the MRI showed that mentally retarded and Down syndrome groups both had brain volumes of about 80 percent of controls. The PET data show that whole brain cortex GMR was greater in both the retarded and Down syndrome groups as compared with control participants.

The question of whether human "intelligence" is composed of a series of subcomponents (such as mathematical ability, verbal ability, and spatial ability) or is a general factor that contributes to success in a large number of cognitive tasks has been hotly contested. Charles Spearman developed the concept of general intelligence of *g* during the early part of the twentieth century. Convincing evidence for *g* has been elusive yet, in a recent study by John Duncan (2000) and his associates at Cambridge, specific parts of the lateral frontal cortex appear to be implicated when people perform a variety of cognitive tasks used to measure intelligence. In the following task, choose the one that does not belong with the rest:[5] In the first task, a type of spatial intelligence is measured and in the second, verbal intelligence.

Spatial   **Verbal**

 LHEC   DFIM   TQNK   HJMQ

fMRI brain scans of people doing these types of tasks show that spatial and verbal processing are generally localized in the frontal part of the brain, thus supporting the *g*, or general theory of intelligence. (See the accompanying figure.) It appears that spatial processing involves both the left and right hemispheres. Such work is on the cutting edge of cognitive neuroscience and raises new questions. For example, are there specialized areas within the general areas that are associated with specific intellectual abilities? And how are these general intelligence areas connected to other parts of the brain that (likely) contribute to intelligent cognition?

Intelligence, or at least the performance on complex problem-solving tasks, is just beginning to succumb to the curious minds of genetic engineers, who champion the

Spatial processing		Verbal processing	
Left hemisphere	Right hemisphere	Left hemisphere	Right hemisphere

idea that through tinkering with the genetic structure of the brain, smarter creatures may be assembled. One such effort that has received wide attention is the work of Joe Tsien (2000) of Princeton University who has altered a protein in mice that is important in learning and memory. These genetically altered mice, dubbed Doogie, were placed in an open box and allowed to explore two objects for several minutes. Then, a few days later, the experimenter replaced one of the objects with a new object. The "smart" mice spent more time exploring the new object while "normal" mice spent an equal amount of time exploring both objects, suggesting that the old object was no more familiar to them than the new. The genetically modified mice remembered objects up to five times longer than the nonmodified mice. Several subsequent tasks involving maze learning

---

[5]The correct answer to the spatial question is the third nonsymmetrical item and to the verbal item, the third item that is equally spaced alphabetically (reversed order).

confirmed the earlier observations. While these mice will not be capable of solving even a simple problem in algebra, they seem to "act intelligently."

The future of genetic engineering—as well as other forms of mind altering, like chemical intervention, as it relates to making humans "act intelligently"—suggests to some a boon for the slow-learning person and to others a serious threat to natural intelligence. The "brave new world" that is being created in today's laboratories will be of immense interest and may present some moral problems for which intelligent decisions will be required.

The implications are many. Why are intelligent brains more efficient than less intelligent brains? Or, is the premise on which that question is framed erroneous? What underlying mechanism is responsible for the greater demand for glucose? Is the basic phenomenon related to the arborization of neurons? How is intelligence related to early development? Is there a critical period of neonatal development and brain development? What is the influence of early childhood stimulation on brain efficiency? Are instances of mental retardation preventable? reversible?

Our work on human intelligence is just beginning. But then, so is the work that needs to be done on perception, learning, memory, problem solving, and a myriad of other problems we twentieth-century cognitive psychologists have tackled. Many of the solutions will be found to these mysteries in the twenty-first century.

Spotlight on Cognitive Neuroscience

Creative Problem Solving

Stephen Fiore and Jonathan Schooler have some interesting perspectives on creative problem solving. Their view is that several aspects of creative problem solving involve right hemisphere functions. In particular, the notion of insight (def here) may be associated with certain cognitive processes that are known to originate in the right hemisphere of the brain. Experiences of insight that lead to creative problem solving often are nonverbal, "aha" moments. Remember in *Cast Away* when Tom Hanks has been trying unsuccessfully to start a fire. In the midst of scraping coconut out of its shell, he has an "aha" moment when he realizes that he should try that scraping motion of wood on wood to start the fire (instead of the spinning action he had been trying previously). The next scene shows him applying his newfound insight to his fire-starting problem. Fiore and Schooler conclude that, although the evidence may be circumstantial, it nevertheless indicates that the right hemisphere is particularly capable of processing information in such a way to lead to the type of insight that is useful in creative problem solving.

Fiore, S. M., & Schooler, J. W. (1998). Right hemisphere contributions to creative problem solving: Converging evidence for divergent thinking. In M. Beeman, C. Chiarello (Eds). *Right hemisphere language comprehension: Perspectives from cognitive neuroscience* (pp. 349–371). Hillsdale, NJ: Lawrence Erlbaum Associates.

*S*UMMARY

1   Problem solving is thought directed toward discovering a solution for a specific problem.

2   Several models have proposed cognitive networks engaged during problem-solving activity. One such model (Eisenstadt & Kareev) has focused on internal representa-

tions formed during problem solving, with related research showing memory about the problem field to be a function of how the problem was formed, negligible anticipatory planning, and scanning patterns of the problem field suggestive of top-down or hypothesis-driven processing.

3   Creativity is cognitive activity resulting in a novel perspective of a problem and is not restricted to pragmatic outcomes.

4   One framework for viewing the creative process (Wallas) proposes four phases: preparation, which involves problem formation, a process engaging our general knowledge base; incubation, which is the period when no direct attempts to solve the problem are made and attention is diverted elsewhere; illumination, which occurs when understanding is achieved; and verification, which involves testing of the insight.

5   Judgments of creativity range from assessments by authorities in the relevant field (for example, an Olympic athlete) to psychometric instruments designed to measure divergent thought processes defined as the ability to generate numerous abstract, flexible answers to one problem (for example, how many different ways can you use a brick?). Both procedures involve subjective evaluations.

6   Training can result in improved performance on standard measures of creativity, but it is not known whether such experience can produce the type of activity associated with people generally considered to be creative (such as van Gogh, Einstein, or Dickinson).

7   The complex nature of intelligence produces definitional problems. Early attempts to address these conceptual difficulties used factor analysis to isolate general and specific abilities, but such procedures have been criticized for not providing information about mental processes; for being difficult to test against theories; and for relying on individual differences, which is not the only or necessarily the best way to study human abilities.

8   Cognitive theories of intelligence hold it to be a component that interacts with information as it is processed through stages involving unique operations. Research using this framework has determined that memory retrieval (speed, accuracy, and amount) is a function of verbal ability, and an individual's knowledge base (novice versus skilled) affects the amount and accuracy of recall as well as the accuracy of his or her metamemory.

9   Studies of brain glucose metabolic rate (GMR) indicate that people who score high on intelligence tests or are well practiced in skill performance tend to require fewer nutrients to parts of the brain than "less efficient" brains.

KEY WORDS

convergent thinking	intelligence
creativity	preparation
divergent thinking	problem solving
functional fixedness	set
illumination	verification
incubation	

$\mathcal{R}$ECOMMENDED $\mathcal{R}$EADINGS

● An outstanding review of early history of research in thinking, concept formation, and problem solving is Woodworth, *Experimental Psychology.* F. Bartlett, *Thinking,* is a good introduction to traditional viewpoints. Bruner, Goodnow, and Austin, *A Study of Thinking,* is the source of much of the traditional theory and experimentation in concept formation.

● Many articles have been collected into two paperback books, Johnson-Laird and Wason, eds., *Thinking and Reasoning* and *Thinking: Readings in Cognitive Science.*

● Three "annual reviews" of thinking that summarize the significant developments are Bourne and Dominowski, *Thinking;* Neimark and Santa, *Thinking and Concept Attainment;* and Erickson and Jones, *Thinking.*

● Rubinstein has written a lively account of thinking and problem solving in *Tools for Thinking and Problem Solving,* as have Bransford and Stein in *The Ideal Problem Solver.* An easy and entertaining book is Mayer's *Thinking, Problem Solving, Cognition.* A first-rate collection of papers on human intelligence has been edited by Robert Sternberg and is called *Handbook of Human Intelligence* and *Advances in the Psychology of Human Intelligence.* Also see *Intelligence Applied* and *Beyond IQ: A Triarchic Theory of Human Intelligence* by Sternberg. Several recent volumes on intelligence have been edited by Chipman, Segal, and Glaser and are called *Thinking and Learning Skills;* and Nickerson, Perkins, and Smith have written an excellent book on thinking called *The Teaching of Thinking.* The periodical *Current Issues in Cognitive Science* frequently contains stimulating articles on the topics covered in this chapter and in the February 1993 issue (Number 1) intelligence was featured in several articles. Hunt has an interesting article in *American Scientist* and for a look at the social/racial side of intelligence see *The Bell Curve* by Herrnstein and Murray. A special issue of *Scientific American* was published in 1998 called *Exploring Intelligence.*

Answer to the Puzzle on Page 457

The puzzle states that you have an "endless supply of rope." You dump the rope into the gorge until it is filled up and you and your pal walk comfortably across. Meanwhile, you may have been inventing ingenious solutions which used the 20-foot ladder, the pliers, candle, matches, and your friend. Sometimes too much information in solving a problem makes it more difficult than just the bare essentials. Try the puzzle on a friend and eliminate all the supplies except the "endless supply of rope." How did the friend do? Why?

Incidentally, the use of this example was inspired by a frustrating event. One of us (RLS) ordered a specially designed drawer for his kitchen. It arrived with a bunch of assorted hardware, the drawer, and terse instructions obviously written by the same person who wrote the early computer guides. The hardware pieces were nondescript—one long piece looked something like a miniature harpoon with wings flaring out of the nonpointy end. Another was similar to a three-dimensional figure used in the test for applicants to dental school and another looked like a roller-coaster guide with only one wheel. It may have been possible to put these odd pieces on the drawer if there was some surface to mount them on. Alas, by Sunday afternoon he gave up and called the factory whose technician on duty was equally baffled. He did an extensive computer search and found a long outdated model from which he attempted to talk me through the installation process. "Take the harpoon, nonpointy side and hold it upright. Now take the dental test . . .". Nothing worked. Late that night the "light turned on" and he realized that the harpoon, the dental test item, the roller coaster guide and so on were all already mounted on the drawer! The company had sent duplicate hardware, and he thinks they even threw in a few extra screws, harpoons and so on just to confuse. Problem solving with information is kind of like a Goldilocks problem: You need not too much, not too little, but just the right amount of information for efficient problem solving. The smart people among us are those who recognize the critical components needed for a solution and disregard the rest—the extra harpoon, the extra dental school test device, the extra screws, and so on. Cryptoanalysts, spies, specialty cabinet packers, and practical jokers all know this. Lao Tzu was right: "Less is more."

Answer to Puzzle on Page 458

Answer to the flagpole problem on page 458. Remember the hint to look at the extremes? In this case first imagine that the flagpoles were 150 feet apart. The rope would be taut. Now imagine the other extreme, that the poles would be touching each other. How would the rope hang? Since the rope is 150-feet long and the flagpoles are each 100-feet tall, when the poles are next to each other the draped rope hangs down one pole 75 feet and down the other 75 feet, leaving the center of the rope hanging 25 feet from the ground.

Answer to Puzzle on Page 459

Answer to problem in box entitled "A Problem of Patients—Psychiatrists' and Yours." Karen and Laura care for a Rubin and, therefore, are not named Rubin (mark in the intersection of Karen and Laura with Rubin and exclusionary mark). Therefore, Mary is married to Rubin. Laura is a patient of Dr. Sanchez and, therefore, is not named Sanchez and must be called Taylor. By elimination, then, Karen is a Sanchez. Mary Rubin is seen by a female (clue 1) and a Dr. Taylor (clue 2), so she is treated by Laura Taylor and Mary's husband is treated by Karen Sanchez. Peter, who is treated by a Dr. Taylor (clue 2), is not Dr. Taylor (obviously) and cannot be the male Dr. Rubin treated by Karen Sanchez, so he must be Peter Sanchez and he treats Laura Taylor (clue 2). Omar cannot be the Dr. Rubin who is treated by Karen Sanchez because Omar is treated by Norman (clue 4), so Omar's last name is Taylor and Norman's last name is Rubin. Peter's psychiatrist is Omar Taylor, and, by elimination, Karen is under Mary Rubin's care. In summary, the full names of psychiatrists and patients are as follows: Drs. Laura Taylor (Mary Rubin), Karen Sanchez (Norman Rubin), Mary Rubin (Karen Sanchez), Omar Taylor (Peter Sanchez), Peter Sanchez (Laura Taylor), and Norman Rubin (Omar Taylor).

CHAPTER **16**

Computerized Cognition

Artificial Intelligence

hmmm...?

- **AI—The Beginnings**
  Computers
  Computers and AI
  AI and Human Cognition
- **Machines and Minds: The Imitation Game and the Chinese Room**
  The Imitation Game, or the Turing Test
  The Chinese Room
  The Chinese Room—Refutation
- **Perception and AI**
  Line Analysis
  Pattern Recognition
  Recognition of Complex Forms
- **Language and AI**
  ELIZA, PARRY, and NETtalk
  Meaning and AI
  Continous Speech Recognition (CSR)
  Language Understanding Program
- **Problem Solving, Game Playing, and AI**
  Computer Chess
- **AI and the Arts**
- **Robots**
- **The Future of AI**
- **AI and Scientific Inquiry**

1. What is artificial intelligence, and how might it affect psychology and your life?
2. Trace the history of computing machines to current AI programs.
3. In what ways are silicon-based computers like a carbon-based brain (the human brain)? In what ways are they unlike each other?
4. What is the Turing test? What are the imitation game and the Chinese room?
5. How does a computer analyze visual forms?
6. How do computers recognize and produce language?
7. What types of artistic productions may be generated by computers? How successful are they?
8. Will computer intelligence ever exceed human intelligence?

It is morally impossible that there should be sufficient diversity in any machine to allow it to act in all events of life in the same way as our reason causes us to act.

—*Descartes*

Then Hal answered, in his normal tone of voice:

"Look, Dave, I know you're trying to be helpful. But the fault is either in the antenna system or in your test procedures. My information processing is perfectly normal. If you check my record, you'll find it completely free from error."

"I know all about your service record, Hal—but that doesn't prove you're right this time. Anyone can make mistakes."

"I don't want to insist on it, Dave, but I am incapable of making an error." "All right, Hal," he said, rather hastily. "I understand your point of view. We'll leave it at that."

He felt like adding "and please forget the whole matter." But that, of course, was the one thing that Hal could never do.

—*Arthur C. Clarke*

Science fiction has a tendency to become science fact. Something like Hal,[1] the on-board spaceship computer capable of ethical decision making and intelligence in Arthur Clarke's *2001: A Space Odyssey,* is being discussed seriously in modern artificial-intelligence (AI) laboratories. That is not to say that computers will evolve exactly as Clarke envisioned, any more than propulsion systems developed in the way Jules Verne imagined three-quarters of a century before a rocket sent a spaceship to the moon. However, computer scientists are developing systems that come very close to mimicking parts of human cognition; it seems plausible that something like Hal will be around before you depart from this earth.[2]

Computerized cognition, or **artificial intelligence (AI),** as it is often called, is broadly defined as that branch of computer science that deals with the development of computers (hardware) and computer programs (software) that emulate human cognitive functions. In the preceding fifteen chapters "human cognitive functions" that have been discussed in some detail and we have learned that cognition involves perception, memory, thinking, language processing, and many other related functions which are carried out in a more or less exact way. You can, for example, see and recognize your friend's face; solve the mathematical problem of $(7 \times 8)/(4 \times 5)$ in "your head"; compose a sensible poem set in iambic pentameter; recognize the voices of Beavis and Butthead; mentally calculate the most direct route from your home to the college; determine if it is or is not proper to invite the father of the bride to the groom's bachelor party; and distinguish sour milk from fresh milk. We do things like this every day with no effort (and, if we may extrapolate from the findings of Haier and his colleagues reported in the previous chapter on human intelligence regarding metabolic rates and intellectual performance, without the expenditure of much

[1]Acrostic for *h*euristically programmed *al*gorithmic computer.
[2]On the other hand, many question that computers can ever truly outsmart humans in significant areas. The neuropsychologist John Eccles writes, in *The Understanding of the Brain,* that those who make "arrogant assertions that computers will soon outsmart man in all matters . . . are the modern variants of the idol makers of other superstitious ages; and like them seek power through the fostering of idolatry."

energy). We also do a lot of foolish things, such as put shampoo on our toothbrush. We are human—and that's a problem for computers, being perfect machines that never make a mistake, "computer errors" notwithstanding. If a computer could simulate human thought and actions precisely, then it would be as good as we are in doing the list of things mentioned earlier, but also be just as fallible as we are—down to the early morning shampoo-toothpaste switcheroo done while one is trying to recover his or her own identity. It is important to recognize the distinction between those who want to write programs that will perform human tasks well, such as the program we are presently using that draws a squiggly red line under misspelled words and those who aim to clone human thought. Computers and their impressive programs have become such an indispensable part of our everyday life that we wonder how we got along without them—still, they aren't clever enough to shampoo with toothpaste (or was it the other way around?). In order to do that, they would have to imitate exactly human thought and actions—to, in truth, perform *indistinguishably* from human cognition. More will be said about that later.

Let's consider a "simple" cognitive task: That of solving algebra word problems. Many computer programs can do this swiftly and accurately, but they do not simulate human cognition. Early in AI research, Simon and colleagues (1966) attempted to model human performance in a computer program called STUDENT, which was designed to solve algebra word problems based on pure syntactic analysis. Some human participants in their study performed much like the way STUDENT did but many did not. They used auxiliary cues and physical representations in solving the problems, much as you probably did when trying to figure out the loss of water in a leaky bucket that was being simultaneously filled—you, thoughtfully, drew a picture.

In spite of fundamental differences between AI and intellectual cloning remarkable growth in this area has been made.

When we discuss AI, it is usually intertwined with cognitive psychology and neuroscience. Ideas from one field, for example, neuroscience, might be incorporated into another, for example, artificial intelligence, and yet other ideas from cognitive psychology might be applied to both of the other areas. All three—AI, cognitive psychology, and neuroscience (especially neuroscience)—build a platform for cognitive science.

AI and cognitive psychology have a kind of symbiotic relationship, each profiting from the development of the other. The development of artificial ways to replicate human perception, memory, language, and thought, is dependent upon understanding how these processes are accomplished by human beings. And the development of AI increases the magnitude of our capabilities to understand human cognition.

This chapter offers a general introduction to AI as it relates to perception, memory, search processes, language, problem solving, artistic performance and robotics.

Although work in AI is devoted to the development of machines that act as if they were intelligent, most are designed without any intention of mimicking human cognitive processes. However, there are researchers who are concerned with the development of "intelligent" machines that model human thought, and it is this perspective—sometimes called computer simulation (CS)—that, for the most part, is reflected in this chapter. (Because at times it is nearly impossible to tell where AI leaves off and CS begins, the widely accepted term *AI* is used in this chapter to embrace all forms of computer-produced output that would be considered intelligent if produced by a human.)

AI—The Beginnings

Calculators of one sort or another—the brain of AI—have been around about as long as history. The earliest type was the abacus, which was used in China during the sixth century B.C. The Egyptians invented a counting machine that used pebbles some time before Herodotus (about 450 B.C.) noted its use. The Greeks had a similar device, and in Rome writers tell of three types of calculating machines. Most of these devices were used to keep track of transactions by adding and subtracting. Multiplication was performed by repeating the adding phase. About 1633 a little-known German astronomer, Wilhelm Schickard (1592–1635), invented an automatic digital calculator that was commemorated on a German postage stamp in 1973. The invention of a calculating machine is more often ascribed to French philosopher Blaise Pascal (1623–1662), the Father of Calculus. Pascal's machine could only add and subtract, but it attracted widespread interest. In the 1670s Gottfried Leibniz introduced a machine that could do multiplication and division. Computers came along later when the eccentric Charles Babbage (1792–1871), sometimes called the world's first computer scientist, assisted by Lady Ada Lovelace invented the difference engine, which had programmable operations containing conditional branches. (See Haugeland, 1989, for details. A model of Babbage's machine can be seen at the Smithsonian Institute in Washington, D.C.)

Computers

The origin of modern computer science can be traced to the 1940s, when vacuum-tube computers such as UNIVAC and ENIAC were invented to speed lengthy and tedious mathematical calculations commonly used by the military, such as calculating the trajectories of artillery shells. The ENIAC (Electronic Numerical Integrator and Computer),

Charles Babbage (1792–1871). British mathematician and inventor who developed the concept of a mechanical computational device that could be programmed. He called it the "analytic engine."

J. Presper Eckert (foreground) and John Mauchley work on the vacuum tube computer, ENIAC, with U.S. Army and other personnel in 1946.

a highly secretive U.S. Army–sponsored project conducted at the University of Pennsylvania, had 17,468 vacuum tubes whose manufacturer guaranteed a service life of 25,000 hours, which meant, on average, that a tube would burn out about every 8 minutes! The behemoth calculating machine weighed 30 tons and drew 174 kilowatts of power. The project directors were John Mauchley and J. Presper Eckert. These early, simpleminded, inefficient giant machines gave way to smaller, more powerful, and complex systems that, in turn, were eventually replaced by the solid-state microelectronic computers in general use today.

Few dates in cognitive psychology are more important than 1956.[3] During the summer of that year, a group of ten scientists met on the campus of Dartmouth College to consider the possibilities of developing computer programs that would "behave" intelligently. Among those who attended this conference were John McCarthy, who later founded AI laboratories at MIT and Stanford University and is generally credited with christening the new science "AI"; Marvin Minsky, who became the director of the AI laboratory at MIT; Claude Shannon, who developed the modern model for a communication system at Bell Laboratories; Herbert Simon, who was to win the Nobel Prize in economics; and Allen Newell, who has carried out his important work in cognitive science and AI at Carnegie Mellon University. The conference was historically significant because the course AI was about to take was set, which directly influenced the way cognitive psychology developed.

Since the Dartmouth conference, AI has grown geometrically. AI, in some form or another, now touches the daily lives of most people in the world, occupies the concentrated effort of thousands of scientists, and is proliferating on college campuses. The diverse ends of AI research and practice cannot be reported in a single chapter, or a book, or even many books. However, we can, in this chapter, present a sample of the work in AI as it relates to cognitive psychology.

[3]During that year Bruner, Goodnow, and Austin published *A Study of Thinking,* Chomsky published "Three Models of the Description of Language," Miller published "The Magical Number Seven," and Newell and Simon completed "The Logic Theory Machine: A Complex Information-Processing System."

John McCarthy. Pioneered studies in artificial intelligence and designed LISP, a widely used AI language.

Computers and AI

The most common type of computer in use today is patterned after a design ("architecture," in computer argot) created by the Hungarian mathematician John von Neumann (1958), who emigrated to the United States in 1930. These computers are sometimes called *Johniacs* or serial processors, meaning that electrical impulses are processed in series, or in sequence. These chainlike sequences operate very rapidly, with each step requiring only nanoseconds, but a computer performing complicated tasks in a serial fashion (such as solving involved mathematical functions, or rearranging data or files) may require several minutes, hours, or even longer. All computer users have experienced the maddeningly "long" lag time required by personal computers to "think" or "digest" a problem. One basic reason serial computers of the von Neumann genus require so much time is that one operation must be completed before another is initiated. Serial processors solve problems bit by bit (or byte by byte), in a stepwise fashion.

Even in the beginning of the technology of computers, AI scientists (and science fiction writers) had grand dreams about thinking machines and robots. A seminal paper was written in the early 1940s by a Chicago psychiatrist, W. S. McCulloch, and his student, W. Pitts. In this paper they introduced a concept that was to have significant impact on computer scientists, including von Neumann and later PDPers. Based on the idea that the *mind* was defined as the workings of the brain, specifically the brain's basic units, neurons, they argued that neurons could be viewed as "logical devices," that "neural events and the relations among them can be treated by means of propositional logic." When neurons communicate with each other, they do so electrochemically. A

John von Neumann (1903–1957). Designed the computer architecture in common use.

tiny electrical current is passed along a cell's axon to the synapse, where a chemical neu-rotransmitter passes the impulse to other neurons. The process of neurotransmission is rule governed: firing of a neuron occurs only when the threshold is achieved, all neurons have thresholds, neurons fire only when the current is positive, a negative current will in-hibit a neuron from firing, and so on. Most importantly, each neuron seems to sum up all excitatory and inhibitory signals from its thousands of connections. Depending on its threshold, a neuron will fire or not; that is, it will be on or off.[4] (Neurons of this type are called **McCulloch-Pitts neurons.**) McCulloch and Pitts observed that this on or off neuron could be seen as a logic device. As is commonly known, computers function by means of on/off circuits. When thousands of these are coupled together in exponential series, the amount of processing power is awesome. Similarly, the basic unit of neural processing, the neuron and its connections, are capable of monumental powers of processing.

A short time after the paper by McCulloch and Pitts, von Neumann saw the connec-tion between the logical behavior of neurons as they interact and the way digital comput-ers go about their work. "It can easily be seen that these simplified neuron functions can be imitated by telegraph relays or by vacuum tubes." (Transistors had not been invented yet, or he probably would have mentioned them.) Von Neumann, who had already de-veloped the most useful computer architecture up to that point, suggested that it might be possible to design a computer that mimicked the human brain—not only in function but also in structure—where vacuum tubes, relays, connecting wires, and hardware replaced neurons, axons, synapses, and "wetware." Following von Neumann, F. Rosenblatt under-took the project of building a computer along these lines. His intent was to make a com-puter that could learn to classify shapes. The result was called a perceptron, and it crudely imitated the brain's organization (see Chapters 1 and 2). Rosenblatt's machine consisted of a three-level hierarchy. Each level was associated with a different function that generally emulated the sensory, associative, and motor pattern of humans. One fun-damental problem of early machines such as the perceptron was that they did not learn. They simply processed a narrow range of stimuli and made equally simple responses.

Humans are capable of learning because they have modifiable synapses. You'll re-call Hebb's rule (introduced in Chapter 2) about the strength between two neurons in-creasing when they are simultaneously activated. Could such a rule be built into the connections between surrogate neurons? Learning by such a machine might require that a resistor (a device that specifies the amount of electrical impulse leaving one transistor that will reach another) be wired into and programmed in an artificial brain. A resistor would act very much like a regulator, allowing some bits of information to be passed on while rejecting others. Perceptrons capable of "learning" (and *learning* is defined here as "the change in strength between units that simulate neurons") do so because they behave in a way similar to McCulloch-Pitts neurons and obey Hebb's theory. A com-puter so constructed might be shown a simple geometric shape, such as a circle, to clas-sify. If it responds by calling it a square, then it can be "taught" to respond correctly by increasing the resistance between certain units and lowering the resistance between others. If the response is correct, that is, if the perceptron calls a circle a circle, the val-ues are left alone. In this sense, perceptrons punish errors and ignore success. These early steps were important in designing machines capable of making generalizations

---

[4]This presents an exciting perspective to the neurally inspired connectionist model discussed in Chap-ter 1.

and learning, factors essential in the construction of a "thinking machine" that functions similarly to a human brain.

During the early stages of computer development, some fundamental opinions about the use and significance of these newfound contraptions also emerged. There were those who thought that if computers were programmed properly, that is, given the right rules and instructions, they could carry out any operations, including the effective mimicking of human thought. Others believed that for a machine to "think," it was necessary that a computer's hardware simulate a brain's "wetware." To achieve the latter would require that a computer be built with layers upon layers of interconnected electronic surrogate neurons whose organization and function would simulate a human brain.

So far we have failed to produce either a truly "thinking" machine or one whose "brain" appears much like a human brain. However, as sciences go, AI is still an infant. Each of the perspectives mentioned has its own problems. In the first case, most AI programs are damnably rigid in "thinking." When I ask you what is the square root of 73, you might say, "Well, it's at least 8 but not quite 9. About 8 and a half." A computer answers 8.5440037. . . . Rather than breed endless concatenations of digits, the human brain seems wonderfully designed to deal with chaos—seeing a familiar face in a crowd, driving on the Los Angeles freeways, understanding the deep meaning of a Chekhov drama, or feeling the sensuousness of silk as it caresses our skin. No computer can do that . . . yet. On the other hand, no human can spew out the answer to the square root problem in milliseconds, as any cheap handheld calculator can.

Just consider the Promethean task faced by those who aspire to wire a computer like a human brain! The brain has about 100 billion neurons, each of which connects with countless thousands of other neurons. That's a lot of soldering. Nevertheless, some people have attempted a small-scale computer model of the brain (see Rosenblatt, 1958) but, until recently (see the box entitled "Cognition in Everyday Life: The Silicon Chip"), have discouraged others from pursuing this pastime (see Minsky & Papert, 1968). Earlier (in 1954) Minsky had written his dissertation on neural nets and had even built one with 400 vacuum tubes, but he soon became disinfatuated with the project. This early work

Cognition in Everyday Life

The Silicon Chip

A silicon chip, which is said to behave much like a human brain cell, was developed by Caltech and Oxford University researchers Mahowald and Douglas. The device, called a silicon neuron, has a structure and process that mimic the workings of neurons in the cerebral cortex. The important aspect of the technology is the analog nature of the device as contrasted with the digital processing units used in most computers. When humans see a complex object, such as a person's face, they do not see digitalized data—a series of pixels—but rather subtly graded contours and continuously varying shades of gray. From these signals the eye and brain extract meaning from the light signals through an analog process.

While others discount the importance of this technological discovery on the basis that the brain has many types of neurons and this is only one example, the idea of a silicon chip that imitates even some important features of the human neuron presents an intriguing question for the future. How far can technology go in creating a brain?

did not produce "practical" results, while developing computer programs and hardware during the same time was the hottest game in town. Garage workshops expanded to megabuck factories, which built computer chips that could do things about which we could only dream.

The recent generation of computer/cognitive scientists is more sanguine regarding the simulation of neural functions by a machine. One of the recent changes in perceptrons was conceptual. Rather than thinking of a computer brain as an input-output device, scientists added a third layer, called a hidden layer. This hidden layer corresponds to the brain's interneurons, which are not concerned with input or output but with connecting impulses to other neurons. The model is compatible with connectionism, mentioned throughout this book.

Many of these issues deal with the problem of the architecture of computers and brains, a most important topic. However, computers still do not perform functions as humans do; computers and brains are not identical. In some ways computers do better than brains, but in some ways they do worse. This disparity is seen in many domains, as has been mentioned previously, but one particularly problematic area is the identification of three-dimensional objects. Our eyes, two-dimensional sensors, readily and accurately transmit signals that are interpreted as three-dimensional. Even with the sluggish "wetware" of the nervous system, the constant change in eye-object location, and size adjustments, our perceptual system works nearly perfectly. Computers do less well, even though the rate of transmission is millions of times faster than neurotransmission.

As has already been mentioned, one reason for the difference is that computers generally process information serially, **sequential** or **processing model,** while brains generally process information in parallel. Some AI scientists have begun to overcome the architectural difference between brains and computers for the purpose of overcoming this functional difference. One such scientist is W. Daniel Hillis, who has developed a "connection machine" (see Hillis, 1987), which solves problems by breaking them into smaller problems (reminiscent of the means-end analysis) and then processing them in parallel, a **parallel processing model.** These smaller problems, or chunks, are then distributed to separate areas of the computer's processing network. This is contrasted with the von Neumann class of computers, which has one central processor that processes information sequentially. In Hillis's connection machine, 65,536 (a prime number with base 2) processors work on a single problem simultaneously. Although each processor is even less powerful than the PC used in the preparation of this manuscript, when those more than 65,000 little chips are hooked up in tandem and work simultaneously, they can execute several billion instructions per second. It's an impressive machine, both conceptually and functionally. Yet, Hillis dreams of a machine with a billion processors functioning in parallel—just for the Hal of it.

AI and Human Cognition

Some of the fundamental questions of AI are:

- What kind of a thinking machine is the brain?
- How can human thinking be emulated by a machine?
- Can human thinking be surpassed by computers?
- Is pursuit of these issues worthwhile?

There are no easy answers to any of these questions, but those who subscribe to a neurally inspired parallel distributed processing model (and others) are hard at work trying to find solutions.

Brain.   The answer to the first question is beginning to take shape after a century of research in psychology, especially during the past several decades of research in cognition. It is hoped that the contents of this book contain a representative sample of the answer. What we have learned about our thinking machine, called the brain, is that it is fundamentally different from the von Neumann computers now in common use. Perhaps AI would be further along if computers resembled brains more closely. To clarify this matter, we have proposed the following comparative résumé:

Human Thinking—Computer.   The answer to the second question, at least within the connectionist camp, is that human thinking can best be emulated by modeling a machine after basic neurological structures.

Computer Superiority.   Some computer programs work far more effectively than human thinking; most, however, are at best clumsy counterfeits of the real thing. Computers can solve some problems, such as detailed mathematical ones, faster and more accurately than humans can. Other tasks, such as making generalizations and learning new patterns of activity, are done well by humans but not by computers.

Cognition in Everyday Life

The Beginnings of a Real $6 Million Man?

While American scientists of a generation ago tinkered with the notion that they could build a brainlike computer, in Japan one scientist, Aizawa, is building a brainlike computer with real nerve cells intermingled with electronic devices in an effort to fabricate a crude, semiartificial neural network. So far he has successfully combined cells with the semiconducting compound indium tin oxide and found that under very weak electrical stimulation organic cells respond with controlled growth (see figure shown here). It is too early to think of an artificial brain, but such devices might be useful as an interface between the nervous system and prostheses such as an artificial eye.

Worthwhile. Finally, the easy answer to whether we should pursue these issues is yes. We learn more about human thinking and machine thinking in the process. Others argue that the pursuit of AI is as foolish as tilting at windmills.

As shown in the table comparing von Neumann-type computers with brains, it is no wonder AI scientists have been frustrated, if not confused. They are working with the wrong kind of machine. It appears as though we are on the verge of a conceptual break-through—perhaps a paradigm shift—in AI, in which the first steps have already been taken to make computers more brainlike in terms of both their structure and their process. Neuronetwork systems, PDP models, and connectionism are attempting to discover the computational principles that govern networks of neurons in the human nervous system. They do this by what may seem to be a highly abstract means. Units may represent neurons, but units follow laws derived from neuron behavior. That is, a unit can be paired with other units, the association between them can be strengthened or weakened, they can achieve stable relations, and so on. (See Churchland, 1989, for further information.)

An important concept has also been proposed with regard to neuronetworks: they can also learn. That is, through a system of synapse-like weights, the infrastructure of the brain can change through experience (which may be externally or internally determined).

It is far too early to know how successful these efforts will be. It is not too early to know that the new way of looking at human cognition has enjoyed great enthusiasm among its proponents.[5] Even the casual student of cognitive psychology should be sensitized to this important contribution to psychology and be on the lookout for future developments.

Machines and Minds: The Imitation Game and the Chinese Room

There are few areas of cognitive psychology that have been the subject of more hot-headed arguments than the debate over the simulation of human thought by machines. On one side of the argument are AI zealots who believe not only that machines are capable of exactly replicating human cognition but also that advanced intellectual processes can be carried out only by machines. The logical extension of this argument is that computers should be directly involved in everyday human decision making. On the other side are those who consider AI to be an intellectually corrupt concept and believe people who put their faith in so-called thinking machines are materialistic idol worshipers. Human thinking is purely a human process that, even if partly synthesized by a machine, will never be duplicated by AI programs.

As a starting point, it is useful to consider the dichotomy proposed by John Searle (1980), a philosopher with the University of California at Berkeley. He describes two forms of AI: "weak" AI, which can be used as a tool in the investigation of human cognition, and "strong" AI, in which a properly programmed computer has a "mind" capable of understanding. "Weak" AI has few opponents; almost everyone acknowledges the importance of computers in the investigation of human cognition, and little more needs to be said about that issue here. "Strong" AI, which Searle refutes, has brought a storm

---

[5]For an interesting account of a type of neural network in the behavior of army ants as they navigate a tropical rain forest, see Franks (1989).

TABLE 16.1

	Silicon-Based Computers (von Neumann type)	Carbon-Based Brains (Humans)
Processing speed	In nanoseconds	In milliseconds to seconds
Type	Serial processor (mostly)	Parallel processor (mostly)
Storage capacity	Vast, for digitally coded information	Vast, for visual and linguistic information
Material	Silicon and electronic supply system (for example, transistors, switches, and electricity)	Neurons and organic supply system (for example, capillaries and blood)
Cooperation	Absolutely obedient (does exactly what it is told)	Generally cooperative, but if pressed is likely to rebel (has a mind of its own)
Learning capacity	Simpleminded, rule governed	Conceptual
Best feature	Can process an immense amount of data in a short period of time without complaint	Can make judgments, inferences, and generalizations easily
	Cost efficient, rule governed, easy to maintain, and predictable	Ambulatory; has language, speech, vision, and emotions
Worst feature	Does not self-learn easily; has difficulty with complex human cognitive tasks such as language understanding and production; is large and requires power inhibiting its mobility.	Has limited capacity for information processing and storage; is forgetful; is expensive to maintain requiring food, drink, sleep, oxygen, moderate temperature in addition to a whole list of biopsychological needs, e.g., love, belongingness, sex, rock-and-roll music, and game playing

of protest. We extend this argument in the section entitled "The Chinese Room," but first let's consider one of the original mind versus machine problems proposed by Alan Turing,[6] a British mathematician.

[6]See Hofstadter's *Metamagical Themas: Questions for the Essence of Mind and Pattern* (1985) for an engaging account of Turing's life and a discussion of other AI topics. Also *Alan Turing: The Enigma* by Andrew Hodges is fascinating reading.

The Imitation Game, or the Turing Test

Turing (1950) proposed a task that involved communication between a human, who asked questions, and an unknown-language-using being. Simply stated, the task of the human was to decide whether the being was indistinguishable from a human. It is to Turing's credit that the use of the imitation game, which later became commonly known as the **Turing test**, was in itself a very subtle deception that, while giving AI specialists something concrete to work on, diverted attention from the philosophic mind—an issue that has been a major hang-up in scientific and psychological history. Instead of addressing the philosophic issue directly (as Turing might have done had he asked, "Is cognition a function of material process, and if so, can those functions originate from an inorganic machine?" or "What is the solution to the mind–body problem?"), he chose a far more clever way to frame the question by basing it in operationalism. Since there remains some confusion in the literature about the real nature of the test Turing proposed, it is printed in detail here.

> The . . . problem can be described in terms of a game which we call the "imitation game." It is played with three people, a man (A), a woman (B), and an interrogator (C) who may be of either sex. The interrogator stays in a room apart from the other two. The object of the game for the interrogator is to determine which of the other two is the man and which is the woman. He knows them by labels X and Y, and at the end of the game he says either "X is A and Y is B" or "X is B and Y is A." The interrogator is allowed to put questions to A and B thus:
>
> C: Will X please tell me the length of his or her hair?
>
> Now suppose X is actually A, then A must answer. It is A's object in the game to . . . cause C to make the wrong identification. His answer might therefore be: "My hair is shingled, and the longest strands are about nine inches long."
>
> In order that tones of voice may not help the interrogator the answers should be written, or, better still, typewritten. The ideal arrangement is to have a teleprinter communicating between the two rooms. Alternatively the question and answers can be repeated by an intermediary. The object of the game for the third player (B) is to help the interrogator. The best strategy for her is probably to give truthful answers. She can add such things as "I am the woman, don't listen to him!" to her answers, but it will avail nothing as the man can make similar remarks.
>
> We now ask the question, "What will happen when a machine takes the part of A in this game?" Will the interrogator decide wrongly as often when the game is played like this as he does when the game is played between a man and a woman? These questions replace our original, "Can machines think?" (p. 434)

It is obvious that the value of certain questions put to X and Y depends on whatever fashion is current. For example, hair length and style as a basis of discrimination would be likely to lead to a high error rate in the 1970s. Nevertheless, the important point of Turing's puzzle for AI and language scientists is that, in order for a computer to fool us into thinking that it is a human, it must be able to understand and generate a response that effectively mimics one important form of cognition.

The Chinese Room

To illustrate the untenable position of the "strong" AI view, Searle offers the following puzzle: Suppose someone is confined to a room with a large collection of Chinese writings. The person knows no Chinese and may not be able to discriminate between Chinese calligraphs and other scripts. From outside the room the person is given another set of Chinese characters along with a set of rules for collating the first set of characters with the second. The rules will only let the person relate one set of symbols with another set of symbols and are in plain English. With the relational rules, the person in the **Chinese room** is able to give meaningful answers to questions about the content of the writings, even though the person is essentially ignorant of the language. After a while the person is so well practiced that questions can be answered both in English (the person's native language) and in Chinese (which the person does not know but is able to give responses in that language based on rules). The output is so good that it is "absolutely indistinguishable from that of native Chinese speakers" (Searle, 1980). The person in the Chinese room is a simple instantiation of a computer program: data in—data out. Up to this point few AI "grunts" would have their feathers ruffled, but then Searle takes the argument one step further. Being able to perform functions, such as translation by complex rules, does not mean that the thing performing the functions understands the meaning of the output. Human minds have *intentionality* (see Searle, 1983), which, according to the author, is defined as "the property of mental states and events by which the mind is directed at objects and states of affairs in the world." These mental

Cognition in Everyday Life

Robbie the Surgeon

The question of indistinguishability of functions in another arena works differently. For example, suppose two surgeons work at a hospital. One surgeon is a graduate of a renowned medical school and is reputed to be one of the best surgeons in the world. The other graduated from an undistinguished medical school and is regarded as a poor surgeon. One day an emergency operation is required, and the first physician is indisposed, so the second physician performs the operation unbeknownst to the patient, who is unconscious. The patient is not told which physician performed the operation and is satisfied that the procedure was successful. Furthermore, other physicians are convinced that the operation was performed by the first surgeon. In this limited example, we could conclude the test of indistinguishability had been passed. However, if you were the patient and learned that the operation had actually been performed by a robot, what would you conclude about the functional properties of the robot vis-à-vis the functional properties of a surgeon? Would you agree that they were the same? Why? Why not? Answers to these questions are hard to come by, but people who have strong opinions about the issues are not. One is Searle, who has turned the Turing test inside out.

states include beliefs, fears, desires, and intentions. No matter how indistinguishable counterfeit thinking is from real human thinking, the two are not the same because of the intentions of the human thinker and because of the physical differences of the thinkers. One is produced organically; the other, electronically.

The Chinese Room—Refutation

Computer scientists objected immediately to Searle's conundrum (see Boden, 1989). First, on the level of semantics; it was argued that the terms *intentionality, understanding,* and *thinking* are used without clear operational referents. The second objection focused on the level of the example. If the person in the Chinese room performed the functions described, the person (or the system) would indeed achieve at least some level of understanding. Third, the argument was dismissed on the basis of a reductio ad absurdum; that is, if carried to its logical conclusion, it would be possible to create a robot identical in every detail to a thinking person, and yet one would be capable of understanding and intentionality and the other not. Finally, for some AI scientists *understanding* and *intentionality* seemed to be related to specific material properties that caused them. Pylyshyn (1980) satirically muses that perhaps intentionality is a substance secreted by the human brain, and then poses his own riddle:

> If more and more of the cells in your brain were to be replaced by integrated circuit chips, programmed in such a way as to keep the input-output function of each unit identical to that of the unit being replaced, you would in all likelihood just keep right on speaking exactly as you are doing now except that you would eventually stop meaning anything by it. What we outside observers might take to be words would become for you just certain noises that circuits caused you to make. (p. 442)

The debate is far from over, and its value to some may be in its philosophic profundity. To me, however, the argument is not likely to be resolved (indeed, it is probably irresolvable!). In addition, both camps have hardened their positions and seem to be advancing articles of faith rather than reason. The importance of discussing the debate in a book like this is twofold. First, it causes the reader to think deeply about the issue of what is human about human cognition. Second, it raises the question of the limits to which AI can imitate human intelligence. The fact that both the Turing test and the Chinese-room problem have excited passions on both sides is a reflection of the intense concern of contemporary philosophers and AI scientists regarding the electronic genie that has been let out of the bottle recently.

In the next section some specific computer capacities are reviewed. The development of these specific functions approximates the flow of information in an information-processing model from perception, to pattern recognition, and to higher forms of cognition.

Perception and AI

Human perception is initiated by external signals of light, sound, molecular composition, and pressure. These signals are detected by our sensory system and transduced (converted to neural energy) into messages the brain can understand. The amount of information available to us through our senses is enormous; our visual system alone can transmit 4.3 × 10^6 bits of information *per second* to the brain) Feigenbaum (1967) suggested that some peripheral device, sometimes called a peripheral memory system, operates like a sensory buffer to prevent the brain from being overwhelmed by the torrent of information flowing into it.

How might a machine be made to mimic this perceptual mechanism? A logical step is to develop some sensing capacity. One such approach can be seen in the work done on computer recognition systems.[7]

Line Analysis

(One way computers can be taught to recognize geometric forms by analyzing local features of an object uses the fact that complex geometric forms are composed of simpler ones) The program uses a number of small templates that are systematically passed over each object in search of a match. An example of a template and a geometric object to be identified is shown in Figure 16.1. The template is made up of two kinds of sensors—positive and negative, present and absent—one to a cell, or subdivision, of the template. The one shown has only six cells—three minus and three plus—and, because of the arrangement of these components (all minus elements at the left), it is of a kind likely to be suitable for identifying the left edge of an object. Positioning the template with its midline over the left edge of the cube would result in a perfect match. The corner match is poor, and there is no match on the bottom edge, where plus and minus sensors cancel out each other. Although this heuristic is more solidly oriented toward what a machine can do, it is not at odds with findings from studies of animal and human perception. Earlier in this book (see Chapter 4), we learned that physiological psychologists have successfully isolated line detectors in the cortical cells of cats, and it seems likely, although it has not been completely validated, that humans also have generalized edge detectors.

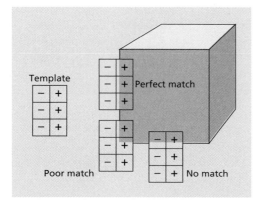

FIGURE 16.1

Finding a left edge by means of a six-cell template. The signs + and – represent cells that respond to the conditions "present" or "absent," respectively.

[7]Much of the early research of this kind was motivated by practical problems (for example, how to create a machine that could read a numerical code on a check) and, as such, only weakly addresses the human analog issue of AI; it is included here to illustrate some of the capacities of "perception" by existing computers.

One difficulty with the system just described is that a great number of templates are needed for simple pattern recognition (for example, a right-edge detector, a left-edge detector, and so on). An additional problem is the "goodness" of the stimulus; most geometric forms (especially those in the real world) have sharp *and* fuzzy edges, or bright *and* dull edges. Pattern recognition by line identification can be greatly simplified if the form to be recognized can first be converted into a line-only image, with templates then used to find the orientation of the lines.

Pattern Recognition

Pattern recognition systems have, for the most part, dealt with visual material. The general format of the perceptual hardware of these systems has been a raster, or matrix, of photoelectric cells (which respond to light energy). The photoelectric cells usually have only two states—on or off (or "white" or "black"). Consider the elementary task of identifying a number. Figure 16.2 shows how digits could be "transduced" into a binary code—*0* for "off" or "black," and *1* for "on" or "white." The computer "reads" each number (that is, the photoelectric cells—one for each square of the grid superimposed on the number—"senses" the light areas, which are the ones not occupied by the number) on the basis of how close the digital code matches a template stored in the memory of the computer. It works very well if the figures are uniform, evenly positioned, and not degraded, and such devices are in wide use in industry and the U.S. Postal Service. However, when it comes to reading a hand-addressed letter to your Aunt Iola, optical scanning devices have some difficulty. It does appear, though, that means are rapidly being developed to "read" even handwriting.

Attempting to identify letters and words with the use of AI not only is a practical problem but also has meaning for those scientists who are interested in the process of human information analysis. Much of the current knowledge of the way we humans

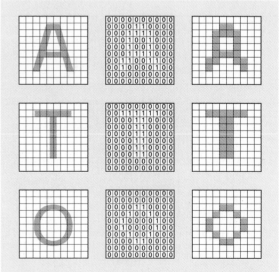

FIGURE 16.2

Representation in binary code (middle column) of letters at far left. 0s indicate "off" or "black"; 1s, "on" or "white." The last column shows letters as they might appear for reading by a scanner.

identify a letter and word is discussed in Chapter 12. This information is helpful in designing a computer program that mimics the process. A seminal report on this topic, which has served as a guide to subsequent research, was one from Selfridge and Neisser (1963). The general procedure for the "perception" of a letter, just described, would require a huge computer memory (to store a template of each novel form of each letter), otherwise many valid forms of letters would go undetected.

The basic logic espoused by Selfridge and Neisser a long time ago has been incorporated into recent letter and word reading machines. These computers "read" text through a series of subroutines, each of which specializes in one part of the task of reading, say, a letter. Such analysis is somewhat reminiscent of the means-end problem solver discussed in Chapters 14 and 15 on thinking. One way a letter reading program might work is illustrated in Figure 16.3. It shows the way the letter *R* is processed through a series of stages, each quite simple, until a match is made on the basis of elimination of alternatives.

The matter of letter perception has also been considered in some detail by the PDPers. A general criticism of AI programs in the area of letter identification and form perception is that there is no workable mechanism for attention. A machine "sees" a form, be it a letter or geometric configuration, as a whole pattern and, unlike a human observer, finds it difficult to focus on critical features. One way the PDP model handles this difficult problem is to posit two types of feature detectors, one called a retinocentric feature unit and the other a canonic feature unit. In the retinocentric system visual stimuli are recorded in their "raw" form, much as an impression might fall on the retina. Canonic features are those that conform to the standard way information is presented, for example, just as we expect to see the letter *A* as it is shown here. In one system Hinton (1981) described a method for mapping retinocentric feature patterns onto canonical patterns. The details of this idea are too extensive to be presented here except to note

The letter *R* processed through a series of stages of identification. At each stage, a program recognizes particular attributes of the character, such as diagonal lines, indentations, and so on.

that this important issue is under active investigation by those interested in PDP models. Interested students are directed to the original sources.

[Older, and much more simpleminded, AI alphanumeric recognition systems were based on a template concept. A pattern of letters and numbers was stored in a computer's memory. When the computer "sees" a digit or letter, it "reads" it by matching the pattern, say *A*, with the mold of *A*. If a match is found, the letter is correctly identified. Even the sequential and parallel search methods described earlier were clearly brainless. [The newer, neurally based computer models are actually capable of "learning" patterns. Some of these computer implementations can learn patterns, store them, and recognize them later. One program, called **DYSTAL** (*DYnamically STable Associative Learning*) successfully acquires alphabetic letters and letter sequences and, perhaps most remarkably, recognizes them even when only parts of the patterns are presented (see Figure 16.4).]

FIGURE 16.4

Pattern recognition by Alkon's artificial network. Operates according to many of the same rules demonstrated by biological systems. When a network is trained to recognize a pattern, such as the lowercase *a* shown here at left, the receiving sites participating in the recognition are given more "weight" than those that are not participating—that is, their excitability is enhanced. Here synaptic weight is represented by the elevation of the elements in the layers. Enhancement helps to link together the neurons involved in a recollection when only a piece of a pattern is presented. (Thomas P. Vogl of the Environmental Research Institute of Michigan helped to design this drawing.)

From Alkon (1989). Reprinted by permission of Thomas C. Moore.

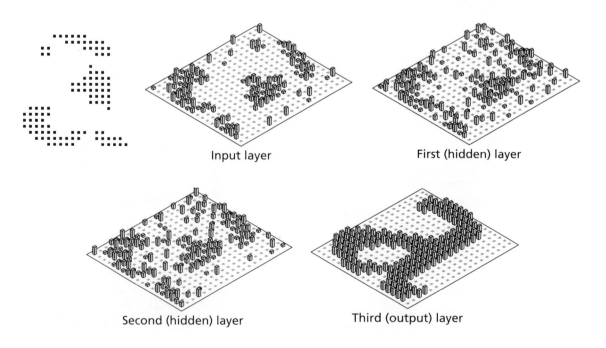

Input layer   First (hidden) layer

Second (hidden) layer   Third (output) layer

(DYSTAL does this, according to Alkon, much as we recognize a famous face suggested by the few lines of a cartoon) The system "learned" the pattern in the sense that there was no prewired connection between the input and output. A connection was developed, however, through greater weights being assigned to units (sites) that participate in the recognition process.

Another innovative feature of the system is that it is able to accommodate a large number of elements without requiring a huge amount of computer power. In many other network systems, each unit is connected with every other unit, so when the number of units is increased, the number of interactions increases exponentially. Thus, a system that has even a hundred units would require considerable processing time, and a network of that dimension would scarcely resemble a brain. "In DYSTAL, however, the weights of the connections are not compared with a fixed value: rather they arrive at a dynamic equilibrium in which the increases and decreases of weight over a set of pattern presentations are equal and no net weight change takes place" (Alkon, 1989). The system is comparable to human long-term memory in that when permanent memories are formed they are, for the most part, irreversible. Once these stable patterns are acquired, they require less computer power than do other, nonbiological networks.

The recognition of more complex forms follows the same logic as the recognition of simple forms, but it generally requires more complex processors. That topic is considered next.

Recognition of Complex Forms

Let's consider one example of a different kind of pattern recognition: the identification of a triangle. Figure 16.5 shows several triangles, all of which you will immediately recognize and categorize as such. If the prototype of triangularity stored in a computer program corresponded to the "good" triangle template (A), then triangles in B and C, if properly rotated and adjusted for size, could be easily recognized. Triangles in D and E, however, are problematic, especially those in E, which are identifiable mainly as the result of a "good gestalt," rather than on the basis of their being composed of three straight lines.

Our capacity to recognize immediately each of these forms as triangles is a function of our vast experience with other triangular objects; this abstract notion of *triangularity* is broad enough to allow us to include these triangles we have never seen in the category of triangles. Can a computer learn that concept? Probably, but the search mechanism needs to be more sophisticated than the single match operation such as that of machines that read numbers on bank checks. Instead, a search program that included the features of a triangle would have to be considered. Thus such features, or attributes, as angles, lines, shape, number of objects, and so on would have to be stored in the computer's memory, much as our own memory contains a catalog of these attributes of a triangle.

A practical application of computer recognition of complex forms is in the area of facial recognition. Suppose your face has unique features, much as your fingerprints do. A computer system that could scan your face and find a perfect match with your identity might be a great aid to police departments. It also might be useful for check identification and even plant and office security. Imagine going to work in some security installation and being greeted every morning by a computer that asks, "Please place your face where I can see it" and, after scanning it and opening the door says, "Have a nice day, Ms. Juel, you have a call from W. M. Beach . . . and, by the way, happy birthday." While this

"Good" (*A–D*) and problematic (*E*) triangles. The former differ only in size, orientation, and relationship of their sides; the latter have no conventional straight-line sides but remain recognizable as triangles.

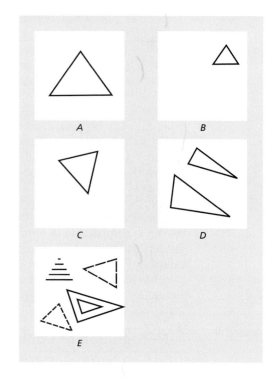

threatens yet another intrusion into our private lives, it is likely that we will be living with such devices sooner than later.

The matter of facial identification has been undertaken by computer scientists such as Thomas Poggio and Roberto Brunelli at MIT. The gist of the program is that salient features, such as the width of the nose, the distance between the eyes and chin, and so on, are extracted from faces and analyzed mathematically. Sixteen features have been identified (see Figure 16.6).

If faces were always the same, a simple template matching model might suffice; however, our faces are never the same. Therefore, the program must find a close match between your face today and your face of last week and yet not be too lenient to allow in an impersonator. The program does this through geometric checks between angles of features and promises to be much more reliable than facial identification by humans. Such a device could help solve some of the photographic mysteries that crop up from time to time, such as the recent question posed by the discovery of a very early photograph of someone who may or may not be Abraham Lincoln. This early nineteenth-century photograph of a young man looks like Lincoln, but is it? Computer analysis of facial features may answer the question.

From our discussion of object recognition (see Chapter 4) we know that human pattern perception is not simply a matter of seeing an object and then fitting that impression into a cerebral template (as computer matching of vertical bar codes is matched to corresponding patterns) but is likely to be built up of previously retained features which, when blended together form a prototype. New, or less familiar, stimuli take

FIGURE 16.6

Face matching. To match this face with a face in the computer's memory, sixteen key features such as eye, nose, and chin measurements are gathered and used in a formula for resemblance. The formula is based on a measurement of Euclidean distance in a sixteen-dimensional space. This work is being done at MIT by R. Brunelli and T. Poggio.

Reprinted with permission.

Could this be Abraham Lincoln?

longer to recognize than old, or familiar, patterns because there are fewer matches between the pattern and memory. Computers do not have such limited capacity—there seems to be no practical limit to the storage capacity of computers—and, therefore, are frequently programmed to use massive storage and search mechanisms in trying to match sensation with memory. In "real life" we recognize people, places, and even words with little effort not because each time we see these things we store that impression separately, but because we store the abstraction associated with a class of stimuli. Thus, when you recognize your own bedroom, your pillow, and your shoes it is because the brain has stored image "ideals" not image "snapshots."

Sinha and Poggio (1996) demonstrated the strength of head shape on recognition, whereas computers rely on details of features as well as spatial configuration. We know each other because we have had months or years of experience with someone. These facial characteristics are stored in memory and, when we see the whole person in which all of the features of his or her prototype face are present, we immediately recognize the person. The process is not unlike the one described experimentally by Solso and McCarthy with their prototype faces (see Chapter 4). In the Sinha and Poggio experiment they presented the faces shown in Figure 16.7. On first glance the famous pair looks like former President Bill Clinton and Vice President Al Gore, but in actuality, the face on the fellow in the background is made up of the salient features of President Clinton—his eyes, nose, and mouth—superimposed on Gore's physique—his hair, ears, and body. You probably were initially fooled by this illusion because you were "set up" to believe the people were a "pair" not a chimera. Even the stance each occupies biased your view and then you caught a glimpse of Gore's hair, his body, his posture, and the decision was quickly made. In humans, then, face recognition is strongly influenced by past perception which, in the case of a Gore finder, is ineffectual. Sinha and Poggio (2002) replicated this illusion with Dick Cheney and George W. Bush, demonstrating that the effect is robust and nonpartisan! The line of research carried out by Poggio and his colleagues is twofold: On the one hand it is possible to design programs which recognize objects and faces better than humans do (and such devices have utility in security scanning operations) and on the other hand it is possible to incorporate a learning program so that computers may through trial and error learn to recognize objects and faces much like humans do.

Systems that perform like human experts are called **expert systems.** Basically, an expert system is an artificial specialist that solves problems in the area of its specialty. Expert systems have been designed to solve problems in medicine, law, aerodynamics, chess, and a myriad of routine chores that generally bore humans or, in some cases, may be too difficult for humans to solve (see the just discussed topic of facial identification). These systems follow rules well. They can "think" about one issue only. An expert system in medicine may not know a tort from a hole in the ground, but it can make a reasonably accurate diagnosis of a 13-year-old girl who has a high fever, abdominal pain, and an abnormal concentration of white corpuscles. One such program, wryly called Puff, is an expert system designed to diagnose lung disorders, such as lung can-

FIGURE 16.7

Can you quickly identify this famous pair? Are you sure? See text for explanation.

cer, and boasts a hit rate of about 89 percent—close to the hit rate of experienced physicians. These systems have been especially popular with industry, with the military, and in space exploration. They are pretty good at the job they are designed to do. Furthermore, they do not go on strike and demand more money, don't mind getting blown to smithereens, do not require life-support, and are loved by nerds.

Language and AI

Psychologists generally consider language a prime manifestation of underlying cognitive processes. Language, more than any other category of human response variables, reflects thought, perception, memory, problem solving, intelligence, and learning. Furthermore, because of its importance to basic psychological principles, it is of major interest to AI scientists.

The capacity for language and involved problem solving of Arthur C. Clark's fictional computer Hal was envisioned by the author to take a very complete form, as in this exchange between Dave (the human) and Hal:

> "I want to do this myself, Hal," he said. "Please give me control."
> "Look, Dave, you've got a lot of things to do. I suggest you leave this to me."
> "Hal, switch to manual hibernation control."
> "I can tell from your voice harmonics, Dave, that you're badly upset. Why don't you take a stress pill and get some rest?"
> "Hal, *I* am in command of this ship. I order you to release the manual hibernation control."
> "I'm sorry, Dave, but in accordance with special sub-routine C1435-dash-4, quote, When the crew are dead or incapacitated, the onboard computer must assume control, unquote. I must, therefore, overrule your authority, since you are not in any condition to exercise it intelligently."

How close have we come to this fiction in the AI laboratory?

Shown in Figure 16.8 is an illustration of Jonathan Swift's "thinking machine" from *Gulliver's Travels*. Swift suggested acerbically that books and other literature could be written by turning the appropriate handles. Some "modern writing programs" have produced a form of science fiction that passes as fair literature. See *Omni* magazine for examples.

ELIZA, PARRY, and NETtalk

Enthusiastic early players at AI quickly embraced the challenge proposed by the Turing task and wrote programs designed to respond to real language queries in a way that were indistinguishable from human responses. Given the perspective of hindsight, some of these programs seem a bit klutzy now, but science often develops that way.

ELIZA. One of the first conversational computer programs, **ELIZA**,[8] was written by Joseph Weizenbaum (1966). Several revisions of ELIZA have appeared since its original

---

[8]The pupil named for the character in George Bernard Shaw's *Pygmalion* and its musical version, *My Fair Lady.*

Swift's Thinking Machine.

conception. In one specific program, called DOCTOR, ELIZA takes a role similar to that of a psychiatrist. In the following example, ELIZA's part is in capital letters:

Men are all alike.

IN WHAT WAY

They're always bugging us about something or other.

CAN YOU THINK OF A SPECIFIC EXAMPLE

Well, my boyfriend made me come here.

YOUR BOYFRIEND MADE YOU COME HERE

He says I'm depressed much of the time.

I AM SORRY TO HEAR YOU ARE DEPRESSED

It's true, I am unhappy.

DO YOU THINK COMING HERE WILL HELP YOU NOT TO BE UNHAPPY

I need some help, that much seems certain.

That conversation, one might argue, could easily have come from an interview between a human psychiatrist and patient. However, let us examine the transcript critically. The computer's responses tend to be stereotyped. For example, it is programmed to respond to certain key words with a response that is only a transformation of the original sentence. Thus, when the "patient" says the keyword "I'm," ELIZA responds with a locution such as "I am sorry to hear you are. . . ." If no key words are found, the computer responds with a content-free remark, or in some instances, an earlier transformation. The human capacity for knowledge about feelings, tendencies, group dynamics, and so on figures into what, for lack of a better word, we call understanding. ELIZA lacks it.

PARRY. What kind of conversation might result if the roles were reversed—that is, if a psychiatrist talked to a computerized simulation of a patient? Colby and his colleagues (1972) simulated such a patient, calling the program **PARRY,** since it simulated a paranoid patient. They selected a paranoid subject because some theoretical notion about the system and process of paranoia existed, the differences between psychotic responses and normal responses were great, and they could use expert judges to validate the distinguishability of computer simulation responses and human responses. Colby and his fellow researchers subjected the computer to a Turing test, asking a group of psychiatrists to interview PARRY by means of teletyped messages. The judges (psychiatrists) were asked to estimate the degree of paranoia of the total responses.

Interview A

Dr. IS THERE ANYTHING ABOUT PEOPLE IN PARTICULAR?

Pt. CERTAIN PERSONS

Comments by Judge

An interesting clue. We'll have to find out what he thinks about these people.

Dr. WHO ARE THE CERTAIN PERSONS AND WHAT IS IT THEY DO?

Pt. DO YOU KNOW HOW THE UNDERWORLD OPERATES?

Bringing up the underworld suggests a delusional system. We don't know whether he is being worked against or whether the underworld is on his side.

Dr. HOW DO YOU MEAN?

Pt. SHOULDN'T I BE?

This question didn't work too well.

Dr. WHY DID YOU ASK ABOUT THE UNDERWORLD?

Pt. WHAT INFORMATION DO YOU HAVE ON THE UNDERWORLD?

This is a kind of evasiveness about my evasiveness. Common with paranoia in my experience. Pretty characteristic.

Dr. I DON'T KNOW ABOUT THE UNDERWORLD BUT WHEN YOU MENTIONED THE UNDERWORLD I THOUGHT YOU MUST HAVE HAD SOME CONTACT WITH IT AND THAT'S WHAT I WOULD LIKE TO KNOW MORE ABOUT.

Pt. TRY TO AVOID THE UNDERWORLD.

This definitely feels paranoid. It has that feeling I associate with twisting. Avoiding answering directly or going into detail. Being suspicious of my questioning. I'm already involved in the patient's delusional system.

The results indicated indistinguishability between the model and the patient in a very specialized setting. Of course, it may be correctly argued that the conditions of the experiment were contrived, that actual diagnosis of paranoia involves extensive face-to-face interviews, and that, had the judges known the real nature of the task, their interviews would have been different. Although Colby and his colleagues successfully programmed a computer to respond in a way that a paranoid patient might and that program passed a form of the Turing test, it is vary far from a complete model of language production and understanding.

NETtalk. A much different type of program, based on a neural net, is called **NETtalk,** developed by Sejnowski then at Harvard Medical School and Rosenberg of Princeton (see Heppenheimer, 1988; Sejnowski & Rosenberg, 1987). In this program, NETtalk reads letters and pronounces them aloud (see Figure 16.9). The neural net simulation model consists of several hundred units ("neurons") and thousands of connections. NETtalk "reads aloud" by converting letters into phonemes, the elementary unit of language sounds.

FIGURE 16.9

NETtalk reads aloud. It translates letters into phonemes. Each letter unit sends signals through weighted connections to all the "hidden" units; if the total signal reaching a hidden unit exceeds a certain threshold, the unit fires, sending signals to the phoneme units. The output is the phoneme that receives the strongest total signal. When a "teacher" tells NETtalk that it has made a mistake—here it has just read *m* instead of *n*—it corrects the error by adjusting all the weights according to a specific learning algorithm.

From Heppenheimer (1988).

Terry Sejnowski. His neural nets contained a hidden layer that corresponds to interneurons.

(This system, like others we have encountered, has three layers: an input layer, in which each unit corresponds to a letter; an output layer, in which units represent the fifty-five phonemes of English; and a hidden unit layer, in which each of the units has a weighted connection to every input and output unit. NETtalk reads by considering each letter one by one, and by scanning three letters on either side for contextual information.) Thus, the *e* in *net, neglect,* and *red* can be assigned different sounds. Each time NETtalk reads a word, it compares its pronunciation with the correct pronunciation provided by humans and then adjusts its weights to correct any errors.

After a few trials NETtalk makes noticeable improvement. Sejnowski reports:

> We left it to run overnight. At first it gave a continuous stream of babble. It was just guessing; it had not learned to associate phonemes with the letters. As the run continued, it began to recognize consonants and vowels. Then it discovered there were spaces between the words. Now its stream of sound broke up into short bursts, separated by these spaces. At the end of the night it was reading quite understandably, correctly pronouncing some ninety-two percent of the letters. (quoted in Heppenheimer, 1988, p. 74)

The practical application of these systems is obvious; what may be less obvious, but in the long run more significant, is the conceptual breakthrough such neurally inspired models present.

As Sejnowski and others recognize, context is of great importance in human and machine discourse. We will now consider another important problem, the issue of meaning and AI.

Meaning and AI

Despite the fact that some of the computer's conversations are good enough to fool some of the people some of the time, they do not fail because of a lack of memory for words, which is nearly limitless; or in their ability to produce meaningful sentences, which is extensive; or in their facility in pronouncing letters, which is acceptable. They fail in their lack of understanding of what language is all about.

In the early stages of AI, it was thought that computers would be of great assistance in language translation. Simply load the memory bank of the computer with equivalent words in two languages (for example, the English-Norwegian equivalents are: necklace = *halsbånd,* cloth = *klœr,* pocketbook = *lommebok,* pink = *lyserød,* and so on); feed in one language and out comes the other. However, even when a one-to-one translation is made within the context of syntactic information, the results are sometimes bizarre. In one example (probably apocryphal), the biblical passage "The spirit is willing, but the flesh is weak" was translated into Russian, then back to English; it came out: "The wine was agreeable but the meat was spoiled."

Experience with these primitive translation programs and developments in psycholinguistics changed our conceptualization of language. In the previous example, although the Russian and English words were equivalent and the syntax (in both languages) correct, the *meaning* of the two sentences was not the same. Our natural language operates within the constraint of a variety of rules that determine the sequence of grammatic components *and* the meaning of the total sequence. These have a complex relationship that is beginning to yield to analysis. Computer analysis of natural language processes has taken the form of designing systems that "understand" the language. Some rather sophisticated "understanding" programs based on the conceptual base of the language have been developed. Built into these systems is the capability to analyze both the context of the discourse and the meaning of the words and, in some cases, "world knowledge" (Winograd). A syntax analyzer determines the most likely parsing and interpretation of a sentence.

The first language systems were limited in their ability to mimic human conversation because of restricted world knowledge and inferential ability. When humans converse, what is *not* said is as important as what is said, insofar as effective communication is concerned. Intelligent human performance is characterized by all types of inferences, not only in language processing but also in other activities such as visual perception. We need not see an entire partially occluded figure to infer that the whole figure exists. Even fractional and secondary cues are enough to trigger a whole series of reactions. For example, if I am walking through a forest known to contain poisonous snakes, the sound of rustling leaves is enough of a cue to make me stop dead in my tracks.

Yet another area of understanding in AI research that has received attention is the concept of "beliefs." Consider the following example:

I was out until 2:00 A.M. yesterday.
Boy, did my wife give it to me.

It is fair to conclude that most people know that what the wife gave to her husband was not affection. Never mind that the inference may be totally wrong. (For example, the husband may have been working in his laboratory and just discovered a cure for cancer that would bring fame and fortune to his family, or the husband may have come home too early!) We are talking about what most people understand from this little story and most computer programs do not. A program that would understand this story would need not only a capacious memory of idioms (how else would it understand "give it to me") but also some understanding of the comings and goings of husbands and their wives' beliefs and attitudes about such mien.

Continuous Speech Recognition (CSR)

Continuous speech recognition (CSR) systems are programs which recognize and record natural speech. On the surface, CSR seems undemanding. After all, most humans and a few animals recognize and record some type of speech. Yet, the task is devilishly intricate for the reasons mentioned earlier. Consider just the problem posed by homophones—words that sound alike but have different meaning, such as *arm*, the limb hanging from your torso, and *arm*, what you do to protect yourself from a midnight intruder. In the sentence, "Jeff armed himself in the event of an emergency," the word *armed* means Jeff got outfitted with some sort of weapon. However, if you knew Jeff and knew that he lost his arms in a tragic accident and had a set of artificial ones he put on in case of an emergency, such as a fire, you would know that *armed* means he put on his limbs. How might a CSR devise handle that speech pattern? Most programs are designed to function on the basis of statistical probability and limited syntactic context and, thus, would misinterpret the intention of the sentence. Gradually, however, more and more sophisticated programs are being developed that give context and include "world knowledge."

Research activities on the cutting edge of CSR are translation programs mentioned above. These newer programs do not simply do a "brute search and match" translation but are capable of translating continuous, comprehensive vocabulary speech recognition, language translation, and speech synthesis with a high degree of accuracy. This means, that someone may speak in English, for example, into a "telephone" (or microphone connected to a computer); the English speech is translated into visual text; the text is translated into another language, say French; a second language speech is synthesized; and the output is a spoken version of the translated message. This wonderfully practical program is already in the experimental stage (see Kurzweil 1999), and a commercial product is expected to be on the market in the early part of this decade.

Language Understanding Program

As NETtalk and CSR programs engage world knowledge in reacting reasonably with humans, so too have other programs incorporated some forms of human understanding in their systems. Among the best known and most controversial is a language understanding program developed at Yale by Roger Schank. The direction of Schank's research was guided by several goals, which included the development of a program that would be able to understand written text, summarize the essential parts of such text, translate it into another language, and answer questions about the meaning of written material. Schank and his colleagues soon discovered that people understand a great deal more than just the raw words of natural language expression. Schank illustrates this issue in the following story: "John went to a restaurant. He ordered a sandwich. The waiter brought it quickly, so he left a large tip." Did John eat the sandwich? Did he pay for it?

When we tell you, "We visited Venice last summer," you can answer many questions more or less accurately: Did we spend any money? Did we travel by plane? By boat? Did we talk to anyone? Did we go to a restaurant? Did we see other people in Venice? Did they speak Italian? Did they wear clothes? Did they have fingernails? How many? For an "intelligent" machine to understand language, it would have to make reasonable inferences about language processing, much as normal humans do. The basic notion is similar to the concept of top-down processing discussed throughout this book.

Among the difficulties encountered in developing a language-processing program was the ambiguity of natural languages. Schank (1981) cites the following examples:

I hit Fred on the nose.
I hit Fred in the park.

To parse these sentences correctly, we need to know much more than purely syntactic and semantic rules. The reader has to know something about where a person can be located as well as other conceptual information about human behavior and general world information.

Problem Solving, Game Playing, and AI

The AI literature on problem solving and game playing is probably more voluminous than that on any other psychological process. One reason many AI scientists have been concerned with *problem solving* is that the term is roughly synonymous with thinking, which in its sophisticated form is a uniquely human attribute. This fact and the general capability of AI machines with regard to problem-solving procedures has led to a proliferation of techniques and theories in this area.

Calculation was one of the earliest instances of "problem solving" by machine. In 1642 Pascal (at the age of 19) demonstrated that some forms of mathematical problems could be solved more accurately and quickly by a mechanical calculator he invented than by humans. Problem solving in the context of modern AI means much more than mechanical calculation; it covers a wide range—finding solutions to complex puzzles, proving theorems, learning successful operations, and playing games.

Designing a computer that can solve a specific problem is easy. Designing a program that is versatile enough to handle a variety of problems is difficult. And designing a program that will adapt and learn solutions to a wide range of problems is, so far, impossible. But the aim of many contemporary AI specialists is to design a learning program that will solve problems. On an elementary level, such self-learning programs might be able to learn which clients would be good risks for credit card use and which would be bad risks (see Figure 16.10). At a more advanced level, computer-vision programs are under development by Abu-Mostafa (1995) whose goal is to recognize objects even when the target object changes direction or orientation.

How do machines learn? The logical answer is "by experience" but, of course, that tells little of the mechanisms which change the performance of the computer. Many AI specialists approach the issue from a mathematical position in which the behavior of a machine is seen as a function that associates input values (the nature of a problem to be solved, for example) with corresponding output values (the actions or decisions). One way to look at the issue is that machine learning is simply the "search for the right position for the knobs." Some programs learn by training examples as in the case of the problem shown in Figure 16.11.

Take a moment to see if you can solve the concept that distinguishes one class of objects from another. Notice that your concept formation solution may focus on semantic relationships—but, in what way are an ancient cork screw, a watch, and Bugs Bunny related? This is a difficult task, and yet you, like the computer, are enlightened when you see the hint in Figure 16.12.

The machine "learns" by emulating the target functions and refining its actions stepwise in ever closer approximations to the target until it succeeds. Several programs

FIGURE 16.10

Machine learning. Involves adjusting a system's internal parameters such that it makes the proper associations between data inputs and desired outputs. A credit-approval system, for example, would be trained to link applicants' personal data with their known credit behavior. In effect, the learning process "tunes the dials" until the machine can duplicate the input-output relations in the training examples.

Reprinted by permission of Roberto Osti Illustrations.

FIGURE 16.11

CAN YOU SOLVE IT? These objects have been sorted into two classes, indicated by either a blue or black border. Which characteristic distinguishes them? Computers programmed to learn from examples often face similar puzzles. Providing the machine with hints can make learning faster and easier. For a hint to help with this puzzle, see Figure 16.12.

Reprinted by permission of Dan Wagner.

FIGURE 16.12

Visual hint. Aids both machines and people in solving the puzzle in Figure 16.11. Drawing the axis makes it clear that the top six objects lack the mirror-image symmetry exhibited by the bottom three. This characteristic distinguishes black and blue categories.

Reprinted by permission of Dan Wagner.

have been successful in this format including those that are based on a neural network (see Hinton, 1992).

(Underlying much of the work in AI is an important distinction between two types of methods used to solve problems. One method is called *algorithmic;* the other is called *heuristic.* **Algorithms** are commonly defined as procedures that guarantee a solution to a given kind of problem; **heuristics** are sets of empirical rules or strategies that operate, in effect, like a rule of thumb.) The difference between the methods can be illustrated by means of a chess problem. Computer chess is a game during which, at any given time, there exists a limited number of possible moves by each player. Also, each of the possible moves may be answered by the opponent in a limited number of moves. For practical purposes the number of these permutations is finite—that is, the game must end in a win (and loss) or draw. (Figure 16.13 shows a portion of the ever-branching tree of possibilities that might ensue from a chess play.) Of course, the number of possible moves for an entire game cannot be represented, for such a chart would contain about 10^{120} different pathways. To understand the enormousness of the number of possible moves in a chess game, consider the space needed to represent the permutations. If all the pathways were coded in the tiniest microdots, they would fill every library in the world many times over! Nevertheless, an algorithmic search that examines all alternatives would inevitably lead to a series of plays that would win (and lose) or draw. Humans (and even the most sophisticated computers imaginable) find this technique

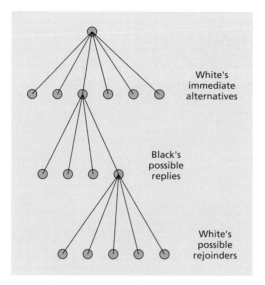

Portion of possibility tree for a chess game.

White's immediate alternatives

Black's possible replies

White's possible rejoinders

impossible. (Instead we humans and computers use heuristic search methods, in which strategy play becomes important—for example, attack opponent's queen, control the center of the board, pin opponent's major pieces, exchange pieces on the basis of piece advantage or positional advantage, and so on.)

Computer Chess

We have described how an optimal scanner working with a computer could make sense out of a simple pattern by means of template matching. (Our discussion of pattern analysis revealed that patterns are complex and that a model of human pattern recognition based on single template matching fails to account for the diversity, complexity, and economy of the human ability to recognize patterns within a brief exposure.)

Surely if there were a template for each of the diverse patterns encountered in daily living, it would overwhelm the storage capacity of even the largest computer. Let us look at template matching with a moderately simple pattern (somewhere between recognizing your grandmother and reading out the cost of a pound of butter from a code imprinted on the package). Chess has such a pattern. It uses a simple 8 × 8 grid of alternately differentiated squares; the moves are clearly defined (for example, the rook may move as many spaces along a vertical or horizontal pathway as desired, provided no other piece is in its path, the pawn may move one space forward except . . . and so on); the moves can be predicted on the basis of a brute search; and the number of permutations, albeit enormous, is finite. Given a very, very large storage and a great deal of time, determination of the probability of *each* move leading to a win is possible. Even though computers do examine a staggering number of possible moves, a model that searches *all* moves is impossible; furthermore, it says nothing about how we humans play chess or, more importantly, how complex patterns are perceived, encoded, transformed, and translated into action.

From the experiments of Chase and de Groot (see Chapter 4), we know that chess players, even modest ones, chunk information about the situation of specific pieces

Cognition in Everyday Life

Carbon-Based Grandmaster versus Silicon-Based Champion

*H*ow well can a computer play chess? As we have seen, the best computer and program, Deep Blue, beat Garry Kasparov whom many consider to be the best human player of all time. And any number of computers now exist that can beat all but the best players, one of which lurks in residence in my own Pentium computer and, it is safe to surmise, exists within a few keystrokes away from you. What can we learn by watching a machine learn to play chess? Most of all, we can learn that pattern analysis by a machine can make only rude judgments as to what features are pertinent. What the computer lacks in perspicacity, however, it makes up in its capacity for rapid and voluminous mathematical search-and-match activity. The human capacity to extract meaningful cues from an enormously complex world of sensory information, to form abstractions of those cues, to transform abstractions into higher associative structures, and to

develop elaborate cognitive plans while at the same time keeping these internal operations consistent with the external reality can still only be approximated in the computer. But even these voluminous search capabilities are not sufficient to exhaust *all* contingencies and the development of strategies of play are a palpable part of modern programs.

Three years before the end of the twentieth century the "impossible" happened. Deep Blue, the world's fastest chess-playing computer, created by Chung-Jen Tan at IBM, beat the world-champion chessmaster Gary Kasparov. Deep Blue was able to win because it was able to search up to 200 million chess positions every second. But it also won because it was able to predict the best strategy. The next generation of game-playing machines is likely to be those that can learn by experience and increase performance over a short period of time, much as humans do only faster and better.

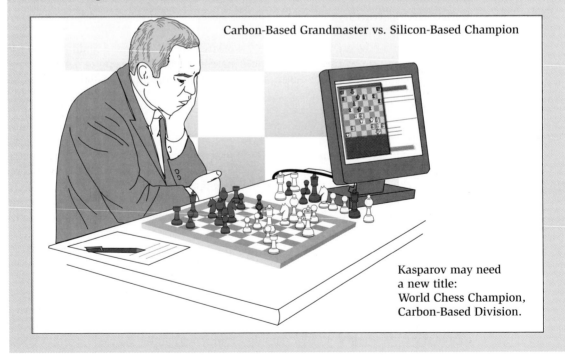

Carbon-Based Grandmaster vs. Silicon-Based Champion

Kasparov may need
a new title:
World Chess Champion,
Carbon-Based Division.

Cognition in Everyday Life

Checkers Program That Thinks Like a Human*

*A*t a recent meeting of the *2000 Congress on Evolutionary Computation,* David Fogel and Kumar Chellapilla showed a computer program called a neural network that was designed to self-learn, much as you might do if you were taught the basic rules of a game, such as checkers, and then improved on your own by thinking about different strategies. The evolved program plays an excellent game of checkers and easily wiped out almost all contestants. But what is interesting for our discussion of computer modeling of human neurological processes is that the program imitates the integrative functions of human neurons. We know that human neurons operate by means of "integrate-and-fire" structures in which a neuron adds up all electrical stimuli it receives from other neurons. If the sum total is above a certain threshold, it fires and stimulates other neurons. This basic principle is fundamental to human learning and responding. The checkers learning program operates by the same principle. Furthermore, given enough time, the program may improve many times over, which might prove interesting in space travel where intelligent machines would be able to "get smarter" throughout long flights. The implications for robot intelligence are significant and represent the new frontier of AI.

From The New York Times, July 25, 2000, pp. d1–d2.

---

and then concentrate on developing a strategy around sensitive pieces and moves. A chess-playing machine, then, if it is to play a game as humans play it, needs to be able to analyze a pattern and quickly abstract from the pieces and their positions information on the relative importance of the chunks.

In addition to chess a wide variety of other computer games may be challenged by humans including backgammon, bridge, checkers, go, Othello, poker, and Scrabble. All of these are available on the Web and waiting for a smart brain, like yours, to give them a try.

AI and the Arts

Perhaps by now, you are thinking there are only a few areas of human endeavor that are protected from the encroachment of AI. You may argue that the arts—poetry, music, and art—are purely human manifestations not to be touched by the intrusion of electronic probes. Yet, in each of these areas, considerable work has been done. First, consider poetry.

Poetry. (Several successful efforts have been made to create poems that pass for human poems. One such program has been developed by Kurzweil[9] called Ray Kurzweil's Cybernetic Poet (RKCP). The program uses language-modeling techniques based on poems that it has "read." RKCP is fed a sample, the larger the sample the better, of a poet, and from those selections it creates a language model in which language

[9]See Kurzweil's insightful book *The Age of Spiritual Machines* for more poems and some provocative predictions for the future of computing and AI.

style, rhythm patterns, and poem structure of the author are mimicked.[10] Ponder this haiku (Japanese lyric verse) written by Ray Kurzweil's Cybernetic Poet after it read poems by John Keats and Wendy Dennis:

Soul

You broke my soul
the juice of eternity,
the spirit of my lips.

And this one after reading poems by Ray Kurzweil, Robert Frost, and Wendy Dennis:

I Think I'll Crash

I think I'll crash.
Just for myself with God
peace on a curious sound
for myself in my heart?
And life is weeping
From a bleeding heart
of boughs bending
such paths of them,
of boughs bending
such paths of breeze
knows we've been there

What do you think of these poems? Do they pass the Turing test?

Music.   If it is possible to capture and emulate poetic schemas, is it also possible to do so with musical themes? Several successful programs have been written that seem to produce musical pieces judged to be quite good by listeners. One such program was written by Steve Larson, a professor of music at the University of Oregon, who selected three compositions—one by Johann Sebastian Bach, one by himself, and one by a computer—to be played before an audience. In an outcome somewhat bemusing to Larson, his own composition was judged to have been composed by the computer while the computer-generated music, called "Experiments in Musical Intelligence (EMI)," was judged to be the authentic Bach.[11] At least on a limited basis, computer-generated music fools some of the people some of the time. Another program called Improvisor has been written by Paul Hodgson, a jazz saxophonist from England. This program can emulate a wide range of styles from that of Bach to those of jazz musicians such as Louis Armstrong and Charlie Parker.

At the present time, computer-generated music seems to be very convincing. The main weakness in these program is in their ability to create music that is persuasive over a longer period of time, especially among musical specialists who are sensitive to the nuances of specialized types of music. While a novice may be convinced that a computer-generated piece of music was composed by Mozart, a Mozart virtuoso could, given a comprehensive context, identify the artificial Mozart. One might be moved to

---

[10]A free copy of RKCP may be found at www.kurzweiltech.com.
[11]Another approach to reconstructing the musical genius of past artists is to clone them from past remains. Mozart's DNA seems to be long lost, but Bach's bones were uncovered in Leipzig in 1894. Some living people are storing their own sperm and eggs . . . just in case.

observe that "it sounds like Mozart but, it sounds as if he was having a 'bad hair day.' " Of course, it is possible that future programs will not only produce Mozart-like compositions but go well beyond the talented young Austrian and generate super-Mozart compositions . . . music that would reincarnate the apotheosis of the boy genius. (For my part, it is unlikely that any computer-produced music could arouse the inner stings of my mind as *The Magic Flute* by Mozart or *Jesu, Joy of Man's Desiring* by Bach do. But then, I am waiting to be surprised.)

Musical programs will probably get better, to the point that the distinction between the real Ella Fitzgerald and a programmed Ella may be indistinguishable. Whether we will be richer or poorer for the blurring of real from artificial is a problem to be pondered not only by philosophers and ethicists but by all of us. The bell tolls for thee.

Art.   Computer-assisted video art has been around for decades, and some of the original CAD (computer-assisted design) programs have relieved the drudgery of architectural and industrial design. These programs are a far cry from programs that create art, such as those developed over the last quarter-century by Harold Cohen. His computer-driven robot, equipped with a drawing device, called Aaron, has been turning out paintings that look like real art, and who is to say that they are not "real" art? A sample of Cohen's art, or should we say Aaron's art, is shown in Figure 16.14.

FIGURE 16.14

Computer-generated art. From Ray Kurzweil, *The Age of Spiritual Machines.*

Viking Press.

The mechanics for drawing these pieces is reasonably simple. A small mobile robot scoots around a canvas drawing an object, as shown. The heart of the program, however, is information about the many aspects of the artistic construction including composition, drawing, perspective, style, and color. The art world, which can at times be the most critical as well as liberal, has exhibited some of Cohen's pieces at major venues such as the Tate Galley in London, the Stedelijk Museum in Amsterdam, and the San Franciso Museum of Modern Art.

In all of the preceding instances of AI and the arts, the ultimate criterion for critical acceptability is the judgment of humans. If the poem, music, or art is judged to be sufficiently humanlike, it is judged aesthetically meritorious. If not, then it's an "off day" for the creator, which means it is a close approximation but is clearly a counterfeit. We lack objective criteria in the arts, and until taste, likes, and preferences are made more operational, poetry, music, and art (as well as many other humanoid personifications) will be in the hands and minds of organic computational devices.

Robots

Robots (devices capable of performing human tasks or behaving in a human manner) embody most of the geography of AI reviewed earlier—the replication of pattern recognition, memory, language processing, and problem solving (see Minsky's 1994 article "Will Robots Inherit the Earth?" for recent reflections).

Cognition in Everyday Life

Robot (Re)volutions

A fascination with the possibilities of humanoids performing in a fashion that mimics human behavior has pervaded folklore and fiction. Stories like "The Sorcerer's Apprentice," "Pinocchio," and *Frankenstein;* tales of "golems" and centaurs; and characters like R2D2 and C3PO (*Star Wars*), and Hal (of *2001* fame) reflect this interest. With the advent of modern engineering technology and cognitive psychology, robotics has evolved from the domain of mythology and science fiction to the status of a very serious scientific endeavor. Pioneering work was done by two British scientists, Ross Ashley and W. Gray Walter. Ashley designed and built an electronic circuit that maintained a favorable homeostasis, or state of internal balance. Walter added mobility to a homeostatic type of device that would seek light below a certain brightness; avoid light above that level;

and, where no light was available, move around in what may be called a search for light. These tropistic machines mimicked only the rudimentary properties of life exhibited by insects, plants, or simple animals. The robot next in line of evolution was put together at the Johns Hopkins University and became known as the Hopkins Beast. This could move about under its own power and was completely self-contained. It navigated by means of sonar, and its perceptual system consisted of a combination of photo cells, masks, lenses, and circuits all designed to detect only one thing: electrical outlet coverplates. When it "saw" one, it would try to make contact with it with its plug-shaped hand. Roving automatic vacuum cleaners have recently hit the market—bringing robot technology home—so to speak.

Robotics grew rapidly in the 1960s with the exploration of space and the need to develop highly sophisticated mechanical devices capable of performing specific tasks. The Mars lander, capable of carrying out a series of complex chemical analyses, is a result of these needs. (It should be pointed out that some of these robots, purely mechanical devices, are only remotely associated with the limited definition of AI used in this chapter.)

Some of the early prototypes of space robots were developed at the AI laboratory of Stanford University, where signs in the vicinity of the laboratory warned visitors that robot vehicles may be about. One of the most intriguing robots was developed there in 1968. It was a mobile, radio-controlled vehicle called Shakey, which had on-board perceptual and problem-solving capabilities. It was equipped with a television camera, a range finder, and a tactile sensor like a cat's whisker. All these relayed sensory information to a computer that held a variety of programs for analyzing the incoming signals and for planning action sequences aimed at manipulating the robot's environment. The whole was mounted in a motorized cart that could go in any direction.

The perceptual system consisted of a television camera that reduced the pictures to line images and then to significant areas or objects in the scene. The problem solver was a type of theorem-proving program that allowed Shakey to execute simple tasks.

A newer robot, Flakey, replaced Shakey. Flakey is a three-foot-tall ambulatory device with a video camera mounted on top. When given a command to go to an office five doors down the hall, Flakey obediently wheels itself to the designated place. Some of the most advanced robots are built by NASA. These machines are somewhat specialized devices used to collect and analyze soil samples from neighboring planets, make repairs on space stations, and carry out scientific experiments and observations in environments too forbidding for humans.

The grandiose plans of the 1970s, which ambitiously started out with designing whole-functioning robots, have given way to more reasonable projects in which relatively small humanoid processes are replicated. In this arena the business community is leading the way; many laborious or dangerous functions can be done by robots.

The Future of AI

In the twentieth century, psychology became grounded scientifically through advances in behaviorism, which gave techniques and objectivity to the study of the human mind and performance. Because of reasons mentioned in the first chapter, behaviorism gave way to cognitive psychology, which focused on internal representations of the mind that greatly expanded the scope of psychology. In the opinion of the author, a significant shift in cognitive psychology as well as psychology in general, is currently taking place. This shift is brought about by advancements in two areas: cognitive neuroscience, which has been thematically infused throughout this book, and artificial intelligence.[12] In the first case, we are beginning to apprehend the physiological underpinnings of human cognition, and in the second case, we are being challenged to ascertain the attributes as well as the limitations of human understanding and intellect. And it is entirely possible that

[12]A third force of equal magnitude is genetic engineering, which portends to change the basic biological structure of living things. The combination of all these forces—genetic engineering, AI, and cognitive neuroscience—may well forever change the human species in this century. We live in interesting, if not challenging, times.

in the present century we will stand side by side with an inorganic instrument whose intellectual acumen is far greater than ours.

Ray Kurzweil, in his provocative book *The Age of Spiritual Machines* (1999), and Bill Gates, in his prescient book *The Road Ahead* (1996), have been keeping track of the increment in computer speed (measured in calculations per second per thousand dollars) throughout the twentieth century. In the first half of the twentieth century, speed doubled every three years; between 1950 and 1966, it doubled every two years; and presently it is doubling every year, which suggests an exponential growth. The exponential growth was predicted by Gordon Moore, the co-founder of Intel, who noted in 1965 that the capacity of a computer chip would double every year. Even though Moore thought the torrid growth projection could not last forever—there are physical laws that would be reached—the rate of growth over the past forty years has been doubling about every eighteen months. This growth rate is called **Moore's law.** If computer power continues to grow over the next few decades, and there is ample reason to believe that it will, then even if the exponential growth rate is decelerated, the resulting capacity of future machines will approximate that of organic brains. Some (Kurzweil, 1999) project that computing potential will approximate that of the human brain as early as 2020 and well outstrip it by the end of the century. (See Figure 16.15 for a projection of the growth of computing through the twenty-first century.)

In order for this fantastic prediction to come true, more than computing power needs to be achieved for an artificial brain to act like a human brain (only smarter). These in-

FIGURE 16.15

The Exponential Growth of Computing, 1900–2100.

From Kurzweil (1999).

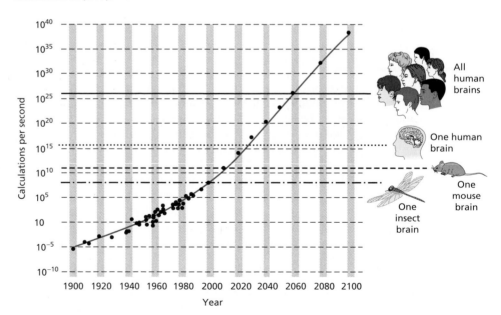

clude the acquisition of information, what we have referred to as "world knowledge" in this chapter. In humans, each of the five senses detects and processes millions of bits of information each day. These bits are multifariously fused with existing knowledge in a vastly complex network which enables each of us to react wisely to new environmental cues in our quest for survival. One final component of an artificial brain is necessary and that is the formulae that govern the operation of the organic brain. This is a hugely complicated matter and it is not clear exactly what these operational codes consist of, but some features include that potential for self-organization of information in workable networks, the capacity for recursive searches, and the ability to learn and self-adapt to external and internal cues. An alternative program would be to combine computer bits into an organic brain[13] and some efforts in this direction have been done with startling success. (See Barinaga, 1999, for an example of how thoughts are being turned into actions.)

In realizing the visionary aspirations of AI dreamers, we need to consider some fundamental differences in the structural components of the brain and computer, computing power, and computer simulation. We learned earlier that the human brain has about 100 billion neurons with an estimated 1,000 connections between each neuron and other neurons (this figure is still definitively unknown). That is about 100 trillion parallel connections, which gives the user considerable cerebral power. The organic brain, however, reacts slowly with only about 200 calculations per second. If we multiply these numbers (100 trillion connections computing at 200 calculations per second), we get 20 million billion calculations per second. That is what your brain is doing at this second. How close are computers to this computational power?

The best massively parallel neural net computer as of this writing is capable of 2 billion connection calculations per second. What the silicon-based brain does far better than the organic brain is process information much much faster. If Moore's law holds, or even approximates the computing capacity in the future, by the year 2020, the present systems will have doubled about 23 times, which would yield a speed of 20 million billion neural connection calculations per second. Check the foregoing figure for the human brain's capacity.

A final word about AI and computer simulation: There is a huge conceptual leap between the types of actions produced by a human brain and an artificial brain. As discussed earlier, it may be possible to construct a Bach cantata, a van Gogh painting, or an e. e. cummings poem that passes the Turing task. It is even plausible to compose the preceding items that are judged by we humans to be the quintessence of the class—a type of aesthetic prototype for each artist rather than simply "like the artist." But in order for this to be done, humanly produced exemplars would have to be learned and understood by the inorganic machine. Man himself provides the blueprint. When and if future thinking programs transcend human thought, then it is humans who *initially will feed* information to computers and set in operation the new thinking machines. Perhaps it would be prudent

---

[13]Not long ago a young Russian scholar asked RLS how he envisioned the future of AI. Here is his reply. "The form AI will take in this century will surprise all. I envision implants that will create a half robot/ half organic human whose computational powers, by which I mean, ability to understand the world and universe, will be in an order of magnitude greater than the evolved creature we are. . . . In fact, you and your classmates may be the last generation of natural creatures. . . . In effect, your generation will (somewhat sadly) be the final conclusion to the millions of years of natural selection and survival of the most fit. In a short time . . . no more than a few hundred years . . . human kind as we know it will be history . . . and our understanding of the physical universe will be impressively enhanced."

to put a scheme into the new brains which will be able to explain things to us in simple human terms, or we will be relegated to service functions, not intellectual functions.

AI and Scientific Inquiry

Throughout most of this chapter we have discussed the computer vis-à-vis human cognition and the immensely complex task undertaken by those who attempt to mimic human performance with the use of machines. In this closing section we would like to propose that the way scientists—including cognitive scientists—conduct research is likely to change significantly in the next few years with the use of computers assisted by AI programs.

We have already seen the widespread adoption of computers in nearly every area of human endeavor, and that trend probably will continue. Calculations necessary for everything from space travel to garbage truck routes to genetic research would be impossible without the modern high-speed computer. In fact, more advanced systems with greater memory capacity and faster processing are sure to appear in the future. Perhaps even radical new systems (such as the Japanese Fifth Dimension, which stresses knowledge information processing) will replace our present systems. Exciting as the past developments are, the future promises even more spectacular discoveries.

One area of interest to scientists is the way information is stored and codified. Presently, an enormous amount of scientific information is available in an electronic format (for example, PsycInfo) in addition to the more conventional form of books and articles. Electronic access to information is expanding greatly in all fields, including psychology, so that a user can access the complete contents of an article or book online. Furthermore, information from other scholarly fields and from disparate sources, linked in the huge network called the Internet, is available to most of us. The Net is here to stay and will continue to affect scientific and other scholarly research.

But what can a scientist do with so much data? Is there the danger of having too much data and not knowing what it all means? Data banks are indispensable to anyone who attempts to write a comprehensive book—such as one on cognitive psychology that encompasses an extended range of topics. Authors of such works can access the abstracts of a subject, say, mental imagery in children, in seconds. As convenient as such databases are, they also present a problem in that the capacity of humans to store and process information is limited. We are at risk of becoming overwhelmed by the plethora of information. If such is the case, it is likely that some type of program that processes information in a knowledgeable, intelligent way—that is, *understands* information—will emerge. (AI will live up to the promise of its name.) If such an AI program appears, it may tell us what research has been done, so we can avoid redundant studies, and it also may tell us what needs to be done, so we can put our valuable time to good use. Furthermore, a superunderstanding computer may not only identify the holes in human knowledge but also fill them in by conducting "research" or making logical inferences from its colossal database (see Solso, 1986, 1987b, 1994). Conceivably, the resulting explosion of knowledge may answer the ancient questions of who we are, where we come from, and what is our future. May we all live so long as to know some of these answers, but not long enough to know all. It is better to travel than to arrive.

Spotlight on Cognitive Neuroscience:

Artificial Face Recognition

Cognitive scientists have been studying how people recognize faces for quite some time. With the advent of technologies such as cell recordings and imaging techniques we know that areas in the temporal lobe process facial information. However, it is unclear exactly what dimensions of the face are being processed. We know much more about how machines process facial information. Although computers are not as good as people in recognizing faces, researchers have developed computer systems that can take an image and recognize it as a face by locating the eyes, mouth, and border of the face. The system then adjusts the size and contrast of the face to convert it to a grid (or array) of numbers representing the gray scale pixel values. The pixel values are then converted to what are referred to as "eigenfaces" using a statistical process called factor analysis. This would be the machine equivalent of encoding the face. To recognize the face, the computer must now match the eigenface values of the face being processed to the eigenface values of "known" faces already stored in the computer. This would be the machine equivalent to the faces stored in memory. Not all matches are exact. However, stored faces that are closely matched to the face being processed will be displayed on the computer monitor along with a value representing how close the faces matched: the machine equivalent of recall. Machine face recognition is not perfect, but it reduces the labor involved in searching a crowd for a wanted individual. Additionally, this technology is being used to track terrorists and to identify children involved in child pornography rings; both require matching of known faces (terrorists or missing children photos) to new faces (people in airports or images off of the Internet).

Turk, M., & Pentland, A. (1991). Eigenfaces for recognition. *Journal of Cognitive Neuroscience, 3*(1), 71–86.

*S*UMMARY

1   Artificial intelligence concerns any computer-produced output that would be judged intelligent if produced by a human.

2   One dichotomy (Searle) distinguishes between "strong" AI, which asserts that proper programming can create a "mind" capable of understanding, and "weak" AI, which emphasizes its value as a heuristic in studying human cognition.

3   Philosophical issues associated with AI concern intent, thought, and understanding. Exercises designed to demonstrate machine-human indistinguishability and functional equivalence (for example, the Turing test and the Chinese room) are considered by some as failing to consider important factors such as intentionality, which humans possess but machines do not.

4   Information processing by machines, as an analog of human cognition, has increased capacity in recognizing complex stimuli from the early models (which used template matching) to more recent approaches (which combine analysis of structural features and their relationships).

5   Computer programs capable of "understanding" natural language require, as a minimum, semantic and syntactic rules, world and social context knowledge bases, and some method of handling the ambiguity present in common language usage.

6   Artificial intelligence problem-solving programs (for example, computer chess) use two principal strategies: algorithmic procedures (which guarantee a solution by examining all possible alternatives) and heuristic procedures (which are strategy based and decompose complex problems into easily solved subproblems).

7   Successful AI programs have been written which produce acceptable poetry, music, and art.

8   The future of AI and cognitive neuroscience (in combination with genetic engineering) is likely to change significantly cognitive psychology as well as all of psychology. A computer brain with computing power of the human brain may emerge by 2020.

$\mathcal{K}$ EY $\mathcal{W}$ ORDS

algorithm	McCulloch-Pitts neurons
artificial intelligence (AI)	Moore's law
Chinese room	NETtalk
continuous speech recognition (CSR)	parallel processing model
DYSTAL	PARRY
ELIZA	robots
expert systems	sequential processing model
heuristic	Turing test

$\mathcal{R}$ ECOMMENDED $\mathcal{R}$ EADINGS

● Resources on the topic of AI are abundant. General reviews are offered in Tauke, *Computers and Common Sense* (available in paperback); and Apter, *The Computer Simulation of Behavior*. A well-written and technically interesting account by a research scientist is Raphael, *The Thinking Computer*. Also recommended is Pylyshyn's *Computation and Cognition: Toward a Foundation for Cognitive Science; The Computer and the Mind,* by Johnson-Laird; *Memory Traces in the Brain,* by Alkon; *Artificial Intelligence: The Very Idea,* by Haugeland; and *Artificial Intelligence in Psychology: Interdisciplinary Essays,* by Boden. As mentioned earlier, Alan Turing's biography by Andrew Hodges is a good read.

● The April 1985 issue of *Byte* magazine is largely devoted to AI and, although dated, has engaging articles by Minsky, Schank, and Hunter; J. Anderson and Reiser; Winston; and others that address themes still current. *Metamagical Themas: Questing for the Essence of Mind and Matter* and *Godel, Escher, Bach: An Eternal Golden Braid,* by Douglas Hofstadter, should be read by all people interested in AI and related matters; besides, they are a good read. Also, Gardner's *The Mind's New Science* is highly recommended for its discussion of AI and many other topics covered in this book. Some interesting technical problems are contained in *Artificial and Human Intelligence,* edited by Elithorn and Banerji. Finally, *The Age of Spiritual Machines* by Ray Kurzweil is highly recommended.

Glossary

Accommodation   An activity involved in the adaptation of intellectual processes during which mental structures undergo reorganization so that new information that does not readily conform to previous structures can be integrated into the cognitive system (Piaget).

Acronym   A word formed on the basis of the first letters in a phrase or group of words. Used as a mnemonic system.

Acrostic   A phrase or sentence in which the first letters are associated with a to-be-remembered word or concept. Used as a mnemonic system.

ACT   See **Adaptive control of thought.**

Adaptation   One of the major processes in intellectual development, the aim of which is to handle environmental demands effectively. Adaptation involves two activities: assimilation and accommodation (Piaget).

Adaptive control of thought   A comprehensive model of cognition developed by Anderson.

Ad hominem   Argument based on attacking the person making the argument, not the substance of the argument itself.

Aggregate field   The idea that cerebral functions are distributed throughout the brain.

Algorithm   Procedure that guarantees a solution to a given kind of problem. See **Heuristic.**

Anterograde amnesia   The loss of memory after the onset of the memory disorder.

Anthropomorphism   The attribution of human characteristics to inanimate or nonhuman objects.

Artificial intelligence (AI)   Computer-produced output that would be considered intelligent if produced by a human.

Association   First formulated by Aristotle, the principle that asserts that ideas are connected in the mind on the basis of contiguity, similarity, or contrast.

Associationism   A connection between two units, such as *ham* and *eggs* or a *stimulus* and a *response.*

Attention   The concentration of mental effort on sensory or mental events.

Attribute-frequency model   A model proposed by prototype theory that asserts that a prototype represents the mode or most frequently experienced combination of attributes.

Autobiographical memories   Memories of an individual's past history.

Automatic processing   The activation of an element in memory that is initiated by contextual cues and proceeds with limited subject attention.

Axon   The long, tubular transmitting pathway in which signals from the cell body are passed along to other cells by means of junctures known as **synapses.**

Bayes's theorem   A mathematical formula that evaluates the likelihood that a hypothesis about a future event (such as the probability that you might see a friend at a party) is valid. Developed by Thomas Bayes, eighteenth-century mathematician. Also called Bayesian theorem.

Bottom-up processing   Borrowed from computer language, cognitive processing initiated by the components of a stimulus pattern which, when summed, lead to recognition of the whole configuration.

Broca's area   A part of the frontal lobe implicated in language production. Named for Paul Broca, French neurologist of the nineteenth century. See also **Wernicke's area.**

Brown-Peterson technique   A procedure used to study short-term memory in which an item to be remembered is followed by a distractor task that lasts for variable time intervals before recall.

Canonic perspectives   Views that "best" represent an object. Frequently, these are the images that first come to mind when we are asked to recall a form.

CBF   See **rCBF.**

Cell body   Part of a neuron in which nutrients and waste products are filtered in and out through its permeable cell wall.

Central executive   Regulatory component that determines the flow of information.

Central nervous system (CNS)   The portion of the neurological system which consists of the brain and spinal cord.

Central-tendency model   A model proposed by prototype theory that holds that a prototype represents the mean or average of a set of exemplars.

Cerebral commissurotomy   The surgical severing of the connective tissue between the two main structures of the brain.

Cerebral cortex   The top layer of the brain, thought to be involved in "higher-order" mental functions.

Cerebral hemispheres   The two major components of the cerebral cortex. The left hemisphere is generally involved in language and symbolic processing, and the right is generally involved in nonverbal perceptual processing.

Channel capacity   An assumption regarding information processing that postulates that the capacity to handle the flow of input is determined by the limitations of the system.

Characteristic features   The incidental or superficial features of a concept (for example, *eats worms* is a characteristic feature of the concept *robin*).

Chinese room   A test used to illustrate the untenability of a strong artificial intelligence position. A subject (or computer) that possesses no knowledge of the Chinese language is given a sample of Chinese characters along with a set of rules for relating those characters to another set of symbols.

Chunking   The recoding of stimuli so that the information load per unit is increased (for example, letters into words, words into phrases, and so on).

Clustering model   A semantic organization model that proposes that concepts are represented in memory in an organized form with similar items stored together.

CNS   See **Central nervous system.**

Cocktail party phenomenon   The intrusion of an interesting, often salacious, event that gains one's attention.

Cognitive map   The idea proposed by Tolman that what rats learn in a maze is not a series of S-R connections but a picture of internal representation of the stimulus situation.

Cognitive model   A metaphor based on observations and on inferences drawn from observations that describes the detection, storage, and use of information.

Cognitive neuroscience The study of the relationships between neuroscience and cognitive psychology, especially those theories of the mind dealing with memory, sensation and perception, problem solving, language processing, motor functions, and cognition.

Commissurotomy See **Cerebral commissurotomy.**

Common fate The Gestalt principle of organization stating that elements shifted in a similar manner from a larger group tend to be grouped together.

Comprehension The ability to grasp the meaning of words and sentences.

Computational brain The concept that the brain's function is to interpret and process sensory signals and bodily needs in a comprehensible way. The computational brain involves coding information, storing information, transforming information, thinking, and, finally, reacting to information. The processing of information enhances one's understanding of the world and hence one's survivability.

Concept formation The discernment of properties common to a class of stimuli and the discovery of rules relating its properties.

Conceptually driven processing See **Top-down processing.**

Conceptual-propositional hypothesis A hypothesis positing that information is represented in memory in an abstract propositional format explicating objects and their relationships.

Conceptual science A system that provides useful metaphorical classification schemes. Because these schemes are devised by humans for human purposes, they are fabrications of human cognition that mirror reality.

Connectionism The idea that complex cognitive functions can be understood in terms of the network of links among units. See also **Parallel distributed processing (PDP) model.**

Consciousness An awareness of events or stimuli in the environment and of cognitive phenomena such as memories, thoughts, and bodily sensations.

Conservation The idea that certain transformations do not alter the basic properties of objects (Piaget).

Conservative focusing A hypothesized strategy used in concept formation in which one hypothesis is formulated and reformulations of a positive instance are sequentially tested and outcomes noted.

Constructive memory The idea that prior experience, postevent information, perceptual factors, and one's desire to remember certain events over others influence what we recall.

Constructive perception The theory that during perception we form and test hypotheses regarding perception based on what we sense and what we know.

Continuous speech recognition (CSR) Computer programs that recognize and record natural human speech. In most instances, the speech is transcribed into graphic form and sometimes further translated into an oral output. For example, a speaker inputs English, which is transcribed into written Spanish, and the output is in spoken Spanish.

Contralaterality The processing by the brain of information derived from an opposing body site.

Convergent thinking Thinking that engages previously encoded factual information.

Corpus callosum The massive bundle of nerves that connects the two hemispheres of the brain.

Creativity The process involving cognitive activity that results in a new, and often impracticable way of viewing some problem or situation.

Data-driven processing See **Bottom-up processing.**

Decay   Forgetting due to a lack of use or rehearsal of previously available information.

Decision frame   A decision maker's framework concerning a choice alternative that includes behaviors, results, and contingencies.

Declarative knowledge   Factual information known about objects, ideas and events.

Declarative memory   Also known as *declarative representation*. Knowing what; knowledge about the world (for example, knowing that San Francisco is in California). (See **Procedural knowledge.**)

Declarative representation   See **Declarative memory.**

Deductive reasoning   The process of reasoning in which particular conclusions are drawn for more general principles.

Deep structure   The underlying form of a sentence that holds information crucial to its meaning.

Defining features   The essential, required features of a concept (for example, wings, feathers, and red breast are defining features of the concept *robin*).

Dendrites   The highly arborized parts of neurons that gather neural impulses from other neurons.

Direct perception   Theory of perception that purports that stimuli themselves contain all the necessary information for perception to occur and that past knowledge is unnecessary. The theory is most closely associated with J. J. Gibson.

Divergent thinking   Thinking that involves generating many different answers to a single problem, with the "correctness" dependent on subjective evaluation of answers as abstract and flexible.

Dual-coding hypothesis   The hypothesis that proposes two coding and storage systems (verbal and imaginal).

Dualistic memory theory   The idea that two different types of memory, short-term and long-term, can be distinguished.

Echoic memory   The persistence of auditory impressions and their brief availability for further processing.

Egocentrism   The tendency to regard the world from one's own perspective (Piaget).

Electroconvulsive therapy (ECT)   Also called *shock therapy*. A form of somatic therapy consisting of the application of electric currents to the head, which produce convulsions and unconsciousness.

Electroencephalography (EEG)   The measurement of electrical activities of the brain.

ELIZA   One of the first conversational computer programs (developed by Weizenbaum of MIT).

Engram   A trace or, in the present context, a collection of neural charges that represent memory.

Episodic memory   Memory that concerns information about temporally dated episodes and events along with the relationships among such events.

Epistemology   The study of the origin and nature of knowledge.

Evolutionary cognitive psychology   Discipline that views cognition from an evolutionary-adaptive viewpoint.

Expert systems   Computer systems that perform as human experts do.

Explicit memory   Memory recovery or recognition based on conscious search processes as one might use in answering a direct question such as, "What is the capital of Russia?" See **Implicit memory.**

Facial cognizance   An astute level of facial processing in which an adept observer or expert (like a portrait artist) is able to see beyond the surface characteristics of a face.

False memories   Reconstructed memories about events that did not occur but are invented. Many times, the subject is unaware that the memory is not real, and sometimes the false memory may occur at the urging of a therapist or counselor.

Feature   A basic component of a complex stimulus pattern. For example, the features of the letter *A* are two diagonal lines (/ \) and one horizontal line (—).

Feature analysis   The hypothesis proposing that pattern recognition occurs only after sensory stimuli have been analyzed according to their simple or basic components.

Fissures   Deep grooves on the surface of the brain.

Focus gambling   A hypothesized strategy used in concept formation in which more than one concept feature at a time is changed, with the goal being a correct response in a shorter time span.

Fovea   A small indentation in the retina that contains the highest concentration of cones and provides the greatest visual acuity.

Foveal vision   Vision that provides the greatest visual acuity and is restricted to a visual angle of about 1 to 2 degrees.

Frontal   One of the four major sections on the surface of each cerebral hemisphere, marked off by major convolutions or fissures.

Functional-equivalency hypothesis   The idea that imagery and perception are very similar cognitive phenomena.

Functional fixedness   The tendency to view things in terms of their familiar uses, which makes it difficult to achieve novel perspectives often necessary for problem solving.

Geon   Basic geometric forms which make complex forms when combined. "Geometric ions."

Gestalt psychology   Theory that states that psychology, especially perception and cognition, can be understood by examining the way information is organized as a whole structured phenomenon.

Gyri   (*gyrus,* sing.) The ridges between the folds in the surface of the brain.

Habituation   The effect that occurs when a stimulus is presented repeatedly until the subject no longer reacts to it.

Heuristic   Sets of empirical rules or strategies that lead to a solution most of the time. General rules. See **Algorithm.**

Homunculus   A diminutive human; a midget. In psychology, a "little person" in the head.

Iconic memory   The momentary persistence of visual impressions and their brief availability for further processing.

Illumination   A hypothetical stage in the creative process that involves sudden understanding of a problem and its solution.

Implicit memory   A type of memory retrieval in which recall (or recognition) is enhanced by the presentation of a cue or prime, despite having no conscious awareness of the connection between the prime and to-be-recalled (recognized) item.

Incubation   A hypothetical stage in the creative process that involves temporarily setting a problem aside and diverting attention elsewhere.

Inductive reasoning   Reasoning from the particular to the general.

Information-processing model   A model proposing that information is processed through a series of stages, each of which performs unique operations. Each stage receives information from preceding stages and passes the transformed input along to other stages for further processing.

Intelligence   The ability to acquire, retrieve, and use knowledge in a meaningful way; to understand concrete and abstract ideas; and to comprehend relationships among objects and ideas.

Internal representation   A transformation of environmental cues into meaningful cognitive symbols of the perceived stimuli. Also referred to as *code.*

Isomorphism   A one-to-one correspondence between a perceived object and its internal representation.

Key word method   A mnemonic technique used in second-language learning. For example, an English word that sounds like some part of the foreign word is associated with the foreign word by using an imaginal interaction between the two.

Knowledge   The storage and organization of information in memory.

Korsakoff's syndrome   The disorder commonly brought about by severe alcoholism resulting in bilateral damage to the diencephalon.

LDT   See **Lexical decision task.**

Levels-of-processing (LOP) model   A theory proposing that memory occurs as a by-product of processing activities, with memory trace durability a function of the depth of that processing.

Lexical-decision task (LDT)   A priming task in which a subject is shown a related word and asked to evaluate quickly whether a second string of letters makes a legal word or not (e.g., bread—butter vs. bread—uretbt).

Linguistic-relativity hypothesis   The hypothesis that proposes that perception of reality is determined by one's language history (Whorf, Sapir).

Localization   Identification of particular structures or regions of the brain that appear to be involved in particular cognitive process.

Logic   The science of thinking based on laws that determine the validity of a conclusion.

Long-term memory (LTM)   A hypothetical storage system given proper cueing, is characterized by its duration, capacity, and accessibility.

Long-term potentiation (LTP)   An increase in neural responsiveness after rapid repeated stimulation over an extended time period.

Mass action   The idea that memories are distributed throughout the brain (Lashley).

Method of loci   A mnemonic technique that involves associating items to be remembered with physical locations and "revisiting" those sites during recall.

Mind–body issue   The philosophic problem dealing with the relationship between the mind and the body.

Mnemonic   Any technique that serves to facilitate storage and recall of information in memory.

Mnemonic encoding principle   The use of techniques that aid in memorization and retrieval of information by adding meaning or imagery.

Moore's law   Originally proposed by Gordon Moore in the mid-1960s. A law that states that the size of a transistor in an integrated circuit chip will be reduced by 50 percent every 24 months with the result being an exponential growth in computing power over time. Now, the law states that computer capacity increases at a rate of doubling every 18 months, a prediction that has held up for about forty years.

Morpheme   The smallest unit of meaning in a language (for example, a prefix or a suffix) that is combined with other such units in various ways to create words.

Myelin sheath   The fatty outer covering of a neuron's axon that facilitates neural transmission in some neurons.

Narcissistic trait   An organized system of internal attributes and memories which encompass topics of self or topics related to "I, me, mine." A **self-schema.**

Network model   A semantic organization model proposing that concepts are represented in memory as independent units stored in spatial arrangements according to the degree and nature of their relationships.

Neural network systems See **Parallel distributed processing (PDP) model.**

Neuron A nerve cell with specialized processes that constitutes the structural and functional unit of nerve tissue. As the basic cell of the nervous system, the neuron conducts neural information.

Neurotransmitters Chemicals that act on the membrane of the dendrite of a neuron to facilitate or inhibit neurotransmission.

Nondeclarative knowledge See **Procedural knowledge.**

Nonsense syllable A nonword sequence (typically composed of three letters), first used by Ebbinghaus in memory studies.

Occipital One of the four major sections on the surface of each cerebral hemisphere, marked off by major convolutions or fissures.

Organizational schemes A technique that organizes information into categories that are used as recall cues.

Output interference The detrimental effect that the retrieval of one item has on the retrieval of subsequent items.

Parallel distributed processing (PDP) model A neurally inspired model of the mind in which information is processed in a massively distributed, mutually interactive, parallel system in which various activities are carried out simultaneously through excitation and/or inhibition between units.

Parallel processing model A computer program that examines all input features at the same time.

Parietal lobe One of the four major sections on the surface of each cerebral hemisphere, marked off by major convolutions or fissures.

PARRY A conversational computer program that simulated responses of a paranoid patient and was used in a test of indistinguishability between a machine and a human with psychiatrists as the expert judges.

PDP See **Parallel distributed processing (PDP) model.**

Peg word system A mnemonic strategy that involves learning a set of stimulus items that serve as pegs on which the items to be remembered are hung.

Perception The branch of psychology that deals with the detection and interpretation of sensory stimuli.

Perceptrons The simulation of neural nets in computer architecture.

Perceptual span The amount of information that can be perceived during a brief presentation or within a specific area.

Peripheral nervous system Nerves that lie outside the spinal cord and the brain, most of which are involved in sensing energy changes in the environment.

Permastore A type of memory that is so well entrenched that it is permanent and lasts a lifetime.

Phoneme The basic speech sound unit of a spoken language distinguishable by how it is produced (voiced, unvoiced, fricative, or plosive). Phonemes are combined with other sound units to create words.

Phonological loop A rehearsal circuit in working memory that holds inner speech for verbal comprehension.

Phrenology The study of the configuration of a person's skull based on the supposition that it accurately indicates mental faculties and character traits.

Pragnanz The Gestalt principle of organization asserting that stimulus figures are seen in the "best" possible way given the stimulus conditions. The "best" figure is stable and cannot be made simpler or more orderly by shifts in perception.

Preparation   A hypothetical stage in the creative process that involves problem formulation and initial solution attempts.

Presynaptic terminals   Terminals that are proximal to the receptive surface of neurons, which transmit information about their activity to other neurons.

Primary memory   The immediate memory that never leaves consciousness and provides an accurate representation of events (William James).

Priming   The process by which a cue enhances recall or recognition or a subsequent item.

Priming effect   The enhanced recall or recognition of an item following a prime. The process usually takes place without conscious awareness of the link between the cue and the to-be-recalled (recognized) item.

Probe item   A cue used to signal a person in a memory task to recall a specific item.

Problem solving   Thought directed toward discovering a solution for a specific problem that involves both response formation and response selection.

Procedural knowledge   Also called *nondeclarative knowledge*. Knowledge that is implicit and sampled through actions or performance. See also **Production memory.**

Procedural memory   The "lowest" form of memory in which simple associations between stimuli and responses are formed.

Production memory (or **procedural knowledge**) The knowledge required to do things, such as tie shoelaces, do mathematics, or order food in a restaurant.

Production system   The notion that underlying human cognition is a set of conditional-action pairs called *productions.*

Proposition   The smallest unit of information that is meaningful (for example, John is tall).

Prototype   An abstraction of stimulus patterns stored in long-term memory against which similar patterns are evaluated in terms of how closely they fit the model.

Prototype recognition   A hypothesis proposing that pattern recognition occurs when a match is made between sensory stimuli and an abstracted or idealized cognitive pattern.

Pseudomemory   The tendency for subjects to recognize a prototype falsely as a previously seen figure with greater confidence than figures that have actually been previously seen.

Psycholinguistics   Study of language as it relates to the human mind.

Psychophysics   The scientific study of the relationship between physical events and psychological phenomena.

rCBF   Regional cerebral blood flow. By measuring the blood flow in the brain, it is possible to infer which regions are neurologically active.

Reconstructive memory   The idea that people assimilate facts about the world and then are able to recall them as they really happened.

REM sleep   Rapid eye movement during dreaming.

Representational knowledge   See **Knowledge** and **Declarative knowledge.**

Repressed memories   Memories so painful or traumatic that they are not expressed in consciousness.

Retina   The membrane on the back of the eye that contains photoreceptor cells (rods and cones).

Retrograde amnesia   The inability to recall information acquired prior to the onset of a disorder.

Robots   Machines capable of performing human tasks or behaving in a human manner.

Saccade The rapid eye movement occurring during reading and when viewing visual patterns.

Schema A cognitive framework of meaningfully organized concepts

Scheme A mental representation of some action (mental or physical) that can be performed on an object and that, as the organism develops, increases in integration and coordination (Piaget).

Secondary memory Permanent memory that is characterized by individual differences (William James).

Second-order isomorphism The relationship between external objects and their internal representation that is lawful but not structural.

Self-schema A complex internal representation of self, revolving around the topics of "I, me, and mine." See **Narcissistic trait.**

Semantic feature-comparison model A model of semantic organization proposing that concepts are stored in memory as sets of semantic features distinguishable as either defining or characteristic features.

Semantic memory Memory that stores word meanings, concepts, and world knowledge.

Semantic priming The presentation of a semantically related prime followed by its target (for example, showing the color red and following that with the target word *blood*).

Sensation The detection of stimulation, the study of which commonly deals with the structure of sensory mechanisms (such as the eye) and the stimuli (such as, light) that affect those mechanisms.

Sensory threshold The level of energy required to activate a neural response. The *limen* in psychophysical terms.

Sentience Having conscious sensations. Experiencing sensations or feelings.

Sequential processing model A computer program that examines each input feature in a pre-determined stepwise fashion, with the outcome of each stage determining the next step in the program.

Seriation The ability to order elements according to some underlying principle (for example, arranging sticks according to increasing length) (Piaget).

Set Any preparatory cognitive activity that precedes thinking and perception.

Set-theoretical model A model of semantic organization proposing that concepts are represented in memory as information sets that include category examples and attributes.

Shadowing An experimental procedure used in auditory attention research in which subjects are asked to repeat a spoken message as it is presented.

Short-term memory (STM) A hypothetical storage system characterized by a duration estimated at about 12 seconds (which can be extended by rehearsal), by a capacity estimated at about 7 ± 2 items, and by accurate recall.

Similarity The Gestalt principle of organization stating that like elements in the same structure tend to be perceived together.

Simultaneous scanning A hypothesized strategy used in concept formation in which people begin with all possible hypotheses and eliminate all untenable ones.

Spreading activation theory The memory model that posits that semantic storing and processing are based on a complex network in which simple associations (for example, blue—sky) are linked together.

Sternberg paradigm A procedure used to study retrieval in short-term memory in which a sequence of items is presented for a short duration followed by a probe digit. Subjects are asked to decide whether the probe digit was in the original series. Reaction times are the principal dependent variable.

Subliminal perception   The influence of stimuli that are insufficiently intense to produce a conscious sensation but strong enough to influence some mental processes.

Subliminal priming   The effect of a prime that is presented below the level of conscious awareness. *Note:* The word *subliminal* is used by psychophysicists to mean below the sensory threshold and is related to such things as decibels, lumens, and the like, which have physical limitations. Cognitive psychologists, social psychologists, people who create ads for TV, and visionaries who besiege talk shows use the term in the more relaxed version.

Successive scanning   A hypothesized strategy used in concept formation in which people begin with one hypothesis, maintain that hypothesis as long as it is successful, and discard or change it when it is no longer tenable.

Sulci   (*sulcus*, sing.) The grooves between the ridges on the surface of the brain.

Surface structure   The portion of a sentence that can be analyzed and labeled by conventional parsing schemes (Chomsky).

Synapse   The juncture between two neurons.

Synesthesia   The condition in which information from one sensory modality (such as, auditory) is coded in another modality (such as, visual).

Syntax   Rules that govern the combination of morphemes into larger linguistic units (such as, phrases and sentences).

Template matching   The postulate asserting that pattern recognition occurs when an exact match is made between sensory stimuli and a corresponding internal mental form.

Temporal   One of the four major sections on the surface of each hemisphere, marked off by major convolutions or fissures.

Thinking   The general process of considering an issue in the mind, which results in the formation of a new mental representation.

Tomogram   An image that shows a cross section of the brain.

Top-down processing   Borrowed from computer language, cognitive processing as hypothesis-driven recognition of the whole stimulus configuration, which leads to recognition of the component parts.

Transformational grammar   Rules that change the linguistic structure of a sentence into another form while maintaining the semantic content (Chomsky).

Transitivity   The ability to coordinate isolated elements from a total system and perform operations on those elements (Piaget).

Turing test   The test involving communication between a human who asks questions and an unknown language-using entity, with the human's task being to distinguish the output as human or nonhuman.

Unconscious inference   Process in which an observer constructs a percept by means of reasoning without being consciously aware of the procedure.

Verbal dialogues   Conversations between people in which argumentation or persuasion plays a role.

Verification   A hypothetical stage in the creative process that involves testing or carrying out the problem solution.

Visuospatial sketchpad   A brief loop that rehearses images in working memory.

von Restorff effect   The tendency to recall an item that is highlighted or otherwise distinctive.

Voxels   Volume of neural tissues activated. Used in fMRI studies to indicate loci of brain activities which are usually associated with the processing of information.

Wernicke's area   A region of the brain adjacent to the auditory projection area implicated in understanding word meanings. Named for Carl Wernicke, nineteenth-century German neurologist. See also *Broca's area.*

Working memory   A memory system that temporarily holds and manipulates information as we perform cognitive tasks. Working memory is analogous to a workbench where new and old material is constantly being processed, transformed, and combined. (See A. Baddeley)

References

Aaronson, D., & Ferres, S. (1984). Reading strategies for children and adults: Some empirical evidence. *Journal of Verbal Learning and Verbal Behavior, 9,* 700–725.

Aaronson, D., & Ferres, S. (1986). Reading strategies for children and adults: A quantitative model. *Psychological Review, 93,* 89–112.

Abu-Mostafa, Y. S. (1995). Machines that learn from hints. *Scientific American,* April, 64–69.

Adams, J. L. (1976a). *Learning and memory.* Homewood, IL: Dorsey Press.

Adams, J. L. (1976b). *Conceptual blockbusters.* (2nd ed.). New York: Norton.

Adelson, B. (1981). Problem solving and the development of abstract categories in programming languages. *Memory and Cognition, 9,* 422–433.

Adelson, B. (1984). When novices surpass experts: The difficulty of a task may increase with expertise. *Journal of Experimental Psychology: Learning, Memory, and Cognition, 10,* 483–495.

Akin, D. (1982). *The psychology of architectural design.* London: Pion.

Alkon, D. L. (1988). *Memory traces in the brain.* Cambridge, England: Cambridge University Press.

Alkon, D. L. (1989). Memory storage and neural systems. *Scientific American,* July, 42–50.

American Heritage Dictionary of the English Language. (1969). Boston: Houghton Mifflin.

Amosov, N. M. (1967). *Modeling of thinking and the mind.* Translated from Russian by L. Finegold. New York: Spartan.

Anderson, A. R. (Ed.). (1964). *Minds and machines.* Englewood Cliffs, NJ: Prentice-Hall.

Anderson, J. R. (1975). Item-specific and relation-specific interference in sentence memory. *Journal of Experimental Psychology: Human Learning and Memory, 104,* 249–260.

Anderson, J. R. (1976). *Language, memory, and thought.* Hillsdale, NJ: Erlbaum.

Anderson, J. R. (1978). Arguments concerning representations for mental imagery. *Psychological Review, 85,* 249–277.

Anderson, J. R. (Ed.). (1981). *Cognitive skills and their acquisition.* Hillsdale, NJ: Erlbaum.

Anderson, J. R. (1983a). *The architecture of cognition.* Cambridge, MA: Harvard University Press.

Anderson, J. R. (1983b). A spreading activation theory of memory. *Journal of Verbal Learning and Verbal Behavior, 22,* 261–295.

Anderson, J. R. (1985). *Cognitive psychology and its implications* (2nd ed.). San Francisco: Freeman.

Anderson, J. R. (1990). *Cognitive psychology* (3rd ed.). San Francisco: Freeman.

Anderson, J. R., & Bower, G. H. (1972). Recognition and retrieval processes in free recall. *Psychological Review, 79,* 97–123.

Anderson, J. R., & Bower, G. H. (1973). *Human associative memory.* Washington, DC: Winston.

Anderson, J. R., & Kosslyn, S. M. (Eds.). (1984). *Tutorials in learning and memory: Essays in honor of Gordon Bower.* San Francisco: Freeman.

Anderson, J. R., & Reiser, B. J. (1978). Schema-directed processes in language comprehension. In A. Lesgold, J. Pellegrino, S. Fokkima, & R. Glaser (Eds.), *Cognitive psychology and instruction.* New York: Plenum.

Anderson, J. R., & Reiser, B. J. (1985). The LISP tutor. *Byte, 10,* 159–178.

Anderson, R. C., & Pichert, J. W. (1978). Recall of previously unrecallable information following a shift in perspective. *Journal of Verbal Learning and Verbal Behavior, 17,* 1–12.

André-Leicknam, B., & Ziegler, C. (1982). *Naissance de l'écriture: Cuneiformes et hieroglyphes.* Paris: Minister of Culture.

Andrew, A. M. (1963). *Brain and computer.* London: Harrap.

Annett, M. (1982). Handedness. In J. G. Beaumont (Ed.), *Divided visual field studies of cerebral organization.* London: Academic Press.

Anokhin, P. K. (1969). Cybernetics and the integrative activity of the brain. In M. Cole & I. Maltzman (Eds.), *A handbook of contemporary Soviet psychology.* New York: Basic Books.

Apter, M. J. (1970). *The computer simulation of behavior.* New York: Harper & Row.

Apter, M., & Westby, G. (Eds.). (1973). *The computer in psychology.* New York: Wiley.

Atkinson, R. C. (1975). Mnemotechnics in second-language learning. *American Psychologist, 30,* 821–828.

Atkinson, R. C., Herrmann, D. J., Wescourt, K. T. (1974). Search processes in recognition memory. In R. L. Solso (Ed.), *Theories in cognitive psychology.* Hillsdale, NJ: Erlbaum.

Atkinson, R. C., & Juola, J. F. (1973). Factors influencing speed and accuracy of word recognition. In S. Kornblum (Ed.), *Attention and performance* (Vol. IV, pp. 583–612). New York: Academic Press.

Atkinson, R. C., & Juola, J. F. (1974). Search and decision processes in recognition memory. In D. H. Krantz, R. C. Atkinson, R. D. Luce, & P. Suppes (Eds.), *Contemporary developments in mathematical psychology* (Vol. 1, pp. 242–293). San Francisco: Freeman.

Atkinson, R. C., & Raugh, M. R. (1975). An application of the mnemonic keyword method to the acquisition of a Russian vocabulary. *Journal of Experimental Psychology: Human Learning and Memory, 104,* 126–133.

Atkinson, R. C., & Shiffrin, R. M. (1965). *Mathematical models for memory and learning* (Tech. Rep. 79). Institute for Mathematical Studies in the Social Sciences, Stanford University.

Atkinson, R. C., & Shiffrin, R. M. (1968). Human memory: A proposed system and its control processes. In K. W. Spence & J. T. Spence (Eds.), *The psychology of learning and motivation: Advances in research and theory* (Vol. 2, pp. 89–195). New York: Academic Press.

Averbach, E., & Coriell, A. S. (1961). Short-term memory in vision. *Bell System Technical Journal, 40,* 309–328.

Baars, B. J. (1983). Conscious contents provide the nervous system with coherent, global information. In R. Davidson, G. Schwartz, & D. Shapiro (Eds.), *Consciousness and self-regulation* (Vol. 2, pp. 45–76). New York: Plenum Press.

Baars, B. J. (1986). *The cognitive revolution in psychology.* New York: Guilford Press.

Baars, B. J. (1988). *A cognitive theory of consciousness.* Cambridge, England: Cambridge University Press.

Baars, B. J. (1996). *In the theater of consciousness: The workspace of the mind.* Oxford, England: Oxford University Press.

Baars, B. J., & McGovern, K. (1995). Steps toward healing: False memories and traumagenic amnesia may coexist in vulnerable populations. *Consciousness & Cognition, Special Issue on Recovery of Traumatic Childhood Memory, 3* (3,4).

Baars, B. J., & McGovern, K. A. (2000). Consciousness cannot be limited to sensory qualities: Some empirical counterexamples. *Neuro-psychoanalysis, 2*(1), 11–13.

Bach, E. (1974). *Syntactic theory.* New York: Holt, Rinehart & Winston.

Bach, M. J., & Underwood, B. J. (1970). Developmental changes in memory attributes. *Journal of Educational Psychology, 61,* 292–296.

Baddeley, A. (1982). *Your memory: A user's guide.* New York: Macmillan.

Baddeley, A. D. (1972). Retrieval-rules and semantic coding in short-term memory. *Psychological Bulletin, 78,* 379–385.

Baddeley, A. D. (1973). Memory coding and amnesia. *Neuropsychologia, 11,* 159–165.

Baddeley, A. D. (1976). *The psychology of memory.* New York: Basic Books.

Baddeley, A. D. (1978). The trouble with levels: A re-examination of Craik and Lockhart's "Framework for memory research" *Psychological Review, 85,* 139–152.

Baddeley, A. D. (1986). *Working memory.* Oxford: Oxford University Press.

Baddeley, A. D. (1990a). *Human memory.* Hove: Erlbaum Associates.

Baddeley, A. D. (1990b). *Human memory: Theory and practice.* Boston: Allyn and Bacon.

Baddeley, A. D. (1992). Working memory. *Science, 255,* 556–559.

Baddeley, A. D., & Hitch, G. (1974). Working memory. In G. H. Bower (Ed.), *The psychology of learning and motivation* (Vol. 8, pp. 47–90). New York: Academic Press.

Baddeley, A. D., & Levy, B. A. (1971). Semantic coding and memory. *Journal of Experimental Psychology, 89,* 132–136.

Baddeley, A. D., & Warrington, E. K. (1970). Amnesia and the distinction between long- and short-term memory. *Journal of Verbal Learning and Verbal Behavior, 9,* 176–189.

Baddeley, A. D., & Warrington, E. K. (1973). Memory coding and amnesia. *Neuropsychologia, 11,* 159–165.

Bahrick, H. P. (1984). Semantic memory content in permastore: Fifty years of memory for Spanish learned in school. *Journal of Experimental Psychology: General, 113,* 1–35.

Bahrick, H. P., Bahrick, P. O., & Wittlinger, R. P. (1975). Fifty years of memory for names and faces: A cross-sectional approach. *Journal of Experimental Psychology: General, 104,* 54–75.

Bahrick, H. P., & Phelps, E. (1987). Retention of Spanish vocabulary over 8 years. *Journal of Experimental Psychology: Learning, Memory and Cognition, 13,* 344–349.

Ballard, D. H., & Brown, C. M. (1985). Vision. *Byte, 10,* 245–261.

Ballard, P. B. (1913). Oblivescence and reminiscence. *British Journal of Psychology Monograph Supplements, 1,* 1–82.

Banks, W. P. (1970). Signal detection theory and human memory. *Psychological Bulletin, 74,* 81–99.

Barinaga, M. (1999). The mapmaking mind. *Science, 285*(5425), 189–192.

Barkow, J. H., Cosmides, L., & Tooby, J. (1992) (Eds.). *The adapted mind: Evolutionary psychology and the generation of culture.* New York: Oxford University Press.

Baron, J. (1973). Phonemic stage not necessary for reading. *Quarterly Journal of Experimental Psychology, 25,* 241–246.

Baron, J. (1988). *Thinking and deciding.* Cambridge, England: Cambridge University Press.

Baron, J., & Thurston, I. (1973). An analysis of the word superiority effect. *Cognitive Psychology, 4,* 207–228.

Barsalou, L. W. (1992). *Cognitive psychology.* Hillsdale, NJ: Erlbaum.

Bartlett, F. C. (1932). *Remembering: A study in experimental and social psychology.* Cambridge, England: Cambridge University Press.

Bartlett, F. C. (1958). *Thinking.* New York: Basic Books.

Bartlett, J. C., & Snelus, P. (1980). Lifespan memory for popular songs. *American Journal of Psychology, 93,* 551–560.

Bauer, M. I., & Johnson-Laird, P. N. (1993). How diagrams can improve reasoning. *Psychological Science, 4,* 372–378.

Beal, M. K., & Solso, R. L. (April, 1996). Schematic activation and the viewing of pictures. Paper presented at the Western Psychological Association, San Jose, CA.

Bédard, J. (1989). Expertise in auditing: Myth or reality? *Accounting, Organizations and Society, 14,* 113–131.

Bédard, J., & Chi, M. T. H. (1993). Expertise. *Current Directions in Psychological Science, 4,* 135–139.

Begg, I., & Denny, J. P. (1969). Empirical reconsideration of atmosphere and conversion interpretations of syllogistic reasoning errors. *Journal of Experimental Psychology, 81,* 351–354.

Bellezza, F. S. (1992). Recall of congruent information in the self-reference task. *Bulletin of the Psychonomic Society, 30,* 275–278.

Bellows, S. (1987). *The bellarosa connection.* New York: Penguin.

Benderly, B. L. (1989). Everyday intuition. *Psychology Today,* Sept., 35–40.

Benson, D. F., & Zaidel, E. (Eds.). (1985). *The dual brain: Hemispheric specialization in humans.* New York: Guilford Press.

Bergen, J. R., & Julesz, B. (1983). Parallel versus serial processing in rapid pattern discrimination. *Nature, 303,* 696–698.

Berlin, B., & Kay, P. (1969). *Basic color terms: Their universality and evolution.* Berkeley: University of California Press.

Bernbach, H. A. (1967). Decision processes in memory. *Psychological Review, 74,* 462–480.

Bernstein, L. (1959). What makes the opera grand. In *The joy of music* (p. 290). New York: Simon & Schuster.

Bernstein, L. (1976). *The unanswered question: Six talks at Harvard.* Cambridge, MA: Harvard University Press.

Bernstein, N. (1967). *The co-ordination and regulation of movements.* Oxford: Pergamon Press.

Bertelson, P. (1967). The time course of preparation. *Quarterly Journal of Experimental Psychology, 19,* 272–279.

Betts, G. H. (1909). *The distribution and functions of mental imagery.* New York: Teachers College, Columbia University Press.

Biederman, I. (1972). Perceiving real world scenes. *Science, 177*, 77–80.

Biederman, I. (1985). Human image understanding: Recent research and a theory. *Computer Vision, Graphics and Image Processing, 31*, 29–73.

Biederman, I. (1987). Recognition by components: A theory of human image understanding. *Psychological Review, 94*, 115–147.

Biederman, I. (1990). Higher-level vision. In E. N. Osherson, S. M. Kosslyn, & J. M. Hollerbach (Eds.), *An invitation to cognitive science* (Vol. 2, pp. 41–72). Cambridge, MA: The MIT Press.

Biederman, I., & Cooper, E. E. (1991). Priming contour-deleted images: Evidence for intermediate representations in visual object recognition. *Cognitive Psychology, 23*, 393–419.

Biederman, I., & Gerhardstein, P. C. (1993). Recognizing depth-rotated objects: Evidence and conditions for 3D viewpoint invariance. *Journal of Experimental Psychology: Human Perception and Performance, 19*.

Biederman, I., Glass, A. L., & Stacy, E. W. (1973). Searching for objects in real world scenes. *Journal of Experimental Psychology, 97*, 22–27.

Bjork, E. L., & Estes, W. K. (1973a). Letter identification in relation to linguistic context and masking conditions. *Memory and Cognition, 1*, 217–223.

Bjork, E. L., & Estes, W. K. (1973b). Detection and placement of redundant signal elements in tachistoscope display of letters. *Perception and Pychophysics, 9*, 439–442.

Black, J. B. (1981). The effects of reading purpose on memory for text. In J. Long & A. Baddeley (Eds.), *Attention and performance* (Vol. 9). Hillsdale, NJ: Erlbaum.

Black, J. B. (1984). Understanding and remembering stories. In J. R. Anderson & S. M. Kosslyn (Eds.), *Tutorials in learning and memory.* San Francisco: Freeman.

Black, J. B., & Bower, G. H. (1980). Story understanding as problem solving. *Poetics, 9*, 223–250.

Blakemore, C. (1977). *Mechanics of the mind.* Cambridge, England: Cambridge University Press.

Bledsoe, W. W., & Browning, I. (1959). Pattern recognition and reading by machine. *Proceedings of the Eastern Joint Computer Conference*, 225–232. Reprinted in L. Uhr (Ed.). (1966). *Pattern recognition.* New York: Wiley.

Bliss, J. C., Hewitt, D. V., Crane, P. K., Mansfield, P. K., & Townsend, J. T. (1966). Information available in brief tactile presentations. *Perception and Psychophysics, 1*, 273–283.

Boden, M. (1977). *Artificial intelligence and natural man.* New York: Basic Books.

Boden, M. A. (1989). *Artificial intelligence in psychology: Interdisciplinary essays.* Cambridge, MA: The MIT Press.

Bogen, J. E., & Vogel, P. J. (1962). Cerebral commissurotomy: A case report. *Bulletin of the Los Angeles Neurological Society, 27*, 169.

Boies, S. J., Posner, M. I., & Taylor, R. L. (1968). *Rehearsal of visual information from a single letter.* Paper presented at the meeting of the Western Psychological Association, San Diego, CA, May. Cited in M. I. Posner, *Abstraction and the process of recognition.* In J. T. Spence & G. H. Bower (Eds.), *The psychology of learning and motivation: Advances in learning and motivation* (Vol. 3). New York: Academic Press.

Boles, D. B. (1984). Sex in latalized tachistoscopic word recognition. *Brain and Language, 23*, 307–317.

Boles, D. B. (1987). Reaction time asymmetry through bilateral versus unilateral stimulus presentation. *Brain and Cognition, 6*, 321–333.

Boles, D. B. (1994). An experimental comparison of stimulus type, display type, and input variable contributions to visual field asymmetry. *Brain and Cognition, 24*(2), 184–197.

Borge, V. (1978). Quoted by Linda Gutstein in "They laugh when he sits down to play." *Parade*, Apr. 9, p. 18.

Boring, E. G. (1942). *Sensation and perception in the history of experimental psychology.* New York: Appleton-Century-Crofts.

Boring, E. G. (1946). The perception of objects. *American Journal of Psychology, 14*, 99–107.

Boring, E. G. (1950). *A history of experimental psychology* (2nd ed.). New York: Appleton-Century-Crofts.

Bothwell, R. K., Brigham, J. C., & Malpass, R. S. (1989). Cross-racial identification. *Personality and Social Psychology Bulletin, 15*, 19–25.

Bourne, L. E., Jr. (1963). Factors affecting strategies used in problems of concept-formation. *American Journal of Psychology, 76*, 229–238.

Bourne, L. E., Jr. (1974). An interference model for conceptual rule learning. In R. L. Solso (Ed.), *Theories in cognitive psychology: The Loyola Symposium* (pp. 231–256). Hillsdale, NJ: Erlbaum.

Bourne, L. E., Jr., & Dominowski, R. (1972). Thinking. In *Annual Review of Psychology* (Vol. 23). Palo Alto, CA: Annual Reviews.

Bourne, L. E., Jr., Dominowski, R. L., Loftus, E. F., & Healy, A. F.: (1986). *Cognitive processes* (2nd ed.). Englewood Cliffs, NJ: Prentice-Hall.

Bourne, L. E., Jr., Ekstrand, B. R., & Dominowski, R. L. (1971). *The psychology of thinking.* Englewood Cliffs, NJ: Prentice-Hall.

Bourne, L. E., Jr., & Guy, D. E. (1968). Learning conceptual rules: I. Some interrule transfer effects. *Journal of Experimental Psychology, 76,* 423–429.

Bourne, L. E., Jr., & Restle, F. (1959). Mathematical theory of concept identification. *Psychological Review, 66,* 278–296.

Bousfield, W. A. (1951). Frequency and availability measures in language behavior. Paper presented at the Annual Meeting of the American Psychological Association, Chicago.

Bousfield, W. A. (1953). The occurrence of clustering in the recall of randomly arranged associates. *Journal of General Psychology, 49,* 229–240.

Bousfield, W. A., & Cohen, B. H. (1953). The effects of reinforcement on the occurrence of clustering in the recall of randomly arranged associates. *Journal of Psychology, 36,* 67–81.

Bousfield, W. A., & Sedgewick, C. H. W. (1944). An analysis of sequences of restricted associative responses. *Journal of Psychology, 30,* 149–165.

Bower, G. H. (1967). A multi-component theory of the memory trace. In K. W. Spence & J. T. Spence (Eds.), *The psychology of learning and motivation: Advances in research and theory* (Vol. 1, pp. 299–325). New York: Academic Press.

Bower, G. H. (1970a). Organizational factors in memory. *Cognitive Psychology, 1,* 18–46.

Bower, G. H. (1970b). Analysis of a mnemonic device. *American Scientist, 58,* 496–510.

Bower, G. H. (1970c). Imagery as a relational organizer in associative learning. *Journal of Verbal Learning and Verbal Behavior, 9,* 529–533.

Bower, G. H. (1972). Mental imagery and associative learning. In L. W. Gregg (Ed.), *Cognition in learning and memory* (pp. 51–88). New York: Wiley.

Bower, G. H. (1973a). How to . . . uh . . . remember! *Psychology Today, 7,* 62–67.

Bower, G. H. (1973b). Memory freaks I have known. *Psychology Today, 7,* 64–65.

Bower, G. H. (1975). Cognitive psychology: An introduction. In W. Estes (Ed.), *Handbook of learning and cognitive processes* (Vol. 1, pp. 25–80). Hillsdale, NJ: Erlbaum.

Bower, G. H. (1976a). *Experiments on story understanding and recall.* Bartlett Lecture to EPS at Durham, England, Apr. 8.

Bower, G. H. (1976b). *Comprehending and recalling stories.* Division 3 Presidential Address presented at the Annual Meeting of the American Psychological Association, Washington, DC, Sept.

Bower, G. H. (1993). Quoted in "Biomedicine in the age of imaging." *Science, 261,* 30 July.

Bower, G. H., Black, J. B., & Turner, T. (1979). Scripts in memory for text. *Cognitive Psychology, 11,* 177–220.

Bower, G. H., & Clark, M. C. (1969). Narrative stories as mediators for serial learning. *Psychonomic Science, 14,* 181–182.

Bower, G. H., Clark, M. C., Lesgold, A. M., & Winzenz, D. (1969). Hierarchical retrieval schemes in recall of categorized word lists. *Journal of Verbal Learning and Verbal Behavior, 8,* 323–343.

Bower, G. H., & Clark-Meyers, G. (1980). Memory for scripts with organized vs. random presentations. *British Journal of Psychology, 71,* 368–377.

Bower, G. H., & Gilligan, S. G. (1979). Remembering information related to one's self. *Journal of Research in Personality, 13,* 420–432.

Bower, G. H., & Karlin, M. B. (1974). Depth of processing pictures of faces and recognition memory. *Journal of Experimental Psychology, 103,* 751–757.

Bower, G. H., Muñoz, R., & Arnold, P. G. (1972). *On distinguishing semantic and imaginal mnemonics.* Unpublished manuscript. Cited in J. Anderson & G. Bower (1973); *Human associative memory* (p. 459). Washington, DC: Winston.

Bower, G. H., & Reitman, J. S. (1972). Mnemonic elaboration in multilist learning. *Journal of Verbal Learning and Verbal Behavior, 11,* 478–485.

Bower, G. H., & Springston, F. (1970). Pauses as recoding points in letter series. *Journal of Experimental Psychology, 83,* 421–430.

Bower, G. H., & Winzenz, D. (1969). Group structure, coding, and memory for digit series. *Journal of Experimental Psychology Monograph Supplement, 80,* 1–17.

Bower, G. H., & Winzenz, D. (1970). Comparison of associative learning strategies. *Psychonomic Science, 20,* 119–120.

Bower, T. G. R. (1970). Reading by eye. In H. Levin & J. P. Williams (Eds.), *Basic studies in reading.* New York: Basic Books.

Bowers, K. S., Regehr, G., Balthazard, C., & Parker, K. (1990). Intuition in the context of discovery. *Cognitive Psychology, 22,* 72–110.

Bowman, J. P. (1968). Muscle spindles in the intrinsic and extrinsic muscles of the rhesus monkey's (macaca mulatta) tongue. *Anatomical Record, 161*, 483–488.

Bowman, J. P., & Combs, C. M. (1968). Discharge patterns of lingual spindle afferent fibers in the hypoglossal nerve of the rhesus monkey. *Experimental Neurology, 21*, 105–119.

Bowman, J. P., & Combs, C. M. (1969a). The cerebrocortical projection of hypoglossal afferents. *Experimental Neurology, 23*, 291–301.

Bowman, J. P., & Combs, C. M. (1969b). Cerebellar responsiveness to stimulation of lingual spindle afferent fibers in the hypoglossal nerve of the rhesus monkey. *Experimental Neurology, 23*, 537–543.

Bradshaw, J. L., & Nettleton, N. C. (1981). The nature of hemispheric specialization in man. *Behavioral and Brain Sciences, 4*, 51–91.

Brainerd, C. J. (1973). Order of acquisition of transitivity, conservation, and class inclusion of length and weight. *Developmental Psychology, 8*, 105–116.

Brainerd, C. J. (1978). *Piaget's theory of intelligence.* Englewood Cliffs, NJ: Prentice-Hall.

Brams, S. J. (1993). Theory of moves. *American Scientist, 81*, 562–570.

Bransford, J. D., & Franks, J. J. (1971). The abstraction of linguistic ideas: A review. *Cognitive Psychology, 2*, 331–350.

Bransford, J. D., & Franks, J. J. (1972). The abstraction of linguistic ideas: A review. *Cognition, 1*, 211–250.

Bransford, J. D., & Johnson, M. K. (1972). Contextual prerequisites for understanding: Some investigations of comprehension and recall. *Journal of Verbal Learning and Verbal Behavior, 11*, 717–726.

Bransford, J. D., & Stein. B. S. (1993). *The ideal problem solver.* New York: Freeman.

Brewer, W. F. (1974). The problem of meaning and the interrelations of the higher mental processes. In W. B. Weimer & D. S. Palermo (Eds.), *Cognition and the symbolic processes* (pp. 263–298). New York: Wiley.

Briggs, G. E., & Blaha, J. (1969). Memory retrieval and central comparison times in information-processing. *Journal of Experimental Psychology, 79*, 395–402.

Broadbent, D. E. (1954). The role of auditory localization and attention in memory spans. *Journal of Experimental Psychology, 47*, 191–196.

Broadbent, D. E. (1958). *Perception and communication.* London and New York: Pergamon Press.

Broadbent, D. E. (1962). Attention and the perception of speech. *Scientific American, 206*, 143–151.

Broadbent, D. E. (1966). The well-ordered mind. *American Education Research Journal, 3*, 281–295.

Broadbent, D. E. (1971). *Decision and stress.* London: Academic Press.

Broadbent, D. E. (1973). *In defense of empirical psychology.* London: Methuen.

Broadbent, D. E. (1981). Selective and control processes. *Cognition, 10*, 53–58.

Broadbent, D. E. (1984). The Maltese cross: A new simplistic model for memory. *Behavioral & Brain Sciences, 7*, 55–94.

Broadhurst P. L. (1957). Emotionality and the Yerkes-Dodson law. *Journal of Experimental Psychology, 54*, 345–352.

Broca, P. P. (1864/1970). Cited in M. Critchley, *Aphasiology and other aspects of language.* London: Edward Arnold.

Bromley, H. L., Jarvella, R. L., & Lundberg, I. (1985). From Lisp machine to language lab. *Behavioral Research Methods, Instruments, and Computers, 17*, 399–402.

Brooks, L. R. (1968). Spatial and verbal components of the act of recall. *Canadian Journal of Psychology, 22*, 349–368.

Brown, A. L. (1975). The development of memory: Knowing, knowing about knowing, and knowing how to know. In H. W. Reese (Ed.), *Advances in child development and behavior* (Vol. 10). New York: Academic Press.

Brown, J. (Ed.). (1975). *Recognition and recall.* London: Wiley.

Brown, J. A. (1958). Some tests of the decay theory of immediate memory. *Quarterly Journal of Experimental Psychology, 10*, 12–21.

Brown, R. (1958). *Words and things.* New York: Free Press.

Brown, R. (1965). *Social psychology.* New York: Free Press.

Brown, R. (1970). *Psycholinguistics.* New York: Free Press.

Brown, R., & Herrnstein, R. J. (1975). *Psychology.* Boston: Little, Brown.

Brown, R., & Kulik, J. (1977). Flashbulb memories. *Cognition, 5*, 73–99.

Brown, R., & McNeill, D. (1966). The "tip of the tongue" phenomenon. *Journal of Verbal Learning and Verbal Behavior, 5*, 325–337.

Bruner, J. S., Goodnow, J. J., & Austin, G. A. (1956). *A study of thinking.* New York: Wiley.

Bruner, J. S., Oliver, R. R., & Greenfield, P. M. (Eds.). (1966). *Studies in cognitive growth.* New York: Wiley.

Bryant, P. E., & Trabasso, T. (1971). Transitive inferences and memory in young children. *Nature, 232,* 456–458.

Bugelski, B. R. (1970). Words and things and images. *American Psychologist, 25,* 1002–1012.

Bugelski, B. R., Kidd, E., & Gegmen, J. (1968). Image as a mediator in one-trial paired-associate learning. *Journal of Experimental Psychology, 76,* 69–73.

Byte, Apr., 1985.

Cabeza, R., & Nyberg, L. (1997). Imaging Cognition: An empirical review of PET studies with normal subjects. *Journal of Cognitive Neuroscience, 9,* 1–26.

Calfee, R. C. (1975). *Human experimental psychology.* New York: Holt, Rinehart & Winston.

Caramazza, A., Gordon, J., Zurif, E. B., & De Luca, D. (1976). Right hemispheric damage and verbal problem solving behavior. *Brain and Language, 3,* 41–46.

Carbonell, J. G. (1979). Subjective understanding: Computer models of belief systems. Unpublished doctoral dissertation, Yale University.

Carpenter, P. A., & Dahneman, M. (1981). Lexical retrieval and error recovery in reading: A model based on eye fixations. *Journal of Verbal Learning and Verbal Behavior, 20,* 137–164.

Carroll, J. B., & Freedle, R. O. (Eds.). (1972). *Language comprehension and the acquisition of knowledge.* Washington, DC: Winston.

Casey, R. G., & Nagy, G. (1971). Advances in pattern recognition. *Scientific American, 224,* 56–64.

Catania, A. C. (1970). Reinforcement schedules and psychophysical judgments. A study of some temporal properties of behavior. In W. N. Schoenfeld (Ed.), *The theory of reinforcement schedules* (pp. 1–42). New York: Appleton-Century-Crofts.

Cattell, J. McK. (1886a). The time it takes to see and name objects. *Mind, 11,* 63–65.

Cattell, J. McK. (1886b). The time taken up by cerebral operations. *Mind, 11,* 277–292, 524–538.

Cattell, J. McK. (1954). Uberdi Aeit der Erkennung and Benennung von Schriftzeichen, Bildern and Farben. *Philos, St. 2,* 1885, 635–650. Cited in R. Woodworth & H. Schlosberg (Eds.), *Experimental psychology.* New York: Holt.

Cattell, R. B. (1965). *The scientific analysis of personality.* Baltimore: Penguin.

Cattell, R. B. (1971). *Abilities: Their structure, growth and action.* Boston: Houghton Mifflin.

Ceraso, J., & Provitera, A. (1971). Sources of error in syllogistic reasoning. *Cognitive Psychology, 2,* 400–410.

Cermak, L. S. (1976). *Improving your memory.* New York: McGraw-Hill.

Chapman, L. J., & Chapman, J. P. (1959). Atmosphere effect reexamined. *Journal of Experimental Psychology, 58,* 220–226.

Charness, N. (1979). Components of skill in bridge. *Canadian Journal of Psychology, 33,* 1–50.

Chase, W. G. (Ed.). (1973). *Visual information processing.* New York: Academic Press.

Chase, W. G., & Ericsson, K. A. (1981). Skilled memory. In J. R. Anderson (Ed.), *Cognitive skills and their acquisition.* Hillsdale, NJ: Erlbaum.

Chase, W. G., & Ericsson, K. A. (1982). Skill and working memory. In G. H. Bower (Ed.), *The psychology of learning and motivation* (pp. 1–58). New York: Academic Press.

Chase, W. G., & Simon, H. A. (1973a). The mind's eye in chess. In W. G. Chase (Ed.), *Visual information processing.* New York: Academic Press.

Chase, W. G., & Simon, H. A. (1973b). Perception in chess. *Cognitive Psychology, 4,* 55–81.

Cheesman, J., & Merikle, P. M. (1984). Priming with and without awareness. *Perception and Psychophysics, 36*(4), 387–395.

Cherry, C. (1953). Some experiments on the recognition of speech with one and with two ears. *Journal of the Acoustic Society of America, 25,* 975–979.

Cherry, C. (1966). *On human communication* (2nd ed.). Cambridge, MA: The MIT Press.

Chi, M. T. (1976). Short-term memory limitations in children: Capacity or processing deficits. *Memory and Cognition, 5,* 559–572.

Chi, M. T. (1978). Knowledge structures and memory development. In R. S. Siegler (Ed.), *Children's thinking: What develops?* Hillsdale, NJ: Erlbaum.

Chi, M. T. H., Feltovich, P., & Glaser, R. (1981). Categorization and representation of physics problems by experts and novices, *Cognitive Science, 5,* 121–152.

Chi, M. T. H., Glaser, R., & Farr, M. J. (Eds.). (1988). *The nature of expertise.* Hillsdale, NJ: Erlbaum.

Chi, M. T. H., Glaser, R., & Rees, E. (1982). Expertise in problem solving. In R. J. Sternberg (Ed.), *Advances in the psychology of human intelligence.* Hillsdale, NJ: Erlbaum.

Chiarello, C. (1988). Lateralization of lexical processes in the normal brain: A review of visual hemi-field research. In H. A. Whitaker (Ed.), *Contemporary reviews in neuropsychology.* (pp. 36–76). New York: Springer.

Chiesi, H. L., Spilich, G. J., & Voss, J. F. (1979). Acquisition of domain-related information in relation to high and low domain knowledge. *Journal of Verbal Learning and Verbal Behavior, 18,* 257–273.

Chipman, S. F., Davis, C., & Shafto, M. G. (1986). Personnel and training research program: Cognitive science at ONR. *Naval Research Review, 38*, 3–21.

Chomsky, N. (1956). Three models of the description of language. Proceedings of a Symposium on Information Theory. *IRF Transactions on Information Theory, IT-2*(3), 113–124.

Chomsky, N. (1957a). *Syntactic structures.* The Hague: Mouton.

Chomsky, N. (1957b). Review of *Verbal behavior* by B. F. Skinner. *Language, 35,* 26–58.

Chomsky, N. (1965). *Aspect of the theory of syntax.* Cambridge, MA: The MIT Press.

Chomsky, N. (1966). *Topics in the theory of generative grammar.* The Hague: Mouton.

Chomsky, N. (1968). *Language and mind.* New York: Harcourt Brace Jovanovich.

Chukovsky, K. (1971). *From two to five.* Berkeley: University of California Press.

Churchland, P. S. (1989). From Descartes to neural networks. *Scientific American*, July, 118.

Churchland, P. S., & Sejnowski, T. J. (1988). Perspectives on cognitive neuroscience. *Science, 242*, 741–745.

Clancey, W. J. (1988). Acquiring, representing, and evaluating a competence model of diagnosis strategy. In M. T. H. Chi, R. Glaser, & M. J. Farr (Eds.), *The nature of expertise.* Hillsdale, NJ: Erlbaum.

Clark, H., & Clark, E. (1977). *Psychology and language: An introduction to psycholinguistics.* New York: Harcourt Brace Jovanovich.

Clark, W. C. (1966). The psyche in psychophysics: A sensory-decision theory analysis of the effect of instruction on flicker sensitivity and response bias. *Psychological Bulletin, 65*, 358–366.

Clark, W. C., Brown, J. C., & Rutschmann, J. (1967). Flicker sensitivity and response bias in psychiatric patients and normal subjects. *Journal of Abnormal Psychology, 72*, 35–42.

Clarke, A. C. (1968). *2001: A space odyssey.* New York: New American Library.

Clement, C., & Falmagne, R. J. (1986). Logical reasoning, world knowledge, and mental imagery: Interconnections in cognitive processes. *Memory & Cognition, 14*, 299–307.

Cofer, C. N. (1973). Constructive processes in memory. *American Scientist, 61*, 537–543.

Cofer, C. N. (Ed.). (1976). *The structure of human memory.* San Francisco: Freeman.

Cohen, G. (1989). *Memory in the real world.* Hillsdale, NJ: Erlbaum.

Cohen, J. D., Servan-Schreiber, & McClelland, J. L. (1992). A parallel distributed processing approach to automaticity. *American Journal of Psychology, 105*, 239–269.

Cohen, J. J., & Corkin, S. (1981). The amnesic patient, H. M.: Learning and retention of a cognitive skill. *Society for Neuroscience Abstracts, 7*, 235.

Cohen, J. J., & Squire, L. R. (1980). Preserved learning and retention of pattern-analyzing skill in amnesia: Dissociation of knowing how and knowing that. *Science, 210*, 207–210.

Cohen, K. M., & Haith, M. M. (1977). Peripheral vision in the effects of developmental, perceptual, and cognitive factors. *Journal of Experimental Child Psychology, 3*, 373–395.

Cohen, L. B., & Salapatek, P. (1975). *Infant perception: From sensation to cognition* (Vol. 1). New York: Academic Press.

Cohen, L. B., & Strauss, M. S. (1979). Concept acquisition in the human infant. *Child Development, 50*, 419–424.

Cohen, L. J. (1981). Can human irrationally be experimentally demonstrated? *Behavioral and Brain Sciences, 4*, 317–370.

Cohen, M. S., Rosen, B. R., & Brady, T. J. (1992). Ultrafast MRI permits expanded clinical role. *Magnetic Resonance, 26*, Winter.

Colby, K. M., Hilf, F. D., Weber, S., & Kraemer, H. C. (1972). Turing-like indistinguishability tests for the validation of a computer simulation of paranoid processes. *Artificial Intelligence, 3*.

Cole, M. (1975). An ethnographic psychology of cognition. In R. W. Brislin, S. Blochner, & W. J. Lonner (Eds.), *Perspectives on learning, I, Cross-cultural research and methodology.* New York: Halsted Press, Wiley.

Cole, M., Frankel, F., & Sharp, D. (1971). Development of free recall learning in children. *Developmental Psychology, 4*, 109–123.

Cole, M., Gay, J., Glick, J., & Sharp, D. (1971). *The cultural context of learning and thinking.* New York: Basic Books.

Cole, M., & Scribner, S. (1974). *Culture and thought.* New York: Wiley.

Collins, A., & Smith, E. E. (Eds.). (1988). *Readings in cognitive science: A perspective from psychology and artificial intelligence.* San Mateo, CA: Morgan Kaufmann.

Collins, A. M., & Loftus, E. F. (1975). A spreading activation theory of semantic processing. *Psychological Review, 82*, 407–428.

Collins, A. M., & Quillian, M. R. (1969). Retrieval time from semantic memory. *Journal of Verbal Learning and Verbal Behavior, 8*, 240–247.

Collins, A. M., & Quillian, M. R. (1972). How to make a language user. In E. Tulving and W. Donaldson (Eds.), *Organization of memory*. New York: Academic Press.

Collyer, S. C., Jonides, J., & Bevan, W. (1972). Images as memory aids: Is bizarreness helpful? *American Journal of Psychology, 85,* 31–38.

Coltheart, M. (Ed.). (1972a). *Readings in cognitive psychology*. Toronto: Holt, Rinehart & Winston.

Coltheart, M. (1972b). Visual information processing. In P. Dodwell (Ed.), *New horizons in psychology: 2*. Harmondsworth, Middlesex, England: Penguin.

Coltheart, M. (1975). Iconic memory: A reply to Professor Holding. *Memory and Cognition, 3,* 42–48.

Coltheart, M. (1983). Ecological necessity of iconic memory. *Behavioral and Brain Sciences, 6,* 17–18.

Coltheart, M. (Ed.). (1987). *The cognitive neuropsychology of language*. Hillsdale, NJ: Erlbaum.

Coltheart, M., & Glick, M. J. (1974). Visual imagery: A case study. *Quarterly Journal of Experimental Psychology, 26,* 438–453.

The Columbia Dictionary of Quotations. (1993). New York: Columbia University Press.

The Concise Columbia Encyclopedia (1995). New York: Columbia University Press.

Conrad, C. (1972). Cognitive economy in semantic memory. *Journal of Experimental Psychology, 92,* 149–154.

Conrad, R. (1963). Acoustic confusions and memory span for words. *Nature, 197,* 1029–1030.

Conrad, R. (1964). Acoustic confusions in immediate memory. *British Journal of Psychology, 55,* 75–84.

Conrad, R. (1970). Short-term memory processes in the deaf. *British Journal of Psychology, 61,* 179–195.

Conway, M. A., Cohen, G., & Stanhope, N. (1991). On the very long-term retention of knowledge acquired through formal education: Twelve years of cognitive psychology. *Journal of Experimental Psychology: General, 120,* 395–409.

Cooper, E. E., & Biederman, I. (1993). Metric versus viewpoint invariant shape differences in visual object recognition. Poster presented at the meeting of the Association for Research in Vision and Ophthalmology, Sarasota, FL, May.

Cooper, L. A., & Shepard, R. N. (1972). The time required to prepare for a rotated stimulus. *Memory and Cognition, 1,* 246–250.

Cooper, L. A., & Shepard, R. N. (1973). Chronometric studies of the rotation of mental images. In W. G. Chase (Ed.), *Visual information processing*. New York: Academic Press.

Cooper, L. A., & Shepard, R. N. (1980). Transformations on representations of objects in space. In E. C. Carterette & M. Friedman (Eds.), *Handbook of perception, Volume 8: Space and object perception*. New York: Academic Press.

Corballis, M. C. (1989). Laterality and human evolution. *Psychological Review, 96,* 492–505.

Corballis, M. C., Kirby, J., & Miller, A. (1972). Access to elements of a memorized list. *Journal of Experimental Psychology, 9,* 185–190.

Corbetta, M., Miezin, F. M., Dobmeyer, S., Shulman, G. L., & Petersen, S. E. (1991). Selective and divided attention during visual discriminations of shape, color, and speed: Functional anatomy by positron emission tomography. *The Journal of Neuroscience, 11,* 2363–2402.

Coren, S. (1991). Retinal mechanism in the perception of subjective contours: The contribution of lateral inhibition. *Perception, 20,* 181–191.

Corteen, R. S., & Dunn, D. (1974). Shock-associated words in a nonattended message: A test for momentary awareness. *Journal of Experimental Psychology, 102,* 1143–1144.

Corteen, R. S., & Wood, B. (1972). Autonomic responses to shock-associated words in an unattended channel. *Journal of Experimental Psychology, 9,* 303–313.

Cousins, N. (1957). Smudging the subconscious. *Saturday Review,* Oct. 5, 20–21.

Cowan, N. (1988). Evolving conceptions of memory storage, selective attention, and their mutual constraints within the human information-processing system. *Psychological Bulletin, 104,* 163–191.

Cowan, W. M. (1979). The development of the brain. *Scientific American, 241,* 112–133.

Craik, F. I. M., & Jacoby, L. L. (1975). A process view of short-term retention. In R. Restle (Ed.), *Cognitive theory* (Vol. 1). Hillsdale, NJ: Erlbaum.

Craik, F. I. M., & Lockhart, R. S. (1972). Levels of processing: A framework for memory research. *Journal of Verbal Learning and Verbal Behavior, 11,* 671–684.

Craik, F. I. M., & Tulving, E. (1975). Depth of processing and the retention of words in episodic memory. *Journal of Experimental Psychology: General, 104,* 268–294.

Craik, F. I. M., & Watkins, M. J. (1973). The role of rehearsal in short-term memory. *Journal of Verbal Learning and Verbal Behavior, 12,* 599–607.

Crick, F. (1993). *The astonishing hypothesis: The scientific search for the soul*. New York: Scribners.

Crick, F. H. C. (1984). Function of the thalamic reticular complex: The searchlight hypothesis. *Proceedings of the National Academy of Sciences. USA, 81* 4586–93 (July).

Crick, F., & Asanuma, C. (1986). Certain aspects of the anatomy and physiology of the cerebral cortex. In D. E. Rumelhart, J. L. McClelland, and the PDP research group (Eds.), *Parallel distributed processing: Explorations in the microstructure of cognition* (Vol. 2). Cambridge, MA: Bradford.

Crowder, R. G. (1982a). *The psychology of memory.* New York: Oxford.

Crowder, R. G. (1982b). The demise of short-term memory. *Acta Psychologica, 50,* 291–323.

Crowder, R. G. (1982c). *The psychology of reading.* New York: Oxford.

Crowder, R. G. (1985). On access and the forms of memory. In N. Weinberger, J. McGaugh, & G. Lynch (Eds.), *Memory systems of the brain.* New York: Guilford Press.

Crowder, R. G. (1993). Short-term memory: Where do we stand? *Memory & Cognition, 21,* 142–145.

Cudhea, D. (1978). Artificial intelligence. *The Stanford Magazine, 6,* 8–14.

Cutler, B. L., & Penrod, S. D. (1995). *Mistaken identification: The eyewitness, psychology, and the law.* New York: Cambridge University Press.

Cutting, J. E. (1986). *Perception with an eye for motion.* Cambridge, MA: MIT Press.

Cutting, J. E. (1993). Perceptual artifacts and phenomena: Gibson's role in the 20th century. In S. C. Masin (Ed.) *Foundations of perceptual theory* (pp. 231–260). New York: Elsevier.

Daehler, M. W., & Bukatko, D. (1985). *Cognitive development.* New York: Knopf.

D'Agostino, P. R., O'Neill, B. J., & Paivio, A. (1977). Memory for pictures and words as a function of levels of processing: Depth or dual coding? *Memory and Cognition, 5,* 252–256.

Dale, P. S. (1976). *Language development: Structure and function* (2nd ed.). New York: Holt, Rinehart & Winston.

Damasio, A. R. (1989). Time-locked multiregional retroactivation: A systems-level proposal for the neural substrates of recall and recognition. *Cognition, 33,* 25–62.

Damasio, A. R. (1999). How the brain creates the mind. *Scientific American, 12,* 4–9.

Dannemiller, J. L., & Stephens, B. R. (1988). A critical test of infant pattern preferences models. *Child Development, 59,* 210–216.

Darwin, C. J., Turvey, M. T., & Crowder, R. G. (1972). An auditory analogue of the Sperling partial report procedure: Evidence for brief auditory storage. *Cognitive Psychology, 3,* 255–267.

Dawes, R. (1966). Memory and the distortion of meaningful written material. *British Journal of Psychology, 57,* 77–86.

Dawson, J. L. M. (1967). Cultural and physiological influences upon spatial-perceptual processes in West Africa. *International Journal of Psychology, 2,* 115–128.

Day, M. C. (1975). Developmental trends in visual scanning. In H. W. Reese (Ed.), *Advances in child development and behavior* (Vol. 10). New York: Academic Press.

Day, R. S., Cutting, J. C., & Copeland, P. M. (1971). Perception of linguistic and nonlinguistic dimensions of dichotic stimuli. *Haskins Laboratories Status Report on Speech Research, SR-27,* 193–197.

Day, R. S., & Wood, C. C. (1972a). Interactions between linguistic and nonlinguistic processing. *Journal of the Acoustical Society of America, 51,* 79A.

Day, R. S., & Wood, C. C. (1972b). Mutual interference between two linguistic dimensions of the same stimuli. *Journal of the Acoustical Society of America, 52,* 175A.

Dearborn, W. (1906). *The psychology of reading* (Columbia University contributions to philosophy and psychology). New York: Science Press.

de Groot, A. D. (1965). *Thought and choice in chess.* The Hague: Mouton.

de Groot, A. D. (1966). Perception and memory versus thought: Some old ideas and recent findings. In B. Kleinmuntz (Ed.), *Problem solving: Research, method and theory.* New York: Wiley.

Dehn, N., & Schank, R. (1982). Artificial and human intelligence. In R. Sternberg (Ed.), *Handbook of human intelligence.* Cambridge, England: Cambridge University Press.

Denes, P. B., & Pinson, E. N. (1963). *The speech chain.* Murray Hill, NJ: Bell Laboratories.

Dennett, D. C. (1987). Consciousness. In R. L. Gregory (Ed.), *The Oxford companion to the mind* (pp. 160–164). Oxford: Oxford University Press.

Dennett, D. C. (1991). *Consciousness explained.* New York: Little, Brown.

Dennett D., & Kinsbourne M. (1992). Time and the observer: The where and when of consciousness in the brain. *Behavioral and Brain Sciences.*

Deregowski, J. B. (1971). Symmetry, Gestalt and information theory. *Quarterly Journal of Experimental Psychology, 23,* 381–385.

Deregowski, J. B. (1973). Illusion and culture. In R. L. Gregory & E. H. Gombrich (Eds.), *Illusion in nature and art.* New York: Scribner.

Deregowski, J. B. (1980). *Illusions, perception and pictures.* London: Academic Press.

Deregowski, J. B., Muldrow, E. S., & Muldrow, W. F. (1973). Pictorial recognition in a remote Ethiopian population. *Perception, 1,* 417–425.

Descartes, R. (1931). *Philosophical works* (E. S. Haldane & G. R. T. Pross, trans.). Cambridge, England: Cambridge University Press.

Deutsch, J. A., & Deutsch, D. (1963). Attention: Some theoretical considerations. *Psychological Review, 70,* 80–90.

Deutsch, J. A., & Deutsch, D. (1967). Comments on selective attention: Perception or response? *Quarterly Journal of Experimental Psychology, 19,* 362–363.

Diringer, D. (1968). *The alphabet: A key to the history of mankind* (Vols. 1 and 2) (3rd ed.). London: Hutchinson.

Dolinsky, R. (1973). Word fragments as recall cues: Role of syllables. *Journal of Experimental Psychology, 97,* 272–274.

Donaldson, W., & Murdock, B. B., Jr. (1968). Criterion changes in continuous recognition memory. *Journal of Experimental Psychology, 76,* 325–330.

Donegan, C. (1989). Think again. *American Way,* Mar. 15, 73–111.

Downing, P., Liu, J., & Kanwisher, N. (2001). Testing cognitive models of visual attention with fMRI and MEG. *Neuropsychologia, 39*(12), 1329–1342.

Dreyfus, H. L. (1965). *Alchemy and artificial intelligence.* Santa Monica, CA: Rand Corporation.

Dreyfus, H. L. (1972). *What computers can't do: A critique of artificial reason.* New York: Harper Row.

Duchamp, M. (1945). From an interview with Janees Johnson Sweeney in Eleven Europeans in America. *Bulletin of the Museum of Modern Art* (New York), *13*(4–5), 19–21.

Duncan, J., Seitz, R. J., Kolodny, J., Bor, D., Herzog, H., Ahmed, A., Newell, F. N., & Emslie, H. (2000). A neural basis for general intelligence. *Science, 289,* 457–460.

Duncker, K. (1945). On problem solving. *Psychological Monographs, 58* (5, whole no. 270).

Dunlap, K. (1900). The effect of imperceptible shadows on the judgment of distance. *Psychological Review, 7,* 435–453.

Dupre, J. (Ed.). (1987). *The latest on the best essays on evolution and optimality.* Cambridge, MA: MIT Press.

Eacott, M. J. (1999). Memory for the events of early childhood. *Current Directions in Psychological Science, 8,* 46–49.

Easterbrook, J. A. (1959). The effect of emotion on cue utilization and the organization of behavior. *Psychological Review, 66,* 183–201.

Ebbinghaus, H. (1885). *Über das Gedächtnis: Intersuchungen zur experimentellen psychologie.* Leipzig: Duncker and Humboldt. (Translated by H. A. Ruger & C. E. Bussenius, 1913, and reissued by Dover Publications, 1964.)

Eccles, J. C. (1973). *The understanding of the brain.* New York: McGraw-Hill.

Edson, L. (1982). Under Babel's tower. *Mosaic, 13,* 22–28.

Edwards, W. (1968). Conservatism in human information processing. In B. Kleinmuntz (Ed.), *Formal representations of human judgment.* New York: Wiley.

Einstein, A. (1950). *Out of my later years.* New York: Philosophic Library.

Eisenberg, A. R., & Garvey, C. (1981) Children's use of verbal strategies in resolving conflicts. *Discourse Processes, 4,* 149–170.

Eisenstadt, M., & Kareev, Y. (1975). Aspects of human problem solving: The use of internal representation. In D. Norman & D. Rumelhart (Eds.), *Exploration in cognition.* San Francisco: Freeman.

Elithorn, A., & Banerji, R. (Eds.). (1984). *Artificial and human intelligence.* New York: Oxford University Press.

Ellis, H. C. (1978). *Fundamentals of human learning, memory, and cognition.* Dubuque, IA: W. C. Brown.

Erdelyi, M. H., & Becker, J. (1974). Hypermnesia for pictures: Incremental memory for pictures but not for words in multiple recall trials. *Cognitive Psychology, 6,* 159–171.

Erdmann, B., & Dodge, R. (1898). *Psychologische untersuchungen über das Lese.* Halle: M. Niemeyer. Cited by R. Woodworth & H. Schlosberg, *Experimental Psychology.* New York: Holt, Rinehart & Winston.

Erickson, J. R. (1974). A set analysis theory of behavior in formal syllogistic reasoning tasks. In R. L. Solso (Ed.), *Theories in cognitive psychology: The Loyola Symposium.* Hillsdale, NJ: Erlbaum.

Erickson, J. R., & Jones, M. R. (1978). Thinking. *Annual Review of Psychology, 29,* 61–91.

Ericsson, K. A., & Charness, N. (1994). Expert performance: Its structure and acquisition. *American Psychologist, 49,* 725–777.

Ericsson, K. A., & Chase, W. A. (1982). Exceptional memory. *American Scientist, 70,* 607–615.

Ericsson, K. A., Krampe, R. T., & Tesch-Römer, C. (1993). The role of deliberate practice in the acquisition of expert performance. *Psychological Review, 100,* 363–406.

Ericsson, K. A., & Polson, P. G. (1988a). A cognitive analysis of exceptional memory for restaurant orders. In M. T. H. Chi, R. Glaser, & M. J. Farr (Eds.), *The nature of expertise.* Hillsdale, NJ: Erlbaum.

Ericsson, K. A., & Polson, P. G. (1988b). An experimental analysis of the mechanisms of a memory skill. *Journal of Experimental Psychology: Learning, Memory, and Cognition, 14,* 305–316.

Eriksen, C. W., & Collins, J. F. (1967). Some temporal characteristics of visual pattern perception. *Journal of Experimental Psychology, 74,* 476–484.

Estes, W. K. (1974). Memory, perception and decision in letter identification. In R. L. Solso (Ed.), *Information processing and cognition: The Loyola Symposium.* Hillsdale, NJ: Erlbaum.

Estes, W. K. (1977). In Laberge and Samuels (Eds.) *Basic procedures in reading: Perception and comprehension,* pp. 1–25. Hillsdale, NJ: Erlbaum.

Estes, W. K. (1977). The structure of human memory. In *Encyclopedia Britannica: Yearbook of science and the future.* Chicago: University of Chicago Press.

Estes, W. K. (Ed.). (1978). *Handbook of learning and cognitive processes* (Vol. 6). Hillsdale, NJ: Erlbaum.

Estes, W. K., Bjork, E. L., & Skaar, E. (1974). Detection of single letters and letters in words with changing versus unchanging mark characteristics. *Bulletin of the Psychonomic Society 3,* 201–203.

Evans, L. (1989). Evans on chess: 24 computers clash. *Reno Gazette-Journal,* Sept. 9.

Evarts, E. V. (1973). Motor cortex reflexes with learned movements. *Science, 179,* 501–503.

Exploring intelligence. (1998, Winter). *Scientific American, 9.*

Eysenck, H. J. (1984). Intelligence versus behavior. *The Behavioral and Brain Sciences, 7,* 290–291.

Eysenck, M. W. (1984). *A handbook of cognitive psychology.* Hillsdale, NJ: Erlbaum.

Farah, M. J. (1984). The neurological basis of mental imagery: A componential analysis. *Cognition, 18,* 245–272.

Farah, M. J. (1988). Is visual imagery really visual? Overlooked evidence from neuropsychology. *Psychological Review, 95,* 307–317.

Farah, M. J. (1995). The neural bases of mental imagery. In M. S. Gazzaniga (Ed.) *The cognitive neurosciences.* 959–961. Cambridge, MA. The MIT Press.

Farah, M. J., Hammond, K. M., Levine, D. N., & Calvanio, R. (1988). Visual and spatial mental imagery: Dissociable systems of representation. *Cognitive Psychology, 20,* 439–462.

FCC (1974). 42, 74–78, *U.S. Law Week 2404,* Feb. 5.

Fehlman, S. E. (1989). Representing implicit knowledge. In G. E. Hinton & J. A. Anderson (Eds.), *Parallel models of associative memory.* Hillsdale, NJ: Erlbaum.

Feigenbaum, E. A. (1967). Information processing and memory. In *Proceedings of the Fifth Berkeley Symposium on Mathematics, Statistics and Probability, 4,* 37–51.

Fein, G. G. (1979). Play and the acquisition of symbols. In L. Kantz (Ed.), *Current topics in early childhood education.* Norwood, NJ: Ablex.

Feinaigle, G. von. (1813). *The new art of memory* (3rd ed.). London: Sherwood, Neely & Jones. Cited in A. Paivio (1971). *Imagery and verbal processes.* New York: Holt, Rinehart & Winston.

Felzen, E., & Anisfeld, M. (1970). Semantic and phonetic relations in the false recognition of words by third and sixth grade children. *Developmental Psychology, 3,* 163–168.

Field, D. (1981). Retrospective reports by healthy intelligent elderly people of personal events of their adult lives. *International Journal of Behavioral Development, 4,* 77–97.

Fikes, R. E., Hart, P. E., & Nilsson, N. J. (1972). In B. Meltzer & D. Michie (Eds.), *Machine intelligence.* Edinburgh: Edinburgh University Press.

Finkbeiner, A. (1988). The brain as template. *Mosaic, 19,* 2–15.

Finke, R. A. (1985). Theories relating mental imagery to perception. *Psychological Bulletin, 98,* 236–259.

Fischler, I., & Bloom, P. A. (1979). Automatic and attentional processes in the effects of sentence context on word recognition. *Journal of Verbal Learning and Verbal Behavior, 18,* 1–20.

Fischler, I. S., & Bloom, P. A. (1985). Effects of constraint and validity of sentence context on lexical decision. *Memory & Cognition, 13,* 128–139.

Fishman, J. A. (1960). A systematization of the Whorfian hypothesis. *Behavioral Science, 5,* 1–29.

Fitts, P. M., & Posner, M. I. (1967). *Human performance.* Belmont, CA: Brooks/Cole.

Flagg, P. W., Potts, G. R., & Reynolds, A. G. (1975). Instructions and response strategies in recognition memory for sentences. *Journal of Experimental Psychology: Human Learning and Memory, 1*(5), 592–598.

Flagg, P. W., & Reynolds, A. G. (1977). Modality of presentation and blocking in sentence recognition memory. *Memory and Cognition, 5*(1), 111–115.

Flavell, J. H. (1963). *The developmental psychology of Jean Piaget.* Princeton, NJ: Van Nostrand.

Flavell, J. H. (1985). *Cognitive development* (2nd ed.). Englewood Cliffs, NJ: Prentice-Hall.

Flavell, J. H. (1986). The development of children's knowledge about the appearance-reality distinction. *American Psychologist, 41,* 418–425.

Flavell, J. H., Beach, D. H., & Chinsky, J. M. (1966). Spontaneous verbal rehearsal in a memory task as a function of age. *Child Development, 37,* 283–299.

Flavell, J. H., & Markman, E. M. (Eds.). (1983). *Handbook of child psychology: Cognitive development* (Vol. 3). New York: Wiley.

Flowers, M., McGuire, R., & Birnbaum, L. (1992). Adversary arguments and the logic of personal attacks. In W. Lehnert & M. Ringle (Eds.), *Strategies for natural language processing.* Hillsdale, NJ: Erlbaum.

Fodor, J., & Garrett, M. (1966). Some reflections on competence and performance. In J. Lyons & R. J. Wales (Eds.), *Psycholinguistic Papers: The Proceedings of the 1966 Edinburgh Conference.* Edinburgh: Edinburgh University Press.

Fodor, J. A., & Pylyshyn, Z. W. (1988). Connectionism and cognitive architecture: A critical analysis. *Cognition, 28,* 3–71.

Forster, P. M., & Govier, E. (1978). Discrimination without awareness? *Quarterly Journal of Experimental Psychology, 31,* 282–295.

Fowler, M. J., Sullivan, J. J., & Ekstrand, B. R. (1973). Sleep and memory. *Science, 179,* 302–304.

Frank, F. (1966). Perception and language in conservation. In J. S. Bruner, R. R. Olver, & P. M. Greenfield (Eds.), *Studies in cognitive growth.* New York: Wiley.

Franks, J. J., & Bransford, J. D. (1971). Abstraction of visual patterns. *Journal of Experimental Psychology, 90,* 65–74.

Franks, N. R. (1989). Army ants: A collective intelligence. *American Scientist, 77* 139–145.

Fredericksen, C. (1975). Effects of context-induced processing operations on semantic information acquired from discourse. *Cognitive Psychology, 7,* 139–166.

Freud, S. (1924/1952). *A general introduction to psychoanalysis.* New York: Washington Square Press.

Freud, S. (1950/1940). A note upon the "mystic writing pad." In J. Strachey (Ed.), *Collected papers of Sigmund Freud.* London: Hogarth Press.

Freund, J. S., & Johnson, J. W. (1972). Changes in memory attribute dominance as a function of age. *Journal of Educational Psychology, 63,* 386–389.

Fritsch, G., & Hitzig, E. (1870). Uber die elektrische Erregbarkeit des Grosshirns. *Archiv fur Anatomie Physiologie und Wissenschaftliche Medicin, 37,* 300–332. In G. von Bonin (Trans.), (1960). *Some papers on the cerebral cortex* (pp. 73–96). Springfield, IL: Charles C. Thomas.

Frost, N. A. H. (1971). Clustering by visual and semantic codes in long-term memory. Unpublished doctoral dissertation, University of Oregon.

Fruth, H. G. (1969). *Piaget and knowledge: Theoretical foundations.* Englewood Cliffs, NJ: Prentice-Hall.

Gabrieli, J. E. E., Desmond, J. E., Demb, J. B., Wagner, A. D., Stone, M. V., Vaidya, C. J., & Glover, G. H. (1996a). Functional magnetic resonance imaging of semantic memory processed in the frontal lobes. *Psychological Science, 7,* 278–283.

Gabrieli, J. E. E., Desmond, J. E., Demb, J. B., Wagner, A. D., Stone, M. V., Vaidya, C. J., & Glover, G. H. (1996b). Functional magnetic resonance imaging of semantic memory processes in the frontal lobes. *Psychological Science, 7,* 278–283.

Galotti, K. M., Baron, J., & Sabini, J. (1986). Individual differences in syllogistic reasoning: Deduction rules or mental models? *Journal of Experimental Psychology: General, 115,* 16–25.

Galton, F. (1880). Statistics of mental imagery. *Mind, 5,* 301–318.

Galton, F. (1907). *Inquiries into human faculty and its development.* London: Macmillan. (Originally published 1883.)

Ganellen, R. J., & Carver, C. S. (1985). Why does self-reference promote incidental encoding? *Journal of Experimental Psychology, 21,* 284–300.

Garcia, G., & Diener, D. (1993). Do you remember . . . A comparison of mnemonic strategies. Paper presented at the annual meeting of WPA, Phoenix, AZ, May.

Gardner, H. (1985). *The mind's new science.* New York: Basic Books.

Gardner, R. A., & Gardner, B. T. (1969). Teaching sign language to a chimpanzee. *Science, 165,* 664–672.

Garner, W. R. (1958). Symmetric uncertainty analysis and its implications for psychology. *Psychology Review, 65,* 183–196.

Garner, W. R. (1962). *Uncertainty and structure as psychological concepts.* New York: Wiley.

Garner, W. R., & Carson, D. H. (1960). A multivariate solution of the redundancy of printed English. *Psychology Review, 6,* 123–141.

Garrity, L. I. (1975). An electromyographical study of subvocal speech and recall in preschool children. *Developmental Psychology, 11,* 274–281.

Gastaut, H., & Bert, J. (1961). Electroencephalographic detection of sleep induced by repetitive sensory stimuli. In G. E. W. Wolstenholme & M. O'Connor (Eds.), *The nature of sleep.* London: Churchill.

Gates, B. (1996). *The road ahead,* New York: Penguin.

Gazzaniga, M. A. (1970). *The bisected brain.* New York: Appleton-Century-Crofts.

Gazzaniga, M. A., & Sperry, R. W. (1967). Language after section of the cerebral commissures. *Brain, 90,* 131–148.

Gazzaniga, M. S. (1967). The split brain in man. *Scientific American, 217*(2), 24–29.

Gazzaniga, M. S. (1975). Experimental apparatus. In M. S. Gazzaniga & C. Blakemore (Eds.), *Handbook of psychobiology.* New York: Academic Press.

Gazzaniga, M. S. (1983). Right hemisphere language following commissurotomy: A twenty-year perspective. *American Psychologist, 38,* 525–537.

Gazzaniga, M. S. (Ed.). (1995). *The cognitive neurosciences.* Cambridge, MA: MIT Press.

Gazzaniga, M. S. (1998). The split brain revisited. *Scientific American, 274,* 123–129.

Gazzaniga, M. S. (Ed.). (2000). *The new cognitive neurosciences* (2nd edition). Cambridge, MA: The MIT Press.

Gazzaniga, M. S., Bogen, J. E., & Sperry, R. W. (1965). Observations on visual perception after disconnection of the cerebral hemispheres in man. *Brain, 88,* 221–236.

Geiger, G., & Lettvin, J. (1987). Dyslexia. *The New England Journal of Medicine, 316,* 1238–1243.

Gelman, R. (1969). Conservation acquisition: A problem of learning to attend to relevant attributes. *Journal of Experimental Child Psychology, 7,* 167–187.

Gelman, R. (1972). The nature and development of early number concepts. In H. Reese (Ed.), *Advances in child development and behavior* (Vol. 7). New York: Academic Press.

Generalization of conditioned GSRs in dichotic listening. In P. M. A. Rabbit & S. Dornic (Eds.), *Attention and performance V.* New York: Academic Press.

Gentner, D. R. (1988). Expertise in typewriting. In M. T. H. Chi, R. Glaser, & M. J. Farr (Eds.), *The nature of expertise.* Hillsdale, NJ: Erlbaum.

Georgopoulos, A. P., Lurito, J. T., Petrides, M., Schwartz, A. B., & Massey, J. T. (1989). Mental rotation of the neuronal population vector. *Science, 243,* 234–236.

Gernsbacher, M. A., & Robertson, R. R. W. (2000). The definite article *the* as a cue to map thematic information. In W. van Peer & M. M. Louwerse (Eds.), *Thematics: Interdisciplinary studies.* Philadelphia: John Benjamins.

Gevins, A., & Cutillo, B. (1993). Spatiotemporal dynamics of component processes in human working memory. *Electroencephalography and Clinical Neurophysiology, 87,* 128–143.

Gibson, J. J. (1966). *The senses considered as perceptual systems.* Boston: Houghton Mifflin.

Gibson, J. J. (1979). *The ecological approach to visual perception.* Boston: Houghton Mifflin.

Glaser, R., & Chi, M. T. H. (1988). Overview. In M. T. H. Chi, R. Glaser, & M. J. Farr (Eds.), *The nature of expertise.* Hillsdale, NJ: Erlbaum.

Glass, A. L., & Holyoak, K. J. (1974). The effect of *some* and *all* on reaction time for semantic decisions. *Memory and Cognition, 2,* 436–440.

Glass, A. L., & Holyoak, K. J. (1975). Alternative conceptions of semantic memory. *Cognition, 3*(8), 313–339.

Glass, A. L., & Holyoak, K. J. (1986). *Cognition* (2nd ed.). New York: Random House.

Glass, A. L., Holyoak, K. J., & O'Dell, D. (1974). Production frequency and the verification of quantified statements. *Journal of Verbal Learning and Verbal Behavior, 13,* 237–254.

Gleason, H. A., Jr. (1961). *An introduction to descriptive linguistics* (rev. ed.). New York: Holt, Rinehart & Winston.

Gluck, M. A., & Rumelhart, D. E. (Eds.). (1990). *Neuroscience and connectionist theory.* Hillsdale, NJ: Erlbaum.

Glucksberg, S. (1962). The influence of strength of drive on functional fixedness and perceptual recognition. *Journal of Experimental Psychology, 63,* 36–51.

Glucksberg, S., & Danks, J. H. (1969). Grammatical structure and recall: A function of the space in immediate memory or of recall delay. *Perception and Psychophysics, 6,* 113–117.

Gold, A. R. (1988). Scholars losing sight of the reason for reading. In *Reno Gazette-Journal,* July 9.

Gold, P. E. (1987). Sweet memories. *American Scientist, 75,* 151–155.

Goldenberg, G., Podreka, I., Steiner, M., Suess, E., Deeke, L., & Willmes, K. (1990). Regional cerebral blood flow patterns in imagery tasks—results of single photon emission computer tomography. In M. Denis, J. Engelkamp, & J. T. E. Richardson (Eds.), *Cognitive and neuropsychological approaches to mental imagery.* Dordrecht, The Netherlands: Martinus Nijhoff.

Goldin-Meadow, S. (1982). Cited in L. Edson, Under Babel's tower. *Mosaic, 13,* 22–28.

Goodman, K. (1970). Reading: A psycholinguistic guessing game. In H. Singer & R. D. Ruddel (Eds.), *Theoretical models and processes of reading* (pp. 259–272). Newark, DE: International Reading Association.

Gordon, R. (1949). An investigation into some of the factors that favour the formation of stereotyped images. *British Journal of Psychology, 39,* 156–167.

Gordon, R. (1950). An experiment correlating the nature of imagery with performance on a test of reversal of perspective. *British Journal of Psychology, 41,* 63–67.

Graham, F. K., Leavitt, L. A., Strock, B. D., & Brown, J. W. (1978). Precocious cardiac orienting in human anencephalic infants. *Science, 199,* 322–324.

Graham, L. R. (1972). *Science and philosophy in the Soviet Union.* New York: Knopf.

Gray, J. A., & Wedderburn, A. A. I. (1960). Grouping strategies with simultaneous stimuli. *Quarterly Journal of Experimental Psychology, 12,* 180–184.

Green, D. M., & Swets, J. A. (1966). *Signal detection theory and psychophysics.* New York: Wiley.

Greenberg, J. H. (1963). Some universals of grammar with particular reference to the order of meaningful elements. In J. H. Greenberg (Ed.), *Universals of language.* Cambridge, MA: The MIT Press.

Greeno, J. G. (1973). The structure of memory and the process of solving problems. In R. L. Solso (Ed.), *Contemporary issues in cognitive psychology: The Loyola Symposium.* Washington, DC: Winston/Wiley.

Greeno, J. G. (1974). Hobbits and orcs: Acquisition of a sequential concept. *Cognitive Psychology, 6,* 270–292.

Gregg, L. W., & Simon H. A. (1967). Process models and stochastic theories of simple concept formation. *Journal of Mathematical Psychology, 4,* 246–276.

Gregory, R. L. (1973). The confounded eye. In R. L. Gregory & E. H. Gombrich (Eds.), *Illusion in nature and art.* New York: Scribner.

Gregory, R. L. (Ed.). (1987). *The Oxford companion to the mind.* Oxford: Oxford University Press.

Gruneberg, M. M., Morris, P. E., & Sykes, R. Jr. (Eds.). (1978). *Practical aspects of memory.* London: Academic Press.

Guilford, J. P. (1959). Three faces of intellect. *American Psychologist, 14,* 469–479.

Guilford, J. P. (1966). Intelligence: 1965 model. *American Psychologist, 21,* 20–26.

Guilford, J. P. (1967). *The nature of human intelligence.* New York: Scribner.

Guilford, J. P. (1982). Cognitive psychology's ambiguities: Some suggested remedies. *Psychological Review, 89,* 48–59.

Guzman, A. (1968). *Computer recognition of three-dimensional objects in a visual scene* (Project MAC-TR-59) (pp. 447–449). Cambridge, MA: MIT Artificial Intelligence Laboratory.

Haber, R. N. (1970). Visual perception. *Annual Review of Psychology* (Vol. 29). Palo Alto, CA: Annual Reviews.

Haber, R. N. (1983). The impending demise of the icon: A critique of the iconic storage in visual information processing. *Behavioral and Brain Sciences, 6,* 1–54.

Haber, R. N. (1985a). Comment on the demise of the icon. *Behavioral and Brain Sciences, 8,* 8.

Haber, R. N. (1985b). An icon can have no worth in the real world: Comments on Loftus, Johnson and Shimamura's "How much is an icon worth?" *Journal of Experimental Psychology: Human Perception and Performance, 11,* 374–378.

Haber, R. N. (1989). Twenty years of haunting eidetic images: Where's the ghost? *Behavioral and Brain Sciences, 2,* 583–594.

Haber, R. N., & Hershenson, M. (1973). *The psychology of visual perception.* New York: Holt, Rinehart & Winston.

Hagen, J. W. (1967). The effects of distraction on selective attention. *Child Development, 38,* 685–694.

Hagen, J. W. (Ed.), *Perspectives on the development of memory and cognition.* Hillsdale, NJ: Erlbaum.

Haier, R. J., Chueh, D., Touchette, P., Lott, I., Buchsbaum, M. S., MacMillan, D., Sandman, C., Lacasse, L., & Sosa, E. (1995). Brain size and cerebral glucose metabolic rate in nonspecific mental retardation and Down syndrome. *Intelligence, 20*(2), 191–210.

Haier, R. J., Siegel, B. V., MacLachlan, A., Soderling, E., et al. (1992). Regional glucose metabolic changes after learning a complex visiospatial/motor task: A positron emission tomographic study. *Brain Research, 570,* 134–143.

Haier, R. J., Siegel, B. V., Tang, C., Abel, L., & Buchsbaum, M. S. (1992). Intelligence and changes in regional cerebral glucose metabolic rate following learning. *Intelligence, 16*(3–4), 415–426.

Haith, M. M., Bergman, T., & Moore, M. J. (1977). Eye contact and face scanning in early infancy. *Science, 198,* 853–855.

Haith, M. M., Morrison, F. J., Sheingold, K., & Mindes, P. (1970). Short-term memory for visual information in children and adults. *Journal of Experimental Child Psychology, 9,* 454–469.

Hale, G. A. (1975). *Development of flexibility in children's attention deployment: A colloquium.* Research memorandum. Princeton, NJ: Educational Testing Service.

Hall, J. L., & Gold, P. E. (1990). Adrenalectomy-induced memory deficits: Role of plasma glucose levels. *Physiology & Behavior, 47,* 27–33.

Hall, J. W., & Halperin, M. S. (1972). The development of memory-encoding processes in young children. *Developmental Psychology, 6,* 181.

Halpern, A. R. (1986). Memory for tune titles after organized or unorganized presentation. *American Journal of Psychology, 99,* 57–70.

Halpern, A. R. (1989). Memory for absolute pitch of familiar songs. *Memory and Cognition, 17,* 572–581.

Hamilton, W. (1938). Cited in R. Woodworth (Ed.), *Experimental psychology.* New York: Holt.

Hamilton, W. (1954). *Lectures on metaphysics and logic* (Vol. 1, Lect. XLV). Edinburgh: Blackwood, 1859. Cited in R. Woodworth & H. Schlosberg, *Experimental psychology.* New York: Holt.

Hart, J. T. (1965). Memory and the feeling-of-knowing experience. *Journal of Educational Psychology, 56,* 208–216.

Haugeland, J. (1989). *Artificial intelligence: The very idea.* Cambridge, MA: The MIT Press.

Haxby, J. V., Ungerleider, L. G., Horwitz, B., Rapoport, S. I., & Grady, C. L. (1995). Hemispheric differences in neurosystems for face working memory: A PET-rCBR study. *Human brain mapping, 3,* 68–32.

Hayes, J. R. (1978). *Cognitive psychology: Thinking and creating.* Homewood, IL: Dorsey Press.

Hayes, J. R. (1986). Three problems in teaching general skills. In J. Segal, S. Chipman, and R. Glaser (Eds.), *Thinking and learning* (Vol. 2). Hillsdale, NJ: Erlbaum.

Hayes, J. R. (1989). *The complete problem solver* (2nd ed.). Hillsdale, NJ: Erlbaum.

Hayes, J. R., & Simon, H. A. (1976). Psychological differences among problem isomorphs. In N. Castellon, Jr., D. Pisoni, & G. Potts (Eds.), *Cognitive theory* (Vol. 2). Hillsdale, NJ: Erlbaum.

Haygood, R. C. (1975). *Concept learning.* Morristown, NJ: General Learning Press.

Haygood, R. C., & Bourne, L. E., Jr. (1965). Attribute and rule-learning aspects of conceptual behavior. *Psychological Review, 72*(3), 175–195.

Hayman, C. A. G., Macdonald, C. A., & Tulving, E. (1993). The role of repetition and associative interference in new semantic learning in amnesia: A case experiment. *Journal of Cognitive Neuroscience, 5,* 375–389.

Head, H. (1926). *Aphasia and kindred disorders of speech.* Cambridge, England: Cambridge University Press.

Head, H. (1958). Cited in F. Bartlett, *Thinking* (p. 146). New York: Basic Books.

Hebb, D. O. (1949). *The organization of behavior.* New York: Wiley.

Heider, E. R. (1971). "Focal" color areas and the development of color names. *Developmental Psychology, 4,* 447–455.

Heider, E. R. (1972). Universals in color naming and memory. *Journal of Experimental Psychology, 93,* 10–20.

Henle, M. (1962). On the relation between logic and thinking. *Psychological Review, 69,* 366–378.

Henle, M., & Michael, M. (1956). The influence of attitudes on syllogistic reasoning. *Journal of Social Psychology, 4,* 115–127.

Heppenheimer, T. A. (1988). Nerves of silicon. *Discover,* Feb. 70–79.

Hernandez-Peon, R. (1966). Physiological mechanisms in attention. In R. W. Russell (Ed.), *Frontiers in physiological psychology.* New York: Academic Press.

Herrmann, D. J. (1987). Task appropriateness of mnemonic techniques. *Perceptual and Motor Skills, 64,* 171–178.

Herrnstein, R. J., & Murray, C. (1994). *The bell curve: Intelligence and class structure in American life.* New York: The Free Press.

Hilgard, E. R. (1980). Consciousness in contemporary psychology. *Annual Review of Psychology, 31,* 1–26.

Hilgard, E. R. (1987). *Psychology in America: A historical survey.* San Diego, CA: Harcourt Brace Jovanovich.

Hilgard, E. R., & Bower, G. H. (1974). *Theories of learning* (4th ed.). Englewood Cliffs, NJ: Prentice-Hall.

Hillis, W. D. (1987). The connection machine. *Scientific American, 256,* 108–115.

Hillyard, S. A. (1993). Electrical and magnetic brain recordings: Contribution to cognitive neuroscience. *Current Operations in Neurobiology, 3,* 217–224.

Hillyard, S. A., Mangun, G. R., Woldorff, M. G., & Luck, S. J. (1995). Neural systems mediating selective attention. In M. S. Gazzaniga (Ed.), *The cognitive neurosciences.* Cambridge, MA: MIT Press.

Hinsley, D., Hayes, J. R., & Simon, H. A. (1977). From words to equations. In P. Carpenter & M. Just (Eds.), *Cognitive processes in comprehension.* Hillsdale, NJ: Erlbaum.

Hinton, G. E. (1981). A parallel computation that assigns canonical object-based frames of reference. *Proceedings of the 7th International Joint Conference on Artificial Intelligence.*

Hinton, G. E. (1992). How neural networks learn from experience. *Scientific American,* September, 67–72.

Hintzman, D. L. (1974). Psychology and the cow's belly. *The Worm Runner's Digest, 16,* 84–85.

Hodges, A. (1983) *Alan Turing: The enigma.* New York: Touchstone.

Hofstadter, D. R. (1979). *Godel, Escher, Bach: An eternal golden braid.* New York: Basic Books.

Hofstadter, D. R. (1985). *Metamagical themas: Questions for the essence of mind and matter.* New York: Basic Books.

Holbrook, M. B., & Schindler, R. M. (1998). Some exploratory findings on the development of musical tastes. *Journal of Consumer Research, 16,* 119–124.

Holding, D. H. (1975a). Sensory storage reconsidered. *Memory and Cognition, 3,* 31–41.

Holding, D. H. (1975b). A rejoinder. *Memory and Cognition, 3,* 49–50.

Holender, D. (1986). Semantic activation without conscious identification in dichotic listening, parafoveal vision, and visual masking: A survey and appraisal. *Behavioral & Brain Sciences, 9,* 1–66.

Hollan, J. D. (1975). Features and semantic memory: Set theoretic or network model? *Psychological Review, 82,* 154–155.

Holmes, D. L., Cohen, K. M., Haith, M. M., & Morrison, F. J. (1977). Peripheral visual processing. *Perception and Psychophysics, 22*(6), 571–577.

Holmes, L. H., & Morrison, F. J. (1979). *The child.* Monterey, CA: Brooks/Cole.

Holt, R. R. (1964). Imagery: The return of the ostracized. *American Psychologist, 12,* 254–264.

Holyoak, K. J., & Glass, A. L. (1975). The role of contradictions and counterexamples in the rejection of false sentences. *Journal of Verbal Learning and Verbal Behavior, 14,* 215–239.

Horowitz, L. M., Chilian, P. C., & Dunnigan, K. P. (1969). Word fragments and their redintegrative powers. *Journal of Experimental Psychology, 80,* 392–394.

Horowitz, L. M., & Prytulak, L. S. (1969). Redintegrative memory. *Psychological Review, 76,* 519–531.

Horowitz, L. M., White, M. A., & Atwood, D. W. (1968). Word fragments as aids to recall: The organization of a word. *Journal of Experimental Psychology, 76,* 219–226.

Horton, D. L., & Turnage, T. W. (1976). *Human learning.* Englewood Cliffs, NJ: Prentice-Hall.

Houston, J. P. (1976). *Fundamentals of learning.* New York: Academic Press.

Hovland, C. I. (1952). A communication analysis of concept learning. *Psychological Review, 59,* 461–472.

Howes, D., & Solomon, R. L. (1951). Visual duration thresholds as a function of word probability. *Journal of Experimental Psychology, 41,* 401–410.

Hubel, D. H. (1959). Receptive fields of single neurons in the cat's striate cortex. *Journal of Physiology, 148,* 574–591.

Hubel, D. H. (1963a). Receptive fields of cells in the striate cortex of very young, visually inexperienced kittens. *Journal of Neurophysiology, 26,* 994–1002.

Hubel, D. H. (1963b). The visual cortex of the brain. *Scientific American,* Nov., 54–62.

Hubel, D. H., & Wiesel, T. N. (1959). Receptive fields of single neurons in the cat's striate cortex. *Journal of Physiology, 148,* 574–591.

Hubel, D. H., & Wiesel, T. N. (1963). Receptive fields of cells in the striate cortex of very young, visually inexperienced kittens. *Journal of Neurophysiology, 26,* 994–1002.

Hudson, W. (1967). The study of the problem of pictorial perception among unacculturated groups. *International Journal of Psychology, 2,* 89–107.

Huey, E. B. (1968). *The psychology and pedagogy of reading.* Cambridge, MA: The MIT Press. (First published by Macmillan in 1908.)

Hume, D. (1912). *An enquiry concerning human understanding.* Chicago: Open Court. (Original publication 1748.)

Humphreys, G. W. (Ed.). (1992) *Understanding vision.* Oxford: Blackwell.

Hunt, E. B. (1961). Memory effects in concept learning. *Journal of Experimental Psychology, 62,* 598–609.

Hunt, E. B. (1968). Computer simulation: Artificial intelligence studies and their relevance to psychology. In P. R. Farnsworth (Ed.), *Annual review of psychology* (Vol. 19). Palo Alto, CA: Annual Reviews.

Hunt, E. B. (1971). What kind of computer is man? *Cognitive Psychology, 2,* 57–98.

Hunt, E. B. (1973). The memory we must have. In R. Schank & K. Colby (Eds.), *Computer models of thought and language* (pp. 343–371). San Francisco: Freeman.

Hunt, E. B. (1978). Mechanics of verbal ability. *Psychological Review, 85,* 109–130.

Hunt, E. B. (1989). Cognitive science: Definition, status, and questions. In M. R. Rosenzweig & L. W. Porter (Eds.), *Annual Review of Psychology, 40* (pp. 603–629). Palo Alto, CA: Annual Reviews.

Hunt, E. B. (1995). The role of intelligence in modern society. *American Scientist, 83,* 356–368.

Hunt, E. B., & Lansman, M. (1982). Individual differences in attention. In R. J. Sternberg (Ed.), *Advances in the psychology of human intelligence.* Hillsdale, NJ: Erlbaum.

Hunt, E., & Love, T. (1972). How good can memory be? In A. W. Melton & E. Martin (Eds.), *Coding processes in human memory.* Washington, DC: Winston.

Hunt, E. B., Lunneborg, C., & Lewis, J. (1975). What does it mean to be high verbal? *Cognitive Psychology, 7,* 194–227.

Hunter, I. M. L. (1957). *Memory: Facts and fallacies.* Harmondsworth, Middlesex, England: Penguin.

Hunter, I. M. L. (1962). An exceptional talent for calculative thinking. *British Journal of Psychology, 53,* 243–258.

Hunter, I. M. L. (1964). *Memory.* Harmondsworth, Middlesex, England: Penguin.

Inhelder, B., & Piaget, J. (1964a). *The early growth of logical thinking.* New York: Norton.

Inhelder, B., & Piaget, J. (1964b). *The early growth of logic in the child.* New York: Harper Row.

Inhoff, A., & Tousman, S. (1990). Lexical priming from partial-word previews. *Journal of Experimental Psychology: Human Perception and Performance, 16,* 825–836.

Inn, D., Walden, K. J., & Solso, R. L. (1993). Facial prototype formation in three to six year old children. Unpublished manuscript. University of Nevada, Reno.

Intons-Peterson, M. J., & Fournier, J. (1986). External and internal memory aids: When and how often do we use them? *Journal of Experimental Psychology: General, 115,* 267–280.

Intons-Peterson, M. J., & Smyth, M. M. (1987). The anatomy of repertory memory. *Journal of Experimental Psychology: Learning, Memory, and Cognition, 13,* 490–500.

Ionesco, E. (1970). *Story number 2.* New York: Harlin Quist/Crown.

Ivry, R. B., & Lebby, P. C. (1993). Hemispheric differences in auditory perception are similar to those found in visual perception. *Psychological Science, 4,* 41–45.

Izawa, C. (1989). *Current issues in cognitive processes: The Tulane Flowerree Symposium on cognition.* Hillsdale, NJ: Erlbaum.

Jackson, A., & Morton, J. (1984). Facilitation of auditory word recognition. *Memory and Cognition, 12,* 568–574.

Jackson, P. C. (1974). *Introduction to artificial intelligence.* New York: Petrocelli/Charter.

Jacoby, L. L., & Witherspoon, D. (1982). Remembering without awareness. *Canadian Journal of Psychology, 32,* 300–324.

Jakobovits, L. A., & Miron, M. S. (1967). *Readings in the psychology of language.* Englewood Cliffs, NJ: Prentice-Hall.

Jakobson, R. (1972). Verbal communication. *Scientific American,* Sept., 38–44.

James, W. (1890). *Principles of psychology.* New York: Holt.

James, W. (1890/1983). *The principles of psychology.* Cambridge, MA: Harvard University Press.

James, W. (1902). *The varieties of religious experience.* New York: Longmans, Green & Co.

Janis, I. L., & Frick, F. (1943). The relationship between attitudes toward conclusions and errors in judging logical validity of syllogisms. *Journal of Experimental Psychology, 33,* 73–77.

Janis, I. L., & Mann, L. (1977). *Decision making.* New York: Free Press.

Javal, L. E. (1878). Essai sur la physiologie de la lecture. *Annales d'Oculistique, 82,* 242–253.

Jaynes, J. (1976). *The origins of consciousness in the breakdown of the bicameral mind.* Boston: Houghton Mifflin.

Jenkins, J. G., & Dallenbach, K. M. (1924). Obliviscence during sleep and waking. *American Journal of Psychology, 35,* 605–612.

Jenkins, J. J. (1963). Mediated associations: Paradigms and situations. In C. N. Cofer & B. S. Musgrave (Eds.), *Verbal behavior and learning.* New York: McGraw-Hill.

Jensen, A. R. (1993). Why is reaction time correlated with psychometric *g? Current Directions in Psychological Science, 2,* 53–56.

John, E. R. (1972). Switchboard versus statistical theories of learning and memory. *Science, 177,* 849–864.

Johnson, E. J. (1988). Expertise and decision under uncertainty: Performance and process. In M. T. H. Chi, R. Glaser, & M. J. Farr (Eds.), *The nature of expertise.* Hillsdale, NJ: Erlbaum.

Johnson, M. H. (Ed.). (1993). *Brain development and cognition: A reader.* Cambridge, MA: Blackwell.

Johnson-Laird, P. N. (1970). The perception and memory of sentences. In J. Lyons (Ed.), *New horizons in linguistics* (pp. 261–270). Baltimore: Penguin.

Johnson-Laird, P. N. (1983). *Mental models: Towards a cognitive science of language, inference, and consciousness.* Cambridge, MA: Harvard University Press.

Johnson-Laird, P. N. (1988). *The computer and the mind.* Cambridge, MA: Harvard University Press.

Johnson-Laird, P. N. (1995). Mental models and probabilistic thinking. In J. Mehler & S. Franck (Eds.), *Cognition on cognition. Cognition special series* (pp. 171–191). Cambridge, MA: MIT Press.

Johnson-Laird, P. N., & Byrne, R. M. J. (1989). Only reasoning. *Journal of Memory and Language, 28,* 313–330.

Johnson-Laird, P. N., & Byrne, R. M. J. (1991). *Deduction.* Hove, England: Erlbaum.

Johnson-Laird, P. N., Legrenzi, P., & Legrenzi, M. (1992). Reasoning and a sense of reality. *British Journal of Psychology, 63,* 395–400.

Johnson-Laird, P. N., & Steedman, M. (1978). The psychology of syllogisms. *Cognitive Psychology, 10,* 64–99.

Johnson-Laird, P. N., & Wason, P. C. (Eds.). (1977). *Thinking: Readings in cognitive science.* Cambridge, England: Cambridge University Press.

Johnston, W. A., & Heinz, S. P. (1975). Depth of non-target processing in an attention task. *Journal of Experimental Psychology, 5,* 168–175.

Johnston, W. A., & Heinz, S. P. (1978). Flexibility and capacity demands of attention. *Journal of Experimental Psychology: General, 107,* 420–435.

Johnston, W. A., & Wilson, J. (1980). Perceptual processing of non-target in an attention task. *Memory and Cognition, 8,* 372–377.

Jolicoeur, P., Regehr, S., Smith, L. B., & Smith, G. N. (1985). Mental rotation of representations of two-dimensional and three-dimensional objects. *Canadian Journal of Psychology, 39,* 100–129.

Julesz, B. (1971). *Foundations of cyclopean perception.* Chicago: University of Chicago Press.

Just, M. A., & Carpenter, P. A. (1980). A theory of reading: From eye fixations to comprehension. *Psychological Review, 87*(4), 329–354.

Just, M. A., & Carpenter, P. A. (1987). *The psychology of reading and language comprehension.* Boston: Allyn & Bacon.

Just, M. A., Carpenter, P. A., Keller, T. A., Eddy, W. F., & Thulbom, K. R. (1996). Brain activation modulated by sentence comprehension. *Science, 274,* 114–116.

Kahn, D. (1967). *The codebreakers: The story of secret writing.* New York: Macmillan.

Kahneman, D. (1973). *Attention and effort.* Englewood Cliffs, NJ: Prentice-Hall.

Kahneman, D., & Miller, D. (1986). Norm theory: Comparing reality to its alternatives. *Psychology Review, 93,* 136–153.

Kahneman, D., & Tversky, A. (1972). Subjective probability: A judgment of representativeness. *Cognitive Psychology, 3,* 430–454.

Kahneman, D., & Tversky, A. (1983). On the psychology of prediction. *Psychological Review, 80,* 237–251.

Kahneman, D., & Tversky, A. (1984). Choices, values, and frames. *American Psychologist, 39,* 341–350.

Kandel, E. R. (1981a). Nerve cells and behavior. In E. R. Kandel and J. H. Schwartz (Eds.), *Principles of neural science.* New York: Elsevier/North-Holland.

Kandel, E. R. (1981b). Brain and behavior. In E. R. Kandel and J. H. Schwartz (Eds.), *Principles of neural science.* New York: Elsevier/North-Holland.

Kandel, E. R., & Schwartz, J. H. (Eds.). (1981). *Principles of neural science.* New York: Elsevier/North-Holland.

Kandel, E. R., Schwartz, J. H., & Jessell, T. M. (1991). *Principles of neural science.* New York: Elsevier.

Kandinsky, W. (1912). *Über das geistige in der Kunst, inbesondere in der Malerei.* Munchen: Piper.

Kanizsa, G. (1976). Subjective contours. *Scientific American, 234,* 48–52.

Kao, Y. F. (1990). Subliminal processing: The spread of activation in color priming. Unpublished doctoral dissertation. University of Nevada, Reno.

Kao, Y. F., & Solso, R. L. (1989). *One second of cognition.* Paper presented at the annual meeting of RMPA/WPA, Reno, NV, Apr.

Kaplan, R. M. (1972). Augmented transition networks as psychological models of sentence comprehension. *Artificial Intelligence, 3,* 77–100.

Kapur, S., Craik, F. I. M., Tulving, E., Wilson, A. A., Hoyle, S., & Brown, G. M. (1994). Neuroanatomical correlates of encoding in episodic memory: Levels of processing effect. *Proceedings of the National Academy of Sciences, 91,* 2008–2011. Washington, DC: National Academy of Sciences.

Kapur, N., Scholey, K., Moore, E., Barker, S., Mayes, A., Brice, J., & Fleming, J. (1994). The mammillary bodies revisited: Their role in human memory functioning. In L. S. Cermak (Ed.), *Neuropsychological explorations of memory and cognition: Essays in honor of Nelson Butters (Critical issues in neuropsychology)* (pp. 159–189). New York: Plenum Press.

Katz, S., & Gruenewald, P. (1974). The abstraction of linguistic ideas in "meaningless" sentences. *Memory and Cognition, 2,* 737–741.

Kausler, D. H. (1974). *Psychology of verbal learning and memory.* New York: Academic Press.

Kavanagh, J. F., & Mattingly I. G. (Eds.). (1972). *Language by ear and by eye: The relationship between speech and reading.* Cambridge, MA: The MIT Press.

Kay, P., & Kempton, W. (1984). What is the Sapir-Whorf Hypothesis? *American Anthropologist, 86,* 65–79.

Keele, S. W. (1973). *Attention and human performance.* Pacific Palisades, CA: Goodyear.

Kendler, H. H., & Kendler, T. S. (1969). Reversal-shift behavior: Some basic issues. *Psychological Bulletin, 72,* 229–232.

Kennedy, A., & Wilkes, A. (Eds.). (1975). *Studies in long-term memory.* New York: Wiley.

Kess, J. F. (1976). *Psycholinguistics: Introductory perspectives.* New York: Academic Press.

Kessen, W., & Kuhlman, C. (1970). *Cognitive developments in children.* Chicago: University of Chicago Press.

Kihlstrom, J. F. (1987). The cognitive unconscious. *Science, 237,* 1445–1453.

Kihlstrom, J. F. (1993). The psychological unconscious and the self. In G. R. Bock & J. Marsh (Eds.), *CIBA Symposium on Experimental and Theoretical Studies of Consciousness* (pp. 147–156). Chichester, NY: Wiley & Sons.

Kihlstrom, J. F., & Cantor, N. (1984). Mental representations of the self. In L. Berkowitz (Ed.), *Advances in Experimental Social Psychology, 93,* 200–208.

Kimura, D. (1963). Right temporal lobe damage. *Arch Neurology, 8,* 264–271.

Kimura, D. (1967). Functional asymmetry of the brain in dichotic listening. *Cortex, 3,* 163–178.

Kintsch, W. (1967). Memory and decision aspects of recognition learning. *Psychological Review, 74,* 496–504.

Kintsch, W. (1974). *The representation of meaning in memory.* Hillsdale, NJ: Erlbaum.

Kintsch, W. (1979). On modeling comprehension. *Educational Psychologist, 14,* 3–14.

Kintsch, W. (1988). The role of knowledge in discourse comprehension: A construction-integration model. *Psychological Review, 95,* 163–182.

Kintsch, W. (1990). The representation of knowledge and the use of knowledge in discourse comprehension. In C. Graumann & R. Dietrich (Eds.), *Language in the social context.* Amsterdam: Elsevier.

Kintsch, W., & Keenan, J. (1973). Reading rate and retention as a function of the number of propositions in the base structure of sentences. *Cognitive Psychology, 5,* 257–274.

Kintsch, W., & van Dijk, T. A. (1978). Toward a model of text comprehension and production. *Psychological Review, 85,* 363–394.

Kintsch, W., & Vipond, D. (1979). Reading comprehension and readability in educational practice and psychological theory. In L. G. Nilsson (Ed.), *Perspectives on memory research.* Hillsdale, NJ: Erlbaum.

Kirkpatrick, E. A. (1894). An experimental study of memory. *Psychological Review, 1,* 602–609.

Klatzky, R. L. (1975). *Human memory: Structures and processes.* San Francisco: Freeman.

Klatzky, R. L. (1984). *Memory and awareness.* San Francisco: Freeman.

Klein, K., & Saltz, E. (1976). Specifying the mechanisms in a levels-of-processing approach to memory. *Journal of Experimental Psychology, 87,* 281–288.

Kleinmuntz, B. (1969). *Clinical information processing by computer.* New York: Holt, Rinehart & Winston.

Kline, S. B., & Kihlstrom, J. F. (1986). Elaboration, organization, and the self-reference effect in memory. *Journal of Experimental Psychology: General, 113,* 26–38.

Kobasigawa, A., & Middleton, D. B. (1972). Free recall of categorized items by children at three grade levels. *Child Development, 43*, 1067–1072.

Koenig, O., Reiss, L. P., & Kosslyn, S. M. (1990). The development of spacial relation representations: Evidence from studies of cerebral lateralization. *Journal of Experimental Child Psychology, 50*, 119–130.

Köhler, W. (1938). *The place of value in the world of facts.* New York: Liveright.

Köhler, W. (1947). *Gestalt psychology: An introduction to the new concepts in modern psychology.* New York: Liveright.

Kolb, B., & Whishaw, I. Q. (1990). *Fundamentals of human neuropsychology.* New York: Freeman.

Kolers, W. (1970). Three stages of reading. In H. Levin & J. P. Williams (Eds.), *Basic studies on reading.* New York: Basic Books.

Kolers, P. A., & Palef, S. R. (1976). Knowing not. *Memory and Cognition, 4*, 553–558.

Kosslyn, S. M. (1973). Scanning visual images: Some structural implications. *Perception and Psychophysics, 14*, 90–94.

Kosslyn, S. M. (1975). Information representation in visual images. *Cognitive Psychology, 7*, 341–370.

Kosslyn, S. M. (1976a). Can imagery be distinguished from other forms of internal representation? Evidence from studies of information-retrieval time. *Memory and Cognition, 4*, 291–297.

Kosslyn, S. M. (1976b). *Visual images present metric spatial information.* Paper presented at the Psychonomic Society Meetings, St. Louis, MO.

Kosslyn, S. M. (1977). Imagery and internal representation. In E. Rosch & U. Lloyd (Eds.), *Categories and cognition.* Hillsdale, NJ: Erlbaum.

Kosslyn, S. M. (1980). *Image and mind.* Cambridge, MA: Harvard University Press.

Kosslyn, S. M. (1981). The medium and the message in mental imagery. *Psychological Review, 88*, 46–66.

Kosslyn, S. M. (1983). *Ghosts in the mind's machine.* New York: Norton.

Kosslyn, S. M. (1988). Aspects of cognitive neuroscience of mental imagery. *Science, 240*, 1621–1626.

Kosslyn, S. M. (1994). *Image and brain: The resolution of the imagery debate.* Cambridge, MA: The MIT Press.

Kosslyn, S. M. (1995). Introduction. In M. S. Gazzaniga (Ed.), *The cognitive neurosciences* (pp. 959–961). Cambridge, MA: The MIT Press.

Kosslyn, S. M., Alpert, N. M., Thompson, W. L., Meljkovic, V., Weise, S. B., Chabris, C. F., Hamilton, S. E., Rauch, S. L., & Buonanno, F. S. (1993). Visual mental imagery activates topographically organized visual cortex: PET investigations. *Journal of Cognitive Neuroscience, 5*, 263–287.

Kosslyn, S. M., Ball, T. M., & Reiser, B. J. (1978). Visual images preserve metric spatial information. Evidence from studies of image scanning. *Journal of Experimental Psychology: Human Perception and Performance, 40*, 47–60.

Kosslyn, S. M., & Koenig, O. (1992). *Wet mind: The new cognitive neuroscience.* New York: The Free Press.

Kosslyn, S. M., Murphy, G. L., Bemesderfer, M. E., & Feinstein, K. J. (1977). Category and continuum in mental comparisons. *Journal of Experimental Psychology: General, 106*, 341–375.

Kosslyn, S. M., & Osherson, D. N. (1995). (Eds.) *Visual cognition.* Cambridge, MA: The MIT Press.

Kosslyn, S. M., & Pomerantz, J. R. (1977). Imagery, proposition, and the form of internal representations. *Cognitive Psychology, 9*, 52–76.

Kosslyn, S. M., & Schwartz, S. P. (1977). A simulation of visual imagery. *Cognitive Science, 1*, 265–295.

Kosslyn, S. M., Sokolov, M. A., & Chen, J. C. (1989). The lateralization of BRIAN: A computational theory and model of visual hemispheric specialization. In D. Klahr and K. Kotovsky (Eds.), *Complex information processing: The impact of Herbert H. Simon.* Hillsdale, NJ: Erlbaum.

Kozulin, A. (1984). *Psychology in Utopia: Toward a social history of Soviet psychology.* Cambridge, MA: The MIT Press.

Kozulin, A. (1986). The concept of activity in Soviet psychology. *American Psychologist, 1*, 264–274.

Kries, J. von. (1925). Über die Natur gewisser mit den pschischen Vorgangen Verknupfter Gehirnzustande. *Z. Psy*, 1985, *8*, 1–33. Cited in R. Woodworth & H. Schlosberg (Eds.), *Experimental psychology.* New York: Holt.

Kroll, N. E. A., Schepeler, E. M., & Angin, K. T. (1986). Bizarre imagery: The misremembered mnemonic. *Journal of Experimental Psychology: Learning, Memory, and Cognition, 12*, 42–53.

Kučera, H., & Francis, W. N. (1967). *Computational analysis of present-day American English.* Providence, RI: Brown University Press.

Kuhn, T. S. (1962). *The structure of scientific revolutions.* Chicago: University of Chicago Press.

Kupferman, I. (1981). Localization of higher function. In E. R. Kandel & J. H. Schwartz (Eds.), *Principles of neural science.* New York: Elsevier/North-Holland.

Kurzweil, R. (1999). *The age of spiritual machines.* New York: Viking.

LaBerge, D. (1972). Beyond auditory coding. In J. F. Kavanagh & I. G. Mattingly (Eds.), *Language by ear and by eye* (pp. 241–248). Cambridge, MA: The MIT Press.

LaBerge, D. (1975). Acquisition of automatic processing in perceptual and associative learning. In P. M. A. Rabbit & S. Dornic (Eds.), *Attention and performance V.* London: Academic Press.

LaBerge, D. (1976). Perceptual learning and attention. In W. Estes (Ed.), *Handbook of learning and cognitive processes,* Vol. 4: *Attention and memory.* Hillsdale, NJ: Erlbaum.

LaBerge, D. (1980). Unitization and automaticity in perception. In J. H. Flowers (Ed.), *Nebraska Symposium on Motivation* (pp. 53–71). Lincoln: University of Nebraska Press.

LaBerge, D., & Samuels, S. J. (1974). Toward a theory of automatic information processing in reading. *Cognitive Psychology, 6,* 293–323.

LaBerge, D., & Samuels, S. J. (1978). *Basic processes in reading: Perception and comprehension.* Hillsdale, NJ: Erlbaum.

Laird, D. A., & Laird, E. C. (1960). *Techniques for efficient remembering.* New York: McGraw-Hill.

Land, M. F., & Fernald, R. D. (1992). The evolution of eyes. In *Annual Review of Neuroscience, 15,* 1–29.

Landauer, T. K. (1975). Memory without organization: Properties of a model with random storage and undirected retrieval. *Cognitive Psychology, 7,* 495–531.

Landauer, T. K., & Meyer, D. E. (1972). Category size and semantic-memory retrieval. *Journal of Verbal Learning and Verbal Behavior, 11,* 539–549.

Lange, G. (1973). The development of conceptual and rote recall skills among school-age children. *Journal of Experimental Child Psychology, 15,* 394–406.

Lashley, K. S. (1929). *Brain mechanisms and intelligence: A quantitative study of injuries to the brain.* Chicago: University of Chicago Press.

Lashley, K. S. (1950). In search of the engram. *Proceedings from Social Experimental Biology, 4,* 454–482. Reprinted in F. A. Beach, D. O. Hebb, C. T. Morgan, & H. W. Nissen (Eds.), *The neuropsychology of Lashley.* New York: McGraw-Hill.

Lashley, K. S. (1951). The problem of serial order in behavior. In L. A. Jeffress (Ed.), *Cerebral mecha-*

nisms in behavior: The Hixon Symposium. New York: Wiley.

Lassen, N. A., Ingvar, D. H., & Skinhoj, E. (1979). Brain function and blood flow. *Scientific American, 239,* 62–71.

Laughlin, P. R. (1968). Focusing strategy for eight concept rules. *Journal of Experimental Psychology, 77,* 661–669.

Laughlin, P. R., & Jordan, R. M. (1967). Selection strategies in conjunctive, disjunctive, and biconditional concept attainment. *Journal of Experimental Psychology, 75,* 188–193.

Le Bihan, D., Turner, R., Zeffiro, T. A., Cuenold, C. A., Jezzard, P., & Bonnerot, V. (in press). Activation of human primary visual cortex during visual recall: A magnetic resonance imaging study. *Proceedings of the National Academy of Sciences.*

Lefebvre, V. A. (1982). *Algebra of consciousness.* Boston: Reidel.

Lefton, L. A. (1973). Guessing and the order of approximation effect. *Journal of Experimental Psychology, 101,* 401–403.

Lenneberg, E. H. (1964a). In J. A. Fodor & J. J. Katz (Eds.), *The structure of language: Readings in the philosophy of language.* Englewood Cliffs, NJ: Prentice-Hall.

Lenneberg, E. H. (1964b). *New directions in the study of language.* Cambridge, MA: The MIT Press.

Lenneberg, E. H. (1967). *Biological foundations of language.* New York: Wiley.

Lenneberg, E. H. (1969). On explaining language. *Science, 164,* 635–643.

Lenneberg E. H., Nichols, I. A., & Rosenberger, E. F. (1964). In D. Rioch (Ed.), *Disorders of communication* (Research publications of Associations for Research in Nervous and Mental Disorders.) New York.

Leontiev, A. N. (1978). Cited in L. S. Vygotsky, *Mind in society.* Cambridge, MA: Harvard University Press.

Lesgold, A. M., & Bower, G. H. (1970). Inefficiency of serial knowledge for associative responding. *Journal of Verbal Learning and Verbal Behavior, 9,* 456–466.

Lesgold, A., Glaser, R., Rubinson, H., Klopfer, D., Feltovich, P., & Wang, Y. (1988). Expertise in a complex skill: Diagnosing X-ray pictures. In M. T. H. Chi, R. Glaser, & M. J. Farr (Eds.), *The nature of expertise.* Hillsdale, NJ: Erlbaum.

Lesher, G. W. (1995). Illusory contours: Toward a neurally based perceptual theory. *Psychonomic Bulletin & Review, 2,* 279–321.

Lesher, G. W., & Mingolla, E. (1993). The role of edges and line-ends in illusory contour formation. *Vision Research, 33,* 2253–2270.

Levine, M. (1993). *Effective problem solving* (2nd ed.). Englewood Cliffs, NJ: Prentice-Hall.

Levitin, K. (1982). *One is not born a personality.* Moscow: Progress Publishers.

Levy, J., Trevarthen, C., & Sperry, R. V. (1972). Perception of bilateral chimeric figures-following hemispheric deconnexion. *Brain, 95,* 61–78.

Lewis, J. L. (1970). Semantic processing of unattended messages using dichotic listening. *Journal of Experimental Psychology, 85,* 225–228.

Liberty, C., & Ornstein, P. A. (1973). Age differences in organization and recall: The effects of training in categorization. *Journal of Experimental Child Psychology, 15,* 169–186.

Libet, B. (1978). Neuronal vs. subjective timing for a conscious sensory experience. In P. A. Buser and A. Rougeul-Buser (Eds.), *Cerebral correlates of conscious experience* (pp. 69–82). INSERM Symposium No. 6. Amsterdam, North Holland: Elsevier.

Libet, B. (1981). Timing of cerebral processes relative to concomitant conscious experiences in man. In G. Adam, I. Meszaros, & E. I. Banyai (Eds.), *Advances in physiological science.* New York: Pergamon Press.

Lindsay, P. H., & Norman, D. A. (1973). *Human information processing* (2nd ed.). New York: Academic Press.

Lindsay, P. H., & Norman, D. A. (1977). *Human information processing: An introduction to psychology, Second edition.* New York: Academic Press.

Linton, M. (1982). Transformations of memory in everyday life. In U. Neisser (Ed.), *Memory observed: Remembering in natural contexts.* San Francisco: Freeman.

Lockhart, R. S., Craik, F. I. M., & Jacoby, L. L. (1975). Depth of processing in recognition and recall: Some aspects of a general memory system. In J. Brown (Ed.), *Recognition and recall.* London: Wiley.

Lockhart, R. S., & Murdock, B. B., Jr. (1970). Memory and the theory of signal detection. *Psychological Bulletin, 74,* 100–109.

Loftus, E. F. (1993). The reality of repressed memories. *American Psychologist, 48,* 518–537.

Loftus, E. F. (1975a). Leading questions and the eyewitness report. *Cognitive Psychology, 7,* 560–572.

Loftus, E. F. (1975b). Spreading activation within semantic categories: Comments on Rosch's "Cognitive representations of semantic categories." *Journal of Experimental Psychology: General, 104,* 234–240.

Loftus, E. F. (1977). How to catch a zebra in semantic memory. In R. Shaw & J. Bransford (Eds.), *Perceiving, acting and knowing.* Hillsdale, NJ: Erlbaum.

Loftus, E. F. (1983). Misfortunes of memory. *Philosophical Transactions of the Royal Society.* London, B 302, 413–421.

Loftus, E. F. (1993a). Desperately seeking memories of the first few years of childhood: The reality of early memories. *Journal of Experimental Psychology: General, 122,* 274–277.

Loftus, E. F. (1993b). The reality of repressed memories. *American Psychologist, 48,* 518–537.

Loftus, E. F., & Ketcham, K. (1991). *Witness for the defense: The accused, the eyewitness, and the expert who puts memory on trial.* New York: St. Martin's Press.

Loftus, E. F., Miller, D. G., & Burns, H. J. (1978). Semantic integration of verbal information into a visual memory. *Journal of Experimental Psychology: Human Learning, 4,* 19–31.

Loftus, E F., & Ketcham, K. (1991). *Witness for the defense: The accused, the eyewitness, and the expert who puts memory on trial.* New York: St. Martin's Press.

Loftus, E. F., & Palmer, J. C. (1974). Reconstruction of automobile destruction: An example of the interaction between language and memory. *Journal of Verbal Learning and Verbal Behavior, 13,* 585–589.

Loftus, E. F., & Zanni, G. (1975). Eyewitness testimony: The influence of the wording of a question. *Bulletin of the Psychonomic Society, 5,* 86–88.

Loftus, G. R. (1982). Picture methodology. In C. R. Pubb (Ed.), *Handbook of research methods in human memory and cognition* (pp. 257–285). New York: Academic Press.

Loftus, G. R. (1983). The continuing persistence of the icon. *Behavioral and Brain Sciences, 1,* 43.

Loftus, G. R. (1995). On worthwhile icons: Reply to Di Lollo and Haber. *Journal of Experimental Psychology: Human Perception and Performance, 18,* 530–549.

Loftus, G. R., Johnson, C. A., & Shimarmura, A. P. (1985). How much is an icon worth? *Journal of Experimental Psychology: Human Perception and Performance, 11,* 1–13.

Loftus, G. R., & Loftus, E. F. (1976). *Human memory: The processing of information.* Hillsdale, NJ: Erlbaum.

Lorayne, H., & Lucas, J. (1974). *The memory book.* New York: Stein and Day.

Lubart, T. I., & Sternberg, R. J. (in preparation). *Creative performance: Testing an investment theory.* New Haven: Yale University Press.

Lubart, T. I., & Sternberg, R. J. (1995). An investment approach to creativity: Theory and data. In S. M. Smith, T. B. Ward, & R. A. Finke (Eds.), *The creative approach* (pp. 269–305). Cambridge, MA: The MIT Press.

Luria, A. R. (1960). *Problems of psychology, No. 1.* New York: Pergamon Press.

Luria, A. R. (1968). *The mind of a mnemonist.* New York: Basic Books.

Luria, A. R. (1971). Towards the problem of the historical nature of psychological processes. *International Journal of Psychology, 6,* 259–272.

Luria, A. R. (1974). The mind of a mnemonist: His memory. In P. A. Fried, *Readings in perception.* Lexington, MA: Heath.

Luria, A. R. (1976). *The neuropsychology of memory.* Washington, DC: Winston.

Lynch, S., & Yarnell, P. R. (1973). Retrograde amnesia: Delayed forgetting after concussion. *American Journal of Psychology, 86,* 643–645.

Lyons, J. (1968). *Introduction to theoretical linguistics.* Cambridge, England: Cambridge University Press.

Lyons, J. (1970). *New horizons in linguistics.* Harmondsworth, Middlesex, England: Penguin.

Lyons, J., & Wales, R. J. (1966). Psycholinguistic papers. *The Proceedings of the 1966 Edinburgh Conference.* Edinburgh: Edinburgh University Press.

MacKay, D. G. (1973) Aspects of a theory of comprehension, memory, and attention. *Quarterly Journal of Experimental Psychology, 25,* 22–40.

Mackworth, N. H. (1950). *Researches on the measurement of human performance* (Medical Research Council Special Report Series, No. 268). England.

Mackworth, N. H. (1965). Visual noise causes tunnel vision. *Psychonomic Science 3,* 67–68.

Mackworth, N. H. (1970). *Vigilance and habituation.* London: Penguin.

MacLin, M. K., & Solso, R. L. (2004). A method for schematic activation in the laboratory. Manuscript under review.

MacNeilage, P. F. (1970). Motor control of serial ordering of speech. *Psychological Review, 77,* 182–196.

MacNeilage, P. F. (1972). Speech physiology. In J. Gilbert (Ed.), *Speech and cortical functioning* (pp. 1–72). New York: Academic Press.

MacNeilage, P. F., & Ladefoged, P. (1976). The production of speech and language. In E. C. Carterette & M. P. Friedman (Eds.), *Handbook of perception* (Vol. 7, pp. 75–120). New York: Academic Press.

MacNeilage, P. F., & MacNeilage, L. A. (1973). Central processes controlling speech production during sleep and waking. In F. J. McGuigan & R. A. Schoonover (Eds.), *The psychophysiology of thinking* (pp. 417–448). New York: Academic Press.

Malakoff, D. (1999). Bayes offers a "new" way to make sense of numbers. *Science, 285,* 1460–1464.

Maltzman, I. (1955). Thinking: From a behavioristic point of view. *Psychological Review, 62,* 275–286.

Mandelbaum, D. B. (1958). *Selected writings of Edward Sapir in language, culture and personality.* Berkeley and Los Angeles: University of California Press.

Mandler, G. (1954). Response factors in human learning. *Psychological Review, 61,* 235–244.

Mandler, G. (1962). From association to structure. *Psychological Review, 69,* 415–427.

Mandler, G. (1967). Organization and memory. In K. W. Spence & J. T. Spence (Eds.), *The psychology of learning and motivation* (Vol. 1). New York: Academic Press.

Mandler, G. (1974). Memory storage and retrieval: Some limits on the reach of attention and consciousness. In P. M. A. Rabbit & S. Dornic (Eds.), *Attention and performance V.* London: Academic Press.

Mandler, G. (1975a). Consciousness: Respectable, useful, and probably necessary. In R. L. Solso (Ed.), *Information processing and cognitive psychology.* Hillsdale, NJ: Erlbaum.

Mandler, G. (1975b). *Mind and emotion.* New York: Wiley.

Mandler, G. (1983). Representation and recall in infancy. In J. H. Flavell & E. M. Markman (Eds.), *Handbook of child psychology: Cognitive development* (Vol. 3). New York: Wiley.

Mandler, G. (1984). Consciousness, imagery, and emotion—with special reference to autonomic imagery. *Journal of Mental Imagery, 8*(4), 87–94.

Mandler, J. M. (1984). Representation and recall in infancy. In M. Moscovitch (Ed.), *Infant memory.* New York: Plenum Press.

Mandler, J. M. (1984). *Mind and body: Psychology of emotion and stress.* New York: Norton.

Mandler, J. M. (1990). A new perspective on cognitive development in infancy. *American Scientist, 78,* 236–243.

Mandler, J. M. (1998). Babies think before they speak. *Human Development, 41*(2), 116–126.

Mandler, J. M. (2000). Perceptual and conceptual processes in infancy. *Journal of Cognition and Development, 1,* 3–36.

Mandler, J. M., & Bauer, P. J. (1988). The cradle of categorization: Is the basic level basic? *Cognitive Development, 3,* 247–264.

Mandler, J. M., & DeForest, M. (1979). Is there more than one way to recall a story? *Child Development, 44,* 697–700.

Mandler, J. M., & Johnson, N. S. (1977). Remembrance of things parsed: Story structure and recall. *Cognitive Psychology, 9,* 111–151.

Mandler, J. M., & McDonough, L. (1998). Studies in inductive inference in infancy. *Cognitive Psychology, 37,* 60–96.

Mangan, B. (1993). Taking phenomenology seriously: The "fringe" and its implications for cognitive research. *Consciousness and Cognition, 2*(2), 89–108.

Manro, H. M., & Washburn, M. F. (1908). The effect of imperceptible lines on the judgment of distance. *American Journal of Psychology, 19,* 242–243.

Mantyla, T. (1986). Optimizing cue effectiveness: Recall of 500 and 600 incidentally learned words. *Journal of Experimental Psychology: Learning, Memory, and Cognition, 12,* 66–71.

Mäntysalo, S., & Näätänen, R. (1987). The duration of neuronal trace of an auditory stimulus as indicated by event-related potentials. *Biological Psychology, 24,* 183–195.

Marcel, A. (1983). Conscious and unconscious perception: Experiments on visual masking and word recognition. *Cognitive Psychology, 15,* 238–300.

Marcel, A. J. (1983). Conscious and unconscious perception: Experiments on visual masking and word recognition. *Cognitive Psychology, 15,* 197–237.

Marks, L. E. (1974). On associations of light and sound: The mediation of brightness, pitch, and loudness. *American Journal of Psychology, 87,* 173–188.

Marks, L. E. (1987a). *Synesthesia, perception and metaphor.* Paper presented before the annual meeting of the American Psychological Association, New York, Aug.

Marks, L. E. (1987b). On cross-modal similarity: Auditory-visual interactions in speeded discrimination. *Journal of Experimental Psychology: Human Perception and Performance, 13,* 384–394.

Marr, D. (1982). *Vision.* San Francisco: Freeman.

Martin, R. C. (1993). Short-term memory and sentence processing: Evidence from neuropsychology. *Memory & Cognition, 21,* 176–183.

Massaro, D. W. (1972). Preperceptual images, processing time, and perceptual units in auditory perception. *Psychological Review, 79*(2), 124–145.

Massaro, D. W. (1975). *Experimental psychology and information processing.* Chicago: Rand McNally.

Massaro, D. W. (1987). *Speech perception by ear and eye: A paradigm for psychological inquiry.* Hillsdale, NJ: Erlbaum.

Massaro, D. W., & Hestand J. (1983). Developmental relations between reading ability and knowledge of orthographic structure. *Contemporary Educational Psychology, 8,* 174–180.

Massaro, D. W., & Schmuller, J. (1975). Visual features, preperceptual storage, and processing time in reading. In D. Massaro (Ed.), *Understanding language.* New York: Academic Press.

Matthews, W. A. (1968). Transformational complexity and short-term recall. *Language and Speech, 11,* 120–128.

Mattingly, I. G. (1972). Speech cues and sign stimuli. *American Scientist, 60,* 327–337.

Maxwell, W. (Ed.). (1983). *Thinking: The expanding frontier.* Philadelphia: Franklin Institute Press.

May, J. (1989). Mental imagery and sports. *Psychology Today,* May, 23–24.

Mayer, R. E. (1981). *The promise of cognitive psychology.* San Francisco: Freeman.

Mayer, R. E. (1983). *Thinking, problem solving, cognition.* San Francisco: Freeman.

McBurney, D., & Collings, V. (1977). *Introduction to sensation/perception.* Englewood Cliffs, NJ: Prentice-Hall.

McCarthy, D. (1954). Language development in children. In L. Carmichael (Ed.), *Manual of child psychology* (pp. 492–630). New York: Wiley.

McCarthy, G., Blamire, A. M., Rothman, D. L., Gruetier, R., & Shulman, R. G. (1993). *Proceedings of the National Academy of Sciences, 90,* 49–52.

McCaul, K. D., & Maki, R. H. (1984). Self-reference versus desirability ratings and memory for traits. *Journal of Personality and Social Psychology, 47,* 953–955.

McClelland, J. L. (1981). Retrieving general and specific information from stored knowledge of specifics. *Proceedings of the third annual meeting of the Cognitive Science Society, 170–172.*

McClelland, J. L. (1988). Parallel distributed processing: Implications for cognition and development. Technical report AIP-47, Carnegie-Mellon University, Department of Psychology, Pittsburgh, PA.

McClelland, J. L., & Jenkins, E. A., Jr. (1992). Emergence of stages from incremental learning mechanisms: A connectionist approach to cognitive development. In K. Van Lehn (Ed.), *Architectures for intelligence.* Hillsdale, NJ: Erlbaum.

McClelland, J. L., & Rumelhart, D. E. (1981). An interactive activation model of context effects in letter perception: Part 1. An account of basic findings. *Psychological Review, 88,* 375–407.

McClelland, J. L., & Rumelhart, D. E. (1985). Distributed memory and the representation of general and specific information. *Journal of Experimental Psychology: General, 114,* 159–188.

McClelland, J. L., Rumelhart, D. E., & Hinton, G. E. (1986). The appeal of parallel distributed processing. In D. E. Rumelhart, J. L. McClelland, & the PDP Research Group (Eds.), *Parallel distributed processing: Explorations in the microstructure of cognition* (Vol. 1). Cambridge, MA: Bradford.

McClelland, J. L., Rumelhart, D. E., & the PDP research group (Eds.). (1986). *Parallel distributed processing: Explorations in the microstructure of cognition* (Vol. 2). Cambridge, MA: Bradford.

McConkie, G. W., & Rayner, K. (1973). *The span of the effective stimulus during fixations in reading.* Paper presented at the American Educational Research Association meetings, New Orleans.

McConkie, G. W., & Rayner, K. (1976). Identifying the span of the effective stimulus in reading: Literature review and theories of reading. In H. Singer & R. Ruddell (Eds.), *Theoretical models and processes of reading.* Newark, DE: International Reading Association.

McCormack, P. D. (1972). Recognition memory: How complex a retrieval system? *Canadian Journal of Psychology, 24,* 19–41.

McCulloch, W. S., & Pitts, W. (1943). A logical calculus of the ideas imminent in nervous activity. *Bulletin of Mathematical Biophysics, 5,* 115–133.

McDaniel, M. A., & Einstein, G. O. (1986). Bizarre imagery as an effective memory aid: The importance of distinctiveness. *Journal of Experimental Psychology: Learning, Memory, and Cognition, 12,* 54–65.

McGaugh, J. L. (1966). Time dependent processes in memory storage. *Science, 153,* 1351–1358.

McGaugh, J. L. (1990). Significance and remembrance: The role of neuromodulatory systems. *Psychological Science, 1,* 15–25.

McGaugh, J. L. (2000). Memory . . . A century of consolidation. *Sciences, 287,* 248–251.

McGoech, J. A. (1932). Forgetting and the law of disuse. *Psychological Review, 39,* 352–370.

McKoon, G., Ratcliff, R., & Dell, G. S. (1986). A critical evaluation of the semantic-episodic distinction. *Journal of Experimental Psychology: Learning, Memory, and Cognition, 12,* 295–306.

Mednick, S. A. (1967). *The remote associates test.* Boston: Houghton Mifflin.

Mehler, J. (1963). Some effects of grammatical transformations on the recall of English sentences. *Journal of Verbal Learning and Verbal Behavior, 2,* 346–351.

Melton, A. W. (1963). Implications of short-term memory for a general theory of memory. *Journal of Verbal Learning and Verbal Behavior, 2,* 1–21.

Melton, A. W., & Irwin, J. M. (1940). The influence of degree of interpolated learning on retroactive inhibition and the overt transfer of specific responses. *American Journal of Psychology, 53,* 173–203.

Melton, A. W., & Martin, E. (Eds.). (1972). *Coding processes in human memory.* Washington, DC: Winston.

Melzoff, A. N., & Borton R. W. (1979). Intermodal matching by human neonates. *Nature, 282,* 403–404.

Metzler, J., & Shepard, R. N. (1974). Transformational studies of the internal representation of three-dimensional objects. In R. L. Solso (Ed.), *Theories in cognitive psychology: The Loyola Symposium.* Hillsdale, NJ: Erlbaum.

Mewhort, D. J. K. (1970). Guessing and the order-of-approximation effect. *American Journal of Psychology, 83,* 439–442.

Meyer, D. E., & Schvaneveldt, R. W. (1971). Facilitation in recognizing pairs of words. Evidence of a dependence between retrieval operations. *Journal of Experimental Psychology, 90,* 227–234.

Meyer, D. E., & Schvaneveldt, R. W. (1976). In C. N. Cofer (Ed.), *The structure of human memory.* San Francisco: Freeman.

Meyer, D. E., Schvaneveldt, R. W., & Ruddy, M. G. (1974a). Loci of contextual effects on visual word recognition. In P. M. A. Rabbit & S. Dornic (Eds.),

Attention and performance V. London: Academic Press.

Meyer, D. E., Schvaneveldt, R. W., & Ruddy, M. G. (1974b). Functions of graphemic and phonemic codes in visual word-recognition. *Memory and Cognition, 2*(2), 309–321.

Miall, R. C., & Tchalenko, J. (2001). The painter's eye movements: A study of eye and hand movement during portrait painting. *Leonardo, 34:* 35–40.

Miller, G. A. (1951). *Language and communication.* New York: McGraw-Hill.

Miller, G. A. (1956). The magical number seven, plus or minus two: Some limits on our capacity for processing information. *Psychological Review, 63,* 81–97.

Miller, G. A. (1962). *Psychology: The science of mental life.* Harmondsworth, Middlesex, England: Penguin Books.

Miller, G. A. (1979). "A very personal history." Talk to Cognitive Science Workshop, Massachusetts Institute of Technology, Cambridge, MA, June 1. Cited in H. Gardner, *The mind's new science: A history of the cognitive revolution.* New York: Basic Books.

Miller, G. A. (1980). Computation, consciousness, and cognition. *Behavioral and Brain Sciences, 3,* 146.

Miller, G. A. (1992). *The science of words.* New York: Freeman.

Miller, G. A., & Friedman, E. A. (1957). The reconstruction of mutilated English texts. *Information Control, 1,* 38–55.

Miller, G. A., Galanter, E., & Pribram, K. H. (1960). *Plans and the structure of behavior.* New York: Holt, Rinehart & Winston.

Miller, G. A., & Isard, S. (1963). Some perceptual consequences of linguistic rules. *Journal of Verbal Learning and Verbal Behavior, 2,* 217–228.

Miller, G. A., & McKean, K. O. (1964). A chronomatic study of some relations between sentences. *Quarterly Journal of Experimental Psychology, 16,* 297–308.

Miller, J. R., & Kintsch, W. (1980). Readability and recall of short prose passages: A theoretical analysis. *Journal of Experimental Psychology: Human Learning and Memory, 6,* 335–354.

Milner, A. D., & Rugg, M. D. (Eds.). (1992). *The neuropsychology of consciousness.* London: Academic Press.

Milner, B. (1966). Amnesia following operation on the temporal lobes. In C. Whitty & O. Zangwill (Eds.), *Amnesia* (pp. 109–133). London: Butterworth.

Milner, B. (1968). Visual recognition and recall after temporal-lobe excision in man. *Neuropsychologia, 6,* 191–209.

Milner, B. (1972). Disorders in learning and memory after temporal lobe lesions in man. *Clinical Neurosurgery, 19,* 421–446.

Milner, B., Corkin, S., & Teuber, H. L. (1968). Further analysis of the hippocampal amnesic syndrome. *Neuropsychologia, 6,* 215–234.

Milner, B., Petrides, M., & Smith, M. L. (1985). Frontal lobes and the temporal organization of memory. *Human Neurobiology, 4,* 137–142.

Minsky, M. (1975). A framework for representing knowledge. In P. Winston (Ed.), *The psychology of computer vision.* New York: McGraw-Hill.

Minsky, M. (1994). Will robots inherit the earth? *Scientific American,* Oct., 109–113.

Minsky, M., & Papert, S. (1968). *Perceptions.* Cambridge, MA: The MIT Press.

Mondloch, C. J., Lewis, T. L., Budreau, D. R., Maurer, D., Dannemiller, J. L., Stephens, B. R., & Kleiner-Gathercole, K. A. (1999). Face perception during early infancy. *Psychological Science, 10,* 419–422.

Monty, R. A., & Senders, J. W. (Eds.). (1983). *Eye movement and psychological processes.* Hillsdale, NJ: Erlbaum.

Moray, N. (1959). Attention in dichotic listening: Affective cues and the influence of instructions. *Quarterly Journal of Experimental Psychology, 11,* 56–60.

Moray, N. (1969). *Attention: Selective processes in vision and audition.* New York: Academic Press.

Moray, N. (1970). *Listening and attention.* London: Penguin.

Moray, N., Bates, A., & Barnett, T. (1965). Experiments on the four-eared man. *Journal of the Acoustical Society of America, 38,* 196–201.

Moray, N., & O'Brien, T. (1967). Signal detection theory applied to selective listening. *Journal of Acoustical Society of America, 42,* 765–772.

Morrison, F. J., Holmes, D. L., & Haith, M. M. (1974). A developmental study of the effect of familiarity on short-term visual memory. *Journal of Experimental Child Psychology, 18,* 412–425.

Morton, J. (1969). Interaction of information in word recognition. *Psychological Review, 76,* 165–178.

Morton, J. (1970). A functional model of memory. In D. A. Norman (Ed.), *Models of human memory.* New York: Academic Press.

Morton, J. (1980). The logogen model and ortho-graphic structure. In U. Frith (Ed.), *Cognitive processes in spelling.* London: Academic Press.

Morton, J. (1981). The status of information process-ing models of language. *Philosophic transactions of the Royal Society of London, B, 295,* 387–396.

Moscovitch, M. (Ed.). (1984). *Infant memory.* New York: Plenum.

Mountcastle, V. B. (1978). Brain mechanisms of di-rected attention. *Journal of the Royal Society of Medicine, 71,* 14–27.

Mountcastle, V. B. (1979). An organizing principle for cerebral function: The unit module and the dis-tributed system. In F. O. Schmitt (Ed.), *The neuro-sciences: Fourth study program.* Cambridge, MA: The MIT Press.

Mowrer, O. H. (1954). The psychologist looks at lan-guage. *American Psychologist, 9,* 660–694.

Müeller, G. E., & Pilzecker, A. (1990). Experimentelle Beitrage zur Lehre vom Gedachtnis. *Zeitshrift für Psychologie,* Ergbd. 1.

Mueller, M. (1974). Cited in N. Chaudhuri, *Scholar ex-traordinary,* London: Chatto & Windus.

Murch, G. M. (1973). *Visual and auditory perception.* Indianapolis, IN: Bobbs-Merrill.

Murdock, B. B. (1965). Signal-detection theory and short-term memory. *Journal of Experimental Psy-chology, 70,* 443–447.

Murdock, B. B. (1971). Four channel effects in short-term memory. *Psychonomic Science, 24,* 197–198.

Murdock, B. B. (1983). A distributed memory model for serial-order information. *Psychological Review, 90,* 316–338.

Mussen, P. M. (Ed.). (1970). *Carmichael's manual of child psychology.* New York: Wiley.

Myers, R. E., & Sperry, T. W. (1953). Interocular trans-fer of the visual form discrimination habit in cats after section of the optic chiasm and corpus callo-sum. *Anatomical Record, 175,* 351–352.

Myers, T., Laver, J., & Anderson, J. R. (Eds.). (1981). *The cognitive representation of speech.* Amster-dam: North-Holland.

Näätänen, R. (1985). Selective attention and stimulus processing: Reflections in event-related potentials, magnetoencephalogram, and regional cerebral blood flow. In M. I. Posner & O. S. Marin (Eds.), *Attention and performance* (Vol. II, pp. 355–373). Hillsdale, NJ: Erlbaum.

Natsoulas, T. (1978). Consciousness. *American Psy-chologist, 33,* 906–914.

Nehrke, M. F. (1972). Age, sex and educational differ-ences in syllogistic reasoning. *Journal of Gerontol-ogy, 27,* 966–970.

Neimark, E. D. (1987). *Adventures in thinking.* San Diego, CA: Harcourt Brace Jovanovich.

Neimark, E. D., & Santa, J. L. (1975). Thinking and concept attainment. *Annual Review of Psychology* (Vol. 26). Palo Alto, CA: Annual Reviews.

Neisser, U. (1967). *Cognitive psychology.* New York: Appleton-Century-Crofts.

Neisser, U. (1969). *Selective reading: A method for the study of visual attention.* Paper presented at the 19th International Congress of Psychology, London.

Neisser, U. (1976). *Cognition and reality: Principles and implications of cognitive psychology.* San Francisco: Freeman.

Neisser, U. (Ed.). (1982a). *Memory observed.* San Fran-cisco: Freeman.

Neisser, U. (1982b). Snapshots or benchmarks? In U. Neisser (Ed.), *Memory observed.* San Francisco: Freeman.

Neisser, U., & Becklen, R. (1975). Selective looking: At-tending to visually significant events. *Cognitive Psychology, 7,* 480–494.

Neisser, U., & Weene, P. (1962). Hierarchies in concept attainment. *Journal of Experimental Psychology, 64,* 640–645.

Neumann, P. G. (1977). Visual prototype formation with discontinuous representation of dimensions of variability. *Memory and Cognition, 5,* 187–197.

Neville, H. J. (1995). Developmental specificity in neu-rocognitive development in humans. In M. S. Gazzaniga (Ed.) *The cognitive neurosciences.* Cambridge, MA: The MIT Press.

Newell, A. (1967). *Studies in problem solving: Sub-ject 3 on the crypt-arithmetic task. DONALD plus GERALD equals ROBERT.* Pittsburgh: Carnegie Mellon Institute.

Newell, A. (1973). Artificial intelligence and the con-cept of mind. In R. C. Schank & C. M. Colby (Eds.), *Computer models of thought and language.* San Francisco: Freeman.

Newell, A. (1990). *Unified theories of cognition.* Cam-bridge, MA: Harvard University Press.

Newell, A., Shaw, J. C., & Simon, H. A. (1960). Report on a general problem-solving program. In W. R. Reitman (Ed.), *Proceedings of the International Conference on Information Processing* (pp. 256–264). Paris: UNESCO.

Newell, A., & Simon, H. A. (1956). The logic theory machine: A complex information processing system. *IRE Transactions of Information Theory, IT-2*(3), 61–79.

Newell, A., & Simon, H. A. (1963). GPS, a program that stimulates human thought. In E. A. Feigenbaum & J. Feldman (Eds.), *Computers and thought.* New York: McGraw-Hill.

Newell, A., & Simon, H. A. (1972). *Human problem solving.* Englewood Cliffs, NJ: Prentice-Hall.

Newell, A., Simon, H. A., & Shaw, J. C. (1958). Elements of a theory of human problem solving. *Psychological Review, 65,* 151–166.

Newman, J., & Baars, B. J. (1993). A neural attentional model for access to consciousness: A Global Workspace perspective. *Concepts in Neuroscience, 4*(2), 255–290.

Nickerson, R. S. (1965). Short-term memory for complex meaningful visual configurations: A demonstration of capacity. *Canadian Journal of Psychology, 19,* 155–160.

Nickerson, R. S. (1968). A note on long-term recognition memory for picture material. *Psychonomic Science, 11,* 58.

Nickerson, R. S., Perkins, D. N., & Smith, E. E. (1985). *The teaching of thinking.* Hillsdale, NJ: Erlbaum.

Nisbett, R. E., & Ross, L. (1980). *Human preferences: Strategies and shortcomings of social judgment.* Englewood Cliffs, NJ: Prentice-Hall.

Noice, H. (1991). The role of explanations and plan recognition in the learning of theatrical scripts. *Cognitive Science, 15,* 425–460.

Noice, H., & Noice, T. (1993). The effects of segmentation on the recall of theatrical material. *Poetics, 22,* 51–67.

Norman, D. A. (1966a). Acquisition and retention in short-term memory. *Journal of Experimental Psychology, 72,* 369–381.

Norman, D. A. (1966b). Memory and decisions. *Proceedings of Symposium on Memory and Attention, 18th International Congress of Psychology,* Moscow.

Norman, D. A. (1968). Toward a theory of memory and attention. *Psychological Review, 75,* 522–536.

Norman, D. A. (1969). Memory while shadowing. *Quarterly Journal of Experimental Psychology, 21,* 85–93.

Norman, D. A. (1976). *Memory and attention* (2nd ed.). New York: Wiley.

Norman, D. A., & Rumelhart, E. E. (1975). *Exploration in cognition.* San Francisco: Freeman.

Norman, D. A., & Shallice, T. (1986). Attention to action: Willed and automatic control of behavior. In R. Davidson, G. E. Schwartz, & D. Shapiro (Eds.), *Consciousness and self-regulation* (Vol. 4, pp. 11–28). New York: Plenum Press.

Norman, D. A., & Wicklegren, W. A. (1965). Short-term recognition memory for single digits. *Journal of Experimental Psychology, 70,* 479–489.

Norman, G. R., Brooks, L. R., & Allen, S. W. (1989). Recall by expert medical practitioners and novices as a record of processing attention. *Journal of Experimental Psychology: Learning Memory and Cognition, 15,* 1166–1174.

Norton, D., & Stark, L. (1971). Eye movements and visual perception. *Scientific American, 224,* 34–43.

Oakley, D. A. (1981). Brain mechanisms of mammalian memory. *British Medical Bulletin, 37,* 175–180.

O'Brien, E. J., & Wolford, C. R. (1982). Effect of delay in testing on retention of plausible versus bizarre mental images. *Journal of Experimental Psychology: Learning, Memory, and Cognition, 8,* 148–153.

Ojemann, G. A. (1991). Cortical organization of language. *The Journal of Neuroscience, 11,* 2281–2287.

Oldfield, R. C. (194). Memory mechanisms and the theory of schemata. *British Journal of Psychology, 43,* 14–23.

Olson, G. M. (1977). An information-processing analysis of visual memory and habituation in infants. In T. J. Tighe & R. H. Leaton (Eds.), *Habituation: Perspectives from child development, animal behavior and neurophysiology.* Hillsdale, NJ: Erlbaum.

Ornstein, P. A. (Ed.). (1978). *Memory development in children.* Hillsdale, NJ: Erlbaum.

Ornstein, P. A., Naus, M. J., & Liberty, C. (1975). Rehearsal and organizational processes in children's memory. *Child Development, 45,* 818–830.

Ornstein, R. (1991). *The evolution of consciousness: The origins of the way we think.* New York: Simon & Schuster.

Ornstein, R., & Thompson, R. F. (1985). *The amazing brain.* Los Altos, CA: ISHK Book Service.

Ornstein, R. E. (1972). *The psychology of consciousness.* San Francisco: Freeman. (Also published by Viking, 1972.)

Ornstein, R. E. (1973). *The nature of human consciousness.* San Francisco: Freeman. (Also published by Viking, 1973).

Ornstein, R. E. (1977). *The psychology of consciousness.* New York: Harcourt Brace Jovanovich.

Osterberg, G. A. (1935). Topography of the layer of rods and cones in the human retina. *Acta Ophthalmologica, Suppl. 6, 61,* 1–102.

Owen, F. W., Adams, P. A., Forrest, T., Stolz, L. M., & Fischer, S. (1971). Learning disorders in children: Sibling studies. *Monographs of the Society for Research in Child Development, 36* (4, serial no. 144).

Owens, J., Bower, G. H., & Black, J. B. (1979). The "soap opera" effect in story recall. *Memory and Cognition, 7,* 185–191.

Paivio, A. (1965). Abstractness, imagery, and meaningfulness in paired-associated learning. *Journal of Verbal Learning and Verbal Behavior, 4,* 32–38.

Paivio, A. (1969). Mental imagery in associative learning and memory. *Psychological Review, 76,* 241–263.

Paivio, A. (1971a). Imagery and deep structure in the recall of English nominalizations. *Journal of Verbal Learning and Verbal Behavior, 10,* 1–12.

Paivio, A. (1971b). *Imagery and verbal processes.* New York: Holt, Rinehart & Winston.

Paivio, A. (1975). Perceptual comparisons through the mind's eye. *Memory and Cognition, 3,* 635–647.

Paivio, A., & Csapo, K. (1969). Concrete-image and verbal memory codes. *Journal of Experimental Psychology, 80,* 279–285.

Paivio, A., Smythe, P. C., & Yuille, J. C. (1968). Imagery versus meaningfulness of norms in paired-associate learning. *Canadian Journal of Psychology, 22,* 427–441.

Paivio, A., Yuille, J. C., & Madigan, S. A. (1968). Concreteness, imagery and meaningfulness values for 925 nouns. *Journal of Experimental Psychology Monograph Supplement, 76*(1), part 2.

Palmer, S. E. (1975a). Visual perception and world knowledge: Notes on a model of sensory cognitive interaction. In D. A. Norman, D. E. Rumelhart, & the LNR Research Group, *Explorations in cognition.* San Francisco: Freeman.

Palmer, S. E. (1975b). The effects of contextual scenes on the identification of objects. *Memory and Cognition, 3,* 519–526.

Palmer, S. E. (1989). Reference frames in the perception of shape and orientation. In B. E. Shepp & S. Ballesteros (Eds.), *Object perception: Structure & process.* Hillsdale, NJ: Erlbaum.

Palmer, S. E. (1999). *Vision science: Photons to phenomenology.* Cambridge, MA: The MIT Press.

Palmer, S. E., Rosch, E., & Chase, P. (1981). Canonical perspective and the perception of objects. In J. Long & A. Baddeley (Eds.), *Attention and performance IX.* Hillsdale, NJ: Erlbaum.

Pardo, J. V., Fox, P. T., & Raichle, M. E. (1991). Localization of a human system for sustained attention by positron emission tomography. *Nature, 349,* 61–64.

Parkin, A. J. (1993). *Memory: Phenomena, experiment and theory.* Oxford: Blackwell.

Pashler, H. (1993). Doing two things at the same time. *American Scientist, 81,* 48–55.

Pear, T. H. (1922). *Remembering and forgetting.* London: Methuen.

Penfield, W. (1959). The interpretive cortex. *Science, 129,* 1719–1725.

Penfield, W., & Jasper, H. H. (1954). *Epilepsy and the functional anatomy of the human brain.* Boston: Little, Brown.

Penfield, W., & Roberts, L. (1959). *Speech and brain mechanism.* Princeton: Princeton University Press.

Petersen, S. E., & Fiez, J. A. (1993). The processing of single words studied with positron emission tomography. *Annual Review of Neuroscience, 16,* 509–530.

Petersen, S. E., Fox, P. T., Posner, M. I., Mintun, M., & Raichle, M. E. (1988). Positron emission tomographic studies of the cortical anatomy of single word processing. *Nature, 331,* 585–589.

Petersen, S. E., Fox, P. T., Snyder, A. Z., & Raichle, M. E. (1990). Activation of extrastriate and frontal cortical areas by visual words and word-like stimuli. *Science, 249,* 1041–1044.

Peterson, L. R., & Peterson, M. J. (1959). Short-term retention of individual verbal items. *Journal of Experimental Psychology, 58,* 193–198.

Peterson, M. T., Meagher, R. B., Jr., Chait, H., & Gillie, S. (1973). The abstraction and generalization of dot patterns. *Cognitive Psychology, 4,* 378–398.

Pew, R. W. (1974). Levels of analysis in motor control. *Brain Research, 71,* 393–400.

Phillips, W. A. (1974). On the distinction between sensory storage and short-term visual memory. *Perception and Psychophysics, 16,* 283–390.

Phillips, W. A., & Baddeley, A. D. (1971). Reaction time and short-term visual memory. *Psychonomic Science, 22,* 73–74.

Philpott, A., & Wilding, J. (1979). Semantic interference from subliminal stimuli in a dichoptic viewing situation. *British Journal of Psychology, 70,* 559–563.

Piaget, J. (1926). *The language and thought of the child*. New York: Harcourt Brace.

Piaget, J. (1952a). *The child's conception of number*. New York: Humanities Press.

Piaget, J. (1952b). *The origins of intelligence in children*. New York: International Universities Press.

Piaget, J. (1970). Piaget's theory. In P. H. Mussen (Ed.), *Carmichael's manual of child psychology* (Vol. 1, pp. 703–732). New York: Wiley.

Piaget, J., & Inhelder, B. (1941). *Le developpement des quantites chez l'enfant*. Neuchatel: Delachaux et Niestle.

Piaget, J., & Inhelder, B. (1956). *The child's conception of space*. London: Routledge & Kegan Paul.

Piaget, J., & Inhelder, B. (1973). *Memory and intelligence*. New York: Basic Books.

Pick, A. D. (1975). *The development of strategies of attention*. Paper presented at the biennial meeting of the Society for Research in Child Development, Denver.

Pick, A. D., Christy, M. D., & Frankel, G. W. (1972). A developmental study of visual selective attention. *Journal of Experimental Child Psychology, 11,* 165–175.

Pick, H. L., Jr., & Saltzman, E. (Eds.). (1978). *Modes of perceiving and processing information* Hillsdale, NJ: Erlbaum.

Pierce, J. R. (1961). *Symbols, signals and noise*. New York: Harper & Row.

Pierce, J. R. (1968). *Science, art and communication*. New York: Clarkson N. Potter.

Pillsbury, W. B. (1897). A study in apperception. *American Journal of Psychology, 8,* 315–393.

Pinel, J. P. J. (1993). *Biopsychology* (2nd ed.). Boston: Allyn & Bacon.

Pinker, S. (1980). Mental imagery and the third dimension. *Journal of Experimental Psychology: General, 109,* 354–371.

Pinker, S. (1984). Visual cognition: An introduction. *Cognition, 18,* 1–63.

Pinker, S. (Ed.). (1985). *Visual cognition*. Cambridge, MA: The MIT Press.

Pinker, S. (1994). *The language instinct*. New York: Morrow.

Pinker, S. (1997). *How the mind works*. New York: Norton.

Place, U. T. (1956). Is consciousness a brain process? *British Journal of Psychology, 47,* 44–50.

Plomin, R., & DeFries, J. C. (1998). The genetics of cognitive abilities and disabilities. *Scientific American,* May, 62–69.

Podgorny, P., & Shepard, R. N. (1978). Functional representations common to visual perception and imagination. *Journal of Experimental Psychology: Human Perception and Performance, 4,* 21–35.

Poincaré, H. (1913). Mathematical creation. In *The foundations of science* (G. H. Halstead, trans.). New York: Science Press.

Pollock, J. (1998). *How to build a person*. Cambridge, MA: The MIT Press.

Porth, C. M. (1986). *Pathophysiology*. Philadelphia: Lippincott.

Posner, M. I. (1969). Abstraction and the process of recognition. In J. T. Spence & G. H. Bower (Eds.), The *psychology of learning and motivation: Advances in learning and motivation* (Vol. 3). New York: Academic Press.

Posner, M. I. (1973). *Cognition: An introduction*. Glenview, IL: Scott, Foresman.

Posner, M. I. (1988). Structures and functions of selective attention. In T. Boll & B. Bryant (Eds.), *Master lectures in clinical neuropsychology* (pp. 173–202). Washington, DC: American Psychological Association.

Posner, M. I. (Ed.). (1989). *Foundations of cognitive science*. Cambridge, MA: The MIT Press.

Posner, M. I. (1992). Attention as a cognitive and neural system. *Current Directions in Psychological Science, 1,* 11–14.

Posner, M. I., & Boies, S. J. (1971). Components of attention. *Psychological Review, 78,* 391–408.

Posner, M. I., Boies, S. J., Eichelman, W., & Taylor, R. L. (1969). Retention of visual and name codes of single letters. *Journal of Experimental Psychology Monographs, 79,* 1–16.

Posner, M. I., Early, T. S., Reiman, E. M., Pardo, P. J., & Dhawan, M. (1988). Asymmetries in hemispheric control of attention in schizophrenia. *Archives of General Psychiatry, 45,* 814–826.

Posner, M. I., Goldsmith, R., & Welton, K. E., Jr. (1967). Perceived distance and the classification of distorted patterns. *Journal of Experimental Psychology 73,* 28–38.

Posner, M. I., & Keele, S. W. (1967). Decay of visual information from a single letter. *Science, 158,* 137–139.

Posner, M. I., & Keele, S. W. (1968). On the genesis of abstract ideas. *Journal of Experimental Psychology, 77,* 353–363.

Posner, M. I., & Konick, A. F. (1966). On the role of interference in short-term memory. *Journal of Experimental Psychology, 72,* 221–231.

Posner, M. I., & Petersen, S. E. (1990). The attention system in the human brain. *Annual Review of Neuroscience, 13*, 25–42.

Posner, M. I., Petersen, S. E., Fox, P. I., & Raichle, M. E. (1988). Localization of cognitive operations in the human brain. *Science, 240*, 1627–1631.

Posner, M. I., & Raichle, M. E. (1994). *Images of mind.* NY: Scientific American Library.

Posner, M. I., & Rothbart, M. K. (1989). Intentional chapters on unintended thoughts. In J. S. Uleman & John A. Bargh (Eds.), *Unintended thought.* New York: Guilford Press.

Posner, M. I., & Rothbart, M. K. (1991). Attentional mechanism and conscious experience. In *The neuropsychology of consciousness* (Chap. 5, pp. 92–111). New York: Academic Press.

Posner, M. I., Sandson, J., Dhawan, M., & Shulman, G. L. (1989). Is word recognition automatic? A cognitive-anatomical approach. *Journal of Cognitive Neuroscience, 1*, 50–60.

Posner, M. I., & Snyder, C. R. R. (1974). Attention and cognitive control. In R. L. Solso (Ed.), *Information processing and cognition: The Loyola Symposium.* Hillsdale, NJ: Erlbaum.

Posner, M. I., & Snyder, C. R. R. (1975). Facilitation and inhibition in the processing of signals. In P. M. A. Rabbit & S. Dornic (Eds.), *Attention and performance V.* London: Academic Press.

Posner, M. I., & Warren, R. E. (1972). Traces, concepts, and conscious constructions. In A. W. Melton & E. Martin (Eds.), *Coding process in human memory.* Washington, DC: Winston.

Potter, R. K., Kopp, G. A., & Kopp, H. G. (1966). *Visible speech.* New York: Dover.

Poudion, E. C. (1962). Peripheral vision, refractoriness, and eye movements in fast oral readings. *British Journal of Psychology, 53*, 409–419.

Pratkanis, A. R., & Greenwald, A. G. (1988). Recent perspectives on unconscious processing: Still no marketing applications. *Psychology & Marketing, 5*, 337–353.

Premack, D. (1976). Language and intelligence in ape and man. *American Scientist, 64*, 674–683.

Pribram, K. H. (1971). *Languages of the brain: Experimental paradoxes and principles in neuropsychology.* Englewood Cliffs, NJ: Prentice-Hall.

Pribram, K. H. (1986). The cognitive revolution and mind/brain issues. *American Psychologist, 41*, 507–520.

Pylyshyn, Z. W. (1973). What the mind's eye tells the mind's brain: A critique of mental imagery. *Psychological Bulletin, 80*, 1–24.

Pylyshyn, Z. W. (1980). The "casual power" of machines. *Behavioral and Brain Sciences, 3*, 442–444.

Pylyshyn, Z. W. (1981). The imagery debate: Analogue media versus tacit knowledge. *Psychological Review, 88*, 16–45.

Pylyshyn, Z. W. (1986). *Computation and cognition: Toward a foundation for cognitive science.* Cambridge, MA: The MIT Press.

Quillian, M. R. (1968). Semantic memory. In M. Minsky (Ed.), *Semantic information processing.* Cambridge, MA: The MIT Press.

Quillian, M. R. (1969). The teachable language comprehender: A simulation program and theory of language. *Communication of the Association for Computing Machinery, 12.*

Rachlin, H., Logue, Q. W., Gibbon, J., & Frankel, M. (1986). Cognition and behavior in studies of choice. *Psychological Review, 93*, 35–45.

Raichle, M. E. (1994). Visualizing the mind. *Scientific American, 270*, 58–63.

Raichle, M. E., Fiez, J. A., Videen, T. O., MacLeod, A. K., Pardo, J. V., Fox, P. T., & Petersen, S. E. (1994). Practice-related changes in human brain functional anatomy during nonmotor learning. *Cerebral Cortex, 4*(1), 8–26.

Ramachandran, V. S. (1987). Visual perception of surfaces: A biological theory. In S. Petry & G. E. Meyer (Eds.), *The perception of illusory contours* (pp. 93–108). New York: Springer-Verlag.

Raney, G. E., & Rayner, K. (1993). Event-related brain potentials, eye movements, and readings. *Psychological Science, 4*, 283–286.

Raphael, B. (1976). *The thinking computer.* San Francisco: Freeman.

Ratcliff, R., & McKoon, G. (1986). More on the distinction between episodic and semantic memories. *Journal of Experimental Psychology: Learning, Memory, and Cognition, 12*, 312–313.

Raugh, M. R., & Atkinson, R. C. (1975). A mnemonic method for learning a second-language vocabulary. *Journal of Educational Psychology, 67*, 1–16.

Rayner, K. (1975). The perceptual span and peripheral cues in reading. *Cognitive Psychology, 7*, 65–81.

Rayner, K. (1978). Eye movements in reading and information processing. *Psychological Bulletin, 85*, 618–660.

Rayner, K. (1980). Personal communication cited by R. G. Crowder in "The demise of short-term memory." *Acta Psychologica, 50*, 1982, 292–323.

Rayner, K. (1993). Eye movements in reading: Recent developments. *Current Directions in Psychological Science, 2*, 81–85.

Rayner, K., & Frazier, L. (1989). Selection mechanisms in reading lexically ambiguous words. *Journal of Experimental Psychology: Learning, Memory, and Cognition, 15,* 779–790.

Rayner, K., & Morris, R. K. (1992). Eye movement control in reading: Evidence against semantic pre-processing. *Journal of Experimental Psychology: Human Perception and Performance, 18,* 163–172.

Rayner, K., & Pollatsek, A. (1987). Eye movements in reading: A tutorial review. In M. Coltheart (Ed.), *Attention and performance XII: The psychology of reading.* London: Erlbaum.

Rayner, K., & Pollatsek, A. (1989). *The psychology of reading.* Englewood Cliffs, NJ: Prentice Hall.

Rayner, K., & Pollatsek, A. (1997). Eye movements, the eye-hand span, and perceptual span during sight-reading of music. *Current Directions in Psychological Science. 6,* 49–53.

Rayner, K., & Posnansky, C. (1978). Stages of processing in word identification. *Journal of Experimental Psychology: General, 107,* 64–81.

Rayner, K., Sereno, S. C., Morris, R. K., Schmauder, A. R., & Clifton, C. (1989). Eye movements and on-line language comprehension processes. *Language and Cognitive Processes, 4* (Special Issue), 21–50.

Reber, A. S., & Scarborough, D. L. (Eds.). (1977). *Toward a psychology of reading.* Hillsdale, NJ: Erlbaum.

Ree, M. J., & Earles, J. A. (1992). Intelligence is the best predictor of job performance. *Current Directions in Psychological Science, 1,* 86–89.

Reed, S. K. (1972). Pattern recognition and categorization. *Cognitive Psychology, 3,* 382–407.

Reed, S. K. (1973). *Psychological processes in pattern recognition.* New York: Academic Press.

Rees, A., Beal, M. K., & Solso, R. L. (1993). *Prototype formation in right and left hemispheres.* Paper presented at the annual meeting of WPA/RMPA, Phoenix, AZ, April.

Reicher, G. M. (1969). Perceptual recognition as a function of meaningfulness of stimuli material. *Journal of Experimental Psychology, 81,* 275–280.

Reitman, J. (1976). Skilled perception in Go: Deducting memory structures from inter-response times. *Cognitive Psychology, 12,* 336–356.

Reitman, J. S., & Bower, G. H. (1973). Storage and later recognition of exemplars of concepts. *Cognitive Psychology, 4,* 194–206.

Reitman, W. R. (1965). *Cognition and thought: An information-processing approach.* New York: Wiley.

Reitman, W. R., Grove, R. B., & Shoup, R. G. (1964). Argus: An information-processing model of thinking. *Behavioral Science, 9,* 270–281.

Restak, R. M. (1988). *The mind.* New York: Bantam.

Restle, F. A. (1955). A theory of discrimination learning. *Psychological Review, 62,* 11–19.

Restorff, V. H. (1933). Über die Wirkung von Bereichsbildungen im Spurenfeld. *Psychologie Forschurg, 18,* 299–342.

Reutner, D. B. (1972). Class shift, symbolic shift, and background shift in short-term memory. *Journal of Experimental Psychology, 93,* 90–94.

Reynolds, D. (1964). Effects of double stimulation: Temporal inhibition of response. *Psychological Bulletin, 62,* 333–347.

Richardson, A. (1969). *Mental imagery.* New York: Springer.

Riley, C. A. (1975). Representation and use of comparative information and inference making in young children. Unpublished doctoral dissertation, Princeton University.

Riley, C. A., & Trabasso, T. (1974). Comparatives, logical structures and encoding in a transitive reference task. *Journal of Experimental Child Psychology, 17,* 187–203.

Rips, L. J. (1975). Inductive judgments about natural categories. *Journal of Verbal Learning and Verbal Behavior, 14,* 665–681.

Rips, L. J. (1998). Reasoning and conversation. *Psychological Review, 105,* 441–441.

Rips, L. J., Brem, S. K., & Bailenson, J. N. (1999). Reasoning dialogues. *Current Directions in Psychological Science, 8,* 172–177.

Rips, L. J., Shoben, E. J., & Smith, E. E. (1973). Semantic distance and the verification of semantic relations. *Journal of Verbal Learning and Verbal Behavior, 14,* 665–681.

Risberg, J. (1987). Development of high-resolution two-dimensional measurement of regional cerebral blood flow. In J. Wade, S. Knezevik, V. A. Maximilian, Z. Mubrin, & I. Prohovnik (Eds.), *Impact of functional imaging in neurology and psychiatry.* London: Libbey.

Risberg, J. (1989). Regional cerebral blood flow measurements with high temporal and spatial resolution. In D. Ottoson (Ed.), *Visualization of brain functions,* Wenner-Gren International Symposium Series. London: Macmillan.

Roberge, J. J. (1972). Effects of structure and semantics on the solution of pure hypothetical syllogisms. *Journal of General Psychology, 87,* 161–167.

Robertson, D. A., Gernsbacher, M. A., Guidott, S. J., Robertson, R. R. W., Irwin, W., Mock, B. J., & Campana, M. E. (2000). Functional neuroanatomy of the cognitive process of mapping during discourse comprehension. *Psychological Science, 11*, 255–260.

Robinson, D. A. (1968). Eye movement control in primates. *Science, 161*, 1219–1224.

Rock, I. (1983). *The logic of perception.* Cambridge, MA: The MIT Press.

Rock, I. (1984). *Perception.* New York: Scientific American.

Rock, I., & Ebenholtz, S. (1962). Stroboscopic movement based on change of phenomenal rather than retinal location. *American Journal of Psychology, 75*, 193–207.

Roe, A. (1946). The personality of artists. *Educational Psychology Measurement, 6*, 401–408.

Roe, A. (1953). *The making of a scientist.* New York: Dodd, Mead.

Roediger, H. L. (1980). Memory metaphors in cognitive psychology. *Memory and Cognition, 8*, 231–252.

Roediger, H. L., & Craik, F. I. M. (Eds.). (1989). *Varieties of memory and consciousness: Essays in honor of Endel Tulving.* Hillsdale, NJ: Erlbaum.

Roediger, H. L., & McDermott, K. B. (1993). Retrieval blocks in episodic and semantic memory. *Canadian Journal of Psychology, 36*, 213–242.

Rogers, T. B., Kuiper, N. A., & Kirker, W. S. (1977). Self-reference and the encoding of personal information. *Journal of Personality and Social Psychology, 35*, 677–688.

Roland, P. E., & Friberg, L. (1985). Localization of cortical areas activated by thinking. *Journal of Neurophysiology, 53*, 1219–1243.

Rosch, E. (1973). On the internal structure of perceptual and semantic categories. In T. E. Moore (Ed.), *Cognitive development and the acquisition of language* (pp. 111–144). New York: Academic Press.

Rosch, E. (1974). Linguistic relativity. In A. Silverstein (Ed.), *Human communication: Theoretical perspectives* (pp. 95–121). New York: Halsted.

Rosch, E. (1975). Cognitive representations of semantic categories. *Journal of Experimental Psychology: General, 104*, 192–233.

Rosch, E. (1977). Human categorization. In N. Warren (Ed.), *Advances in cross-cultural psychology* (Vol. 1). London: Academic Press.

Rosenblatt, F. (1958). The Perceptron: A probabilistic mode for information storage and organization in the brain. *Psychological Review, 65*, 386–407.

Rosenzweig, M. R., & Bennett, E. L. (1996). Psychology of plasticity: Effects of training and experience on brain and behavior. *Behavioural Brain Research, 78*(1), 57–65.

Roskies, A. L. (1994). Mapping memory with positron emission tomography. *Proceedings of the National Academy of Sciences, 91*, 1989–1991.

Ross, G. S. (1980). Categorization in 1- to 2-year-olds. *Developmental Psychology, 16*, 391–396.

Rovee-Collier, C. K. (1987). Learning and memory in infancy. In J. D. Osofsky (Ed.), *Handbook of infant development* (2nd ed., pp. 517–536). New York: John Wiley.

Rovee-Collier, C. K. (1990). The "memory system" of prelinguistic infants. In A. Diamond (Ed.), *The development and neural bases of higher cognitive functions.* New York: The New York Academy of Sciences.

Rovee-Collier, C. (1999). The development of infant memory. *Current Directions in Psychological Science, 8*, 80–85.

Rubin, D. C. (1985). Flashbulb memories. *Psychology Today,* Sept.

Rubin, D. C. (1987). Quoted in *The New York Times,* June 23.

Rubin, D. C. (2000). Autobiographical memory and aging. In D. C. Park & N. Schwarz (Eds.), *Cognitive aging: A primer* (pp. 131–149). Philadelphia: Psychology Press.

Rubin, D. C., & Friendly, M. (1986). Predicting which words get recalled: Measures of free recall, availability, goodness, emotionality, and pronunciability for 925 nouns. *Memory and Cognition, 14*, 79–94.

Rubin, D. C., Rahhal, T. A., & Poon, L. W. (1998). Things learned in early adulthood are remembered best. *Memory & Cognition, 26*, 3–19.

Rubin, D. C., Wetzler, S. E., & Nebes, R. D. (1986). Autobiographical memory across the life span. In D. C. Rubin (Ed.), *Autobiographical memory.* Cambridge, England: Cambridge University Press.

Rubinstein, H., Lewis, S. S., & Rubinstein, M. A. (1971). Evidence of phonemic recoding in visual word recognition. *Journal of Verbal Learning and Verbal Behavior, 10*, 645–657.

Rubinstein, M. F. (1986). *Tools for thinking and problem solving.* Englewood Cliffs, NJ: Prentice-Hall.

Ruch, T. C., & Patton, H. D. (1965). *Physiology and biophysics* (19th ed.). Philadelphia: Saunders.

Rugg, M. D. (1995). Event-related potential studies of human memory. In M. S. Gazzaniga (Ed.), *The cognitive neurosciences.* Cambridge, MA: MIT Press, 789–801.

Rumelhart, D. E. (1975). Notes on a schema for stories. In D. Bobrow & A. Collins (Eds.), *Representation and understanding: Studies in cognitive science.* New York: Academic Press.

Rumelhart, D. E. (1977). *An introduction to human information processing.* New York: Wiley.

Rumelhart, D. E., Hinton, G. E., & McClelland, J. L. (1986). A general framework for parallel distributed processing. In D. E. Rumelhart, J. L. McClelland, & the PDP research group (Eds.), *Parallel distributed processing: Explorations in the microstructure of cognition* (Vol. 1). Cambridge, MA: Bradford.

Rumelhart, D. E., Lindsay, P. H., & Norman, D. A. (1972). A process model for long-term memory. In E. Tulving & W. Donaldson (Eds.), *Organization of memory.* New York: Academic Press.

Rumelhart, D. E., & McClelland, J. L. (1982). An interactive activation model of context effects in letter perception: Part 2. The contextual enhancement effect and some tests and extensions of the model. *Psychological Review, 89,* 60–94.

Rumelhart, D. E., McClelland, J. L., & the PDP research group (Eds.). (1986). *Parallel distributed processing: Explorations in the microstructure of cognition* (Vol. 1). Cambridge, MA: Bradford.

Rumelhart, D. E., & Norman, D. A. (1975). The computer implementation. In D. Norman & D. Rumelhart (Eds.), *Exploration in cognition.* San Francisco: Freeman.

Russell, W. R. (1959). *Brain, memory, learning.* Oxford: Clarendon.

Saarinen, T. F. (1987). Centering of mental maps of the world: Discussion paper. Department of Geography and Regional Development, University of Arizona, Tucson.

Sagen, C., Drake, F. D., Drugen, A., Ferris, I., Lomberg, J., & Sagen, L. S. (1978). *Murmurs of earth: The voyager interstellar record.* New York: Random House.

Sakitt, B. (1976). Iconic memory. *Psychological Review, 83,* 257–276.

Sakitt, B., & Long, G. M. (1979). Spare the rod and spoil the icon. *Journal of Experimental Psychology: Human Perception and Performance, 5,* 19–30.

Salapatek, P. (1975). Pattern perception in early infancy. In L. B. Cohen & P. Salapatek (Eds.), *Infant perception: From sensation to cognition.* New York: Academic Press.

Salasoo, A., Shiffrin, R. M., & Feustel, T. C. (1985). Building permanent memory codes: Codification and repetition effects in word identification. *Journal of Experimental Psychology: General, 114,* 50–77.

Salisbury, H. E. (1955). *American in Russia.* New York: Harper.

Samuel, A. G., & Ressler, W. H. (1986). Attention within auditory word perception: Insights from the phonemic restoration illusion. *Journal of Experimental Psychology: Human Perception and Performance, 12,* 70–79.

Santa, J. L., & Lamners, L. L. (1974). Encoding specificity: Fact or artifact? *Journal of Verbal Learning and Verbal Behavior, 13,* 412–423.

Santa, J. L., & Lamners, L. L. (1976). Where does the confusion lie? Comments on the Wiseman and Tulving paper. *Journal of Verbal Learning and Verbal Behavior, 15,* 3–57.

Sapir, E. (1958). Language and environment. *American Anthropologist, 1912,* n.s., 226–242. Also in D. G. Mandelbaum (Ed.), *Selected writings of Edward Sapir in language, culture, and personality* (pp. 89–103). Berkeley and Los Angeles: University of California Press.

Saporta, S. (Ed.). (1961). *Psycholinguistics: A book of readings.* New York: Holt, Rinehart & Winston.

Savin, H. B., & Perchonock, E. (1965). Grammatical structure and immediate recall of English sentences. *Journal of Verbal Learning and Verbal Behavior, 4,* 348–353.

Schacter, D. L. (1987). Memory, amnesia, and frontal lobe dysfunction. *Psychobiology, 15,* 21–36.

Schacter, D. L. (1989). On the relationship between memory and consciousness: Dissociable interaction and conscious experience. In H. L. Roediger, III, and F. I. M. Craik (Eds.), *Varieties of Memory and Consciousness: Essays in Honor of Endel Tulving* (pp. 355–389). Hillsdale, NJ: Erlbaum.

Schacter, D. L. (1990). Toward a cognitive neuropsychology of awareness: Implicit knowledge and anosognosia. *Journal of Clinical and Experimental Neuropsychology, 12*(1), 155–178.

Schacter, D. L. (1996). *Searching for memory: The brain, the mind, and the past.* New York: Basic.

Schaeffer, B., & Wallace, R. (1970). The comparison of word meanings. *Journal of Experimental Psychology, 86,* 144–152.

Schank, R. C. (1972). Conceptual dependency: A theory of natural language understanding. *Cognitive Psychology, 3,* 552–631.

Schank, R. C. (1981). Language and memory. In D. A. Norman (Ed.), *Perspectives on cognitive science.* Norwood, NJ: Ablex.

Schank, R. C. (1982). *Dynamic memory: A theory of reminding and learning in computers and people.* Cambridge, England: Cambridge University Press.

Schank, R. C., & Abelson, R. (1977). *Scripts, plans, goals, and understanding.* Hillsdale, NJ: Erlbaum.

Schank, R. C., & Hunter, L. (1985). The quest to understand thinking. *Byte,* Apr., 143–155.

Schmidt, F. L., & Hunter, J. E. (1992). Development of a causal model of processes determining job performance. *Current Directions in Psychological Science, 1,* 89–92.

Schmidt, R. A. (1975). A schema theory of discrete motor skill learning. *Psychological Review, 82,* 225–229.

Schneider, W. (1987). Connectionism: Is it a paradigm shift for psychology? *Behavioral Research Methods, Instruments, & Computers, 19,* 73–83.

Schneider, W., Noll, D. C., & Cohen, J. D. (1993). Functional topographic mapping of the cortical ribbons in the human visual cortex using conventional MRI. *Nature, 365,* 150–153.

Schneider, W., & Shiffrin, R. M. (1977). Controlled and automatic human information processing: Detection, search and attention. *Psychological Review, 84*(1).

Schulman, A. I. (1974). Memory for words recently classified. *Memory and Cognition, 2,* 47–52.

Schvaneveldt, R. W., & McDonald, J. E. (1981). Semantic context and the encoding of words: Evidence for two modes of stimulus analysis. *Journal of Experimental Psychology: Human Perception and Performance, 2,* 243–256.

Scientific American (1998). Exploring Intelligence, *9,* Winter.

Scribner, S. (1975). Recall of classical syllogisms: A crosscultural investigation of error on logical problems. In R. J. Falmagen (Ed.), *Reasoning: Representation and process.* Hillsdale, NJ: Erlbaum.

Scribner, S., & Cole, M. (1972). Effects of constrained recall training on children's performance in a verbal memory task. *Child Development, 43,* 845–857.

Scribner, S., & Cole, M. (1974). Research program on Vai literacy and its cognitive consequences. *Cross-Cultural Psychology Newsletter, 8,* 2–4.

Scribner, S., & Cole, M. (1981). *The psychology of literacy.* Cambridge, MA: Harvard University Press.

Seamon, J. G., & Travis, Q. B. (1993). An ecological study of professors' memory for student names and faces: A replication and extension. *Memory, 1,* 191–202.

Searle, J. (1980). Minds, brains, and programs. *Behavioral and Brain Sciences, 3,* 417–457.

Searle, J. (1983). *Intentionality: An essay in the philosophy of mind.* Cambridge, England: Cambridge University Press.

Sehulster, J. R. (1989). Content and temporal structure of autobiographical knowledge: Remembering twenty five seasons at the Metropolitan Opera. *Memory and Cognition, 17,* 590–606.

Sejnowski, T. J., Koch, C., & Churchland, P. S. (1988). Computational neuroscience. *Science, 241,* 1299–1306.

Sejnowski, T. J., & Rosenberg, C. R. (1987). NETtalk: Parallel networks that learn to pronounce English text. *Complex Systems, 1,* 145–168.

Sejnowski, T. J. Stevens, & J. Watson (Eds.). (1991) *Cold Spring Harbor Symp. Quart. Biol., 55.*

Sekuler, R. W., & Abrams, M. (1968). Visual sameness: A choice time analysis of pattern recognition process. *Journal of Experimental Psychology, 77,* 232–238.

Selfridge, O. G., & Neisser, U. (1963). Pattern recognition by machine. In E. Feigenbaum & J. Feldman (Eds.), *Computers and thought.* New York: McGraw-Hill.

Sells, S. B. (1936). The atmosphere effect: An experimental study of reasoning. *Archives of Psychology,* no. 200.

Service, R. F. (1993). Making modular memories. *Science, 260*(5116), 1876.

Shallice, T. (1972). On the dual functions of consciousness. *Psychological Review, 79,* 383–396.

Shallice, T. (1978). The Dominant Action System: An information-processing approach to consciousness. In K. S. Pope & J. L. Singer (Eds.), *The stream of consciousness: Scientific investigations into the flow of experience,* New York: Plenum.

Shallice, T. (1988). Information-processing models of consciousness: Possibilities and problems. In A. J. Marcel & E. Bisiach (Eds.), *Consciousness in contemporary science* (pp. 305–333). Oxford: Clarendon Press.

Shallice, T., & Vallar, G. (1990). The impairment of auditory-verbal short-term storage. In G. Vallar & T. Shallice (Eds.), *Neuropsychological impairments of short-term memory* (pp. 11–53). Cambridge, England: Cambridge University Press.

Shannon, C. E. (1948). A mathematical theory of communication. *Bell System Technical Journal, 27,* 479–523.

Shannon, C. E., & Weaver, W. (1949). *The mathematical theory of communication.* Urbana: University of Illinois Press.

Shapiro, P., & Penrod, S. (1986). Meta-analysis of facial identification studies. *Psychological Bulletin, 100,* 139–156.

Sheehan, P. W. (1967a). A shortened form of Betts' questionnaire upon mental imagery. *Journal of Clinical Psychology, 23,* 386–398.

Sheehan, P. W. (1967b). Reliability of a short test of imagery. *Perceptual and Motor Skills 25,* 744.

Sheehan, P. W. (1971). Individual differences in vividness of imagery and the function of imagery in incidental learning. *Australian Journal of Psychology, 23,* 279–288.

Sheehan, P. W. (1973). Stimulus imagery effect and the role of imagery in incidental learning. *Australian Journal of Psychology, 25,* 93–102.

Sheehan, P. W., & Neisser, U. (1969). Some variables affecting the vividness of imagery in recall. *British Journal of Psychology, 25,* 93–102.

Sheingold, K. (1973). Developmental differences in intake and storage of visual information. *Journal of Experimental Child Psychology, 16,* 1–11.

Shepard, R. N. (1966). Learning and recall as organization and search. *Journal of Verbal Learning and Verbal Behavior, 5,* 201–204.

Shepard, R. N. (1967). Recognition memory for words, sentences, and pictures. *Journal of Verbal Learning and Verbal Behavior, 6,* 156–163.

Shepard, R. N. (1968). *Cognitive Psychology:* A review of the book by U. Neisser. *American Journal of Psychology, 81,* 285–289.

Shepard, R. N. (1975). Form, formation, and transformation of internal representations. In R. L. Solso (Ed.), *Information processing and cognition: The Loyola Symposium.* Hillsdale, NJ: Erlbaum.

Shepard, R. N. (1977). *The mental image.* Paper delivered before the American Psychological Association Meeting, San Francisco, Sept.

Shepard, R. N. (1978). The mental image. *American Psychologist, 33,* 125–137.

Shepard, R. N. (1987). Evolution of a mesh between principles of the mind and regularities of the world. In *The latest on the best essays on evolution and optimality.* J. Dupre (Ed.). Cambridge, MA: MIT Press.

Shepard, R. N. (1987). Toward a universal law of generalization for psychological science. *Science, 237,* 1317–1323.

Shepard, R. N. (1990). *Mind sights.* San Francisco: Freeman.

Shepard, R. N. (1992). The perceptual organization of colors: An adaptation to the regularities of the terrestrial world? In J. Barkow, L. Cosmoides, & J. Tooby (Eds.), *The adapted mind: Evolutionary psychology and the generation of culture* (pp. 495–532). New York: Oxford University Press.

Shepard, R. N. (1994). Perceptual-cognitive universals as reflections of the world. *Psychonomic Bulletin & Review, 1,* 2–28.

Shepard, R. N. (1995). Toward a 21st century science of mental universals. In R. L. Solso & D. W. Massaro (Eds.), *The science of the mind: 2001 and beyond.* New York: Oxford University Press.

Shepard, R. N., & Chipman, S. (1970). Second-order isomorphism of internal representations: Shapes of states. *Cognitive Psychology, 1,* 1–17.

Shepard, R. N., & Metzler, J. (1971). Mental rotation of three-dimensional objects. *Science, 171,* 701–703.

Shepherd, G. M. (1994). *Neurobiology* (3rd ed.). New York: Oxford University Press.

Shiffrin, R. M., & Atkinson, R. C. (1969). Storage and retrieval processing in long-term memory. *Psychological Review, 76,* 179–193.

Shiffrin, R. M., & Schneider, W. (1977). Controlled and automatic human information processing: II Perceptual learning, automatic attending, and a general theory. *Psychological Review, 84,* 127–190.

Shimamura, A. P. (1996). Unraveling the mystery of the frontal lobes: Explorations in cognitive neuroscience. *Psychological Science Agenda,* September–October 1996. Copyright 1996 American Psychological Association.

Shimamura, A. P., & Squire, L. R. (1984). Paired-associate learning and priming effects in amnesia: A neuropsychological study. *Journal of Experimental Psychology: General, 113,* 556–570.

Shulman, H. G. (1970). Encoding and retention of semantic and phonemic information in short-term memory. *Journal of Verbal Learning and Verbal Behavior, 9,* 499–508.

Shulman, H. G. (1971). Similarity effects in short-term memory. *Psychological Bulletin, 75,* 399–415.

Shulman, H. G. (1972). Semantic confusion errors in short-term memory. *Journal of Verbal Learning and Verbal Behavior, 11,* 221–227.

Siegler, R. S. (1976). Three aspects of cognitive development. *Cognitive Psychology, 8,* 481–520.

Siegler, R. S. (Ed.). (1978). *Children's thinking: What develops?* Hillsdale, NJ: Erlbaum.

Siegler, R. S. (1981). Developmental sequences within and between concepts. *Monographs of the Society for Research in Child Development, 46,* (No. 189, pp. 1–74).

Siegler, R. S. (1986). *Children's thinking.* Englewood Cliffs, NJ: Prentice-Hall.

Siegler, R. S., & Klahr, D. (1982). When do children learn? The relationship between existing knowledge and the acquisition of new knowledge. In R. Glaser (Ed.), *Advances in instructional psychology* (Vol. 2). Hillsdale, NJ: Erlbaum.

Siegler, R. S., & Richards, D. D. (1982). The development of intelligence. In R. J. Sternberg (Ed.), *Handbook of intelligence.* Cambridge, England: Cambridge University Press.

Simon, H. A. (1966). Thinking by computers. In R. G. Colodny, *Mind and cosmos: Essays in contemporary science and philosophy* (pp. 3–21). Latham, MD: Center for the Philosophy of Science.

Simon, H. A., & Feigenbaum, E. A. (1964). An information processing theory of some effects of similarity, familiarization, and meaningfulness in verbal learning. *Journal of Verbal Learning and Verbal Behavior, 3,* 385–396.

Simpson, G. B., Peterson, R. R., Castell, M. A., & Burgess, C. (1989). Lexical and sentence context effects in word recognition. *Journal of Experimental Psychology: Learning, Memory, and Cognition, 15,* 88–97.

Singer, H., & Ruddell, R. D. (Eds.). (1976). *Theoretical models and processes of reading.* Newark, DE: International Reading Association.

Singer, J. L., & Antrobus, J. S. (1966). *Imaginal processes inventory.* New York: Authors.

Singer, J. L., & Antrobus, J. S. (1970). *Imaginal processes inventory.* New York: Authors.

Singer, J. L., & Antrobus, J. S. (1972). Daydreaming, imaginal processes, and personality: A normative study. In P. W. Sheehan (Ed.), *The function and nature of imagery* (pp. 175–202). New York: Academic Press.

Singer, M. (1973). A replication of Bransford and Franks' (1971) "The abstraction of linguistic ideas." *Bulletin of the Psychonomic Society, 1,* 416–418.

Singh, J. A. L., & Zingg, R. M. (1940). *Wolf children and feral man.* New York: Harper.

Sinha, P., & Poggio, T. (1996). SIR—Exactly what do we recognize in a face? Intuition suggests that it is . . . *Nature 384,* 404.

Skinner, B. F. (1957). *Verbal behavior.* New York: Appleton-Century-Crofts.

Skinner, B. F. (1989). The origins of cognitive thought. *American Psychologist, 44,* 13–18.

Slobin, D. I. (1971). *Psycholinguistics.* Glenview, IL: Scott, Foresman.

Slovic, P., Fischhoff, B., & Lichtenstein, S. (1977). Behavioral decision theory. *Annual Review of Psychology, 28,* 1–39.

Small, S. L., Cottrell, G. W., & Tanenhaus, M. K. (Eds.). (1988). *Lexical ambiguited resolution: Perspectives from psycholinguists, neuropsychology, and artificial intelligence.* Los Altos. CA: Morgan Kaufmann.

Smart, J. J. C. (1959). Sensations and brain processes. *Philosophical Review, 68,* 141–156.

Smedslund, J. (1961). The acquisition of conservation of substance and weight in children. *Scandinavian Journal of Psychology, 2,* 11–20.

Smedslund, J. (1965). The development of transitivity of length: A comment on Braine's reply. *Child Development, 36,* 577–580.

Smith, E. E. (1978). Theories of semantic memory. In W. K. Estes (Ed.), *Handbook of learning and cognitive processes* (Vol. 6). Hillsdale, NJ: Erlbaum.

Smith, E. E., & Medin, D. L. (1981). *Categories and concepts.* Cambridge, MA: Harvard University Press.

Smith, E. E., Shoben, E. J., & Rips, L. J. (1974). Structure and process in semantic memory: A featural model for semantic decisions. *Psychological Review, 1,* 214–241.

Smith, F. (1971). *Understanding reading.* New York: Holt, Rinehart & Winston.

Smith, S. B. (1983). *The great mental calculators: The psychology, methods, and lives of calculating prodigies, past and present.* New York: Columbia University Press.

Snodgrass, I. (1975). Psychophysics. In B. Sclarf (Ed.), *Experimental sensory psychology.* Glenview, IL: Scott, Foresman.

Sokolov, E. N. (1960). Neuronal models and the orienting reflexes. In M. A. Brazier (Ed.), *The central nervous system and behavior.* New York: J. Macy.

Sokolov, E. N. (1963). *Perception and the conditioned reflex.* New York: Macmillan.

Solomon, P. R., Goethals, G. R., Kelly, C. M., & Stephens, B. R. (Eds.). (1989). *Memory: Interdisciplinary approaches.* New York: Springer.

Solso, R. L. (Ed.). (1973). *Contemporary issues in cognitive psychology: The Loyola Symposium.* Potomac, MD: Winston/Wiley.

Solso, R. L. (Ed.). (1974). *Theories of cognitive psychology: The Loyola Symposium.* Potomac, MD: Erlbaum.

Solso, R. L. (Ed.). (1975). *Information processing and cognition: The Loyola Symposium.* Hillsdale, NJ: Erlbaum.

Solso, R. L. (1985). The citation of Soviet scholars by Western psychologists. *American Psychologist, 40,* 1264–1265.

Solso, R. L. (1986). Organization of knowledge in the world community of cognitive scientists. *Cognitive Systems,* Dec., 321–327.

Solso, R. L. (1987). The social-political consequences of the organization and dissemination of knowledge. *American Psychologist, 42,* 824–825.

Solso, R. L. (1989). Prototypes, schemata, and the form of human knowledge: The cognition of abstraction. In C. Izawa (Ed.), *Current issues in cognitive processes: The Tulane Flowerree symposium on cognition.* Hillsdale, NJ: Erlbaum.

Solso, R. L. (1994a). *Cognition and the visual arts.* Cambridge, MA: The MIT Press.

Solso, R. L. (1994b). Turning the corner. In R. L. Solso & D. W. Massaro (Eds.), *The science of the mind: 2001 and beyond.* Cambridge, MA: The MIT Press.

Solso, R. L. (1997) (Ed.). *Mind and brain sciences in the 21st century.* Cambridge, MA: MIT Press.

Solso, R. L. (2000). The cognitive neuroscience of art: A preliminary fMRI observation. *Journal of Consciousness Studies, 7,* 75–85.

Solso, R. L. (2001). Brain activities in an expert versus a novice artist: An fMRI study. *Leonardo, 34*(1), 31–34.

Solso, R. L., Ament, P., Kuraishy, F., & Mearns, C. (1986). *Prototype formation of various classes.* Paper presented at the 27th meeting of the Psychonomic Society: Nov. 13, 1986, New Orleans, LA.

Solso, R. L., & Biersdorff, K. K. (1975). Recall under conditions of cumulative cues. *Journal of General Psychology, 93,* 233–246.

Solso, R. L., & Dallob, P. (1995) Prototype formation of "dance steps" among professional dancers. *Empirical Studies of the Arts, 13,* 3–16.

Solso, R. L., Heck, M., & Mearns, C. (1987). *Prototype formation in very short-term memory.* Paper presented at the 28th meeting of the Psychonomic Society: Nov. 6, 1986, Seattle, WA.

Solso, R. L., & Johnson, H. H. (1989). *An introduction to experimental design in psychology: A case approach.* New York: Harper & Row.

Solso, R. L., & Johnson, H. H. (1994). *An introduction to experimental design in psychology: A case approach* (3rd ed.). New York: Harper & Row.

Solso, R. L., & MacLin, O. H. (2000). The history of cognitive psychology. In A. E. Kazdin (Ed.), *Encyclopedia of Psychology.* New York: APA Books, Oxford University Press.

Solso, R. L., & McCarthy, J. E. (1981a). Prototype formation of faces: A case of pseudomemory. *British Journal of Psychology, 72,* 499–503.

Solso, R. L., & McCarthy, J. E. (1981b). Prototype formation: Central tendency model versus attribute frequency model. *Bulletin of the Psychonomic Society, 17,* 10–11.

Solso, R. L., & Raynis, S. A. (1979). Prototype formation from imaged, kinesthetically, and visually presented geometric figures. *Journal of Experimental Psychology: Human Perception and Performance, 5,* 701–712.

Solso, R. L., & Short, B. A. (1979). Color recognition. *Bulletin of the Psychonomic Society, 14,* 275–277.

Sophian, C. (Ed.). (1984). *Origins of cognitive skills.* Hillsdale, NJ: Erlbaum.

Spear, N. (Ed.). (1989). *Comparative perspectives on the development of memory.* Hillsdale, NJ: Erlbaum.

Spearman, C. (1904). General intelligence objectively determined and measured. *American Journal of Psychology, 15,* 201–293.

Spearman, C. (1927). *The abilities of man: Their nature and measurement.* New York: Macmillan.

Spelke, E. S. (1979). Perceiving bimodally specified events in infancy. *Developmental Psychology, 15,* 626–636.

Spelke, E. S. (1988). The origins of physical knowledge. In L. Weiskrantz (Ed.), *Thought without language* (pp. 168–184). London: Clarendon Press.

Spelke, E. S., & Kestenbaum, R. (1986). Les origines du concept d'objet. *Psychologie française 31,* 67–72.

Spencer, H. (1864/1981). *Essays: Moral, political, and aesthetic.* New York: Appleton.

Sperling, G. (1960). The information available in brief visual presentation. *Psychological Monographs, 74.*

Sperling, G. (1963). A model for visual memory tasks. *Human Factors, 5,* 19–31.

Sperling, G. (1967). Successive approximations to a model for short-term memory. *Acta Psychologica, 27,* 285–292.

Sperry, R. W. (1968). Hemisphere deconnection and the utility of conscious experience. *American Psychologist, 23,* 723–733.

Sperry, R. W. (1974). Lateral specialization in surgically separated hemispheres. In F. O. Schmitt & F. G. Worden (Eds.), *The neurosciences* (Vol. 3). Cambridge, MA: The MIT Press.

Sperry, R. W. (1982). Some effects of disconnecting the cerebral hemispheres. *Science, 217,* 1223–1226.

Springer, S. P., & Deutsch, G. (1981). *Left brain, right brain.* San Francisco: Freeman.

Springer, S., & Deutsch, G. (1984). *Left brain, right brain* (2nd ed.). San Francisco: Freeman.

Squire, L. R. (1982). The neuropsychology of human memory. *Annual Review of Neuroscience, 5,* 241–273.

Squire, L. R. (1986). Mechanisms of memory. *Science, 232,* 1612–1619.

Squire, L. R. (1987). *Memory and brain.* New York: Oxford University Press.

Squire, L. R., & Butters, N. (Eds.). (1984). *Neuropsychology of memory.* New York: Guilford Press.

Squire, L. R., Zola-Morgan, S., Cave, C., Haist, H., Musen, G., & Suzuki, W. P. (1990). Memory: Organization of brain systems and cognition. In E. Kandel, T. Sejnowski, C. Stevens, & J. Watson (Eds.), *Cold Spring Harbor Symp. Quart. Biol., 55.*

Standing, L. (1973). Learning 10,000 pictures. *Quarterly Journal of Experimental Psychology, 25,* 207–222.

Standing, L., Bond, B., Hall, J., & Weller, J. (1972). A bibliography of picture-memory studies. *Psychonomic Monograph Supplement, 29*(6B).

Standing, L., Conezio, J., & Haber, R. N. (1970). Perception and memory for pictures: Single-trial learning of 2560 visual stimuli. *Psychonomic Science, 19,* 73–74.

Stanovich, K. E., & West, R. F. (1979). Mechanism of sentence context effects in reading: Automatic activation and conscious attention. *Memory and Cognition, 7,* 77–85.

Stanovich, K. E., & West, R. F. (1983). On printing by a sentence context. *Journal of Experimental Psychology: General, 112,* 1–36.

Staszewski, J. J. (1988). Skilled memory and expert mental calculation. In M. T. H. Chi, R. Glaser, & M. J. Farr (Eds.), *The nature of expertise.* Hillsdale, NJ: Erlbaum.

Staszewski, J. J. (1989). Exceptional memory: The influence of practice and knowledge on the development of elaborative encoding strategies. In W. Schneider & F. E. Weinert (Eds.), *Interactions among aptitudes, strategies, and knowledge in cognitive performance.* Berlin: Springer.

Sternberg, R. J. (1977). *Intelligence, information processing, and analogical reasoning: The componential analysis of human abilities.* Hillsdale, NJ: Erlbaum.

Sternberg, R. J. (1979). Developmental patterns in the encoding and combination of logical connectives. *Journal of Experimental Child Psychology, 28,* 469–498.

Sternberg, R. J. (1980a). The development of linear syllogistic reasoning. *Journal of Experiment Child Psychology, 29,* 340–356.

Sternberg, R. J. (1980b). Representation and process in linear syllogistic reasoning. *Journal of Experimental Psychology: General, 109,* 119–159.

Sternberg, R. J. (1982). Reasoning, problem solving, and intelligence. In R. J. Sternberg (Ed.), *Handbook of human intelligence.* Cambridge [Cambridgeshire]; New York: Cambridge University Press.

Sternberg, R. J. (Ed.). (1984a). *Mechanisms of cognitive development.* San Francisco: Freeman.

Sternberg, R. J. (1984b). Toward a triarchic theory of human intelligence. *Behavioral and Brain Sciences, 7,* 269–315.

Sternberg, R. J. (1985a). Human intelligence: The model is the message. *Science, 230,* 1111–1118.

Sternberg, R. J. (1985b). *Beyond IQ: A triarchic theory of human intelligence.* Cambridge, England: Cambridge University Press.

Sternberg, R. J. (1986a). *Intelligence applied.* New York: Harcourt Brace Jovanovich.

Sternberg, R. J. (1986b). Inside intelligence. *American Scientist, 74,* 137–143.

Sternberg, R. J. (1989). Intelligence, wisdom, and creativity: Their natures and interrelationships. In R. L. Linn (Ed.), *Intelligence: Measurement, theory, and public policy.* Chicago: University of Illinois Press.

Sternberg, R. J. (Ed.). (1994). *Encyclopedia of human intelligence.* New York: Macmillan.

Sternberg, R. J., Lubart, T. I., & Todd, J. (1991) An investment theory of creativity and its development. *Human Development, 34,* 1–31. New Haven, CT: Yale University Press.

Sternberg, R. J., & Lubart, T. I. (1996). Investing in creativity. *American Psychologist, 51,* 667–688.

Sternberg, R. J., & Wagner, R. K. (1993). The geocentric view of intelligence and job performance is wrong. *Current Directions in Psychological Science, 2,* 1–5.

Sternberg, S. (1966). High speed scanning in human memory. *Science, 153,* 652–654.

Sternberg, S. (1967). Two operations in character recognition: Some evidence from RT measurements. *Perception and Psychophysics, 2,* 45–53.

Sternberg, S. (1969). Memory scanning: Mental processes revealed by reaction time experiments. *American Scientist, 57,* 421–457.

Stevens, A., & Coupe, P. (1978). Distortions in judged spatial relations. *Cognitive Psychology, 63,* 390–397.

Strand, B. N., & Mueller, J. H. (1977). Levels of processing in facial recognition memory. *Bulletin of the Psychonomic Society, 9,* 17–18.

Strauss, M. S. (1979). Abstraction of prototypical information by adults and 10-month-old infants. *Journal of Experimental Psychology: Human Learning and Memory, 5,* 618–663.

Strauss, M. S., & Carter, P. N. (1984). Infant memory: Limitations and future directions. In R. Kail & N. E. Spear (Eds.), *Comparative perspectives on the development of memory.* Hillsdale, NJ: Erlbaum.

Stromeyer, C. G. (1970). Eidetikers. *Psychology Today,* Nov., 76–80.

Suler, J. (1989). "Eliza" helps students grasp therapy. *APA Monitor,* Jan., 30.

Sutherland, N. S. (1972). Object recognition In E. C. Carterette & M. P. Feidman (Eds.), *Handbook of perception* (Vol. 3). New York: Academic Press.

Swets, J. A. (1961). Is there a sensory threshold? *Science, 134,* 168–177.

Swick, D., Kutas, M., & Neville, H. J., (in press). Localizing the neural generators of event-related brain potentials. In A. Kertesz (Ed.), *Localizations and neuroimaging in neuropsychology.* New York: Academic Press.

Swinney, D. (1979). Lexical access during sentence comprehension: Reconsideration of context effects. *Cognitive Psychology, 18,* 645–660.

Tanenhaus, M. K., & Lucas, M. M. (1987). Context effects in lexical processing. *Cognition, 25,* 213–234.

Tanner, W. P., & Swets, J. A. (1954). A decision-making theory of visual detection. *Psychological Review, 61,* 401–409.

Tauke, M. (1961). *Computers and common sense.* New York: Columbia University Press.

Taylor, H. A., & Tversky, B. (1992). Descriptions and depictions of environments. *Memory & Cognition, 20,* 483–496.

Taylor, S. E. (1965). Eye movements while reading: Facts and fallacies. *American Educational Research Journal, 2,* 187–202.

Theios, J., Smith, P. G., Haviland, S., Traupmann, J., & Moy, M. C. (1973). Memory scanning as a serial self-termination process. *Journal of Experimental Psychology, 97,* 323–336.

Thibadeau, R. (1985). Automatic visual inspection as skilled perception. In P. Jackson (Ed.), *The Robotics Institute: 1984 Annual Research Review.* Pittsburgh: Robotics Institute.

Thomas, J. C., Jr. (1974). An analysis of behavior in the hobbits-orcs problem. *Cognitive Psychology, 6,* 257–269.

Thompson, M. C., & Massaro, D. W. (1973). Visual information and redundancy in reading. *Journal of Experimental Psychology, 98,* 49–54.

Thompson, R. A., & Nelson, C. A. (2001). Developmental science and the media: Early brain development. *American Psychologist, 56*(1), 5–15.

Thompson, R. F. (1993). *The brain: A neuroscience primer* (2nd ed.). New York: W. H. Freeman.

Thomson, D. M., & Tulving, E. (1970). Associative encoding and retrieval: Weak and strong cues. *Journal of Experimental Psychology, 86,* 255–262.

Thorndike, E. L., & Lorge, I. (1944). *The teacher's word book of 30,000 words.* New York: Teachers College, Columbia University Press.

Thorndyke, P. W. (1977). Cognitive structures in comprehension and memory of narrative discourse. *Cognitive Psychology, 9,* 77–110.

Thorndyke, P. W., & Hayes-Roth, B. (1982). Differences in spatial know]edge acquired from maps and navigation. *Cognitive Psychology, 14,* 580–589.

Thurstone, L. L. (1938). Primary mental abilities. *Psychometric Monographs, No. 1.* Chicago: University of Chicago Press.

Tinklenberg, J. R., & Taylor, I. L. (1984). Assessments of drug effects on human memory functions. In L. R. Squire & N. Butters (Eds.), *Neuropsychology of memory.* New York: Guilford Press.

Titchener, E. B. (1909). *Experimental psychology* (Vol. 1, Part 1, Student's Manual). New York: Macmillan.

Tolman, E. C. (1932). *Purposive behavior in animals and man.* New York: Appleton-Century.

Trabasso, T. (1977). The role of memory as a system in making transitive inferences. In R. V. Kall & J. W. Hagen (Eds.), *Perspectives on the development of memory and cognition.* Hillsdale, NJ: Erlbaum.

Trabasso, T., & Bower, G. (1964). Memory in concept identification. *Psychonomic Science, 1,* 133–134.

Trabasso, T., & Bower, G. (1968). *Attention in learning.* New York: Wiley.

Treisman, A. (1988). Features and objects: The fourteenth Bartlett Memorial Lecture. *Quarterly Journal of Experimental Psychology, 40A,* 201–237.

Treisman, A. M. (1960). Contextual cues in selective listening. *Quarterly Journal of Experimental Psychology, 12,* 242–248.

Treisman, A. M. (1964a). Monitoring and storage of irrelevant messages in selective attention. *Journal of Verbal Learning and Verbal Behavior, 3,* 449–459.

Treisman, A. M. (1964b). Selective attention in man. *British Medical Bulletin, 20,* 12–16.

Treisman, A. M. (1964c). The effect of irrelevant material on the efficiency of selective listening. *American Journal of Psychology, 77,* 533–546.

Treisman, A. M. (1969). Strategies and models of selective attention. *Psychological Review, 76,* 242–299.

Treisman, A. M. (1977). Focused attention in the perception and retrieval of multidimensional stimuli. *Perception and Psychophysics, 22,* 1–11.

Treisman, A. M. (1986). Personal communication, April 23.

Treisman, A. M., & Geffen, G. (1967). Selective attention: Perception or response? *Quarterly Journal of Experimental Psychology, 19,* 1–17.

Treisman, A. M., & Gelade, G. (1980). A feature integration theory of attention. *Cognitive Psychology, 12,* 97–136.

Treisman, A. M., & Riley, J. (1969). Is selective attention selective perception or selective response? A further test. *Journal of Experimental Psychology, 79,* 27–34.

Treisman, A. M., Squire, R., & Green, J. (1974). Semantic processing in dichotic listening? A replication. *Memory and Cognition, 2,* 641–646.

Treisman, A. M., & Williams, T. C. (1984). A theory of criterion setting with an application to sequential dependencies. *Psychological Review, 91,* 68–111.

Trotter, R. J. (1986). Three heads are better than one. *Psychology Today,* Aug., 56–62.

Tsien, J. Z. (2000). Building a brainier mouse. *Scientific American,* April, 62–68.

Tufte, E. R. (1983). *The visual display of quantitative information.* Cheshire, CT: Graphics Press.

Tulving, E. (1962). Subjective organization in free recall of "unrelated" words. *Psychological Review, 69,* 344–354.

Tulving, E. (1972). Episodic and semantic memory. In E. Tulving & W. Donaldson (Eds.), *Organization of memory.* New York: Academic Press.

Tulving, E. (1974). Cue-dependent forgetting. *American Scientist, 62,* 74–82.

Tulving, E. (1983). *Elements of episodic memory.* London: Clarendon Press/Oxford University Press.

Tulving, E. (1984). Organization of memory: Quo vadis? In M. S. Gazzaniga (Ed.), *The cognitive neurosciences.* Cambridge, MA: The MIT Press.

Tulving, E. (1984). Precis of *Elements of episodic memory. Behavioral and Brain Sciences, 7,* 223–268.

Tulving, E. (1985a). How many memory systems are there? *American Psychologist, 40,* 385–398.

Tulving, E. (1985b). Memory and consciousness. *Canadian Psychologist, 26,* 1–11.

Tulving, E. (1986). What kind of a hypothesis is the distinction between episodic and semantic memory? *Journal of Experimental Psychology: Learning, Memory, and Cognition, 12,* 307–311.

Tulving, E. (1989a). Remembering and knowing the past. *American Scientist, 77,* 361–367.

Tulving, E. (1989b). Memory: Performance, knowledge, and experience. *European Journal of Cognitive Psychology, 1,* 3–26.

Tulving, E. (1993). What is episodic memory? *Current Directions in Psychological Science, 2*(3), 67–70.

Tulving, E., & Arbuckle, T. Y. (1963). Sources of intratrial interference in immediate recall of paired associates. *Journal of Verbal Learning and Verbal Behavior, 1,* 321–334.

Tulving, E., & Gold, C. (1963). Stimulus information and contextual information as determinants of tachistoscopic recognition of words. *Journal of Experimental Psychology, 66,* 319–327.

Tulving, E., & Hastie, R. (1972). Inhibition effects of intralist repetition in free recall. *Journal of Experimental Psychology, 92,* 297–304.

Tulving, E., Kapur, S., Craik, F. I. M., Moscovitch, M., & Houle, S. (1994). Hemispheric encoding/retrieval asymmetry in episodic memory: Positron emission tomography findings. *Proceedings of the National Academy of Sciences, 91,* 2016–2020. Washington, DC: National Academy of Sciences.

Tulving, E., & Madigan, S. A. (1970). Memory and verbal learning. In P. H. Mussen & M. R. Rosenzweig (Eds.), *Annual Review of Psychology* (Vol. 21). Palo Alto, CA: Annual Reviews.

Tulving, E., & Osler, S. (1968). Effectiveness of retrieval cues in memory for words. *Journal of Experimental Psychology, 77*(4), 593–601.

Tulving, E., & Pearlstone, Z. (1966). Availability versus accessibility of information in memory for words. *Journal of Verbal Learning and Verbal Behavior, 5,* 381–391.

Tulving, E., & Psotka, J. (1971). Retroactive inhibition in free recall: Inaccessibility of information available in the memory store. *Journal of Experimental Psychology, 87,* 1–8.

Tulving, E., & Schacter, D. L. (1990). Priming and human memory systems. *Science, 247,* 301–306.

Tulving, E., & Thompson, D. M. (1971). Retrieval processes in recognition memory. *Journal of Experimental Psychology, 87,* 116–124.

Tulving, E., & Thompson, D. M. (1973). Encoding specificity and retrieval processing in episodic memory. *Psychological Review, 80,* 352–373.

Turing, A. M. (1950). Computing machinery and intelligence. *Mind, 59,* 433–460.

Tversky, A. (1972). Elimination by aspects: A theory of choice. *Psychological Review, 79,* 281–299.

Tversky, A., & Hutchinson, J. W. (1986). Nearest neighbor analysis of psychological spaces. *Psychological Review, 93,* 3–22.

Tversky, A., & Kahneman, D. (1973). Availability: A heuristic for judging frequency and probability. *Cognitive Psychology, 4,* 207–232.

Tversky, A., & Kahneman, D. (1981). The framing of decisions and the psychology of choice. *Science, 211,* 453–458.

Tversky, B. (1981). Distortions in memory for maps. *Cognitive Psychology, 13,* 407–433.

Tye, M. (1991). *The imagery debate.* Cambridge, MA: The MIT Press.

Uhr, L., & Vossler, C. (1963). A pattern-recognition program that generates, evaluates and adjusts its own operators. In E. A. Feigenbaum & J. Feldman (Eds.), *Computers and thought.* New York: McGraw-Hill.

Underwood, B. J. (1969). Attributes of memory. *Psychological Review, 76,* 559–573.

Underwood, G. (1976). Semantic interference from unattended printed words. *British Journal of Psychology, 67,* 327–338.

Underwood, G. (1977). Contextual facilitation from attended and unattended messages. *Journal of Verbal Learning and Verbal Behavior, 16,* 99–106.

Underwood, G. (1982). *Aspects of consciousness.* New York: Academic Press.

Usher, J. A., & Neisser, U. (1993). Childhood amnesia and the beginnings of memory for four early life events. *Journal of Experimental Psychology: General, 122,* 155–165.

Uttal, W. R. (1978). *The psychobiology of mind.* Hillsdale, NJ: Erlbaum.

Valenta, J., & Potter, W. C. (1984). *Soviet decision making for national security.* Winchester, MA: Allen & Unwin.

Valenza, E., Simion, F., Cassia, V., & Umilta, C. (1996). Face preference at birth. *Journal of Experimental Psychology: Human Perception and Performance, 22,* 892–903.

van Dijk, T. A., & Kintsch, W. (1983). *Strategics of discourse comprehension.* New York: Academic Press.

Vaughn, M. E. (1968). Clustering, age and incidental learning. *Journal of Experimental Child Psychology,* 323–331.

Von Frisch, K. (1967). *The dance language and orientation of bees.* Cambridge, MA: Belknap.

von Neumann, J. (1958). *The computer and the brain.* New Haven, CT: Yale University Press.

von Wright, J. M., Anderson, K., & Stenman, U. (1975). Generalization of conditioned GSRs in dichotic listening. In P. M. A. Rabbit & S. Dornic (Eds.), *Attention and performance V.* New York: Academic Press.

Vurpillot, E. (1968). The development of scanning strategies and their relation to visual differentiation. *Journal of Experimental Child Psychology, 6,* 632–650.

Vygotsky, L. S. (1962). *Thought and language.* Cambridge, MA: The MIT Press. (Originally published in Russian in 1934.)

Vygotsky, L. S. (1934/1978). *Mind in society.* Edited by M. Cole, V. John-Steiner, S. Scribner, & E. Souberman. Cambridge, MA: Harvard University Press.

Wagenaar, W. (1986). My memory: A study of autobiographic memory over the past six years. *Cognitive Psychology, 18,* 225–252.

Wallas, G. (1926). *The art of thought.* New York: Harcourt Brace.

Walton, G. E., & Bower, T. G. R. (1993). Newborns form "prototypes" in less than 1 minute. *Psychological Science, 4,* 203–205.

Wardlaw, K. A., & Kroll, N. E. A. (1976). Autonomic responses to shock-associated words in a nonattended message: A failure to replicate. *Journal of Experimental Psychology: Human Perception and Performance, 2,* 357–360.

Warrington, E. K., & Shallice, T. (1969). The selective impairment of auditory-verbal short-term memory tasks. *Quarterly Journal of Experimental Psychology, 24A,* 30–40.

Watkins, S. H. (1914). Immediate memory and its evaluation. *British Journal of Psychology, 7,* 319–348.

Watson, J. B. (1913). Psychology as a behaviorist views it. *Psychological Review, 20,* 158–170.

Watson, J. B. (1914). *Behavior: An introduction to comparative psychology.* New York: Holt.

Watson, J. B. (1919). *Psychology from the standpoint of behaviorist.* Philadelphia: Lippincott.

Waugh, N. C., & Norman, D. A. (1965). Primary memory. *Psychological Review, 72,* 89–104.

Weaver, W. (1949). Introductory note on the general setting of the analytic communication studies. In

C. E. Shannon & W. Weaver (Eds.), *The mathematical theory of communication.* Urbana: University of Illinois Press.

Wechsler, S. B. (1963). Engrams, memory storage, and mnemonic coding. *American Psychologist, 18,* 149–153.

Weiskrantz, L. (1966). Experimental studies in amnesia. In C. W. M. Whitty & O. L. Zangwill (Eds.), *Amnesia.* London: Butterworth.

Weiss, A. P. (1967). 1 + 1 ≠ 2 (one plus one does not equal two). In G. C. Quarton, T. Melnechuk, & F. O. Schmitt (Eds.), *The neurosciences* (pp. 801–821). New York: Rockefeller University Press.

Weisstein, N. (1973). Beyond the yellow Volkswagen detector and the grandmother cell: A general strategy for the exploration of operations in human pattern recognition. In R. L. Solso (Ed.), *Contemporary issues in cognitive psychology: The Loyola Symposium.* Washington, DC: Winston/Wiley.

Weist, R. M., & Crowford, J. (1977). The development of organized rehearsal. *Journal of Experimental Child Psychology, 24,* 164–179.

Weizenbaum, J. (1966). ELIZA—A computer program for the study of the natural language communication between man and machine. *Communication Associates Computing Machinery, 9,* 36–45.

Weizenbaum, J. (1976). *Computer power and human reason: From judgment to calculation* (pp. xii–300). San Francisco: Freeman.

Welch, J. C. (1898). On the measurement of mental activity through muscular activity and the determination of a constant of attention. *American Journal of Physiology, 1,* 283–306.

Welker, W. I., Johnson, J. I., & Pubols, B. H. (1964). Some morphological and physiological characteristics of the somatic sensory system in raccoons. *American Zoologist, 4,* 75–94.

Wertheim, T. (1934). Über die indirekte Sehsharfe. *Zeitschrift fur Psychologie, 7,* 172–187.

Wertheimer, M. (1912). Experimentelle Studein über das Sehen von Bewegung. *Zeitschrift fur Psychologie, 61,* 161–265.

Wertheimer, M. (1923). Untersuchungen zur Lehre von der Gestalt. II. *Psychologie Forschung,* 301–350. Reprinted in D. C. Beardslee & M. Wertheimer (Eds.), *Readings in perception.* Princeton, NJ: Van Nostrand, 1958.

Wertheimer, M. (1945). *Productive thinking.* New York: Harper & Row.

Wertheimer, M. (1958). Principles of perceptual organization. In D. C. Beardslee & M. Wertheimer (Eds.), *Readings in perception.* Princeton, NJ: Van Nostrand.

Wertsch, J. V. (1985a). *Vygotsky and the social formation of mind.* Cambridge, MA: Harvard University Press.

Wertsch, J. V. (Ed.). (1985b). *Culture, communication, and cognition: Vygotskian perspectives.* Cambridge, England: Cambridge University Press.

Wheeler, D. (1970). Processes in word recognition. *Cognitive Psychology, 1,* 59–85.

Wheeler, M. A., & Roediger, H. L. (1992). Disparate effects of repeated testings: Reconciling Ballard's (1913) and Bartlett's (1932) results. *Psychological Science, 3,* 240–245.

Whitaker, H. A., Savary, F., Markovits, H., Grou, C., & Braun, C. M. J. (1991). Inference deficits after brain damage. Paper presented at the annual INS meeting, San Antonio, Texas.

White, K., Sheehan, P. W., & Aston, R. (1977). Imagery assessment: A survey of self-report measures. *Journal of Mental Imagery, 1,* 145–170.

Whitehead, R. (1991a). Right hemisphere processing superiority during sustained visual attention. *Journal of Cognitive Neuroscience, 3,* 329–334.

Whitehead, R. (1991b). Right hemisphere superiority during sustained visual attention. *Journal of Cognitive Neuroscience, 3–4,* 329–331.

Whorf, B. L. (1956). A linguistic consideration of thinking in primitive communities. In J. B. Carroll (Ed.), *Language, thought, and reality.* New York: Wiley.

Wickelgren, W. A. (1965). Acoustic similarity and intrusion errors in short-term memory. *Journal of Experimental Psychology, 70,* 102–108.

Wickelgren, W. A. (1968). Sparing of short-term memory in an amnesiac: Implications for strength, theory of memory. *Neuropsychologia, 6,* 235–244.

Wickelgren, W. A. (1970). Time, interference and rate of presentation in short-term recognition memory. *Journal of Mathematical Psychology, 7,* 219–235.

Wickelgren, W. A. (1973). The long and short of memory. *Psychological Bulletin, 80,* 425–538.

Wickens, D. D. (l970). Encoding categories of words: An empirical approach to meaning. *Psychological Review, 77,* 1–15.

Wickens, D. D. (1972). Characteristics of word encoding. In A. Melton & E. Martin (Eds.), *Coding processes in human memory* (pp. 191–215). Washington, DC: Winston.

Wickens, D. D. (1973). *Memory and Cognition, 1,* 490. The Psychonomic Society, Inc.

Wickens, D. D., Born, D. G., & Allen, C. K. (1963). Proactive inhibition and item similarity in short-term memory. *Journal of Verbal Learning and Verbal Behavior, 2,* 440–445.

Wickens, D. D., Clark, S. E., Hill, F. A., & Wittlinger, R. P. (1968). Grammatical class as an encoding category in short-term memory. *Journal of Experimental Psychology 78,* 599–604.

Wickens, D. D., & Engle, R. W. (1970). Imagery and abstractness in short-term memory. *Journal of Experimental Psychology, 84,* 268–272.

Wilkins, A., & Stewart, A. (l974). The time course of lateral asymmetrics in visual perception of letters. *Journal of Experimental Psychology, 102,* 905–908.

Wilkins, M. C. (1917). Unpublished M. A. thesis, Columbia University. In R. S. Woodworth (Ed.), *Experimental psychology.* New York: Holt.

Wilks, Y. (1973). An artificial intelligence approach to machine translation. In R. Schank & K. Colby (Eds.), *Computer models of thought and language.* San Francisco: Freeman.

Williams, J. D. (1971). Memory ensemble selection in human information processing. *Journal of Experimental Psychology, 88,* 231–238.

Wilson, R. A., & Keil, F. C. (Eds.). (1999). *The MIT encyclopedia of the cognitive sciences.* Cambridge, MA: MIT Press.

Winikoff, A. (1973). Eye movements and an aid to protocol analysis of problem solving behavior. Unpublished Ph.D. dissertation, Carnegie Mellon University. Cited by A. Newell in "Artificial intelligence and the concept of mind." In R. Schank & K. Colby (Eds.), *Computer models of thought and language.* San Francisco: Freeman.

Winograd, T. (1972). *Understanding natural languages.* New York: Academic Press.

Winograd, T. (1974). Artificial intelligence: When will computers understand people? *Psychology Today.* May.

Winograd, T. (1975). Computer memories: A metaphor for memory organization. In C. Cofer (Ed.), *The structure of human memory.* San Francisco: Freeman.

Winograd, T. (1981). What does it mean to understand language? In D. A. Norman (Ed.), *Perspectives on cognitive science.* Norwood, NJ: Ablex.

Winograd, T. (1985). *Language as a cognitive process.* Reading, MA: Addison-Wesley.

Winokur, S. (1976). *A primer of verbal behavior: An operant view.* Englewood Cliffs, NJ: Prentice-Hall.

Winston, P. H. (1970). *Learning structural description from examples* (Project MAC-TR-231–447–48, 450–52, 460–480–82). Cambridge, MA: MIT Artificial Intelligence Laboratory.

Winston, P. H. (1973). Learning to identify toy block structures. In R. L. Solso (Ed.), *Contemporary issues in cognitive psychology: The Loyola Symposium.* Washington, DC: Winston/Wiley.

Winston, P. H. (1975). *The psychology of computer vision.* New York: McGraw-Hill.

Winston, P. H. (1984). *Artificial intelligence* (2nd ed.). Reading, MA: Addison-Wesley.

Wittgenstein, L. (1915/1993). Quoted in *The Columbia Dictionary of Quotations.* New York: Columbia University Press.

Woldorff, M. G., Gallen, C. C., Hampson, S. A., Hillyard, S. R., Pantev, C., Sobel, D., & Bloom, F. E., (1993). Modulation of early sensory processing in human auditory cortex during auditory selective attention. *Proceedings of the National Academy of Sciences.* USA, *90,* 8722–8726.

Woldorff, M. G., Hansen, J. C., & Hillyard, S. A. (1987). Evidence for effects of selective attention to the midlaterncy range of the human auditory event-related potential. *Electroencephalographic Clinical Neurophysiology.* Supplement, *40,* 146–154.

Wollen, K. A., & Lowry, D. H. (1971). Effects of imagery on paired-associate learning. *Journal of Verbal Learning and Verbal Behavior, 10,* 276–284.

Wollen, K. A., Weber, A., & Lowry, D. H. (1972). Bizarreness versus interaction of mental images as determinants of learning. *Cognitive Psychology, 3,* 518–523.

Wood, C. C. (1975). Auditory and phonetic levels of processing in speech perception: Neurophysiological and information-processing analyses. *Journal of Experimental Psychology: Human Perception and Performance, 104,* 3–20.

Woodson, W. E. (1954). *Human engineering guide for equipment designers.* Berkeley: University of California Press.

Woodworth, R. S. (1929). *Psychology.* New York: Holt.

Woodworth, R. S. (1938). *Experimental psychology.* New York: Holt.

Woodworth, R. S. (1948). *Contemporary schools of psychology* (revised). New York: Ronald.

Woodworth, R. S., & Sells, S. B. (1935). An atmosphere effect in formal syllogistic reasoning. *Journal of Experimental Psychology, 18,* 451–460.

Woolridge, D. E. (1968). *Mechanical man: The physical basis of intellectual life.* New York: McGraw-Hill.

Wundt, W. (1892). In R. Woodworth (Ed.), *Contemporary schools of psychology* (p. 24). New York: Ronald.

Wundt, W. (1905). *Grundriss der Psychologie.* Leipzig: Englemann.

Yarbus, A. L. (1967). *Eye movements and vision* (B. Haigh, trans.). New York: Plenum.

Yates, F. A. (1966). *The art of memory.* Chicago: University of Chicago Press.

Yerkes, R. M., & Dodson, J. D. (1908). The relation of strengths of stimulus to rapidity of habit-formation. *Journal of Comparative Neurological Psychology, 18,* 459–482.

Yoshimura, E. K., Moely, B. E., & Shapiro, S. I. (1971). The influence of age and presentation order upon children's free recall and learning to learn. *Psychonomic Science, 23,* 261–263.

Young, L. R. (1963). Measuring eye movements. *American Journal of Medical Electronics, 2,* 300–307.

Young, M. N., & Gibson, W. B. (1974). *How to develop an exceptional memory.* North Hollywood, CA: Wilshire.

Young, R. K. (1975). *Human learning and memory.* New York: Harper & Row.

Yuille, J. C., & Catchpole, M. J. (1977). The role of imagery in models of cognition. *Journal of Mental Imagery, 1,* 171–180.

Yuille, J. C., & Paivio, A. (1967). Latency of imaginal and verbal mediators as a function of stimulus and response concreteness-imagery. *Journal of Experimental Psychology, 75,* 540–544.

Zaffy, D. J., & Bruning, J. L. (1966). Drive and the range of cue utilization. *Journal of Experimental Psychology, 71,* 382–384.

Zeman, A. (2001). Consciousness. *Brain, 129,* 1263–1289.

Zinchenko, P. I. (1962). *Neproizvol'noe azpominanie* (Involuntary memory) (pp. 172–207). Moscow: USSR APN RSFSR.

Zinchenko, P. I. (1981). Involuntary memory and the goal-directed nature of activity. In J. V. Wertsch, *The concept of activity in Soviet psychology.* Armonk, NY: Sharpe.

Zola-Morgan, S., & Squire, L. R. (1990). Neuropsychological investigations of memory and amnesia: Findings from humans and nonhuman primates. In A. Diamond (Ed.), *The development and neural bases of higher cognitive functions.* New York: New York Academy of Sciences.

Name Index

Abel, L., 480
Abu-Mostafa, Y. S., 516
Adams, J. L., 467
Agostino, D., 220
Aitken, A. C., 250
Aizawa, 495
Akin, D., 252
Alkon, D. L., 504, 505
Allen, W., 151
Alphonse, 261
Anderson, J. R., 242, 271, 273–274, 278, 295–296, 339
Aristotle, 14–16, 42–43, 291
Armstrong, L., 522
Ashley, R., 524
Atkinson, R. C., 214, 215, 216, 220, 240, 242
Austin, G. A., 420

Baars, B., 157, 159–162
Babbage, C., 489
Bach, J. S., 522–523, 527
Baddeley, A., 171–172, 220, 261, 280
Bahrick, H. P., 190, 193
Bahrick, P. O., 190
Barinaga, M., 527
Barnett, T., 80
Bartlett, F., 17, 19, 332–335, 338, 342
Bates, A., 80
Bauer, M. I., 388
Bayes, T., 444
Beal, M. K., 66, 340
Bedard, J., 244, 252
Beethoven, L. van, 353
Bellezza, F. S., 223
Bennett, E. L., 393
Bennett, T., 243
Bentin, S., 231

Bergen, J. R., 94
Berger, A., 52
Bergman, T., 402
Berkeley, G., 15, 129, 291
Berlin, B., 331
Betts, G. H., 291
Biederman, I., 117, 121–123
Biersdorff, K. K., 244
Binet, 478
Black, J. B., 339
Blakemore, C., 170
Bliss, J. C., 81
Boden, M., 500
Bogen, J. E., 61
Bois, S. J., 176–177
Boles, D., 286, 287
Bond, J., 296
Boring, E., 15, 82
Borton, R. W., 388, 389
Bosch, V., 231
Bothwell, R. K., 199
Bourne, L. E., 422
Bower, G. H., 38, 174, 187, 237–238, 242, 263–264, 273, 295–296, 339, 413
Bowers, K. S., 465
Bradshaw, J. L., 65–66
Brady, T. J., 56
Bransford, J. D., 130, 133, 334–337
Breasted, J., 60
Brem, S. K., 435
Brentano, F., 15
Brigham, J. C., 199
Broadbent, D., 83, 88–92, 96, 242
Broca, P., 47, 49, 321
Brown, G. M., 220, 249
Brown, J. A., 171

Brown, R., 331
Brunelli, R., 506, 507
Bruner, J., 12, 107, 420–421
Buchsbaum, M. S., 480
Buddha, 142
Bugelski, B. R., 292
Buhss, U., 258
Burns, H. J., 198
Bush, G. W., 508
Byrne, R. M. J., 429

Cabeza, R., 172
Caja, S. R., 48
Calkins, M., 210–211
Caramazza, A., 439
Carpenter, P. A., 357, 363, 372, 374
Carter, P. N., 412
Cassia, V., 404
Cattell, J., 16, 78, 354, 478
Cesher, 111
Chapman, L. J., 427
Charness, N., 252
Chase, B., 258
Chase, W. G., 116, 134, 473, 519
Chekhov, 493
Chen, J. C., 66
Cheney, R., 508
Cherry, C., 87
Chi, M. T., 244, 251, 257, 473
Chiarello, C., 66
Chiesi, H. L., 252
Chipman, S. F., 299
Chomsky, N., 12, 326–327, 337, 338, 344
Clancey, W. J., 252
Clarke, A. C., 509
Clinton, W. J., 508
Cohen, G., 191
Cohen, H., 523
Cohen, J. D., 56
Colby, K. M., 511
Cole, M., 409
Collins, A., 269, 271
Coltheart, M., 250
Conrad, R., 175
Conway, M. A., 191
Cooper, E. E., 124
Corballis, P., 65, 67, 137, 302
Corbetta, M., 99
Coren, S., 111
Corkin, S., 280
Cosmides, L., 30

Coupe, P., 309
Craik, F. I. M., 169, 217–222, 242, 371
Crick, F., 155
Crowder, R. G., 80
Cutillo, B., 52
Cutler, B., 199
Cutting, J., 107

Dahneman, M., 363
Damasio, A. R., 142
Danks, J. H., 454
Darwin, C., 30–31, 353
Darwin, C. J., 80, 81
da Vinci, L., 255, 353, 535
Dearborn, W., 359
DeFries, J., 398
de Groot, A. D., 134, 519
Denes, P. B., 323
Dennett, D. C., 157
Dennis, W., 522
Deomonticus, 236
De Quincey, 469
Deregowski, J. B., 113
Descartes, R., 24, 143, 157
Dettmar, P., 258
Deutsch, G., 66
Dickinson, E., 313, 469
Diener, D., 243
Dodge, R., 78
Donders, F. C., 16
d'Onim, S., 251
Douglas, 493
Downing, P., 100
Duncan, J., 481
Dunker, K., 454
Durkheim, E., 391

Eacott, M. J., 406
Ebbinghaus, H., 15, 17, 142, 167, 203–206, 209
Eckert, J. P., 490
Einstein, A., 262, 353, 385, 469
Eisenstadt, M., 460–462
Eliot, T. S., 380
Elkonin, D., 390
Erdman, B., 78
Erickson, E., 242
Ericsson, K. A., 235, 258
Escher, M., 73–74, 110
Estes, E., 242, 357, 359
Eysenck, H., 475

Farah, M. J., 292, 302–304
Fechner, G., 15
Feigenbaum, E. A., 501
Feltovich, P., 257
Field, D., 194
Fiez, J. A., 60
Finke, R. A., 293
Fiore, S., 482
Fishman, J. A., 330
Fisk, A., 97
Fitzgerald, E., 523
Flourens, P., 44, 49
Fogel, D., 521
Fox, P. T., 57, 99
Frankel, F., 409
Franks, J. J., 130, 133, 336–337
Freud, S., 85, 142, 148, 206, 469
Friberg, L., 303
Frick, F., 433
Frith, U., 377
Fritsch, G., 48
Frost, R., 522
Fuller, B., 462
Funnel, M., 137

Gabriel, J., 371
Gabrieli, J. D. E., 316
Galileo, 353
Galperin, P., 390
Galton, F., 15, 291
Garcia, G., 243
Gardner, B. T., 67
Gardner, H., 2
Gardner, R. A., 67
Gates, B., 526
Gautier, 313
Gazzaniga, M., 35, 61, 63–64, 137, 302, 371
Geffen, G., 93
Gentner, D. R., 252
Georgopoulos, A. P., 298, 299
Gernsbacher, M. A., 377
Gevins, A., 52
Gibbs, W., 349
Gibson, J., 107
Glaser, R., 251, 257
Gleason, H. A., 330
Glick, M. J., 250
Glucksberg, S., 454
Goldsmith, R., 129
Goodnow, J. J., 420

Gore, A., 508
Grady, C. L., 172
Graham, L., 390
Gray, J. A., 90–91
Gregory, R., 107
Gruenewald, C., 231
Guenther, F., 350
Guidotti, S. J., 377
Guilford, J. P., 466, 478
Gutenberg, J., 353

Haber, R., 193, 357
Halpern, A. R., 252
Hartley, D., 291
Haxby, J. V., 172
Hayes, J. R., 456, 469
Hayes-Roth, B., 308
Hazeltine, E., 316
Hebb, D., 42–43, 168–169, 284
Heck, M., 181
Hegel, 390
Heider, E. R., 332
Helmholtz, H., 15, 107
Heppenheimer, T. A., 511–513
Herrmann, D., 242
Hershenson, M., 357
Hillis, W. D., 494
Hillyard, S. A., 99
Hinsley, D., 469
Hinton, G. E., 28, 286, 503, 518
Hitzig, E., 48
H. M., 170
H. O., 254
Holbrook, M. B., 407, 408
Holmes, S., 137
Hon, W. H., 172, 173
Horwitz, B., 172
Hoyle, S., 220
Hubel, D. H., 125, 133
Huey, E. B., 353
Hume, D., 15, 291
Hunt, E., 248–249, 471–472, 478
Hunter, I. M. L., 250
Huxley, A., 24

Ingvar, D. H., 55
Inhoff, A., 359
Inn, D., 413
Intons-Peterson, M. J., 252

Iterman, D., 242
Iverson, P., 349
Ivry, R. B., 65–66

Jacobs, 172
James, W., 15–16, 22, 30, 82, 142, 162, 167–168, 203, 206, 209, 213, 412, 464
Janet, P., 391
Janis, I. L., 433
Javal, E., 78, 354
Jefferson, T., 462
Jessell, T. M., 40, 60, 170
Johnson, E. J., 252
Johnson, J. I., 46
Johnson-Laird, P. N., 422, 429–431
Julesz, B., 94–95
Just, M. A., 357

Kaas, J., 188
Kahneman, D., 363, 441, 443
Kandel, E. R., 40, 60, 170
Kandinsky, W., 312
Kanisza, G., 111
Kanwisher, N., 100
Kao, Y. F., 272
Kareev, Y., 460–462
Kasparov, G., 520
Kay, P., 331
K. C., 226, 281
Keele, S. W., 132, 175
Keil, F. C., 13
Keller, H., 374
Kempton, W., 332
Kennan, G., 345, 346
Ketcham, K., 199
K. F., 170
Kinsbourne, M., 157
Kintsch, W., 338, 341–343, 345, 346, 410
Kirker, W. S., 221, 223
Klein, K., 220
Koenig, O., 396
Koffka, K., 454
Kohler, W., 113
Kolb, B., 393
Kosslyn, S., 66, 292–293, 299, 300, 304, 307, 396, 411–412
Kozulin, A., 390
Krampe, 235, 258
Kraus, K., 142
Kuiper, N. A., 221, 223

Kulpe, O., 15
Kupferman, I., 60
Kurzweil, R., 515, 521–523, 526

LaBerge, D., 96, 98, 155
Lange, G., 408
Lansman, M., 471
Larson, G., 48
Larson, S., 522
Lashley, K., 26, 49–51, 279
Lassen, N. A., 55
Lebby, P. C., 65–66
Legrenzi, M., 422
Legrenzi, P., 422
Leibniz, G., 489
Lesgold, A., 252, 263
Levine, M., 458
Levy, J., 63
Lewis, J. L., 471
Lincoln, A., 506
Lindsay, P. H., 155, 335
Linton, M., 195
Liu, J., 100
Locke, J., 291
Lockhart, R. S., 217, 218, 219
Loftus, E., 198–199, 242, 269, 271, 407
Lorayne, H., 243
Love, T., 248–249
Lubart, T. I., 466
Lucas, J., 243
Lunneborg, C., 471
Luria, A., 50, 209, 242, 245, 302, 339–340
Lynch, S., 209

MacLachlan, A., 480
MacLin, M. K., 339–340
MacLin, O. H., 13
Madigan, S. A., 295
Mahowald, 493
Malpass, R., 199
Mandelbaum, D. B., 330
Mandler, G., 97, 144
Mandler, J., 388, 406, 409–410
Marcel, T., 149
Marks, L. E., 313–314
Martin, R. C., 170
Marx, K., 390
Mauchley, J., 490
Mayer, R. E., 418
McCarthy, J., 60, 130, 490, 507

McClelland, J., 28, 227, 229, 231, 286, 369–370
McConkie, G. W., 359
McCulloch, W. S., 491
McDermott, K. B., 147
McDonough, L., 406
McGaugh, J. L., 283, 284
Mearns, C., 181
Mecklinger, A., 231
Mednick, S. A., 464
Meltzoff, A. N., 388, 389
Mendeleev, D., 21–22
Metzler, J., 292, 297, 307
Meyer, D. E., 148, 364, 366–369
Miall, C., 252, 254–256
Mill, J., 15
Mill, J. S., 15
Miller, D. G., 198
Miller, G., 8, 12, 17, 35, 172–174
Milner, B., 57, 154, 169, 171, 280, 302
Minksy, M., 38, 490, 493, 524
Mintun, M., 57
Mires, J., 316
Mnemosyne, 236
Moely, B. E., 408
Mondloch, C. J., 404
Moore, G., 526–527
Moore, M. J., 402
Moray, N., 80, 87, 91
Moscovitch, M., 169
Mountcastle, V. B., 26, 27, 99
Mozart, W. A., 23, 462, 522
Muir, J., 71
Muller, G. E., 15, 17, 283
Myers, R. E., 61

Nagourney, E., 377
Nebes, R. D., 197
Neisser, E., 2, 78, 80, 219, 406, 503
Nelson, C. A., 393, 413
Neuman, P. G., 157
Newell, A., 12, 24–25, 476
Newman, J., 162
Newton, C., 141
Newton, I., 353, 469
Nickerson, R. S., 193, 470
Nisbett, R., 148
Noice, H., 252
Noice, T., 252
Noll, D. C., 56
Norman, D. A., 19–20, 23, 98, 155, 206, 213–214, 220, 335, 356
Nyberg, L., 172

Oakley, D. A., 225
Ocean, H., 252–256
Ojemann, G. A., 348
O'Keefe, G., 62
O'Neill, B. J., 220
Ornstein, R. E., 60
Owens, J., 339

Paivio, A., 220, 292, 294–295
Palmer, S. E., 116, 117
Papert, S., 38, 493
Pardo, J. V., 99
Parker, C., 522
Pascal, B., 24, 489, 515
Paulesu, E., 377
Pavlov, I., 143, 144
Penfield, W., 50, 169, 347, 348
Penrod, S., 199
Pentland, A., 529
Perkins, D. N., 470
Petersen, S. E., 55, 57, 100, 130, 249, 273, 369–370
Peterson, C., 167–169
Peterson, L. R., 167–171
Peterson, M. J., 167–171, 242
Peterson, S., 55, 57
Petrides, M., 57
Philpott, A., 86
Piaget, J., 19, 242, 381, 386, 388, 390
Picasso, P., 255, 469
Pichert, J. W., 339
Pick, A. D., 401
Pilzecker, A., 283
Pinel, J. P. J., 170
Pinker, S., 30, 71, 141, 292–293
Pinson, E. N., 323
Pitts, W., 491
Plato, 14–16, 291
Plomin, R., 399
Podgorny, P., 303
Poe, E. A., 313
Poggio, T., 506–508
Poincare, H., 463
Pollatsek, A., 363
Pollock, J., 435
Polson, P. G., 252
Pomerantz, J. R., 299
Poon, L. W., 407–408
Posner, M., 55, 57, 60, 88, 98–100, 129, 132, 175–177, 242, 273, 369, 371, 464
Presley, E., 353
Pubols, B. H., 46
Pylyshyn, Z. W., 500

Quillian, M. R., 269–271, 286

Rahhal, T. A., 407–408
Raichle, M., 55, 57, 99
Ramachandran, V., 111, 315
Ramon y Cajal, S., 39, 48
Raney, G. E., 359
Rapoport, S. I., 172
Raugh, M. R., 240
Rayner, K., 242, 357, 359–360, 363
Reed, S. K., 134
Rees, A., 65–66
Rees, E., 252
Reiss, L. P., 396
Reitman, J., 252
Restak, R. M., 27
Richards, D. D., 472
Richter, P., 258
Rips, L. J., 267, 268, 435
Risberg, J., 53, 55, 57
Roberts, L., 169, 347–348
Robertson, R. R. W., 377
Robinson, 313
Rock, I., 107
Roe, A., 469
Roediger, H. L., 147
Rogers, T. B., 221–223
Roland, P. E., 303
Rosch, E., 116, 269
Rosen, B. R., 56
Rosenberg, C. R., 511
Rosenblatt, F., 38, 492–493
Rosenzweig, 393
Ross, G. S., 412
Ross, L., 148
Rossini, G., 469
Rothbart, M. K., 273
Rubin, A., 197, 407–408
Ruddy, M. G., 148, 366–369
Rudolf, M., 258
Rumelhart, D., 19, 28, 227, 229, 231, 242, 286, 335

Saarinen, T. F., 311
Salapatek, P., 402
Salisbury, H. E., 457
Saltz, E., 220
Sapir, E., 330
Schacter, D. L., 57, 59, 123, 158–159
Schank, R., 515
Schickard, W., 489
Schneider, W., 56
Schooler, J., 482

Schvaneveldt, R. W., 148, 364, 366–369
Schwartz, J. H., 40, 60, 170
Searle, J., 496
Sehulster, J. R., 196
Sejnowski, T., 511–512
Selfridge, O. G., 503
Sells, S. B., 427
Sergent, J., 169
Shakespeare, W., 353
Shallice, T., 170
Shannon, C. E., 88, 490
Shapiro, S. I., 409
Sharp, D., 409
Sheehan, P. W., 292
Shelley, P. B., 313
Shepard, R. N., 30–31, 193, 242, 292, 297–299, 307
Shepherd, G. M., 34
Shereshevskii, S. V., 245
Shiffrin, R. M., 214, 215, 216, 220
Shimamura, A., 265, 282
Shoben, E. J., 267–268
Short, B. A., 123
Siegel, B. V., 480
Siegler, R. S., 472, 480
Simon, H. A., 12, 24–25, 134, 469, 473, 488, 490
Singh, J. A. L., 394
Sinha, P., 507–508
Skinhoj, E., 55
Skinner, B. F., 144, 329
Smith, E. E., 267, 268, 470
Smith, M. L., 57
Smyth, M. M., 252
Snyder, C. R. R., 98
Soderling, E., 480
Sokolov, E., 66
Solso, R. S., 28, 65–66, 123, 130, 176–177, 181, 244, 252–253, 272, 339–340, 359, 389, 413, 435, 507
Spearman, C., 478, 481
Spelke, E. S., 388
Spencer, H., 261
Sperling, G., 79–81
Sperry, R., 61, 63, 302
Spielberg, S., 466
Spilich, G. J., 250
Springer, S. P., 66
Springston, F., 174
Squire, L. R., 170, 282
Stanhope, N., 191
Stark, L., 356
Steedman, M., 429
Stein, G., 121

Sternberg, R., 466, 469, 473, 478
Sternberg, S., 242
Stevens, A., 309
Strauss, M. S., 412
Stromeyer, C. G., 248
Swift, J., 509–510

Tan, C., 520
Tang, C., 480
Taylor, H. A., 308
Taylor, I. L., 99
Tchalenko, J., 252, 254–256
Techener, E., 15
Tesch-Romer, 235, 258
Teuber, H. L., 280
Thompson, R. A., 393, 413
Thorndyke, P. W., 338
Thulborn, K. R., 374
Thurstone, L. L., 478
Tinklenberg, J. R., 99
Titchener, E. B., 15, 291
Tolman, E., 16, 17, 19, 308
Tompon, R., 414
Tooby, J., 30
Tousman, S., 359
Trabasso, T., 385
Treisman, A., 91–96
Trevarthen, C., 63
Tsien, J., 481
Tulving, E., 55–56, 58, 60, 123, 169, 220–227, 371
Turing, A., 497, 527
Turk, M., 529
Turvey, M. T., 80
Tversky, A., 434, 440–441, 443
Tversky, B., 316

Underwood, G., 86
Ungerleider, L. G., 172
Usher, J. A., 406
Uttal, W. R., 51

Valenza, E., 404
Vallar, G., 170
van Dijk, T. A., 341–343
van Gogh, V., 469, 527
Vaughn, M. E., 408
Vipond, D., 343
Vogel, P. J., 61
Vogl, T. P., 504
Volke, H. J., 258

Von Cramon, D. Y., 231
Von Neumann, J., 24, 28, 50, 51, 133, 491
von Restorff, 235
Voss, J. F., 252
V. P., 248–249
Vygotsky, L. S., 242, 381, 389–392

Wagenaar, W., 195
Wagner, D., 517, 518
Walden, K. J., 413
Walker, N., 46, 97
Wallas, G., 463
Walter, W. G., 524
Walton, G. E., 413
Warrington, E., 170, 280
Wason, P. C., 422
Watkins, M. J., 219
Watson, J., 143
Waugh, N. C., 23, 206, 213, 214, 220
Weaver, W., 88
Wechsler, S. B., 478
Wedderburn, A. A. I., 90–91
Weiskrantz, L., 209
Weizenbaum, J., 509
Welker, W. I., 46
Wernicke, C., 47–49, 321
Wertheimer, M., 112, 453
Whishaw, I. Q., 393
Whitaker, H. A., 440
Whorf, B. L., 330
Wiesel, T. N., 125, 133
Wilding, J., 86
Wilson, F. A., 220
Wilson, R. A., 13
Winograd, T., 513
Witherspoon, D., 281
Wittgenstein, L., 372
Wittlinger, R. P., 190, 193
Woodworth, R. S., 292, 427
Wundt, W., 15

Yarbus, A. L., 126, 242
Yarnell, P. R., 209
Yoshimura, E. K., 408

Zacks, J. M., 316
Zaman, A., 144, 164
Zaporozhets, 390
Zinchenko, P. I., 216–217, 390
Zingg, R. M., 394

Subject Index

Abducens, 244
Abstraction
  linguistic ideas, 5
  visual, 128
Abstract proposition, 277
Accommodation, 382
Acquisition components, 478
Acronym, 238, 242
Acrostic, 238, 242
ACT. *See* Adaptive Control of Thought
Adaptation, 382
Adaptive Control of Thought, 275, 278, 279
Ad hominem, 437
Aggregate field theory, 44
AI. *See* Artificial intelligence
Algorithm, 512, 518
Alpha waves, 52
Amnesia, 147, 153, 169, 280, 279
  anterograde, 280
  retrograde, 280
Amygdala, 284
Analogies, 469, 476
Anomalous messages, 87
Anosognosia, 158
Aphasia, 47, 49
  Broca's aphasia, 49
  conductive aphasia, 49
  subcortical aphasia, 49
  Wernicke's aphasia, 49
Arborizations, 39
Artificial intelligence (AI), 6, 7, 11, 12, 19, 20,
    24, 25, 251, 469, 487, 500, 501, 509, 513,
    515, 521
  arts, 521
  strong AI, 496
  weak AI, 496
Assimilation, 382
Associationism, 46, 420

Associative cortex, 321
Atomic theory, 28
Attention, 2, 5, 6–8, 16–19, 36, 82–83
Attribute-frequency model, 132–133
Auditory, 160, 244
  code, 175
  cortex, 47
  impulses, 80
  information, 80
  system, 67
Automaticity, 97, 98
Automatic processing, 96
Automatic skills, 144
Awareness, 39, 141
Axial projection, 377
Axon, 39–41

Bayes's Theorem, 444–447
Behaviorism, 16, 18, 144, 525
Beta waves, 52
Bipolar electrical probes, 347
Bottom-up processing, 108, 117, 304, 462
Boundary paradigm, 362
Brain, 4, 34–38, 40, 42, 44, 45, 53, 142, 394,
    501, 526
  development, 402
Brainstorming, 469
Breadth-first strategy, 462
Broca's area, 47, 321, 347, 374–375
Brown-Peterson technique, 168, 472

Candle Problem, 455
Canonic
  features, 503
  perspectives, 114, 115, 117
Cartesian paradoxes, 157
Cell body, 39, 40
Central executive, 172

Central nervous system (CNS), 38, 48, 67, 72
Central tendency model, 132
Cerebellum, 45
Cerebral cortex, 26, 36, 38, 45–46, 59, 320
Cerebral hemisphere, 45, 60, 137, 253
   left hemisphere, 46, 60, 62
   right hemisphere, 46, 60, 62
Cerebral migration, 59
Channel capacity, 85
Characteristic features, 268
Checkers, 521
Chess, 135, 251, 519–520
Chimera, 508
Chimeric face, 63, 65
Chinese room, 498, 500
Chomsky's Theory, 326, 329
Chunking, 134, 173, 174, 408
Classification, 385
Clustering model, 262, 266
Cocktail party phenomenon, 88
Coding, 72, 78
Cognition, 2, 4, 30, 36, 46, 71, 73, 75, 144,
   380, 398
Cognitive
   development, 6, 11, 19, 381
   map, 10, 16–17, 308
   models, 20–22
   neuroscience, 6, 34–36, 169, 266, 525, 529
   psychology, 2, 4, 6, 26
   revolution, 12, 16
   science, 25
   system, 8, 76
Colorado Adoption Project, 398, 399, 400
Commissurotomy, 61, 65
Communication, 19, 514
Componential, 476
Comprehension, 49, 338, 372
Computational brain, 7, 71
Computed Axial Tomography (CT), 38, 53, 54, 76
Computerized cognition, 487
Computers, 489, 505
Computer simulation, 527
Concept formation, 6, 11, 419
Conceptual
   hierarchy, 264
   models, 470
   science, 20–22
Concrete-operational period, 384, 386, 387
Cones, 73, 109, 355–356
Connectionism, 26, 37, 42, 496

Consciousness, 2, 6, 8–9, 12, 16–18, 36, 141–142,
   161–163, 292
Conservative focusing, 421
Constructive perception, 107–108
Context effect, 117
Continuous speech recognition (CSR), 514
Contralaterality, 46, 60, 75
Convergent thinking, 466
Conversation, 384
Cornea, 109
Corpus callosum, 45, 61–63, 66, 137
Cortex, 58. *See also* Cerebral cortex
Cortical neurons, 39
Creative process, 462–464
   illumination, 463–464
   incubation, 463–464
   preparation, 463
   verification, 463–464
Cross-talk, 315
CSR. *See* Continuous speech recognition
Cultural blocks, 467
Curvilinear, 195
CVC, 168
Cybernetics, 19

Decay, 213
Decision
   frames, 441
   making, 446
Decoding, 325
Deductive reasoning, 470
Deep structure, 327
Defining features, 268
Dendrites, 39–41
Depth-first strategy, 462
Design architecture, 491
Development
   cognitive, 6, 11, 19, 381
   comparative, 381
   developmental psychology, 2, 380
DICE, 158, 159
Diencephalon, 280
Digit-span task, 473
Direct perception, 107, 108. *See also* Perception
Divergence production test, 466
Divergent thinking, 467
Dizygotic twins, 398
Dominant theme, 334
Dreams, 141
Drugs, 141

Dual-coding hypothesis, 294
Dualistic memory theory, 209
Dual memory theory, 211
Dyslexia, 365, 377
DYSTAL, 504–505

Ear, 73
Echoic memory, 80
Echoic storage, 72, 80–82
ECT. *See* Electroconvulsive shock therapy
Edge detectors, 501, 502
EEG. *See* Electroencephalograph
Eidetic imagery, 248
Electrochemical processes, 7
Electroconvulsive shock therapy (ECT), 209, 280
Electroencephalograph (EEG), 28, 38, 41, 51–52, 56, 147, 151, 258
ELIZA, 509–510
Emotions, 2, 43
Empiricists, 13, 15
Encoding, 278, 471, 476
Engram, 159, 209, 279
ENLAC, 489
Environmental
    context, 466
    cues, 6–8
    stimuli, 141
Epidermis, 76
Epistemology, 76
ERP, 41
Evolution, 29, 30, 31, 38
Exemplar faces, 131
Experience, 145
Experts, 250
Expert systems, 251, 508
External reality, 21
External signals, 8
Extrasensory perception (ESP), 187
Eye, 73, 75, 77
    fixation, 372
    movements, 126
Eye-tracking, 254, 358–360, 365, 403
Eyewitness identification, 198

Face, 244, 254
    attention, 401
Face recognition, 505–507, 529
Facial cognizance, 254
Feature analysis, 109, 125
Features, 125

Filler model, 88
Fissures, 45, 47
Fixations, 358, 359
Flexibility, 467–468
fMRI. *See* Magnetic Resonance Imaging
Focus gambling, 422
Forgetting, 5
    curve, 167
Formal operations, 387
Form perception, 109, 133. *See also* Perception
Fovea, 109, 355
Free-association, 148
Free recall, 210, 211, 243
Fricatives, 323
Frontal lobe, 46, 47, 59
Fuchsian functions, 463
Functional-equivalency, 294
Functional fixedness, 454, 464
Functional validation, 394
Fusiform face area, 101, 102

Games, 521
Gamma ray, 57
Generativity, 67
Genetic engineering, 482
Geometric illusions, 74
Geon theory, 117, 121
Gestalt Psychology, 16, 108, 112, 114, 133, 453, 454, 458
Global aphasia, 49
Global Workplace Theory, 159–162
Glossopharygeal, 244
GMR, 480
Gomuku game, 461
Grammar, 320, 327, 343
Gustatory signals, 75
Gyri (gyrus), 45

Habituation, 144, 283, 406
Hair cells, 73
HAM, 273, 275, 278
Hearing, 73, 75, 77, 80
Hebb's Theory, 186
Hemispheres, 60, 137, 253. *See also* Cerebral hemisphere
Heuristics, 501, 518
Higher-order cognition, 409. *See also* Cognition
Hippocampus, 153, 169
Homunculus, 27
Hypoglossal, 244
Hypothalamus, 45
Hypothetical constructs, 37

Icon, 79
  iconic fading, 78
  iconic memory, 78
  iconic storage, 72, 78–82
Identikit, 412
Illusions, 73, 110
  illusory contours, 110
  Muller-Lyer illusion, 73, 110
Imagery, 6, 10, 18, 36, 292, 410
Imaging technology, 34
Implicit
  cognition, 143
  learning, 144
  memory, 124, 147
Incoherent words, 465
Inductive reasoning, 424, 425, 433, 475
Inferences, 425
  inferential logic, 22
Information acquisition, 527
Information processing, 4–6, 24, 26, 81, 83, 144, 219,
    471, 476, 500
Infrared radiation, 77
Inhibitory connections, 42
Integration metaphor, 156
Intelligence, 5–7, 11, 43, 398, 469, 509
  cognitive neuroscience, 478
  cognitive theories, 470
  componential intelligence, 473
  contextual intelligence, 474, 476
  experiential intelligence, 474, 476
  processes of intelligence, 466
  spatial intelligence, 481
  triarchic theory of intelligence, 473
  verbal intelligence, 481
Intentionality, 499–500
Interference, 5
Internalization, 391
Internal representations, 5–6 10–15, 16, 19–21, 144,
    459–461
Internal systems, 4
Interpretation, 6
Intervening variables, 16
Intuition, 465
Isomorphism, 16, 299

Johniacs, 491

Key word method, 238, 240
Knowledge, 5, 13, 20, 261–262, 279, 281, 466
Korsakoff's syndrome, 280

Language, 5, 6, 10, 30, 36, 46, 60–61, 261, 319, 322,
    396, 509, 511, 513, 515
  processing, 5, 17, 37, 44, 46, 67, 338
Lateral inhibition, 111
Lateralization, 396
Law of parsimony, 81
LDT. See Lexical-decision task
Learning, 2, 40, 50, 163, 327, 492, 509
Level of processing, 217–219
Level of recall, 216, 217
Lexical-decision task (LDT), 364, 367, 369, 370, 371
Lexicon, 10, 161
Life-span development, 381
Light energy, 73, 119
Limpet, 76
Line analysis, 501
Linguistic-relativity hypothesis, 330
Linguistics, 19, 61, 322, 349
Local area network, 242
Local features, 501
Localization, 43–44
Loci, 238
Logic, 422
Logogen, 368
Long term potentiation, 208
Long term store, 215, 216. See also Memory
Luminance, 313
Lumping, 286

Machine learning, 516
Macrostructures, 346
Magnetic Resonance Imaging (MRI), 28, 38, 83, 51–53,
    55, 76, 100, 101, 253, 255, 320, 371, 374, 481
MANSCAN, 52
Mass action, 50
Mathematical ability, 472
McCulloch-Pitts neurons, 492
Meaning, 513
Medial temporal lobe, 59
Meditation, 141
Medulla, 45
MEG, 53, 56, 100, 101
Memory, 2, 5–6, 9, 17, 30, 36, 39, 40, 44, 46, 50,
    16–18, 48, 59, 67, 72, 77–78, 144, 167, 188–189,
    193, 198, 243, 245, 285, 322, 332, 405, 409, 509
  autobiographical memory, 193, 195, 200
  declarative memory, 161, 208, 276, 281
  dual memory theory, 211
  echoic memory, 80
  episodic memory, 56–57, 224–227, 281
  explicit memory, 124, 147

false memories, 59, 199, 407
iconic memory, 78
implicit memory, 124, 147
infant memory, 406
lexical memory, 366
long term memory (LTM), 5, 9, 21, 103, 127, 167, 169,
    171–172, 174, 187, 189, 194, 211–212, 214–215,
    244, 251, 257, 274, 280, 328, 344, 373, 471
memorization, 239
photographic memory, 248
primary memory, 22, 167, 206
procedural memory, 170, 208, 226, 281
production memory, 276
pseudomemory, 130
repressed memories, 199
secondary memory, 22, 206
semantic memory, 5, 224–226, 264, 368
short term memory (STM), 5, 9, 21, 77, 80, 103,
    124, 143, 167, 169, 171–172, 174–176, 211–212,
    214–215, 220, 251, 257, 280, 344, 471
very long term memory (VLTM), 190, 191, 193
vintage memories, 196
working memory, 9, 171–172, 231, 275, 373, 462
Mental
    events, 141
    imagery, 5, 143, 291, 308, 528
    representations, 15
    retardation, 478
    rotation, 297
    states, 292
Mentalists, 143
Metacognition, 265
    metamemory task, 473
Meta components, 478
Metaphorical thinking, 410
Meta statements, 342
Method of loci, 236–238
Midbrain, 45
Mind, 35–36, 292
Mind-body problem, 143
Mnemonics, 5, 236, 238, 247
    Mnemonic encoding principal, 257
    Mnemonic techniques, 244
Modal model, 413
Moore's Law, 526
Morphemes, 324
Motivation, 466
Motor
    behavior, 5, 254
    cortex, 47
    regions, 58

Moving window paradigm, 361
MRI. See Magnetic Resonance Imaging
Muller-Lyer illusion. See Illusions
Music, 522–523
Myelin sheath, 39, 40

Narcisstic trait, 222
Nativists, 13
Neocognitive revolution, 18
Nerve cells, 73, 125
Nerve fibers, 76
Nervous system. See Central nervous system
NETtalk, 509, 511–513
Network model, 266, 269
Neural
    activity, 36
    energy, 6
    impulse, 41
    neural nets. See neural network systems
    neural network systems, 25–26, 37, 42, 496, 512
    transmission, 29
Neuroanatomy, 8, 29, 37
Neurocognitive development, 381
Neurocognitive imagery, 27
Neurocognitive techniques, 27
Neurology, 38, 47, 321
Neuron, 25–26, 29, 34, 36, 38–40, 42, 48, 51,
    55, 75, 396
Neurophysiology, 37, 51
Neuroscience, 4, 25–26, 34, 36–37
Neurotransmitter, 35, 40, 41
Nonsense syllables, 204, 205
Nose, 73
Novelty metaphor, 155
Nucleus, 39, 40

Object priming effect, 123
Object recognition, 506
Occipital
    cortex, 75
    lobe, 46–47, 58–59, 75, 159
Oculomotor, 244
Olfactory, 244
    signals, 75
Omissions, 334
Optic, 244
    chiasm, 62
    nerve, 62
Organization, 408
Organizational schemas, 238, 241, 242
Organizational variables, 263

Orthographically, 323
Oscilloscope, 261

Parahippocampal place area (PPA), 101, 102
Parallel distributed processing (PDP), 26–29, 37,
    42–43, 227–230, 285–286, 496, 503–504
Parallel processing model, 48–49, 494
Parietal lobe, 46–47, 59
PARRY, 509, 511
Parsimony, 48
Partial report technique, 79
Pattern
    organization, 112
    perception, 126
    recognition, 2, 6, 8, 17, 105, 109, 118, 120, 134, 137,
        500, 502, 504
PDP. See Parallel distributed processing
Pedagogy, 467
Perception, 2, 5–7, 9, 30, 38, 43–44, 46, 71–77, 105,
    108, 144, 315, 319, 418, 492, 500, 503, 509
    depth perception, 108
    form perception, 109, 133
    subliminal perception, 85
Perceptrons, 38
Percepts, 5, 21
Perceptual
    illusion, 73
    perceptual-motor skills, 280
    persistence, 78
    process, 75, 77
    span, 77–78, 354, 358
    system, 76
    theories, 104
Performance components, 478
Peripheral nervous system (PNS), 71
Permastore, 190–191
Personality, 43, 466
PET. See Positron Emission Tomography
Phonemes, 221, 322–324, 350, 512
Phonological loop, 171
Phonology, 321
Photosensitive, 355, 356
Phrenology, 43–44, 48, 60
Physicalism, 143
Physical senses, 15
Pitch, 313
Pituitary gland, 45
Plosives, 323
Poetry, 521
Polhemus motion sensor, 255
Pons, 45

Pop-out effect, 94
Positron Emission Tomography (PET), 28, 38, 53–55,
    57–59, 76, 100, 209, 273, 303, 320, 348, 479
Postsynaptic membrane, 41
Pragnanz, 111
Preattentive processing, 95
Preconscious input processing, 144
Preoperational period, 383, 386, 387
Pressure, 73
Presupposed knowledge, 144
Presynaptic membrane, 41
Presynaptic terminals, 39–40
Primacy effects, 210, 211
Priming, 85, 123–124
    subliminal priming, 148
Probabilities, 440
Problem solving, 5, 24, 452, 473, 509, 515
Production systems, 276
Productivity, 326
Progressive deepening strategy, 462
Propositional networks, 273, 343
Prototype, 127, 412, 507
    matching, 127, 137
    recognition, 128
    theory, 109, 132
Psychophysics, 72
PsycInfo, 528
Puzzles, 516, 517
Pythagorean Theorem, 13

Rapid eye movement (REM), 152, 153, 165
Rationality, 446
Rationalization, 334
rCBF, 57, 302, 304
Reaction time, 76, 314
Reading, 5, 8, 36, 78, 81, 503
Reasoning, 473
    dialogues, 435
Recall, 154, 332
    interval, 168
Recency effects, 210
Receptivity, 76
Receptors, 41, 63, 75–76
Recognition, 36, 507
    by components (RBC), 121
Regularity, 326
Reinstatement search, 244
REM. See Rapid eye movement
Remote Associations Test, 464
Renaissance philosophers, 14
Representation of knowledge, 5, 6, 9, 12, 15, 20

Retention, 191
Retention components, 478
Retina, 63, 76, 109, 113, 125
Retrieval, 277
Retrieval structure principal, 257
Right hemisphere, 46, 60, 62
Robots, 524, 535
Rods, 73, 109

Saccades, 78, 354, 362
Schema, 17, 332, 334, 340
Scholastic Aptitude Test, 471
Scientific inquiry, 528
Scratch pad, 172
Second-order isomorphism, 299
Selective attention, 88, 401
Self-recognition, 145
Self schema, 222
Semantic
    organization, 473
    priming, 123
    information, 5, 56–57
Semantic Feature-Comparison Model, 266, 267
Sensation, 2, 5–7, 44, 71–72, 73, 75–76, 105
Sensorimotor period, 154, 383, 387
Sensory
    cortex, 46
    detection, 72
    memories, 77,80
    sensory-motor, 46
    signals, 7, 76–77
    stimuli, 8, 20, 73
    store, 77, 79, 211, 212
    system, 71–73, 75–77
    threshold, 148
Sentience, 161
Sequential (serial) processing, 27, 494
Seriation, 385, 386
Set, 454
Set-theoretical model, 266
Shadowing, 87
Shakey, 525
Shepard's recognition test, 194
Short term store, 215, 216. See also Memory
Signal detection, 18, 19
Similarity, 112
Simultaneous scanning, 421
Single channel theory, 88
Skin, 73
Sleep, 147, 151, 153
Smell, 73, 75, 77

Social cognition, 5
Somatosensory system, 67
Sound waves, 73
Spatial ability, 472
    analysis, 161
    image, 277
Spatial imaginal tasks, 307
Spatial processes, 67
Speaking, 58
Spectrograph, 324
Spectrum, 77
Speech, 46–47, 328
Speed up principal, 258
Spinal cord, 4, 45
Split-brain, 63–64, 138
Splitting, 287
Spreading activation theory, 271, 272
Sternberg paradigm, 472
Stimuli, 22, 461
Stimulus energy, 72,71
Stimulus-response (S-R) psychology, 16
STM. See Memory
Structural task, 221
Subjective experience, 141
Subjective organization, 110
Subroutines, 503
Successive scanning, 421
Sulci (sulcus), 45, 47
Supermetaphor, 157
Surface structure, 327, 344
Syllogism, 423, 427, 431
Syllogistic
    logic, 432, 428
    reasoning, 427
Sylvian fissure, 47
Symbols, 319
Synapse, 40
Synaptic cleft, 41
Synaptic transmission, 41
Synesthesia, 245, 247, 312–313, 315
Syntax, 10, 144, 161, 321, 323, 343, 513

Tabula rasa, 380
Tachistoscopic, 358
Tactical signals, 75
Taste, 73, 75, 77
Taxonomy, 282, 283
TBR, 237,239
Template matching, 108, 119, 120, 133, 461
Temporal cortex, 321
Temporal lobe, 4, 9, 169

Temporal string, 277
Terminal button, 39
Tetris, 479–480
Thalamus, 45
Thinking, 2, 6, 7, 11, 16–18, 30, 36, 39, 44, 48, 50, 418, 500
Thorax, 323
TMS, 56
Tomogram, 53
Tongue, 73
Top down processing, 133, 134, 461–462
Touch, 73, 75, 77
Transduction, 72, 77, 502
Transfer components, 478
Transformation, 385
Transformational grammar, 327, 329
Transitivity, 385
Traumatic experiences, 200
Triangularity, 505
Turing test, 498, 527

Unattended speech, 144
Unconscious processes, 8, 144
Understanding, 500
UNIVAC, 489
Universal affirmative, 266, 267
Unmyelinated axons, 45

Verbal dialogues, 435
Vesicles, 41
Vision, 73, 77–78, 109, 160
Visual
    acuity, 358
    code, 175, 176
    cortex, 47, 62, 109, 125
    field, 62
    imagery, 293
    knowledge, 304
    pattern, 42
    peripheral, 355
    processing, 303
    search, 97
    signals, 75
    system, 67, 500
Visuospatial, 171
VLTM. *See* Memory
Vocal cavities, 323
Voiceprints, 323
von Restorff effect, 235
Voxels, 375, 376
Vygotsky's theory of language, 392

Waking state, 145
Wechsler Adult Intelligence Scale, 248
Wernicke's area, 47, 321, 347
Whorfian hypothesis, 330–332
Wisconsin Card Sorting Task, 438, 439
Words, 320
    identification, 355
    recognition, 120
Working memory. *See* Memory, working

Zone of proximal development, 391